HANDBOOK OF TEACHING AND LEARNING IN TOURISM

Handbook of Teaching and Learning in Tourism

Edited by

Pierre Benckendorff

The University of Queensland, Australia

Anita Zehrer

Management Center Innsbruck, Austria

EE Edward Elgar
PUBLISHING

Cheltenham, UK • Northampton, MA, USA

Published by
Edward Elgar Publishing Limited
The Lypiatts
15 Lansdown Road
Cheltenham
Glos GL50 2JA
UK

Edward Elgar Publishing, Inc.
William Pratt House
9 Dewey Court
Northampton
Massachusetts 01060
USA

A catalogue record for this book
is available from the British Library

Library of Congress Control Number: 2016949965

This book is available electronically in the **Elgar**online
Social and Political Science subject collection
DOI 10.4337/9781784714802

ISBN 978 1 78471 479 6 (cased)
ISBN 978 1 78471 480 2 (eBook)

Typeset by Servis Filmsetting Ltd, Stockport, Cheshire
Printed and bound in Great Britain by TJ International Ltd, Padstow

Contents

Contributors

David Airey is Emeritus Professor at the University of Surrey. He has been involved in tourism as a subject for study for more than 40 years as an academic and as a government official with national responsibility for tourism programmes in England. He co-edited the first book on tourism education and has recently co-edited the 500-page Routledge *Handbook* on the same topic. He has been involved in many research studies related to tourism education, many of which have appeared in academic journals. In 2006 he received the United Nations World Tourism Organization's Ulysses Prize for his work in the creation and dissemination of knowledge. Since retiring from his full-time position at Surrey he has continued to teach, research and write, based both in the UK and internationally, where he holds a number of visiting professorships.

Kathleen Andereck is Director of School of Community Resources and Development and Director of Curricular Initiatives in the College of Public Service and Community Solutions at Arizona State University where she also holds the rank of Professor. She serves on several university level advisory committees including the Study Abroad, Graduate Education, and Social Science Research Advisory Committees. Her research focuses on the tourism experience from the perspective of both visitors and residents particularly as it applies to sustainable tourism. Andereck has done research work with a diversity of organizations and agencies at the federal and state level including the Bureau of Land Management, the USDA Forest Service, the Arizona Office of Tourism and the Arizona Department of Transportation. She has published this work in numerous academic journals including the top-tier publications in tourism studies. She has also presented many papers at national and international conferences. Andereck is active in a number of local and national organizations. She is an associate editor for three academic journals.

Charles Arcodia is an Associate Professor within the Department of Tourism, Sport and Hotel Management. He joined Griffith University in 2012 and has held previous full-time positions at the University of Queensland and the Queensland University of Technology. He has also had part-time/visiting academic positions at various other Australian and overseas universities. Arcodia's research interests are generally in the field of event management and tourism management education, particularly approaches to experiential learning. The outcomes of his research have appeared in a variety of books and academic journals. Arcodia is the Executive Editor of the *International Journal of Event Management Research* and is an editorial board member of four other scholarly journals.

Florian Aubke is an Assistant Professor/Senior Lecturer for Hotel Management at the Department of Tourism and Service Management at MODUL University Vienna. He has substantial operational experience in the hospitality industry as well as national and international event management. Florian received his Bachelor of Business in Marketing and Hospitality Management as well as a Master of Business by Research from Victoria University, Melbourne, Australia. Since his doctoral studies (completed in 2012 with distinction at the Vienna University of Economics and Business), his research has focused on the analysis of social networks, both within and between organizations, with a particular application to the hospitality and tourism industry. Florian is an active member of the International Network for Social Network Analysis (INSNA) as well as the European Chapter of the International Council on Hotel, Restaurant and Institutional Education (EuroCHRIE).

Roy Ballantyne is a Professor at the University of Queensland. He has over 35 years' experience in teaching and researching in tertiary institutions and has an established international reputation for his work and publications in higher education, environmental interpretation and education, free-choice environmental learning, and visitor research in museums, wildlife and ecotourism settings. He is the joint author of *Reflecting on University Teaching: Academics' Stories* and *Designing Effective Interpretive Signs and Exhibits: Principles in Practice*; and is joint Editor of *Contemporary Issues in Heritage and Environmental Interpretation* and *The International Handbook on Ecotourism*. He has won national and international awards for his teaching, including the Australian National Teaching Fellowship (1997) and is an Honorary Fellow of the Australian Learning and Teaching Council.

J.E. (Joe) Barth is an Associate Professor in the School of Hospitality, Food & Tourism Management at the University of Guelph. Dr Barth's research interests are in the area of wine, bundling, yield management and pricing. Recent publications are about wine list inventory optimization, wine label marketing and the efficiency of wine retailing. He has also co-authored journal and conference papers with his MBA graduate students about location models for the Ontario gaming industry, market segment profitability analysis, cruise line rating systems, automated telephone systems and special event promotions. Joe is the HTM MBA Graduate Coordinator and President of the University Club. He is a lifetime member of the Honor Society of Phi Kappa Phi, and is the recipient of several teaching awards.

Pierre Benckendorff is an educator and scholar at The University of Queensland, Australia and has more than 15 years' experience in education and research in the tourism field. Pierre's passion for travel and tourism has taken him to some of the world's leading theme parks and airports, the major cities of Europe and North America, the African Savannah and the bustling streets of Asia. He has also travelled extensively around Australia and New Zealand. His interests include visitor behaviour, tourism information technologies, and tourism education and training. Pierre is also an award-winning university lecturer and has held several teaching and learning leadership positions at both The University of Queensland and James Cook University. In 2007 he received a national Carrick (now Office for Learning and Teaching) citation for outstanding contributions to student learning. He has developed and taught undergraduate and postgraduate courses in introductory tourism management, international tourism, tourist behaviour, tourism and leisure futures, tourism transportation, tourism operations, tourism technologies, tourism analysis, business skills and marketing communications.

Pedro Bingre do Amaral has graduated in Forestry (MSc) and Regional and Urban Planning (MSc). He is currently doing his PhD research on Land Use Policies applied to Forestry and Nature Conservation. He is an Assistant Professor at the Higher School of

Agriculture, Polytechnic Institute of Coimbra, Portugal, where he teaches several courses related to applied ecology to Ecotourism and Environmental Engineering undergraduates. He is a member of the coordinating committee of a Master's degree in Ecotourism and has published several articles and reports in his areas of interest.

Monika Birkle is a Senior Lecturer at HAAGA-HELIA University of Applied Sciences, Porvoo Unit. She has been actively involved in the renewal of the curriculum and pedagogical processes at Porvoo Campus. In addition to pedagogical issues, her main research interests and subject areas in teaching cover event planning and management, service design and developing services.

Anna Blackman's areas of expertise include business coaching effectiveness, Human Resource Management, Business Management and Wellbeing. She is specifically interested in building capacity with regional and rural businesses. She has published her work in journals, book chapters and case studies and has presented at local, national and international conferences and forums. She has successfully won a number of competitive grants (one being JCU's Rising Star ECR Leadership Program) and a citation for outstanding contributions to student learning. Dr Blackman has worked in small business management for approximately eight years in Australia and has worked for a large multinational corporation in the UK. She is currently employed as a Senior Lecturer for James Cook University in their College of Business, Law and Governance. She is the Course Coordinator for the Graduate Certificate in Australian Rural Leadership for the Australian Rural Leadership Foundation and is a Fellow and Queensland Councillor for the Australian Human Resources Institute.

Andrea Boyle has over 15 years' tourism teaching experience in the higher education and vocational education training sectors. Originally from England, Andrea gained an undergraduate award in law (LLB, Hons) and travelled to Australia where she managed a retail travel office before entering the field of tourism education. She has taught and coordinated a wide range of tourism subjects, and as a member of two teaching teams in the School of Business and Tourism at Southern Cross University, Australia, received two Vice Chancellor's Awards for Teaching Excellence and a national ALTC Award for Outstanding Contribution to Student Learning. After completing a Graduate Certificate in Higher Education (Learning & Teaching), Andrea's PhD explored 'education for sustainability' within Australian tourism higher education. She is currently working as a Project Coordinator in Southern Cross University's Equity and Diversity Office. Andrea's research interest and publications focus on sustainability education, transformative education, critical perspectives within curricula and critical pedagogy. She is a guest co-editor for a Special Edition on Critical Perspectives in Tourism Education for the *Journal of Hospitality, Leisure, Sport and Tourism*.

Julia Caldicott is the Work-Integrated Learning (WIL) Coordinator with the School of Business and Tourism at Southern Cross University, Australia. The WIL team, of which Julia has been a part for many years, was awarded an Australian Learning and Teaching Council citation for pioneering and sustaining student-centred, transformative, work-enriched experiential learning opportunities in tourism and hospitality management. With a long-term interest in student development, Julia is currently completing a PhD, which examines the current role and further potential of WIL in fostering tourism students' self-authorship development. Julia holds a Graduate Certificate in Higher Education (Teaching and Learning) in addition to tourism and nursing degrees. Prior to academia, Julia facilitated experiential learning for university students as a workplace supervisor and preceptor whilst in tourism and nursing positions.

Lorenzo Cantoni is Full Professor at the Università della Svizzera italiana (USI), Lugano, Switzerland, Faculty of Communication Sciences, where he served as Dean of the Faculty in the academic years 2010–14. He is currently Director of the Institute for Communication Technologies and scientific director of the laboratories webatelier.net, NewMinE Lab: New Media in Education Lab, and eLab: eLearning Lab. He is chairholder of the UNESCO chair in ICT to develop and promote sustainable tourism in World Heritage Sites, established at USI, and president of the International Federation IT and Travel and Tourism (IFITT). His research interests are where communication, education and new media overlap, ranging from eLearning to eTourism, and from ICT4D to eGovernment.

Vivina Almeida Carreira is an Associate Professor at the Higher School of Agriculture, Polytechnic Institute of Coimbra, Portugal, where she has been teaching several subjects in the areas of specialized languages, communication, tourism products and cultural tourism as well as being engaged in institutional positions and in supervising students' training and research. She is presently the coordinator of a Bachelor's degree in Ecotourism and a member of the coordinating committee of a Master's degree in Ecotourism. She is a referee for a few international journals and has published several papers in proceedings of national and international conferences, as well as in peer-reviewed scientific journals.

Debbie Cotterell is a PhD candidate within the Department of Tourism, Sport and Hotel Management at Griffith University, Australia. Debbie has a background of experience within the tourism and hospitality industry in Australia as well as Europe, Africa and Asia. Her career in teaching started as a secondary school teacher and workplace trainer. More recently she has been a regular tutor for tourism courses at Griffith University and Lecturer at Griffith College, Australia in an introductory research course. Her PhD is exploring the teaching and learning of sustainable tourism courses within higher education with a particular interest in the concept of 'strong sustainability' and the use of phenomenography as a research approach in education.

Ruth Craggs is a Lecturer at Dublin Institute of Technology, School of Hospitality Management and Tourism, Ireland. Ruth lectures in event management and tourism and is part of the 'Students in Action' initiative at DIT. She received her PhD from the University of Salford and has lectured in a number of Higher Education Institutes in the Republic of Ireland and the UK. Her research interests include business tourism, event fundraising and sponsorship, the social and economic impacts of events and consumer behavior in tourism.

Émilie Crossley is a recent graduate of Cardiff University whose work explores tourist subjectivity from the perspective of psychosocial studies and critical psychology. Her doctoral research presented an in-depth, qualitative study of British volunteer tourists in Kenya, focusing on postcolonial constructions of the toured Other, understandings of care in a tourism context, and the development of 'ethical' identities over time. As an interdisciplinary scholar, Émilie has taught on a variety of degree programmes, including social psychology and tourism studies, and has a strong interest in pedagogical innovation. Her research interests include volunteer tourism, tourists' perceptions of poverty, spatialities of care, and longitudinal methods. She currently works in Communications at Otago Polytechnic in New Zealand.

John C. Crotts is a Professor of Hospitality and Tourism Management in the School of Business at the College of Charleston, located in Charleston, South Carolina, USA. Prior to this position, he lectured in the Advanced Business Programme on tourism subjects at Otago University, Dunedin, New Zealand and was Director of the Center for Tourism Research and Development at the University of Florida, USA. His research encompasses the areas of economic psychology, sales and negotiation strategy, and the management of cooperative alliances. He also serves as the North American Editor of *Tourism Management*. Crotts is an active consultant with both large and small organizations, most recently including Hyatt North America, Starbucks, the South Carolina Ports Authority, the US Department of Energy, and the cities of Grand Island, LA and Charleston, SC. Educated at Appalachian State, Minnesota State, and the University of Oregon, John earned a PhD in Leisure Studies and Services from the University of Oregon in 1989.

W. Glen Croy is a Senior Lecturer and Director of Education in the Department of Management, Monash University, and visiting researcher at the Oxford School of Hospitality Management, Oxford Brookes University. His teaching and research interests are in tourism, with special research interests in the role of media in tourism, higher education, and tourism in natural and protected areas. Reflecting the tourism and media interest, he focuses primarily on the complex and subtle roles of film in tourism image formation and destination planning, and is a co-convener of the International Tourism and Media (ITAM) conferences. Glen's interest in higher education is in three areas: first, the development, delivery and maintenance of authentic-experiential assessment and learning; second, students' research skills development; and third, student peer-learning. Merging the interests in tourism, media and natural and protected areas, Glen has been involved in a number of projects partnered with protected area agencies including on pre-visit communication, partnerships and non-use of parks.

Violet V. Cuffy holds a PhD in Sustainable Tourism Management from the University of Surrey, and is a Fellow of the Higher Education Academy, UK. Violet is currently a Senior Lecturer in Tourism and Events at Bedfordshire University, United Kingdom. She is a former Commonwealth Scholar and also a former Scholar of the Organization of American States. She has taught a wide range of Tourism and Hospitality courses, Operations Management, Professional Development for Strategic Managers, Small Business Management and Business Research Methods. She has a strong research interest in Island Tourism, Carnival Tourism, Heritage and Cultural Tourism, Diaspora Tourism, Destination Development and Marketing, Tourism Policy and Product Development, Tourism Education and Training, and Lifelong Learning. She also has a background in Tourism Consultancy at both the small business and government level with an emphasis on community tourism, and eco-tourism planning and development. Violet is the author of *The Book on Guest Houses*; editor of the forthcoming book *Carnival, Culture and Tourism* (CABI) and co-editor of *Lifelong Learning for Tourism: Key Concepts, Policy and Implementation* (Routledge).

Johan R. Edelheim is a dual citizen of Finland and Australia. He started his working career working in the tourism and hospitality industries and changed later to both vocational and higher education in the same fields. Johan's cross-disciplinary education includes diplomas and degrees from hospitality, business, education, philosophy and cultural studies. He directed the Multidimensional Tourism Institute (MTI), an innovative combination of tourism education and research at three different educational institutions representing three different educational dimensions, from August 2011 until August 2016, and continues working there now as a Research Fellow. Behind most of Johan's research lies a deeply rooted aim for humanism and equality. He looks at society and events with a purpose to highlight inequality in order to bring issues to common awareness. These matters of inequality can be found in all fields of studies and a conscious use of different theoretical lenses allows him to investigate matters. The majority of his research focuses on tourism, hospitality, leisure, education and society, quite often using different popular culture sources for data collection. Three distinct categories can be distinguished from his publications; culturally critical tourism and hospitality studies; tourism and hospitality education studies; and clarifications of tourism and hospitality concepts.

Chris Fanning has had a long involvement with the tourism industry as practitioner and tourism lecturer. As Lecturer and Coordinator of Tourism Industry Work-Integrated Learning at Flinders University, Chris has formed strong business relationships with a wide range of industry partners and has been able to combine her excellent practical knowledge of the sector with the mentoring of aspiring young professionals and students looking to have a career in tourism and events. Chris has placed over 1000 students with the tourism industry, primarily within South Australia but also across Australia and internationally. Chris regularly runs professional development workshops for the tourism industry on Customer Service, Tour Guiding and Interpretation. Her research interests include interpretation for children, destination management and work-integrated learning. Chris has a diverse background including 20 years' experience in the Finance Industry and experience as a tour guide, site interpreter, tourism officer, conference secretary, event organizer and as a visitor information centre officer. As a tourism educator Chris is acutely aware of the importance of educating work-ready students and working with the tourism and event industry to ensure their workforce needs are recognized.

Jo-Anne Ferreira is Associate Professor and Deputy Head of School (Teaching and Learning) in the School of Education at Southern Cross University, Gold Coast, Australia. Jo-Anne's research field is sociology of education, with a special interest in post-structuralist theories of identity, embodiment and power, and environmental and sustainability education. Recent research focuses on systems-based change in teacher education and strategies and techniques deployed by environmental and sustainability educators to empower learners to become environmental citizens.

Babu P. George has more than fifteen years of university teaching, research, and administrative service experience, in the US and internationally. Currently, he is Associate Professor of Management at Fort Hays State University, USA. In the recent past, he served as Professor of Business Research Methods in the Swiss Management Center University, faculty for DBA programme in the University of Liverpool, and as Visiting Professor in the University of Nevada Las Vegas. He is the editor of the *International Journal of Qualitative Research in Services*. He holds a PhD in Management, focusing on tourism marketing. Challenges in institution building in international settings is one of his current research interests.

Rebekka Goodman received her PhD from the University of Exeter in Human Geography with a focus on sustainable tourism. Her current academic interests include sustainable tourism development, community-based eco-tourism, power and politics of development and qualitative research methods. She is currently a Lecturer at the School of Community Resources and Development at Arizona State University. Goodman has nearly six years of experience in curriculum development in sustainability and tourism including the creation and implementation of study abroad programmes in Switzerland, Mexico, Chile, Guatemala and Australia. She runs two programmes focused on enhancing ASU's School of Community Resources and Development's existing curriculum.

Catherine Gorman lectures in sustainable tourism, culture and heritage, tourism marketing and sustainable facilities management at the School of Hospitality Management and Tourism at the Dublin Institute of Technology, Ireland. Prior to lecturing, Catherine gained significant sectoral experience working with the National Tourist Board, where she was involved in development and marketing tourism at local, regional and national level. This connection with the industry acted as one of the catalysts for the Students in Action initiative first rolled out in 2012. Academic outputs and research interests relate to evaluating collaborative strategies, aspects of cultural and heritage tourism, environmental tourism and ecotourism. Catherine is a member of Campus Engage, which promotes civic engagement as part of education in tertiary institutions and universities in Ireland and is a member of ICOMOS Ireland.

Kevin Griffin is a Lecturer and former Head of Tourism at the Dublin Institute of Technology. His academic and teaching interests are quite eclectic and his key activity spans religious tourism and pilgrimage, sustainable tourism, cultural tourism, heritage interpretation, local history and education. He has written, presented and edited a range of work on various topics in the sphere of tourism, events and local studies, being keen to undertake research of both an applied and a theoretical nature. Kevin actively participates in a number of international tourism networks including the European Tourism Futures Institute, the UNESCO-UNITWIN Culture Tourism and Development network and the International Religious Tourism and Pilgrimage Group, which he has led through the production of numerous publications and foundation of an international journal. He recently worked on a three-year, fifteen-partner, one million euro EU-funded Tempus IV project entitled NETOUR, which aims to support the development of tertiary tourism education in Russia. Kevin has also developed an international profile in the area of sustainable tourism, and the DIT-ACHIEV Model for Sustainable Tourism Planning, which he developed with his colleague Sheila Flanagan, is recognized internationally as an exemplar of best practice in the area of sustainable tourism indicators.

Anja Hergesell is a Research Assistant at the University of Technology Sydney and a PhD student at Vienna University of Economics and Business. Her PhD studies examine the determinants of environmentally friendly tourist behaviour and opportunities for behaviour change. Anja holds a Master's degree in European Tourism Management from Bournemouth University and has previously worked as a Researcher and Lecturer at MODUL University Vienna and the University of Southern Denmark. Anja has been involved with the B.E.S.T. Education Network since 2003, serving first as secretary and currently as executive committee member.

Freya Higgins-Desbiolles is a Senior Lecturer in Tourism in the School of Management at the University of South Australia. She has researched and taught on Indigenous tourism for more than a decade; her work involves an Indigenous rights approach and is based on Indigenous community engagement and collaborations. Her work through the course Tourism and Indigenous Peoples has received numerous awards for community engagement, teaching and research, including an Australian national award, the Australian Teaching and Learning Council's Citation Award for Outstanding Contributions to Student Learning in 2009.

Anne-Mette Hjalager is Professor and Research Director at the Danish Centre for Rural Research, University of Southern Denmark. Her areas of interest and publication are, among others, local development, innovation and labour market issues in tourism. She is involved in transnational research in the fields of rural outdoor activities, well-being and ecosystems services and in the exploration of innovation issues in tourism. She is editor-in-chief for the recently launched research journal *Gastronomy and Tourism*. Anne-Mette Hjalager is the co-creator of the tourism learning platform www.innotour.com.

Patrick J. Holladay is an Assistant Professor in the School of Hospitality, Sport and Tourism Management at Troy University. He received his PhD from Clemson University in Parks, Recreation & Tourism Management. His research focuses on eco- and sustainable tourism, community development through tourism, tourism planning and global issues in tourism. He has worked in conservation, environmental education, ecotourism, national park management, sustainability and community-based tourism development in Eastern Europe, the Caribbean, South-East Asia, Central and South America, as well a myriad of projects in the United States.

Eva Holmberg is a Senior Lecturer of Tourism and Methods at Haaga-Helia University of Applied Sciences. She teaches students on both Bachelor's and Master's courses such as brand management, responsible tourism and destination management. Her research interests are mainly related to destination management and development, branding and responsible tourism. In the EAKR-funded Tourism Co-opetion Network Project (TOUNET), she was the project manager for the study related to the economic impacts of tourism in Uusimaa region.

Laurel Horton-Tognazzini is with the Australian School of Management as an adjunct research associate. She graduated from Florida State University with an undergraduate degree in education and from Rollins College with a Master's degree in counseling. Laurel is a Licensed Mental Health Counselor in the state of Florida with an extensive clinical work history including a private practice in Winter Park, Florida. She also is a national peer reviewer for Prevention Child Abuse: Healthy Families America. Her research focuses on education, with an emphasis on MOOCs.

Cathy H.C. Hsu is a Chair Professor in the School of Hotel and Tourism Management at The Hong Kong Polytechnic University (PolyU). Prior to joining PolyU, she was teaching at Kansas State University and Iowa State University, USA. She is the Editor-in-Chief of the *Journal of Teaching in Travel & Tourism*. She also serves on 10 journal editorial boards. She is the editor of the book, *Global Tourism Higher Education: Past, Present, and Future* (2005) and co-editor of the book, *Tourism Education: Global Issues and Trends* (2015). Her research focuses have been hotel branding, hospitality marketing, tourist behaviours, service quality, and the economic and social impacts of casino gaming. She has obtained numerous extramural and intramural grants and has over 200 refereed publications. She received the John Wiley & Sons Lifetime Research Achievement Award in 2009 and the International Society of Travel and Tourism Educator's Martin Oppermann Memorial Award for Lifetime Contribution to Tourism Education in 2011.

Karen Hughes is a Senior Lecturer and Programme Leader for the Bachelor of International Hotel and Tourism Management programme at the University of Queensland. She has been teaching and researching in tourism for approximately twenty years, specializing in the areas of environmental interpretation, visitor management and sustainable tourism. Karen has a practical and creative approach to teaching, one that is informed by her research interests and expertise in the design and evaluation of visitor learning experiences in museums, zoos, national parks and heritage settings. She believes that as in visitor settings, the key to successful learning experiences is to provide practical examples, interactive classroom exercises, and opportunities that encourage students to discuss, dissect and extend their in-class learning to 'real world' situations. Karen is currently working on several research projects investigating the impact of interpretation on visitors' environmental behaviour, as well as exploring ways of using interpretation to familiarize Chinese visitors with Australian landscapes.

Gayle Jennings is the Director of Research, Imagine Consulting Group International Pty Ltd. She is also an Adjunct Professor of Tourism Management, Department of Tourism, Sport and Hotel Management, Griffith University, Gold Coast Campus. Gayle has a variety of experiences across various sectors associated with education, training and research. She is a qualified educator and experienced educational change consultant. Gayle has worked in a national government agency responsible for natural and marine area management, in planning and management as well as in research and monitoring. Gayle's research agenda focuses on practical and applied research for business and industry, research training and education, qualitative methodologies, and quality tourism experiences. She has been the sole author and editor of a number of books and has written book chapters and journal articles across a range of topics relating to education, theoretical paradigms that inform research processes, water-based tourism, and quality tourism experiences.

Olga Junek is a Lecturer in Tourism and Events Management at Victoria University. Her lengthy overseas work experience in education and her early work experience in tourism have given her a broad international perspective in these study areas as well as an understanding of international students. Using grounded theory methodology in her PhD thesis on international students and their leisure time provided her with a good understanding of this methodology and its strengths in qualitative research. Further research interests include crisis and tourism, tourism and events management education and curriculum design and volunteering among international students.

Ulrike Kachel is a Lecturer in Business Management and Marketing at Charles Darwin University in Sydney, Australia. Ulrike has a strong background in both the information technology (IT) and tourism sectors, including online marketing and platform development, touristic events management as well as working in dive tourism in the Caribbean. Ulrike's research interests include sustainable tourism management and marketing, consumer behaviour, climate change, environmental practices and learning, conservation volunteering, online research, as well as higher education research. In her PhD from Griffith University in Australia, she developed the grounded theory of 'Mediating Climate Change', exploring tourists' climate change perceptions and influences on travel behaviours.

Magdalena Kachniewska is the Dean of Master Studies and Associate Professor in Tourism Department, Warsaw School of Economics (WSE). She is a member of the Scientific Council of World Economy Collegium in WSE and a member of the Tourism Research Working Group at the Polish Ministry of Sport and Tourism. She is an expert of the Hotel Market Institute. She is an honorary member of the Gdansk Agrotourism Society, senior consultant of the Polish Tourism Organisation and Mazovia District Regional Tourism Organisation. Magdalena has been the leading consultant at the opening stage of 26 hotels in Poland and Slovakia. She is a juror in numerous competitions of HoReCa enterprises, propagator of the concept of e-marketing and new technologies in tourism, a member of the Scientific Council of e-TravelForum and Chairperson of the competition committee in 'New Technologies in Travel Sector Tech. Travel Award' contest. Until 2010 she was the president of Efekt Hotele Co., General Manager of Best Western Krakow Premier Hotel, General Manager of Express by Holiday Inn Hotel. Until 2012 she was a member of the Supervisory Board at the European Mortgage Fund (managing four hotels in Poland). She is a member of the Scientific Council of *Folia Turistica* and *Journal of Eastern European and Central Asian Research*.

Nadzeya Kalbaska is a Lecturer and Postdoctoral Researcher at the Faculty of Communication Sciences at the Università della Svizzera italiana (USI), Lugano, Switzerland. Her research focus is on the intersection of eLearning and eTourism, specifically on the use of Information and Communication Technologies for Human Resource Management in the hospitality and tourism industry. In USI she leads the content creation team of 'eTourism: Communication Perspectives' MOOC, launched in October 2015. Nadzeya manages various applied research projects at the webatelier.net laboratory. She serves at the IFITT-International Federation for IT and Travel and Tourism as General Secretary.

Marina Karlqvist is a Senior Lecturer in Marketing at Haaga-Helia University of Applied Sciences, Porvoo Unit. She is a Master of Science in Economics. Her main interests in marketing focus on service marketing, visual marketing and design. She has worked for many years with different projects. She also functions as thesis coordinator at Haaga-Helia.

Sandra Kensbock is a Lecturer in the Department of Tourism, Sport and Hotel Management at Griffith University. She teaches international tourism and hotel management related courses. Sandie's research interests are predicated on a socialist feminist philosophical perspective investigating the sociological aspects of tourism, hospitality and events. Her specific research interests are in the fields of hospitality employment relations, sustainable tourism and tourism entrepreneurship. Her research appears in leading tourism management, research and tourism education journals. Sandie has a keen interest in theoretical aspects of qualitative research and especially in grounded theory methodologies.

Brian King is Professor and Associate Dean at The Hong Kong Polytechnic University. He was previously Professor of Tourism at Victoria University in Australia (1998–2012) and is originally from Scotland. In addition to his academic roles he has occupied various university leadership positions in Australia including Pro Vice-Chancellor (Industry and Community) and Pro Vice-Chancellor (Students). His research expertise is in tourism marketing with an emphasis on cultural dimensions and emerging Asia-Pacific markets, particularly China. He has published several books on tourism marketing, VFR travel, resorts and Asia-Pacific tourism. He is joint editor-in-chief of *Tourism, Culture & Communication* and has held visiting professorships in Italy, Fiji, the UK and USA. He has consulted for international agencies on tourism, human resource development and marketing. His industry experience includes manager and/or director roles in airlines, tour operations, destination management, cruise operations and hotels. He is a Fellow of the International Academy for the Study of Tourism (IAST) and of the Council of Australasian Tourism and Hospitality Education (CAUTHE). He chairs the assessment panel for the International Centre of Excellence for Tourism and Hospitality Education (THE-ICE).

Janne J. Liburd is Professor of Tourism and Director of the Centre for Tourism, Innovation and Culture at the University of Southern Denmark. She is a cultural anthropologist and her research interests are in the fields of higher education, innovation and sustainable tourism development. She is the co-founder of the European Master in Tourism Management and the INNOTOUR platform. Professor Liburd is the former Chair of the BEST Education Network (2005–10) and present Chair of the UNESCO World Heritage Wadden Sea National Park.

Kevin Lyons is a Professor of Tourism and Management at the University of Newcastle, Australia and was recently appointed Deputy Head of the Faculty of Business and Law. His research focuses upon the intersections between volunteering, tourism and community engagement, regional tourism planning and management, and transformational learning through travel.

Ceri Macleod is an experienced specialist in providing cross-faculty support and leadership in the development and delivery of effective work-integrated learning practices in higher education. Ceri worked in the Australian higher education sector for many years, prior to which she worked in the UK public sector. She has a professional and academic background in economic development, specializing in the promotion of long-term economic growth and employment. She has an Honours degree in Industrial Economics and a Master's in Local and Regional Economic Development. She now lives in New Zealand, after switching from academia to the tourism sector in the country's beautiful South Island.

Amy Maguire is a Senior Lecturer in Public International Law at the University of Newcastle Law School, Australia. Amy's doctoral research and subsequent work considers the right of self-determination under international law, with particular focus on the right's capacity to address the legacies and experience of colonialism in settler societies. In this context, Amy is particularly interested in the relationships between international and domestic law and Indigenous peoples in Australia. She also conducts research in the fields in public international law, human rights, climate change law, refugee rights, Indigenous legal issues, and the Indigenization of law curricula. Amy is interested in the social impacts and potential of law, and seeks to explore inter-disciplinary approaches to law reform. As a teacher of law to undergraduate and postgraduate students, Amy is committed to the exploration of Indigenous experiences, perspectives and laws and the benefits this brings for her students, both Indigenous and non-Indigenous.

Ady Milman is a Professor in the Rosen College of Hospitality Management at the University of Central Florida. He earned a Master's degree in Tourism Planning and Development from the University of Surrey in England, and a PhD in Business Administration from the University of Massachusetts. His background includes extensive research, consulting, publications, public speaking, and presentations in the fields of marketing, strategic management, hospitality and tourism. Following his practice as the Disney Sabbatic Professor, he developed a curriculum in Theme Park and Attraction Management. Ady Milman is often invited to offer lectures in Austria, Canada, France, Israel, the Netherlands, Puerto Rico and Portugal. In 2014, he spent his sabbatical at the Management Center Innsbruck, Austria as a Fulbright Scholar. He was also the recipient of ISTTE's Martin Oppermann Memorial Award, the Canadian Pacific Visiting Scholar grant at the University of Calgary, and the Rosen College Faculty Award for Outstanding Service.

Massimo Morellato is a Lecturer at the Department of Tourism and Events at Auckland University of Technology, New Zealand. Massimo has conducted his doctoral research on mega events at the Centre for Tourism Policy and Research, Simon Fraser University, Canada. Massimo holds a PhD in Marketing and Management, a Doctor Magistrale degree in Computer Science and a Postgraduate Certificate in Education and Pedagogy. Massimo's research interests span across tourism, marketing and leisure studies and he is particularly attracted by interdisciplinary studies that lead to more sustainable use of natural and cultural resources. Massimo has acquired extensive teaching experience at different levels of education. In Italy, he renewed didactical and educational programmes according to European Commission guidelines on digital competence. In New Zealand he introduced an experiential and digital-enhanced learning project in the Bachelor of Arts in Event Management. His involvement in digital and mobile learning initiatives is driven by the possibility to empower students as active creators of knowledge.

Claudia Mössenlechner has been active in the field of teaching and higher tourism education for some 20 years, focusing on English as a second language, communication skills, intercultural training and leadership. Her courses and coaching sessions focus on language, communication and leadership and management for tourism and hospitality businesses. In her function as a head of MCI Learning Solutions, Claudia is responsible for developing and overseeing eLearning solutions and online graduate programmes including curriculum development. She has conceptualized courses for tertiary education as well as for private and public companies in Austria and Italy. In addition, she has extensive experience as an examiner and accreditor (European Higher Education Space).

Ziene Mottiar is a Lecturer in the School of Hospitality Management and Tourism, College of Arts and Tourism, Dublin Institute of Technology, Ireland. Her key areas of research interest in tourism are in the areas of entrepreneurship, destination development and regional development. She has published in a variety of books and journals including *Journal of Vacation Marketing*, *Tourism Planning & Development*, *Leisure Studies* and *International Small Business Journal*. From an educational perspective she is particularly interested in innovative teaching methods, student feedback, video in education and the dissertation experience for students and supervisors, and has researched, published and created teaching materials in these areas.

Jamie Murphy is a Professor and Research Director at the Australian School of Management. His background includes European Marketing Manager for PowerBar and Greg Lemond Bicycles, Lead Academic for the Google Online Marketing Challenge, and a PhD from Florida State University. Professor Murphy's industry and academic experience spans continents and includes hundreds of academic publications and presentations, as well as dozens of *New York Times* and *Wall Street Journal* stories. His research focus is on the effective use of the Internet for citizens, businesses and governments, particularly MOOCs.

Aliisa Mylonas has extensive experience teaching in both secondary and higher education settings. In 2009, she joined Tourism at The University of Queensland as a Learning Manager, enabling her to make a significant contribution to improving students' learning experiences. This has been achieved by directly supporting academics with initiatives linked to programme and course design, curriculum alignment, first year and capstone experiences, revamped teaching approaches and the creation of authentic assessment tasks. Aliisa is also an accomplished facilitator, education consultant, and 'critical friend' and mentor to university academics keen to reflect on, and share, their practice. She particularly enjoys supporting early career academics as they transition into the demands, rewards and challenges of teaching, learning and assessment in higher education.

Ara Pachmayer is an Assistant Professor at the Humboldt State University. She received her PhD from Arizona State University in the School of Community Resources and Development. Her research interests include international education, impact of tourism development on perception of community life, sustainable and community-based tourism development and qualitative research methods, the common thread in the research being how hosts and travellers experience tourism and the resulting impacts on communities and individuals. She has 15 years of experience in the field of international education and has created and assisted in the development of numerous study abroad programmes in many locations. Pachmayer has also led multiple groups of university students on educational programmes abroad.

Georgios C. Papageorgiou is Head of the International Tourism and Hospitality Management Department at Deree – the American College of Greece. Having completed studies in tourism business administration, tourism policy and management, and academic practice in Greece and the UK, he was previously a Lecturer in Tourism at the University of Surrey and the Academic Dean of Alpine Center in Greece. His experience focuses on academic quality assurance and programme design in the areas of tourism and hospitality, and his research interests include tourism marketing, tourism policy planning and development, tourism education, qualitative research methodologies, and the relationship between tourism and popular culture – in particular music, film and literature.

Anna Para is a PhD candidate in the Collegium of World Economy at the Warsaw School of Economics (WSE) and is currently working on her PhD thesis. Her research interests include: tourism management, HR management, innovativeness, competitiveness, CSR and sustainable development. She graduated from the Warsaw School of Economics in 2011, where she studied International Relations as well as Management. In 2011 she took part in a one-semester exchange programme in Germany at Johannes Gutenberg University in Mainz. She has gained professional experience in different tourism companies.

Philip L. Pearce is the first Professor of Tourism in Australia and is based at James Cook University. He holds a First Class Honours degree in Psychology and a Diploma of Education from the University of Adelaide and earned a Doctorate from the University of Oxford studying tourists in Europe. He has held a Fulbright scholarship at Harvard University. In 2008 he won a national level award from the Australian Learning and Teaching Council (ALTC) for advancing tourism education and for the supervision of Doctoral level students, having now successfully supervised 40 such students. He is the author of 250 publications and 15 books on tourism. He was awarded the James Cook University President's Award for overall research excellence in 2012. In 2016 Philip Pearce became the first social science researcher to be recognized as a Distinguished Professor of James Cook University. He is a frequent keynote speaker at tourism conferences, particularly in Asia. His special interest areas are tourist behaviour, including positive psychology applied to tourism, and Chinese tourism. He has taught multiple international specialist tourism courses in Bangkok, Thailand; Sardinia and Milan, Italy; Innsbruck, Austria and in Singapore. He supervises a large number of current PhD students and has been the principal supervisor for successful graduates from 12 countries. He currently supervises PhD students from Australia, China, Malaysia, Russia, Singapore and Thailand.

Bernadette Quinn is a Human Geographer working in the Department of Tourism at the Dublin Institute of Technology, Ireland. She teaches a number of modules relating to tourism studies, tourism policy and international event management to students on undergraduate and postgraduate tourism programmes and is Programme Tutor for the DIT's MSc Event Management. Bernadette is an active researcher with a particular interest in festivals and cultural events, cultural and heritage tourism, as well as women and leisure. She has a strong publications track record, having published her first book *Key Concepts in Event Management* in 2013, and numerous articles in journals such as the *Annals of Tourism Research*, *Journal of Sustainable Tourism*, *Urban Studies*, *Tourism Geographies* and the *Journal of Policy Research in Tourism, Leisure & Events*.

Sarah Rawlinson joined the University of Derby 20 years ago after a career in the travel industry where she specialized in group travel. She is passionate about experiential learning and making sure that students have the skills and knowledge that employers are seeking in today's graduates. Sarah is currently Head of Department, Hotel, Resort & Spa Management at the University.

Dirk Reiser is Professor of Sustainable Tourism at the Rhine-Waal University of Applied Sciences in Kleve, Germany. He is a social scientist. His primary research interests include sustainable tourism, wildlife tourism, events, and globalization. He is a member of the expert panel for the European Tourism Indicator System (ETIS) and of the Deutsche Gesellschaft für Tourismuswissenschaft (DGT).

Jarmo Ritalahti is a Principal Lecturer of Tourism at HAAGA-HELIA University of Applied Sciences. His main research interests in tourism focus on intermediation and business tourism and pedagogical development and pedagogy in higher education. He was responsible for the new pedagogical approach and curricula development at HAAGA-HELIA's Porvoo Campus project in 2007–11. Ritalahti is also doing regional tourism research and development projects.

Peter Ryan is the founder of the Higher Education Leadership Institute. Over the past 20 years Peter has assisted a number of organizations to navigate the complex regulatory framework which ensures the quality of Australia's higher education providers, specializing in the areas of regulatory approvals, quality assurance, and corporate and academic governance. Peter has also undertaken academic due diligence on a number of acquisitions on behalf of prospective purchasers and provided strategic advice in relation to regulatory matters associated with takeover and merger activity in the Australian private higher education sector. Peter maintains a bank of research and statistical data on the size and make-up of the Australian private higher education sector. Peter's current research focuses on the commercialization of MOOCs.

Theresa Ryan is a Lecturer and Researcher in the College of Arts and Tourism at the Dublin Institute of Technology Ireland. Her background is in marketing and international business and her current research interests include tourism, memory and interpretation, tourism history, destination development and entrepreneurship. She has an avid interest in exploring and adopting interactive and innovative approaches to learning and sees this as an essential part of her role as a lecturer. This has included the adoption of new technologies for teaching, learning and assessment purposes, including wikis, blogs and ePortfolios. She is particularly interested in facilitating collaborative, problem-focused, generative learning. She has been involved in 'The Students in Action' Programme in DIT since its inception in 2012 and sees this as a key means of encouraging learners to become fully immersed in learning, to develop new strategies and to solve problems in a real-time situation to the benefit of both the learners and the tourism communities with which they engage.

Nicolai Scherle is Professor of Tourism Management and Intercultural Communication at the BiTS, University of Applied Sciences in Iserlohn, Germany. He is a cultural geographer and is head of the International Management for Service Industries programme. His primary research interests include entrepreneurship and internationalization, intercultural communication and diversity, and tourism media. He is a Fellow of the Royal Geographical Society, as well as a member of the Center for Corporate Citizenship and the advisory network for intercultural communication FORAREA.

Stephen Schweinsberg is a Lecturer in Sustainable Management in the UTS Business School. Stephen coordinates the core unit Integrating Business Perspectives, which is completed by all first year students in the Bachelor of Business degree. He also teaches in a range of research methods and other subjects across the Bachelor of Management and Master of Management degree programmes. Stephen's current research interests are in the areas of Honours pedagogy in business education, the social impacts of coal seam gas development in Australian rural communities and national park-based tourism management.

Mary-Anne Smith has over twenty years of industry experience in most sectors of the tourism and hospitality industry, within Australia and internationally. Her frontline managerial experience in travel agencies and hotels developed her customer focus, while her airline and tour wholesaling practice developed managerial and corporate skills. Mary-Anne began studies at Griffith University, Gold Coast, Queensland, Australia in 1999, completing an MBA followed by a MITHM (with Honours) and a MEDL (Higher Ed) through Macquarie University, Sydney. She is a recent PhD graduate, whose thesis focused on Quality Tourism Experiences. For Mary-Anne, education is the key to employability. Having both industry knowledge and academic understanding, she changed careers. She has taught for over ten years in technical colleges and at postgraduate level at Griffith University. Mary-Anne intends to continue teaching, publishing from her PhD and furthering her quality experiences studies in teaching and tourism.

Dimitrios P. Stergiou holds a PhD from the University of Surrey. Currently he is Assistant Professor of Tourism Management at the Hellenic Open University. He also holds appointments as Adjunct Assistant Professor at the Technological Educational Institutes of Athens and Thessaloniki, Greece. He has over 10 years of experience in teaching, learning and research in the wider areas of tourism education and tourism management. Alongside his academic duties he has worked with several government and private organizations on tourism project work.

Michael A. Tarrant is Josiah Meigs Distinguished Teaching Professor at the University of Georgia in Athens, GA, USA. He is the founding Director of Global Programs in Sustainability (www.DiscoverAbroad.uga.edu) started in 2001, which provides study abroad programmes for approximately 400 students a year throughout the South Pacific and South-East Asia. He maintains a campus-wide research programme addressing the global learning outcomes of international education and his research interests extend to the human dimensions of natural resources, educational travel and tourism, and attitude–behaviour correspondence.

Lynn Vanzo is an experienced Work-Integrated Learning (WIL) administrator in the School of Humanities & Creative Arts at Flinders University, Adelaide, Australia. Her position requires strong working relationships with key stakeholders, including industry professional organizations and government agencies, enabling placement and project opportunities for a diverse range of students. WIL programmes in the school occur in the areas of International Tourism, Screen & Media, Archaeology, Creative Writing, Languages and High Achievers programme (Bachelor of Arts). Her position entails providing high-level advice to academics, students and placement providers, ensuring that WIL policy and procedures, WH&S and insurance requirements are adhered to. Lynn has worked at Flinders University for 12 years. She has a Bachelor's degree in Cultural Tourism and a Master of Teaching (Secondary). Most recently her research has focused on employability and the student benefits of undertaking placements and research into WIL leadership.

Catherine Vertesi began her academic career in 1980 at the University of British Columbia in Marketing and Strategic Management. She was one of the first in Canada to introduce mobility programmes for students and grew them to become 25 per cent of the BBA U/G and 50 per cent of the MBA students' experience. She joined the President's team to work on a variety of internationalization initiatives including ESL pathway programmes and professional education undertakings. In 2001 she became Dean of Business at Capilano University and was named Vice President, Education with a portfolio that included management, tourism and international programmes in 2006. Catherine has been active in the international education associations worldwide, assuming leadership positions and promoting excellence in international education practices. She received awards from UBC for teaching, curriculum innovation and student service and in 2003 received the CBIE International Leadership Award for Canada. In 2012 she was awarded the Woman of Distinction Award for Education in Vancouver and in 2013 she was given the Distinguished International Leadership Award for the Province of British Columbia. Since beginning at Capilano she has initiated exchanges and field schools, introduced internationalization elements into Capilano courses and led the international centre in developing greater integration of the international students attending Capilano. In partnership with Switzerland's FHNW, Catherine has four times led Canadian faculty from 17 institutions to Europe for professional development.

Stephen Wearing is at the University of Newcastle, Australia. He has conducted numerous projects and lectures worldwide and is the author of 13 books and over 100 articles dealing with issues surrounding leisure and sustainable tourism. His practical experience as an environmental and park planner at local, state and international level has provided him with real world experiences that he brings to his teaching and research. His research interests include ecotourism, community based and volunteer tourism, environmentalism, sociology of leisure and tourism and social sciences in protected area management.

Alan Williams is the former CEO and Managing Director of the Australian School of Management, and past President of the Asia Pacific Council of Hotel, Restaurant and Industry Educators (APacCHRIE). He is current Director of the International Centre of Excellence in Tourism and Hospitality Education (THE-ICE), a not-for-profit international hospitality and tourism accreditation agency and global network of leading quality education institutions. Alan has been in the hospitality and tourism education industry for more than 26 years. He is passionate about education at the vocational and higher education levels and has presented at numerous conferences. A recent focus is successful development and use of Massive Open Online Courses (MOOCs) in hospitality and tourism.

John Willison is a Senior Lecturer in the School of Education, University of Adelaide and teaches in the Master's in Education programme. He is currently using and evaluating interactive learning modules in advance of face-to-face sessions to flip the classroom for educators enrolled in the Master's. He collaborates closely with colleagues across the university and this work has led to rich and varied aspects of curriculum design and assessment, including at national and international levels. John's principal research interest centres on the ways that academics conceptualize and implement the explicit development of their students' research skills in content-rich courses. He leads an initiative considering Research Skill Development (RSD) and assessment in the curricula of disciplines in all faculties across whole undergraduate and postgraduate degrees. This long-term project focuses on degree-programme outcomes of RSD use and draws heavily on interviews with graduates, academics and, in the future, with industry partners.

Erica Wilson is Associate Professor and Deputy Head, Teaching and Learning in the School of Business and Tourism at Southern Cross University, Australia. She has taught across a range of subject areas, including special interest tourism, research methods, and sustainable tourism. Erica's research publications focus on gender and tourism, slow tourism, and critical approaches and methodologies in tourism. Following her interest in critical theory, Erica has applied this lens more recently to the scholarship of teaching, exploring the potential of critically reflective practice (CRP) and transformative change through Education for Sustainability.

Peter Wiltshier is Senior Lecturer and Programme Leader for Tourism Management at the University of Derby. He conducts research to ensure that the public and private sector work together to develop resources and skills for communities to take charge of their own destinies. It is the pursuit of bottom-up planning and policy development that is sought and is to be enabled through his work and teaching.

Nicholas Wise has lectured in the areas of tourism and recreation management and his academic background and PhD is in human geography from Kent State University in Ohio, USA. Nicholas has conducted research focusing on sport in the Dominican Republic and Argentina and tourism in Croatia and Serbia, publishing broadly across several disciplines. His academic interests involve urban and regional regeneration, sports geography, sports tourism, competitiveness and place image/identity. For his teaching, he regularly uses Google Earth in his lectures, especially in classes focusing on sustainable regeneration and tourism planning as part of his spatial perspective and emphasis in his visual method of lecturing. He has also published articles on the use of Google Earth in research in the *Journal of Community Psychology* and *Cityscape: A Journal of Policy Development and Research.*

Tamara Young is a Senior Lecturer in Tourism Studies in the Newcastle Business School at the University of Newcastle, Australia. Tamara combines critical tourism theory and cultural methodologies to examine the role of tourism media as an interface between traveller cultures and travelled cultures, and the role that cultural learning in travel experiences plays in the shaping of traveller identities. Recent work includes examining representations of Aboriginal Australia in tourism media and backpacker experiences of Indigenous cultures and Indigenous cultural landscapes. Tamara is co-author of *Tourist Cultures: Identity, Place and the Traveller* (Sage, 2010), interrogating the experiential and educational aspects of tourism cultures and their significance in contemporary global society. These longstanding interests complement and inform her current research agenda focused on critical perspectives and pedagogies in tourism education, particularly the incorporation of non-Western knowledges in curriculum design and development.

Anita Zehrer is Professor and Head of the Family Business Center at MCI Management Center Innsbruck, Deputy Head of the MCI Academic Council, Adjunct Professor at the University of Notre Dame in Sydney as well as Vice-President of the German Association for Tourism Research. Since 2014 she has also been a Member of the Tourism Advisory Board of the Federal Ministry of Foreign Affairs and Energy, Germany and, since 2016, she is tourism expert at the EU Committee of Regions in Brussels. Her research interests are diverse and include family business management, service experiences and service design, entrepreneurship and leadership, tourism epistemology and tourism education. Anita has fifteen years of experience in education (both undergraduate and graduate level) and research in the tourism field.

Hanqin Qiu Zhang is a Professor of International Tourism at Hong Kong Polytechnic University. She received her BA from Nankai University in Mainland China, her MA from the University of Waterloo in Canada, and her PhD from the University of Strathclyde in the UK. She has been teaching Chinese tourism-related subjects at both undergraduate and graduate level. Her research interests are tourism studies, consumer behaviour, and Chinese hotel and tourism development and policy issues.

Preface

The notion of universities as places of learning began over a thousand years ago and some universities rightly claim that they are amongst the oldest continuous institutions in the world, perhaps only surpassed by a handful of businesses and religious institutions. While the curriculum has changed dramatically over the last thousand years, with the introduction of new disciplines and fields, teaching and learning techniques have changed little until very recently. Arguably teaching and learning has changed more in the past 30 years than the previous 1000 years. While several books have been devoted to tourism education, this *Handbook* represents the most comprehensive attempt to address the more focused topic of teaching and learning. The purpose of this *Handbook* is to provide an international perspective on contemporary issues and future directions in teaching and learning in tourism.

The various contributions in this *Handbook* draw on a wide range of disciplinary perspectives and focus on the full spectrum of teaching and learning techniques in higher education, from undergraduate programs to the supervision of research students. Key themes include:

- the knowledge, skills, capabilities and values needed by tourism graduates;
- the assimilation and assurance of standards and threshold learning outcomes in curriculum design, pedagogy and assessment;
- the diversity and complexity of the tourism curriculum space and the importance of alternative disciplinary perspectives;
- the impact of technology-enhanced learning on teaching and learning paradigms;
- internationalization and student mobility in tourism education; and
- work-integrated learning, co-op education and other pedagogies that enhance employability outcomes and bridge the gap between theory and practice.

Chapters are organized into eight major sections:

- 'Part I: Understanding and Developing Graduate Capabilities' focuses on the capabilities expected from graduates and techniques for developing some of these capabilities.
- 'Part II: Technology-enabled Learning' starts with the idea that educators need to rethink the role of technology in tourism education, before presenting several innovative applications of technology in teaching and learning.
- 'Part III: Experiential Learning' commences with a discussion of the principles and practice of experiential learning in tourism, with subsequent chapters providing examples of linking learning with paid work experience, work-integrated learning, action learning, learning laboratories and fieldtrips.
- 'Part IV: Internationalization' includes three contributions that examine strategic frameworks and approaches to internationalizing the tourism curriculum.

- 'Part V: Critical Perspectives and Education for Sustainability' presents a series of thought-provoking chapters that illustrate how teaching and learning can foster critical awareness and concern about economic, social, cultural, political and ecological interactions in tourism.
- 'Part VI: Teaching, Learning and Research' examines the nexus between teaching and research and the often neglected role of teaching and learning in research supervision.
- 'Part VII: Contemporary Issues in Teaching and Learning' examines a range of topics including standards and quality assurance, the role of industry advisory boards, social capital building, and innovation and change.
- 'Part VIII: Conclusions' includes two final chapters that attempt to summarize and synthesize the key themes across the entire volume.

Editing this *Handbook* has provided us with a truly remarkable insight into the diversity of innovative teaching and learning approaches used by educators in our field. While the winds of change that sweep across higher education are accelerating, the many creative ideas and thought-provoking debates presented in this *Handbook* fill us with optimism. We hope the many contributions from educators around the world will enrich discussions about the future of teaching and learning in tourism.

Pierre Benckendorff
Anita Zehrer

Acknowledgements

We would like to thank the many tourism educators who are passionate about innovation in teaching and learning. Your patience and professionalism during a lengthy editorial process made this a very enjoyable project. When we initially planned this *Handbook* we anticipated a much smaller volume but the response to our call for chapters revealed a healthy enthusiasm and appetite for the scholarship of teaching and learning in our field. Your willingness to share the many perspectives and examples found in this book is indicative of the creativity and commitment to teaching and learning in tourism.

We would especially like to thank Alex O'Connell and the team at Edward Elgar for first raising the possibility of a handbook of teaching and learning in tourism, and for patiently supporting us with words of encouragement and advice throughout the project.

PART I

UNDERSTANDING AND DEVELOPING GRADUATE CAPABILITIES

1 Tourism education and industry expectations in Greece: (re)minding the gap

Dimitrios P. Stergiou and David Airey

1. INTRODUCTION

The tourism industry in Greece is experiencing growth even in the midst of the current economic crisis. In 2013, international visitors consumed more than €11 billion worth of goods and services produced by the Greek economy, which accounted for 26.5 percent of the country's total exports (World Travel and Tourism Council (WTTC), 2013). The level of arrivals to Greece increased by 6.1 million (38.2 percent) between 2008 (the year the crisis hit) and 2014 (SETE (Association of Greek Tourism Enterprises, 2014; World Bank, 2015), with revenues reaching €13.4 billion (Bank of Greece, 2015). Moreover, in 2014 tourism directly supported 340 500 jobs (9.4 percent of total employment). According to the latest WTTC (2015) research, this was expected to rise at an annual rate of 2.4 percent to 446 000 jobs (10.4 percent of total employment) in 2025.

From an educational perspective, this growing demand for tourism employees can be translated into a growing need of tourism education to adequately prepare the workforce to serve present and future needs of the industry. As Ladkin (2005) points out, tourism higher education, as a major platform for human capital development for the tourism industry, has a mission to provide graduates with the particular skills and attributes necessary for successful operation in tourism workplaces. In other words, tourism education needs to enhance the employability of tourism graduates. Indeed, students enrolling in tourism programs of study are motivated by anticipated career outcomes (Airey and Johnson, 1999). However, employability of the future graduates is not likely to increase unless they demonstrate their ability to cope with the circumstances of the business world.

Yet there appears to be a considerable gap between what is taught in tourism education and what is actually needed by the industry (Amoah and Baum, 1997; Zehrer and Mössenlechner, 2009). In this respect, tourism education has often been criticized for over-emphasizing theoretical knowledge, at the expense of practical application (Dale and Robinson, 2001; Koh, 1995). At the same time, the tourism industry tends to discount students' formal qualifications on the grounds of insufficient knowledge and expectations about tourism employment conditions and lack of experience (Hjalager, 2003; Jugmohan, 2010; Kusluvan and Kusluvan, 2000). Similar results are reported by a set of evaluative studies of the Greek tourism education system, presented later in this chapter. However, findings from these studies are almost exclusively based on the views of hotel managers and graduates working in hotels and are, therefore, of limited scope because they are confined to a single sector of the tourism industry. To this end, this chapter takes an interest in tourism industry expectations of tourism graduates in Greece. The scope of these earlier studies is broadened by using empirical material from an interview study of tourism managers in Athens, representing a wider range of tourism organizations.

These concerns are explored in four sections. First, some observations are made regarding the development of tourism education and its links with tourism employment, particularly drawing on the UK experience. The second section reviews the tourism curriculum in Greece at undergraduate level, with the purpose of illuminating the nature of provision and its relevance to industry needs. This is followed by a presentation of the study's methodology and findings. The conclusion presents a summary of the outcomes of the study and considers inferences from the data obtained.

2.   INDUSTRY AND TOURISM EDUCATION: AN EXPECTATION GAP

Education for the tourism sector is a relatively recent arrival in the education system. Although the study of tourism can trace its origins back to the 1930s or earlier (Airey et al., 2015a), it was not until the 1960s that it was established as an 'area of study in its own right and as a subject of study up to degree and diploma level' (Airey, 2005, p. 13). It was developed against a background of the recognition of the link between an educated work force and economic prosperity; a rapid expansion of higher education, including the development of many new universities and other institutions; and a growth in tourism itself (Airey, 2015). Tourism was identified, particularly by these new institutions that were relatively free from the constraints of older academic disciplines, as a new area of study that would attract students. Tourism was seen as providing a direct link to employment in a growing activity. Ayikoru et al. (2009) have pointed to the extent to which the expansion of further and higher education generally in the UK in the 1960s was very much driven by the need for an educated workforce and tourism was very much a part of this. As noted by Airey and Johnson (1999, p. 233), the consequential tourism programs placed great emphasis on the subsequent employment opportunities that they provided with 'Career Opportunities' and 'Employment/Employers Links/Work' being among the top aims of such programs.

This link between higher education and employment has remained a key theme for higher education institutions, and if anything it has been thrown into sharper focus by the more recent changes in the funding of higher education. Airey et al. (2015b) point to the extent to which students (and their parents), rather than the state, are increasingly responsible for funding their higher education. As a result, students leaving higher education, often with considerable debts, are increasingly conscious of their employment prospects and associated money-earning opportunities. Hence employment opportunities have become a key factor in students' decisions about which subjects to study. With this influence, employment success rates have become one of the important drivers of the league tables in which the performance of subjects and of whole universities is compared. Subject areas such as Medicine achieve almost 100 percent graduate employment records. By contrast other subjects have much lower post-graduation employment rates. For example, Airey et al. (2015b) quote figures from Australia of 34 percent unemployment for tourism graduates four months after graduation compared with 32 percent for sciences and 30 percent for economics (Hobsons, 2012). For the UK, six months after graduation, they give employment figures for tourism graduates as 45 percent compared with 66 percent for economics and 67 percent for mathematics (*The Guardian*, 2012). Further, they draw on Walmsley (2012) to indicate that only about one-half of employed tourism graduates in the UK were employed in the tourism sector itself and on Hobsons (2012) to suggest that starting salaries for tourism graduates in Australia lag behind other subject areas.

This brief account points to a number of dimensions in which the link between tourism education and tourism employment is important. First, in many ways, employment stands as one of the important reasons why tourism first appeared in the academy. Secondly, success in graduate employment is a key indicator of the success of tourism education programs and this is becoming increasingly important. And thirdly, there are clearly some doubts as to the success of the link between tourism and employment. As Ladkin (2005, p. 437) puts it, 'the vocational element of tourism education necessitates that it is considered in the wider labour market context'. Given this importance from its very beginning, it is in many ways surprising that attention to post-graduation employment and careers in tourism came in for so little attention at an early stage. Ladkin (2005, p. 440) voiced her surprise about this some ten years ago, writing 'surprisingly little is known about careers and employment in the tourism industry' and Petrova (2015, p. 392) continued in a similar vein, suggesting that 'there is a dearth of systemized large scale research focusing on recent graduates and their transition to employment'.

Early writings on this topic seem to be confined to studies setting out employment opportunities and directions (Chester, 1985; Hebblethwaite, 1973) for those contemplating a career in tourism. However, notwithstanding its relatively limited development, Ladkin (2005) is able to identify themes in the literature. Notably, in relation to progression from education to employment, she draws attention to the work of Ross and others (Airey and Frontistis, 1997; Ross, 1997), who write on interest and motivations for careers in tourism. She also points to work on the values of tourism degrees to employers (Petrova and Mason, 2004) and on career progression, especially in relation to the hospitality sector, which she suggests is rather better documented than tourism (Ladkin, 2002; Ladkin and Riley, 1996). Since Ladkin's account, and very much influenced by the focus on the employment potential of graduates from different subject areas, far more information is now readily available, at least about first employment positions. For example, the subject association in the UK, the Association for Tourism Higher Education, has produced a series of reports that include statistics on career progression (Walmsley, 2009, 2012).

At the same time the link between education and tourism has continued to be explored. Most recently, for example, Petrova (2015, p. 386) explores the employability of tourism graduates and, drawing on the work of various authors (Airey, 2005; Churchward and Riley, 2002; Cooper, 1993; Dale and Robinson, 2001; Evans, 1993), makes the point that 'Research capturing employers' perspectives claimed that there was a mismatch between skills and knowledge required by industry and those provided by universities'.

Notably, in examining the issues that influence the take-up of graduate employment in tourism, Petrova refers to the extent to which academics prioritize research over working with industry, the lack of agreement over the nature of skills or even of content provided by tourism degrees, the size structure and sheer diversity of the tourism industry, the predominance in tourism of small and medium sized enterprises, the low proportion of managers educated to degree level, and entry points to the industry not requiring graduate-level qualifications. She also suggests that the moves to widen participation in higher education which have been successful in many tourism programs may have influenced some employers' perceptions of tourism graduates and further that the strong intake of female students, who have often found it more difficult to secure employment than their male counterparts, may have had an overall effect on progression to employment. In brief, as she puts it, 'the vocational link of tourism and hospitality courses, which is often featured in the way these courses are advertised, and is part of tourism and students' considerations when embarking on their HE studies, is contested' (Petrova, 2015, p. 387).

What is clear from the literature, as presented by Petrova (2015), is that there is a gap between tourism education and tourism employment. This is reflected in the metrics of graduate employment in which, as noted above, tourism tends to perform relatively less well than other subject areas. This is surprising not only because it is obviously important that there should not be a gap but also because tourism itself, as a subject for study, has such a clear vocational link to a particular sector of the economy and, what is more, most tourism programs build upon this link in the form of inviting guest speakers, and providing for field trips and supervised work experience, all of which directly bring industry and education together (Busby, 2005). Petrova's work gives some pointers to the nature of the gap from a UK perspective. This study now seeks to explore this further in the context of a country where tourism is relatively very important.

3.   TOURISM EDUCATION IN GREECE

After about 45 years of development, Greece has a fairly well-developed higher education system in tourism, even though recent educational reforms cast doubts over its future. More specifically, according to Greek legislation, public higher education comprises two parallel sectors (Papazoglou, 2006).[1]

The first sector includes universities, polytechnics, and the Athens School of Fine Arts. Within this sector, degree-level modules with a tourism management component (but not degrees on tourism) are offered by the Business Administration Departments of the University of the Aegean and the University of Patras. Also in the university sector, three Universities (University of the Aegean, University of Piraeus, and the Hellenic Open University) offer postgraduate programs in tourism, leading to Master's or PhD degrees, established during the past sixteen years.

The second sector includes the Technological Educational Institutions (TEIs). It should be emphasized that TEIs are very similar to the former British polytechnics (Christou, 1999) and were fully integrated into the higher education system in 2001. Up until recently, there were seven TEIs offering courses leading to an undergraduate degree in tourism management. In all cases, these courses were offered by independent departments of tourism management. However, recent reforms initiated by the government in response to the ongoing economic crisis that has struck Greece have changed the map of tourism education. Space precludes details but suffice it to say that the latest educational reform, named 'Athena', took effect in the academic year 2013–14 and aimed to curtail state expenditures by reducing the number of higher education departments (Tsiligiris, 2012). Accordingly, under the Athena plan tourism departments have either been abolished, merged with other departments, or will only continue to operate until currently enrolled students have graduated. The situation is still very unclear as tourism departments are trying to come to terms with the full impact of these changes. In any case the result of these developments is that tourism management is now offered only as a degree specialization in TEIs and the number of tourism modules has been drastically reduced.[2] For example, the specialization 'Tourism and Hospitality Management' offered by the Department of Business Administration at the TEI of Thessaly stems from the merger of three pre-existing departments (Department of Business Administration, Department of Tourism Management, Department of Project Management). In the same TEI this transition from a tourism course to a tourism specialization also meant that the number of tourism-related modules has gone down from 26 to 18. These changes have been met with skepticism and hostility by tourism educators and students, who perceive them as degrading tourism education. The most telling criticism to be leveled against the plan in this respect is that the shrinkage of tourism education will render it unable to respond to growing industry needs, thereby raising questions about its usefulness for future employment.

The remainder of this section now turns to a consideration of the nature of tourism education in the technological sector, which still acts as the sole provider of tourism education at the undergraduate level. However, many of the issues presented are also relevant to the wider tourism educational system of Greece.

To a large extent the development of tourism education in Greece has been driven by what Tribe (1997) has referred to as a 'vocational action' approach. As Tribe (1999, p. 123) explains, vocational actions 'are activities or performances in the world and generally involve exercise of a skill or technique'. It follows logically that within the context of tourism, vocational actions refer to the actions of those employed in the tourism industry. So, for example, the preparation of a profit and loss account, the operation of a reception desk and the marketing of an attraction involve vocational actions. In this connection, the aims of a tourism education for vocational action are defined as preparation for employment in tourism workplaces (Tribe, 2005).

Considering its origins and development, this vocational emphasis is not surprising. Greek tourism education originated as a response to the remarkable growth of the tourism industry during the last 40 years and the associated employment needs of this growing sector. It was given added impetus by students anxious about future employment (Christou, 1999). The result of these developments was that formal qualifications became, at least in principle, the main route for potential workers to gain employment in the tourism industry. Not surprisingly tourism courses offering these qualifications were strongly geared towards employment needs. This vocational orientation was further supported by a strong national vocational ethos, which emphasized, and continues – at least in principle – to do so even today, the important links between an educated workforce and a strong tourism industry.

This industry influence was seen in the initial establishment of technological educational institutions in the 1970s as Centres of Professional Technological Education. Today it can be felt in that the location of tourism specializations in all TEIs is in Schools of Business Administration. This organizational arrangement played a pivotal role in setting out a vocational orientation for tourism education, which subsequently exerted strong influence in the content of degree programs. A relevant comment on this in the UK was made by Tribe (1999, p. 29), who pointed out that 'the importance of this [organization] for the process of curriculum development is that the curriculum is born into, nurtured, and developed in departments which have an established culture and community of business orientation'.

Table 1.1   Tourism modules included in a four-year program in Business Administration with a specialization in tourism

1st semester	5th semester
Introduction to Tourism	Organisation and Operations of Travel Agencies
	Food and Beverage Management
	English for Tourism
2nd semester	**6th semester**
Front-desk Management	Alternative Forms of Tourism
Hotel Procurement	Tourism Economics
	Professional Cooking
	Bartending-Oenology
3rd semester	**7th semester**
Tourism Geography	Customer Relationship Management in Tourism
Clients Record Keeping	Hospitality Management
	Global Reservation Systems
	Graduate Seminar
4th semester	**8th semester**
Sociology of Tourism	Dissertation
Events Management	Six-month industrial placement

Note: Modules in italics include a laboratory component.

Source: Table developed by the authors, based on Technological Educational Institute of Thessaly (2015).

The outcome of this process can be seen in the list of the tourism modules provided in Table 1.1. These are part of a four-year program on Business Administration with a specialization in tourism management, spread progressively throughout the semesters of study and starting from the first semester after entrance. The emphasis on industry-oriented content is apparent in module titles such as *Tourism Economics*, *Customer Relationship Management in Tourism* and *Hotel Procurement*. The prevalence of laboratories in *Front Desk* and *Professional Cooking*, and six-month industrial placements as part of the students' experience, also provide evidence of this focus. The industry influence is also demonstrated clearly in the 2013 prospectus of the TEI of Athens (2013, p. 55), which states that the aim of the offered tourism curriculum is 'to prepare and form highly qualified professionals in the field of tourism management'. This theme is also echoed in an earlier study conducted by Christou (1999, p. 687), who argues that tourism graduates gain 'knowledge and practical skills in food and beverage operations, accommodation services and front-office operations'.

What all this adds up to is an orientation that produces a vocational curriculum. This is to be expected as in many ways the vocational orientation fits the needs of the key stakeholders in tourism education: the employers, the students and the educators. As Airey (2003) explains, the emphasis on vocational actions helps meet employers' immediate workforce needs, thus providing students with fairly good initial employment prospects. It also ensures that the educators have a good student demand for their programs. Indeed, this combination is often seen as one of the strengths and successes of this aspect of education.

Yet despite its vocational orientation, there is debate about whether tourism education in Greece is responsive to the needs of the tourism industry. This is reflected in the results of a number of studies relative to the vocational link of tourism courses. An early study was that of Christou (1999), who explored perceptions of tourism graduates employed in the hospitality industry about their educational preparation for the workplace. This found that graduates had problems in applying their knowledge to real-life working situations and concluded that tourism graduates in Greece 'are not fully prepared for the requirements of the hotel and tourism industry' (Christou, 1999, p. 689). In a study on the employment status of tourism graduates, Moira et al. (2004) came to the conclusion that holding a tourism degree does not necessarily ensure gaining entry to the industry, with only 34 percent of respondents being employed in tourism with similar salaries to non-graduate employees. A later study of hotel managers' expectations found that tourism graduates may not be able to cope with the demands of employment, suggesting 'a clear gap between education and the reality of the industry' (Prinianaki, 2005, p. 6). More recently, Diplari and Dimou (2010) reported a need for tourism education to respond to industry needs by adding more practical elements in the curriculum, as expressed by a group of hotel and travel agency managers. Based on these results, all of these studies highlight the need for nurturing closer industry/academic interaction.

One attempt to actually create an interface between what educational institutions offer and what is needed by the industry is to look at practitioner expectations of employees who are graduates of tourism education programs as well as perceptions of current provision. For the purpose of this case, in March 2013 an interview study of tourism managers took place in Athens, Greece. The results are presented below as they provide one of the few accounts of how tourism professionals perceive tourism education issues in Greece.

4.   THE STUDY

Data for this analysis were taken from an interview study with tourism managers in Athens. The tourism industry of the city covers a broad array of sectors including accommodation, food service, transportation, attractions, entertainment and tours (Asprogerakas, 2007). This broad representation made Athens an appropriate context to undertake industry-related empirical research. A personal invitation to participate was emailed to people who worked in tourism companies that employ tourism graduates and were personal acquaintances of one of the authors. The email included a request for the recipient to refer the researcher to three other potential interviewees among their professional acquaintances. The interviews asked respondents about: their educational background and their experience in hiring/supervising tourism graduates; their perceptions of tourism education; knowledge, skills and attitudinal qualities expected from tourism graduates; and the preparedness of tourism graduates to enter professional practice. The participants were also invited to make additional comments at the end of the interviews.

In order to broaden the scope of earlier studies, an attempt was made to identify respondents closely mirroring the classifications of tourism activities presented in the International Recommendations for Tourism Statistics 2008 (see Annex 3, United Nations Statistics Division, 2008). This proved to be unattainable, as it was either not possible to identify respondents from certain sectors or some sectors did not appear to hire tourism graduates. Still, the sampling procedure resulted in 22 participants employed in the following sectors: accommodation (n = 6), food and beverage services (n = 2), water and air passenger transport (n = 5), travel agencies and other reservation service activities (n = 7), cultural activities (n = 1), and sports and recreational activities (n = 1). The respondents were well-qualified to answer the interview questions, having experience in hiring between five and over 80 employees, and in supervision of between four and over 100 employees. Twelve respondents had a Bachelor's degree, three a Master's degree, and seven a post-secondary (non-tertiary) diploma. The degrees/diplomas were mostly in management-related fields (n = 15); six respondents had a degree in tourism management, and one in statistics.

All interviews took place at the offices of the respondents at a time convenient for them as respondents had indicated limited time availability for the study. Accordingly, interviews were relatively short (average: 30 minutes, longest: 45 minutes) to fit into the respondent's working day. This resulted in much less exploration of expectations than had been planned. The interviews were not tape-recorded as participants indicated that they were uncomfortable with the idea. Rather, the first author took hand-written notes using a form of shorthand. Following the interviews, the interviewer typed up the interview notes and emailed participants a summary of responses for clarification to ensure accurate representation of the interview content. This process was followed as a means to validate interview responses (Rose, 2013). The researchers read through the typed notes several times in order to identify recurrent unifying concepts or statements. This analysis was conducted independently by each researcher to serve the purpose of establishing inter-rater reliability. During this iterative process it was discovered that key emerging issues could be conveniently grouped into three main headings: graduates' preparedness, expectations from tourism graduates, and additional comments. The remainder of this section is structured around these headings. Moreover, since interviews were not recorded, the quotations presented here were reconstructed from the interview notes and might therefore be approximations of the respondents' comments.

4.1   Graduates' Preparedness for the Workplace

Participants in the interview process all painted a negative picture of tourism education struggling to cope with industry needs. This is clearly illustrated in common statements relating to 'irrelevant content', 'over-theoretical knowledge', and 'unprepared graduates'. When asked explicitly to rate the preparedness of graduates entering the workforce, all respondents unanimously agreed that this should be rated as merely adequate or inadequate. More specifically, respondents repeatedly emphasized that new graduates generally lack specialized knowledge. As they said, 'Educational institutions provide knowledge which is of limited use in the workplace' and 'Institutions provide tourism knowledge, but they do not specialize on the use of that knowledge'. However, these comments should not be taken to totally disregard the importance of theory in tourism studies. Several participants were of the opinion that some theoretical principles of tourism and tourism management are desirable to industry as long as they advance the practical skills of graduates.

Respondents involved in job interviewing also expressed concerns about the degree of professionalism displayed by tourism graduates. Some of the 'unprofessional' traits cited were inappropriate attire, poor personal appearance, and being overconfident. They further emphasized that most graduates were unprepared for the interview and unable to provide coherent responses to company or industry-specific questions. In the study by Christou (1999) referenced earlier in this chapter, new tourism professionals also indicated transferable skills, such as the ability to 'sell oneself', to be the area in which they felt least prepared upon entering the workforce. If this is still the case today, it might explain the unpreparedness of graduates for their job interviews. On-the-job complaints from supervisors included poor punctuality, lack of care, poor work ethic, and being uninterested. Taken as a whole, the industry agreed that it is the responsibility of educational institutions to undertake this aspect of education. In the words of one respondent, 'Educational institutions should be prepared to teach the business standards of dress and conduct'. The issue of unprofessionalism among tourism graduates is also generally raised by Prinianaki (2005) and Diplari and Dimou (2010), even though no details on specific unprofessional behaviors or traits are offered.

Outdated educational content was also identified as a weakness of tourism education. This was particularly evident in the case of sectors requiring the use of specialized software. For example, one respondent explained, 'By the time students graduate, the front-office applications they were taught are not used anymore'. Another one said, 'Taught computer reservation systems modules are clearly outdated and need significant changes to reflect current industry practices of travel professionals'. Although these comments are more directly related to front-office activities and reservation services, the lesson may be equally applicable to other tourism modules concerning Information Technology (IT) applications. Also in relation to the use of software, respondents cautioned that new graduates often know how to use a particular type of software but are not aware of the analytical principles that are applied. This means that they are often unable to make the transition from one software system to another. It can also lead to overreliance on packaged programs and inability to develop creative solutions to problems. This lack of creativity seems to extend beyond the use of IT. Several participants were of the opinion that tourism graduates are accustomed to working standard problems with a standard approach, looking for an, often unrealistic, textbook solution.

Industry participants in the interview process also stated that many graduates enter the tourism industry unprepared for 'real life', with glamorous expectations of fun, excellent wages, and important managerial responsibilities. When confronted with the realities of employment they are severely disappointed. However, as one participant argued, 'New graduates should not expect to take on managerial responsibilities immediately, but must learn business fundamentals from the bottom up'. In connection with this, it was also noted that some graduates seem to resent being supervised by managers who lack formal education and have 'come up through the ranks'. Research by Airey and Frontistis (1997), conducted many years ago, concluded that Greek pupils had unrealistic expectations of tourism employment fueled by their impractical views about the tourism industry and limited knowledge of tourism employment. It appears that this 'rosy' representation of the industry is still present today at the level of higher education.

4.2   Expectations from Tourism Graduates

In an open question, respondents were asked to identify important skills expected from new graduates entering the workplace. To a large extent the respondents produced a list that was similar to their responses in the previous section. In this context, it seems reasonable to suggest that these responses are related, since areas in which tourism graduates have been found wanting are also areas sought from the industry. Accordingly, specific skills and desirable characteristics included the ability to apply knowledge to real life situations, the ability to approach problems creatively, to demonstrate professional behavior and appearance, and to be current with the industry.

In addition, the respondents all agreed that foreign language competence is extremely important. There is little doubt that foreign languages are invaluable when communicating with people from other countries, as is often the case in the cross-cultural interface between tourism organizations and tourists. Tourism graduates must also have excellent verbal and written communication skills and be able to understand the needs of diverse groups of customers. Taken together, these skills are necessary if the graduate is to manage guest problems effectively. This suggests that tourism employers do not simply seek graduates to provide basic service to customers, but to be able to manage the service encounter. Interestingly, in a study of desirable graduate competencies according to the views of Greek hotel managers, the ability 'to manage guest problems with understanding' emerged as the single most important skill (Christou, 2002, p. 30).

Participants in the interviews also felt that tourism graduates must be patient, committed and motivated in pursuing a tourism career. The industry reality is that tourism employees must be prepared to work unsocial hours, such as weekends, holidays and evenings. These conditions might require greater commitment and self-motivation than other jobs (Zehrer and Mössenlechner, 2009). As reinforcement of their earlier comment, respondents added that these characteristics are clearly linked to the issue of having realistic employment expectations. The industry perception was also that most work is undertaken as a team effort and graduates should be able to function as team members. The ability to accept criticism, willingness to learn, and a strong work ethic were also valued. Altogether, these personal competences were perceived by respondents as equally important to other occupational requirements of tourism jobs.

4.3   Additional Comments

The usefulness of industrial placement as a means for acquiring employability skills and putting graduate knowledge to a real-life test was acknowledged by all respondents. However, they also raised concerns about the way the undergraduate placement scheme is implemented. As one respondent stated, 'As far as I am concerned, students are not always able to undertake their placement in their desired field, but often have to settle for available employers'. Others commented that industrial placement is not adequately supported by educational institutions, with academics not monitoring students during their placement. Further on the issue of work experiences, participants strongly recommended opportunities for part-time employment for graduating students. They believe that these would provide students with a real feel of employment conditions prior to graduation, thus reducing the possibility of unpleasant surprises for both employers and new employees.

Finally it should be stressed that several participants were surprised and appreciative that people working in academia were interested in their input with regard to the evaluation of tourism education and its graduates. For most of them, the only interaction with educational institutions was limited to scarce meetings and phone conversations with industrial placement coordinators. Taking this opportunity, they registered a willingness to reinforce their company's links with tourism education by providing guest lecturers, hosting student visits, and providing material for study projects, for example. However, despite this willingness to nurture closer interaction with educational institutions, it was clear that the industry does not look to academia for new sources of knowledge or research assistance. Given respondents' perceptions of tourism education and the fact that tourism graduates do not seem to bring new skills and ideas to the workplace, this is hardly unexpected.

5. CONCLUSIONS

From the results of this interview study, which was undertaken with tourism managers who hire and supervise tourism graduates, a clear picture emerges of the demands for knowledge and skills of tourism graduates. Some desired skills are generic. Communication and team skills are not specific to tourism studies, but tourism curricula should provide students with ample opportunities to develop them. Other expectations, such as the ability to apply tourism knowledge in practical situations, should be integral in tourism education courses, yet it was raised as a specific inadequacy of tourism graduates during the interviews. Personal characteristics, such as being patient and self-motivated, were also regarded as essential to achieve career success. There is an important lesson here for tourism educators and graduates that tourism employers look for both specific knowledge/skills and personality.

These findings replicate and complement the findings of previous studies. These efforts were in response to concerns over the vocational link of tourism courses in Greece. Their basic purpose was to create an interface between tourism education and the tourism industry. These studies have now surveyed or interviewed tourism graduates (Moira et al., 2004), new tourism professionals in their jobs after graduation (Christou, 1999), and tourism and hospitality managers (Diplari and Dimou, 2010; Prinianaki, 2005). This study has broadened the scope of these earlier undertakings by including wider representation of respondents from diverse tourism sectors. All these studies paint the same picture, that there is a clear mismatch between skills and knowledge required by industry and those provided by educational institutions. Taken together they therefore have cumulative validity that compensates for problems in aligning data from the different methods employed.

These findings here very much hark back to one of the longstanding issues raised in one of the earliest studies of tourism career profiles and knowledge (Airey and Nightingale, 1981) that there is a mismatch between what employers are seeking and what educators are offering. Petrova's (2015) work is one of the most recent offerings on this theme. Clearly Greece is not alone in experiencing the longstanding perceived gap between the dynamics that drive higher education and those that drive the world of work.

At one level the 'take-home' message from this strand of research, including this study, is quite clear: educational institutions in Greece need to bridge the gap between what is taught in tourism education and the needs of the industry. Receiving industry input is very important in this respect. This raises the wider question of how to create a proper interface for information about expectations from tourism employers to tourism educators.

This study has found that the industry is willing to contribute input to tourism education and respondents have suggested ways to involve industry professionals in the educational process. However, the use of interviews and surveys for the purpose of this case is clearly not ideal. These methodological approaches provide only snapshots of a given situation in a given time. They should therefore be repeated frequently to provide a continuous flow of information and knowledge to tourism educators, keeping them up to date with changing industry needs and developments. This may be impractical due to the costs involved in conducting these types of research. Future researchers are therefore challenged to develop better methods for bridging the communication gap between industry and academia.

The findings also prompt a deeper level of query about the role of tourism education in an increasingly complex world and the extent to which such education has a role to play in preparing students and in providing opportunities for employers. This is a theme that has most recently been picked up by Dredge et al. (2015). In a world of increasing complexity, for students and for employers, higher education cannot simply be judged on how well it meets current industry needs. It must prepare students to make decisions for a complex world. Tourism as a multi-dimensional, multi-disciplinary and multi-methodological area of study lends itself well to dealing with the complexities presented by a post-industrial and post-disciplinary world. Such an education has relevance for all employment and especially for tourism employment where the proper stewardship of an activity that crosses economic, environmental, sociological, political and many other boundaries needs multi-talented employees. In this context, perhaps the most important point is for tourism educators to be aware of what they can offer to meet the needs of the future tourism world and to make sure that the communication with industry explains this as well as responding to more immediate employment needs.

Given the undeniable challenges facing Greek tourism education and industry today, it is imperative for educational institutions to re-examine existing curricula, revising them where necessary in response to changes in industry needs. Of course, given the shrinkage of tourism education in the course of the current financial crisis in Greece, it is a fact that the industry desires academia to cover more material than can be adequately covered in an undergraduate tourism curriculum. But at the same time, this suggests that the industry has high expectations of tourism graduates and, as Christou (2002) observes, tourism managers in Greece may be more demanding than their international counterparts. In this context, students wishing to pursue a tourism career should be able to rely on their education to guide their skill development in a way that allows them to fulfill industry expectations and successfully perform their professional roles. Graduating without the skills necessary to carry out their professional responsibilities is damaging for both students and the industry. We therefore invite tourism professionals to think of ways of effectively communicating their needs to tourism educators, and urge educators to be open to the expressed industry needs.

NOTES

1. Private colleges can also offer undergraduate and postgraduate programs of study in Greece, under proper registration with the Greek Ministry of Education and Religious Affairs. The emphasis of this chapter is on public higher education for tourism.

2. A Greek version of the Athena plan can be found at http://www.minedu.gov.gr/publications/docs2013/130305_ telikh_protash_athhna.pdf.

REFERENCES

Airey, D. (2003), 'Tourism education: from practice to theory', paper presented at the WTO 15th General Assembly, Beijing, China, 19–24 October.

Airey, D. (2005), 'Growth and development', in D. Airey and J. Tribe (eds), *An International Handbook of Tourism Education*, Oxford: Elsevier, pp. 13–24.

Airey, D. (2015), '40 years of tourism studies: a remarkable story', *Tourism Recreation Research*, **40** (1), 6–15.

Airey, D. and A. Frontistis (1997), 'Attitudes to careers in tourism: an Anglo-Greek comparison', *Tourism Management*, **18** (3), 149–58.

Airey, D. and S. Johnson (1999), 'The content of degree courses in the UK', *Tourism Management*, **20** (2), 229–35.

Airey, D. and M. Nightingale (1981), 'Tourism occupations, career profiles and knowledge', *Annals of Tourism Research*, **8** (1), 52–68.

Airey, D., D. Dredge and M. Gross (2015a), 'Tourism, hospitality and events education in an age of change', in D. Dredge, D. Airey and M. Gross (eds), *The Routledge Handbook of Tourism and Hospitality Education*, London: Routledge, pp. 3–14.

Airey, D., J. Tribe, P. Benckendorff and H. Xiao (2015b), 'The managerial gaze: the long tail of tourism education and research', *Journal of Travel Research*, **54** (2), 139–51.

Amoah, V. and T. Baum (1997), 'Tourism education: policy versus practice', *International Journal of Contemporary Hospitality Management*, **9** (1), 5–12.

Asprogerakas, E. (2007), 'City competition and urban marketing: the case of tourism industry in Athens', *Tourismos*, **2** (1), 89–114.

Ayikoru, M., J. Tribe and D. Airey (2009), 'Reading tourism education: neoliberalism unveiled', *Annals of Tourism Research*, **36** (2), 191–221.

Bank of Greece (2015), *Tourism Balance of Payments 2014*, accessed 22 April 2016 at http://www.bankofgreece. gr/Pages/el/Bank/News/PressReleases/DispItem.aspx?Item_ID=4945&List_ID=1af869f3-57fb-4de6-b9ae-bdfd83c66c95&Filter_by=DT [in Greek].

Busby, G. (2005), 'Work experience and industrial links', in D. Airey and J. Tribe (eds), *An International Handbook of Tourism Education*, Oxford: Elsevier, pp. 93–107.

Chester, C. (1985), *Careers in the Holiday Industry*, London: Kogan Page.

Christou, E. (1999), 'Hospitality management education in Greece: an exploratory study', *Tourism Management*, **20** (6), 683–91.

Christou, E. (2002), 'Revisiting competencies for hospitality management: contemporary views of the stakeholders', *Journal of Hospitality & Tourism Education*, **14** (1), 25–32.

Churchward, J. and M. Riley (2002), 'Tourism occupations and education: an exploratory study', *International Journal of Tourism Research*, **4** (2), 77–86.

Cooper, C. (1993), 'An analysis of the relationship between industry and education in travel and tourism', *Teoros*, **1** (1), 65–75.

Dale, C. and N. Robinson (2001), 'The theming of tourism education: a three-domain approach', *International Journal of Contemporary Hospitality Management*, **13** (1), 30–34.

Diplari, A. and I. Dimou (2010), 'Public tourism education and training in Greece: a study of the necessity for educational restructuring', *Industry & Higher Education*, **24** (2), 115–20.

Dredge, D., D. Airey and M. Gross (2015), 'Creating the future: tourism hospitality and events education in a post-industrial, post-disciplinary world', in D. Dredge, D. Airey and M. Gross (eds), *The Routledge Handbook of Tourism and Hospitality Education*, London: Routledge, pp. 535–50.

Evans, J. (1993), 'Current issues: the tourism graduates: a case of overproduction', *Tourism Management*, **14** (4), 243–6.

The Guardian (2012), *The Guardian University Guide*, accessed 9 September 2012 at www.guardian.co.uk/ education/table/2012/may/2021/university-league-table-2013.

Hebblethwaite, R. (1973), *Just the Ticket: the Travel Industry*, Reading: Educational Explorers Ltd.

Hjalager, A.M. (2003), 'Global tourism careers? Opportunities and dilemmas facing higher education in tourism', *Journal of Hospitality, Leisure, Sport and Tourism Education*, **2** (2), 26–37.

Hobsons (2012), 'The good universities guide to universities, TAFEs and higher education providers', accessed 11 September 2014 at www.gooduniguide.com.au.

Jugmohan, S.N. (2010), 'Curriculum responsiveness in tourism programmes', *The Journal of Independent Teaching and Learning*, **5**, 34–41.

Koh, K. (1995), 'Designing the four-year tourism management curriculum: a marketing approach', *Journal of Travel Research*, **24** (1), 68–72.

Kusluvan, S. and Z. Kusluvan (2000), 'Perceptions and attitudes of undergraduate tourism students towards working in the tourism industry in Turkey', *Tourism Management*, **21** (3), 251–69.

Ladkin, A. (2002), 'Careers analysis: a case study of hotel general managers in Australia', *Tourism Management*, **23** (4), 379–88.

Ladkin, A. (2005), 'Careers and employment', in D. Airey and J. Tribe (eds), *An International Handbook of Tourism Education*, Oxford: Elsevier, pp. 437–50.

Ladkin, A. and M. Riley (1996), 'Mobility and structure in the career patterns of UK hotel managers: a labour market hybrid of the bureaucratic model', *Tourism Management*, **17** (6), 443–52.

Moira, P., D. Milonopoulos and S. Anastasiou (2004), 'Producing graduates for the tourism industry in Greece: a case study', *Journal of Hospitality, Leisure, Sport and Tourism Education*, **3** (2), 55–60.

Papazoglou, M. (2006), 'The Greek education system: structure and recent reforms', accessed 17 August 2014 at http://video.minpress.gr/wwwminpress/aboutgreece/aboutgreece_education_system.pdf

Petrova, P. (2015), 'The evolution of the employability skills agenda in tourism higher education', in D. Dredge, D. Airey and M. Gross (eds), *The Routledge Handbook of Tourism, Hospitality and Events Education*, Oxford: Routledge, pp. 383–94.

Petrova, P. and P. Mason (2004), 'The value of tourism degrees: a Luton based case study', *Education and Training*, **46** (3), 153–61.

Prinianaki, E. (2005), 'An assessment of hospitality management study programmes in Greece: industry's perspectives', *Proceedings of the International Conference on Tourism Development and Planning*, Patras: TEI of Patras, pp. 4–21.

Rose, P. (2013), 'Factors predicting the conversion of interns into regular employees: an empirical study of business internships in China', unpublished doctoral dissertation, Curtin University, Perth.

Ross, G.F. (1997), 'Tourism/hospitality industry employment acquisition strategies, higher education preferences and the work ethic among Australian secondary school graduates', *Managing Leisure*, **2**, 82–93.

SETE (Association of Greek Tourism Enterprises) (2014), *International Tourist Arrivals 2000–2013*, accessed 19 August 2014 at http://sete.gr/_fileuploads/entries/Statistics/Greece/International%20Tourist%20Arrivals%20%28Non-Residents%29/catID48/EN/140416_Afikseis%20Mi%20Katoikon-Ellada%202000-2013_new%20layout.pdf.

Technological Educational Institute of Athens (2013), *Prospectus*, accessed 13 August 2014 at www.teiath.gr/userfiles/khitas/documents/en/odigos_spoudon_eng.pdf.

Technological Educational Institute of Thessaly (2015), *Business Administration Program: Tourism Specialization Modules*, available at www.teilar.gr. Tribe, J. (1997), 'The indiscipline of tourism', *Annals of Tourism Research*, **24** (3), 638–57.

Tribe, J. (1999), 'The philosophic practitioner: tourism knowledge and the curriculum', unpublished doctoral dissertation, University of London.

Tribe, J. (2005), 'Tourism, knowledge and the curriculum', in D. Airey and J. Tribe (eds), *An International Handbook of Tourism Education*, Oxford: Elsevier, pp. 47–60.

Tsiligiris, V. (2012), 'Can Greek HE survive?', accessed 13 August 2014 at www.scienceguide.nl/201212/can-greek-he-survive.aspx.

United Nations Statistics Division (2008), *International Recommendations for Tourism Statistics 2008*, accessed 12 August 2014 at http://unstats.un.org/unsd/trade/IRTS/IRTS%202008%20unedited.pdf.

Walmsley, A. (2009), *ATHE Report on Tourism in Higher Education in the UK 2009*, London: Association for Teachers in Higher Education.

Walmsley, A. (2012), *Tourism Intelligence Monitor: ATHE Report on Tourism Higher Education in the UK 2012*, Brighton: Association for Tourism in Higher Education.

World Bank (2015), *International Tourism: Number of Arrivals*, accessed 22 April 2016 at http://data.worldbank.org/indicator/ST.INT.ARVL.

World Travel and Tourism Council (2013), *Travel & Tourism: Economic Impact 2013: Greece*, accessed 5 August 2014 at www.wttc.org/site_media/uploads/downloads/greece2013_1.pdf.

World Travel and Tourism Council (WTTC) (2015), *Travel & Tourism: Economic Impact 2015: Greece*, accessed 22 April 2016 at https://www.wttc.org/-/media/files/reports/economic%20impact%20research/countries%202015/greece2015.pdf.

Zehrer, A. and C. Mössenlechner (2009), 'Key competencies of tourism graduates: the employers' point of view', *Journal of Teaching in Travel & Tourism*, **9** (3–4), 266–87.

2 Hospitality employers' expectations towards the higher education system in Poland
Magdalena Kachniewska and Anna Para

1. INTRODUCTION

Tourism is considered to be one of the largest and fastest growing global industries. According to data published by the World Travel and Tourism Council, nearly 266 million jobs were supported by the travel and tourism industry in 2013. The travel and tourism sector generated in excess of 100 million jobs directly in 2013 (3.4 percent of total employment). It is estimated that by 2024, the industry will account for over 126 million direct jobs, an increase of 2.0 percent over the next ten years (WTTC, 2014). As a result, there is an increasing need for highly educated, qualified professionals who possess professional knowledge and employability skills. In the highly volatile global tourism industry, the development of human resources seems to be crucial in achieving competitive advantages. Tourism is a multi-faceted phenomenon involving many variables, activities and interest groups. For this reason training and education in tourism needs to be approached in an integrated and holistic manner.

The past decades have seen an expansion of subjects such as tourism and hospitality in higher education. Higher education in the field of tourism and recreation in Poland has a long tradition. Jagiellonian University introduced the first tourism studies program in Poland in 1936. In the 1970s and 1980s more universities introduced tourism into their educational offerings.

In 2013 there were 70 universities and colleges that offered education in the fields of tourism and recreation (Wartecka-Ważyńska, 2014). Most of these were located in the Mazovian Province around Warsaw (11 institutions) and the Greater Poland Province around Poznan (also 11 institutions). Nearly half of the universities offering programs in the fields of tourism and recreation (34 units) are public universities. Bachelor's studies are offered in 67 universities, whereas Master's studies are only at 30 universities (Wartecka-Ważyńska, 2014). Universities and colleges offering tourist studies operate mostly in big cities, where the demand for qualified graduates is substantial. Tourism and recreation have enjoyed considerable popularity among students. In 2002, the number of graduates of tourism and recreation amounted to 4188, whereas in 2013 as many as 12 300 graduated in the field of tourism in Poland while the majority of studies in social sciences have remained stable or have recorded a considerable fall in recruitment. The level of staff, their qualifications and capacity for innovation influences the development of the tourism industry and improves the level of customer service.

The teaching standards for tourism and recreation programs determine the profile of the graduates. According to the Polish Ministry of Science and Higher Education, graduates should possess general knowledge in the social, economic and natural sciences (for example economics, psychology, law). They should be prepared to pursue business activities in the field of tourism and recreation. Graduates should be able to organize their work as well as prepare tourism offers for different customers, and should be able to establish contacts as well as speak at least one foreign language (MNiSW, 2007). Unfortunately, these skills and competences for tourism and recreation graduates are described in general terms, without detailed explanation.

The existing curriculum seems to be detached from the reality of the labor market and future professions. Degree courses such as 'Tourism and Recreation' and 'Tourism Economics' are becoming less popular due to outdated knowledge and low demand from employers. Nonetheless, graduates who study other economic fields of study do not possess sufficient knowledge of the tourism market and its entities, which discredits them in the employers' opinion. Therefore the gap between employers' needs and labor supply widens. This contributes to an increase in structural unemployment.

The system of education should not only meet the students' needs and expectations but also correspond with future employers' requirements. However, despite increased development in tourism education and training, there are no strategic plans for the development of tourism curriculum frameworks and training approaches. Higher education that is adjusted to the needs of employers is a crucial factor in increasing the chances of graduates' employment and future career development. This cannot happen without cooperation between universities and business (DeMicco and Williams, 1999). The role of collaboration between business and science institutions was highlighted in the Lisbon Strategy (Erixon, 2010). The main goal of the cooperation is to boost innovation in the European economy.

The aim of the study presented in this chapter is to determine hospitality entrepreneurs' expectations towards skills and knowledge of graduates and to indicate the possible changes that should be made in tourism and hospitality education. A descriptive analysis method was applied in the study. The authors used Polish and foreign literature. The fieldwork was conducted in 103 hotels and included 147 hotel managers. Despite the fact that the hotel industry represents only a narrow slice of the tourism market, this group of companies was selected for research purposes. Graduates of 'Tourism and recreation' find employment in the hotel industry (as a future possible place of work) interesting (62 percent of responses). The vast majority of graduates (84 percent of responses) make at least one attempt to work in the hospitality sector. This attempt often fails because of the discrepancy between hospitality entrepreneurs' expectations and the range of skills and knowledge provided by the higher education system (SGH, 2010).

2.   LITERATURE REVIEW

A number of studies have explored the nature of the relationship between tourism and hospitality education, the tourism industry and the student. The main theme of this research is providing the industry with graduates that possess the necessary skills and attitudes essential for careers in the tourism industry. The debate on discrepancies between industry requirements regarding skills and competences and the actual educational curriculum has been the focus of a range of studies (Lewis, 1993; Gunn, 1998; Busby and Fiedel, 2001; Morgan, 2004; Raybould and Wilkins, 2005; Barron, 2008; Ring et al., 2009).

Ring et al. (2009) noted that tourism education initially started out as training courses for staff in specific sectors. These courses subsequently led to the establishment of technical and vocational schools, which, in turn, have evolved into undergraduate and graduate programs. However, meeting the industry's requirements and expectations is still a basic aim of tourism curricula (Smith and Cooper, 2000; Ernatawi, 2003; Raybould and Wilkins, 2005) and industry needs still are the predominant factor when it comes to curriculum design (Gunn, 1998; Dale and Robinson, 2001; Morgan, 2004; Inui et al., 2006). At the same time, the need for balancing vocational and liberal aspects in curricula has become increasingly important (Morrison and O'Mahony, 2003; Inui et al., 2006).

The discussion about the curriculum in the field of tourism started many years ago. In 1993 Lewis stated that curricula are tailored to what the industry has needed in the past, not what it needs today, or what it will need in the future (Lewis, 1993). Many educators are out of touch with the business world and consequently are unaware of its evolving needs and continue to provide outdated solutions. Although this opinion was expressed more than twenty years ago it continues to be valid and relevant. Tourism and hospitality education, like all professional education, should lead the industry rather than follow it. Graduates need to be prepared for a changing environment because, at the time of education, the future needs of the industry and levels of complexity cannot be predicted. Tourism and hospitality educators must anticipate the future needs of the industry and respond as quickly as possible.

Ring et al. stress that:

> a program creating graduates who just 'function' in the current tourism environment has to be questioned since it does not embrace the needs of education for an industry of constant change . . . . Students have to be educated to think critically, be analytical, and be able to use creative and new ways of thinking to solve problems and adapt easily to changes. . . . they have to actively participate in creating and shaping the future of tourism. (Ring et al., 2009, p. 2)

Meeting the tourism and hospitality industry's needs and expectations is the basic goal when developing tourism curricula (Raybould and Willkins, 2005). Yet most curricula are ill-equipped to be sensitive and adaptive to changes in business environment (Jayawardena, 2001). Understanding of the latest trends and problems faced by the industry is significant for the universities offering tourism and hospitality degree programs. Tourism companies need professionals with up-to-date knowledge, who have skills and competencies that are necessary in the contemporary, dynamic workplace. Changes and developments in the industry require new skills that enable graduates to cope with changing circumstances of the business world. Managers are increasingly required to assume more diverse responsibilities. Recent changes in the tourism industry have a direct impact on the industry's expectations regarding specific competencies and knowledge of employees (Zehrer et al., 2006).

To prepare tourism and hospitality leaders for future jobs, educators should look outside the box when creating new educational programs. Amoah and Baum (1997) argue for more real in-depth understanding of the industry – theoretical and conceptual interpretations of human resource management – issues to be provided to students before operational and presumptive models. Amoah and Baum (1997, p. 6) state that 'When the main features of tourism education arise through initiatives by the tourism environment on the one hand and the world of education on the other, with no consensus between the two, problems arise for those on the receiving end of tourism education'. If education does not comply with industry requirements, the students and graduates will not be equipped with skills and competencies relevant for future jobs in tourism and hospitality. This includes a strong focus on generic skills, which are described as 'those transferable skills which are essential for employability at some level' (Raybould and Wilkins, 2005, p. 204). One attempt to increase the chances for graduates to obtain employment is to take a look at diverse skills and competencies that enhance the employability of graduates.

Undoubtedly it is important that the tourism industry and education institutions respect and are aware of each other's needs. Gilbert and Guerrier (1997) found significant differences between the perceptions of the industry and academics' views on the skills, knowledge and attitudes required by graduates to pursue successful careers in the industry. Industry criticized educators for overemphasizing theoretical concepts and identified deficiencies in certain practical skills. On the other side, educators were of the opinion that the industry did not make the best use of students, both during their practical training and after graduation. This problem is a sign of urgent need for discussion between both sides.

Several studies have revealed that employers do pay attention to skills such as: communication, empathy, motivation, decision-making, planning and improvisation (Cassidy, 2006; Zinser, 2003; Bagshaw, 1996). Mössenlechner and Zehrer (2008) also identified the skills and competences that are important to employers. The skills were divided into four categories. The most important skills were: (1) language competence, problem-solving skills, conceptual skills (professional and methodological competences); (2) communication competencies, active listening, social and team skills (social and communicative competences); (3) self-motivation, willingness to learn, willingness and personal commitment, ability to work under pressure (personal competencies); (4) decision-making abilities, initiative and proactiveness, creativity (activity and action-oriented competencies). Other research has also found that the ability to communicate with clients and colleagues, foreign language skills, the ability to work in a multicultural team, a positive attitude to work, organizational skills, the ability to apply theoretical knowledge in practice, foreign language skills, IT skills, initiative, strategic approach to entrepreneurship and creativity are important to the tourism and hospitality industry (Luka and Donina, 2012; Raybould and Wilkins, 2005, Ring et al., 2009).

The Hotel and Catering International Management Association (HCIMA) in cooperation with the University of Surrey undertook a study to identify the future skill needs of managers in the hospitality industry. They discovered that language skills, people management, communication skills and managing cultural differences were important requirements (Battersby, 1996). In addition, Fallows and Steven (2000) revealed that when recruiting, employers pay attention not only to specific academic skills and knowledge, but also to the capability to be proactive, to identify and respond to problems in a creative and individual way. Similarly, Raybould and Wilkins (2005) determined that the most highly valued skills were dealing effectively with customers' problems, reacting effectively and calmly in critical situations and maintaining professional and ethical standards at work. The results of another study indicated that because the industry is constantly changing, employers were also looking for more flexible and adaptable staff who would be able to transform their companies into more flexible and adaptable businesses (Cox and King, 2006).

In the Polish literature significant research on training requirements was conducted by Szymańska (2009). The author revealed the greatest deficiencies in tourism education.

Table 2.1   Skills required by the employers

Skill	Battersby (1996)	Cox & King (2006)	Fallows & Steven (2000)	Luka & Donina (2012)	Mössenlechner & Zehrer (2008)	Raybould & Wilkins (2005)	Szymańska (2009)
Ability to work under pressure					●		
Communication skills	●			●	●		
Creativity			●	●	●		
Customer service						●	●
Flexibility		●					
Foreign languages	●			●	●		●
Knowledge of tourism			●	●	●		●
Maintaining professional and ethical standards						●	
Managing cultural differences	●			●			
People management	●						
Proactiveness			●	●	●		
Problem-solving			●		●		
Teamwork skills					●		●
Willingness to learn					●		

Entrepreneurs indicated that more attention needed to be paid to foreign language skills, practical knowledge of tourism industry, team work skills and customer service.

As we can see in Table 2.1, some skills (such as foreign languages, communication skills, flexibility, creativity, organization and planning skills) appear repeatedly in several studies. Nevertheless, skills requirements can vary from country to country and from region to region. It must be noted that the quality of the higher education as well as the development of the tourism and hospitality industry are at different stages in each country.

3.   TOURISM EMPLOYMENT IN POLAND

It is difficult to estimate the scale of employment in the Polish tourism industry because of its heterogeneity. Moreover, not all companies operating in the tourism market identify themselves with this industry. The Tourism Satellite Account (TSA) is believed to be the most advanced way (in terms of methodology) of measuring the economic effects of tourism (including employment in tourism). According to the latest available edition (2011), the total number of people working in specific types of tourism activities in Poland amounted to nearly 518 000, accounting for almost 6 percent of the Polish workforce (Dziedzic et al., 2014). However, these numbers refer to the total number of employees in the so-called specific types of tourism. The actual direct rate of employment in tourism is estimated at 138 000 people. Since 2003 there has been slow growth in employment in the tourism industry. This was partially caused by the fact that in the period of economic recession the group of self-employed (18 percent) grew more dynamically, whereas the number of employed decreased.

The global financial crisis also affected the Polish tourism industry. The recession resulted in lay-offs (within the employment) in many companies (Dziedzic et al., 2009). On the other hand, the crisis contributed to an increased tendency to pursue independent economic opportunities. The number of micro-enterprises (employing up to nine people) is gradually growing. Those companies are perceived to be the source of self-created jobs. In 2011 entities employing more than nine people accounted for 67 percent of employment. This means that in 2011 medium and large companies offered twice as many jobs as micro-enterprises (33 percent) (Kachniewska, 2012).

The trend toward an increase in the average number of employees in micro tourism enterprises (observed in 2005–06) stabilized under the influence of the recession (after 2007). The growing number of micro-enterprises combined with a low average employment reflects the negative phenomenon of 'crowding out' the employees working for large companies towards registration of sole proprietorships. This solution was used during the financial crisis by many companies as a way to reduce labor costs.

As no data regarding employment for subsequent years exists, it is impossible to make comparisons on unemployment in the catering and hospitality industries. In the first half of 2014, the unemployment rate in this group amounted to 52 900. At the same time, the number of new job openings announced by labor offices amounted to 25 500. This means that there were two unemployed people for every job vacancy in the catering and hospitality sector (MSiT, 2011).

The share of unemployed in catering and hospitality compared to the total number of people registered as unemployed amounted to 3.9 percent in 2014. Moreover, the share of job vacancies offered in this sector amounted to 4.2 percent (compared with all jobs offered). This means that there is demand for skilled workers in the catering and hospitality industry. This phenomenon can be also explained by the high level of employee turnover in tourism enterprises.

Chefs, waiters, tourist guides, maids, tour leaders, kitchen maids, catering service managers and travel agents are the most sought-after professions in the catering and hospitality sector. The number of job vacancies for these professions exceeded the number of registered unemployed in labor offices. The above-mentioned professions are characterized by relatively low remuneration and short-term job contracts, contributing to the high employee turnover.

Tourism companies are not the only stakeholders who have an interest in improving the quality of vocational training and in-service training for tourism employees. Organizations and public institutions related to the state and local administration (at various levels) play an equally important role. Their service complements and supports the activities of tourism companies in many aspects (for example tourist information offices to promote the city/region or local convention centers). The quality of human resources in the public administration units determines the quality of the business environment and conditions for the development of tourism companies. Moreover, the quality of work determines the effective functioning of the whole tourism market (MSiT, 2011).

Global trends in the tourism market and the process of globalization are the main factors determining the need to create and develop new tourist professions (including, for example, tourism entertainers, tourism brokers and consultants as well as so-called 'tourism business angels'). Newly emerging professions in the tourism business can be perceived as a result of changing lifestyles of Polish society (far more consumptive and dynamic). Poles travel more eagerly and have become more demanding (especially in the areas of business tourism, MICE sector, health and wellness tourism).

The above-mentioned trends and remarks provide useful contextual information to support the development of a curriculum framework at a higher educational level. There are two reasons for this. First, particular occupational groups need to develop different skills and competencies. Second, graduates should be aware of the range of possibilities provided by higher education as well as of the requirements they will need to fulfill in the event of occupational retraining. This will ensure the desired flexibility of graduates on the labor market.

Modern human resources management theories should also play an important role while developing the curriculum framework. Delegation of authority is one of the most important concepts. On the one hand, it requires the managerial skill to relinquish part of the power and to empower the employees. On the other hand, giving the power and imposing an obligation to solve guests' or tourists' problems immediately requires specific skills from employees (for example, interpersonal skills). This requirement exceeds the professional service within the scope of the job. Such skills are particularly essential in tourism services (including hospitality) because of the key role of employees in ensuring customer satisfaction.

Employability is another special feature required in the modern labor market. It refers to a person's capacity to gain and maintain employment (Hillage and Pollard, 1998). This ability derives from a certain combination of knowledge, skills and competencies acquired in the process of learning (not only during formal education). Employability depends also on the ability to present skills properly to the employer. Partially, employability depends on environmental factors such as the candidate's life situation and conditions in the labor market (Hind and Moss, 2011).

It should not be overlooked that fierce competition between the various players in tourism supply forces candidates to compete more actively on the labor market. The process of rewarding the employees (compensation, benefits and so on) as well as the process of motivation should aim at achieving two goals. They aim to meticulously select their personnel as well as making great efforts to keep the most valuable workers within the company. In practice, this means that entrepreneurs are more often looking for and striving to retain the most creative workers, who have strong adaptability skills. Employers also redefine the previously existing requirements for employees (Jasiński and Smolbik-Jęczmień, 2005).

Management staff, especially middle and senior managers, are being retrained in order to develop and improve skills such as future-based thinking, the capacity to work in teams, an ability to assess their own work, creativity, flexible approaches to problem-solving, good communication skills, and ability to motivate employees effectively and dynamically influence staff.

Moreover, dismissal of employees who do not perform well, employing and retaining the best employees, introduction of healthy competition between workers (to undermine confidence of having a secure 'job for life') should be perceived as a natural and effective approach to human resource management. In practice, this is reflected by widespread use of trial periods of employment as well as short-term contracts. This particular approach to testing employees reveals basic deficiencies in their education. The cost of these short-comings is borne by the entrepreneur, either by paying for the necessary training, or by retaining a badly performing employee, or finally by deciding to find a better candidate for the job.

4.   METHOD

The research into hoteliers' opinions about their requirements regarding the quality of higher education in tourism was based on a survey and in-depth interviews. The study covered the whole country and was conducted in 2013 and 2014 among 147 entrepreneurs and hotel managers. The group of respondents consisted of representatives of chain and non-chain hotels of all categories. Among the respondents there were 61 managers of business hotels located in the cities (from eight Polish cities), 72 managers of wellness hotels, and 14 managers of transit hotels. The hotels were divided into two groups: newly created hotels (running for less than two years) and hotels functioning for a longer time in the market (85 percent).

The set of questions concerned the shortcomings in education as well as employees' aptitude for working in the tourism industry. The following issues were investigated:

1.   theoretical knowledge of the tourism market and its structure;
2.   knowledge of the structure of the hospitality product;
3.   knowledge of basic tools (including software) used in the management and marketing of hotel services (including catering);
4.   skill to deliver impeccable customer service;
5.   command of foreign languages;
6.   social competencies;
7.   managerial skills.

Managers were asked to indicate the answers best reflecting (in their opinion) shortcomings of employees' knowledge.

5.   FINDINGS

5.1   Inadequacies of Higher Education in the View of Hospitality Entrepreneurs

Management responses to each of the above seven issues are summarized in Table 2.2. Only 16 percent of respondents indicated just one answer. Others respondents provided two to six replies. All respondents identified item 3 as a shortcoming (knowledge of basic tools used in the management and marketing of hotel services).

From the in-depth interviews, it was found that employees' sales skills (including nego-tiation, up-selling and cross-selling) as well as proficiency in software applications used at reception or in hotel catering were particularly limited. Sales staff (marketing staff) did not have knowledge of modern promotional tools and techniques. Moreover, sales people were not able to manage public relations efficiently. Lastly employees had only limited

Table 2.2   Types of shortcomings in employees' education and aptitudes for working in the tourism industry

Skill category	Responses	%
1. Theoretical knowledge of the tourism market	135	92
2. Knowledge of hospitality product	140	95
3. Knowledge of basic tools used in management and marketing	147	100
4. Skill to deliver impeccable customer service	62	42
5. Command of foreign languages	103	70
6. Social competencies	105	71
7. Managerial skills	96	65

knowledge of new technologies and their applicability in hotel marketing (for example mobile applications).

Lack of knowledge of the hotel product structure (item 2) caused most of the sales problems. The people employed in the particular hotel divisions did not perceive that these hotels offered a complex product. They perceived the product rather selectively and approached their responsibilities directly (for example accommodation, catering, conference facility, wellness, recreation). Employees were not able to identify opportunities to create packages and to react to consumer expectations in a flexible way. Such an attitude has a negative impact on the finances of their company.

Theoretical knowledge of the tourism market and its structure (response no. 1) was also frequently ticked by respondents. This factor can cause a decline in profitability and contributes to poor PR performance. Employees cannot 'move' in the intricate structure of the tourism market and can easily 'get lost' in the net of institutional ties that exist in the market. Workers do not know how to build and sustain a mutually beneficial relationship. This affects the company image as well as operational issues (for example use of outsourcing, selection of contractors, expanding their business with the help of external entities).

A large proportion of respondents (71 percent) selected response item 6 (social competencies). Respondents underlined the problems regarding teamwork and cooperation, knowledge and information sharing (the tendency to knowledge appropriation), low levels of assertiveness, vulnerability to stress as well as sense of responsibility and duty. Lack of employees' entrepreneurship and creativity, low sense of responsibility regarding team performance as well as lack of innovative spirit and no habit of lifelong learning were indicated to be the greatest deficiencies.

A low level of managerial skill was the least frequently selected response. Deficiency in managerial skill makes it difficult to organize work properly. In this industry some tasks and duties are only temporary projects that should be coordinated by only one person, for example one employee selected from the group of reception or marketing workers. Respondents emphasized that it is extremely difficult to find a person with the proper skills and experience to manage the project or to be a team leader (for example reception). Graduates cannot even cope with such challenges as maintaining discipline in the team, task division, work schedules, conflict management, motivation and so on.

5.2   Analysis of Training Needs in the Hotel Industry

Clearly there is a discrepancy between the formal education that graduates obtain in the 'tourism' schools, and the expectations of employers. Entrepreneurs take various measures to attract and retain the best employees available. Employees perceive this strategy as a kind of deployment of their weak market position. In fact, this weak position of candidates is conditioned by poor preparation for entering the labor market, both in terms of knowledge quality and also in terms of skills and competences they acquired during their studies. According to the entrepreneurs who participated in the survey, secondary schools and universities often deliver inadequate knowledge (for example outdated knowledge, poorly adapted to trends and changes in today's tourism market). Additionally, inadequate methods and techniques are being used during the teaching process. Teaching methods raise many concerns: there is not enough professional training and there is a lack of appropriate teaching aids such as software used in modern tourism enterprises.

Moreover, universities do not follow the emergence of new professions in the tourism market (for example concierge, front office manager, area coach, personal trainer, leisure time manager). Because of this, universities are not able to integrate the training of new skills and knowledge (which are vital for the profession) into the curriculum. This is especially important at the first level of higher education (Bachelor's studies), which should operate as higher vocational education.

On the other hand, there are many unconventional marketing campaigns where entrepreneurs (mainly hotels, airlines and travel agents) evoke the impression that the labor market is offering more and more new forms of employment, or even professions (for example 'bed tester', 'airline tester', 'travel assistant'). In fact, these are rather one-off promotional activities, often announced with the help of famous bloggers or amateur photographers, published only for marketing purposes. In this case 'new jobs' remain an illusion. However, universities should take into consideration such kinds of phenomena happening on the market in order to develop the market awareness of future graduates.

The research aimed to identify the areas of employees' education in the hotel industry that are most requested by hospitality managers (see Table 2.3). Training in the field of tourism service marketing was the most often sought after (90 percent of all responses). A similar rate was recorded for active sales and negotiation training (88 percent) and tourism management (85 percent) as well as for revenue management training (87 percent). Customer service training was indicated by 70 percent of respondents, and front office training received a similar response (73 percent).

Table 2.3   Training needs requested by hospitality managers (% of responses)

Training needs requested by hospitality managers	%
Tourism service marketing	90
Active sales and negotiation	88
Revenue management	87
Tourism management	85
Front office	73
Customer service	70

In non-chain hotels, the need for management training (86 percent) was identified more frequently than average. An in-depth analysis revealed that the following skills are fundamental: time management, work organization, effective authority delegation, motivation, setting goals and standards, planning, scheduling, controlling of operation and performance, building good interpersonal relations, negotiating, problem-solving, decision-making, change management, communication skill, career and development planning. The vast majority of these skills are officially included in the training curriculum (for example within the subject Human Resources Management). However, respondents emphasized that the knowledge obtained at university is strictly theoretical and concerns human resources management rather from an academic perspective, rarely from the perspective of labor law and extremely rarely from the perspective of business practice.

The case of personnel training and motivation seems to be exceptional. The diversity of hotel organizational units as well as jobs and skills of particular employees does not allow housekeepers, catering and sales people to be treated equally. They require the use of different assessment tools and motivation techniques. Education programs and training offered on the training market seem to omit these kinds of nuances.

The leisure hotels pointed to the need of training for a new job – namely 'leisure assistant' (53 percent). The trend for this type of tourism service appeared in Poland along with the popularity of trips to the so-called tourist enclaves, where leisure-time animation has long been an important element of this destination's distinction. There are few professional leisure assistants in Poland. The majority of them are trained by well-known tourist multinationals, where they also find employment. In Polish hotels the leisure-time animation service is often replaced by newly popular sports such as Nordic walking (special marching technique using poles), jogging, swimming or aqua-aerobics training.

Training of waiters (51 percent) and chefs (47 percent of responses) was also mentioned by many respondents. It should be noted that it is very rare for graduates from higher education programs to start working in these particular positions. Furthermore, employers made relatively few remarks about hard skills of catering employees, whereas they assessed the interpersonal skills of waiters to be very poor. This finding indicates that the titles of degrees and programs may poorly reflect the perceptions of entrepreneurs who contract business trainers and training companies. It is not uncommon that only in the course of an in-depth interview does it become clear that 'waiters' training' is focused on the ability to establish contact with the guest, up-selling and cross-selling, because hotel employers believe that employees do not possess these skills. However, the basic principles of waiters' service are well-developed in the course of school education. Lack of foreign language skills seems to be another widely reported problem (over 70 percent of employers organized short language courses).

The same applies to marketing training, which in reality often overlaps (in terms of scope and entrepreneurs' expectations) with training in the field of active sales and negotiation. Given the fact that marketing is a compulsory subject in many 'tourist' fields of study (both 'Tourism and Recreation' and 'Tourism Economy'), it is surprising that graduates employed in hotels are not able to conduct business talks, draft (lawful) contracts, specify payment conditions, manage pricing and so on. These skill deficiencies were frequently mentioned by employers.

Almost all of the respondents believed that reducing the curriculum content stems from the desire to preserve some relevant areas of expertise for commercial use only. This assumption is based on monitoring the training sector. Ninety-two percent of respondents mentioned that in the private training industry there were a large number of university lecturers and training companies as well as a broad offering of postgraduate studies which did not differ greatly from the standard university curriculum. Sixty percent of respondents stressed that during their university studies they or their employees were offered opportunities to participate in commercial courses. The course syllabi for these courses covered the same knowledge and skills that were included in the full-time university courses.

Ninety-two percent of hospitality entrepreneurs were of the opinion that there were not enough courses that enabled contact with business practitioners. This is not so much a matter of apprenticeship training, which is included in most of the tourist university curriculum, but rather of contact with entrepreneurs, local authorities and representatives of institutions. These people, through their attitudes and activity, influence the shape of the tourism business environment. These types of meetings and contacts are regarded as a crucial factor in the development of entrepreneurial attitudes and skills that are indispensable if individuals are to move around comfortably in the reality of the market economy.

6.   CONCLUSION

The study of the industry expectations regarding the higher education curriculum framework confirms the outcomes of other research within the tourism education sector. The similarity of tourism entrepreneurs' expectations indicates that changes to tourism education should strengthen the employability and flexibility of graduates. Respondents unanimously emphasized the huge importance of and the need for social skills training. Social skills contribute to improving the quality of customer service, help create the spirit of entrepreneurship and creativity, determine the adaptability of workers and their efficiency as well as their ability to work together and achieve effects of synergy. Meanwhile, these features and skills seem to be particularly neglected by the higher education system. This problem should not be justified by curriculum reductions, as these skills can and should be developed in the course of learning any academic subject using appropriate teaching tools (group work, practical exercises, case study analysis, webquesting) and by implementing a modified grading system in which creativity and teamwork will be rewarded more highly than individual achievements.

REFERENCES

Amoah, V. and Baum, T. (1997), 'Tourism education: policy versus practice', *International Journal of Contemporary Hospitality Management*, **9** (1), 5–12.
Bagshaw, M. (1996), 'Creating employability: how can training and development square the circle between individual and corporate interest?', *Industrial and Commercial Training*, **28** (1), 16–18.
Barron, P. (2008), 'Education and talent management: implications for the hospitality industry', *International Journal of Contemporary Hospitality Management*, **20** (7), 730–42.
Battersby, D. (1996), 'The challenge and the opportunity facing the hospitality industry', in R. Kotas, R. Teare, J. Logie, C. Jayawardena and J. Bowen (eds), *The International Hospitality Business*, London: HCIMA/Casell, pp. 107–11.
Busby, G. and Fiedel, D. (2001), 'A contemporary review of tourism degrees in the United Kingdom', *Journal of Vocational Education and Training*, **53** (4), 501–21.
Cassidy, S. (2006), 'Developing employability skills: peer assessment in higher education', *Education+Training*, **48** (7), 508–17.

Cox, S. and King, D. (2006), 'Skill sets: an approach to embed employability in course design', *Education+Training*, **48** (4), 262–74.

Dale, C. and Robinson, N. (2001), 'The theming of tourism education: a three-domain approach', *International Journal of Contemporary Hospitality Management*, **13** (1), 30–34.

DeMicco, F.J. and Williams, J.A. (1999), 'The strategic power of partnerships for university hospitality and tourism management programmes', *Journal of Hospitality and Tourism Education*, **2** (3), 75–8.

Dziedzic, E., Kachniewska, M., Łopaciński, K. and Skalska, T. (2014), 'Rachunek satelitarny turystyki dla Polski', Warsaw: Instytut Turystyki.

Dziedzic, T., Łopaciński, K., Saja, A. and Szegidewicz, J. (2009), 'Wpływ światowego kryzysu gospodarczego na stan i perspektywy rozwoju sektora turystyki w Polsce', accessed on 10 March 2015 at http://dms.msport. gov.pl/app/document/ file/1054/raport_nt_kryzysu.pdf?field=file1.

Erixon, F. (2010), 'The Europe 2020 strategy: time for Europe to think again', *European View*, **9** (1), 29–37.

Ernatawi, D.B. (2003), 'Stakeholder's view on higher tourism education', *Annals of Tourism Research*, **30** (1), 255–8.

Fallows, S. and Steven, C. (2000), 'Embedding a skills programme for all students', in S. Fallows and C. Steven (eds), *Integrating Key Skills in Higher Education*, London: Kogan Page, pp. 17–31.

Gilbert, D. and Guerrier, Y. (1997), 'UK hospitality managers past and present', *The Service Industries Journal*, **17** (1), 115–32.

Gunn, C.A. (1998), 'Issues in tourism curricula', *Journal of Travel Research*, **36** (4), 74–7.

Hillage, J. and Pollard, E. (1998), 'Employability: developing a framework for policy analysis', *Research Brief No. 85*, Department for Education and Employment.

Hind, D. and Moss, S. (2011), *Employability Skills*, Sunderland: Business Education Publishers.

Inui, Y., Wheeler, D. and Lankford, S. (2006), 'Rethinking tourism education: what should schools teach?', *Journal of Hospitality, Leisure, Sport and Tourism Education*, **5** (2), 25–35.

Jasiński, Z. and Smolbik-Jęczmień, A. (2005), 'Nowe tendencje w kształtowaniu rozwoju zawodowego pracowników wobec integracji Polski z Unią Europejską', in A. Pocztowski (ed.), *Praca i Zarządzanie Kapitałem Ludzkim w Perspektywie Europejskiej*, Kraków, Oficyna Ekonomiczna.

Jayawardena, C. (2001), 'Challenges in international hospitality management education', *International Journal of Contemporary Hospitality Management*, **13** (6), 310–31.

Kachniewska, M. (2012), 'Wpływ kryzysu gospodarczego na metody zarządzania obiektami hotelowymi', *Zeszyty Naukowe Kolegium Gospodarki Światowej*, **35**, 61–75.

Lewis, R.C. (1993), 'Hospitality management education: here today, gone tomorrow', *Hospitality Research Journal*, **17** (1), 273–83.

Luka, I. and Donina, A. (2012), 'Challenges of tourism education: conformity of tourism curriculum to business needs', *Academica Turistica*, **5** (1), 85–101.

MNiSW, Ministerstwo Nauki i Szkolnictwa Wyższego (2007), 'Standardy kształcenia dla kierunków studiów: turystyka i rekreacja', accessed 10 March 2015 at https://www.nauka.gov.pl/g2/oryginal/2013_05/711ad3fb8 2fb85614b1786c7823d797d.pdf.

Morgan, M. (2004), 'From production line to drama school: higher education for the future of tourism', *International Journal of Contemporary Hospitality Management*, **16** (2), 91–9.

Morrison, A. and O'Mahony, G.B. (2003), 'The liberation of hospitality management education', *International Journal of Contemporary Hospitality Management*, **15** (1), 38–44.

Mössenlechner, C. and Zehrer, A. (2008), 'Competence requirements of tourism employees: the industry point of view', in C. Hu (ed.), *ISTTE Conference Proceedings: The Future Success of Tourism: New Directions, Challenges and Opportunities*, ISTTE, pp. 159–79.

MSiT (Ministerstwo Sportu i Turystyki) (2011), 'Rejestrowane bezrobocie w zawodach gastronomiczno-hotelarskich w I półroczu 2010 r.', accessed 17 September 2014 at http://www.msport.gov.pl/article/1720-Rejestrowane-bezrobocie-w-zawodach-gastronomiczno-hotelarskich-w-I-polroczu-2-1-roku.

Raybould, M. and Wilkins, H. (2005), 'Over qualified and under experienced: turning graduates into hospitality managers', *International Journal of Contemporary Hospitality Management*, **17** (3), 203–16.

Ring, A., Dickinger, A. and Wöber, K. (2009), 'Designing the ideal undergraduate program in tourism: expectations from industry and educators', *Journal of Travel Research*, **48** (1), 106–21.

SGH (2010), 'Plany zawodowe absolwentów kierunku Turystyka i Rekreacja', unpublished research, Warsaw School of Economics, Polish Ministry of Tourism.

Smith, G. and Cooper, C. (2000), 'Competitive approaches to tourism and hospitality curriculum design', *Journal of Travel Research*, **39**, 90–95.

Szymańska, E. (2009), 'Oczekiwania rynku turystycznego w zakresie kształcenia kadr', *Ekonomia i Zarządzanie. Kwartalnik Wydziału Zarządzania*, **1** (1), Białystok: Politechnika Białostocka.

Wartecka-Ważyńska, A. (2014), *Absolwenci Uczelni Wychowania Fizycznego na Rynku Pracy w Polsce*, Poznań: Akademia Wychowania Fizycznego w Poznaniu.

WTTC (World Travel and Tourism Council) (2014), *Travel and Tourism: Economic Impact: World. The Economic*

Impact of Travel & Tourism 2014, accessed 10 March 2015 at http://www.wttc.org/-/media/files/reports/economic%20impact%20research/regional%20reports/world2014.pdf.

Zehrer, A., Ailler, H. and Altmann, A. (2006), 'A module system in tourism and leisure education: theoretical and practical perspectives', in C. Ho (ed.), *Imagining the Future of Travel and Tourism Education*, Proceedings of the ISTEE Conference 2007 in Las Vegas, pp. 276–85.

Zinser, R. (2003), 'Developing career and employability skills: a US case study', *Education+Training*, **45** (7), 402–10.

3 The case for a return to the prevalence of examinations in student evaluation

J.E. (Joe) Barth

1. INTRODUCTION

On 11 May 2010 the Faculty of Arts and Sciences at Harvard adopted the motion, 'unless an instructor officially informs the Registrar by the end of the first week of the term the assumption shall be that the instructor will not be giving a final examination' (*Harvard Magazine*, 2010, pp. 64–5). Prior to this motion, it was officially assumed that all courses would have a final examination and instructors were required to petition for an exemption. The motion passed easily because the original policy had been ignored for many years. Out of 1137 undergraduate courses only 259 final examinations (23 percent) were scheduled; and an even smaller proportion (7 percent) of graduate courses had final examinations.

The author has informally observed similar reductions in the number of final examinations at several institutions over time, and suggests that this has been happening for many years throughout the post-secondary education system in Canada and abroad. The modern pedagogical reality is that instructors are choosing other methods of evaluation such as final papers, projects or so-called take-home examinations far more often than in the past. Most contemporary assessment design is based on the practice of constructive alignment (Gibbs and Simpson, 2004), which suggests that educators should select the most appropriate assessment task for the outcomes they wish to examine. The problem is not that there is a lack of exams, but rather in many cases educators are using other types of assessment when an exam may in fact be the best tool in that particular context.

While many instructors have abandoned the examination as an evaluation tool, it is interesting to note that most professions (medical doctors, lawyers, accountants, actuaries and so on) require candidates to write comprehensive written examinations in order to practice. Automobile driver's licenses, and permits such as pleasure craft operator, firearms possession and acquisition permits (in Canada), even citizenship, all involve a written examination. Equally interesting is the fact that many academic institutions continue to require examination scores (GMAT, LSAT, SAT) as part of the admission process.

The preferential use of written examinations in the past has largely been explained as an educational tradition. Written examinations have been extensively used to determine grades, classify and promote students, and sometimes to determine or compare the efficiency of teaching techniques. Aggregated student results obtained from standardized examinations have been used in some schools to evaluate the quality of education, teaching performance and adherence to curricula.

This chapter does not suggest classroom assignments should be replaced by examinations. It is proposed that examinations have an important role to play in both learning and assessment, and should not be abandoned as they have been in such a large proportion of course offerings.

2.   LITERATURE REVIEW

Teachers have been concerned with learning evaluation for many years. The tradition of sitting for examinations has been questioned on the basis of efficacy, validity and contribution to learning. As new ideas about teaching and pedagogy have emerged, researchers have sought to find methods of assessment that feature a greater contribution to learning, not just a measurement of how much has been learned.

2.1   Examinations

Early studies have provided evidence that written examinations stimulated student achievement to a significant degree (Johnson, 1938). Meyer (1936) found that the use of completion (essay) examinations yielded higher retention than recall (memory) examinations due to student differences in study methods. Evidence was found that subjective (essay) and objective (short answer) examinations are equally effective in evaluating the student's learning and retention (Vallance, 1947). These early researchers were very much aware of the benefits of written examinations in the process of student learning, retention and as a motivator to do well.

There has been research on the question of whether examinations should be cumulative (a comprehensive final exam) or sequential. Szpunar et al. (2007) found that students in courses with cumulative final exams retain information in a more accessible state, making it easier to retrieve during the final exam. They also proposed that not having a final examination serves as a cue for students to forget the material. Recent results (Lawrence, 2013) show that there is no effect on gifted students' retention two months after a cumulative final exam, while challenged students retained more material.

As shown by the results obtained in a study by Tynjala (1998), the measured difference between assignments and examinations can be small among the same students, and despite arguments to the contrary, we may infer that assessments using examinations are more or less equal to those obtained in other ways.

2.2   Un-invigilated Assessments

Un-invigilated assessments include individual and group assignments, take-home examinations and online examinations.

There is research that suggests the traditional, invigilated written examination has sub-optimal learning outcomes. Gibbs and Simpson (2004) present a comprehensive literature review which provides evidence that higher grades are achieved when assignments are used. There is also evidence that higher levels of learning are accomplished when classroom assignments and extensive feedback are provided. Gibbs and Simpson report that assessment using examinations fails to engage students with appropriate types of learning. Students cram (rote memorization) for exams rather than following a regimen of repetition and response to instructor feedback on assignments that is optimal for retention and more complete understanding.

Particularly in the case of distance or e-learning, invigilated examinations are often not an option unless they can be administered in a secure classroom setting at an institution near the student's home. Williams and Wong (2007) investigated the effectiveness of open book or open web (OBOW) examinations in this context. Their findings report that student perceptions of this examination instrument compared to the invigilated, closed book type exam are positive. This evidence in favor of un-invigilated assessments must be tempered by recognizing a number of other factors that may be in play.

It is known that grade inflation is more likely to take place if examinations are not used. When assignments are a significant fraction of the course mark instead of examinations, the failure rates are one third of what they are when the course mark is based solely on exam scores (Bridges et al., 2002).

Students prefer courses that do not have an examination. Bishop (1994) found that when exams are absent many students choose courses that have the reputation of not requiring much work to get a good grade. He also found that when exams are absent, students spend an average of 40 minutes more watching television per day. Kornell (2010) proposes that the cumulative final exam provides students with an incentive to do well, changes the way most students study for the better, and causes a greater expenditure of effort.

Faculty often prefer assignments (particularly group assignments) to final exams because there is less time pressure to grade the examinations promptly and report grades at the end of the term.

2.3   Group Projects

Group projects (also known as cooperative learning) are a very popular teaching and evaluation tool. Bolton (1999) found that 72 percent of instructors used group work in their courses. Instructors have attributed the popularity of group projects as a method of coping with an ever-increasing workload and declining resources (Morris and Hayes, 1997). Others profess that group work links classroom learning with the way tasks are performed in the work environment and that problem-based group research projects have the ability to develop critical thinking, interpersonal and communication skills (Candy et al., 1994, p. 140).

There are very serious concerns about group work. Student concerns about non-participation, free-riders and group composition are frequently voiced, but few solutions other than faculty intervention are available. When students choose their own groups, inevitably some students find themselves in groups with less talented participants and are doomed to receiving lower marks. Another serious issue is how marks are allocated among team members who may not contribute equally to the assignment in terms of quality, quantity and even attendance at group meetings. High achievers inevitably do most of the work, and are often dissatisfied with receiving the same grade as those who contribute less. Despite these serious issues and drawbacks, group work is very common, and continues to be practiced in many courses.

2.4   Academic Misconduct

Academic misconduct is rampant in post-secondary institutions, and instructors have an obligation to take steps to reduce this threat to the integrity of the educational system (Christensen-Hughes and McCabe, 2006). Particularly in the case of un-invigilated assessments on web-based courses, a high percentage of students have been involved in academic dishonesty (Chapman et al., 2004). Plagiarism, copying, the outright purchase of essays, padding bibliographies, collaboration on individual work assignments, and asking for extensions on the basis of false pretenses are a few of the means by which students can (and do) cheat (Mullens, 2000).

Essays, projects and assignments (including take-home examinations) provide students with much opportunity for academic misconduct despite plagiarism-checking tools such as Turnitin.com, not to mention vigilant professors who know their subject (and often students) very well. In an unsupervised environment, students have ample opportunity to collaborate, plan and find ways to cheat that would not be possible in a well-proctored examination environment.

When cheating is suspected, it is time-consuming, and often difficult to prove. In the case of group work, it is typical that one or two group members will assemble, edit and submit the final report close to the due date. It is common for the majority of students in a group not to have read their final group submission before it has been submitted. Very serious questions arise when plagiarism takes place. Who is responsible when plagiarism is found? Is plagiarism by one group member attributed to everyone, given that the assignment is jointly submitted? Is everyone in the group punished? How is responsibility for an academic misconduct infraction determined?

Examinations provide a number of advantages in discouraging and managing academic misconduct. Examinations can provide a controlled environment in which evaluation takes place. Provided good examination practice is followed, students have less opportunity to cheat, and cheating is much easier to detect and control. Citations and plagiarism are not ordinarily part of examination questions; however, students may be asked to discuss or describe the contributions of various authors when the instructor deems this an important learning outcome.

Universities have well-designed policies for proctoring examinations. These include selection of a room with plenty of table space for each student, a clearly visible clock, student identification checks, printing examinations on randomly chosen non-white paper (so that disallowed materials stand out), assigned seating, attendance mapping (where students sit in relation to each other) and a procedure for verifying that all students have turned in exams and no exam papers (completed or otherwise) are missing. Digital document handling allows instructors to easily randomize the order of questions so that students sitting adjacent to each other can less easily copy their answers. However, despite the existence of good examination proctoring procedures, opportunities for cheaters are created every time one or more of the policies are contravened.

2.5   Performance Stress and Test Anxiety

All students experience some degree of stress while studying for exams and anxiety when they write exams. Many educators believe that test anxiety reduces academic performance (grades). However, Hunsley (1985) analyzed the relationship between test anxiety and academic performance in a class of 62 students. He found evidence that suggests that students who suffer from anxiety at the beginning or end of the semester obtain the strongest debilitative effects on test performance (about 10 percent). He concluded that test-anxious students experienced the most doubt and concern early in the term (and not during final exams).

Test anxiety is not different from other types of time and performance stress. Time and performance stress is common in many life situations. It is the basis of most athletic competitions and provides reality show producers with endless opportunity to ramp up excitement in their programs. Time and performance stress exists in most jobs, particularly in management positions. Students need to learn how to cope with this kind of stress, and examinations are a good way to do that. As students write more examinations, they have the opportunity to learn to cope with stress and can become more confident performers.

While stories abound about high suicide rates among students, no empirical evidence has been found to support these widely held beliefs. Morton Silverman (1993) states that 'multiple-site collaborative studies done in the United States since 1960 strongly suggest a campus student suicide rate significantly less than in the matched control population' (Silverman, 1993, p. 329). A study by Yip (1998) found that student suicide was not linked to academic performance or examinations stress, but was highly correlated to depression and drug abuse.

3.   EXAMINATION TRADE CRAFT

Instructors can improve examinations with a view to increasing student satisfaction with the examination experience, reducing test anxiety, discouraging cheating and making examinations a more valid way to evaluate student learning.

Students' satisfaction with the examination experience and the effectiveness of examinations in assessment are highly related to gaps between what is taught in the classroom, course materials and the examination questions. The proposed 'Gap model of examination validity' shown in Figure 3.1 illustrates how the gaps between these three components affect examination validity and student satisfaction with the examination.

1.   Gap between course materials and what is examined: Students should have required course materials (textbooks, course packs, reading lists, library materials on reserve, handouts/notes online, and so on) that include the sources needed to answer every question on the examination. Notes taken in class may not be adequate to review concepts a few weeks after the lecture, and students must be able to refer to the course materials to supplement their notes and provide a more complete presentation of the material.

Instructors should ensure that they can direct a student to the exact place or places in the course material where the answer to each question on the examination can be found. Examination questions that are not fully supported with course materials prevent students from studying the material thoroughly and doing well in the examination.

2.   Gap between course materials and what is taught: Instructors must ensure that the

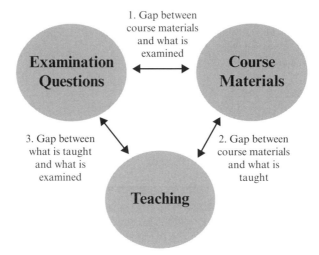

Figure 3.1   The gap model of examination validity

course materials cover what is taught in the classroom. Further to coverage issues, instructors must also ensure that what is taught is consistent with what the course materials say about the subject. If the course materials are not consistent with what the instructor teaches, students become confused, and ask, 'in an examination, which is the correct answer?'. It has been said that repetition is the mother of study. Having students read the course material, have it taught in class, and then make notes supports this ancient wisdom.

3. Gap between what is taught and what is examined: Instructors must ensure that students have been taught everything needed to answer the questions in the examination. While this seems simple enough, it is quite common for an instructor to miss something during a lecture, or to expect students to study material on their own. A good way for instructors to eliminate this gap is to prepare a set of potential examination questions (similar to learning objectives, but more specific) prior to each class, and to review these after the class to ensure that the material has been covered well. Only questions that have been well covered should be in the examination.

3.1   Performance Stress and Anxiety Reduction

Performance stress and testing anxiety can be reduced without compromising the effectiveness of the examination in several ways.

3.1.1   Examination lottery effects

Examinations should have even coverage of the course material so that all parts of the course need to be studied in order to do well. A lottery approach (some things are examined, others are not) is unpopular with students, and does not provide a comprehensive evaluation of student learning. For example, students need to know what material they will be responsible for in the examination. The author is well known for in-class review sessions that consist of reading the exam questions (but not the answers) a week prior to the examination. Student anxiety is greatly reduced, and they know exactly what they are expected to know. Class averages and the range of grades are similar to courses where this is not done.

3.1.2   Memory aids

Another stress reduction technique is to allow students to bring a one-page, handwritten memory aid into the examination room. Affectionately known as a 'cheat sheet', the preparation of this memory aid is highly valuable in learning the course material, and serves as a security blanket for those who suffer from testing anxiety. The 'cheat sheet' also eliminates the temptation to cheat by smuggling notes into the examination room. In the experience of the author, the one-page memory aid does not affect the class average or grade dispersion. Better students don't consult their cheat sheets very much, and challenged students (or those who bring a copy of a cheat sheet prepared by someone else) do not find them a useful alternative to knowing the material.

Preparing the 'cheat sheet' is an excellent learning and review activity. Post-examination interviews with students clearly revealed that they found preparing the cheat sheet to be a better way of study than simply reviewing notes.

3.1.3   Structured examination design

Testing anxiety can be further reduced by good examination design. Examinations should be structured so that 50 percent of the questions are straightforward, 25 percent are challenging and the rest somewhere in between. Easier questions should be at the beginning of the exam, so that students gain confidence as they write their answers. Nothing sets off an anxiety attack better than a 'killer' question right at the start of the exam.

Never include 'gotcha' questions in an examination. 'Gotchas' are questions that are counter-intuitive, unexpected and tricky; they invite mistakes because they appear easy but have a complex solution. Gotcha questions have very little useful value in most courses, with the possible exception of enhancing the instructor's ego! Detailed knowledge, special situations or exceptions should be tested in a straightforward manner.

Multi-part questions should be unbundled so that a student who gets a preceding question wrong will not lose their chance to answer a following part correctly. A secondary benefit of unbundling multi-part questions (particularly in the case of numerical questions) is that grading is much easier and more consistent.

3.1.4   Take-home examinations

Some instructors espouse the opinion that higher order learning (Bloom's Taxonomy) is not well evaluated using examinations. Essays or lengthy discussions that demonstrate integration of concepts and logical presentation of ideas often take longer than a typical 2–3 hour examination period. The so-called 'take-home examination' is actually an assignment, not an examination. However, the same assignment can readily be administered as an examination. It is simply a matter of informing students of the examination question several days prior to the examination, and having them write their answer in the examination room. Students prepare for this kind of examination by writing their paper at home, rehearsing and perfecting it, and then producing the final text in the controlled environment of the examination room. Even if they choose to discuss the material with other students, what they write in the examination room will be their own work.

3.2   Grading Exams

Grading examinations is a time-consuming and time-pressured activity for most instructors. An early study confirmed substantive disparity in grades among and within the same examiner (Hartog and Rhodes, 1936). More recently, studies have shown that student perceptions of unfairness remain highly associated with grading inconsistencies (Yorke, 2000).

Instructors should have a comprehensive answer key for their examinations. In the case of essay questions, a grading rubric should be used so that students understand the relationship between their work and the grade given. This ensures that all answers will be graded consistently, and student inquiries about their exam grades can be answered uniformly after the results have been returned. A well-graded paper with feedback is a second learning opportunity for students, from both subject knowledge and exam writing skill perspectives. In general, examination questions that are more subjective in nature require more detailed and comprehensive feedback than questions of a more objective or quantitative nature.

When class sizes are large, instructors often use teaching assistants or graduate students to assist with grading. When one or more individuals will be involved in some or all of the grading work, several strategies can be used to minimize grading inconsistencies. Each marker should grade the same questions across all examinations, thereby reducing inter-item variability. Not only does this make the grading easier and more accurate, but it also enables inconsistencies to be addressed to the individual responsible.

Regardless of whether grades are obtained by a single grader or a team, an instructor should perform an analysis and review of the grades for each question. This is easily accomplished using spreadsheet software. A grade breakdown with student names down the side and questions (or parts of questions) across the top should be filled in by graders as they go (in addition to marking grades on the exams). By sorting each question from highest to lowest, an audit of the grade consistency and inter-item variation becomes easier to do. For example, by sorting the grades from highest to lowest for a particular question, instructors can quickly review the answers for students with similar or different grades. For large class sizes, a sample of such comparisons is often enough to determine whether grading has been done consistently.

The best course feedback about their course an instructor can get is to grade their own examinations. Examination validity is readily improved when instructors grade their own exams. Instructors will quickly learn which examination questions are well worded and which should be changed the next time around. Instructors can reflect on the topics that are well taught (students seem to answer these questions well) and those that are not so well understood. When errors are the same for a significant number of students, one can reflect on whether it was taught incorrectly, or whether there was inconsistency between the materials and the question. Perhaps a change in the way the material is taught, the course materials or the examination questions is in order.

3.3   Examination Security

In addition to proctoring methods mentioned in section 2.4, instructors should consider whether to re-use examinations, or whether to change them every time the course is offered.

Using the same examination over a period of years has the advantage of allowing direct comparisons with previous classes, the refinement of questions, grading rubrics, teaching materials and how the material is taught in the classroom.

However, if the same examination is used more than once, there is an increasing risk that the examination will be circulated during a future offering of the course. Students may remove a copy of the examination from the room, or reconstruct the questions from memory after the exam has taken place. This provides future students with an opportunity to gain an advantage over students who do not have access to the examination paper and/or inflate grades overall. Instructors who decide to use the same examination each year must be particularly vigilant to ensure that each printed examination is accounted for before and after the examination. Randomizing the order of the questions, changing numerical values and/or making minor changes to questions can also be helpful in reducing the chance that exam security is breached.

With advanced document processing, instructors can develop a bank of questions over time, and create a different exam each time the course is offered by drawing from the bank. Many textbook publishers provide instructors with test banks from which to create examinations, making that task easier. If an instructor teaches the same course for many years, developing a test bank, along with grading rubrics and so on, is a worthwhile investment that captures both examination security and the benefits mentioned earlier.

4.   NEW IDEAS FOR EXAMINATIONS

A relatively new concept used for both individual student evaluation and enhanced student learning in groups is the two-stage exam. Pioneered by the University of British Columbia's physics department, two-stage exams test the student's individual performance by first administering an examination in the normal way. After the examination is completed, the same examination is administered again to a group of 3–5 students. In the second, 'collaborative' examination, students have the opportunity discuss the question, obtain consensus and submit a group answer. In addition to evaluating students' individual knowledge in the first stage, students learn from each other and improve their understanding of the material in the second stage. It was found that students' retention scores were significantly higher after completing the second examination, with the potential limitation of learning gain due to low group examination scores. It was also found that all students benefit equally in collaborative testing (Gilley and Clarkson, 2013).

Immediate Feedback Assessment Technique (IF-AT) is an assessment technique that both assesses student knowledge and improves student learning (Dibattista et al., 2004). Based on multiple choice examinations, the answer sheet is similar to scratch and win lottery tickets. If students identify the correct answer, a 'star' symbol is revealed. If they choose a wrong answer, they can choose again until they obtain the correct answer (star). Aside from providing immediate feedback on performance, the IF-AT system teaches students the correct answer by identifying their wrong answer selections as they go. IF-AT score sheets can be used to give partial marks for answers that are partially correct. Enhanced learning obtained by using IF-AT exams has been demonstrated empirically with improved retention as much as six months after the examinations have been administered (Brosvic et al., 2006).

5.   SUMMARY AND CONCLUSIONS

The use of written examinations in student evaluation has decreased over time, and many instructors have chosen to use un-invigilated forms of assessment almost exclusively. While there is no standard or 'optimal' mix of examination and assignment grades, instructors should reconsider the benefits of examinations when making decisions about the teaching, learning and assessment of students. Assignments, group projects, take-home examinations and so on have significant problems with plagiarism, copying, unauthorized collaboration and other forms of academic misconduct. Cheating is rampant among students and is more difficult to discourage, detect, control or assess in an unsupervised environment.

Examinations have been shown to be an effective evaluative tool and motivate students to do well. In many cases, examination grades and assignment grades for the same student are comparable. The controlled environment provided by the examination process makes cheating more difficult, discourages students from doing so and vastly improves detection of academic misconduct. Examinations enhance the integrity of the evaluation system.

Instructors can learn a great deal from examinations. Gaps between examination questions, course materials and classroom teaching that undermine learning, reduce examination validity and degrade the students' examination experience are readily identified. Instructors can do many things to reduce examination stress, increase the validity of examinations and improve students' satisfaction with the examination itself. Several new ideas have been developed that show promise in using the examination as a teaching tool, as well as for assessment purposes.

While there are valid reasons why assignments should play a role in the pedagogy of learning and assessment, instructors are urged to reconsider the mix of un-invigilated work and examinations in their teaching practice.

REFERENCES

Bishop, John H. (1994), *The Impact of Curriculum-Based Examinations on Learning in Canadian Secondary Schools*, Center for Advanced Human Resource Studies, Working Paper, ILR Cornell, accessed 20 July 2012 at http://digitalcommons.ilr.cornell.edu/cgi/viewcontent.cgi?article=1254&context=cahrswp.

Bolton, M.K. (1999), 'The role of coaching in student teams: a "just-in-time" approach to student learning', *Journal of Management Education*, 23 (3), 233.

Bridges, P., Cooper, A., Evanson, P., Haines, C., Jenkins, D., Scurry, D., Woolf, H. and Yorke, M. (2002), 'Coursework marks high, examination marks low: discuss', *Assessment and Evaluation in Higher Education*, 27 (1), 36–48.

Brosvic, G.M., Epstein, M., Dihoff, R. and Cook, M. (2006), 'Acquisition and retention of Esperanto: the case for error correction and immediate feedback', *The Psychological Record*, 56 (2), 205–18.

Candy, P.C., Crebert, G. and O'Leary, J. (1994), *Developing Lifelong Learners through Undergraduate Education*, Canberra: Australian Government Publishing Service.

Chapman, K.J., Davis, R., Toy, D. and Wright, L. (2004), 'Academic integrity in the Business School environment: I'll get by with a little help from my friends', *Journal of Marketing Education*, **26** (3), 236–50.

Christensen-Hughes, J. and McCabe, D. (2006), 'Understanding academic misconduct', *Canadian Journal of Higher Education*, **36** (1), 49–63.

Dibattista, D., Mitterer, J. and Gosse, L. (2004), 'Acceptance by undergraduates of the immediate feedback assessment technique for multiple choice testing', *Teaching in Higher Education*, **9** (1), 17–28.

Gibbs, G. and Simpson, C. (2004), 'Conditions under which assessment supports student learning', *Learning and Teaching in Higher Education*, **1**, 3–31.

Gilley, Brett and Bridgette Clarkson (2013), 'Does collaborative testing increase students' retention of concepts?', Carl Weiman Science Education Initiative, University of British Columbia, accessed 12 September 2014 at www.cwsei.ubc.ca/Files/EOY/EOY2013/Posters/Gilley-Clarkston_TwoStageExams_CWSEI-EOY2013.pdf.

Hartog, Sir Philip and Rhodes, E.C. (eds) (1936), *The Marks of Examiners*, London: Macmillan.

Harvard Magazine (2010), 'Bye bye, blue books', *John Harvard's Diary*, July–August, accessed 19 July 2012 at http://harvardmagazine.com/2010/07/bye-bye-blue-books.

Hunsley, John (1985), 'Test anxiety, academic performance and cognitive appraisals', *Journal of Educational Psychology*, **77** (6), 678–82.

Johnson, Bess E. (1938), 'The effect of written examinations on learning and on the retention of learning', *Journal of Experimental Education*, **7** (1), 55–62.

Kornell, Nate (2010), 'Everybody is stupid except you', *Psychology Today*, accessed 20 July 2012 at http://www.psychologytoday.com/blog/everybody-is-stupid-except-you/201012/study-better-the-benefits-cumulative-exams.

Lawrence, N. (2013), 'Cumulative exams in the introductory psychology course', *Teaching of Psychology*, **40** (1), 15–19.

Meyer, G. (1936), 'The effect of recall and recognition on the examination set in classroom situations', *Journal of Educational Psychology*, **27**, 81–99.

Morris, R. and Hayes, C. (1997), 'Small group work: are group assignments a legitimate form of assessment?', in Pospisal, R. and Willcoxson, L. (eds), *Learning Through Teaching*, pp. 229–33. Proceedings of the 6th Annual Teaching Learning Forum, Murdoch University, Perth, February 1997, accessed 30 August 2016 at http://clt.curtin.edu.au/events/conferences/tlf/tlf1997/morris.html.

Mullens, A. (2000), 'Cheating to win', *University Affairs*, December, pp. 22–8.

Silverman, M.M. (1993), 'Campus student suicide rates: fact or artifact?', *Suicide and Life-Threatening Behavior*, **23** (4), 329–42.

Szpunar, K.K., McDermott, K.B. and Roediger III, H.L. (2007), 'Expectation of a final cumulative test enhances long-term retention', *Memory & Cognition*, **35**, 1007–13.

Tynjala, P. (1998), 'Traditional studying for examination vs constructivist learning tasks: do learning outcomes differ?', *Studies in Higher Education*, **23** (2), 173–91.

Vallance, T. (1947), 'A comparison of essay and objective examinations as learning experiences', *Journal of Educational Research*, **41** (4), 279–88.

Williams, J.B. and Wong, Amy (2007), 'Closed book, invigilated exams versus open book, open web exams: an empirical analysis', *Proceedings Ascilite 2007*, accessed 19 July 2012 at http://www.ascilite.org.au/conferences/singapore07/procs/williams-jb.pdf.

Yip, Paul (1998), *Youth Suicides in Hong Kong*, Hong Kong: Befrienders International, pp. 15–27.

Yorke, M. (2000), 'The quality of the student experience: what can institutions learn from data relating to non-completion?', *Quality in Higher Education*, **6**, 61–75.

4 Teaching sales and negotiations
John C. Crotts

1. INTRODUCTION

A well-staffed sales team is critical for business success, but surprisingly most hospitality and tourism management (HTM) programs fail to offer any sales-related courses. It is true that virtually all HTM programs offer courses in marketing. Marketing, as currently taught, is framed by the marketing mix paradigm, which under promotion involves, at best, a chapter reading and lecture on sales usually focused at the retail level. Take a look at virtually any company and you will see that only a small fraction of the careers available in our industry have *marketing* in their title. For those that do – such as the chief marketing officer or marketing manager – their focus is primarily on promotion, which in today's context involves working with advertising agencies in the design and placement of paid space advertising, sales promotions, publicity, and the social media. For every one job in marketing you identify, you will find many more in sales. The reality is that the salesperson is responsible for implementing the marketing strategies of their firms (Javier et al. 2014). In business-to-business sales, on which this chapter is focused, it is the salesperson, supported by marketing collateral, who is entrusted with a firm's most precious asset: its customers.

Given that all HTM programs purport themselves to be gateways for students to the middle class and that sales managers are the most highly compensated individuals in any tourism organization (Kefgen and Mahoney 2006), educators should question why such courses have been omitted from our curriculum. Until recently HTM programs might have been justified in skipping over sales. Time was that success in sales was composed of two parts personality and one part product knowledge, and formal education could add very little (Fogel et al. 2012). People skills are often thought of as unteachable in any conventional sense and best learned experientially. Product knowledge is unique to each firm and therefore handled best by internal training.

Personal selling and sales management has come a long way since the days when most HTM programs were developed. In short, there are plenty of substantial materials to be taught but they require teaching methods that extend beyond the traditional lecture method. The intent of this chapter is to expand educators' awareness not only of the importance of the topic in our field, but also how to teach it to our students. My recommendations are based on more than a decade of research and teaching in personal selling skills gleaned from countless interviews with effective sales professionals. Moreover, they have been validated through interviews with the buyers they serve as to what makes a salesperson effective. What collectively they tell us is that the skills required to be a successful salesperson can be learned and always improved.

It is my hope that sales education will be improved, and that more HTM faculty will be drawn to the field of sales and negotiations, not only for teaching but also for rigorous research. Drawing from the broader sales literature, research has shown that sales professionals who graduated from formal sales courses that are aligned with industry best practices reached their break-even point in their territories faster, are more satisfied with their jobs, and their tenure with the company lasted much longer, saving companies significant amounts of money in training costs (Bolander et al. 2014; Leasher and Moberg 2008). Perhaps an even stronger argument for increasing the number of courses in sales and negotiations is that our industry suffers from a lack of capable sales professionals. Many sales positions go unfilled due to a lack of qualified applicants. Moreover, many more sales positions are filled by those who are unprepared to excel in them, creating lost opportunties for business growth and development.

The study of personal selling and sales negotiations is a relatively young but mature field of study (50 years). It draws from practice and theory from the fields of marketing, psychology, and behavioral economics. This chapter will attempt to do more than simply synthesize the practice by expanding educators' awareness of the importance of the topic in our field and the pedalogical tools available to teach it to our students effectively.

2.   ATTRACTING STUDENTS TO SALES

Build a course and they will come is an approach I first took that ultimately proved successful. However, over the years I have put a system into place that reasonably assures me that the instructional approach I am taking is valid and student demand is high. Consider adopting or adapting any and all aspects as you see fit.

The field of sales seems to be a good fit for students who are marketing-oriented, strategic, self-motivated, and can manage pressure. The things that can help attract them to a course, and ultimately a career, in sales are several. There are reasonable working hours – you work during those times when you can call upon your customers, which generally means Monday to Friday 8:00 am–5:00 pm; a decent and motivational compensation package; and advancement opportunities. Given that the framework I apply to sales training is consultative in nature, hospitality management majors who are naturally service-oriented are also drawn to sales due to the problem-solving, needs-based approach to helping customers.

In today's highly connected environment, graduates from the class who obtain well-paying and satisfying sales jobs after graduation help to ensure that the sales classes are filled each semester. Today, I work with a select group of companies who provide me with feedback on the curriculum, and use the class and the network of former graduates for recruitment purposes. In addition to the director of sales for a hotel chain and a convention center, the list of partners includes a wholesale food supplier to the restaurant industry, a wine wholesaler/distributor, a catering company, and a realtor. Since these are busy people, the commitment I can expect from them is limited. In addition to gaining an awareness of my approach to sales training and offering me advice, they assist me in developing role-plays in their sectors, allow me to mystery shop their sales managers, and to call upon them to judge student sales competitions. As a result the placement rate for students who decide to go into sales is reasonably high, and the word spreads that it is a useful, challenging and arguably a fun course to take.

3.   A SHORT PRIMER OF SALES AND NEGOTIATIONS

Sales, at least the way I and others teach it, is business-to-business (B2B) focused, as opposed to retailing or business-to-consumer (B2C) focused. It's about calling on organizational buyers who purchase what we have to sell in reasonably large volumes. In the hotel and convention business, group sales managers call on customers who are meeting planners, conference or tradeshow managers, corporate travel offices, and tour operators. Group sales is not limited to hotels and convention centers. The very same meeting planner who has reserved a room block in a convention hotel has probably also bought related services from off-premise caterers, special event consultants, entertainment agents and speaker bureaux. Looking backward one step will remind us that the meeting planner more often than not sold his/her services to the association's board of directors, which required using his/her own skills in prospecting, personal selling and negotiating. In essence, B2B relations and the sales managers who develop them permeate our industry.

In the world of hospitality sales, hotels are not only sellers but also organizational buyers. What they buy includes furnishings, fixtures and equipment, interior design services, computerized property management systems, back office accounting systems, landscape and golf greens maintenance – and on and on. The same is true for the restaurant industry. Restaurants who sell to individuals and groups are just the final stage of a series of buyer–seller relationships. Between 25 and 35 percent of the revenue made from restaurant patrons goes to suppliers to pay for wholesale food costs. Explore even deeper and one will see that the restaurant owner or manager has been a buyer in another sense. He/she has purchased (or leased) the real estate and building for the restaurant, as well as everything required to operate it efficiently such as kitchen equipment, furnishings, linens, point of sales system, and a host of services such as book-keeping, time-and-attendance systems, grounds maintenance, contract services and so on.

Meet the salespersons of our industry's suppliers, and you will find that the best have previous experience working directly with the final end-user in the hospitality and tourism industry (that is, the guest). Why? One of the first truisms in sales is to know your product *and* your customer's industry better than your competitors. Who better to sell a new restaurant account for a food wholesaler than a salesperson with culinary or restaurant management experience? The same is true for virtually all other buyer–seller dyads in the hospitality and tourism industry.

Selling requires far more skills than order taking. Even when the prospect initiates the contact, it is likely that he/she is contacting several other firms simultaneously and weighing all options to identify the best solution or value. In addition, most firms cannot afford to wait for customers to come looking for them. More often firms realize that to compete, they must proactively go after new business and thereby create new demand. In these instances the sales professional wears the hat of a marketer and will:

- Identify sources of leads or prospects within his/her territory. Prioritize specific leads that offer the highest quantity and quality of prospects.
- Determine the best method to make an initial contact with prospects.
- Stimulate the prospect's interest with an initial contact for purposes of scheduling a meeting, during which the prospect's needs can be investigated and the benefits of the seller's service highlighted.

- Ask for the prospect's business.
- Build and continue to develop the relationship for mutual gain.

Organizational buyers are considerably more sophisticated than buyers in the consumer marketplace. They have to be very careful in considering the costs and technical requirements of what is being purchased. Often the organizational buying decision involves more than one individual. The decision as to what vendor to use in renovating a hotel may be influenced by the hotel's owner(s), its management company and the franchiser. Knowing who are the gatekeepers, decision influencers and ultimately the decision makers is the responsibility of the salesperson.

Organizational buyers have a more involved buying process as well. More often than not, virtually all non-recurring purchase decisions (for example, re-orders) require a formal request-for proposals (RFP) from multiple suppliers. Suppliers that make the initial cut will often be invited to make a formal sales presentation to the buyer's team. The potential buyer then analyzes the pros and cons of the alternative sources and suppliers, and will try to work through any perceived shortcomings. Once the decision of who to buy from is reached and a contract signed, post-sale implementation is the next important step.

Over the years I have progressively added more to the second half of the class in negotiation skills. Issues frequently arise with clients where there are no clear or established methods for reaching a decision. To reach a satisfactory resolution requires the sales person at times to be accommodating to the will and demands of another party; at other times they must be distributive and hold firm, prepared to walk away from making a deal; and hopefully more often they find integrative solutions that create win–win solutions for both buying and selling organizations. There are many good negotiation role-plays and case studies I will later share with you, including short readings that can provide students with a needed foundation. I wish to press upon students the natural tension that exists in the role of sales professionals. On the one hand, research has shown that empathetic people have a strong ability to recognize others' interests, which is key to reaching negotiated sales agreements. On the other hand, the trait of assertiveness contributes to negotiation outcomes as well, insuring that a selling organization's interests are not undermined. Remember that there are distributed aspects in even integrative negotiations. The point is that people are generally stronger in one trait than the other, but in order to be an effective negotiator one must develop both skills.

4.   TEACHING A COURSE IN SALES AND NEGOTIATIONS

A course on personal selling, I argue, should be a core component of all HTM curriculums. Paraphrasing Lewicki (1986), personal selling is a *learnable and teachable skill.* Effective sales persons *are made, not born*, and skills can be improved and relearned throughout one's career. Changes and improvements in sales abilities require *a combination of intellectual training and behavioral skill development*. Hence, an effective approach to teaching such a course generally integrates analysis and skill development exercises into a single course.

My approach to teaching sales involves a flipped classroom approach. Students, on their own time outside of class, are quizzed on weekly reading assignments using an online course management system. Class times are used for mystery shops, role-plays and case studies, as they provide a useful experiential means to enact selling in a variety of environments.

Textbooks on personal selling skills specific to the tourism and hospitality industry are limited. Abbey (2008) provides a useful text in hotel group sales with an emphasis on the role of a director of sales. The career ladder to a director of sales starts as a sales manager, so my approach is to provide students with the foundational skills in personal selling needed to begin such a career path. There are a number of quality textbooks on personal selling that are B2B focused in the general business literature. In addition, Rich McNeil and I co-authored a textbook in 2005 that is HTM-oriented and I believe is still quite valid (McNeil and Crotts 2005). Over the past several years I have gravitated to a shorter eBook that I am happy to make available (Crotts 2014). Though I know of HTM faculty who make their courses totally experiential, I see value in giving the students readings that introduce the key concepts I expand upon in the classroom experientially.

A typical class will begin with a ten-minute introduction where my students can ask me any questions they have on the day's reading and quiz, followed by a brief perspective on the topic. Periodically I will share with them a mystery shop with a sales manager either live or audio recorded over the telephone. Effective learning can occur through hearing good as well as bad techniques. Most of my live telephone calls to a sales manager are to former graduates of the class. Though students in the class believe otherwise, these calls are always prearranged. The advantage is that after the call has progressed to an appropriate point and I expose the ruse, the former student can provide some prepared words of advice to the students.

This naturally leads us to engage in a role-play. Role-plays are an effective way to develop competencies and are relatively easy to construct. In Appendix 4A.1 of this chapter you will find two examples. All require students in teams of two to engage in a sales call where one takes on the role of the buyer and the other the seller. The point of the role-play is for the selling student to manage the flow of the sales call. As the instructor, I will observe as time permits a few teams' role-plays for coaching purposes, and call upon the best to repeat the role-play in front of the class. Arguably a useful extension of role-playing would be to engage teams in a role-play conducted soley by email or Skype. For those faculty whose class sizes are too large, making it difficult to observe all students, consider requiring students to complete a reflective self-analysis of their own, as well as their partner's, performance as they switch roles in the role-play (see Appendix 4A.2).

The approach to sales skill development involves creating a structure which the sales person employs in managing the flow of the conversation. Though students start off feeling overly scripted by the structures, over time they learn to make the conversation their own. The framework of sales models can vary, but all that I have witnessed have similar elements. The framework I use is called Personal Selling Skills (PSS), which has been widely adopted in the hospitality industry. If you feel more comfortable in a different model, then use it. I have found this five-step framework easy for students to comprehend and eventually follow. It involves:

1. *Call Opening* (warm friendly greeting, thanking the customer for the call, proposing the agenda, stating the value of the agenda, checking for acceptance).
2. *Probing* (identifying a customer's needs through good questions and listening).

3. *Supporting* (presenting relevant features as benefits to the customer).
4. *Closing* (advancing the sell, asking for the business).
5. *Handling Objections* (misunderstandings, doubts, shortcomings).

The first role-plays of the semester stop after the call opening. Subsequent role-plays are progressive in nature, and include all previously learned steps. Later-stage role-plays are designed to challenge the selling student's ability to think on his or her feet, where the buyer will raise objections at any step in the process. This, in essence, is the first half of the semester, which culminates with a mid-term oral exam. The oral exam is on a one on one basis in which they are asked to sell me something which I video for playback coaching purposes.

   The second half of the semester involves students in more complex negotiation role-plays and sales case studies. Foundational readings and quizzes expose them to important new topics on ethics, organization and management of a sales office, technology, and sales channels, which all can be reinforced experientially. Northwestern University's Dispute Resolution Center (http://www.kellogg.northwestern.edu/research/drrc.aspx) has what I have found to be a wonderful repository of role-plays on bargaining that are surprisingly rich in hospitality and tourism management settings. Most require students, in teams of two, to attempt to negotiate an agreement following an outlined scenario which later can be compared with other team outcomes in the exercise debrief led by the faculty member. Two to three case studies from Harvard Business School have also proven to be helpful.

5.   CLASS STRUCTURE

Developing a course on sales requires some practical considerations in its set-up as well as in your role as professor in the course. Allow me to turn my final attention to these concerns.

- *Class size.* Teaching such a course experientially requires a classroom of moderate size – this is big enough to have multiple teams that will produce different results, small enough to orchestrate the experience in a limited time. I generally prefer class sizes of 25–35 students. Classes larger than 35 effectively bar a single instructor from observing and coaching every student at least once during the semester.
- *Facilities.* Role-playing, with multiple teams simultaneously participating in the learning activity, means that each team requires a reasonably private place to stand and engage one another. A classroom can suffice, but the noise level becomes high and I find it difficult to navigate around desks for coaching purposes. Outdoors is better on either a lawn, patio or parking lot that is immune to bystanders. I prefer to teach this course in the daytime as well.
- *Class time.* It is very difficult to teach this class in a number of short 50-minute class periods. Class times of 120 minutes meeting twice a week allow students to prepare for and carry out most exercises. I recommend that you avoid scheduling this class once a week for three to four hours. Student fatigue is not the issue – it is that a seven-day gap between classes disrupts the progressive building block aspect

Table 4.1   Grading of sales and negotiation

Task	Weight (%)
Online chapter quizzes (10)	20
Cvent exam	10
Mid-term exam	10
Book review	10
One paperclip exercise	10
Case studies (3)	15
Semester project	15
Class participation/attendance	10
Total	100

of role-playing. With this said, a two to three-day intensive workshop format is also quite effective.

- *No electronic device policy.* A mutually supportive learning environment depends on active attention and engagement. For this reason, I enforce a no use of laptops, phones or any electronic devices policy during classroom sessions. The value of any legitimate use of laptops is far outweighed by the distraction that they create. I inform students that their grade will be reduced by two points for every time they use an electronic device during class time and seldom have to enforce it.
- *Guest speakers.* Though guest speakers add much value to the classroom, in the case of classes in personal selling most faculty use them sparingly. As Wheeler (2006) noted, sales and negotiations is a *wicked* learning environment and as an illustration, a guest speaker who purports to students that (s)he is an effective sales person because they close every deal may be misleading themselves and others. Instead, my approach has been to interview local industry leaders, and, with their permission, draft my own case exercises from their experiences. As previously mentioned, I also bring them in through in-class mystery shops or having them assist me in a role-play.
- *Grading.* Faculty assess student progress using a variety of assessment strategies. The assessment strategy shown in Table 4.1 has worked well for me.

Cvent Exam

The online request-for-proposal (RFP) process has been adopted by many meeting planners and organizational buyers. In order for your students to gain an in-depth understanding of these systems, I encourage you to contact Cvent (Cvent.com), who will provide you the details of this service. They will provide each student with a password and login information, giving them access to a study guide and tutorial of their RFP system. At the assigned date set by you, students can take a 25-question multiple choice certification exam which will serve them well on their résumé.

Mid-term Exam

Many would suggest (and I would concur) that personal selling skills are best assessed through role-plays as opposed to exam questions. Hence, the mid-term exam I employ is on an individual basis where they attempt to sell me an item of their choosing using all the steps in the consultative selling process. I video each role-play using a tablet for coaching playback purposes. I set aside 20–25 minutes for each oral exam. Add up the figures and you will see this requires of me a grueling two-week schedule during mid-terms.

Book Review

I typically add an assignment requiring a three-page critique of a book I select. There are several you may wish to consider, but my favorite is *Influence: Science and Practice* (5th edition, authored by Robert Cialdini, 2009). *The Art of Woo* (by Richard Shell and Mario Moussa, 2007) is worth considering as well. I ask the students to critique the central thesis of the book, its strategies and tactics, as well as to provide me with their opinions on the approach. I find it effective to introduce the One Paperclip Exercise on the day we discuss the book review in class.

One Paperclip Exercise

This is a sales competition for which instructions can be sourced through Harvard Business School Case Studies. It involves handing each student a paperclip and giving them the task of trading it with others for something of higher value. A total of five trades must occur over the course of a two-week period. I highly recommend incorporating this into your class.

Case Studies

I generally incorporate three case studies during the second half of the semester to enhance students' understanding of sales strategy and management. Some are conducted in class while others include take-home assignments. Grades are based upon student responses to the assigned questions, where they apply what they are learning to complex situations requiring the synthesis of information and a fair amount of reasoning, creativity and innovation. From Northwestern University's Dispute Resolution Center, I like using Negotiating a Salary and Sugar Bowl. Daktronics and Gallo Wine are the two cases I have used from Harvard Business School (http://hbsp.harvard.edu/) case studies.

Semester Project

In lieu of a final exam, I require a semester project. The project asks each student to prepare a sales plan focused on how each will pursue finding a job after graduation. Their ideal job can be in any field, just so long as they have aimed reasonably high, which means no entry-level positions. If they already have a position secured for after graduation, I ask them to complete a plan anyway as a plan B. What I am looking for is a demonstration of a realistic sales plan that covers every aspect of this course, starting from prospecting and the stating of your value proposition, to presenting their features as benefits with supporting proof devices.

Though it is obvious that the course as outlined is grading intensive for the instructor, adding one more written assignment in lieu of a final exam can be considered extreme. For a time I dropped the semester project, only to be convinced by former graduates to include it once again. Their reason: the importance of learning the art of lead generation, prospecting, lead nurturing and pre-approach research which the semester project clearly requires. Since most students are graduating seniors, the timeliness of the exercise is not lost on them either. As their careers advance to director of sales, some basic understanding of how to write a sales plan will be warranted as well.

6.   CONCLUSION

In closing, I hope you will take up this challenge to craft your own course on sales and negotiations. However, understand that if you draw from my framework, your role as faculty member will change and you will face some unique challenges as to the dynamics in the classroom. Allow me to briefly summarize them for you.

In a traditional academic course, the instructor has clear-cut roles in structuring a logical course outline, lecturing, facilitating class discussions, and evaluating student performance. However, by virtue of the variety of educational experiences described earlier, instructors in personal selling courses are placed in multiple roles. Instructors must continue to act as formal educators, but also take on enhanced responsibilities as classroom managers and coaches. The following are some guidelines for each role.

- *Educator/Evaluator*. The instructor's responsibilities are, as just outlined, to structure the course, to be well versed in the conceptual foundations of sales and negotiations, to convey that expertise through lectures and assigned readings, to facilitate classroom discussion, and to evaluate student learning and performance.
- *Classroom Manager*. The instructor's job is to orchestrate the learning experience. Role-plays need to be planned with regard to preparation and distribution of materials, securing adequate facilities, time scheduling, and organizing students into groups. Before an exercise is concluded, students should discuss the exercise and abstract key points. Simulations are useless activities without this analysis.
- *Coach*. Students often become overly self-conscious and freeze up in role-plays as well as the mid-term. For the educational process to proceed, students must be able to detach themselves sufficiently from being observed to complete the activities. The instructor's job is to help the student achieve this balance, which frequently requires encouragement, role reversals, and at times a degree of humor.

Expect from time to time that a student will try to argue that role-playing is *not real* because people play artificial roles and there are no actual outcomes. This argument is often used to avoid taking responsibility for their behavior or its consequences. Moreover, they argue that they certainly would have behaved differently had this been a *real* situation involving a product or service about which they have extensive knowledge. Instructors will recognize this behavior as defensive, yet feel frustrated by an inability to persuade the student that this is a limited and perhaps distorted view. Instead of becoming enmeshed in such a argument, it is usually easier to have students accept on the first day of class the premise that all behavior in the course is *real*, that they make choices on the way they behave, that behavior has consequences, and they must be willing to live with them. The stakes may be different outside the classroom, but the behavior is no less real.

Good luck!

REFERENCES

Abbey, J. (2008), *Hospitality Sales and Marketing* (5th edn), Lansing, MI: American Hotel and Lodging Association.

Bolander, W., Bonney, L. and Satornino, C. (2014), 'Sales education efficacy: Examining the relationship between sales education and sales success', *Journal of Marketing Education*, **36** (2), 169–81.

Cialdini, R. (2009), *Influence: Science and Practice* (5th edn), New York: Pearson.

Crotts, J. (2014), *Selling Hospitality: A Consultative Sales Approach*, Author.

Fogel, S., Hoffmeister, D., Rocco, R. and Strunk, D. (2012), 'Teaching sales', *Harvard Business Review*, **90** (7/8), 94–9.

Javier, M., Critten, P., Squire, P. and Speakman, J. (2014), 'Enhancing the professional mindset of future sales professionals: Key insights from a master in sales transformation', *Journal of Marketing Education*, **36** (2), 144–55.

Kefgen, K. and Mahoney, R. (2006), *Compensation and Benefits in the Hotel Industry*, Mineola, NY: HVS International Executive Search.

Leasher, L. and Moberg, C. (2008), 'Evaluating the impact of collegiate sales training and education on early salesperson performance', *Journal of Selling and Major Account Management*, **32** (4), 32–45.

Lewicki, Roy (1986), 'Challenges of teaching negotiation', *Negotiation Journal*, **2** (1), 15–30.

McNeil, R. and Crotts, J. (2005), *Selling Hospitality: A Situational Approach*, Clifton Park, NY: Delmar/ Thompson Publishing.

Shell, R. and M. Moussa (2007), *The Art of Woo: Using Strategic Persuasion to Sell your Ideas*, New York: Penguin Group.

Wheeler, M. (2006), 'Is teaching negotiations too easy, too hard, or both?', *Negotiations Journal*, **22** (2), 187–97.

APPENDIX 4A.1   SAMPLE ROLE-PLAYS

Selling Skills Role-play

Association Market
Salesperson's Role

Background Information:

You are on the phone with: The meeting planner for ISPA (International Spa Association).

How the call came about: Your sister facility in Munich sent a lead out that ISPA is looking at your convention center and 3 competitive sites/destinations for their annual EU trade show and educational congress. The show is always held over five days, mid-week, during a shoulder season when you would really like the business. The show would utilize all of your space for meetings and exhibits, sell out your city's hotels, and would bring in much needed rental and food and beverage income to your center.

Your sales call objective: To familiarize yourself with the ISPA's needs for this event and to have the Executive Director come to your destination for a site visit.

Purpose of the Role-play

To practice and receive feedback on the following skills:
Call Openings
Probing
Supporting
Closing Skills

Before you begin, write your call opening statement (Agenda, Value, Check for Acceptance) and at least 3 questions that you might have of the new Executive Director.

You may call a TIME OUT if you get stuck and need help during the role-play, ask your professor and he will offer you guidance.

Selling Skills Role-play

Association #2 Role-play
Customer's Role

Background information: You are the meeting planner for ISPA (International Spa Association) and your office is located in Washington, DC.

You are on the phone with: A sales representative from a convention center.

How the call came about: You sent out a lead to the Director of Sales at the Munich Expo Centre that ISPA is looking at 4 competitive destinations (convention centers) for your annual EU trade show and educational congress. The show is always held over five days, mid-week, during a shoulder season (off-peak season) when you know they would really like the business. You would utilize all of their space for meetings and exhibits and would bring in much needed rental and food and beverage income.

Needs: If the sales person asks you closed-probe questions only answer yes or no or maybe! If they ask open probes, elaborate on your needs which are listed below. You may also make up needs if they are appropriate and consistent with the role-play.

#1. A convention center that is in good shape and is kept in good repair
Need behind the need:
To impress your picky membership, the word of mouth will not be good unless the facility is in great shape, as your members operate high quality facilities and tend to be high maintenance.

#2. Twenty small meeting rooms that are quiet and flexible for theater style seating
Need behind the need:
You offer a lot of educational topics and although you ask your members to sign up in advance, they never seem to attend the sessions that they sign up for and some sessions are more popular than others, so you need to work with staff that can react quickly to last minute requests for more chairs, etc. Also, the attendees need to be able to hear the speaker talk so they get the full value of the sessions.

#3. A facility that can offer interesting spa-like cuisine
Need behind the need:
Because your membership is in the health field, their expectations of food and beverage are that it will consist of low-calorie, interesting and unique food. In other words, this group is not impressed with donuts and coffee. They prefer things like green tea and carrot and yogurt muffins.

Purpose of the Role-play

Call Opening (warm friendly greeting, thanking the customer for the call, proposing the agenda, stating value, checking for acceptance)
Probing
Supporting
Closing Skills

Selling Skills Role-play

Corporate Meeting Planner
Salesperson's Role

Background Information:

You are at the office of: The meeting planner for the Pfizer Pharmaceutical Company.

How the call came about: You are a group sales manager for a downtown hotel making a prospecting call on the meeting planner. You know that she/he holds several large meetings throughout the year, ranging from meetings of the Board of Directors, Annual Stockholders' meeting, and training sessions for their field sales force. All of these typically use 4 to 5 diamond hotels with meeting facilities. Given the current economic environment (their stock price is down by two-thirds in value), you believe they may be interested in your 3 diamond hotel.

Your sales call objective: To familiarize yourself with the needs of the meeting planner, provide initial support for these needs, and to invite the planner for a site tour of your property.

Purpose of the Role-play

To practice and receive feedback on the following skills:
Call Openings
Probing
Supporting
Closing

Before you begin write your call opening statement (Warm friendly greeting, Agenda, Value, Check for Acceptance) and at least 3 questions that you might have of the meeting planner.

Selling Skills Role-play

Corporate Meeting Planners
Customer's Role

You are: The meeting planner for Pfizer Pharmaceutical Company.

How the call came about: You have agreed to meet for five minutes in your office with the group sales manager of a 3 diamond downtown hotel who contacted you. You hold several large meetings throughout the year ranging from meetings of the Board of Directors, Annual Stockholders' meeting, and training sessions for your field sales force which typically use 4 to 5 diamond hotels with meeting facilities. Given the current economic environment (your company's stock price is two-thirds its normal value), you may be interested in a 3 diamond hotel in a nice destination.

Needs: If the sales person asks you closed-probe questions only answer yes or no or maybe! If they ask open probes elaborate on your needs which are listed below. You may also make-up needs if they are appropriate and consistent with the role-play.

#1. A facility that offers a quality experience but at a budget price.
Need behind the need:
To have those in attendance have a great experience but not at the level of extravagance

#2. Nice destination in which your people can enjoy a variety of low key things to do after hours.
Need behind the need:

#3 A hotel that is near a variety of 3 and 4 star restaurants . . . your members are used to Michelin rated restaurants but due to the economy are more price sensitive.

APPENDIX 4A.2   SELF ANALYSIS FORM

Name: _____   Partner's Name:_____

When I took on the role as the sales manager, what did I do well?

What I can do more effectively next time.

My Key Learning:

When my partner took on the role as the sales manager, what did he/she do well?

What he/she can do more effectively next time.

Note: In addition to managing the flow of the sales conversation, include some feed-back on non-verbal cues (facial expressions, body language, eye contact, tone of voice, gestures, etc.)

5 Research skill development in tourism
W. Glen Croy and John Willison

1.   INTRODUCTION

This chapter presents an approach to assessing and evaluating knowledge, skill and capability outcomes needed by tourism graduates. More specifically, it is about explicitly embedding research skill development within tourism university educational programmes. The chapter starts by evidencing the nature of tourism higher education as largely employment orientated and then demonstrating the skill profile of graduates. From the skill profile, the importance of research is established. Research, as a skill set, is analysed. The component skills clarify research operationally, and an autonomy dimension adds further clarity. Together, the component skills and autonomy comprise the Research Skill Development (RSD) framework. Implementing the RSD in tourism programmes provides opportunities to explicitly develop, practise and assess these crucial skills.

A specific implementation across an undergraduate degree in tourism is presented in three parts: skill assessment; enhancement; and learning environment design. Reflections of using the RSD framework over seven years in the tourism programme are provided from the lecturer, tutor and student perspectives. Future directions and considerations for the implementation of the RSD in tourism are presented. Finally, the conclusion draws together key points.

2.   TOURISM PROGRAMME OUTCOMES

Tourism programmes have grown with the industry. As such, it is not surprising that, in their study of tourism education in the United Kingdom (UK), Airey and Johnson (1999, p. 233) highlighted that the most common objective of tourism programmes was to cater for career opportunities and the second was for employment, employer links and work. The next five most common objectives also had clear connections to industry. While these were not universal objectives, the high priority speaks of provision and demanded aspects of undergraduate degrees. Pearce (2005) too, in the Australian context, notes that often tourism degrees are promoted for tourism industry and career outcomes. Students are selecting degrees as paths to career and employment opportunities, and this is also what universities are providing. Fidgeon's (2010) study further highlighted that the employment outcome emphasis of tourism courses remained in the UK. Zhang and Fan (2005), commenting on the development of tourism programmes in China, also noted the main driver to be industry development needs. These developments, outcomes and challenges facing tourism programmes appear to be relatively common around the globe (McKercher, 2002; Hsu, 2005).

While the main objectives of tourism programmes have been industry orientated, there is disagreement about whether this should be the sole purpose of such programmes.

Harkison et al. (2011, p. 378) state that tourism and hospitality are inherently vocational qualifications, 'in that they prepare graduates for a particular vocation', where 'vocational' has also been widely interpreted as just providing graduates with work-ready skills. The apparent vocational trend has led to concerns. Tribe (2002), for example, argued that a focus on the vocation and maximizing business would limit graduates' ability to conceptualize and deal with externalities. He proposed a space for the 'philosophical practitioner', being a combination of reflective and action-orientated modes of study, and vocational and liberal outcomes in the tourism curriculum. He concludes that the graduate of the philosophical practitioner curriculum 'will intervene in the simple, yet potentially dangerous cycle of reproduction of the world "as is" where students learn passive adaptation to the world that exists' (Tribe, 2002, pp. 354–5). Stuart-Hoyle (2003) further describes the divide as education *about* tourism versus education *for* tourism, the former reflecting the more liberal, and the latter the more vocational.

Dredge et al. (2012) further highlight the limits of a solely vocational education and present a need for programmes that integrated vocational and liberal aspects. However, they emphasize the constrained environment within which curriculum design takes place, and the trade-offs made to deliver a 'philosophical practitioner'. Similarly, MacLaurin (2005) describes how in Canada tourism programmes are constrained by government emphasis on tourism, which influences university investment and availability of staff and student demand. Dredge et al. (2012) add the capacity for institutions to adjust the balance between vocational and liberal aspects to meet the needs of their students and stakeholders within a 'force-field' bound by knowledge (liberal) and capability (vocational) outcomes. They argue that through the tourism curriculum students should move from basic skills and simple knowledge to developing and transforming their capabilities and knowledge to the institutional standards of 'practical wisdom' (Dredge et al., 2012, pp. 2167–8).

Clearly, while vocational outcomes are crucial, the development of graduate liberal knowledge and skills is also recognized as important. This combination as a graduate 'philosophical practitioner' or of 'practical wisdom' highlights general qualities, and as Dredge et al. (2012, p. 2172) state, the models 'are abstractions of reality . . . they simplify complex relationships and provide a graphic tool to provoke further thought and understanding'. This draws the question as to what these graduate profiles actually look like.

2.1   Graduate Profiles

Tourism programme graduate profiles aspired to, demanded and achieved vary along with institutional and contextual demands (Dredge et al., 2012). Within these constrained environments, studies have indicated that tourism programme graduate profiles, in the most part, do demonstrate a combination of vocational and liberal ends. For example, Cho and Kang (2005, p. 236) identified that 'tourism education in Korea, thus, has been developed according to the tourism industry's growth and labor demands' and has used a cooperative approach 'to balance between academic principles and technical knowledge and vocational skills'.

When analysing studies of attribute profiles in tourism and hospitality the authors noted that these are generally investigating graduate profiles, skill profiles, employment profiles or employability profiles. While these terms are sometimes used interchangeably, there are differences (Table 5.1). *Graduate attributes* as a term refers to the institution-prescribed

Table 5.1   Attribute profile focus and distinctions

Attribute Profiles	Focus and Distinctions
Graduate attributes	Profile of graduates from the institution and/or the program of study
Skill profile	Profile of skills that the individual student has
Employment profile	Profile needed for employment in a specific position
Employability profile	General profile needed for employment

outcomes of graduates (the profile of students who exit a course or institution). A *skill profile* is what a person has, and understandably, people exiting the same course can have variations in their profiles. An *employment profile* is prescribed by employers, in the form of essential and desirable attributes of prospective employees. Finally, the *employability profile* is the broader set of attributes generally expected of those seeking employment.

These profiles and the attributes that comprise them frequently overlap yet they do not always align. Graduate attribute statements often include broad scale and aspirational aspects including, for example, 'global citizenship'. This can be compared to, say, employment profiles, which are often very specific, for example 'two years in a tourism marketing role'. The potential variance between graduate attributes and employability attributes has been an increasing concern for universities as employment measures from specific institutions and courses are more publicly available, and students are looking for higher education opportunities to open career pathways. As such, most universities are further facilitating student achievement of the graduate profile and an employability profile. As noted, these profiles have many attributes that do indicate an overlap, as also proposed by Tribe (2002) and Dredge et al. (2012). The emphasis has drawn an explicit focus, in addition to the tourism knowledge foundation, on a series of generic cognitive, transferable and practical skills to be developed, practised and assessed (Fidgeon, 2010).

Table 5.2 presents an overview of the attributes, indicating where the attribute has been reported. These have been collected from tourism and hospitality studies of graduate attributes, employability attributes and employment attributes.

Critical thinking, analytical and problem-solving skills was the attribute most commonly noted across the previous studies, followed by interpersonal, team and human relations skills. Of note was the infrequent identification of discipline knowledge and academic qualifications and performance. Understandably, when assessing graduates, there is a necessary discipline knowledge and subsequent qualification recognizing this. More broadly, the attributes presented in Table 5.2 show obvious similarities across the studies, and appear relevant to both the educational context within they are expected to be developed, as well as the employment environment where it is expected they continue. For the former point, Pearce (2005, p. 260) noted, however, that 'for many tourism programmes, the task of building these skills into the content subjects . . . is an ongoing and critical issue'. He continues in identifying: 'there is certainly a challenge here to all educators to think about exactly what students are gaining in an enduring long-term sense from content-based subjects and courses'.

The Table 5.2 profile also readily reflects the general graduate and employability attribute profiles. For example, Litchfield et al. (2010, p. 521) in their study of multiple disciplines' work-ready graduates identified: 'ethics and professionalism, a global perspec-

Table 5.2   Tourism and hospitality graduate, employability and employment attributes

Attribute	No. of Studies	Contributors
Critical thinking, analytical and problem-solving skills	9	Busby et al. (1997); Pearce (2005); Zhang and Fan (2005); Yuan et al. (2006); Weiler and Goyal (2007); Sheldon et al. (2008); Fidgeon (2010); Harkison et al. (2011); Kwok (2012)
Interpersonal, team and human relations skills	8	Busby et al. (1997); Pearce (2005); Masberg et al. (2004); Weiler and Goyal (2007); Sheldon et al. (2008); Fidgeon (2010); Harkison et al. (2011); Kwok (2012)
Communication, writing, presenting, listening skills	7	Busby et al. (1997); Masberg et al. (2004); Pearce (2005); Weiler and Goyal (2007); Sheldon et al. (2008); Fidgeon (2010); Harkison et al. (2011)
Information gathering, numeracy, inquiry and research skills	6	Busby et al. (1997); Masberg et al. (2004); Pearce (2005); Zhang and Fan (2005); Weiler and Goyal (2007); Fidgeon (2010)
Information technology skills	4	Masberg et al. (2004); Pearce (2005); Weiler and Goyal (2007); Sheldon et al. (2008)
Academic performance and qualifications	3	Yuan et al. (2006); Harkison et al. (2011); Kwok (2012)
Leadership and preparedness	3	Yuan et al. (2006); Sheldon et al. (2008); Kwok (2012)
Negotiation, advocacy and lobbying skills	3	Busby et al. (1997); Masberg et al. (2004); Sheldon et al. (2008)
Personal qualities and personality	3	Busby et al. (1997); Yuan et al. (2006); Harkison et al. (2011)
Discipline knowledge	3	Zhang and Fan (2005); Weiler and Goyal (2007); Harkison et al. (2011)
Work experience	3	Yuan et al. (2006); Harkison et al. (2011); Kwok (2012)
Autonomy, self-evaluation and management skills	2	Fidgeon (2010); Harkison et al. (2011)
Business skills	2	Masberg et al. (2004); Sheldon et al. (2008)
Civic responsibility and ethical skills	2	Pearce (2005); Sheldon et al. (2008)
Commercial and policy awareness	2	Busby et al. (1997); Zhang and Fan (2005)
Extra-curricular activities	2	Yuan et al. (2006); Kwok (2012)
Flexibility	2	Sheldon et al. (2008); Kwok (2012)
Social and cultural awareness and stewardship skills	2	Pearce (2005); Sheldon et al. (2008)
Foreign language abilities	1	Yuan et al. (2006)
Interview behaviors	1	Kwok (2012)
Job pursuit intention	1	Kwok (2012)
Lifelong learning orientation	1	Pearce (2005)
Person–organization and person–job fit	1	Kwok (2012)
University attended	1	Yuan et al. (2006)
Willingness to relocate	1	Yuan et al. (2006)

tive, communication capacity, ability to work well in a team, ability to apply knowledge, and creative problem solving and critical thinking skills'. Moreover, a review of Australian university graduate employability skills noted another similarly reflective graduate profile (Precision Consultancy, 2007). The profile identified:

> Communication skills that contribute to productive and harmonious relations between employees and customers; Teamwork skills that contribute to productive working relationships and outcomes; Problem solving skills that contribute to productive outcomes; Self-management skills that contribute to employee satisfaction and growth; Planning and organizing skills that contribute to long-term and short-term strategic planning; Technology skills that contribute to effective execution of tasks; Life-long learning skills that contribute to ongoing improvement and expansion in employee and company operations and outcomes; Initiative and enterprise skills that contribute to innovative outcomes. (p. 10)

Whilst Table 5.2 and generic lists provide an indication of the commonness of attributes, they do not always reflect the importance of each. In their comparative study of business and tourism graduates, in response to the open-ended question 'what aspects of university study have been helpful in doing the job you are currently doing?', Weiler and Goyal (2007) found that the top four responses were communication skills (28 percent of respondents), marketing knowledge skills (21 percent), nothing in particular (20 percent), and research skills (18 percent). Yuan et al. (2006) found that managers rated, in order, problem-solving abilities, work experience and personal qualities as the top three most important. Recruiters and students rated the same three attributes, in a different order, as their top three most important, though students did not value these as much. Reflecting the prominence of research, a study of graduates in other fields found that research skills were frequently required in their working environment (Willison, 2014).

Research skills are commonly and importantly evident in tourism graduate and employability attributes, though not always explicitly. Given the apparent ambiguity and ill-defined concept, questions are raised as to how research skills are developed, and how educators demonstrate that students have acquired these skills.

3.   WHAT IS RESEARCH, AND WHAT ARE RESEARCH SKILLS?

As Brew (1988, cited in Brew and Boud, 1995, p. 267) put simply: 'research is a process of learning'. Leedy and Ormrod (2010, p. 2) further emphasized the 'process' to state that 'research is a systematic process of collecting, analysing, and interpreting information (data) in order to increase our understanding of a phenomenon about which we are interested or concerned'. They further clarify that research is a process involving intention to enhance understandings, through to the communication of findings. Brew and Boud (1995) similarly state that research is a systematic production of knowledge. Willison and O'Regan (2007, p. 394) note there is a continuum of knowledge production, 'from knowledge new to the learner to knowledge new to humankind, moving from the commonly known, to the commonly not known, to the totally unknown'. All students and academics are on this continuum, framing the facilitation of students' movement to develop their knowledge production skills, generating new knowledge for themselves and others. Importantly,

Table 5.3 Research skills and descriptions

Research Skill	Description
a. Embark and Clarify	Respond to or initiate research and clarify or determine what knowledge is required, heeding ethical/cultural and social/team considerations
b. Find and Generate	Find and generate needed information/data using appropriate methodology
c. Evaluate and Reflect	Determine and critique the degree of credibility of selected sources, information and of data generated, and reflect on the research processes used
d. Organize and Manage	Organize information and data to reveal patterns and themes, and manage teams and research processes
e. Analyze and Synthesize	Analyze information/data critically and synthesize new knowledge to produce coherent individual/team understandings
f. Communicate and Apply	Write, present and perform the processes, understandings and applications of the research, and respond to feedback, accounting for ethical, social and cultural (ESC) issues.

Source: Willison and O'Regan (2007).

research is more inclusive than just 'research methodology' and 'primary data collection'. As such, the skills needed for research would likewise be necessarily more inclusive.

Each of the definitions of research highlights many of the most common graduate and employability attributes from Table 5.2. Similarly, the component research skills reflect the attributes from Table 5.2. Willison and O'Regan (2007) present six interrelated research skills, presented as a sequential cyclical process of continuous feedback loops. These six skills are presented with a brief description in Table 5.3. The research skills were derived from Australian and New Zealand Institute for Information Literacy (ANZIL) (2004) *Information Literacy Framework* and Bloom and colleagues' (1956) *Taxonomy of Educational Objectives* (Willison and O'Regan, 2007).

As previously noted, the six research skills strongly reflect a number of the graduate and employability attributes presented in Table 5.2, including critical thinking, analytical and problem-solving, communication, writing, presenting, listening, information gathering and numeracy skills.

In addition to a continuum of 'knowing', it is implied that there is also a continuum of research autonomy. As each of these research skills is developed, the skill holder is more autonomous in applying this skill.

4. AUTONOMY

The second and core component of having research skills is, moreover, being able to apply them in new settings and ways. This translates to having autonomy in the application of the skills. Willison and O'Regan (2007) initially presented five autonomy levels, from prescribed research through to open research (Table 5.4).

Table 5.4   Research skill autonomy level and description

Research Autonomy Level		Description
Level 1 Prescribed Research	Supervisor initiated	Highly structured directions and modeling from educator prompt student research
Level 2 Bounded Research		Boundaries set by and limited directions from educator channel student research
Level 3 Scaffolded Research		Scaffolds placed by educator shape student independent research
Level 4 Student-initiated Research	Researcher initiated	Students initiate the research and this is guided by the educator
Level 5 Open Research		Students research within self-determined guidelines that are in accord with discipline or context

Source: Willison and O'Regan (2007).

5.   RESEARCH SKILL DEVELOPMENT FRAMEWORK

Combining the research skills and levels of autonomy, Willison and O'Regan (2007) presented their framework for students becoming researchers: the Research Skill Development (RSD) Framework. The RSD is presented as 'a conceptual framework for the explicit, coherent, incremental and spiralling development of students' research skills' (Willison and O'Regan, 2007). The research skills form a matrix with increasing levels of student autonomy, from lecturer-specified closed inquiry with high degrees of guidance to student-specified with self-determined guidelines (Willison and O'Regan, 2007) (Figure 5.1, RSD 5).

The RSD framework articulates together these two dimensions of the facets of research and the varying levels of student autonomy. The framework can be used to identify and diagnose students' progression, to design learning tasks, and to inform subject and course design. One key to explicitly developing student research skills is through the framing or reframing of assessment marking rubrics with the RSD (Willison and O'Regan, 2007). The rubrics make research skills explicit to students and direct their demonstration of these within their assessment items.

In a 2010 review of RSD framework implementation in 28 subjects/units/papers/ courses, from a variety of faculties across five Australian universities, Willison et al. (2010) reported:

● measured improvements in student research skills through the use of the RSD;
● students reported being better prepared for and more interested in research generally, and in higher degrees by research after use of the RSD;
● students reported a more satisfying learning environment, including greater skill development as compared to subjects not using the RSD;
● the RSD was transferable across disciplines and different groups of universities;
● students identified transferability of research skills to employment (89 percent), and to other subjects (76 percent).

Research Skill Development Framework

For educators to facilitate the explicit, coherent, incremental and cyclic development of the skills associated with researching, problem solving, critical thinking and clinical reasoning.

RSD

www.rsd.edu.au
john.willison@adelaide.edu.au

Students' Autonomy when Researching

Facets of Research

Facets of Research / Disposition	Prescribed Researching — Highly structured directions and modeling from educator prompt researching, in which…	Bounded Researching — Boundaries set by and limited directions from educator channel researching, in which…	Scaffolded Researching — Scaffolds placed by educator shape independent researching, inwhich…	Open-ended Researching — Students initiate research and this is guided by the educator…	Unbounded Researching — Students determined guidelines for researching that are in accord with discipline or context…
Students develop a research mindset through engagement with content and increasing awareness of ethical, cultural, social and team (ECST) aspects, when they…					
Embark and Clarify (Curious) — *What is our purpose?* Students respond to or initiate research and clarify whatknowledge is required, considering ECST issues.	Students respond to questions/tasks arising explicitly from a closed inquiry. Use a provided structured approach to clarify questions, terms, requirements, expectations andECST issues.	Students respond to questions/tasks required by andimplicit in a closed inquiry. Choose from several provided structures or approaches to clarify questions, terms, requirements, expectations and ECST issues.	Students respond to questions/tasks generated from a closed inquiry. Choose from a range of provided structures or approaches to clarify questions, requirements, expectations and ECST issues.	Students generate questions/aims/hypotheses framed within structured guidelines*. Anticipate andprepare for ECST issues.	*Students generate questions/aims/hypotheses based on experience, expertise and literature*. Delve into and prepare for ECST issues.
Find and Generate (Determined) — *What do we need?* Students find andgenerate needed information/data using appropriate methodology.	Students collect andrecord required information/data using a prescribed methodology from a prescribed source in which the information/data is evident.	Students collect andrecord appropriate information/data using given methodology from pre-determined source/s where information/data is not obvious.	Students collect and record appropriate information/data from self-selected sources using one of several provided methodologies.	Students collect and record self-determined information/data choosing an appropriate methodology based on parameters set.	Students collect and record information/data from self-selected sources, choosing or devising an appropriate methodology with self-structured guidelines.
Evaluate and Reflect (Discerning) — *What do we trust?* Students determine the credibilityof sources, information anddata, andmake own research processes visible.	Students evaluate sources/information/data using simple prescribed criteria to specify credibility andto reflect on the research process. See patterns. *Ask emergent questions of clarification/curiosity*.	Students evaluate a choice of provided criteria to specify credibility andto reflection the research process.	Students evaluate sources/information/data and inquiry process using criteria related to the aims of the inquiry. Reflect insightfully to improve own processes used.	Students evaluate information/data and the inquiry process usingself-determined criteria developed within parameters given. Reflect to refine others' processes.	Students evaluate information/data and inquiry process rigorously using self-generated criteria based on experience, expertise and the literature. Reflect insightfully to renew others' processes.
Organize and Manage (Harmonising) — *How do we arrange?* Students organize information anddata to reveal patterns/themes, managing teams and processes.	Students organize information/data using prescribed structure. Manage linear process provided (with pre-specified team roles).	Students organize information/data using a choice of given structures. Manage a process which has alternative possible pathways (and specify team roles).	Students organize information/data using recommended structures. Manage self-determined processes (including teams) with multiple possible pathways.	Students organize information/data using self-determined structures, and manage the processes (including team function) within the parameters set.	Students organize information/data using self-determined structures and management of processes (including team function).
Analyze and Synthesize (Creative) — *What does it mean?* Students analyze information/data critically and synthesize new knowledge to produce coherent individual/team understandings.	Students interpret given information/data and synthesize knowledge into prescribed formats.	Students interpret several sources of information/data and integrate knowledge into standard formats. Apply the knowledge developed to a similar context and follow prompts on ECST issues.	Students analyze trends in information/data and synthesize to integrate component parts in structures appropriate to task. *Ask rigorous, researchable questions based on new understandings*.	Students analyze information/data and synthesize to fully integrate components, consistent with parameters set. Fill knowledge gaps that are stated by others.	Students analyze and synthesize information/data to generate or abstract knowledge that addresses self-or-group-identified gaps in understanding.
Communicate and Apply (Constructive) — *How will we relate?* Students discuss, listen, write, respond to feedback andperform the processes, understandings and applications of the research, heeding ECST issues and needs of audiences.	Students communicate with each other and relate their understanding throughout set task. Use prescribed genre to develop and demonstrate understanding to a prescribed audience. Apply to a similar context the knowledge developed. Follow prompts on ECST issues.	Students use prescribed genre to develop anddemonstrate understanding to a pre-specified audience. Apply the knowledge developed to a similar context and follow prompts on ECST issues.	Students use some discipline-specific language and prescribed genre to demonstrate understanding from a stated perspective and/or a specified audience. Apply to several similar contexts the knowledge developed and specify ECST issues.	Students use discipline -specific language andgenres to demonstrate scholarly understanding for a specified audience. They apply the knowledge developed to diverse contexts and specify ECST issues in initiating, conducting and communicating.	Students use appropriate language and genre to extend the knowledge of a range of audiences. Apply innovatively the knowledge developed to multiple contexts. Probe and specify ECST issues that emerge broadly.

What characterizes the move from 'search' to 'research'? Gathering more information and generating more data is merely a 'biggasearch'? Research is when students engage in all the above facets, time and again.

Research Skill Development (RSD), a conceptual framework for Primary School to PhD, developed by John Willison and Kerry O'Regan, with much trailing by Eleanor Peirce and Mario Ricci. October 2006, revised March 2016. Facets based on: ANZIL (2004) Standards and Bloom's et al. (1956) Taxonomy. Extent of Synthesis informed by SOLO taxonomy (Biggs and Collis, 1982). * Framing researchable questions often requires a high degree of guidance and modeling for students, resulting from their synthesis (Red, Orange, Yellow) then initiating their research (Green and Blue). The six facets are often used directly with students as a learning routine (Richthart andPerkins 2008). The bold italicfont reflects dispositions towards research. Framework, resources and references available at www.rsd.edu.au. Information: john.willison@adelaide.edu.au.

Source: Willison and O'Regan (2006 [2016]).

Figure 5.1   Research skill development framework

In a follow-up study of graduates' perceptions of research skills in employment and further study, Willison (2014) identified that in degrees using RSD marking rubrics:

- research skills developed across degree programmes are perceived by a substantial majority of graduates (25/27) to be useful in their employment context;
- a substantial majority of Honours students (20/23) recommended that the RSD framework be used to inform courses earlier in the degree programme as well;
- use of the RSD framework in multiple courses of degree programmes was recommended by the majority of graduates and by Honours students interviewed.

Evidenced by these two projects is that the RSD framework, when applied in individual subjects or across a degree generally, has a positive influence on students' achievement of research skill awareness and development.

6.   APPLICATION IN TOURISM

In the tourism education context, approaches to assessing and evaluating skill outcomes have not always been explicit at university level. Predominantly there is a focus on knowledge acquisition, and assumed skills through the demonstration of acquired knowledge. Nonetheless, higher education institutions have a greater emphasis on achieving graduate outcomes by needing to demonstrate employability, adoption of threshold learning outcomes, assurance of learning, and, for many in business schools (where tourism, in the Australian context, often sits), accreditation purposes (for example AACSB and EQUIS) (Taylor et al., 2009; DEEWR, 2010). The RSD provides an explicit framework to develop, enhance and assess students' research skills. The framework is used in three main ways: for designing learning engagements, for skill enhancement, and for skill assessment. Each of these three uses will be discussed within the context of an undergraduate tourism major within a business degree at an Australian university.

The RSD was first used in the introductory subject of the tourism major in 2008, as a marking rubric in one assessment item. In the next offering of the subject, the use of the RSD rubrics was extended to all assessment items in the subject. In 2010 two additional subjects in the tourism major also adopted RSD rubrics for the internal assessment items, and by 2014, six of the eight subjects in the major used RSD rubrics (a quarter of the 24 subjects in the degree). Additionally, as the research skills were being made more explicit, specific efforts to enhance students' research skills were also being implemented in the subjects. Furthermore, in 2011, the entire major was offered with a Problem-Based Learning (PBL) orientation. The PBL pedagogy is closely aligned with the philosophy of the RSD, which was therefore useful for designing student engagement with problems.

The precursor to the adoption of the RSD was exposure to the clarity of process and expectations it provided to students, tutors and staff. At a workshop where initial findings and experiences of the RSD were presented, it was evident that the lecturers had been assessing students on all of these skills but had not necessarily made this explicit to their students. The RSD provided the opportunity to make the first author's expectations explicit to students, while at the same time providing a common conversation piece to discuss appropriate evidence of these expectations. The next three subsections will outline the adoption as research skill assessment, enhancement, and learning environments.

6.1 Research Skill Assessment

Initially, the RSD was introduced to assess students' demonstration of research skills. The RSD was introduced as rubrics, using the six facets as a basis, individualized for each of the assignments. In the most part, existing assessment items were maintained, and the change was moving from the previous content-focused marking guides (specifically, allocating marks and expectations to the introduction, body, conclusion, referencing and the like) to a focus on the evidence of the processes employed in making and communicating the product.

In terms of the learning objectives being assessed, further consideration was given to student autonomy, to specific evidence required and to the extent of alignment with learning objectives. As an overview of the process, first, the minimum level of autonomy or student choice was determined for each learning objective. Second, specific evidence to demonstrate learning objective achievement was articulated as one or more criteria for each of the research skills. Third, the alignment of these articulated criteria, autonomy and the learning objectives were scrutinized. Through these considerations, the original assessment criteria and items required changes to be made. Particularly, the changes included making the stated performance expectations much more explicit to students and clearly connecting them to each facet of research. These changes were a collaborative and reiterative process that occurred over a short time period. Feedback was sought from tourism and RSD-active colleagues, reflections upon student understanding and performance were observed, and changes made to the rubrics and instructions.

To address these three aspects in detail, first, we identified how autonomous we expected students to be in the demonstration of the learning objectives. The decision on student autonomy was informed by student engagement with the skills within the context of the assessment item. If students had not previously engaged with the skills in the assessment item context, then the expected demonstration of the skills would be lower (supervisor initiated). If students had high degrees of familiarity with the skills in the assessment context, then higher levels of autonomy could be expected. It was expected that students would demonstrate varying levels of autonomy, and so criteria standards from unacceptable dependence (fail), to top-end demonstration of autonomy were specified. For example, in an assignment, it may be identified that to pass, students need to demonstrate evidence at Level 2, and at the top end, students need to demonstrate evidence at Level 4. Level 1 demonstration would be unacceptable (fail), and Level 3 would be a mid-point of success. This would then provide the scope of the rubric (Table 5.5).

Second, to evidence the skills, each facet of the RSD was addressed in turn. We started with considering what evidence we were expecting for the best demonstration of the learning objectives for each skill. For example, for students' evidence of embarking and clarifying, did we expect the knowledge requirement would be specified, did we expect its importance to be justified, did we expect support from a range of literature, and did we expect ethical scope to be stated? In expressing the expectations, we attempted to be specific so that students and others would also share the same interpretation, whilst at the same time not over-prescribing or creating undue limits. Continuing the example, the criteria for this facet at the top end were stated as:

Table 5.5   Autonomy levels for the assignment

Research Skills	Level 1 Fail	Level 2 Pass	Level 3 Mid-point	Level 4 Top end
a. Embark and Clarify				
b. Find and Generate				
. . .				

Source: Authors.

- justified and ethically scoped own knowledge gap;
- supported by a range of appropriate sources.

Once the top end was clarified, we then completed the same process for a 'pass' assignment, making sure to maintain the same measures. For example:

- justified *or* ethically scoped supplied knowledge gap;
- supported by one or two appropriate sources.

Then, the 'fail' demonstration was stated, and the gaps between pass and top end were also filled in (see Table 5.6 for an example). Writing down these expectations made explicit what we were expecting of students and enabled conversations as to alignment between teaching staff and across subjects. This process was repeated for each of the different research skills.

The third step was to review the rubric for consistency between the skill demonstration criteria and the level of autonomy. In addition, importantly, did it actually reflect the learning objectives and the expected assignment? In completing the third step, we found it ideal for external eyes to facilitate conversation-based review of the proposed rubric by RSD-active and or discipline colleagues unfamiliar with the specific process undertaken. The reviewer identified any items needing further clarification, described what they

Table 5.6   Embark and clarify demonstration expectations

Research Skill	Level 1 Fail	Level 2 Pass	Level 3 Mid-point	Level 4 Top end
a. Embark and Clarify	Replicated a supplied knowledge gap without justifying or ethically scoping Not supported or supported by inappropriate sources	Justified or ethically scoped supplied knowledge gap Supported by one or two appropriate sources	Justified and ethically scoped supplied knowledge gap Supported by three or four appropriate sources	Justified and ethically scoped own knowledge gap Supported by a range of appropriate sources

Source: Authors.

expected needed to be demonstrated, however not currently in the rubric, and clarified misconceptions which were changed on the spot.

When sharing the completed rubrics with students, we found that this third step was continually repeated. The rubrics were presented and discussed with students, and peer-group conversations were initiated for common understanding of the expected demonstration. Where student peer-groups identified items that needed clarifying, these were discussed at an all-of-class level. The rubric was the conversation topic, though the understanding was developed through the shared language and discussion. With each conversation, and each assessment round, iterations were made to the instructions and rubric to emphasize and clarify different aspects, with each cycle requiring fewer and fewer changes.

6.2   Research Skill Enhancement

To note that research skill enhancement was only identified once the assessment items were completed understates what is identified when creating the rubrics. When identifying desired levels of autonomy and demonstration of the skills it also becomes clear that some of these skills would need targeted development. Nonetheless, the need to prioritize skill enhancement becomes especially evident through the assessment process. Depending on the breadth of skill enhancement needs (that is, some, half, or all of the class), we made decisions on how to deliver the skill enhancement opportunities. If it were just a small number of students that needed skill enhancement, then they would be referred to library and/or learning skills advisors. If it were about half the students needing skill enhancement, then co-curricular workshops would be developed for the subject in partnership with the library and/or learning skills advisors. If most or all the students needed skill enhancement, then the workshop would be embedded in the class, and generally in class time. Examples of skill enhancement activities included database use to develop students' finding and generating skills, journal article reading guides to develop students' finding and analysing skills, and referencing workshops to enhance students' communicating skills.

6.3   Research Designed Learning Environments

A change to a Problem-Based Learning (PBL) approach for the degree in which the tourism major was situated introduced the opportunity to design the learning environments based upon the research skills. PBL was adopted for the degree, meaning that students were actively engaged in solving problems as their process of learning, and inherently undertaking research. The seven-step jump approach of PBL was adopted, and students were further guided in their problem solving by an RSD skill checklist (see Figure 5.2 example). Students, in peer-groups, developed the RSD checklist based upon their conversation of the assessment rubrics. The learning team's leader would then use the checklist as staged checkpoints during the problem-solving process.

Whilst the problem solving was not assessed, their translated learning from this process was. The assessment programme used RSD rubrics, and the explicit alignment meant students practised the skills to the necessary demonstration of the assessment. Students also received feedback from within the peer-group, other groups and the facilitator on their demonstration of skills in the presented solutions, further preparing their practice and

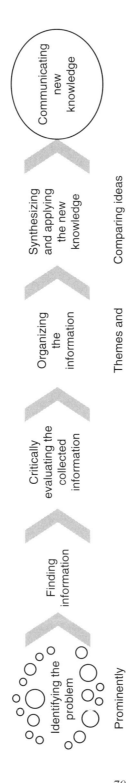

Identifying the problem

Prominently includes learning objective keywords

Finding information

Textbook + 3–5 other sources

Critically evaluating the collected information

Credible and relevant

Organizing the information

Themes and structure emerging from the information

Synthesizing and applying the new knowledge

Comparing ideas and supporting with a range of sources

Communicating new knowledge

Formal and referenced

Source: Authors.

Figure 5.2 Student team RSD checklist for problem solving

judgement for the assessment items. Adopting the RSD to design the learning environments then made the assessment, skills, skill enhancements and demonstration explicit in every class.

7.   REFLECTIONS ON RSD IN TOURISM

The reflections on implementing the RSD in tourism are presented in three sections: the lecturer, the tutor and the student. The reflections are derived from seven years (2008–14) of student surveys, student feedback, tutor feedback, and lecturers' observations and reflections. The general findings found from the overall RSD project were observed, to varying degrees, in the tourism implementation. The reflections provide implications for the use of the RSD framework in tourism learning. Overall, the reflections are largely positive, encouraging the adoption of the RSD framework. All the same, the reflections also highlight points for consideration in this adoption.

7.1   Lecturer

Comparing the new RSD instructions and rubrics to the original marking guides, it was evident that we had previously assessed students against uncommunicated criteria, and had preferred particular research skills to the exclusion or only implicit inclusion of others. The RSD rubrics specifically guided students through the research process to prepare, complete and submit their assessment, and explicitly set expectations for each skill of their research. The clarity in expectations greatly assisted in the communication and moderation between teaching staff and instruction to students. This resulted in greater consistency in student guidance and marking. There was still varying student performance across the assessment items, though there was greater targeted performance to the skills assessed.

All the same, it was noticeable that some students still did not engage with the rubric, and hence their performance did not align with the assessed criteria. We now require students to submit a self-assessment, using the rubric, with their assignment to make sure they explicitly engage with the rubric. In early subjects, students are required to complete peer-feedback on a draft section using a relevant component of the rubric. This, the lecturers found, engages students in their assessment programme earlier, it enhances their performance, and it also enhances their judgement as to demonstration of the criteria. Importantly, the peer-feedback process was implemented on students' second assignment after they had received feedback on their first assignment (so it had been role modelled first). A structured feedback guide with an example was provided together with a video outlining the process.

Having skill enhancement activities further enhanced student performance on these aspects. When a skill has been addressed, other skill gaps then become more obvious. Of note is that once a skill gap is identified and addressed in one class, it is likely that this skill gap will also need to be addressed in the next cohort. Be wary of automatically moving to the next skill gap for the next offering of the subject without continuing to address the traditional gap. A benefit of having the RSD embedded across so many subjects in the major has been that specific skill enhancements can be targeted to specific subjects. This allows for planned skill development as students progress through the degree. A key reflection in skill enhancement is the opportunity to undertake a skill diagnostic early in the semester. A diagnostic can more accurately direct skill enhancement activities for embedding, co-curricular or individually targeted (depending on student honesty and self-awareness).

Finally, adopting the RSD as a design tool in the learning environments has targeted students' effort within class to match with the assessment programme. Skill gaps and rubric clarifications are also a consistent part of the learning conversation in class. In the PBL context, giving the checklist responsibility to the learning team has also meant that there is greater ownership of the process, skills and outcomes, and students have taken responsibility for this. Even those students that may not usually engage with the rubric are forced to engage with the research skills and their demonstration by the learning team.

7.2   Tutor

Tutor feedback especially noted the time saved due to the RSD rubrics. First, time was saved in providing instruction and guidance to students, as this was much clearer and explicit in the assignment instructions and rubric. Tutors noted the value of the rubric as a consistent reference for student guidance. The tutors were able to refer students to the rubric to contextualize questions about the assignment, and to again use the rubric to contextualize responses. Second, time was saved during marking, as students had targeted their performance, and feedback for formative improvements was to a large degree already included in the rubric.

For marking, tutors also reflected that they felt more confident in the grading consistency between assignments. The consistency was also evident during lecturer–tutor team marking calibration and moderation sessions, where past grading discrepancies were largely reduced. Tutors not familiar with the RSD rubrics also noted that they felt confined in their judgement and marking, although they felt that the end grade matched what they would have expected. As such, they often concluded that the confinement saved them time as it focused what they were looking for and their comments.

In the enhancement of skills, tutors often reflected that they wished such sessions had been available to them when they were students. Whilst the tutors were generally very capable students (many being current PhD students), they recalled that skill development was often in response to errors, as compared to active development. As in-class skill enhancement activities were contextualized with subject learning, and in cases supported by library or learning skills advisors, tutors also felt comfortable with the dual focus (knowledge and skill enhancement).

7.3   Students

Student feedback noted that they appreciated the explicit assignment instructions provided through the rubric, setting explicit performance expectations. The instructions meant they felt more confident to embark on their assignment and complete it to a satisfactory level. Students also highlighted the consistency in skills assessed across the subjects, that an assessed skill deficiency in one assignment meant there was reward for improving that skill for the next assignment.

As highlighted by the tutors, the skill enhancement activities were often well received, especially as they were directly linked to assessment performance. Nonetheless, some students did not appreciate class time being dedicated to perceived remedial skills, even though the assessment programme evidenced that these were under-demonstrated skills. As such, it is necessary to carefully contextualize skill enhancements as development (and everyone undertakes development activities), as compared to addressing a deficiency.

In the PBL environment, where students used their self-defined checklist, the team leaders liked the structure the checkpoints provided. As the leader role rotated for each class, the structure also provided consistency for the team. It was often observed when a team had skipped a checkpoint that another member would remind the leader.

The reflections from lecturers, tutors and students have been generally positive. Some students need active engagement for their ownership of the learning and assessment process, especially as they are often exposed to so many different types of assessment marking guides and rubrics. The consistency in conversations created by the rubrics, then reinforced in the skill enhancement activities and learning environment design, has provided a common reference point and terminology between the three groups (and with the library and learning skills). Additionally, the consistency in conversation pieces across the subjects reinforces the development of research skills and rewards students for doing so.

8.   FUTURE DIRECTIONS AND CONCLUSION

The RSD framework has already been implemented across a range of disciplines, including health sciences, engineering, arts, languages, business, pharmacy and tourism. Its success in each of these disciplines has been due to the explicit conversations and connections it creates between students, lecturers, and library and learning skills. The main implementation has been in the form of marking rubrics. Developments in skill enhancements and designed learning environments are emerging.

In the range of disciplines, the implementation of the RSD framework has generally been subject-specific. That is, students' engagement with explicit research skill development has been isolated within their learning programme. As in the case presented in this chapter, exposure through six subjects in the major, a quarter of the subjects in the degree, has still ensured engagement at each year level, and rewards for enhancements within the major. This has been possible due to the small and aligned team, and the challenge in bigger programmes is getting lecturer buy-in across the programme.

In conclusion, tourism programmes, and universities more broadly, increasingly need to ensure that their proposed degree outcomes are achieved. These 'philosophical practitioner' outcomes include knowledge and skill attributes, embedding employability skills as well. A university education provides a means to continue learning and the capacity for lifelong learning is encapsulated in the development of students' research skills. Prominently, students and employers have additionally noted these skills as important for career success. Research is a systematic process of learning, a process in which students and lecturers alike are involved.

Six research skills were identified, namely to embark and clarify, find and generate, evaluate and reflect, organize and manage, analyse and synthesize, and communicate and apply. For each of these skills, there were five levels of autonomy, from supervisor initiated prescribed research, to researcher initiated research. Research skills and levels of autonomy were conceptually combined in the Research Skill Development framework, and its implementation across different disciplines and universities has demonstrated improvement in research skills, transferability of skills to other disciplines, and transferable and useful skills in employment.

The application of the RSD in tourism has occurred within the broader adoption to assess and enhance research skills, and as a basis for designing learning environments. Three steps of identifying expected student autonomy, descriptors of expected skill performance, and checking the match with objectives determined the rubric design. Skill enhancement was, in cases, a response to assessment-evidenced gaps, though it was also identified during the design of rubrics. With the change in pedagogy, a more explicit research-focused learning approach was used, giving student teams ownership and responsibility in the assessment aligned process. The key reflections were of clarity in expectations and then students' performance in relation to these expectations, time saved in explanations, marking and directed feedback, and an explicit reward for skill enhancement in future assignments.

Future directions are to provide students with multiple exposures to the RSD and to provide them with explicit opportunities to enhance and demonstrate their research skills. Overall, the RSD framework explicitly guides the development of research skills. The implementation of the RSD framework has provided evidenced benefits within the tourism curriculum. Reflections on the use of RSD in tourism highlight positives, though consideration is also needed for its effective implementation.

REFERENCES

Airey, D. and S. Johnson (1999), 'The content of tourism degree courses in the UK', *Tourism Management*, **20** (2), 229–35.
Brew, A. and D. Boud (1995), 'Teaching and research: establishing the vital link with learning', *Higher Education*, **29** (3), 261–73.
Busby, G., P. Brunt and S. Baber (1997), 'Tourism sandwich placements: an appraisal', *Tourism Management*, **18** (2), 105–10.
Cho, M.H. and S.K. Kang (2005), 'Past, present, and future of tourism education: the South Korean case', *Journal of Teaching in Travel & Tourism*, **5** (3), 225–50.
Department of Education, Employment and Workplace Relations (DEEWR) (2010), *Mission-based Compacts for Universities*, accessed 23 November 2010 at http://www.deewr.gov.au/HigherEducation/Policy/Pages/Compacts.aspx.
Dredge, D., P. Benckendorff, M. Day, M.J. Gross, M. Walo, P. Weeks and P. Whitelaw (2012), 'The philosophic practitioner and the curriculum space', *Annals of Tourism Research*, **39** (4), 2154–76.
Fidgeon, P.R. (2010), 'Tourism education and curriculum design: a time for consolidation and review?', *Tourism Management*, **31** (6), 699–723.
Harkison, T., J. Poulston and J.H.G. Kim (2011), 'Hospitality graduates and managers: the big divide', *International Journal of Contemporary Hospitality Management*, **23** (3), 377–92.
Hsu, C.H.C. (2005), 'Preface', *Journal of Teaching in Travel & Tourism*, **5** (1–2), xxvii–xxix.
Kwok, L.C. (2012), 'Exploratory-triangulation design in mixed methods studies: a case of examining graduating seniors who meet hospitality recruiters' selection criteria', *Tourism and Hospitality Research*, **12** (3), 125–38.
Leedy, P.D. and J.E. Ormrod (2010), *Practical Research: Planning and Design* (9th edn), Upper Saddle River: Pearson Education.
Litchfield, A., J. Frawley and S. Nettleton (2010), 'Contextualising and integrating into the curriculum the learning and teaching of work-ready professional graduate attributes', *Higher Education Research & Development*, **29** (5), 519–34.
MacLaurin, D. (2005), 'Tourism education in Canada: past, present and future directions', *Journal of Teaching in Travel & Tourism*, **5** (1–2), 1–25.

Masberg, B.A., D.M. Chase and M.S. Madlem (2004), 'A Delphi study of tourism training and education needs in Washington State', *Journal of Human Resources in Hospitality & Tourism*, **2** (2), 1–22.

McKercher, B. (2002), 'The future of tourism education: an Australian scenario?', *Tourism and Hospitality Research*, **3** (3), 199–210.

Pearce, P.L. (2005), 'Australian tourism education: the quest for status', *Journal of Teaching in Travel & Tourism*, **5** (3), 251–67.

Precision Consultancy (2007), *Graduate Employability Skills*, accessed 23 November 2010 at http://www.dest. gov.au/NR/rdonlyres/E58EFDBE-BA83-430E-A541-2E91BCB59DF1/20214/GraduateEmployabilitySkills FINALREPORT1.pdf.

Sheldon, P., D. Fesenmaier, K. Woeber, C. Cooper and M. Antonioli (2008), 'Tourism education futures, 2010–2030: building the capacity to lead', *Journal of Teaching in Travel & Tourism*, **7** (3), 61–8.

Stuart-Hoyle, M. (2003), 'The purpose of undergraduate tourism programmes in the United Kingdom', *Journal of Hospitality, Leisure, Sport and Tourism Education*, **2** (1), 49–74.

Taylor, T., D. Thompson, L. Clements, L. Simpson, A. Paltridge, M. Fletcher, M. Freeman, L. Treleaven, R. Lawson and F. Rohde (2009), '*Facilitating* staff and student engagement with graduate attribute development, assessment and standards in business faculties', Sydney: Australian Learning and Teaching Council Ltd, DEEWR.

Tribe, J. (2002), 'The philosophic practitioner', *Annals of Tourism Research*, **29** (2), 338–57.

Weiler, B. and M. Goyal (2007), 'Exploring the relationships between university course branding, length of study and employment outcomes in undergraduate tourism education', *Tourism Recreation Research*, **32** (2), 7–19.

Willison, J. (2014), *Outcomes and Uptake of Explicit Research Skill Development across Degree Programs*, Sydney: Office for Learning and Teaching.

Willison, J. and K. O'Regan (2006[2016]), *Research Skill Development Framework*, accessed 24 April 2016 at http://www.adelaide.edu.au/rsd/framework/.

Willison, J., K. Le Lievre and I. Lee (2010), *Making Research Skill Development Explicit in Coursework*, Sydney: Australian Learning and Teaching Council Ltd, DEEWR.

Willison, J.W. and K. O'Regan (2007), 'Commonly known, commonly not known, totally unknown: a framework for students becoming researchers', *Higher Education Research and Development*, **26** (4), 393–410.

Yuan, J.X.J., K. Houston and L.A. Cai (2006), 'Foreign language ability: a core attribute of hospitality graduates' competency?', *Journal of Human Resources in Hospitality & Tourism*, **5** (1), 77–90.

Zhang, W. and X. Fan (2005), 'Tourism higher education in China: past and present, opportunities and challenges', *Journal of Teaching in Travel & Tourism*, **5** (1–2), 117–35.

6   Lifelong tourism education: current and future trends in Scottish universities
Violet V. Cuffy

1.   INTRODUCTION

Tourism is the fastest-growing industry, generating over 266 million jobs and 9.5 percent of global GDP in 2013. By 2024 international tourist arrivals are forecast to exceed 1.7 billion, generating over USD2 trillion in revenue (World Travel and Tourism Council, 2014). Increased travel across the globe has been driven by: growth in real incomes; greater amounts of leisure time; improved and highly accessible transportation systems; ongoing globalization of business linkages, including supply chains; highly effective communication systems that facilitate marketing; and a significant number of new tourism services (Turner and Sears, 2013).

Unquestionably tourism continues to make a significant contribution to national growth and development worldwide. In the United Kingdom, the tourism industry's cumulative growth in employment between 2009 and 2013 is 5.4 percent and in non-tourism related industries 4.8 percent. In that regard much effort must be placed in developing a skilled and educated labor supply for the industry at all levels of the sector. Consequently, Higher Education (HE), while adapting to the changing demands of the education system, must continue to hold a pivotal role in producing tourism graduates who can be future industry leaders.

Internationally, lifelong learning has been championed as a key strategy to education provision. Accordingly, education policies and strategies are universally employed to reflect and implement the core concepts of learning throughout life. Remarkably the debate surrounding lifelong learning in tourism has only been recent (Cuffy et al., 2012, 2014; Su, 2015) and quite sparse. Therefore, this chapter seeks to examine the provision and approach to tourism higher education to ascertain current alignment to the lifelong learning paradigm and to proffer an appropriate approach for future engagement within the Scottish context and further afield.

The Scottish government through its education system has embraced the Curriculum for Excellence (CfE) as the main vehicle for advancing lifelong learning. Overall, at the level of Higher Education (HE), much effort has been placed in adapting program offerings and widening access to allow for institutional changes which the CfE demands. However, in the area of tourism higher education, there has been very little engagement and adoption of lifelong learning approaches. In that regard the chapter focuses on the approach of tourism higher education programs to the Scottish government's policies of increased access and participation in HE as demarcated within the CfE lifelong learning principles.

2.　THE LIFELONG LEARNING (LLL) PARADIGM

2.1　History and Development of the Lifelong Learning (LLL) Agenda in the EU

Lifelong learning has its roots as early as the 1970s in the policy oriented United Nations Educational, Scientific and Cultural Organization (UNESCO), the Organisation for Economic Co-operation and Development (OECD) and the European Union (EU) (Rubenson, 2006; Milana, 2012). Rubenson (2006) reports that LLL owes its conceptual formation mainly to the OECD and UNESCO, resulting from their response to existing educational and societal crises, with the European Commission (EC) championing implementation in EU countries.

In 1970 the Director General of UNESCO mandated the Faure Commission in response to the increasing demand for adult education (Rubenson, 2006). Its main precepts were those of lifelong education and the creation of a learning society. For UNESCO the humanistic approach to education and the need for broadening of democratic processes in society were pivotal. This demanded a more open and flexible system catering to the needs of the individual to access educational services (Rubenson, 2006) and keep learning throughout life (Medel-Anonuevo et al., 2001).

In contrast to UNESCO, from its inception in 1948 the focus of the OECD was on developing strategies to allow expansion of education for economic prosperity. From this perspective the OECD, through its Centre for Educational Research and Innovation (CERI), advocated the concept of recurrent education as a strategy for the long-term planning of educational provision (Leader, 2003; Tuijnman and Boström, 2002). The understanding and expectation was that such a system would yield economic gains, benefit the labor market, lead to increasing equality and stimulate students' search for knowledge, arguably framing lifelong learning largely in economistic and employability terms (Medel-Anonuevo et al., 2001).

Further, Haggar-Guénette (1991) contends, as alluded to earlier, that lifelong learning was mainly championed by the OECD as a strategy for providing new educational opportunities for adults. Thus, in the 1980s the phenomenon became popular as a large number of working adults returned to education at colleges and universities. During the same period, building a knowledge-economy and innovative society were heralded as key governmental goals (Gibb and Walker, 2011). However, Rubenson (2006) argues that LLL was largely promoted as a fit between students profiling the competences of the labor force, and the needs of the labor market.

Regardless, globally LLL was adopted as a central organizing concept in education and training (McKenzie, 1998), focusing on the core concepts of breadth, progression and continuity (DFID–World Bank, 2009) throughout schooling and beyond. For many proponents it is a social prerogative (Leader, 2003) and a master education concept (Tight, 1998; Blaxter et al., 2002) for achieving continuing employment and economic success (Brennan et al., 2000; Parnham, 2001; Vargas, 2005; Marshall et al., 2008). These precepts are still upheld today as reflected in the key education strategies of the CfE currently employed within the Scottish education system.

Here it is important to highlight two noteworthy efforts (among others) for adopting the lifelong learning agenda at the European level. First, 1996 was declared the European year of lifelong learning (Larson, 2011). Second, much later on in 2000 in Lisbon, the meeting of the European Council launched the Memorandum of Lifelong Learning, which affirmed LLL as a vehicle for making the EU the most competitive and dynamic knowledge-based economy in the world, capable of sustainable economic growth with more and better jobs and greater social cohesion (EC, 2000).

Over the development of LLL the key themes shaping the lifelong paradigm are the strong link to economic advancement, creation of a knowledge-driven society and the lifetime engagement of learners with their learning and development. An additional central element is the focus on addressing the government's education policy in skill and knowledge development throughout life for betterment of society. However, Leader (2003) cites some ongoing challenges between the framework for lifelong learning and education structures:

- the far-reaching impacts of widening participation at the institutional level;
- the goals of social inclusion in education and the complex factors surrounding lifelong learning opportunities;
- issues of accessibility and implementation of initiatives by individual institutions.

The question this chapter seeks to examine is how these abovementioned precepts of lifelong learning have been adopted within tourism higher education. Furthermore, it aims to ascertain the effectiveness of tourism higher education in addressing the government's agenda of creating a knowledge-economy and a society equipped for life, work and industry.

2.2   Adoption of the Lifelong Learning (LLL) Paradigm in Scotland

The concept of learning from cradle to grave (OECD, 1996; Medel-Anonuevo et al., 2001) and womb to tomb (Cuffy et al., 2012) is not novel. In fact, lifelong learning is considered both a social priority and an economic necessity (Anderson, 1999). More significantly the fact that learning begins at birth and continues throughout life is a precept long held at the heart of the Scottish government's education policies. Furthermore the government of the United Kingdom over the years issued a number of documents (DfEE, 1998a, 1998b, 1998c, 1999) advocating policy positions on lifelong learning (Hyland, 2003).

By illustration, with the Education (Scotland) Act 1872 education became compulsory in Scotland and was managed by the Scotch Education Department. Until 1918 offices were located in London. They then moved to Edinburgh and were renamed the Scottish Education Department. In 1991 the department received another name change, the Scottish Office Education Department, and later on the Scottish Office Education and Industry Department in 1995. With the onset of devolution in 1999 the Scottish Executive Education Department was launched and thereafter managed school education, whilst the Scottish Executive Enterprise and Lifelong Learning Department had responsibility for full-time higher education. However, these departments were all abolished in 2007 with the election of the Scottish National Party.

Throughout these reiterations of the education department in the Scottish system, the various governments through their education strategy always recognized that learning is lifelong, and therefore continuously aimed to help learners develop the skills needed for learning, life and work. In that regard, within the current Scottish government, lifelong learning falls under the portfolio of the Cabinet Secretary for Education and Lifelong Learning. The secretary is responsible for all levels of education from nursery to higher education. Additionally, the office of the Cabinet Secretary is supported by the Minister for Learning, Science and Scotland's Languages and the Minister for Children and Young People.

What has remained evident is that lifelong learning is an emergent process (Rogers, 1996) impacted by changing and cyclical government structures and corresponding political philosophies. Lifelong learning therefore requires the engagement of learners at the heart of government's agenda, for establishing a knowledge-driven society and a sustainable culture of lifelong learning (Leader, 2003). The key is to ensure clarity of government policy and its broad goals and objectives and to understand the implications for implementation at the institutional level throughout the entire education system, but of more relevance here in HE.

2.3 Lifelong Learning Perspectives

As highlighted previously, lifelong learning is linked to the concept of a knowledge-based economy, which engenders the need for learning to take place throughout a person's lifetime (Marshall and Marrett, 2008). As such, lifelong learning entails the establishment of a 'learning society' (Antonacopoulou, 2000; Parnham, 2001) with the key aims of education providers focused around making learning easier for the learner. According to McKenzie (1998) the complexities of modern societies, with rapidly increasing knowledge and information-intensive economies, demand one to predict and adapt to change, or risk marginalization.

Recognizing this, lifelong learning champions the case for broad and continuous learning through a wide range of platforms and formats allowing for flexibility in education provision and structure, as relevant to the learner at various stages of life. In so doing, based on the following key concepts offered by the Department for International Development–World Bank (DFID–WB) (2009), lifelong learning seeks to:

- alter methods and contexts of teaching and learning to promote efficiency in foundation skill acquisition;
- create access, recognize or certify skills and competences acquired through formal, informal or non-formal learning;
- introduce incentives that leverage investment by providers and third-parties, and participation and investment by learners;
- provide information on learning opportunities.

Further, the ethos of lifelong learning is equally concerned with concepts of personal development, quality of life of the individual, self-evaluation, self-awareness and self-directed learning (Rubenson, 2006). This high level of learner engagement was also emphasized in the 2000 EC memorandum on LLL, which highlights the responsibility of the individual for vigorously pursuing their own learning (EC, 2000). Moreover, the emphasis is on learning through active participation in society all through the lifetime of the learner (Medel-Anonuevo et al., 2001). As such, throughout their working lives, individuals are encouraged to take up a more self-directed role and make meaningful choices about their learning and development (Leader, 2003). The underlying principle here is the shift to 'learner-oriented life span learning'.

2.4   Lifelong Learning in Higher Education

The core principles of higher education have long been with producing graduates who are critical thinkers and possess employability skills. In his seminal works, Barnett (1990) postulates that the search for truth, discovery, character formation, a certain degree of academic freedom, knowledge advancement, and the preservation of society and its intellectual culture are all fundamental principles of the education product at this level. Barnett (1997) further argues that higher education must produce graduates of high criti-cal thought, reflexive capacity, rich imagination, capacity for change and critical action. If one upholds this philosophy, any absence of these pivotal elements within higher edu-cation programs arguably would negatively influence an institution's ability to contribute in the reshaping of modern society, a central role of higher education. What is of interest here is how engagement with the lifelong learning paradigm facilitates these high levels of learning and educational development at the heart of HE.

Equally important is higher education's role in producing graduates with employability attributes, self-presentational ability and continuing learning dexterity (Harvey, 2001) who can become leaders and managers in the tourism industry (Holder, 2001; Poon, 2001). However, according to Fallows and Steven (2000, p. 75), modern higher education universities face several challenges as itemized below:

- there is increasing recognition that the transition from the world of higher educa-tion into the world of employment is not always straightforward;
- the academic curriculum is essentially a vehicle through which attributes delivered are constant regardless of subject studied;
- the world of employment is changing rapidly.

Nevertheless, higher education is expected to produce graduates with the appropriate levels of critical thinking skills, expertise, and personal and professional qualities to func-tion efficiently in the environment of the 'learning age' and/or 'learning society'.

This view is also held by Knapper and Cropley (2000), who point out that lifelong learning demands a specific kind of knowledge, skills, attitudes and values from learners. For them LLL at the level of higher education is simply not just about catering to mature learners and designing special adult programs (as mentioned before, an earlier tenet of LLL), providing increased budgets for continuing education, and provision of increased part-time programs. They remind us that full-time students entering university directly from secondary school continue to form a major part of the HE clientele. Hence address-ing the needs of both groups of students within the lifelong learning agenda is a major challenge for universities.

As such, lifelong learning has been defined as a process and philosophy for educational provision and a set of organizational and procedural guidelines for educational practice (Knapper and Cropley, 2000). Moreover, in an era of widespread knowledge explosion, an increasingly rapid pace of change and technological advances, the need for lifelong learning has become more evident, particularly to the ever equally rapidly growing tourism industry. Consequently, the possible challenges for adoption for a LLL approach within tourism higher education programs are now examined.

2.5   Tourism Higher Education

There is much debate on the nature of and the provision of tourism higher education (Airey and Johnson, 1999; Airey, 2008; Zagonari, 2009). Further, it was acknowledged that tourism touches on every aspect of society and is therefore interdisciplinary in nature, encompassing a broad range of knowledge, skills and attitudes (Tribe, 2000). Historically, tourism programs have developed from an instrumental perspective, focused largely on employability skills and addressing the direct needs of industry.

Though there has been much growth and advancement over the last few decades, there still remain some core concerns due to the diverse nature of the tourism industry itself. As such, tourism education continues to be part of a range of other disciplines such as geography, anthropology, business, law, sociology and management, leading to different program structures, delivery modality and durations. This phenomenon allows for different educational pathways for individual learners, depending on how each institution's curriculum is framed (Tribe, 2002). It is no surprise, then, that decisions about programs and curriculum structure as well as approaches to course delivery have become central to the success and survival of institutions (Dredge et al., 2015).

Simultaneously, significant changes in the work environment, increased competition, demanding and increasingly sophisticated clientele, advances in technology and changing expectations of investors, employers and employees have all influenced tourism education provision at the university level (Scotland, 2006). Moreover, political and government policy decisions play a major role in funding, access, research agendas and ultimately program structures.

Regardless, the key foundations of tourism higher education revolve around establishing the right balance between liberal and vocation education (Lewis, 2005), notwithstanding the widespread preoccupation with the traditional instrumental view upheld about tourism programs. As Holder (2001) and Poon (2001) caution, tourism higher education should not only focus on employability skills but also produce tomorrow's leaders and managers for the industry. Interestingly, in keeping with the LLL agenda, Fallows and Steven (2000) earlier affirm that at higher education the preparation of graduates with the required expertise to function professionally within the learning age and/or learning society is vital.

The key challenge that remains in adopting the LLL paradigm within the tourism education curriculum is ensuring:

> The development of learning at each education level, forging connections between levels and the provision of open access to learning, all leading to continuous learning and ultimately contributing to the advancement the learner and the learned about (tourism) and the development of an informed society with vocational and critical skills. (Cuffy et al., 2012, p. 1406)

However, what is striking throughout the literature debate is that the level of discourse around the provision of lifelong tourism education within higher education is almost non-existent barring the work of Cuffy et al. (2012) and Su (2015). In that regard, this chapter will proceed to examine the tourism education provision in Scotland's universities to determine which current approaches and trends align themselves with and address the life-long learning agenda. In so doing, discussions will proceed around both the institutional dimension, by examining two case studies, and the policy dimension, by reflecting on the relevant aspects of the core education policy in place in Scotland.

3.   LIFELONG LEARNING AND TOURISM HIGHER EDUCATION: THE CASE OF SCOTLAND AND THE POLICY DIMENSION

A review of the tourism programs offered in universities in Scotland confirmed that, as highlighted in the Association for Tourism in Higher Education (ATHE) Report on tourism higher education in the UK in both 2007 and 2009, the availability of accurate data on tourism higher education is sparse. Nevertheless, secondary research that has been conducted focused on the following three areas:

1.   What were the main areas of curriculum focus in tourism higher education?
2.   What were the modes of access into tourism higher education?
3.   What were the main structure and modality of delivery of tourism higher education?

By way of context, in general, it is important to note here that the definition of 'higher education' is complex, dynamic, and quite variable internationally; notwith-standing the harmonization efforts ongoing through the Bologna process (see European Commission, 2009). Specifically in Scotland, higher education is defined by reference to levels 7 and above of the Scottish Credit and Qualifications Framework (SCQF). In the UK as a whole, for the purpose of the Higher Education Statistics Agency (HESA's) data collection, higher education students are those students on courses for which the level of instruction is above level 3 of the Qualifications and Curriculum Authority (QCA) National Qualifications Framework (NQF) (for example, courses at the level of Certificate of HE and above).

Providing further background, the HESA published an approximate correspondence between the NQF levels and those of the SCQF. HESA distinguishes the course aim of students entering HE as postgraduate, first degree and other undergraduate. In Scotland the term 'sub-degree' is used synonymously with 'other undergraduate'. The category 'other undergraduate' covers foundation degrees, Higher Education Diploma (HND), Higher National Certificate (HNC), Diploma of Higher Education (Dip. HE), Certificate of Higher Education (Cert. HE) and a variety of professional and other qualifications. Higher Education courses are delivered in Higher Education Institutions (HEIs). Further, in Scotland there is also substantial delivery of Higher Education courses in colleges. In the rest of the UK a much smaller proportion of Higher Education is delivered outside HEIs.

In December 2009, the Lifelong Learning Analytical Services Unit commissioned research on behalf of the Scottish Funding Council and the Scottish Government to examine current approaches to the measurement of participation in Higher Education (HE) and to advise on possible options for further development (Cohen et al., 2010). Table 6.1 shows the parameters employed by the research team for determining participation in higher education in Scotland.

Table 6.1   Domains relevant to the assessment of measures of participation

Type of Factor	Domain Categories
Level	Sub-degree/First degree/Postgraduate degree
Mode	Full-time/part-time/distance learning
Institutional	Type of Institution HEI/College
Age	Specific years or age bands
Gender	Male/Female
Ethnicity	Census groupings
Previous	Education SCQF or QCA level attained
Domicile	Scotland/UK/EU/non-EU
Area	Deprivation SIMD levels
Socio	Economic Group NS-SEC 1–7
Individual	Local area local authority areas; Wards; or other small area statistics

Source: Adapted from Cohen et al. (2010, p. 23).

As reflected in Table 6.1, higher education in Scotland is provided at the sub-degree, degree and postgraduate levels. Hence programs are offered both at colleges and higher education institutions, and either full-time, part-time or via distance learning. Generally, undergraduate degrees last three years, with an additional year for Honours degrees. There is much flexibility to access via the split degree, which allows direct entry at various university levels dependent on previous education and professional certification obtained. In addition, the Scottish Index of Multiple Deprivation (SIMD) policy stipulates that preferential entry is allocated to prospective students who are residents of underprivileged areas referenced by specific postcodes. The SIMD 20 and 40 are strategic measures and identifiers employed by government in widening access to students and refer to neighborhoods in the most deprived two quintiles in Scotland.

New National Qualifications are now replacing the previous Standard Grade qualifications, and the existing Access, Intermediate, Higher and Advanced Higher qualifications. National 1, National 2, National 3, National 4, National 5 and Higher are now being delivered in schools and colleges across Scotland. The new Advanced Higher was earmarked for introduction in August 2015. Table 6.2 presents information on current changes being implemented across Scottish universities. This structure is unique to the Scottish education system and worthy of mention here in underpinning the lifespan approach to education and the implication for the tourism higher education curriculum.

At both the institutional and sector level, great effort has been employed to widen access to higher education in Scotland. Professor Pete Downes OBE, Convener Access All Areas, Universities Scotland, reports that more students are entering university from socially disadvantaged backgrounds and through non-traditional entry routes. In recent years, he continues, there has been an 11 percent increase in the number of students at university who are drawn from areas identified as being in the 20 percent most deprived neighborhoods according to the Scottish Index of Multiple Deprivation (SIMD20).

Additionally, strides have been made in increasing the number of non-traditional entry pathways into university. Efforts observed include articulation from college straight into

Table 6.2   *National Qualifications replaces the previous/existing National Qualifications, and differences in grading*

SCQF level	Previous National Qualifications	Grades	Replaced by	New Qualifications	Grades
7	Advanced Higher	A to D	>	Advanced Higher	A to D
6	Higher	A to D	>	Higher	A to D
5	Intermediate 2	A to D	>	National 5	A to D
	Standard Grade (Credit level)	1 or 2			
4	Intermediate 1	A to D	>	National 4	Not graded
	Standard Grade (General level)	3 or 4			
3	Standard Grade (Foundation level)	5 or 6	>	National 3	Not graded
	Access 3	Not graded			
2	Access 2	Not graded	>	National 2	Not graded
1	Access 1	Not graded	>	National 1	Not graded

Source: Scottish Qualification Authority (SQA) (2014).

the second or third year of university. The Access All Areas 2013 report indicates that more than 16 000 students had used this alternative route into higher education over the five previous years. Furthermore, a number of institutions have launched a range of initiatives as part of their individual strategies to widen access. Among outstanding examples of these are:

- University of Glasgow participation in REACH, a national program focused on widening access to the professions;
- Glasgow Caledonian University programs working with senior pupils in partner secondary schools facilitated through a new Schools and Colleges Engagement and Transition Team.

Though this section reveals the technical elements at work within the Scottish education system it serves to contextualize the prevailing approach to tourism within HE that follows.

4.   LEARNING FOR TOURISM EDUCATION (LLLFTE) IN SCOTTISH UNIVERSITIES: THE INSTITUTIONAL DIMENSION

4.1   Tourism Education Provision Across Scottish Universities

At the time of this research, under the system discussed above, nine out of Scotland's 19 universities offered 34 tourism degrees in Scotland. As discussed previously, the program structure and modality over these few universities is as wide and varied as the departments

Table 6.3   Tourism education provision at Scotland's universities

Institution	Full/Part-Time	BA	MSc
Edinburgh Napier University	FT & PT	9	8
Glasgow Caledonian University	FT & PT	1	1
Heriot-Watt University	FT & PT	0	2
University of Glasgow	FT & PT	0	2
University of Highlands & Islands	FT & PT	1	1
University of Strathclyde	FT & PT	11	2
University of West Scotland	FT & PT	1	1
Queen Margaret University	FT & PT	2	0
Robert Gordon University	FT & PT	1	1

Source: Compiled for universities across Scotland, 2014, online.

and disciplines within which they are located. Programs range from combined degrees (twinned with hospitality, law, business, accounting, marketing, management, languages and anthropology) to specialized courses (Tourism Management, Adventure Tourism Management, Tourism Marketing, Tourism Heritage and Development, Heritage and Cultural Tourism, Ecotourism and International Tourism Management).

Also of interest was the type of degree and mode of delivery among the universities. As reflected in Table 6.3, tourism education is largely provided in Scotland within the framework of the new universities implemented in the 1990s to increase access to higher education in the UK. Programs are mostly offered full-time or part-time across the nine universities. Other modes of delivery not measured in the participation instrument include virtual learning, online/blended learning, distance learning programs, international collaborations, adult learning programs, continued professional development training, and opportunities for doctoral studies. As discussed earlier, the Scottish Government education strategy recognizes that learning is lifelong, and as such through its Curriculum for Excellence (CfE) aims to help learners develop the skills they need for learning, life and work as captured and delineated in its core four capacities. As such, the purpose of the curriculum is to enable each child or young person to be (1) successful learners; (2) confident individuals; (3) responsible citizens; and (4) effective contributors to society.

Aligned with the principles of lifelong learning, the CfE aims to achieve transformation of education in Scotland by providing a coherent, more flexible and enriched curriculum from age 3 to 18. A key objective is to provide a framework by which all young people in Scotland are enabled in acquiring the knowledge and skills for learning, skills for life and skills for work necessary for survival in a modern society and economy. The curriculum encapsulates experiences that are planned for children and young people through their education, at whatever level or institution. Of particular significance here is how new curriculum models for the senior phase could be delivered and how young people could progress from the senior phase into higher education. As a result and in response to the CfE program, all Scottish universities have adopted policy statements on how they seek to engage and facilitate smooth transition in learning from secondary to higher education (accessible by prospective students on university websites).

Now special emphasis turns to two universities with exemplary programs aligned with the ethos of the lifelong learning agenda. In that regard Queen Margaret University and Strathclyde University are singled out for their relevance to the objectives of this chapter.

4.2   Queen Margaret University: The Academy Model

Apart from its international hospitality and tourism undergraduate degree, which follows the standard entry procedures as elsewhere in Scotland, Queen Margaret University (QMU) is part of a collaboration aimed at widening access to higher education to students who may not have attained the required entry qualifications via the normal route.

The university has established four Academies to take forward progression to university degrees, one of which is in Hospitality and Tourism. As part of a consortium comprising Edinburgh College and four local authorities (Edinburgh, Mid and East Lothian and Scottish Borders), a pioneering and innovative model has been developed for smoothing the transition for senior school pupils between school, college, university and work.

Universities Scotland (2013), in the 'Access All Areas' document, reports that students take classes at school, college and university during their senior years and must be committed to the Academy over and above the demands of their normal school curriculum. Moreover, at the end of one year in operation, the first cohort of the Hospitality and Tourism Academy's 16 to 18-year-olds are reaping the rewards. Some have benefited from a guaranteed place in a related subject at Edinburgh College. Meanwhile, others have advanced to complete the full two-year Academy program by transferring directly into the second year of the BA (Hons) International Hospitality and Management at Queen Mary University (QMU). The words of Professor Alan Gilloran, Deputy Principal at QMU, best express the significance of this innovative approach:

> At the core of this ground-breaking model is the total buy-in from industry partners. By working with industry experts, for example hotel groups such as Novotel, The Point Hotel and the Marriott, we are creating a dynamic young workforce which is fit for purpose – a ready-made source of young talent equipped with the right skills and knowledge to hit the ground running when entering the industry. With employers providing work placement opportunities and industry overviews, we are hoping to inspire youngsters to be the next generation of skilled individuals who are helping Scotland remain as world leaders in food and drink, raise standards in healthcare and the hospitality sector, or contribute to Scotland's growing creative industries. (Gilloran, 2013, p. 39)

As is evident in this statement, the Queen Margaret University and Edinburgh College Academy Model creates real education and job opportunities while simultaneously supporting the growth and development of Scotland's key industries. What seems to be equally evident, as elsewhere, is the under-provision or -emphasis of tourism '*specific*' opportunities and industry engagement.

Nevertheless, like other universities across Scotland, the university is fully engaged with Scotland's curriculum for excellence agenda as published on the university's website, www.qmu.ac.uk. The policy delineates the university's efforts in structural adjustment in enabling widening of access and participation of learners, a cornerstone on which LLL is built (see excerpt in Appendix 6A.1).

4.3   Lifelong Learning: The Strathclyde Model

In contrast to Queen Margaret University, which offered a single combination degree in International Hospitality and Tourism Management, the University of Strathclyde offered 11 programs as follows:

- Hospitality and Tourism and Management Science;
- Management and Hospitality and Tourism;
- HRM and Hospitality and Tourism;
- Italian and Hospitality and Tourism;
- French and Hospitality and Tourism;
- Spanish and Hospitality and Tourism;
- Economics and Hospitality and Tourism;
- Business Law and Hospitality and Tourism;
- Business Entrepreneurship and Hospitality and Tourism;
- Accounting and Hospitality and Tourism;
- Marketing and Hospitality and Tourism.

As previously indicated in Table 6.3, these are offered both part-time and full-time at undergraduate and postgraduate levels. Of particular interest is the Centre for Lifelong Learning established at Strathclyde University (see excerpt in Appendix 6A.2). According to Dr Rob Mark (2014) (Head of the Centre for Lifelong Learning), the aim of the program is to provide the people of Greater Glasgow and the surrounding areas access to university-level education.

Arguably, the Lifelong Learning Centre at Strathclyde needs to be commended for embracing the agenda of lifelong learning in its comprehensive program offerings. Again, what is striking here in the lifelong learning offerings is the absence of tourism opportunities. At the time of this publication, there was no distinct lifelong learning course offered in tourism or travel-related subjects. Nevertheless, it must be noted that there were a few courses closely linked to the tourism industry, which could be advanced and packaged as tourism programs. Among these are: Wine Appreciation, Glasgow's History, Scottish Heritage, and Genealogy.

Arguably, in making a case for adopting the LLL agenda within the tourism curriculum space, there is the possibility of offering courses in niche tourism under the umbrella of wine tourism, ancestral tourism, heritage tourism and genealogy tourism respectively. Additionally, based on the full-time program offering previously delineated above, there is also scope for tour guide training, travel, and sustainable tourism business, to name a few. The question raised here is why tourism-specific courses are not offered.

4.4   Location of Lifelong Learning in Tourism Curriculum

What needs to be answered is why the key facets of the LLL agenda are not actively and literally embraced across the universities, as evidenced at Strathclyde University? But more significantly, why is tourism not represented in a distinctive manner within the curriculum space at Strathclyde's Lifelong Learning Centre? Understandably, a number of considerations such as staffing, resources and demand go into determining an institution's program structure and delivery. Nevertheless, upon reflection, a clear question is whether tourism as an area of study is being marginalized or whether it is simply a matter of lack of demand on the part of prospective students or due to lack of supply in terms of staffing? Certainly, there is a void of tourism options within the lifelong learning package that remains to be addressed.

Clearly, the academy approach at QMU bridges the gap from formal schooling into university life for school leavers. Embracing the CfE program and through its collaboration with Edinburgh College, local government and high schools, it engages with the core principle of LLL in facilitating continuity of education after formal schooling. This model allows students who may not have had the opportunity to enter university education through the normal route to gain access via an alternate approach to entry.

Although both universities are identified as good models for duplication elsewhere, certain questions typical of the ongoing tourism debate remain. A concern that both cases have highlighted through this work is the absence of a distinct tourism program offering along the lifelong learning route. What seems to be lacking in both cases is a distinctive strategy to engage with the precepts of lifelong learning within the tourism curriculum space and program delivery.

Undoubtedly, Strathclyde University can boast of being one of the two universities alongside the University of the Highlands and Islands offering the largest number and most varied program offering in tourism in Scotland within its traditional route of studies. Equally, QMU rightfully can boast of having developed, through its Academies, an exemplary non-traditional entry route for the largest group of higher education clientele, school leavers. What is missing is a holistic approach to provision of tourism education as a discipline in its own right along the guidelines of LLL. One may argue that a combination of both approaches engaged by the individual universities would be ideal. Nevertheless, some fundamental policy, planning and implementation challenges would need to be addressed.

In that regard, and in keeping with the core concepts proffered by Cuffy, Tribe and Airey (2012) and revisited by Su (2015), this chapter now proffers an approach for embracing the strategies of both universities for Lifelong Learning for Tourism Higher Education (LLLfTHE).

5.   FUTURE DIRECTIONS: LIFELONG LEARNING FOR TOURISM HIGHER EDUCATION (LLLFTHE)

A new type of university and industry collaboration has become a global pattern (Istance et al., 2002) and in the process of economic globalization, employability is expected to depend on continually mastering new skills. Simultaneously, individuals and the private sector now increasingly take responsibility for their continuous learning. These factors all have significant impact for the provision of tourism at the level of higher education.

In Scotland, going forward, university entrants who have experienced CfE through schools and colleges will have had a different experience of learning and teaching and different pathways through qualifications. In accordance with the concept of lifelong learning for tourism (Cuffy et al., 2012, 2014), universities now need to adopt a collaborative approach to tourism education. As suggested by Cunningham (2012), maximizing the opportunities that CfE provides requires a partnership approach across sectors to ensure that young people experience a smooth transition, building on prior learning and preparing for future learning.

> Because of the nature of developments so far, it is only recently that awareness has been publicly raised of how the new senior student pathways will impact on the higher education sector. Higher education has always had an involvement in CfE development but we have now moved into a new phase where regular and open communications across the sectors is essential . . . with commitment to collaboration and communication on the part of schools, universities, colleges, and the Scottish Government, the prospects of Scotland's young people as they move to future study should be assured. (Cunningham, 2012, p. 1)

As is highlighted in Universities Scotland's (2012) 'Beyond the senior phase' report, the first group of young people to have experienced CfE throughout their secondary education will enter university in 2015. Due to the flexibility of qualification pathways, new challenges will be faced in the teaching and learning process. What then are the implications for tourism higher education?

According to CfE, progression is now defined in terms of breadth, challenge and application of learning. Notwithstanding the challenges of the 'indiscipline of tourism' (Tribe, 1997) evidenced in early discussions and the absence of a core tourism curriculum (Airey, 1997) combined with the philosophical decisions around liberal versus vocational approaches (Lewis, 2005), critical issues for lifelong tourism curriculum planning and program delivery remain.

No longer can tourism curriculum planners and stakeholders sit on the fence within the safety net of university walls of the once traditional elitist higher education model. Universities now more than ever need to take up a collaborative approach with partners at the lower levels of education (within high schools and further education). Besides, globalization, international competition and the forces of change campaigned for by CfE demand a new approach – Lifelong Learning for Tourism Higher Education (LLfTHE).

What is required is a national tourism education framework that addresses key competencies at the various levels of education from 'cradle to grave'. For Scotland this must be aligned to the four capacities of the CfE as well as the principles of education for each age and learning stage along formal and non-formal education (Cuffy et al., 2012). Furthermore, as illustrated in Table 6.4, within the lifelong learning tourism curriculum space it is necessary to adopt a holistic collaborative approach to tourism education.

Lifelong Learning for Tourism Education (LLLfTHE) entails addressing the needs of society, the economy, industry, and government's educational policies and strategy as outlined in the CfE. The role of the universities as drivers of knowledge creation and advancement of a learning society is pivotal. Higher education has long served as the hub of innovation, life-changing discoveries and creation of new ways of knowing and learning. As universities move to embrace the core capacity pillars of CfE and adapt their institutional structure and program design, a more holistic and collaborative approach is necessary. Thus, it is essential that more active and participatory approaches are employed. This requires deeper engagement between and with external stakeholders such as schools, further education institutions, industry stakeholders and policy makers. The main objective here is to ensure that learning at all levels prior to higher education is indeed addressing the lifelong learning principles at the relevant and appropriate level

Table 6.4   Lifelong Learning for Tourism Higher Education (LLLfTHE)

Core principles and functions of Higher Education	Core principles Lifelong Learning focused on	4 core capacity pillars of CfE	Key collaborators creating a holistic approach	Tourism programs full/part-time
Critical Thinkers	Creation of a learning society	Successful Learners	Government University	BSc BA
Managers and Leaders	Creation of a knowledge-economy	Confident Individuals	Policymakers and relevant institutions	MSc MScRes MPhil
Skilled Professionals	Prepare citizenry for learning, life and work	Responsible citizens Effective contributors	Learner engagement	PhD PGCert PGDip Continuing Education

Source: Adapted from Cuffy et al. (2012) and CfE 2014 online.

(see Cuffy et al., 2012) to facilitate smooth transition and continuity of learning into tourism degrees and other non-professional tourism HE programs.

The QMU Academy model, coupled with the exemplary Strathclyde's Lifelong Learning Centre program, can serve as a platform upon which such a national lifelong approach within the tourism curriculum space is designed and advanced. What is needed and necessary within the tourism education agenda is adoption of that lifespan approach. Employing such an approach would allow for the learner, the university and all relevant stakeholders to collaborate in creating a learning society and knowledge economy well equipped to address the future demands of the ever-changing and growing tourism industry with all its vast and wide ranging dimensions.

6.   CONCLUSION

As highlighted earlier, there is very little discourse among scholars on lifelong tourism education. Nevertheless, many do argue that tourism is a sector that permeates all aspects of life and the economy. As such, this chapter sought to examine the role lifelong learning plays at the level of higher education and how existing tourism education practices in Scotland are aligned to the lifelong learning agenda and could be advanced in the future.

Currently in Scotland, as elsewhere, tourism education is suffering from the customary curriculum, structure and delivery problems previously discussed. Nevertheless, Scotland can be highlighted for championing lifelong learning precepts at both the government and institutional level. Accordingly, it is hoped that the proposed Lifelong Learning for Tourism Higher Education (LLLfTHE) approach can be a springboard for designing and developing a national holistic and collaborative agenda within the tourism higher education space in Scotland and beyond.

REFERENCES

Airey, David (1997), 'After twenty-five years of development: A view of the state of tourism education in the UK', in E. Laws (ed.), *The ATTT Tourism Education Handbook*, London: The Tourism Society, pp. 9–13.
Airey, D. (2008), 'Tourism education: Life begins at 40', *Teoros*, **27** (1), 27–32.
Airey, D. and S. Johnson (1999), 'The content of tourism degree courses in the UK', *Tourism Management*, **20** (2), 229–35.
Anderson, D. (1999), 'Navigating the rapids: The role of educational and careers information and guidance in transition between education and work', *Journal of Vocational Education and Training*, **21** (3), 371–99.
Antonacopoulou, E. (2000), 'Reconnecting education, development and training through learning: A holographic perspective', *Education and Training*, **42** (4/5), 255–63.
Barnett, Robert (1990), *The Idea of Higher Education*, Buckingham: The Society for Research into Higher Education and Open University Press.
Barnett, Robert (1997), *Higher Education: A Critical Business*, Buckingham: The Society for Research into Higher Education and Open University Press.
Blaxter, Loraine, Christina Hughes and Malcolm Tight (2002), *How to Research*, Buckingham: Open University Press.
Brennan, J., J. Mills, T. Shah and A. Woodley (2000), 'Lifelong learning for employment and equity: The role of part-time degrees', *Higher Education Quarterly*, **54** (4), 411–18.
Cohen, Geoff, Antony Fielding and Jennifer Waterton (2010), *Measurements of Participation in Scottish Higher Education Report*, Social Research, Education Analytical Services, Lifelong Learning Research, Glasgow: Scottish Government.
Cuffy, V., J. Tribe and D. Airey (2012), 'Lifelong learning for tourism', *Annals of Tourism Research*, **39** (3), 1402–24.
Cuffy, V., J. Tribe and D. Airey (2014), 'Collaborating planning for lifelong tourism education and training', in Proceedings of Council for Hospitality Management Education Annual Research Conference, 28–30 May, Buxton: CHME.
Cunningham, Ken (2012), 'Foreword', in 'Beyond the senior phase: University engagement with Curriculum for Excellence', Report commissioned by Universities Scotland.
Curriculum for Excellence (CfE), accessed November 2014 at http://www.curriculum-for-excellence.co.uk/.
DfEE (1998a), *The Learning Age: A Renaissance for a New Britain*, Green Paper Consultation, London: Department for Education and Employment.
DfEE (1998b), *University for Industry: Pathfinder Prospectus*, Green Paper Consultation, London: Department for Education and Employment.
DfEE (1998c), *Further Education for the New Millennium*, Green Paper Consultation, London: Department for Education and Employment.
DfEE (1999), *Learning to Succeed: A New Framework for Post 16-Learning*, Green Paper Consultation, London: Department for Education and Employment.
Department for International Development (DFID)–World Bank (2009), *Collaboration on Knowledge and the Skills for the New Economy,* White paper DFID-WB.
Dredge, Dianne, David Airey and Michael J. Gross (eds) (2015), *The Routledge Handbook of Tourism and Hospitality Education*, London: Routledge, pp. 322–34.
European Commission (EC) (2009), Council Conclusions of 12 May 2009 on a strategic framework for European cooperation in education and training (ET 2020), Brussels: Council for the European Union.
EC (2000), 'Presidency conclusions', Lisbon European Council, 23–24 March, Brussels: European Council.
Fallows, S. and C. Steven (2000), 'Building employability skills into the higher education curriculum: University-wide initiative', *Education and Training*, **42** (2), 75–82.
Gibb, T. and J. Walker (2011), 'Educating for a high skills society? The landscape of federal employment, training and lifelong learning policy in Canada', *Journal of Educational Policy*, **26** (3), 381–98.
Gilloran, Allan (2013), *Access All Areas*, Universities in Scotland, accessed November 2014 at www.universities-scotland.ac.uk.
Haggar-Guénette, C. (1991), 'Lifelong learning: who goes back to school?', *Perspectives on Labour and Income*, **3** (4), 24–30.
Harvey, L. (2001), 'Defining and measuring employability', *Quality in Higher Education*, **7** (2), 97–109.
Holder, Jean (2001), 'Meeting the challenge for change', address delivered by Secretary General of the Caribbean Tourism Organisation, CARICOM Tourism Summit, 8–9 December 2001, Nassau, The Bahamas: Press release 149/2001, 10 December, accessed November 2014 at www.caricom.org.
Hyland, Terry (2003), 'Learning, work and community, vocational studies and social values in the learning age', in J. Field and M. Leicester (eds), *Lifelong Learning, Education Across the Lifespan*, London: RoutledgeFalmer, pp. 119–33.

Istance, David, Hans G. Schuetze and Tom Schuller (2002), *International Perspectives on Lifelong Learning: From Recurrent Education to the Knowledge Society,* The Society for Research into Higher Education and Open University Press.

Knapper, Christopher K. and Arthur J. Cropley (2000), *Lifelong Learning in Higher Education*, 3rd edn, London: Kogan Page.

Larson, Anne (2011), 'Lifelong learning: From European policy to national legislation', paper presented at the ECER conference in Berlin, 12–16 September, Department of Education, Aarhus University.

Leader, G. (2003), 'Lifelong learning policy and practice in further education', *Education and Training*, **45** (7), 361–70.

Lewis, A. (2005), 'Rationalizing a tourism curriculum for sustainable tourism development in small island states: A stakeholder perspective', *Journal of Hospitality, Leisure, Sport and Tourism Education*, **4** (2), 4–15.

Mark, Rob (2014), 'Bringing learning to life, 2014–2015', Centre for Lifelong Learning, evening and weekend classes for adults, University of Strathclyde, Glasgow, accessed November 2014 at www.strath.ac.uk/cll

Marshall, Stewart and Christine Marrett (2008), 'External providers of tertiary education in the Commonwealth Caribbean', in Stewart Marshall, Ed Brandon, Michael Thomas, Asha Kanwar and Tove Lyngra (eds), *Foreign Providers in the Caribbean: Pillagers or Preceptors? Perspectives on Distance Education*, Vancouver: Commonwealth of Learning, pp. 1–10.

Marshall, Stewart, Ed Brandon, Michael Thomas, Asha Kanwar and Tove Lyngra (eds) (2008), *Foreign Providers in the Caribbean: Pillagers or Preceptors? Perspectives on Distance Education*, Vancouver: Commonwealth of Learning.

McKenzie, Phillip (1998), *Lifelong Learning as a Policy Response*, ACER Centre for the Economics of Education and Training and ACER, Monash University.

Medel-Anonuevo, Carolyn, Toshio Ohsako and Werner Mauch (2001), *Revisiting Lifelong Learning for the 21st-century,* Hamburg: UNESCO Institute for Education.

Milana, Marcella (2012), 'Political globalisation and the shift from adult education to lifelong learning', *European Journal for Research on the Education and Learning of Adults*, **3** (2), 103–17.

OECD (1996), 'Lifelong learning for all: Meeting of the education community at ministerial level', 16–17 January, Paris: OECD.

Parnham, J. (2001), 'Lifelong learning: A model for increasing the participation of non-traditional adult learners', *Journal of Further and Higher Education*, **25** (1), 57–65.

Poon, Auliana (2001), 'The Caribbean', in A. Lockwood and S. Medlik (eds), *Tourism and Hospitality in the 21st Century*, Oxford: Reed Educational and Professional Publishing, pp. 143–53.

Queen Margaret University (n.d.), Website accessed November 2014 at www.qmu.ac.uk.

Rogers, Alan (1996), *Teaching Adults*, Milton Keynes: Open University Press.

Rubenson, Kjell (2006), 'Constructing the lifelong learning paradigm: Competing visions of the OECD and UNESCO', in Soren Ehlers (ed.), *Milestones Towards Lifelong Learning Systems*, Copenhagen: Danish University of Education Press, pp. 151–70.

Scotland, Miriam (2006), *The Higher Education Program Curricula Models in Tourism and Hospitality Education: A Review of the Literature*, Texas A&M University.

Scottish Qualification Authority (SQA) (n.d.), Website accessed November 2014 at www.scqf.org.uk.

Strathclyde University (n.d.), Website accessed November 2014 at www.stathclyde.ac.uk.

Su, Yahui (2015), 'Lifelong learning in tourism education', in Dianne Dredge, David Airey and Michael J. Gross (eds), *The Routledge Handbook of Tourism and Hospitality Education*, London: Routledge, pp. 322–34.

Tight, M. (1998), 'Education, education, education! The vision of lifelong learning in the Kennedy, Dearing and Fryer Reports', *Oxford Review of Education*, **24** (4), 473–85.

Tribe, J. (1997), 'The indiscipline of tourism', *Annals of Tourism Research*, **24** (3), 638–57.

Tribe, J. (2000), 'Balancing the vocational: The theory and practice of liberal education in tourism', *Tourism and Hospitality Research*, **2** (1), 9–25.

Tribe, J. (2002), 'The philosophical practitioner', *Tourism and Hospitality Research*, **29** (2), 338–57.

Tuijnman, A. and A.K. Boström (2002), 'Changing notions of lifelong education and lifelong learning', *International Review of Education*, **48** (1–2), 93–110.

Turner, Rochelle and Zachary Sears (2013), 'Travel & tourism as a driver of employment growth', in J. Blanke and T. Chiesa (eds), *The Travel & Tourism Competitiveness Report 2013*, Geneva: World Economic Forum, pp. 63–9.

Universities Scotland (2012), 'Beyond the senior phase: University engagement with Curriculum for Excellence', Report commissioned by Universities Scotland.

Universities Scotland (2013), 'Access All Areas', accessed November 2014 at www.universities-scotland.ac.uk.

Vargas, F. (2005), *Key Competencies and Lifelong Learning*, The Inter-American Centre for Knowledge Development in Vocational Training, International Labour Office (ILO).

World Travel and Tourism Council (2014), *World WTTC Travel & Tourism Economic Impact 2014*, World Travel & Tourism Council.

Zagonari, F. (2009), 'Balancing tourism education and training', *International Journal of Hospitality and Management*, **28** (1), 2–9.

APPENDIX 6A.1   MARGARET'S UNIVERSITY STATEMENT ON ENGAGEMENT WITH CURRICULUM FOR EXCELLENCE

Queen Margaret University and the Curriculum for Excellence

Queen Margaret University welcomes the Curriculum for Excellence. The University is committed to ensuring that pupils undertaking the new curriculum in Scotland will be able to progress to its courses in a way that best suits their needs. The increased emphasis within the Curriculum for Excellence on skills development in preparation for employment is consistent with our Graduate Attributes. These are the core transferable (social and personal) skills that we expect all QMU students to acquire through the course of their degree or diploma to equip them for work and life after university.

Source: Adapted from Queen Margaret University, 2014, online.

APPENDIX 6A.2   LEARNING AT STRATHCLYDE UNIVERSITY

Strathclyde University Lifelong Learning Program

Strathclyde University through its Centre for Lifelong Learning offers an exemplary lifelong learning program with a varied portfolio of approximately 200 classes delivered on evenings and weekends throughout the year. According to the centre's manager this is in keeping with the University's mission of making learning open to all who may benefit from it and in so doing maintains its tradition of making available to the public an interesting and stimulating selection of study opportunities (Dr Rob Mark, Head of Centre for Lifelong Learning, 2014).
  Accordingly the core objectives of the program are:

● to encourage the intellectual growth of adult learners;
● to link university provision to the wider community;
● to provide learning opportunities for those who seek career progression;
● to provide an environment in which curiosity can be satisfied and skills can be mastered.

Our classes have:

● open entry, no qualifications necessary;
● liberal teaching and learning methods;
● the opportunity to accumulate credit, enabling progression to undergraduate study.

Open to all, the diverse program provides a wide choice to inform and entertain. Credits can be accumulated towards a University of Strathclyde Open Studies Certificate

Source: Adapted from Strathclyde University, 2014, online.

7   Enhancing tourism graduates' soft skills: the importance of teaching reflective practice
Karen Hughes, Aliisa Mylonas and Roy Ballantyne

1.   INTRODUCTION

Tourism education is a relatively new field in tertiary education (Tribe, 2005), and in many institutions curricula have tended to respond to the demands of the industry. Thus, instruction in academic skills has often been accompanied by the more vocational skills required to succeed in the tourism and hospitality workforce. While most programs incorporate some form of coaching on soft skills, few focus on the importance of being able to critically self-assess one's own communication skills and to adjust these to suit particular situations and audiences. Reflecting on what did or did not work well in a given scenario is an important aspect of guest relations, yet where do graduates learn these skills and how should these be developed?

Tourism is a service-oriented industry that relies heavily on communication skills in all their guises – written, oral, aural and interpersonal. To communicate well, individuals need to be able to assess their role in particular situations and respond in a way that is going to enhance the interaction (either immediately or by changing subsequent approaches). While communication skills are important, individuals also need to be able to reflect, gauge what went well or badly, assess their role in the interaction, determine what could have been done differently, and develop strategies and plans should the situation arise in future.

Reflection is a process that requires the unveiling of self. Through self-examination, we reveal the real and raw 'me' in a given circumstance or situation and, in the process, progress towards self-development (Ross, 2014). Self-reflection is therefore a process of baring our souls and looking at things from different perspectives; essentially, it's a 'warts-and-all' approach to understanding why we reacted in particular ways and why this did or did not lead to particular outcomes. Such abilities are essential in the tourism industry, where service personnel regularly interact with guests with a range of dispositions, attitudes, issues and requests. The ability to self-assess one's performance is critical in these interactions and, in many cases, can be the difference between a positive or negative service encounter.

In this chapter we propose that self-reflection is one of those 'hidden' skills embedded and implicit in effective performance of many other 'soft' skills required by employers. We argue that unless graduates have the ability to critically reflect on their own practice, their success in situations that require effective interpersonal communication is likely to be compromised (Schön, 1983; Tribe, 2002).

2.   LITERATURE

2.1   Development of Graduate Attributes in Higher Education

Within the higher education sector, universities have developed their own statements of graduate attributes which are reflected and embedded in all degree programs offered by that institution. In identifying the generic knowledge, skills, abilities and attributes learners are expected to develop during their studies – and ultimately achieve as demonstrable graduate outcomes – inevitably institutions will include statements reflecting the need for their graduates to be effective communicators, problem solvers, and critical and creative thinkers (or similar themed descriptors). When 'drilling down' into the meaning of these particular attributes, you often find many 'common ground' statements espousing an ability for graduates to interact effectively with others, identify problems and create solutions, apply critical reasoning to problems, and reflect critically on decisions made. While it is beyond the scope of this chapter to address how well institutions are *assuring* the attainment of these graduate outcomes, there is an expectation from both universities and industry that our graduates will be effective communicators, problem solvers and reflective thinkers (Barrie, 2006; Oliver, 2010).

2.2   What is Reflective Practice?

There are two models of reflection that dominate the literature. The first, building on the influential thinking of John Dewey's 'making sense of the world' reflection process (1933), is Schön's (1983) notion of *reflection-in-action and reflection-on-action*. Reflection-in-action is immediate and short term. It requires the ability to 'think on one's feet', to analyze situations and to react accordingly. Because reflection-in-action draws on tacit knowledge (Morrison, 1996), it tends to be used more by experienced employees than by graduates (Finlay, 2008). Reflection-on-action, conversely, is more systematic and involves logical analysis of the antecedents and consequences of the situation under consideration. Thus, the practitioner seeks to gain a full understanding of the situation by applying rules, theories and principles after a particular incident has occurred (Morrison, 1996). Such an approach is more typically associated with new employees (Finlay, 2008), while reflection-in-action is more likely to be associated with the essential skills identified by employers (that is, confronts problems early, anticipates obstacles and develops plans).

The second model of reflection focuses on the development and empowerment that emerges from reflective practice. This approach acknowledges that through the process of reflection, the reflective practitioner develops plans and strategies for future action and thereby becomes empowered (Bain et al., 2002a; 2002b). The argument is that this process creates in practitioners 'autonomy, informed professional judgement, decision-making and existential self-realization – individually and collectively, contributing to an egalitarian democracy' (Morrison, 1996, p. 319). It requires individuals to consider what they did, what it means, why they reacted as they did, and what they might do differently next time (Morrison, 1996). While both models have had their critics, Morrison (1996) argues that they are complementary, and can be embedded in curricula.

2.3   Why is Reflective Practice Important for Tourism Graduates?

Researchers in higher education have consistently highlighted the importance of ensuring that graduates' skills and competencies are relevant, current and match what is required by employers (Knight and Yorke, 2004; Oliver et al., 2011; Ferns, 2012; Dredge et al., 2012). Today, employers are seeking a workforce that is flexible and adaptable, one with the skills and abilities to respond to a wide range of customer needs. More than a decade ago, Bennett (2002) gathered over one thousand advertisements for general managerial, marketing, finance and human resource management positions in UK graduate recruitment databases over a two-year period. Analysis revealed that recruiters for general management vacancies were significantly more likely to focus on initiative, motivation, leadership and communication skills than those recruiting for finance and human resource management positions.

A more recent analysis of skill competencies in educational contexts has highlighted the development of graduates' generic or transferable skills. This change in emphasis acknowledges the dynamic nature of employment and careers in the twenty-first century, and the importance of developing skills that enable employees to transfer from one role or workplace to another (Raybould and Wilkins, 2005). The possession of so-called transferable skills (for example, communication skills, organizational skills, self-motivation, initiative, creativity, the capacity to solve problems, and leadership) is highly prized by prospective employers as these skills enable graduates to make 'an immediate contribution to a business' (Bennett, 2002, p. 458).

In tourism and hospitality, employment options cover a wide variety of job opportunities, which makes collating a list of essential graduate attributes challenging. However, most roles involve relating to, and interacting with, guests or customers; as such, 'soft skills' (interpersonal communication skills, empathy, emotional intelligence and so on) are likely to be highly prized by potential employers.

Zehrer and Mössenlechner's (2009) review of studies exploring tourism graduate employability reveals that when recruiting graduates, the tourism industry values both academic skills and 'soft' skills such as interpersonal communication, creativity, empathy, improvisation, and being proactive and responsive. Based on this review, Zehrer and Mössenlechner surveyed 48 domestic and international partners of the Management Centre Innsbruck about the attributes and skills graduates required if they were considering employment in the tourism industry. Skills rated most important included: overall communication abilities (4.79 on a 5-point scale where 5 equals most important), language competence (4.75), self-motivation (4.77), personal commitment (4.73), conceptual skills (4.73), problem-solving skills (4.71), decision-making (4.64), initiative (4.61), and ability to work under pressure (4.61). Though not at the top of the list, self-reflection was also seen as important by potential employers (4.23 on a five-point scale).

In exploring the changing nature of industry requirements of graduates, Raybould and Wilkins (2005) surveyed 371 general managers, human resource managers and operations managers in four and five star hotels across Australia. The top ten qualities required of employees could be classified as generic skills and covered key domains such as interpersonal skills, problem solving and self-management. We contend that the use of reflective practice is one way to overtly develop these skills in tourism.

In 2009 Ring et al. (2008) investigated the design of an ideal undergraduate tourism program that meets the expectations of both industry and educators. They employed adaptive conjoint analysis to assess the subject themes of 64 bachelor's programs which included 'tourism' in the program title. From a total of 19 levels of subject areas and themes, generic skills – personal and social skills; and creativity, reflection and entrepreneurship – were ranked fourth in importance by industry professionals and third in importance by educators.

In 2010, Cheung et al. explored whether academic institutions offering hospitality education in Hong Kong produce 'industry ready' graduates. Surveys from 38 hotel departmental managers (four and five star properties) revealed that managers felt that the most important dimensions were leadership, industry knowledge and communication. In terms of specific competencies, the top five essential competencies were soft skills: work as a member of a team (6.08 on a seven-point scale), treat people with respect (6.00), protect confidential information (5.97), confront problems early (5.97) and anticipate obstacles and develop contingency plans (5.92).

We argue that underlying the ability to excel in soft skills is the capacity to step back from the situation and systematically analyze one's own and others' thoughts, reactions and behavior. In other words, employees in the tourism and hospitality industry need the skills to reflect on a given situation, dissect their own – and others' – contribution and then respond, either at the time of the incident or in future similar situations. Accordingly, it is not surprising that discussion of learners' reflective skills is now starting to emerge in tourism and hospitality curricula.

Arendt and Gregoire (2008) explored the relationship between reflective practice and leadership skills by surveying 345 hospitality management students attending eight US universities. They found that students who reported reflecting on their classroom behavior had significantly higher scores in two out of five leadership practices than those who did not reflect. Likewise, those who reflected in the work environment also had significantly higher scores on three of these leadership practices than those who did not. The authors suggest that incorporating reflection into classroom practice is likely to enhance leadership skills both in the classroom and workplace. However, they caution that students are also likely to require appropriate stimuli and support to develop their reflective skills.

More recently, Robinson et al. (2014) analyzed 488 reflective journal entries of 124 undergraduate students enrolled in a food and beverage course at an Australian university. They found that entries improved (that is, became more reflective) with successive iterations of the task. The authors suggest that scaffolding reflective activities is likely to produce more reflective practitioners and facilitate the integration of classroom-based theory activities and students' personal experiences.

2.4   Program/Curriculum Design

While there appears to be consensus that both academic skills and 'soft' skills are necessary to excel as an employee in the tourism industry, there is still considerable debate about which particular soft skills should be developed and whether or not this should be the role of higher educational institutions (Zehrer and Mössenlechner, 2009).

Barr and Tagg (1995) argue that tertiary education is subtly changing towards a Learning Paradigm in which higher education institutions provide an environment and experiences that support and encourage students to become active learners who seek to discover and construct knowledge for themselves. To do this effectively, learners need to master how to learn and work towards becoming lifelong learners. As such, the 'learning' of reflection should be a natural part of this process.

Ryan (2013) asserts that 'learners are not often taught how to communicate their disciplinary knowledge through reflection' and stresses that 'students can and should be taught how to reflect in deep and transformative ways' (p. 144). This notion is supported by Maresse et al. (2012), who propose that 'how reflective writing is managed throughout a program is important in determining how students can advance their reflective capabilities, and thus develop their professional understandings and thinking processes' (p. 35). We also can't expect students to just 'go and reflect' (Welch, 1999). Rather, 'they need help with connecting their experiences to course material, with challenging their beliefs and assumptions, and with deepening their learning' (Ash and Clayton, 2004, p. 138).

Ryan and Ryan (2012), in their role as lead researchers of an Australian national teaching project, used Bain et al.'s (2002a) 5Rs Reflective Thinking Framework (reporting/responding, relating, reasoning and reconstructing) as a cross-faculty framework to scaffold teaching design, student work and assessment descriptions. The project resulted in the creation of resources to support a community of educators embedding pedagogical changes for teaching and assessing reflective learning.

With reference to the Reflective Thinking Framework (Bain et al., 2002a) and Ryan and Ryan's TARL Model (2012), the following summaries and practical examples are presented as a guide for helping tourism academics structure and scaffold the development of reflection for students studying within a tourism context. Importantly, in situations where reflective practice is being assessed, consideration must be given to choosing an appropriate assessment item that not only aligns with learning outcomes, but also aligns with the level of reflective practice embedded within that course. The practical examples listed below also provide some assistance with this aspect. It is important to note that while the reflection levels are not designed to 'match' the different year levels of a degree program, planning should be undertaken to introduce these levels sequentially.

Level 1: Reporting/responding
For developing reporting and responding as the first level of reflective thinking (Box 7.1):

- teach learners to identify and discuss specific aspects of their practice;
- guide learners in their ability to form an opinion or have an emotional reaction to an issue or incident relevant to their area of study;
- as reporting and responding are foundational to higher levels of reflection, provide opportunities for learners to understand how to clearly articulate the focus of their reflection, that is, a specific incident or issue.

Level 2: Relating
For developing relating as the second level of reflective thinking (Box 7.2):

- guide learners to think about the chosen issue/incident in terms of their previous experiences with similar or related issues or situations;
- prompt learners to examine their skills, knowledge, values and priorities, and consider how these relate to those of key stakeholders involved;

BOX 7.1   LEVEL 1 PROMPTS FOR RELATING/RESPONDING

Level 1 Prompts/Applications

Guiding Questions/Prompts for Students

- Choose an incident or issue that either supported or challenged your learning, and describe what happened.
- Make observations, express an opinion, ask further questions about the incident or issue.

Practical Applications for Tourism Students

- Select a critical incident (positive or negative) that occurred during your industry placement. Describe where it was, what happened, who was involved, and how you reacted.
- Select a topic that was discussed in class that interested, inspired or annoyed you. Explain why it caught your attention. Describe what was discussed and your initial reaction to the topic.

HINT: For classes with high numbers of international students, ask students to consider the topic in relation to their home environment.

- Peruse a problem-based scenario, then identify and describe the relevant topics or issues. Discuss these with your peers, and select one that has the most potential to lead to new actions or ideas. As a group, construct a flowchart to map out the key points, examples and literature that will form the basis for subsequent levels of reflections about this issue or incident.

- help learners to evaluate whether they have the ability to deal with the issue themselves or whether they need to consult others.

Level 3: Reasoning
For developing reasoning as the third level of reflective thinking (Box 7.3):

- assist learners to progress from thinking about their own personal response in a particular situation to a consideration of broader issues;
- explore different interpretations of the scenarios and issues under consideration by undertaking a thorough analysis of the context so that issues and possible impacting factors are produced.

Level 4: Reconstructing
For developing reconstructing as the highest level of reflective thinking (Box 7.4):

- guide learners in developing new ways of approaching problems and thinking about issues;
- encourage learners to consider future actions and predict the impacts and benefits these may have for themselves and/or others;
- expect learners to support decisions about future actions with reference to what is considered 'best practice' in the discipline.

BOX 7.2   LEVEL 2 PROMPTS FOR RELATING

Level 2 Prompts/Applications

Guiding Questions/Prompts for Students

- Clearly describe how this incident or issue relates to other experiences you have previously encountered.
- Determine whether you have the ability to deal with the issue or incident, and explain why or why not.

Practical Applications for Tourism Students

- Peruse recent media articles that relate to tourism, hospitality or events issues and select those that particularly appeal to you. In small groups, explore and discuss the underlying issues, making reference to the notes, readings, audio-visual materials and case studies provided in class. **HINT**: For an assessment item, you can extend this activity by asking learners to write a reflective essay responding to one of the media articles, based on their own and others' input.
- In groups of three, analyse a key journal article relating to your area of study. As a group, present a summary of the article that demonstrates your understanding of the article's main message/s and implications for practice. Design and conduct a class activity which supports the class's learning with regard to the topic/s discussed.
- In groups of six, debate the likely impacts of a fictitious tourism development. Choose one of the six stakeholder roles (3 'for' and 3 'against') and argue for or against development from your stakeholder's perspective. You need to get into character and present your case using examples adapted from the literature and the media. Use artifacts (costumes, props etc.) and persuasive language to convince the audience of your views. At the end of the debate, students in the audience will be invited to add any further arguments and vote on the winning side. **HINT**: To overcome potential repetitiveness of arguments within the same group, encourage group members to individually develop their own case based on their specific stakeholder role, before regrouping with the two others on their side to check that a range of arguments will be presented.

Ryan asserts that 'unless all levels [of reflection] are scaffolded, students are unlikely to produce succinct, rigorous and transformation reflections in their assessment tasks' (2013; p. 153). As such, the following points can assist in guiding a tourism teaching team's approach to developing levels of reflective practice across all year levels of a degree program:

1. *Agree on a definition of reflection best suited to your field and institutional context.* Agreeing on your own definition of reflection allows it to become 'common language' and, thus, able to be more clearly and consistently communicated to learners so that they, too, share your team's understanding of the meaning of reflective practice within your discipline/context.
2. *Holistic curriculum planning.* Within your discipline/field, most learners tend to follow a similar pathway of study across the years of their degree program. Taking a more holistic 'helicopter' view of the curriculum, the teaching team can agree on the types – and timing – of learning experiences that they believe will best scaffold the development of the levels of reflection.

BOX 7.3   LEVEL 3 PROMPTS FOR REASONING

Level 3 Prompts/Applications

Guiding Questions/Prompts for Students

- What are the key factors contributing to the issue or incident?
- Explain why these factors are important in understanding what is happening.
- Support your analysis with theory and literature.
- How would other people respond to this issue or incident?

Practical Applications for Tourism Students

- After each week's class, write a one-page reflection on key elements/issues that you found personally relevant, interesting and/or thought-provoking in some way (even if you disagreed with the points made). Why did you select these and what is your personal understanding of the key issues discussed?
  HINT: As an extension of this activity, advise learners that their draft reflections will be discussed in pairs in class the following week. This gives learners an opportunity to share thoughts and ideas, seek feedback from their peers/teacher and extend their thinking about course content before finalizing their reflections (which could be submitted as part of a reflective portfolio at the end of the semester).
- Prepare an industry standard report in response to a current industry issue/problem presented by an industry guest speaker. Include an assessment of the issue in terms of its impact on the industry sector and a review of relevant literature. Based on your literature review, provide a minimum of five recommendations as to how the industry could overcome the issue or problem.
  HINT: As an extension of this activity, the industry guest presenter can be invited to select the best recommendations. The group can then be presented with a certificate acknowledging this achievement.
- During industry placement, write a daily reflective diary that clearly documents tasks completed, observations made, your ideas/emotions/reactions to events in the workplace, issues discussed with others, and notes relating to what you have learnt about the job (including a self-assessment of strengths/weaknesses in relation to this position).
  HINT: As an extension of this activity, encourage learners to collect and collate relevant artifacts that express and/or illustrate their experiences (for example, photos, sketches, poems, objects collected from their workplace).
- Either via an industry-based scenario (provided by your teacher) or an actual industry-based experience, choose one issue that you believe has ethical implications for the industry. Access relevant sources of information to assist you in 'unpacking' this issue, and form an opinion on your response to this issue. Be prepared to justify your stance when this issue is raised in class.
  HINT: To add depth to this activity, ask students to prepare an annotated bibliography of the five key sources of information they used to inform their opinion.
- Visit a tourism/hospitality or event site and conduct a critique of the facilities and/or services from a visitor/guest perspective. What are your thoughts and feelings? Why do you think you reacted like this? Compare your responses with other students – did they feel the same way? Identify what led to these differences/similarities.
  HINT: As an extension of this activity, learners could postulate why management designed the experience in this way, analyze how well it works, and provide recommendations for improving the site/experience.

BOX 7.4   LEVEL 4 PROMPTS FOR RECONSTRUCTING

Level 4 Prompts/Applications

Guiding Questions/Prompts for Students

- If this issue or incident were to re-occur, how would you react? What would you do and why?
- Identify different responses and describe the likely outcomes for self and others.
- Make links to relevant theory.

Practical Applications for Tourism Students

- Create a service log of three service encounters by reflecting upon your own experiences as a customer. Select one and briefly describe what happened from your own customer perspective. From the list of key service concepts provided in class, choose the one you consider to be most relevant to your service experience. Undertake a literature review of articles related to the service concept chosen. Once completed, use these articles to, first, reflect on your service experience and, second, provide relevant managerial recommendations.
- Reflect upon how you have grown/changed as a result of your workplace experience. Write a reflective portfolio addressing the following:
  - What were your initial feelings, beliefs and assumptions prior to your work placement, and how have these changed?
  - What are your strengths?
  - What might you need to improve?
  - What have you learnt about your chosen industry?
  - Does the industry/profession match your initial expectations?
  - Do you think you will continue working in this industry? How has this experience impacted on your post-graduation career plans?

HINT: Prior to the industry placement, students should be expected to outline their career plans/ambitions, and complete a self-assessment of strengths/weaknesses. They can then use this information to inform their reflections, post-placement (along with any verbal or written feedback received from their workplace supervisor/mentor).

- Over the duration of your program you have heard presentations from industry and past students about industry's expectations and requirements of graduates. Using these conversations and presentations as a guide, reflect upon your readiness to enter the workforce. Do you consider yourself a good 'fit' for your chosen industry – why/why not? Is it what you expected/hoped? What further skills or training might you need and how will you obtain these? When applying for positions after graduation, what qualifications and experiences will you highlight?
- You will be given annotated exemplars of past assignments. Peruse the examples then analyze the feedback on your own piece of work. Identify key similarities/differences between your work and the exemplars, and highlight places where you could have achieved higher marks. Use this analysis to develop a response to the assessor. In your response, explain a detailed course of action, with justifications, on how you intend to improve your work.
- After a class debate of an ethical issue, take time to self-reflect on the arguments used during the discussion. Decide which argument/s require further thought/(re)construction, and develop a plan for reconstructing the argument.

HINT: You could extend this activity by asking learners to pair up and take turns providing peer feedback regarding their self-analysis and decision for reconstructing a particular argument. The pair could then work together to complete this task.

3. *Levels of reflection reflected in learning outcomes.* While we hope that the love of our field drives learning, most academics would agree that the practical reality is that most learners are driven by the set assessment tasks. As such, those key courses targeted as supporting the development of reflective practice must have learning outcomes and assessment tasks that make this intention explicit.

4. *Variety of learning experiences.* There are a variety of learning experiences that can support the development of reflection. Again, adopting a holistic view of planned learning experiences (and assessment tasks) over the program can highlight where best to consolidate learning (via similar types of tasks), as well as extend the level of reflection via new or varied approaches/tasks.

5. *Appropriate choice of assessment.* The type of assessment chosen must align with the planned learning outcome linked to the level of reflective practice embedded in your course. For example, a course focused on developing reasoning (Level 3) won't be supported by a task that only requires learners to identify and discuss an issue (Level 1) or consider how an issue relates to their own personal experience or opinion (Level 2). Clearly described assessment criteria will also assist learners in understanding the level of reflection expected, and the evidence required to demonstrate their reflective learning.

6. *Consistent message.* As a teaching team, you have agreed on the importance of learners developing reflection across a number of levels. You have intentionally planned for the inclusion of activities that will support this development, and designed assessment tasks that will give learners the opportunity to demonstrate their capacity to reflect at a particular level. However, like all of us, learners need to understand not only what you require of them, but also *why*. For this reason, it is vital that all members of your teaching team can 'sell' to learners the benefits and importance of developing levels of reflection within your discipline/context, and that this message – along with planned support and scaffolding – is consistent across the program. Importantly, there needs to be an understanding that reflective practice can't be 'done to students'; rather, it is learning that needs to be mutually constructed within a co-creative, supportive space (Pavlovich et al., 2009).

7. *Reflection on reflection.* Reflective practice takes time and effort; in 'practicing what we preach', make time each semester to meet with your team to discuss how well the planned approaches to teaching and assessing reflective processes are working. This also provides a good opportunity to bring new team members into the conversation, ensuring a smoother transition for them into understanding your discipline's approach to scaffolding and assessing the levels of reflection.

3.   CONCLUSION

In the tourism industry, it is critical that personnel ensure that their interactions with guests result in a positive service experience. For this reason, 'soft skills' are highly valued by employers, including communication and interpersonal skills. While these skills are essential, the difference between a positive or negative service encounter often depends on how well employees can reflect and self-assess their actions. Without the ability to 'stand back' and reflect on what worked well or could have been done differently, how will the employee develop further strategies for application to similar – or more challenging – encounters in the future?

In this chapter, we assert that tourism graduates require the ability to critically reflect on their practice; however, the development of this highly valued 'soft' skill should not be left to chance. By adopting and applying the ideas of Bain et al.'s (2002a) Reflective Thinking Framework and Ryan and Ryan's (2012) TARL Model across an area of study or entire degree program, tourism educators can proactively plan for the scaffolded and ongoing development of learners' reflective thinking skills.

Using the reflective framework, learning experiences, resources and assessment tasks can be designed around the level of reflective thinking applicable to the unit being taught. Ideally, a 'whole of course' team approach is adopted, enabling educators to have confidence in the types of reflective thinking experiences learners have encountered prior to entering their class.

We live in a world where international travel and cross-cultural interactions (and the corresponding potential for conflict and misunderstanding) are increasing. Our graduates need to be able to deconstruct situations and accurately analyze how their input and reactions contribute to the outcome (whether positive or negative). They also need the skills and confidence to act upon their analysis: the best way to ensure their development of reflective thinking is by providing numerous opportunities for practice during their studies, in a safe and supported learning environment.

REFERENCES

Arendt, S.W. and Gregoire, M.B. (2008), 'Reflection by hospitality management students improves leadership practice scores', *Journal of Hospitality and Tourism Education*, **20** (2), 10–15.
Ash, S.L. and Clayton, P.H. (2004), 'The articulated learning: An approach to guided reflection and assessment', *Innovative Higher Education*, **29** (2), 137–54.
Bain, J.D., Ballantyne, R., Mills, C. and Lester, N. (2002a), *Reflecting on Practice: Student Teachers' Perspectives*, Flaxton: Post Pressed.
Bain, J.D., Mills. C., Ballantyne, R. and Packer, J. (2002b), 'Developing reflection on practice through journal writing: Impacts of variations in the focus and level of feedback', *Teachers and Teaching – Theory and Practice*, **8** (2), 171–96.
Barr, Robert B. and Tagg, J. (1995), 'From teaching to learning: a new paradigm for undergraduate education', *Change: The Magazine of Higher Learning*, **27** (6), 12–26.
Barrie, Simon C. (2006), 'Understanding what we mean by the generic attributes of graduates', *Higher Education*, **51** (2), 215–41.
Bennett, R. (2002), 'Employers' demands for personal transferable skills in graduates: A content analysis of 1000 job advertisements and an associated empirical study', *Journal of Vocational Education and Training*, **54** (4), 457–76.
Cheung, C., Law, R. and He, K. (2010), 'Essential hotel managerial competencies for graduate students', *Journal of Hospitality and Tourism Education*, **22** (4), 25–32.
Dewey, J. (1933), *How We Think: A Restatement of the Relation of Reflective Thinking to the Educative Process* (revised edn), Boston: D.C. Heath and Company.
Dredge, D., Benckendorff, P., Day, M., Gross, M.J., Walo, M., Weeks, P. and Whitelaw, P. (2012), 'The philosophic practitioner and the curriculum space', *Annals of Tourism Research*, **39** (4), 2154–76.
Ferns, S. (2012), 'Graduate employability: Teaching staff, employer and graduate perceptions', *Proceedings ACEN National Conference Melbourne/Geelong 2012*.
Finlay, L. (2008), 'Reflecting on reflective practice', PBPL CETL, Open University, accessed 2 November 2014 at www.open.ac.uk/cetl-workspace/cetlcontent/documents/4bf2b48887459.pdf.
Knight, P. and Yorke, M. (2004), *Learning, Curriculum and Employability in Higher Education*, London: Routledge Farmer.
Maresse, S., McKay, J. and Grellier, J. (2012), 'Supporting and promoting reflective thinking processes in an

undergraduate Medical Imaging Program', in Brown, N., Jones, S.M. and Adam, A. (eds), *Research and Development in Higher Education: Connections in Higher Education*, **35**, 160–69.

Morrison, K. (1996), 'Developing reflective practice in higher degree students through a learning journal', *Studies in Higher Education*, **21** (3), 317–32.

Oliver, B. (2010), *Teaching Fellowship: Partnerships for Graduate Employability*, Final Report: Australian Learning and Teaching Council.

Oliver, B., Whelan, B., Hunt, L., Hammer, S., Jones, S., Pearce, A. and Henderson, F. (2011), *Introducing the Graduate Employability Indicators*, Sydney: Australian Learning and Teaching Council.

Pavlovich, K., Collins, E. and Jones, G. (2009), 'Developing students' skills in reflective practice: Design and assessment', *Journal of Management Education*, **33** (1), 37–58.

Raybould, M. and Wilkins, H. (2005), 'Over qualified and under experienced', *International Journal of Contemporary Hospitality Management*, **17** (3), 203–16.

Ring, A., Dickinger, A. and Wöber, K. (2008), 'Designing the ideal undergraduate program in tourism: Expectations from industry and educators', *Journal of Travel Research*, **48** (1), 106–21.

Robinson, R.N.S., Kralj, A., Brenner, M.L. and Lee, A.H. (2014), 'Reflective practice in food and beverage education', *Journal of Hospitality and Tourism Education*, **26** (4), 166–77.

Ross, J. (2014), 'Performing the reflective self: Audience awareness in high-stakes reflection', *Studies in Higher Education*, **39** (2), 219–32.

Ryan, M. (2013), 'The pedagogical balancing act: Teaching reflection in higher education', *Teaching in Higher Education*, **18** (2), 144–55.

Ryan, M. and Ryan, M. (2012), *Developing a Systematic, Cross-Disciplinary Approach to Teaching and Assessing Reflective Writing in Higher Education,* Sydney: Australian Learning and Teaching Council.

Schön, D.A. (1983), *The Reflective Practitioner: How Professionals Think in Action*, London: Temple Smith.

Tribe, J. (2002), 'The philosophic practitioner', *Annals of Tourism Research*, **29** (2), 338–57.

Tribe, J. (2005), 'Tourism, knowledge and the curriculum', in D. Airey and J. Tribe (eds), *An International Handbook of Tourism Education*, Chicago: Routledge.

Welch, M. (1999), 'The ABCs of reflection: A template for students and instructors to implement written reflection in service learning', *NSEE Quarterly*, **25**, 22–5.

Zehrer, A. and Mössenlechner, C. (2009), 'Key competencies of tourism graduates: The employers' point of view', *Journal of Teaching in Travel and Tourism*, **9** (3–4), 266–87.

8   Student motivation in inquiry learning: lessons from a service development project

Monika Birkle, Eva Holmberg, Marina Karlqvist and Jarmo Ritalahti

1.   INTRODUCTION

Motivation is regarded as a key to success of human beings in the fields of sports, music and education. Motivation and interest are also the key elements in inquiry learning, which is the pedagogical approach implemented on Haaga-Helia Porvoo Campus. In inquiry learning students are expected to actively create and share knowledge in real life development projects, requiring them to take responsibility for their own learning process.

During a semester project of the degree program in tourism in autumn 2011 it became clear that not all students were very interested in the current project, which was to develop service experiences for a historical gunboat. The project was challenging due to its historical setting and its complexity, and from the teachers' point of view it was recognized that the motivation of the students was low at certain times. It was realized that there is a need for a deeper understanding of the factors influencing motivation in inquiry learning. The role of the teacher or coach is to provide tools and guidance for students who are responsible for creating the knowledge needed in the project themselves. If students are unmotivated to actively proceed in the project, teachers have to find tools to enhance the process.

This chapter explores factors influencing the motivation in a group of students working in an inquiry learning project. The aim is to identify motivational factors that should be considered in designing successful learning situations.

2.   INQUIRY LEARNING AS A PEDAGOGICAL STRATEGY AT HAAGA-HELIA UNIVERSITY OF APPLIED SCIENCES

Haaga-Helia University of Applied Sciences is one of the leading universities of applied sciences in Finland, with a mission of offering high-quality expertise, regeneration and innovation needed for competitiveness, particularly in the service sector and entrepreneurship in the Helsinki Metropolitan area, Finland. Haaga-Helia is a university with some 10 500 students and 650 employees on six campuses: four in Helsinki, one in Vierumäki and one in Porvoo. The fields of education are business, tourism and hospitality, information technology, journalism, management assistant training, sports management and vocational teacher training (Haaga-Helia, 2012a). Porvoo Campus, where this semester project took place, offers six different degree programs in tourism and business management in three languages. The Porvoo unit has approximately 1000 students and 60 employees (Haaga-Helia, 2012a).

2.1   Haaga-Helia Porvoo Campus's Pedagogical Approach

Porvoo Campus is a new kind of learning and competence center with a new curriculum established in 2010. The pedagogical method and the new way of working on Porvoo Campus are based on inquiry learning. Inquiry learning and a joint curriculum project between the six degree programs aim at implementing real life projects where cooperation focuses on the fields of tourism, well-being, Knowledge Intensive Business Services (KIBS), and the creative sector. Learning takes place in projects where it is facilitated in many different ways: studying literature, participating in lectures, seminars and various workshops, as well as by looking for solutions individually or through joint efforts (Porvoo Campus, 2012).

The starting point of the Haaga-Helia Porvoo Campus curriculum is learning together with the industry. The learning tasks are carried out in conjunction with companies, teacher teams and students. These tasks are intended to enhance the meta-skills required for employment, such as project management, research and development, coaching, creative problem-solving and innovation (Porvoo Campus, 2012). The aim is that the student should grow into a proactive and self-driven professional who is motivated to develop the personal level as well as to develop his or her job and workplace community. Students set learning objectives for themselves and also participate in planning their study processes within the framework of the curriculum. A teacher functions as a planner, enabler, advisor, motivator and learner, as well as a professional consultant when required. Teachers cooperate with students, business representatives and other stakeholders, and guide the learning process. The professional identities of both teachers and students are built via social interaction in a learning environment. Partners enrich the learning process and also provide motivation and support for it. Participation in the learning community also develops competencies and operations of chosen partners (Haaga-Helia, 2012b).

For the students the new way of learning means a change from being an object to becoming a subject. This changes the role of a student from an individual learner to a team member with a role that varies depending on the learning task. As all the learning takes place in real-life projects, the versatile learning outcomes require the students to actively seek different roles in order to gain the knowledge and skills expected from a graduate. Learning outcomes can be achieved in various ways and the student is expected to take the initiative in reaching them. There are individual aims but the students are also responsible for collective achievement and the success of the whole team (Ritalahti and Lindroth, 2010).

2.2   Inquiry Learning

Collaborative inquiry-based learning, often organized as project work in schools, is playing an increasingly prevalent role in education. This form of learning differs from traditional settings in several ways. Instead of learning individually through short and specific subject-related tasks, students have to work with others in teams and therefore learning outcomes depend not only on individual efforts but also on team collaboration. Instead of learning with goals defined by teachers, students have to cope with many uncertainties in their inquiry processes and often have to determine their own goals (Chow and Law, 2005).

Inquiry-based learning is student-centered and based on John Dewey's philosophy that education begins with the curiosity of the learner. It is an approach to learning whereby students find and use a variety of sources of information and ideas to increase their understanding of a problem, topic or issue. It incorporates the experience, thinking and actions of the student. Education is not about telling and being told but an active and constructive process (Kuhlthau et al., 2007, p. 14).

Motivation and interest are the key elements in inquiry-based learning. The inquiry learning approach used on the Porvoo Campus has borrowed most of its ideas from the theory presented by Finnish education specialists Hakkarainen, Lonka and Lipponen in the late 1990s (Ritalahti, 2015). The main ideas are learning together, shared expertise and reflection. Students form their own understandings through conversations and writing. During the process students gain a sense of ownership and accomplishment in the work they are producing that gradually leads to development of competences and expertise. Existing research shows that active learning is a powerful tool. Benefits for students are the development of abilities that are crucial for lifelong learning, such as critical thinking, teamwork and tools for information search. Inquiry learning encourages students to be self-directed, which is an important skill that students need in order to be successful in the future work environment. Inquiry-based learning can improve students' enthusiasm and motivation for learning (Kuhlthau et al., 2007).

In traditional classroom learning situations learning goals are often clear, concrete and mainly set up by the teacher. In an inquiry learning class, students have to self-generate their learning agenda and are also responsible for setting up goals. Consequently, the learning task may not be clearly defined but rather complex and open. Such responsibility could cause problems for those students who are used to a teacher-directed learning process. Therefore, it is important that the students know the model and the process of inquiry learning in order to gain the most advantages out of it (Hakkarainen et al., 2004a).

Most courses on Porvoo Campus are tied to projects planned by the teaching staff and implemented in collaboration with students and work life representatives. Work life representatives are staff members of companies and other organizations that commission projects to student groups. All projects should comprise the following six steps (Porvoo Campus, 2012):

1. Defining the development task and problem;
2. Constructing the aims and content of the implementation plan;
3. Agreeing on theoretical framework;
4. Working together to build knowledge;
5. Reflection;
6. Knowledge sharing.

In the projects, the teaching staff, the participating company and organizational representatives and the students are all learners. The methods intended to enhance learning are used in a versatile way, taking into account the current state of studies and capabilities of individual students (Porvoo Campus, 2012).

The core of the learning activity is collaboration. Collaboration between the different actors in the project enhances equality, respect and creativity. The prerequisites for successful learning are trust between the actors involved in the project and commitment to the common goals. Everyone involved in the project is expected to facilitate the process. This is not only about aiming at joint goals, but also about adopting an active and entrepreneurial role to support the aims of the process (Porvoo Campus, 2012).

Learning in inquiry learning is often independent of time and place and allows for individual decisions and interpretations that support the students' ability to cope in challenging projects as graduates. The learning tasks are supposed to be challenging in order to awaken the students' curiosity and interest in the topic in question (Porvoo Campus, 2012).

3.   THE GUNBOAT PROJECT

Suomenlinna, a historical maritime fortress, is one of the most important cultural heritage sites in Finland and is situated on a group of islands off Helsinki. Today, it is a UNESCO World Heritage Site and it attracts over 700 000 visitors every year. Suomenlinna was built during the Swedish era as a maritime fortress to defend the eastern part of the Swedish Empire. Work on the fortress began in the mid-eighteenth century (Suomenlinna, 2012a). Suomenlinna has played a key role in many turning points in Finland's history. It has been the property of three sovereign states. The majority of its buildings date from the late eighteenth century, the end of the Swedish era. From the early nineteenth century to the early twentieth century, Suomenlinna was part of Russia, along with the rest of Finland. When Finland became independent the fortress was used as a garrison until the 1970s (Suomenlinna, 2012b).

In the eighteenth century, Swedish shipbuilder and scientist Fredrik Henrik af Chapman invented a new ship to counter attacks from the Russian navy. It was a gunboat that could be rowed as well as sailed. Designed for the narrow straits of the Finnish coast, the gunboats with their massive firepower changed the tactical way of thinking about naval warfare (Tykkisluuppi, 2012b; Wikipedia, 2012).

Two organizations recently active at Suomenlinna, the Ehrensvärd Society and the Viapori Dockyard Society, decided a few years ago to rebuild the traditional gunboat. After public funding for the project, the gunboat was built in Suomenlinna according to the drawings made by F.H. af Chapman. The gunboat is equipped with sails and 15 pairs of oars. The length of the hull is 20 meters. The main aims of the shipbuilding project were to employ and instruct young people, maintain and revive skills for building traditional wooden ships and liven up the history of the maritime fortress. The gunboat was expected to be ready for operating cruises in the surroundings of Suomenlinna in spring 2013 (Uolamo, 2011; Tykkisluuppi, 2012a).

The commissioners of the project carried out by the students at Haaga-Helia were the Ehrensvärd Society and the Viapori Dockyard Society. The task of the project was to develop authentic tourism products for different customer groups interested in cruises with the gunboat. A significant part of the development task was related to the creation of tourism packages that could give the customers unique historical experiences. Moreover, authentic narratives related to the Swedish time of Suomenlinna were to be developed in order to provide potential tourists a deeper insight into the historical time of the gunboat.

The project was carried out as a semester project for a group of second-year tourism students. The project started in August 2011 and was finished in March 2012. At the start

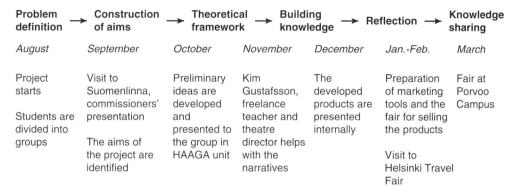

Problem definition	Construction of aims	Theoretical framework	Building knowledge	Reflection	Knowledge sharing
August	September	October	November	December	Jan.-Feb.	March
Project starts Students are divided into groups	Visit to Suomenlinna, commissioners' presentation The aims of the project are identified	Preliminary ideas are developed and presented to the group in HAAGA unit	Kim Gustafsson, freelance teacher and theatre director helps with the narratives	The developed products are presented internally	Preparation of marketing tools and the fair for selling the products Visit to Helsinki Travel Fair	Fair at Porvoo Campus

Figure 8.1   The main stages of the project and stages in inquiry learning

of the project the group of 20 students was divided into smaller groups of four to five students, all focusing on developing their own tourism product for a certain segment of tourists such as seniors, pupils and Russian visitors. The final stage of the project was a fair on Porvoo Campus through which the different gunboat experiences were sold. Figure 8.1 shows the timeframe of the project as well as its main stages according to the phases of an inquiry learning project.

4.   MOTIVATION AND INQUIRY LEARNING

Many contemporary authors have defined the concept of motivation. As a concept the word *motivation* comes from Latin, with the meaning of 'moving on' (Hamjah et al., 2011). Motivation is generally seen as something causing people to act in a certain way (Schwartz, 2003).

   Drivers of motivation were explored by Freud as early as the beginning of the twentieth century. According to Freud the main motivational drivers of human beings are sex and aggression. It is a general tendency to believe that motivation, or more conscientiousness, is a personal trait. Some people have it and others do not. In practice, some are labelled as lazy because they do not display any outward signs of motivation. However, individuals differ in their basic motivational drives as well as areas of interest. The concept of motivation is situational and its level varies between different individuals and at different times. If you understand what motivates people, you have at your command the most powerful tool for dealing with them (Deci and Ryan, 2004).

   In the late 1950s a paper arguing that individuals are not driven only by external impulses but also internal mechanisms was published (Deci and Ryan, 2004). This idea was described as energy of the ego. This energy of the ego is often referred to as intrinsic motivation. According to the view of many researchers the root to the intrinsic motivation of human beings is the need for being competent and self-determining (Deci and Ryan, 2004). The opposite of intrinsic motivation driven by an individual need for fulfilment is extrinsic motivation. This means that people are seen as being motivated by mainly external stimuli, such as rewards or punishments (Sansone and Harackiewicz, 2000).

4.1   Motivation and Learning

When there is no motivation to learn, there is no learning (Wlodowski, 2008; Järvelä and Niemivirta, 1999; Hamjah et al., 2011). Moreover, motivated students are prepared to put more time into completing their courses and are more likely to graduate (Wijnia et al., 2011). From a 'simple' point of view the motivation of a student is related to two things: the fact that the student perceives that the topic is important and valuable to learn and that the task is challenging but not too difficult for existing capabilities (Lindholm-Ylänne et al., 2002).

The self-regulated theory is the most commonly used theory for explaining the motivation of students to learn (Lin et al., 2003). According to this theory, self-regulated students are successful and have the ability to apply different learning strategies (Hakkarainen et al., 2004b; Järvelä and Niemivirta, 1999). These students are characterized by intrinsic motivation, which means that they perceive that activities are rewarding by themselves. For example, students may be prepared to work on projects in order to develop themselves without external drivers such as rewards (Hakkarainen et al., 2004a; Lin et al., 2003). Extrinsic motivation, on the other hand, means that the student is regulated by rewards and/or punishment, that is, the aim of the studying is to gain something concrete like credits or an exam (Lin et al., 2003). These students can also perform well in traditional study settings by learning a lot of facts before an exam.

Deep learning takes place when students are able to use the knowledge gained in the long term. In order to achieve deep learning, students need to be self-motivated because as long as motivation to learn is extrinsic, learning is likely to be superficial. Students have the responsibility to develop intrinsic motivation, since this kind of motivation is often not innate. On the other hand, these issues have to be reflected upon at educational institutions and those who work with students have to find strategies for how students can be inspired in order to foster intrinsic motivation (Elmgren and Henriksson, 2010). According to Lindblom-Ylänne et al. (2002), good students mostly possess both intrinsic and extrinsic motivation.

Many factors influence the motivation of students. Learning motivation also varies from time to time. The seminal study by Turner and Paris (1995) identified six Cs for a motivating educational experience:

1. *Choice*: when students are allowed to choose the tasks by themselves according to their own interest they will put more effort into understanding and executing the task.
2. *Challenge*: the tasks given to the students should be challenging but not too complex.
3. *Control*: students should be allowed to control the learning themselves.
4. *Collaboration*: interaction in order to solve a task enhances inspiration and offers the possibility to consider several perspectives.
5. *Constructing meaning*: if students perceive the knowledge they are acquiring as important it will improve their motivation to learn.
6. *Consequences*: feedback from others, reflection and information sharing support students' motivation to perform.

The above list of factors indicates that the way students are motivated varies and students who are normally intrinsically motivated can sometimes be unmotivated because they find a certain class or a certain project uninteresting. The teacher has a responsibility to use strategies that enhance the intrinsic motivation of students by being inspiring, enthusiastic and by trying to find solutions that ensure the working atmosphere of the students becomes as positive as possible.

4.2   Motivation in Inquiry Learning

Due to the nature of inquiry learning as a pedagogical approach where students are supposed to actively look for solutions themselves, students with intrinsic motivation usually take a more active role in the projects. All projects will not be interesting for all students; however, it is important to identify strategies for developing the intrinsic motivation of students showing little interest, otherwise these students may simply aim for the lowest effort necessary to pass.

Teaching and learning strategies that enhance the motivation of unmotivated students are not discussed extensively in the literature on inquiry learning. However, it is clear that students who are learning-oriented (that is, have intrinsic motivation) tend to have a more active cognitive engagement in learning activities. For instance, a study by Tapola et al. (2001) shows that low learning-oriented students produce less knowledge in an inquiry learning project. The challenge for the teacher is to consider how the motivation of low learning-oriented students can be improved. According to the existing literature the following factors could be considered: the project itself, the commitment and support of teachers and team members involved.

4.3   Nature of the Project

Generally, it is perceived that the more interesting a task or assignment is, the more it will support students' process of knowledge construction, and it is more likely that intrinsic motivation will develop (Järvelä and Niemivirta, 1999). Compared, for instance, to projects solved in project-based learning, the challenge of finding a suitable project for inquiry learning is more demanding. The starting point is that it should be possible to define interesting and deepening research questions, otherwise the key features of inquiry learning cannot be met. The team of teachers considering the project have to consider the age of the students, university timetables, the curriculum as well as internal and external resources related to knowledge, money and skills. It is important that the nature of the project inspires students not to study only for grades. The projects should be real life projects that are important to be solved, for instance, from a scientific, cultural or human point of view (Hakkarainen et al., 2004b).

4.4   The Role of the Educator

Although students are supposed to actively search for new knowledge in an inquiry learning project, the importance of teachers guiding the process should not be underestimated (Hakkarainen et al., 2004b). Students with low motivation will need structured supervision and feedback in order to complete the project successfully (Tapola et al., 2001). Moreover, students with weak self-regulation ability might be completely destructive if they are left alone in the learning situation. Thus, shared control between teachers and students is often recommended in inquiry learning. Teachers also have to develop an understanding of self-regulation of different students in the group in order to be able to provide appropriate support during the learning process (Hakkarainen et al., 2004b).

4.5   Team Members

In many contemporary learning paradigms interaction between students is seen as a major contribution to learning. By discussing and problem solving through collaboration it is possible to work with complex issues from different angles (Elmgren and Henriksson, 2010; Järvelä and Niemivirta, 1999). The starting point of inquiry learning is also that the work is done by the whole group and then the group may be divided into smaller teams. The teams should be created in such a way that they comprise students with different types of knowledge and capabilities, since a team can create synergies and outcomes that are not possible when students work individually. On the other hand, it is recommended that the more mature the students are, the more they should be allowed to influence at least to some extent with whom they work (Hakkarainen et al., 2004b).

Repo-Kaarento and Levander (2002) identify several prerequisites for a successful outcome of a group working with a cooperative learning task. First of all, the group members should be positively interdependent on each other at the same time as all group members have individual accountability. This means that when all group members work together and take responsibility for the proceeding of the project they will realize that by working together they will gain more. Moreover, the task to be solved must be such that all group members have equal possibilities to contribute. This will reduce the risk of 'free riders', which is a common challenge in all group work. Finally, the students should be in open and direct interaction with each other.

5.   METHODS

Qualitative research seeks out the 'why', not the 'how' of its topic through an analysis of unstructured information. Typical data collected and analysed in a research project conducted by qualitative research methods are interview transcripts, emails, notes, feedback forms, photos and videos (Silverman, 2005; Veal, 2006).

In this research project two different kinds of qualitative data were collected and analysed. First of all students participating in the project wrote essays reflecting on their own motivation. Secondly, the teachers involved in the project conducted focus groups where the project and its ups and downs in motivation were discussed. The interviews were tape recorded and transcribed as suggested in the literature on qualitative interviewing (for example, Trost, 2005; Veal, 2006).

The data collection took place in two phases. In December 2011 the students were asked to write essays on motivation and to analyse the factors influencing their own personal motivation and that of their team in the project. Furthermore, the students were asked to focus especially on the importance of teachers, team members and team leader as factors influencing their motivation in the project. Ten essays were analysed for this chapter. At this point, the first part of the project was finished, and the theory part and the product development phase were concluded.

The second phase of data collection took place in March 2012, after a more practical part of the project where students focused on promoting and selling the products they developed in the previous semester. The second part of the study was performed by conducting focus groups with team members (three groups of four to five students). The students were first asked to visualize the process from a motivational point of view. They were given a timeline to fill in and the sheet was divided into a positive and a negative field. Thereafter, the students were asked to reflect on feelings at the beginning of the project, critical turning points (both positive and negative) during the process, and the challenges they faced and how these were resolved. Finally, they were asked to discuss their learning and insights.

6.   MOTIVATION OF STUDENTS IN THE GUNBOAT PROJECT

The analysis of the learning stories identifies which factors influence students' motivation positively and which negatively. The analysis also reveals that extrinsic motivation plays a much more important role in the project work than intrinsic motivation. The main issues highlighted by the students as key issues for their motivation were extrinsic factors such as the team, the nature of the project, the teacher, other team members and technical factors. Some intrinsic factors were also identified.

6.1   Functionality of the Teams

The most discussed topic in the learning stories was the role of the teams. Factors such as support from other team members, group meetings, the feeling of working effectively together, taking responsibility, hardworking and positive attitude, good communication and solving problems together influenced motivation in a positive way. Issues related to teamwork that had a negative influence on students' motivation were personal conflicts and lack of conflict management skills to solve these, absence of team members, lack of team spirit, lack of interest and concentration, some team members having difficulty in receiving negative feedback from peers. For example: 'The motivation of our group was very low at the beginning of the project. All group members were seldom present at the meetings and we had difficulties in co-operating. The problems were caused by different personalities and different ways of working' (Learning story 2).

In the learning stories a majority of the students felt that the division into groups was not successful, because it was made by the teachers and did not correspond with the level of ambition of the different students in the group. The students also felt that disciplinary action towards students often absent should have been taken at an early stage by the teachers to ensure a fair treatment towards those who did their work.

> After a while the motivation sank and in some groups the team leader was replaced and little later the motivation rose again because some really unmotivated students were replaced and some students who didn't do anything were excluded from the project. This was good for the whole class and motivation returned because you knew that those who remained did their tasks properly. (Learning story 5)

6.2   The Commission and Task

The commission itself influenced the students' motivation both in a positive and negative way. The idea of the project was to create historically authentic experiences around the gunboat at the Suomenlinna fortress, which is one of the UNESCO World Heritage Sites. The fact that this project required research into the history, culture and military history of the eighteenth century influenced motivation in a very negative way. Most of the students had a negative attitude towards history and the few students who had an interest in the topic could not inspire their team members. The project was characterized by a 'fuzzy front end', meaning that many things were unclear at the beginning and the starting point was quite abstract. What clearly increased the students' motivation was the visit to Suomenlinna fortress where the gunboat plan was presented and the students saw a miniature model of the boat and the construction hall were the boat was being built. The meeting with the commissioners helped the students to clarify the task and this influenced all students' motivation very positively.

> When we went to Suomenlinna and met the commissioners and got to ask questions and heard what they had to say about the task and what they expected from us, then the task became suddenly much clearer. The visit to Suomenlinna gave us a lot of ideas and we got a lot of valuable information that we could make use of when we started working with the project. (Learning story 6)

The fact that the project was a real life case with external commissioners helped the students to realize the importance of professional reporting. At the beginning of the project they also had the feeling they were doing something valuable and meaningful and they thought that their input was of great importance.

> The three of us in our group who were motivated realized that it is important to do a good job because we have a real commissioner and it's good for us to put a report together, to mark the sources properly, correct the texts of others and to receive feedback. (Learning story 2)

In addition, the students were motivated by the fact that they could influence the process and could, within the given framework, freely come up with and develop their ideas. Later on, however, the lack of contact with the commissioner and the lack of feedback resulted in low motivation. The commissioner was difficult to reach and communication problems contributed to a lack of motivation at certain points in the project. A lack of key information led to anxiety and frustration among the students.

6.3   Role of Educator/Advisor

There were several teachers involved in advising and counseling the students in the gunboat project. The role of the teacher in motivating students was seen as important. In their learning stories the students mention as positive factors influencing their motivation: acknowledgement, encouragement, a positive attitude towards the project, positive feedback, helpfulness, and providing needed information. Some students mentioned that the teachers reminded them of the importance and learning possibilities of the project and this helped them go on in the work. For example: 'The motivation of the teachers has been good, they didn't give up on us' (Learning story 1), and 'During the project I think that the teachers were helpful and gave a lot of counselling. It was of great importance how the teacher gave support when we got stuck' (Learning story 5).

On the other hand, some of the students were confused by contradictory information and advice provided by different teachers and this contributed to decreased motivation. Follow-up meetings and presentations of different phases in the process organized by the teachers mainly supported the students in their work. What increased motivation was the time for discussions of personal conflicts in the teams and help from the teacher in solving these issues. Developmental discussions with tutor teachers were mentioned by some students and they helped to clear the thoughts and to find new motivation. During the project, several presentations were held to share knowledge and to get feedback on ideas. This was mainly helpful for the students and it often resulted in higher motivation. But some of the students thought that these presentations were organized too often and the teams had no time to deliver anything new to the following meeting. This resulted in decreased motivation for some students. On the other hand, the second-year students were also aware of their own responsibility for the success of the project as one of the students highlighted during the interview: 'The teachers are not supposed be our mums' (interview 1).

6.4   Role of the Team Leader

The role of the team leader was discussed in the learning stories. The stories show that the students were not satisfied with the team leaders and the leaders themselves felt that they could not motivate their teams. The team leaders were seen as insecure, passive and unable to organize and delegate the work, unable to acquire needed information and lacking motivation. Some students mentioned that team leaders had a negative attitude towards the whole project and it had an impact on the team. There was also some confusion about who the actual team leader was, since the official leader did not take any responsibility for leading the group. The challenge of a team leader incapable of leading the team was described by several students: 'Our team leader had difficulties in delegating and in planning of team meetings. This resulted in that the rest of the team became frustrated and another student had to take responsibility for dividing the work between the members in the group' (Learning story 2); and 'The team leader did not at all act as a team leader is supposed to do. He did not take any action for the project to proceed, he did not delegate and he did not put himself into the project and the information needed to finish it' (Learning story 3).

6.5   The Influence of Other Teams

The role of other teams was significant for students' motivation. The eagerness to perform at least as well as the other teams was a trigger to work harder and get things done. Also the feedback given by other teams was considered valuable. Almost all students mention the meeting with the other degree program on another campus working on the same project as a milestone. They compared their performance with the other student group and felt somewhat ashamed of their presentation and were inspired by that experience to do even better. For example, one respondent wrote: 'In this project I received a lot of motivation of all the members in our group, not only those in my team. I realized that we are all in the same situation and facing the same challenges which gave me a lot of support' (Learning story 1).

6.6   Other Extrinsic Factors

Students also mentioned other external factors influencing their motivation positively such as deadlines, getting credits and in the final end a degree with good grades. As one student stated: 'The fact that I knew that I will receive credits for the project and thereby able to graduate in a shorter time was motivating me' (Learning story 8).

   Some students also mentioned that the will to just get the whole thing done and over with motivated them to go on. The breaks were also important; almost the whole group went to Lisbon in October, and of course the Christmas break also divided the project into two parts. It was also difficult for some of the students to continue with the same project in spring when they had already worked on the project the entire autumn. On the other hand, the tone and character of the project changed: after writing the report describing the whole tourist package including the narrative, the focus was now on more practical issues: 'In spring we were planning a fair for selling our products, it was nice' (Interview 3). The huge workload both in the project as well as in some other courses together with lack of time were mentioned as external factors influencing motivation negatively.

6.7   Intrinsic Factors

In the instructions for the essays on motivation given to students, the focus was on the external factors such as the role of the teacher, team and team leader, but a few internal factors driving the students to better performance were also evident in the learning stories. A few students mentioned the mental satisfaction of getting things done and the rewarding feeling when you do well in different phases. The satisfaction of overcoming difficulties was also mentioned as an intrinsic factor influencing the motivation positively. Understanding the task, 'getting the whole picture' and learning new things were also mentioned by the students. The possibility of being creative can also motivate students, for instance: 'When the theory was written and we were allowed to be more creative the project was more meaningful' (Learning story 7). The feeling of being under stress and pressure were internal factors that influenced motivation negatively.

6.8   Central Turning Points Influencing Motivation During the Project

These above-mentioned factors emerged in different phases of the project. In the interviews done in March the students visualized the ups and downs (Figure 8.2) in motivation on a timeline stretching from September 2011 to March 2012. The interviews and the timelines show where the critical points are and can be helpful to teachers when planning the process of advising students.

   In the interviews all students agreed that in the beginning the motivation was high and it was even strengthened by the visit to Suomenlinna at an early stage of the process. The idea phase and brainstorming phase are described as fun and creative, which had a positive impact on motivation.

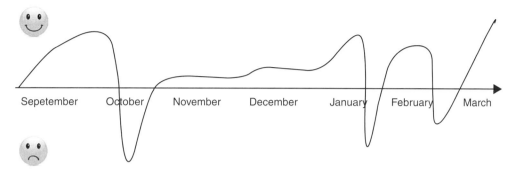

Figure 8.2   Perceptions of motivation during the Gunboat Project

Some of the students, however, had difficulties generating new ideas and felt stuck at the early stage of the process. After the brainstorming phase the lack of information and unclearness were the main reasons for a big loss of motivation. The majority of the students felt totally lost and had great difficulty in motivating themselves and their team members. At this stage the commissioners were also hard to reach and could not offer any support and the lack of information led to frustration and decrease in motivation. In Bruce Tuckman's (1965) stages of group development, students' behavior is related to the storming stage where participants are able to express discontent and challenge others' opinions. Furthermore, the discontent can be contentious and unpleasant, especially for those members who try to avoid conflict.

In October a mid-term presentation was held on another campus together with students from another degree programme and the student group of this study felt that they failed and were very self-critical of their own performance. For some students this event decreased their motivation, whereas other students were energized to perform better.

As the understanding of the task and the goal became clearer, the motivation also grew stronger. The support of other team members, a good team spirit, positive feedback from teachers and other teams and regular presentations and deadlines kept the teams working during the autumn. Personal conflicts, negative attitudes towards the project, absent students, lack of leadership in the teams and difficulties in communication with the commissioner were the most important negative factors mentioned in the interviews.

At the beginning of November, the students cooperated with a theatre director to develop stories for their products. This was an important turning point in the process where the students felt relieved and got on with one of the most challenging tasks, to create a story based on authentic, historical facts. The motivation rose towards the end of term because of the approaching deadline, the upcoming Christmas break, and for some students a strong will to get things completed.

After the Christmas holidays motivation decreased, because some of the students had not realized that the project's second phase was to be introduced in the spring term. These students had expected to start with a new project and were disappointed to hear that this was not the case.

During the spring term several factors boosted motivation, for example a visit to the annual travel fair in Helsinki and the learning task connected to this. The students also found it very challenging and interesting to arrange a Gunboat Fair on Porvoo Campus to present their products. This was clearly a more concrete, practical, and motivational part of the project, including creating brochures and planning the market stalls for the fair. One thing that caused loss of motivation was the fact that the plans the students completed for the Gunboat Fair had to be revised several times.

The fair was successful and the commissioners were satisfied with the end result. The students would have liked more feedback and confirmation from the commissioners about the next steps. Some students commented in the interviews that it would be nice to know what happened to their ideas.

In their closing comments some students stated that they felt proud of being part of a project that sought to animate history, and others thought that the given framework, the history of the eighteenth century, made it easier to find the focus of the product. During the fair, the students realized that they knew a lot about the history of the gunboat, Suomenlinna, and life in the eighteenth century, and they were glad to be able to answer questions posed by visitors.

7.   DISCUSSION

What are then the main issues related to motivation that teachers and supervisors have to reflect upon when working with students in inquiry learning projects? First, it is important to consider how the teams should be formed. Meredith Belbin (2010) discusses how this can be done. According to her, project teams can be created, for example, based on free choice of members or by combining different kind of personalities who are identified by psychological tests. Monica Lööw (2009) states that project organization is based on the needs of the project. Both literature and results from this study show that it is more likely that students are more motivated if they are allowed to work with team members they have chosen themselves. Self-determination theory applied in this context indicates that the more possibilities students have to influence decision-making related to their learning situations, the more motivated they are (for example, Deci and Ryan, 2004). This project involved a group of heterogeneous students and in the planning phase it was perceived that there is a need to deliver several good ideas to the commissioner. Thus, the groups were planned in such a way that they comprised at least one student who had performed very well in earlier projects. Accordingly, the students who showed a lack of commitment to previous projects were separated. The outcome of this thinking was five rather good product ideas delivered to the commissioners, but on the other hand it contributed to a lot of frustration among the students eager to produce good results and thereby being able to gain a good grade.

Secondly, it is important to find real-life projects that interest students and that are challenging but not too difficult to manage from the students' point of view. The Gunboat Project was challenging because the ship was under construction when the project took place and it was difficult for the students to get an idea of how it could really work as a tourism product in practice. Moreover, even if the commissioners of this project were interested in cooperation from the start, they were too busy to actively commit themselves to the product development process. Students perceived that their motivation could have been improved if they had received more feedback on their ideas from the commissioners during the process. On the other hand, students appreciated that they were allowed to work with external commissioners and develop real tourism products. In the future it is important to find commissioners who are committed to give students support during the whole project process, not only at the very beginning.

Thirdly, the role of the teacher(s) is also important in projects. The challenge is to be actively supportive but not to give too much guidance, which limits the students' possibilities for creative solutions. In this project students were given clear information on what kind of models they were supposed to use in the product development process and rather strict advice related to what the report should look like. Some students perceived these strict instructions demotivating: on the other hand most students were happy to receive clear advice on how the project should proceed.

The fourth key issue to think about is the appointment of the leader in the teams. In this project students were divided into five teams, all having their own leader with the main responsibility for the success of the product development process as well as the reporting of the process. The students in each team were allowed to choose the team leader themselves, with the starting point that such students who had been team leaders in earlier projects should not be the first choice. All students managed to choose a leader for themselves at the beginning of the project but the leaders did not actually change the team leaders in the middle of the project. From the point of view of the supervisor it is important to acknowledge that some students are less suitable as team leaders in certain projects. Moreover, it is important to discuss and clarify the responsibilities of a team leader at the very beginning of the project. At the same time the team members could prepare guidelines for what is expected of the other members of the team. According to Belbin (2013), it is especially important to consider mental abilities, communication skills, and possession of self-discipline of potential team leaders before they are appointed.

The fifth issue that has to be considered is the sharing of knowledge between teams. In projects like the Gunboat Project where several teams developed new tourism services for the same commissioner, it is important that the different teams meet and have the opportunity to share both their ideas but also their feelings with the other students in the cohort. Especially in this project it became clear that every team struggled with the same challenges such as low commitment to the project by some team members, as well as a lack of view of what the final product could be, which helped many students to proceed. On Porvoo Campus Mondays are usually so-called project days when students work independently on their projects. It would be important to collect all students to class for instance every second week in order to let them discuss their feelings and their progress in order to increase peer support.

The last important extrinsic factor clearly influencing the motivation in inquiry learning projects was the load of work in other projects and/or courses during the semester. The students in the Gunboat Project felt that when there were a lot of other deadlines coming up, the motivation for proceeding with the projects was low. This challenge was also observed during other semesters and highlights the need for a discussion about how much time students should invest in the project compared to other more traditional learning assignments. Typically students receive between 6 and 12 credits for a semester project at Porvoo Campus. If the project is as extensive as 9 or 12 credits, the other work during the semester must be adjusted to allow for the huge work involved with the project.

Only a limited number of students discussed their intrinsic motivation in the Gunboat

Project in their essays or in the group interviews. This is not surprising taking into consideration that the project as a whole was perceived as boring. Some students, though, stated that they found it interesting to learn more about product development in tourism and that they really felt relieved and rewarded when they got things done. For the teachers it is a challenge to influence the intrinsic motivation of the students, especially when it comes to students with low ability for self-regulation. This challenge is probably related to the nature of the project. When students are allowed to work with projects and tasks they are really interested in they are more likely to find strategies to motivate themselves. On the other hand, if the purpose of inquiry learning is to prepare students for working life, they also have to learn strategies to force themselves to finish demanding and sometimes even, in their opinion, boring projects.

8.   CONCLUSIONS

The aim of the study was to identify motivational factors in student projects implemented through inquiry learning. Motivation is one of the key elements in successful implementation of inquiry learning as well as in all learning situations.

This study comprises different types of data: student essays and three focus group interviews, as well as visual presentations of motivation curves during the project. The findings from the analysed data support previous research results. Students should be allowed to choose between projects and topics according to their own interests. Freedom to choose will enhance both commitment and motivation. Moreover, the tasks given to students should be challenging, but not too complex. Finally, collaboration and interaction between students working in sub-teams of the same project have a clear positive impact on motivation and creativity.

This study brings in new perspectives into inquiry learning: the commissioners from the industry have a great impact on the motivation of the students. As outlined above, the other teams, or sub-teams of the same project, play a role especially in the creation of motivation in the early stages of the project process.

More research related to student motivation in inquiry learning is needed when developing this pedagogical approach since the enhancement of motivation of students is a constant challenge in higher education. This challenge exists in both traditional and more student oriented pedagogical approaches. Inquiry-based learning, as it is implemented on Porvoo Campus, is one tool to make students more motivated to learn competences needed in business life. Inquiry-based learning is implemented in semester projects where students work and create knowledge in teams. These teams also cooperate with educators, commissioners and other possible stakeholders.

According to this study, one can conclude that giving students more ownership of the project process will increase their motivation to reach the project aims. It is crucial to appoint an efficient project manager from the student group, and if the student group is divided into several teams, the team leaders should have a suitable personality for the task.

Finally, the role and responsibilities of commissioners must be discussed and defined clearly before the project is presented to the students. There is a clear demand from the students' side to get commissioners more engaged in the different stages of the project.

REFERENCES

Belbin, Meredith R. (2010), *Team Roles at Work*, Oxford: Butterworth-Heinemann.

Belbin, Meredith R. (2013), *Management Teams. Why they Succeed or Fail,* New York: Routledge.

Chow, A. and N. Law (2005), 'Measuring motivation in collaborative inquiry-based learning contexts', *Proceedings of The 2005 Conference on Computer Support For Collaborative Learning: Learning 2005: the Next 10 Years!* (Taipei, Taiwan, 30 May–4 June), International Society of the Learning Sciences, pp. 68–75.

Deci, Edward L. and Richard M. Ryan (2004), *Handbook of Self-Determination Research*, Rochester, NY: University of Rochester Press.

Elmgren, Maja and Ann-Sofie Henriksson (2010), *Universitetspedagogik*, Stockholm: Nordsteds.

Haaga-Helia (2012a), 'Haaga-Helia in a nutshell', accessed 31 March 2015 at http://www.haaga-helia.fi/en/about-haaga-helia/haaga-helia-in-a-nutshell.

Haaga-Helia (2012b), 'Pedagogical strategy', accessed 31 March 2015 at http://www.haaga-helia.fi/en/students-guide/welcome-to-haaga-helia/pedagogical-strategy?searchterm=Pedag.Hakkarianen, Kai, Kirsti Lonka and Lasse Lipponen (2004b), *Tutkiva Oppiminen Järki, Tunteet ja Kulttuuri Oppimisen Sytyttäjänä*, Porvoo: WSOY.

Hakkarainen, Kai, Marianne Bollström-Huttunen, Riikka Pyysalo and Kirsti Lonka (2004a), *Tutkiva Oppiminen Käytännössä. Matkaopas Opettajille*, Porvoo: WS Bookwell Oy.

Hamjah, S.H., Z. Ismail, R.M. Rasit and E.H. Rozali (2011), 'Methods of increasing learning motivation among students', *Procedia Social and Behavioral Sciences*, **18**, 138–14.

Järvelä, S. and M. Niemivirta (1999), 'The changes in learning theory and the topicality of the recent research on motivation', *Research Dialogue in Learning and Instruction*, **1**, 57–65.

Kuhlthau, Carol, Leslie Maniotes and Ann Caspari (2007), *Guided Inquiry Learning in the 21st Century*, Westport, CT: Libraries Unlimited.

Lin, Y.-G., W.J. McKeachie and Y.C. Kim (2003), 'College student intrinsic and/or extrinsic motivation and learning', *Learning and Individual Differences*, **13**, 251–8.

Lindholm-Ylänne, Sari, Anne Nevgi and Taina Kaivola (2002), 'Opiskelu yliopistossa', in Sari Lindholm-Ylänne and Anne Nevgi (eds), *Yliopisto- ja Korkeakoulu Opettajan Käsikirja*, Helsinki: WSOY, pp. 117–38.

Lööw, Monica (2009), *Att Leda och Arbeta i Projekt*, Malmö: Liber.

PorvooCampus(2012),Website,accessed31March2015athttp://porvoocampus.fi/en/learning-on-porvoo-campus.

Repo-Kaarento, Saara and Lena Levander (2002), 'Oppimista edistävä vuorovaikutus', in Sari Lindholm-Ylänne and Anne Nevgi (eds), *Yliopisto- ja Korkeakoulu Opettajan Käsikirja*, Helsinki: WSOY, pp. 140–70.

Ritalahti, J. (2015), 'Inquiry learning in tourism', in P. Sheldon and S. Hsu (eds), *Tourism Education: Global Issues and Trends*, Bingley: Emerald, pp. 135–51.

Ritalahti, J. and K. Lindroth (2010), 'Porvoo Campus: Living lab for creativity, learning and innovations', *Proceedings of the New Zealand Tourism and Hospitality Research Conference 2010*, 24–26 November, Aukland.

Sansone, Carol and Judith M. Harackiewicz (2000), *Intrinsic and Extrinsic Motivation: The Search for Optimal Motivation and Performance*, San Diego, CA: Academic Press.

Schwartz, Andrew E. (2003), *Motivation: Linking Performance to Goals*, Waverley, MA: A.E. Schwartz & Associates.

Silverman, D. (2005), *Doing Qualitative Research*, London: Sage Publications.

Suomenlinna (2012a), 'Visitor's guide', accessed 31 March 2015 at http://www.suomenlinna.fi/visitors_guide.

Suomenlinna (2012b, 'Fortress', accessed 31 March 2015 at http://www.suomenlinna.fi/en/fortress

Tapola, Anna, Kai Hakkarainen, J. Syri, Lasse Lipponen, Tuire Palonen and Markku Niemivirta (2001), *Motivation and Participation in Inquiry Learning Within a Networked Learning Environment,* accessed 31 March 2015 at http://Helsinki.fi/science/networkedlearning/texts/ tapolaetal2001.pdf.

Trost, J. (2005), *Kvalitativa Intervjuer*, Lund: Studentlitteratur.

Tuckman, Bruce W. (1965), 'Developmental sequence in small groups', *Psychological Bulletin*, **63** (6), 348–99.

Turner, J. and S.G. Paris (1995), 'How literacy tasks influence children's motivation for literacy', *The Reading Teacher*, **48** (8), 662–73.

Tykkisluuppi (2012a), Website, accessed 31 March 2015 at http://www.tykkisluuppi.fi/.Tykkisluuppi (2012b), 'Lyhyesti Tykkisluupeista', accessed 31 March 2015 at http://www.tykkisluuppi.fi/lyhyesti-tykkisluupeista/.

Uolamo, T. (2011), 'Presentation of the Tykkisluuppi project', Suomenlinna, Helsinki.

Veal, A.J. (2006), *Research Methods for Leisure and Tourism*, Harlow: Pearson Education.

Wijnia, L., S.M. Loyens and E. Derous (2011), 'Investigating effects of problem-based versus lecture-based learning environments on student motivation', *Contemporary Educational Psychology*, **36** (2), 101–13.

Wikipedia (2012), 'Gunboat', accessed 31 March 2015 at http://en.wikipedia.org/wiki/Gunboat.

Wlodowski, Raymond J. (2008), *Enhancing Adult Motivation to Learn: A Comprehensive Guide for Teaching All Adults*, San Francisco, CA: Jossey-Bass.

PART II

TECHNOLOGY-ENABLED LEARNING

9 Rethinking technology-enhanced learning: disconnect passive consumers, reconnect active producers of knowledge
Massimo Morellato

1. INTRODUCTION

Digital technologies and mobile systems have become protagonists of pedagogical transformation, new learning styles, and the re-design of curricula at every level of education, in tourism as well as in other disciplines. Universities around the world have rapidly adopted content learning systems, software platforms and mobile 'apps' to fulfill the educational promise of enabling new learning experiences. Unfortunately, in many situations, this promise seems to devolve into attempts and practices that involve students in a meager way as passive end-users of institutionally adopted platforms and tools. Attention is often focused on the features and functionality of the digital instruments adopted for producing assignments, and the learning outcomes remain confined to the sphere of digital literacy. The important goal of fostering the development of skills in knowledge management and knowledge mobilization is more challenging to attain, is seldom achieved, and requires going beyond training that emphasizes the technological features in the usage of digital tools. The debate around the integration of digital technologies in education is continuously evolving and many universities are now experimenting with how to improve critical reflective thinking and ethical practices amongst students in order to achieve collaborative and creative teamwork.

1.1 Changing the Trend

The involvement of the author in collaborative educational projects in Italy and New Zealand contributes to this transition and aims to sustain a new student-centered perspective and to create learning experiences that empower students as content producers, administrators of the digital instruments, authors and generators of layers of information, and protagonists of collaborative practices. Empowered students can shift from being passive consumers of the latest technology to being active participants in the co-construction of knowledge. This shift is of particular importance among the generation of digital natives who are confident with pervasive technology and ubiquitous access to information but demonstrate a lack of awareness of the implications of the use of digital technology.

1.2 What this Chapter is About

This chapter explores a student-centered perspective in the adoption of digital technology in education. It first introduces the current state of technology-enhanced learning and the typical scenario of contemporary universities under the wave of digital innovation, and then presents a project conducted at the School of Hospitality and Tourism at a New Zealand University. The project reconceptualizes technology-enhanced learning and the students' online presence. It includes an array of different digital instruments employed under a strategy rooted in three domains: pedagogical, ethical and technological. The strategy follows the belief that the pedagogical process has to lead technological adoption in education and not the opposite. The chapter provides details of the learning experience over the three domains and discusses outcomes, emerging issues and students' comments. The last part of the chapter presents considerations for future initiatives and for stimulating further discussion.

2. THE CURRENT ACADEMIC CONTEXT

The transformation of educational systems under the influence of an exaggerated respect for the information and communication technologies (ICT) brought new modes of educational delivery, new learning domains, new principles of learning, new learning processes and outcomes, and new educational roles and entities (Harasim, 2000). At the turn of the twenty-first century, this transformation also brought a phenomenal level of financial investments and educators' expectations for changing pedagogic strategies and stimulating better and more creative use of digital technologies in all forms of education (Kirschner et al., 2004). The goal was, and it seems still to be, to ensure that students and teachers are equipped with skills and capacities needed in the knowledge society (Bolstad et al., 2012; Kirschner et al., 2004). In a knowledge-based, networked economy, it is considered essential for graduates to have attained skills in collaborative teamwork and competencies to deal with new situations and ever-changing environments, where the management of knowledge is a key to success for economic development (Benckendorff, 2009; Bruns and Humphreys, 2005; Cooper, 2006) and employability (Zehrer and Mössenlechner, 2009).

2.1 Digital Innovation in Contemporary Education

Digital technologies offer a number of opportunities for developing knowledge management skills and social/communicative competencies, and higher-education institutions are experimenting with the adoption of the latest technology in the instructional design and in the various attempts to create learning communities (Istance and Kools, 2013; Shapiro and Levine, 1999). Furthermore, the new ubiquitous technologies are resetting the boundaries of educational possibilities (Dumont and Istance, 2010) and are associated with future-oriented education in many people's minds (Bolstad, et al., 2012). They also 'look good' in institutional marketing campaigns and investment plans. However, significant investments in digital resources have not revolutionized learning environments (Dumont and Istance, 2010) and furthermore 'these highly funded projects have often resulted in either short lived or local successes or outright failures' (Kirschner et al., 2004, p. 359). Several scholars are enriching the debate on the role of new technologies in higher education with the analysis of failures and success factors identified in educational ICT projects (Kirschner et al., 2004); interesting critiques of technological determinism and 'technopositivism' (Cuban, 2001; Robertson, 2003); alternative stories about digital schools (Brown and Murray, 2003); and critical views of a possible overemphasis on technology in the classroom (Oppenheimer, 2003).

The enthusiasm for technological innovations in contemporary education is still high, but it is also acknowledged that mere provision of digital instruments is not enough to meet the needs of twenty-first-century learning and teaching objectives. As Bolstad et al. (2012) state, 'For the most part, educational thinking about ICT has moved on from the idea that simply introducing new ICT tools and infrastructure into school will trigger beneficial and meaningful educational change' (p. 55). Today it is recognized that integrated strategies are required for ensuring sufficient ICT infrastructures and for improving teachers' capabilities with these tools; for inspiring teachers and school leaders with regard to what it is possible to do; and for supporting the integration of ICT into teaching and learning practice (Bolstad et al., 2012). In the last decade almost every school, college and university has experienced rapid changes in web-based tools, software platforms and institutional learning management systems (LMS). Educators have found themselves at the center of this innovation/transformation. Some educators have sustained a growing community of digital enthusiasts by taking opportunities to network and share practices through traditional forums as well as on social media (Liburd et al., 2011). Not surprisingly, others have demonstrated a conservative resistance to the introduction of ICT in education when such introduction would radically alter their conditions, status and identity (Robertson, 2003). More educators have taken part in ICT professional development and they have gained experience (and certifications) in knowing why and how to use such software tools in their teaching.

2.2   Digital Migrant Teachers in Digital Natives' Classes

We are living at a crucial point of twenty-first-century learning. The last generation of 'digital migrants', led by 'digital enthusiasts', is dealing with the technological transformation of modern education to meet the needs of 'digital natives'. 'Digital' has become more than an adjective and seems to carry differences across generations as well as confusion in the related implications and applications of latest technology. It is likely that generational differences in thinking and processing information, highlighted by Prensky (2001), will disappear when digital natives themselves become the educators. When this occurs, both educators and learners may exhibit the same ability to deal with multiple simultaneous stimuli and, unfortunately, with a shorter attention span. For now, technology-enhanced learning mainly follows the inclination of digital-migrant teachers who incorporate digital tools into existing educational models. The consequence is that the ICT instruments are generally used in teacher-initiated projects for finding and presenting existing knowledge and students are passive spectators in relation to knowledge (Bosltad et al., 2012). Quite often students are end-users of learning management systems hosted by the institutions where teachers are conveying class material and students are uploading assignments. They are passive consumers of platforms and prototypes created by the teachers in their attempts to participate in the technological transformation.

2.3   Transformational Learning Over Technological Transformation

Technological transformation is a term used by Puentedura (2006) to identify the highest level of technology integration in education. He distinguishes four levels:

1. Substitution: the technology acts as a direct substitute for traditional tools with no functional change (for example read an online text);
2. Augmentation: the technology acts as a direct substitute for traditional tools with functional improvement (for example spellchecking, linked sites);
3. Modification: the technology allows for significant task redesign (for example multimedia tools for creating contents);
4. Redefinition: the technology allows for the creation of new tasks, previously inconceivable (for example tools integrated with work group and content management software).

According to Puentedura (2006), the first two levels are part of technological enhancement and the other two levels are part of technological transformation. Transformation in this sense is a term related to the possibility that an educator can redefine practice and assessments in a way that would not be available without the use of technology. The stream in the literature that focuses on the adoption of mobile phones and tablets in education is referring to Puentedura's (2006) level of redefinition and argues that new technologies are enabling new pedagogies (Harasim, 2000; Cochrane and Rhodes, 2013). It is important to draw a distinction here, because the availability of a new technological infrastructure does not automatically lead to new pedagogies. Although we are in the middle of a technological transformation it is important to understand that digital technology can support new pedagogies, but only if cognitive development and ethical practice are the drivers of transformation. As Calvani et al. (2010) point out, the integration of all technological, cognitive and ethical dimensions is essential for understanding the potential offered by technologies in enabling individuals to build new knowledge (Calvani et al., 2010).

The word 'transformation' itself should be considered in the context of a pedagogical perspective rather than a synonym of technological innovation. In the literature on adult education, the term 'transformation' acquires significance in Mezirow's Transformative Learning Theory where learners use critical reflection and rational discourse as vehicles to articulate ideas and to question the validity of their personal world-view (Mezirow, 1991, 1997; Cranton, 1994). The emphasis is on an advanced cognitive development that conveys the ability to engage in reflective discourse with others and to examine alternative perspectives. Mezirow considered critical reflection to be the distinguishing characteristic of adult learning, and saw it as the vehicle by which one questions the validity of a personal world-view. He identified rational discourse as a catalyst for transformation, as it induced the various participants to explore the depth and meaning of their various world-views, and to articulate those ideas to their instructor and classmates (Mezirow, 1997). All of these activities required a level of interactions between students that might be better to leverage in the classroom before cyberspace.

2.4   The Need for a Student-centered Approach

Are we really sure that inducing students to leave some comments in a forum or to write a paragraph in a wiki as part of their assignments will stimulate the reflection advocated by Mezirow's process of transformational learning? In Italy, I became aware of students who created a script to refresh their Internet browser automatically in order to simulate their presence on the software platform used by the university to monitor their 'active time' in front of class material delivered online. Other students confessed to me that they felt annoyed by the request forwarded from a colleague to leave posts in the forum, so they simply wrote comments to satisfy the minimum assignment requirements. Used in this way the technology does not seem to stimulate a reflective process.

Adopting technology effectively in education is not simple for today's educator. Many efforts are commendable and the brief history of integration of new technologies in education is rich with interesting initiatives. However, there is a need to move to a more student-centered approach. Several scholars have argued that technology-enhanced learning should empower students as authors and creators of content as well as managers and administrators of employed instruments (Cochrane and Rhodes, 2013; Morellato, 2014; Herrington and Herrington, 2007). Student-centered projects should aim to involve students as active producers of knowledge rather than passive consumers (Bigum, 2003; Gilbert, 2007; Morellato, 2014). Gilbert recommends the adoption of ICT tools to 'allow learners to "play" with different ways of making meaning' (p. 121), and she envisions learners 'exploring the use of different knowledge systems for different purposes' (p. 122). Cochrane and Rhodes (2013) underline the importance in changing the focus from teacher-generated content to student-generated content as part of pedagogical change. Morellato suggests an experiential learning approach that allows students to have the role and the responsibilities of 'administrators' of the digital instruments employed in their education. When students are awarded greater autonomy, they develop critical thinking and ethical attitudes not only in the use of the instruments but also in the management of personal online presence and participation in communities of the modern information society.

3.   CASE STUDY: THE AUT LEARNING DEVELOPMENT PROJECT

The Learning Development Project conducted in 2014 at the Auckland University of Technology (AUT) in New Zealand experiments with a new 'student-centered' perspective in the integration of digital technology in learning. A hundred students enrolled in the Bachelor of Arts in Event Management and four lecturers were involved for the first time in an experiential learning project with digital and mobile technologies employed to reinforce, support and build on traditional learning activities. During the four weeks, Event Management course students analyzed a range of major events in order to develop their knowledge of historical and contemporary events and the interdisciplinary principles that underpin event management. Each student became the creative author of contents related to the course and the administrator of an online personal space wherein the student collected, organized and presented knowledge and personal reflection developed during the course. 'First in class, later online' was the course's motto for any discourse or group activity. Following a problem-based learning model, students went through problem-solving experiences and collaboratively identified how and where to access new information, how to combine individual analysis in a participative construction of knowledge, and how to include in their assignments reflections on decisions taken. A quick overview of two proposed assignments should help to clarify the implementation of this learning approach.

Assignment 1: Investigation Map of Information Sources

Students produced a personal investigation map of the academic literature and other online sources of information in the form of a wiki as a collaborative assessment. They composed web-navigation maps whose purpose was to support other learners to explore efficiently the growing volume of information on the topics they were analyzing. By using a simplified hypertext format, students linked articles, websites, images, videos and information they found relevant in their study. By using mobile apps such as Storify and Flipboard they curated and aggregated a selection of content. Students were free to organize and present the information in ways they considered most effective: however, they were required to provide:

- the characteristics considered relevant for selecting the sources of information;
- a brief description of the selected sources with an assessment of their reliability;
- the identification of 'gateway' websites, as hubs that link to a list of other websites and attract visitors' attention on the topic.

Assignment 2: Producing and Publishing Content Online

Students prepared essays on subject matter and participated in the analysis of case studies by using a variety of mobile and digital technologies (for example iBook, video clips, micro-blogging, slideshow, mobile apps and augmented reality). Empowering learners to produce online content is not new. Many universities have experimented with different tools and technologies. However, the novelty of this project resides in the approach used and the attention on ethical issues rather than in the technological resources employed.

Regardless of their preferred digital instrument, students were challenged in solving problems related to copyright and licensing. The intention was not to create or explore new instruments but to use the technology already available at the university and make that technology 'more available' to the students. The strategy for pursuing this goal is articulated in initiatives in three domains: pedagogical, ethical and technological.

3.1   Technological Domain

Simplification, aggregation and usability are the key factors that underpinned the technological domain of the project. The information society is evolving towards seamless ICT solutions and mashup applications to aggregate contents in fast and fashionable ways (Polillo, 2013). Unfortunately, learning management systems do not follow the same path. Although LMSs usually display the architecture of a web application, they do not offer many possibilities of integration and aggregation. Therefore, students are required to move between different platforms adopted at the institution and to follow different access paths created by educators to reach class material or upload assignments. The 'three click rule' concerning the design of web navigation with intuitive, logical hierarchical structures (Zeldman, 2001) is usually employed in commercial sites to avoid having frustrated visitors leave the site but this rule is ignored in the online learning spaces for students. Blackboard and Mahara were the learning platforms available at the university and several efforts have been dedicated to link them as an 'aggregated learning system' able to incorporate additional external contents and to reduce the sequential steps needed to reach a content. Blackboard, the principal LMS at the university, can easily manage a wiki. Mahara, the open source platform for handling e-portfolios, can embed social media resources and uploaded files. Mahara's e-portfolio was presented to the students as a potential solution for administrating their own online space, and several templates were prepared for students not interested in customizable options. Alternative solutions such as blogs or websites proposed by students were equally welcomed.

The very limited time dedicated to the use of technology was a characteristic of this project, with only two hours in a computer lab during one tutorial, and about ten hours on self-directed activities. The intention was to 'build technology into learning, not learning into technology'. Encouraging freedom of choice and experimental play with the instruments was another important characteristic of the project. This was achieved by allowing learners to select the digital tools they wanted to use to produce, present and share their content. Artifacts, posters and paintings were also welcomed and, in these cases, students published a sequence of images or a movie with their personal comments. Several learners decided to create an iBook, many chose to prepare slideshows or video clips, and some experimented with micro blogging, augmented reality and mobile apps. The requirement to dedicate only a few hours to the production of the content remained for all the experiments. Students were also discouraged from using commonly used tools such as PowerPoint and Prezi.

3.2   Ethical Domain

The rapid penetration of smart-phones and tablets has dramatically increased the possibilities of ubiquitous access to information and has further enabled the creation of user-generated content (UGC). Today's students have an innate expectation of instantaneous access to information, and many have generated and published content on the Internet since their childhood. But these learners also demonstrate a lack of awareness about issues such as privacy, legality and security. Immediacy and confidence are not always accompanied by an adequate appreciation of the possible consequences of producing and consuming information. In the last decade, and increasingly today, more attention is being devoted to ethical behavior and responsible social practice in virtual communities and online spaces. Calvani et al. (2010) advocate for a better consideration of the ethical dimension of digital competence. They also highlight the importance of fostering awareness of one's own personal responsibilities and respect of reciprocal rights/obligations (Calvani et al., 2010). These ethical aspects are often not obvious to contemporary learners, and educators therefore have an important role to play in stimulating students to manage digital technology responsibly (Morellato, 2014). A practical context would help to clarify how a teacher can influence the raising of awareness and ethical behavior in learners and will serve to unfold these issues further.

The evolution of Web 2.0 technologies and the mobile web are offering unprecedented opportunities for the development of collaborative skills amongst students (Benckendorff, 2009; Parker and Chao, 2007). Educators now have a variety of social software tools at their disposal (Alexander, 2006). Learners can produce assignments based on podcasts, they can publish in blogs, they can share content using shared drives and they can use instant messaging systems to converse. But how often is the practice of inviting students to publish their assignments supported by considerations of privacy and respect for copyright? How often are ethical considerations receiving adequate attention in the activities proposed in collaborative spaces? Unfortunately, very little attention is generally dedicated to ethical issues and students are mainly trained on the features of the instruments.

In this project, students experimented with the use of Creative Commons Aotearoa New Zealand for licensing any content they created. Creative Commons provides free licenses that copyright holders can use to allow others to share, reuse and remix the material, legally (McGregor, 2013). Other ethical issues have been addressed by asking students to identify solutions to the following problems:

- how to recognize credits to other authors' work in using their material;
- how to decide where to store personal content and grant access to others;
- how to assess the reliability of information found in the Internet.

3.3   Pedagogical Domain

Some of the elements from the pedagogical domain have already emerged in the previous sections: the project promotes discovery (Barr and Tagg, 1995), experiential learning (Kolb, 1984) and the use of a problem-solving learning approach (Woods, 1996). The overarching perspective is oriented around knowledge co-construction during collaborative learning but with the intention to stimulate individual cognitive development from the collaboration (Bruner, 1966). There are clearly aspects of Vygotsky's (1978) zone of proximal development in considering participation as part of personal development. Students shared the information found on the subject studied but they also shared their critical reflections. They engaged with others in discourses for examining alternative solutions to problems and to widen their points of view by incorporating other students' assumptions and critical reflections. For example, in a video clip as well as in an augmented reality mobile app, students presented all team members' assumptions on the cultural and sociological reasons for hosting a festival, and later they showed a subset of assumptions collectively selected and refined. The variety and diversity of contributions in personal portfolios and wikis illustrated the value of using these digital tools. The number of comments and other indicators typically available on the software platform were not taken into account at all. Students generated meanings and representation of the materials analyzed (Roschelle, 1992) through a combination of self-construction and co-construction of explanations (Jeong and Chi, 1997).

The idea of shifting from seeing technology as a cognitive delivery system to seeing it as an instrument to support collaborative conversations and building understanding of a topic is something that Brown (1990) identified 25 years ago. Gilbert (2007) sustains this principle and claims the importance of using ICTs for connecting minds and generating new knowledge rather than storing and presenting existing knowledge. She envisions education systems in the Knowledge Age with a focus on:

- developing new knowledge;
- developing multi-modal literacy (understanding and using non-print modes of making meaning);
- relationships, connections and interactions between different knowledge systems and different modes of representation;
- difference and diversity, not sameness and/or one-size-fits-all approaches;
- process not product (Gilbert, 2007, p. 121).

The project conducted in the Event Management program at AUT aimed to create a learning environment based on this vision and students were members of communities of learners that made discoveries and solved problems (Barr and Tagg, 1995). They actively administered their portfolios and built knowledge using a variety of digital channels. Moreover, they used instruments for collaborating and supporting the generation of explanations. It is a student-centered project aligned with the change from the instruction paradigm to the learning paradigm (Barr and Tagg, 1995; Cochrane and Rhodes, 2013; Rogers, 2000). Students are empowered content producers guided by expert teachers in making decisions during individual and group activities. They need to understand how subjects are constructed and engage with the teachers, their peers and the content matter.

4.   OUTCOMES

The project demonstrated the possibility of engaging students as creative authors instead of passive consumers. The level of engagement demonstrated by the students in reviewing the literature and producing the investigation map was noticeably higher than the involvement presented in the previous semester during a similar secondary data analysis. The adoption of digital technology facilitated students' engagement with the content and in the development of the assignments. This was reflected in an overall better accuracy in the final reports produced and, more importantly, in enriching class discussions during the tutorials. This 'window effect' has been observed in another project in Italy and demonstrates that students will dedicate more attention in preparing an assignment when they know their work will be published in an online 'window' accessible to other students. An improved participation in group activities and class discussion has been observed by the educators; however, a proper assessment will be needed in the future. A meta-cognitive survey would help to collect students' considerations.

4.1   Two Types of Knowledge Construction

The knowledge construction in most of the groups was driven by a convergence of explanations and answering questions posed by group members and educators (for example: why has a particular event evolved as it has and which characteristics remain from the original event in the past?). In some groups the process of knowledge generation was driven by the integration of different meanings generated individually (for example cultural assumptions provided by students from different ethnic/cultural backgrounds on the Diwali festival hosted in Auckland).

4.2   Owning the Digital Learning Environment

The amount of multimedia content produced by students in a relatively short time was surprising. Even more surprising was the transformation that occurred in the use of learning platforms in some classes. The page prepared in Blackboard to collect entry points to the personal portfolios allowed fast access to all the students' portfolios. In two classes (out of four), students started to develop interconnections and links to other students' portfolios and used this evolving network for exchanging drafts and comments. It became a resource for merging and remixing material 'under construction'. Some lecture content available on Blackboard (the official learning management system) was curated by the students in this new space. The web of personal portfolios was clearly the dominant online learning system for those students. In other classes this never happened and the students considered their portfolios as instruments to just 'showcase individual assignments'. 'It is a nice way to present work' was one of the comments that emerged in the students' evaluation of the course. In the same class, some students also expressed negative comments on the adoption of digital instruments. For example: 'I don't believe it enhances our learning', 'It is just a different way of submitting work', 'I don't enjoy the portfolio', and 'it just distracts from what is really important'. It appears that students' perceptions were significantly different across classes, as analyzed further in the next section.

4.3   Considerations on Outcomes

There is a discrepancy between those comments and the comments collected in a different class facilitated by another educator. Four lecturers and tutors were involved in this project in four different classes. Examples of positive comments included: 'It makes the learning experience more interesting', 'Get to see how other people are doing', 'Helpful for the learning process', 'It allows us to have a lot of interesting class discussions', and 'It helped to share resources between students'.

The adoption of the same technology in parallel classes of the same course produced different perceptions and probably also different learning outcomes. Indeed, educators have an important influence on the creation of meaningful learning experiences in the integration of digital technologies in education. Being a trained teacher on the use of a particular technology does not guarantee automatic success. The analysis of students' comments in their evaluations of the course, combined with the direct observations during class activities, give rise to several considerations:

- Supporting and empowering learners in the exploration of possible usages of digital technologies can lead to the ownership of digital learning environments that can sometimes also be reconfigured by the learners.
- Learners' interactions with these environments seem to positively influence the way in which they generate new knowledge and achieve course learning outcomes. It would be interesting to research the conditions that favor learner ownership of

digital learning environments and to assess the influences (if any) on the learning outcomes.

● Learner perceptions of the use of digital tools need to be monitored during the learning experience to understand attitudes toward technology usage and also to identify educators' shortcomings and difficulties in implementing a learner-centered perspective. The adoption of digital instruments can be overwhelming in certain situations.

● The project confirmed that learners need to dedicate more consideration to the respect of copyright and licensing in the production of content as well as protecting their privacy. Half of the students declared that they had never considered these issues before.

● The project highlighted the importance of group discussions and face-to-face spaces for forging content reflection on the experience of using digital tools for studying subject matters and for creating new knowledge.

4.4   The Successful Use of Mobile Augmented Reality Browser

One instrument was particularly appealing to the students: the mobile augmented reality browser Layar. Augmented reality (AR) is considered to be a new medium of creative expression that enriches the manner in which human beings experience reality (Marimom et al., 2010). AR is the overlaying of digital information on an image of something viewed through a device such as a smart-phone camera. It is becoming increasingly popular due to the availability of sensors and computing power available on hand-held devices connected to the Internet. A mobile AR browser allows the user to superimpose geo-tagged information from the web to images captured by the device in real time. In tourism, context-aware applications able to provide location-based services and tailored information are already widely popular.

The interesting aspects of mobile AR browsers in education are related to the creation of content rather than the consumption of existing content. In this sense the adoption of a mobile AR browser sustained the core aim of the project to involve learners as active authors. Layar is one of the available AR browsers (Wikitute, Junaio and Tagwhat are other examples). Layar offers a 'creator platform' for creating layers of information in a simple and easy way. Text and images link to online content, and video can be easily associated to an image for creating an interactive print.

Students were able in a few minutes to play with the instrument to generate layers of information related to the subject of their study and upload them in the Layar system. Once uploaded, everyone with a Layar app installed on a smart-phone or tablet could consume the information created by simply pointing the camera on the mobile device toward the image that the author chose to make interactive. Although the generation of levels of layers is quite basic, students were highly engaged in preparing and refining the information. The new technological toy generated enthusiasm and fostered participation in the process to prepare and elaborate material. It also raised issues on behavioral changes that students addressed in the class discussion:

● the generated content was hosted on a server external to the university intranet and owned by a private company;

- the enthusiasm to quickly produce, curate and deploy the content in the online system was the major cause for a lack of consideration of copyright and licensing practice adopted with other platforms;
- the new media contained new limitations on contents under construction and constraints for a communication that was more appealing but less rich in information;
- the integration with the existing learning system was not possible.

All of these are elements are important to consider in future implementations.

5. CONCLUSIONS

The learning experiences trialed in the Event Management program can be explored further in other courses and in other universities. Much needs to be investigated in the area of adoption of digital technology in education for creating effective and meaningful learning experiences. The project demonstrated the possibility of engaging students as creative authors and responsible administrators instead of passive consumers. This experimentation of 'rethinking' technology-enhanced learning and the students' online presence raises more questions than providing definitive answers. The issues that emerged during the project are challenges that universities are facing all around the world. A change in how the latest technology is used today in education is needed to 'help learners to build a sense of themselves as active knowledge-builders' (Gilbert, 2007, p. 121).

Learners and educators need to become aware of what they are doing and how they are doing it when the technology enters class. This requires advancement not only in the technological domain but also in the ethical domain and the pedagogical domain. Mobile devices and mobile web are already part of the learning experience and are already offering personal ubiquitous features within a new set of context-aware applications and services hosted directly on the devices. Students are producing content in the mobile web and using these applications in their daily routines and any attempt to confine them to the intranet of a university is anachronistic. Empowering students as authors and administrators of personal online spaces carries a set of problems in terms of privacy, safety and copyright. Teachers have an important role in supporting learners in solving these problems and in stimulating the development of ethical practices. They also have an important role to keep the focus on learners' cognitive development in adopting ICTs in education. As Krumsvik (2008) highlights, the emphasis on subject content instead of technical skills requires 'extended competence on the part of the teacher in terms of seamlessly incorporating subject, pedagogy and digital competence' (p. 285).

The insights gained from this project also highlighted the value of traditional offline, face-to-face interactions in class. The group activities and the discussions orchestrated by the teachers between students in class were determinants for enabling a more effective and critical use of digital instruments in generating knowledge on the subject studied. In the technological enhanced learning initiatives, it is time to stop considering classroom face-to-face experiences and technology delivered experience as dichotomistic solutions. Creating opportunities for the students to collaborate in online and asynchronous environments does not mean forgetting the value and importance of the interaction conducted in person, in class.

REFERENCES

Alexander, B. (2006), 'Web 2.0: A new wave of innovation for teaching and learning', *Educause Review*, **41** (2), 1–7.

Barr, R.B. and Tagg, J. (1995), 'From teaching to learning: A new paradigm for undergraduate education', *Change: The Magazine of Higher Learning*, **27** (6), 12–26.

Benckendorff, P. (2009), 'Evaluating wikis as an assessment tool for developing collaboration and knowledge management skills', *Journal of Hospitality and Tourism Management*, **16** (1), 102–12.

Bigum, C. (2003), 'The knowledge-producing school: Moving away from the work of finding educational problems for which computers are the solution', *Computers in New Zealand Schools*, **15** (2), 22–6.

Bolstad, R., Gilbert, J., McDowall, S., Bull, A., Boyd, S. and Hipkins, R. (2012), *Supporting Future-oriented Learning & Teaching: A New Zealand Perspective*, Wellington: Ministry of Education.

Brown, J.S. (1990), 'Toward a new epistemology for learning', in Frasson, C. and Gauthier, G. (eds), *Intelligent Tutoring Systems: At the Crossroad of Artificial Intelligence and Education*, Norwood, NJ: Ables Publishing, pp. 266–82.

Brown, M. and Murray, F. (2003), 'Whose line is it anyway? Alternative stories about the digital world', *Computers in New Zealand Schools*, **15** (2), 10–15.

Bruner, J.S. (1966), *Toward a Theory of Instruction*, Cambridge, MA: Harvard University Press.

Bruns, A. and Humphreys, S. (2005), 'Wikis in teaching and assessment: The M/Cyclopedia project', in *Proceedings of the 2005 International Symposium on Wikis*, New York: ACM Press, pp. 25–32.

Calvani, A., Fini A. and Ranieri, M. (2010), *La Competenza Digitale nella Scuola: Modelli e Strumenti per Valutarla e Svilupparla*, Trento: Erickson.

Cochrane, T. and Rhodes, D. (2013), 'iArchi [tech] ture: Developing a mobile social media framework for pedagogical transformation', *Australasian Journal of Educational Technology*, **29** (3), 372–86.

Cooper, C. (2006), 'Knowledge management and tourism', *Annals of Tourism Research*, **33** (1), 47–64.

Cranton, P. (1994), *Understanding and Promoting Transformative Learning: A Guide for Educators of Adults*, San Francisco, CA: Jossey-Bass.

Cuban, L. (2001), 'Why are most teachers infrequent and restrained users of computers in their classrooms?', in Woodward, J. and Cuban, L. (eds), *Technology Curriculum and Professional Development*, Thousand Oaks, CA: Corwin Press.

Dillenbourg, P., Järvelä, S. and Fischer, F. (2009), 'The evolution of research on computer-supported collaborative learning', in Balacheff, N., Ludvigsen, De Jong, T., Lazonder, A. and Barnes, S. (eds), *Technology-Enhanced Learning*, Enschede: Springer, pp. 3–19.

Dumont, H. and Istance, D. (2010), 'Analyzing and designing learning environments for the 21st century', in Dumont, H., Istance, D. and Benavides, F. (eds), *The Nature of Learning, Using Research to Inspire Practice*, Paris: OECD, pp. 19–34.

Gilbert, J. (2007), 'Knowledge, the disciplines, and learning in the Digital Age', *Educational Research for Policy and Practice*, **6** (2), 115–22.

Harasim, L. (2000), 'Shift happens: Online education as a new paradigm in learning', *The Internet and Higher Education*, **3** (1), 41–61.

Herrington, A. and Herrington, J. (2007), 'Authentic mobile learning in higher education', paper presented at the AARE 2007 International Educational Research Conference, 13–14 June, Fremantle, Australia, accessed 31 March 2015 at http://researchrepository.murdoch.edu.au/5413/1/authentic_mobile_learning.pdf.

Istance, D. and Kools, M. (2013), 'OECD work on technology and education: Innovative learning environments as an integrating framework', *European Journal of Education*, **48** (1), 43–57.

Jeong, H. and Chi, M.T. (1997), 'Construction of shared knowledge during collaborative learning', in *Proceedings of the 2nd International Conference on Computer Support for Collaborative Learning*, International Society of the Learning Sciences, pp. 130–34, accessed 31 March 2015 at http://www.webmail.isls.org/cscl/1997/papers/jeong.pdf.

Kirschner, P.A., Hendricks, M., Paas, F., Wopereis, I. and Cordewener, B. (2004), 'Determinants for failure and success of innovation projects: The road to sustainable educational innovation', Association for Educational Communications and Technology, accessed 31 March 2015 at http://eric.ed.gov/?id=ED485042.

Kolb, D. (1984), *Experiential Learning*, Upper Saddle River, NJ: Prentice-Hall.

Krumsvik, R.J. (2008), 'Situated learning and teachers' digital competence', *Education and Information Technologies*, **13** (4), 279–90.

Liburd, J.J., Hjalager, A-M. and Christensen, I-M.F. (2011), 'Valuing tourism education 2.0', *Journal of Teaching in Travel and Tourism*, **11** (1), 107–30.

McGregor, M. (2013), 'Free to Mix, Creative Commons Aotearoa NZ Resources', accessed 31 March 2015 at http://creativecommons.org.nz/wp-content/uploads/2013/03/Free-to-Mix.pdf.

Marimon, D., Sarasua, C., Carrasco, P., Álvarez, R., Montesa, J., Adamek, T. and Gascó, P. (2010), 'MobiAR:

Tourist experiences through mobile augmented reality', *Telefonica Research and Development*, Barcelona, Spain, accessed 31 March 2015 at http://nem-initiative.org.

Mezirow, J. (1991), *Transformative Dimensions of Adult Learning*, San Francisco, NJ: Jossey-Bass.

Mezirow, J. (1997), 'Transformative learning: Theory to practice', *New Directions for Adult and Continuing Education*, **74**, 5–12.

Morellato, M. (2014), 'Digital competence in tourism education: Cooperative-experiential learning', *Journal of Teaching in Travel & Tourism*, **14** (2), 184–209.

Oppenheimer, T. (2003), *The Flickering Mind: False Promise of Technology in the Classroom and How Learning can be Saved*, Toronto: Random House.

Parker, K. and Chao, J. (2007), 'Wiki as a teaching tool', *Interdisciplinary Journal of e-learning and Learning Objects*, **3** (1), 57–72.

Polillo, R. (2013), 'La didattica al tempo di Twitter', lecture conducted at Bicocca University of Milan, Italy.

Prensky, M. (2001), 'Digital natives, digital immigrants', *On the Horizon*, **9** (5), 1–6.

Puentedura, R. (2006), 'Transformation, technology, and education', presentation delivered at the Strengthening Your District Through Technology workshops, accessed at http://hippasus.com/resources/tte/part1.html.

Robertson, H.J. (2003), 'Toward a theory of negativity: Teacher education and information and communications technology', *Journal of Teacher Education*, **54** (4), 280–96.

Rogers, D.L. (2000), 'A paradigm shift: Technology integration for higher education in the new millennium', *Educational Technology Review*, **1** (13), 19–33.

Roschelle, J. (1992), 'Learning by collaborating: Convergent conceptual change', *The Journal of the Learning Science*, **2** (3), 235–76.

Shapiro, N.S. and Levine, J.H. (1999), *Creating Learning Communities: A Practical Guide to Winning Support, Organizing for Change, and Implementing Programs*, San Francisco, CA: Jossey-Bass.

Vygotsky, L. (1978), 'Interaction between learning and development', in *Mind and Society*, Cambridge, MA: Harvard University Press, pp. 79–91, reprinted in Guvain, M. and Cole, M. (1997), *Readings on the Development of Children*, New York: Freeman and Company, pp. 29–36.

Vygotsky, L.S. (1992), *Educational Psychology*, Boca Raton, FL: St Lucie Press.

Woods, D.R. (1996), 'Problem-based learning: Helping your students gain most from PBL', in D.R. Woods, *Instructor's Guide for Problem-based Learning: How to Gain the Most from PBL*, 3rd edn, accessed 31 March 2015 at http://chemeng.mcmaster.ca/sites/default/files/media/PBL-chap2.pdf.

Zehrer, A. and Mössenlechner, C. (2009), 'Key competencies of tourism graduates: The employers' point of view', *Journal of Teaching in Travel & Tourism*, **9** (3), 266–87.

Zeldman, J. (2001), *Taking your Talent to the Web: A Guide for the Transitioning Designer*, Thousand Oaks, NJ: New Riders Publishing.

10 Pedagogy for online tourism classes
Patrick J. Holladay

1. INTRODUCTION

The world is shrinking. Technology is growing. The classroom is evolving. These are all facts and this reality is penetrating deeply into tourism management (Buhalis and Law 2008). Thus, new learning spaces – particularly online – are growing in scope and popularity (Cantoni et al. 2009). Online teaching, blended learning, and flipped classrooms are becoming more important as digital technologies are expanding rapidly (Delich 2005). This means that it is incumbent upon institutions of higher learning to equip both instructors and learners with digital literacy along with delivering course content (Dagada and Chigona 2013). The benefits of teaching online include flexibility (Lomine 2002), delivery of formative feedback (Halupa and Bolliger 2013), ease of access (Hogan and Nimmer 2013), particularly for those with disabilities (Betts and Edgell 2013), rapid and equitable information sharing (Lee and Tsai 2011), asynchronous independent learning (Murphy et al. 2011), opportunities for multidisciplinary contexts in learning, and connections to the vast array of online resources useful to educational outcomes. Technology and the internet are changing global societal structures and digital connections are rapidly becoming a common social norm. Recognizing that most learners are deeply embedded in this digital world means that educators must embrace these new vehicles of knowledge delivery for communities of learners (McQuiggan 2012; Russell 2011).

The online teaching and educational environment has expanded into the realm of tourism (Cantoni et al. 2009). Additionally, a strong push has been made by the Tourism Education Futures Initiative (TEFI) to build a values-based framework for tourism education (Sheldon and Fesenmaier 2015; TEFI 2010). These TEFI values – stewardship, mutuality, ethics, professionalism and knowledge – can easily be incorporated into online teaching. This chapter will first examine why online teaching in tourism is important and some theoretical underpinnings to support this assertion, as well as explaining the TEFI values framework. Next, applications to the curriculum with appropriate technologies will be folded together using TEFI values and their intersection with the eLearning Technology Compass (Moss 2014).

2. LITERATURE

2.1 Online Teaching

Online teaching should not be considered different from traditional teaching – with the obvious exception of the technology needed. Both a social presence and a teaching presence are required (Bair and Bair 2011). Interaction between the instructor and the learner enhances satisfaction and dedication to coursework (Jacobs 2013). Therefore, facilitating learner engagement through course design (Crawford-Ferre and Wiest 2012) and appropriate technology is needed (Bair and Bair 2011). Dynamic, diverse faculty with high levels of professional development, innovative curricula and fully engaged learners are keys to the foundations of online education (Betts and Edgell 2013). Meeting the needs of online instructors through appropriate training in technology and institutional support, such as quality equipment, is vital (Crawford-Ferre and Wiest 2012).

Instructors that are used to teaching in traditional structured classrooms will have to re-learn teaching methodologies to accommodate the growing online learner populations (Barrett 2010). Global perspectives of faculty to online teaching include the necessity of interactive activities, solid evaluation criteria and defined self-expectations (Hsieh 2010). Factors for success in online courses include intimate knowledge of course content, design to eliminate unanticipated problems, reduced emotional gaps, timely feedback, and a demonstrated teaching presence (Baran et al. 2013). Other ways to facilitate online learning include access and motivation, socialization, information exchange, knowledge construction and personal development (Salmon 2002).

2.2   Theory

This chapter recognizes that there must be inherent theoretical pluralism when addressing online learning. Cercone (2008) reviewed several learning theories and found that none comprehensively addressed adult learning, which has consequences for online learning. Indeed, most learners will exhibit different learning styles (Felder and Brent 2005). That said, however, the theoretical foundations of this chapter draw largely from the constructivist learning model (Schell and Janicki 2012), as well as transformative learning (Mezirow 1991, 1997), experiential learning (Kolb 1984) and authentic e-learning (Herrington et al. 2010).

The constructivist learning model rejects the notion that knowledge is transferred from the expert to the learner. Rather, the learner 'constructs' their own knowledge and learning through idea formulation, critical thinking and active description (Guthrie and McCracken 2010). The implication of a social constructivist paradigm in online learning is that the online environment should be used to encourage learners who may not be co-located to interact with each other to create knowledge. Moreover, within online environments learner-centered collaborative and constructivist environments are posited to promote higher learning (Sigala 2002).

Although Mezirow's transformative learning theory has evolved over the years (Kitchenham 2008; Taylor 2007), its focus on how adults interpret the world (Mezirow 1981) and how instructors teach their educational philosophies (Taylor 2008) are important to online learning. The theory postulates that it is the role of the educator to equip the learner with the skills to critically evaluate their own assumptions to become a more effective learner, thus leading to a change in perspective (Mezirow 1991, 2003).

Transformative learning is induced by change but also by experience (Kolb 1984). As Kolb (1984, p. 38) stated, 'Learning is the process whereby knowledge is created through the transformation of experience'. This experiential learning is represented in a four-stage cycle: (1) concrete experience; (2) reflective observance; (3) abstract conceptualization; and (4) active experimentation.

Experiential learning, transformative learning and social constructivism all must be supported by authentic e-learning environments. Herrington et al. (2010) produced a model for authentic e-learning using nine key elements to create an authentic e-learning environment. These are: (1) provide authentic contexts that reflect the way the knowledge will be used in real life; (2) provide authentic tasks and activities; (3) provide access to expert performances and the modeling of processes; (4) provide multiple roles and perspectives; (5) support collaborative construction of knowledge; (6) promote reflection to enable abstractions to be formed; (7) promote articulation to enable tacit knowledge to be made explicit; (8) provide coaching and scaffolding by the teacher at critical times; and (9) provide for authentic assessment of learning within the tasks.

2.3   Teaching Education Futures Initiative Framework

There has been a recent shift in corporate and societal values that has influenced tourist values such that it needs to be reflected in tourism education (Sheldon et al. 2008). Tourism Education Futures Initiative (TEFI) went through a rigorous visioning process to formulate a values-based educational framework to address this issue (TEFI 2010). These principles are designed to shape tourism learners into responsible leaders and are composed of five value sets (Sheldon et al. 2011; TEFI 2010). These five values are stewardship, mutuality, ethics, professionalism and knowledge (see Figure 10.1). Sheldon et al. (2011) give a thorough treatise on the definitions, content and learning objectives for these value-based principles. Folding in these values with transformative, experiential and authentic learning – using technology – should create quality tourism education into the future.

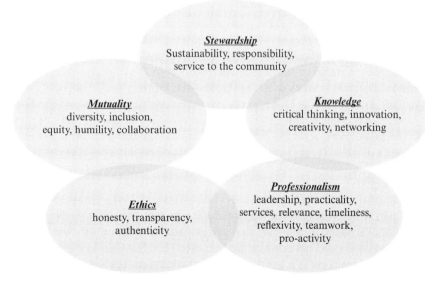

Source: Sheldon et al. (2011, p. 8).

Figure 10.1   Tourism Education Futures Initiative values

3.   TEACHING APPROACHES

Teaching online should not be overly foreign or intimidating. The process of lesson planning and assessment is the same as in a traditional classroom. The most important thing to remember is that the learning outcomes, the activities to facilitate learning outcomes and the assessment of learning outcomes are the same as in a traditional setting. The development of curriculum comes first and then the appropriate technology to deliver the curriculum is selected – never the other way around. This will ensure the constructive alignment of learning outcomes, activities and assessments (Biggs 2014).

Equally important to planning is an understanding of the technology used to deliver the course materials. Digital literacy can be a challenge to both learners and instructors. Not all learners are fluent in technology (Jacobs 2013) and even heavy users of personal online technologies may not be able to apply these technologies skillfully to learning and professional outcomes (for example the number of learners with a Facebook account who do not have a LinkedIn profile). Some keys to consider when selecting online delivery tools are: (1) will learners know how to use the technology; (2) will instructors know how to use the technology and be able to demonstrate how to use the technology; and (3) is this technology accessible to all the learners in the course. Instructor-created videos embedded within the course are a very simple way to demonstrate how to use a particular type of internet tool.

There are a variety of innovative and engaged ways to teach online content. The choices will depend on the tools and/or platform of choice. The eLearning Technology Compass (Figure 10.2) gives a snapshot of many of the technologies available and how they relate to assessments and competencies (Moss 2014). The eLearning Technology Compass is used by (1) identifying a goal in the center and then (2) moving out to find performance assessment and then potential technology tools.

Many universities are using Learning Management Systems (LMS), web-based software for online and hybrid courses. There are quite a variety of both open source (for example Canvas) and proprietary (for example Blackboard) LMS options. Regardless of the LMS used, they generally allow an instructor a method to organize, deliver and assess course materials, as well as flexible learner access via desktop and laptop computers and mobile devices (Jacobs 2013). The remainder of this section will discuss the five TEFI value sets – stewardship, mutuality, ethics, professionalism and knowledge – as they relate to online teaching. There will also be explicit connections between these five value sets and the theories of constructivist, transformative, experiential and authentic e-learning.

3.1   Stewardship

Within the TEFI framework stewardship involves sustainability, responsibility and service to communities (TEFI 2010). The fact that learners are interfacing with the course via an online environment should never preclude the instructor from using experiential education. Service-based learning is a great experiential education tool that promotes responsibility and community interaction (Sedlak et al. 2003). Requiring learners to engage in a minimum number of hours of service in an organization working in the tourism field or closely affiliated industry will force them away from the computer.

Online technologies such as blogs, VoiceThread and reflection journals will support

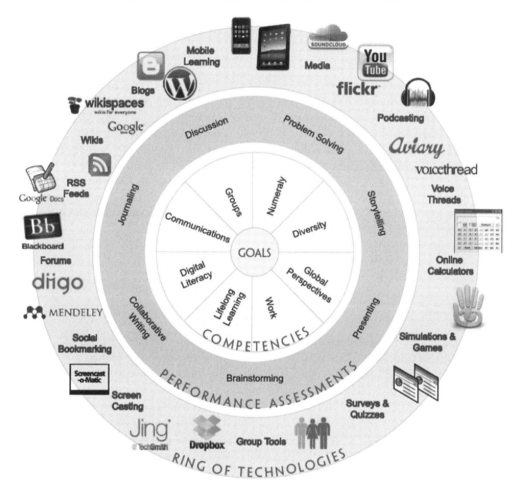

eLEARNING TECHNOLOGY COMPASS

Source: Moss (2014), online.

Figure 10.2   eLearning Technology Compass

service learning activities' educational outcomes. One suggestion is to have learners keep a journal of their experiences (Hatcher et al. 2004). Journals can act as a reflective exercise both during and after the service learning experience (Connor-Greene 2000) and are meaning-making (Hubbs and Brand 2005). Meaning-making reflections are an opportunity for learners to critically evaluate new learned information, tie it to course materials and analyze how this information helps them in becoming better tourism professionals. These journals are an instructor's 'window' into learner thinking and help build the learner relationship with the instructor (Spalding and Wilson 2002), which is of importance in the online environment.

Journaling should support learner growth and development (Hiemstra 2001). This type of exercise stimulates constructivist, transformative thinking and is both experiential – as learning takes place away from the 'classroom' – and authentic in that it represents real life knowledge acquisition. Journals could include a brief account of activities, skills and knowledge gained, the effect the service had and a synthesis of the experiences with class materials (Holladay 2014).

Related to journaling are blogs and VoiceThread. Blog is short for weblog and is similar to an online journal except that it is usually more public and readers can post comments below a blog entry. Blogs represent a method of co-learning (Williams and Jacobs 2004), wherein learners not only reflect on their service learning experience but with the addition of peer comments there is a collaborative opportunity (Sigala 2002) that promotes constructivist learning (Guthrie and McCracken 2010). Slightly more complex – but not complicated – is the use of VoiceThread. VoiceThread is an online educational tool that is interactive and may incorporate images, documents and videos that a learner narrates (Brunvand and Byrd 2011). VoiceThread supports learners' – both their own and others' – thoughts, integrates collaborative groups and advances understanding of self, task and other (Augustsso 2010). This provides multiple perspectives, collaborative knowledge construction, reflection and abstraction, which are all dimensions of authentic e-learning (Herrington et al. 2010).

3.2   Mutuality

According to the TEFI framework, mutuality integrates diversity, equity, inclusion, humility and collaboration (TEFI 2010). All of these values may be promoted in an online class with the use of discussion forums. The discussion forum is an opportunity to incorporate the material presented in the course and offer views and opinions on the topic at hand. The discussion forum allows learners to post a response to a topic the instructor has posed. Since learners come from all types of demographic backgrounds, the responses tend to be diverse in nature. This stimulates self-awareness that questions 'I versus Them' attitudes and could lead to acceptance of different viewpoints and inclusivity (TEFI 2010). In essence, this is transformative learning as learners are challenging their own assumptions, which leads to changes in viewpoints (Mezirow 1991; 2003).

In general, learners perceive the benefits of online discussion forums (Hamann et al. 2012). Posting to weekly discussion forums (or discussion boards) allows the instructor to interface with learners by posing a question related to the week's materials. It is imperative to explain the role of discussions, set rules for participation and create a social environment as reminiscent of a traditional classroom as possible (Nilson 2003). This type of online social atmosphere inspires interaction with learners who are not co-located and constructivist learning through collaboration (Guthrie and McKracken 2010).

One method is the twice-weekly posting. For example, the instructor will open a discussion forum on a Sunday of the week and close it the following Sunday. Learners then must post a response by Wednesday evening at midnight. They then must also respond to one of their classmates' posts by Sunday evening at midnight. The lag-time between Wednesday and Sunday posts allows the learners to read through their peers' posts and select one they wish to respond to. This type of peer-to-peer interaction allows learners to appreciate each other's viewpoints (Costen 2009) and provides a good example of a social constructivist approach in the online space.

3.3   Ethics

The TEFI framework indicates that ethics are comprised of honesty, transparency, authenticity and authentic self (TEFI 2010). By extension, this ethic value must also be a part of the other four TEFI value sets. Instructors always strive to ensure that learners are ethical in their coursework and should adopt best practices for online pedagogical design, delivery, engagement and assessment that support ethical behavior (Collins et al. 2014). Cheating, plagiarism and other such behaviors are not tolerated and specific penalties are meted out by policy for such actions. Further, such activities undermine all of the theoretical benefits of constructivist, transformative, experiential and authentic e-learning.

Olt (2002) described four strategies for minimizing academic dishonesty in an online environment. These are: (1) use of log-ins in an LMS – web-based software for online and hybrid courses that allows instructor and learner access to a course – coupled with short assessments; (2) effectively designed online assessments; (3) creation of original curricula from class to class; and (4) provision of an academic integrity/dishonesty policy. This type of policy would certainly describe plagiarism. In an online classroom the best technology to defeat plagiarism is plagiarism-detection software, through which all written learner assignments are processed for comparison with material published in traditional sources (books, journals, magazines), on the internet (to include essays for sale), and papers turned in by learners in the same and other classes in current and all class periods. Most, if not all, LMS have built-in plagiarism-detection tools.

For example, the Blackboard LMS incorporates a system called 'Turnitin'. Although Turnitin has received mixed reviews from instructors (Bruton and Childers 2015; Park 2014), it does function to detect plagiarism. Some learners experience anxiety about unintended plagiarism but this stress can be shifted by guiding learners away from plagiarism-detection to a more positive focus on academic writing skills (Bostock and Taylor 2014), a function of authentic e-learning (Herrington et al. 2010). Plagiarism-detection services exist in other LMS, such as Desire2Learn's (D2L) use of Dropbox's plagiarism tool and Moodle's integration of a variety of plug-ins, which include Turnitin.

3.4   Professionalism

TEFI stipulates that the professionalism value should incorporate leadership, practicality, service, reflexivity, teamwork and pro-activity (TEFI 2010). Group projects support all of these factors because of the amount of time spent working with a team on a project. Communication skills are a realized benefit because of the interactions among class project members through cooperative learning (Johnson and Johnson 2009). Group projects increase learners' effort and commitment (Johnson et al. 1998), which is important in an online class where there is a lack of social connection. By creating this social connection an authentic e-learning environment is established through collective construction of knowledge (Herrington et al. 2010).

Learners may resist group work because they feel they can do as well or better on their own. Another caution is that since the pace of classes is generally faster and learners may sign up for online courses because they want to work in their own time, the instructor may encounter resistance. Therefore, the benefits of group work and collaborative learning (Guthrie and McCracken 2010; Herrington et al. 2010) must be illustrated (Moore 2005). It is important to establish group guidelines, break the project into phases, assign (preferably randomly and diverse) group members, and create an assessment rubric (Delich 2011). Ongoing instructor management is also important to manage conflict in the case that a learner does not believe all members are cooperating equally (Roberts and McInnerney 2007).

The LMS that is used will typically have (a) group working space(s). Moodle is a very popular open-source LMS (Cole and Foster 2008). Moodle has private and shared group spaces. There are options for both visible groups – learners interact with members of their group, can read other groups' materials but not interact with other groups – or separate groups, wherein there is no group interaction of any kind. Within the Blackboard LMS there is a function called Blackboard Collaborate, which allows multi-functionality with tools like web conferencing and break-out rooms for group work (Blackboard 2011).

3.5   Knowledge

This component of the TEFI values set addresses creativity, critical thinking and networking (TEFI 2010). Online video lectures act as a supporting mechanism to reinforce creativity and advance critical thinking. Video lectures allow more time for challenging topics (Brecht and Ogilby 2008). Notably, video lectures help create instructor-to-learner connections (Kay 2014) in an environment where the instructor and learner do not normally interact. This leads to authenticity of e-learning through coaching, performance and modeling (Herrington et al. 2010).

Learners have found short summary lectures useful for reviewing materials, exam study aids, self-tutoring and better grades (Brecht and Ogilby 2008; Whatley and Ahmad 2007). Moreover, online lectures reduce withdrawal rates (Brecht 2012), particularly in difficult courses that learners tend to avoid (Geri 2012). Emerging evidence suggests that optimal video length is six minutes or shorter and engagement shortens for videos that are longer than 12 minutes (Guo, 2013).

There are a variety of open source and proprietary recording tools available. It is up to the individual lecturer to choose based their own preferences, comfort and digital literacy. A video lecture does not necessarily mean that the lecturer captures their own image. Video lectures with voice-only are quite common. An open source audio editor and recorder (for example Audacity) allows an educator to record their voice, as well as edit out long pauses, 'umms' and the like. These audio clips can be inserted from files into slide-sharing software (for example PowerPoint) in the appropriate slides. The slides can then be saved as video. More robust software (for example Camtasia) exists for screen recording, video capture, clickable links, and embedding assessments (for example quizzes) into the lectures.

These types of interactive video lecture tools like Camtasia allow for effects, creativity and enhanced user–lesson interface. A cautionary note must be made on doing due diligence when deciding to use video lectures in the online classroom. It is not possible to simply save your video into your course in most LMS platforms. An embed code step is needed. Code is created by uploading the slide presentation into a video-sharing site (for example YouTube). The HTML code that is created is what is needed to insert the video into the course. As with any online tool, users must familiarize themselves with the tools they are using to create the best end-product, such as an online video lecture. Finally, it is imperative to explain to learners the benefits of watching the video lectures. Some learners conditioned to traditional lectures may be resistive to online lectures unless the assessment design provides an 'incentive' for learners to view them.

4.   FUTURE DIRECTIONS

4.1   Web 2.0

Web 2.0 consists of a set of rapidly evolving and emerging tools that people use to interact with each other and learn (Anastasiades and Kotsidis 2013). Blogs, wikis and social media are all examples of Web 2.0 tools (Anderson 2007). In the future, online educators must tap into the ways that online social media tools enable users to communicate, collaborate and create dynamic content in social networks (Delich 2005). All of these Web 2.0 tools can be embedded in the course unit through an LMS or used as a complementary external tool to the LMS. Imagine using Twitter through the online course in such a way that when someone accesses the course they can see the latest tweets (and archived tweets) of other users of the course that are related to the course. This allows for social interaction, rapid feedback, and knowledge sharing (Tsai et al. 2013).

There are some inherent limitations and cautions for using Web 2.0. Web 2.0 usage must be planned thoroughly, assessed rigorously, limited to appropriateness and the instructor must be cognizant of learner self-regulated learning skills (Yen et al. 2013). Using Web 2.0 may indicate 24/7 availability of the instructor because of the immediacy most learners attribute to online social media tools. The instructor must set parameters and instruct learners that they should not expect immediate feedback – the use of online office hours during specified times of the week are appropriate. On a cautionary note, Web 2.0 tools may be a barrier to some learners who do not use them. To coincide with whichever Web 2.0 tools are selected by the instructor, there should also be a set of training materials (for example video lecture) from the instructor to explain the use of the tool(s).

Most people are now familiar with Wikipedia as an open online collaborative encyclopedic effort. That said, however, the use of a wiki does not have to be of that magnitude. A wiki is simply a collaborative tool that lets someone contribute to the content. Wikis can be effective for allowing tourism learners to develop knowledge management skills, as well as consensus building (Benckendorff 2009). Thus, a wiki for an individual class or set of classes (for example all the tourism classes offered) could be used for collaboration and learning (Deters et al. 2010), which is in-line with social constructivism (Guthrie and McCracken 2010).

4.2   Other Technologies

Other technologies and/or platforms to be aware of are curated content tools, learning analytics and Massively Open Online Courses (MOOCs). Curated content tools allow for filtering, contextualizing, reflecting on, personalizing and illustrating relevant information about a specific topic for a specific audience (Waters 2014). Popular curation tools include Diigo, Twitter, Evernote, Pinterest and Scoop.it! (Waters 2014). Learning analytics focus on learner-produced data, analysis models and optimization of learning environments and have been compared to data mining (Wikipedia 2015). By far the behemoth of new technologies/platforms is the MOOC. A MOOC is an online open access course with unlimited participation. The major players in this arena include edX, Coursera, Udacity and Udemy. Finally, there is an ongoing strong transition of many of these and the earlier discussed technologies to mobile/portable devices. MOOCs, like Coursera, and LMS platforms, like Blackboard, are completely available and functional as apps. Learners no longer need – or in some cases want – a traditional classroom. They can now be fully engaged with the course on a smart-phone, tablet or other mobile device while riding a train, relaxing in a park or reading content in a coffee shop.

5.   SUMMARY AND CONCLUSION

The growth of online education requires that learning environments within the realm of tourism education keep pace and seek to innovate (Betts and Edgell 2013). While technology can be intimidating to some faculty that are used to traditional classrooms, with proper attitude and training, online teaching can be mastered (Barrett 2010). Online classroom planning and assessment are no different in e-learning than in the face-to-face classroom. Technology and technological tools should never drive course development. Course content – curriculum – comes first and then the appropriate technology to deliver the content should be selected. Digital literacy and access to technology should also be emphasized when choosing the online teaching tools. Further, much of the interface between instructor and learner typical of a traditional classroom is needed. Finding ways to create a social and teaching presence – through online discussion, formative feedback and thoughtful communication – reduces emotional gaps and bolsters learner academic success (Baran et al. 2013). Online video lectures have the power to both teach and to create instructor-to-learner connections (Brecht 2012). Shaping learners' learning and worldviews through self-constructed knowledge (Schell and Janicki 2012) and experiential (Kolb 1984), transformative learning (Mezirow 1981; 1991; 1997) and authentic e-learning (Herrington et al. 2010) have been recognized as necessary for supporting online learning outcomes. Educational tools related to service-learning (Sedlak et al. 2003), personal reflections (Spalding and Wilson 2002), discussion forums (Hamann et al. 2012) and group projects/cooperative learning (Johnson and Johnson 2009) are all recommended for online tourism education. Moving beyond the more familiar, online teaching platforms will begin to use evolving instruments such as Web 2.0 tools: blogs, wikis and social media are all examples. As research and understanding grow about online teaching, exciting new methodologies and technologies will emerge that will be ideal for maximizing online education. Examples include content curation and learning analytics. Those teaching within the tourism industry must not only embrace these ideas but seek to adapt and grow them for our own dynamic pedagogies.

REFERENCES

Anastasiades, P.S. and K. Kotsidis (2013), 'The challenges of Web 2.0 for education in Greece: a review of the literature', *International Journal of Web-Based Learning and Teaching Technologies*, **8** (4), 19–33.

Anderson, P. (2007), 'What is Web 2.0?: ideas, technologies and implications for education', *JISC Technology & Standards Watch*, **1** (1), Bristol: JISC.

Augustsso, G. (2010), 'Web 2.0, pedagogical support for reflexive and emotional social interaction among Swedish learners', *The Internet and Higher Education*, **13** (4), 197–205.

Bair, D.E. and M.A. Bair (2011), 'Paradoxes of online teaching', *International Journal for the Scholarship of Teaching and Learning*, **5** (2), 1–15.

Baran, E., A. Correia and A.D. Thompson (2013), 'Tracing successful online teaching in higher education: voices of exemplary online teachers', *Teachers College Record*, **115**, 1–41.

Barrett, B. (2010), 'Virtual teaching and strategies: transitioning from teaching traditional classes to online classes', *Contemporary Issues in Education Research*, **3** (12), 17–20.

Benckendorff, P. (2009), 'Evaluating wikis as an assessment tool for developing collaboration and knowledge management skills', *Journal of Hospitality and Tourism Management*, **16**, 102–12.

Betts, K. and D.L. Edgell Sr (2013), 'Online education and workforce development: ten strategies to meet current and emerging workforce needs in global travel and tourism', *Journal of Tourism & Hospitality*, **2** (1), 1–9.

Biggs, J. (2014), 'Constructive alignment in university teaching', *HERDSA Review of Higher Education*, **1**, 1–18.

Blackboard (2011), '10 cool ways to engage with Blackboard Collaborate', accessed 15 March 2015 at http://www.blackboard.com/CMSPages/GetFile.aspx?guid=f1dab0b6-c2bc-47d3-adc9-7c90f45713d2.

Bostock, J. and L. Taylor (2014), 'Using Turnitin as a formative assessment tool to support academic writing', paper presented at SOLSTICE/CLT Conference, 5–6 June 2014, Edge Hill University.

Brecht, H.D. (2012), 'Learning from online videos', *Journal of Information Technology Education*, **11**, 227–50.

Brecht, H.D. and S.M. Ogilby (2008), 'Enabling a comprehensive teaching strategy: video lectures', *Journal of Information Technology Education*, **7**, 71–86.

Brunvand, S. and S. Byrd (2011), 'Using VoiceThread to promote learning engagement and success for all students', *Teaching Exceptional Children*, **43** (4), 28–37.

Bruton, S. and D. Childers (2015), 'The ethics and politics of policing plagiarism: a qualitative study of faculty views on learner plagiarism and Turnitin', *Assessment & Evaluation in Higher Education*, (ahead-of-print), 1–15.

Buhalis, D. and R. Law (2008), 'Progress in information technology and tourism management: 20 years on and 10 years after the internet – the state of eTourism research', *Tourism Management*, **29** (4), 609–23.

Cantoni, L., N. Kalbaska and A. Inversini (2009), 'E-learning in tourism and hospitality: a map', *Journal of Hospitality, Leisure, Sport and Tourism Education*, **8** (2), 148–56.

Cercone, K. (2008), 'Characteristics of adult learners with implications for online learning design', *AACHE Journal*, **16** (2), 137–59.

Cole, J. and H. Foster (2008), *Using Moodle: Teaching with the Popular Open Source Course Management System*, Sebastopol: O'Reilly Media, Inc.

Collins, D., J. Weber and R. Zambrano (2014), 'Teaching business ethics online: perspectives on course design, delivery, learner engagement, and assessment', *Journal of Business Ethics*, **125**, 513–29.

Connor-Greene, P. (2000), 'Making connections: evaluating the effectiveness of journal writing in enhancing learner learning', *Teaching of Psychology*, **27** (1), 44–6.

Costen, W.M. (2009), 'The value of staying connected with technology: an analysis exploring the impact of using a course management system on learner learning', *Journal of Hospitality, Leisure, Sport and Tourism Education*, **8** (2), 47–9.

Crawford-Ferre, H.G. and L.R. Wiest (2012), 'Effective online instruction in higher education', *Quarterly Review of Distance Education*, **13** (1), 11–14.

Dagada, R. and A. Chigona (2013), 'Integration of e-learning into curriculum delivery at university level in South Africa', *International Journal of Online Pedagogy and Course Design*, **3** (1), 53–65.

Delich, P. (2005), 'Pedagogical and interface modifications: what instructors change after teaching online', Malibu: Pepperdine University.

Delich, P. (2011), 'Designing learner collaborative projects for online courses', accessed 15 March 2015 at http://elearningnetworks.com/materials/.

Deters, F., K. Cuthrell and J. Stapleton (2010), 'Why wikis? Learner perceptions of using wikis in online coursework', *Journal of Online Learning and Teaching*, **6** (1), 1–15.

Felder, R.M. and R. Brent (2005), 'Understanding learner differences', *Journal of Engineering Education*, **94** (1), 57–72.

Geri, N. (2012), 'The resonance factor: probing the impact of video on learner retention in distance learning', *Interdisciplinary Journal of E-Learning and Learning Objectives*, **8**, 1–13.

Guo, P. (2013), 'Optimal video length for learner engagement', accessed 15 March 2015 at https://www.edx.org/blog/optimal-video-length-learner-engagement.

Guthrie, K.L. and H. McCracken (2010), 'Reflective pedagogy: making meaning in experiential based online courses', *The Journal of Educators Online*, **7** (2), 1–21.

Halupa, C. and D.U. Bolliger (2013), 'Learner perceptions on the utilization of formative feedback in the online environment', *International Journal of Online Pedagogy and Course Design*, **3** (2), 59–76.

Hamann, K., P.H. Pollock and B.M. Wilson (2012), 'Assessing learner perceptions of the benefits of discussions in small-group, large-class, and online learning contexts', *College Teaching*, **60** (2), 65–75.

Hatcher, J.A., R.G. Bringle and R. Muthiah (2004), 'Designing effective reflection: what matters to service learning', *Michigan Journal of Community Service Learning*, 11 (1), 38–46.

Herrington, J., T.C. Reeves and R. Oliver (2010), *A Guide to Authentic E-learning*, New York: Routledge.

Hiemstra, R. (2001), 'Uses and benefits of journal writing', *New Directions for Adult and Continuing Education*, No. 90 (special issue: *Promoting Journal Writing in Adult Education*), pp. 19–26).

Hogan, R. and N. Nimmer (2013), 'Increasing access to effective education across Oceania', *International Journal of Web-Based Learning and Teaching Technologies*, **8** (1), 17–31.

Holladay, P.J. (2014), *Efficacy of Reflection Journals for Learner Learning in an Online Environment*, Proceedings from the Georgia Education Research Association 39th Annual Meeting, Savannah, Georgia, available at http://digitalcommons.georgiasouthern.edu/gera/2014/2014/44/.

Hsieh, P. (2010), 'Globally-perceived experiences of online instructors: a preliminary exploration', *Computers & Education*, **54**, 27–36.

Hubbs, D. and C. Brand (2005), 'The paper mirror: understanding reflective journaling', *The Journal of Experiential Education*, **28** (1), 60–71.

Jacobs, P. (2013), 'The challenges of online courses for the instructor', *Research in Higher Education Journal*, **21**, 1–18.

Johnson, D.W. and R.T. Johnson (2009), 'An educational psychology success story: social interdependence theory and cooperative learning', *Educational Researcher*, **38** (5), 365–79.

Johnson, D.W., R.T. Johnson and K.A. Smith (1998), 'Cooperative learning returns to college: what evidence is there that it works?', *Change: The Magazine of Higher Education*, **30** (4), 26–35.

Kay, R.H. (2014), 'Exploring applications for using video podcasts in online learning', *International Journal of Online Pedagogy and Course Design*, **4** (2), 64–77.

Kitchenham, A. (2008), 'The evolution of John Mezirow's transformative learning theory', *Journal of Transformative Education*, **6** (2), 104–23.

Kolb, David A. (1984), *Experiential Learning: Experience as the Source of Learning and Development*, Englewood Cliffs, NJ: Prentice Hall.

Lee, S. and C. Tsai (2011), 'Learners' perceptions of collaboration, self-regulated learning, and information seeking in the context of Internet-based learning and traditional learning', *Computers in Human Behavior*, **27**, 905–14.

Lomine, L.L. (2002), 'Online learning and teaching in hospitality, leisure and tourism: myths, opportunities and challenges', *Journal of Hospitality, Sport & Tourism Education*, **1** (1), 43–9.

McQuiggan, C.A. (2012), 'Faculty development for online teaching as a catalyst for change', *Journal of Asynchronous Learning Networks*, **16** (2), 27–61.

Mezirow, J. (1981), 'A critical theory of adult learning and education', *Adult Education*, **32** (1), 3–34.

Mezirow, Jack (1991), *Transformative Dimensions of Adult Learning,* San Francisco: Jossey-Bass.

Mezirow, Jack (1997), 'Transformative learning: theory to practice', *New Directions for Adult and Continuing Education*, **74**, 5–12.

Mezirow, J. (2003), 'Transformative learning as discourse', *Journal of Transformative Education*, **1** (1), 58–63.

Moore, J. (2005), 'Is higher education ready for transformative learning: a question explored in the study of sustainability', *Journal of Transformative Education*, **3** (1), 76–91.

Moss, J. (2014), 'eLearning technology compass', accessed 15 March 2015 at http://iteachu.uaf.edu/online-training/grow-skills/choosing-the-best-technology/.

Murphy, E., M.A. Rodriguez-Manzanares and M. Barbour (2011), 'Asynchronous and synchronous online teaching: perspectives of Canadian high school distance education teachers', *British Journal of Educational Technology*, **42** (4), 583–91.

Nilson, L.B. (2003), *Teaching at its Best: a Research-based Resource for College Instructors*, Bolton, MA: Anker Publishing Company.

Olt, M.R. (2002), 'Ethics and distance education: strategies for minimizing academic dishonesty in online assessment', *Online Journal of Distance Learning Administration*, **5** (3).

Park, J. (2014), 'Instructors' firsthand experience toward the Turnitin embedded onto the course', *Society for Information Technology & Teacher Education International Conference*, **1**, 151–3.

Roberts, T.S. and J.M. McInnerney (2007), 'Seven problems of online group learning (and their solutions)', *Educational Technology & Society*, **10** (4), 257–68.

Russell, Alicia K. (2011), *Catalysts for Re-examining Pedagogical Assumptions: a Phenomenological Inquiry into Higher Education Faculty Designing and Teaching Online Courses*, Boston, MA: Northeastern University.

Salmon, G. (2002), *E-tivities: the Key to Active Online Learning*, London: Kogan Page.

Schell, G.P. and T.J. Janicki (2012), 'Online course pedagogy and the constructivist learning model', *Journal of the Southern Association for Information Systems*, **1**, 26–36.

Sedlak, C.A., M.O. Doheny, N. Panthofer and E. Anaya (2003), 'Critical thinking in learners' service-learning experiences', *College Teaching*, **51** (3), 99–103.

Sheldon, P. and D. Fesenmaier (2015), 'Tourism Education Futures Initiative: current and future curriculum influences', in D. Dredge, D. Airey and M.J. Gross (eds), *The Routledge Handbook of Tourism and Hospitality Education* (pp. 155–70). New York: Routledge.

Sheldon, P.J., D.R. Fesenmaier and J. Tribe (2011), 'The Tourism Education Futures Initiative (TEFI): activating change in tourism education', *Journal of Teaching in Travel & Tourism*, **11** (1), 2–23.

Sheldon, P.J., D. Fesenmaier, K. Woeber, C. Cooper and M. Antonioli (2008), 'Tourism education futures, 2010–2030: building the capacity to lead', *Journal of Teaching in Travel & Tourism*, **7** (3), 61–8.

Sigala, M. (2002), 'The evolution of internet pedagogy: benefits for tourism and hospitality education', *Journal of Hospitality, Leisure, Sport & Tourism Education*, **1** (2), 29–45.

Spalding, E. and A. Wilson (2002), 'Demystifying reflection: a study of pedagogical strategies that encourage reflective journal writing', *Teachers College Record*, **104** (7), 1393–421.

Taylor, E.W. (2007), 'An update of transformative learning theory: a critical review of the empirical research (1999–2005)', *International Journal of Lifelong Education*, **26** (2), 173–91.

Taylor, E.W. (2008), 'Transformative learning theory', *New Directions for Adult and Continuing Education*, **119**, 5–15.

Tourism Education Futures Initiative (TEFI) (2010), 'A values-based framework for tourism education: building the capacity to lead', accessed 15 March 2015 at http://www.tourismeducationfutures.org/publications.

Tsai, C., P. Shen and Y. Chiang (2013), 'The application of social networking sites (SNSs) in e-learning and online education environments: a review of publications in SSCI-indexed journals from 2004–2013', *International Journal of Web-Based Learning and Teaching Technologies*, **8** (3), 18–23.

Waters, S. (2014), 'Curation: creatively filtering content', accessed 15 March 2015 at http://www.theedublogger.com/2014/06/12/curation/.

Whatley, J. and A. Ahmad (2007), 'Using video to record summary lectures to aid students' revision', *Interdisciplinary Journal of Knowledge and Learning Objects*, **2**, 185–96.

Wikipedia (2015), 'Learning analytics', accessed 15 March 2015 at http://en.wikipedia.org/wiki/Learning_analytics#What_is_Learning_Analytics.3F.

Williams, J.B. and J. Jacobs (2004), 'Exploring the use of blogs as learning spaces in the higher education sector', *Australasian Journal of Education Technology*, **20** (2), 232–47.

Yen, C., C. Tu, L.E. Sujo-Montes, S.W.J. Armfield and J.Y. Chan (2013), 'Learner self-regulation and Web 2.0 tools in management in personal learning environment', *International Journal of Web-Based Learning and Teaching Technologies*, **8** (1), 46–65.

11 Massive Open Online Courses (MOOCs) in hospitality and tourism

Jamie Murphy, Nadzeya Kalbaska, Lorenzo Cantoni, Laurel Horton-Tognazzini, Peter Ryan and Alan Williams

1. INTRODUCTION

The tourism industry, interesting and challenging, faces structural human resource problems such as skills shortages and staff turnover, seasonality and a high percentage of small to medium enterprises whose employees have limited time for training or education. Large tourism enterprises often span countries and continents, such as hotel chains, airlines, cruise companies and car rentals, where the employees need similar training – a costly activity. Although hospitality and tourism educational resources have expanded and evolved during the last two decades, online courses – particularly free and open courses – remain limited. Electronic learning (eLearning) can help address some of these training issues (Cantoni et al., 2009; Kalbaska, 2012; Kuttainen and Lexhagen, 2012; Sigala, 2002).

Throughout history, pundits have heralded new communication innovations as revolutionizing education (Gumport and Chun, 1999). Massive Open Online Courses (MOOCs), a recent education innovation, are gaining momentum, controversy, confusion, accolades and participation across industry and academia (Daniel, 2012; Murphy et al., 2014). The *New York Times*, for example, proclaimed 2012 as the 'Year of the MOOC', noting thousands to hundreds of thousands of learners taking a single MOOC from prestigious universities, for free (Pappano, 2012).

Despite MOOCs' free aspect and subsequent business model concerns (Dellarocas and Van Alstyne, 2013), the number of MOOCs on offer keeps growing, doubling – 2112 to 4277 – from March 2014 to March 2015 (openeducationeuropa.eu/en/european_scoreboard_moocs). Despite no immediate income, higher education institutions might offer MOOCs for altruistic motives, educational research, as a testing ground and hothouse for other online learning initiatives and marketing motives (Daniel, 2012). The motives, and MOOC ecosystem, seem an evolving work in progress.

Universities, and organizations such as the National Geographic Society and World Bank, are queuing to offer MOOCs via an emerging genre of providers that offer MOOC *platforms* and *marketplaces* (Klobas et al., 2014). Platforms help house and manage MOOC content and learners. MOOC marketplaces help interested learners locate open online courses. The marketplace often helps individuals and organizations build and manage MOOCs. The growing number of MOOC providers suggests a large, diverse MOOC supply. Similarly, millions of MOOC participants suggest demand for diverse and varied MOOCs.

Table 11.1 highlights six such platforms and marketplace providers, and their June 2015 statistics from the platform's website and Class-Central.com.

Perhaps the leading for-profit platform and marketplace provider, Coursera, lists over

Table 11.1   MOOC platforms and marketplace providers

Provider	Number of participants	Number of MOOCs	Languages
Alison.com	5 million	750	8
Coursera.org	13 630 million	1,041	12
edX.org	400 000 certificates	539	6
Floofl.com	Unknown	6	2
FutureLearn.org	1 725 579	163	3
NovoEd.com	600 000	165	2

13 million participants and 1041 MOOCs in 12 languages from 117 universities and other organizations. Alison, an Irish for-profit, offers 35 000 basic education topics in eight languages and 750 MOOC-like workforce certificate courses and diploma qualifications. Alison lists five million learners in 200 countries, 400 000 course graduates, and 200 000 monthly enrolments. A leading not-for-profit, edX, lists 539 MOOCs across six languages from 53 schools and organizations, with over 400 000 certificates earned (edx.org/schools-partners). FutureLearn from Open University, which collaborates with 60 universities and other organizations, launched in 2013 and lists almost two million participants to date (futurelearn.com). NovoEd, a for-profit platform, is one of the few that provides a predominantly collaborative online learning environment. NovoEd lists 600 000 learners, 165 courses and cites a 35–65 percent MOOC completion rate (novoed.com/educators). Finally, Floofl provides free travel and tourism education, listing five academic MOOCs in English, an industry MOOC in both English and German and one simulation: *Rooms Management*.

Four factors help distinguish MOOCs from traditional online higher education: open access, cost, recognition and scale. The initial 2011 massive MOOC enrolments, such as MIT and Stanford's 150 000+, however, have scaled down. A recent study of 91 MOOCs found a median enrolment of 42 844 students (Jordan, 2014). Anyone in the world with Internet access can register for a MOOC, for free, without meeting any admission requirements such as course prerequisites or prior education.

This openness goes beyond enrolment to include participation. MOOC registrants choose or omit content – such as videos, readings or assessment – as they want and in any order they wish (Breslow et al., 2013). Registrants that complete the MOOC, including satisfactory assessments and homework, usually obtain a certificate of completion but no formal credit from the offering institution. In addition, some MOOCs offer a verified certificate for a nominal fee.

MOOCs are an evolving concept, particularly in their pedagogy, business models and definitions (Dellarocas and Van Alstyne, 2013; Dolan, 2014; Klobas et al., 2014; Martin, 2012). This chapter defines MOOCs as open online courses that provide assessment and subsequent recognition of satisfactory completion, with no financial cost to the participants. The next section, a brief history of distance learning, helps position MOOCs as the latest in a long line of educational innovations.

2.   DISTANCE LEARNING

2.1   Communication and Learning

Formal and informal learning happens throughout our existence, ranging from earning an institutional degree to being able to cook Italian spaghetti al dente thanks to a conversation in a friend's kitchen (Hager and Halliday, 2006). In every learning experience, communication plays a major role (Cantoni, 2006). Communication can help outline learning needs and goals, provide new information or content, negotiate meanings and manage teaching/learning strategies and processes.

Because of communication's importance within teaching/learning experiences and practices, educators and administrators continually test the integration of available communication technologies within education and training. The outcome of this testing is that technologies impact words and subsequently shape a corresponding teaching/learning environment (Ong, 2012). Furthermore, testing communication technologies in education can be controversial at the time, and humorous decades or millennia later.

In the 5th century BC, education faced a seemingly major technological impediment and controversy. 'Written materials would undermine the learning process and diminish the quality of the personal relationship between tutor and student' (Gumport and Chun, 1999, p. 6). Learners would rely on external written characters rather than memory. Two millennia later, in 1841, the inventor of the blackboard was hailed among the best contributors to learning and science (Daniel, 2012).

From the rise of writing, communication technology has affected learner relationships, both between learners and teachers, and between learners and intellectual content. Concerning learners and teachers, written communication bridges distance through the availability of the documented word. With learners and intellectual content, the extensive available written communication for learning and teaching embodies a broad range of discipline-specific content.

2.2   Evolution of Distance Learning

The Apostle Paul's writings to Christians were a forerunner of distance teaching (Peters, 2003). In addition to his missionary travels, he used technology, writing and transportation for his evangelizing. Paul supplemented face-to-face preaching and teaching with written letters for sharing with current and potential followers, that is, 'mediated and asynchronous preaching and teaching. And, it was a technology-based, but still "pre-industrial" approach. At that time nobody could imagine the outstanding importance which would be attached to this very approach all over the world in the twentieth century and, it appears, even more so in the twenty-first century' (Peters, 2003, p. 14).

With the emergence of the printing press and postal services, academic institutions started to offer, especially to people who left their country for a colony, correspondence teaching (Holmberg, 1995). Distance learning blossomed, combining the technologization of the word – printed materials first, then radio, cinema, television and information and communication technologies – with newly available reliable and fast transportation.

Only late last century did distance education emerge as a global phenomenon. Four converging factors driving this emergence were: (1) social needs – people want to study in an institution, but cannot attend full-time; (2) political and cultural views of higher education as an individual right; (3) technological advances, especially digital media that make it possible to scale the offer and add extensive interactivity to the distance-learning experience; and related to the third point, (4) improved access to information facilitated by declining technology costs and the growth of the Internet.

These four factors have led to the birth of so-called eLearning, using 'multimedia technologies and the Internet to improve the quality of learning by facilitating access to resources and services as well as remote exchanges and collaboration' (CEC, 2001, p. 2). Research of information technologies and learning, especially informal learning, has accelerated thanks to the latest generation of digital technologies, such as mobile devices (Donner, 2008; Traxler, 2009), social media (Bull et al., 2008) and digital games (Gee, 2003; Prensky, 2006). According to Kapp (2012), gamification and game-based learning are effective for changing behavior and creating positive learning outcomes.

2.3 Evolution and Types of Online Learning in Hospitality and Tourism

Distance education via the Internet, eLearning, has evolved into different approaches and strategies that rely upon three types of interaction: Student/learner to Content (S2C), Student/learner to Student/learner (S2S) and Student/learner to Teacher/trainer/tutor (S2T) (Negash and Wilcox, 2008; Piccoli et al., 2004). A meta-analysis of 1034 articles found that increasing S2C interaction showed the greatest learning effect, followed by S2S and S2T (Bernard et al., 2009). S2C interaction examples include frequently asked questions (FAQs), automated testing and simulations (Anderson, 2003; Daniel et al., 2009). Such interactions, along with costs, recognition and structure of the learning materials, result in four progressive categories of online learning: online resources, online tutorials, online courses and MOOCs.

Online resources

Online resources provide rich educational materials but usually lack the structure of a traditional higher education course. Such resources typically have no lecturer, tutor or subsequent S2T interactivity. Resources may have some S2C interactivity such as the ability to comment on items, search and access Frequently Asked Questions (FAQs), but lack other S2C interaction such as quizzes and S2S interactivity, for instance forums. Online educational resources typically have no fees, no registration and are open to everyone.

Publishing resources online makes it easy to share them – provided those interested have reliable Internet access and are on the privileged side of the digital divide (Cantoni and Tardini, 2006). The resources category resembles online libraries: documents available for consultation, with the advantage of eliminating space, time and shelf-availability issues, while adding multimedia affordances and S2C interactivity. The International Federation for IT and Travel & Tourism's (IFITT) *Digital Library* (ifitt.org/resources/digital-library) and *eTourism Wiki* (ifitt.org/resources/wiki) are two such online resources. IFITT's policy of social corporate responsibility and supporting lifelong learning motivated the creation of the Digital Library and Wiki. These resources help learners, globally, develop their knowledge and career opportunities in today's multicultural and technology-driven working society.

Online tutorials
Similar to online resources, tutorials have limited S2C interaction such as FAQs and the ability to comment. Likewise, tutorials usually lack a tutor or a lecturer, and both S2T and S2S interactions. Online tutorials tend to have more course structure than online resources, such as a linear progression of content, learning objectives and evaluation activities. Tutorials usually have no fees but may require or limit registration. Three tourism tutorial examples follow.

Tourism Australia's e-Kits (tourismekit.atdw.com.au) for travel industry professionals comprise 60 tutorials across nine subject areas with similar pedagogical materials, including evaluation activities.

The Building Excellence in Sustainable Tourism (BEST) Education Network, a collaborative network of tourism academics and practitioners, develops and shares sustainable tourism resources and tutorials with video, slides, literature, case studies and assignments (besteducationnetwork.org/Teaching_Materials). A related BEST initiative, INNOTOUR, is an experimental meeting place for academics, students and enterprises to share and collaborate with case studies and other academic resources (innotour.com).

Finally, in late 2013 The University of Central Florida offered *Tourism Industry Analysis* (canvas.net/courses/tourism-industry-analysis), an eight-week tutorial with videos and a forum (S2S). Unlike other tutorials, *Tourism Industry Analysis* required purchasing a textbook. Furthermore, and discussed later, *Tourism Industry Analysis* now resembles a MOOC more so than a tutorial or online course.

Online courses
Online courses (OCs) differ from tutorials and resources in that OCs typically restrict registration to qualified entrants, such as at a university, and charge direct or indirect fees to the students. In return, course content extends beyond resources and tutorials to include formal assessment, recognition such as university credit, and S2T, S2C and S2S interactions. Academic institutions provide OCs from a Bachelor's degree (for example the Hospitality and Tourism Management degree program at Sheffield Hallam University) up to an MBA (for example Glion Online MBA in International Hospitality and Service Industries Management).

Ahead of academia, the hospitality and tourism industry has been using online training for the last twenty years (Miralbell et al., 2014). Companies, especially those with an expanded geographical distribution, use OCs rather than in-house training to update existing staff or to induct new staff. Industry educational initiatives include hotels, such as Hilton University or Accor Academy, cruise companies (for example Royal Caribbean Cruise Lines Corporate University) and transportation providers (for example Hertz Academy). Moreover, 75 Ministries of Tourism (elearning4tourism.com), as of October 2014, provide online training and certification, such as Tourism Australia's Aussie Specialist (www.aussiespecialist.com/about.aspx).

Two recent online course advancements are online simulations and serious gaming. Educators and industry globally use these tools to deliver knowledge while increasing audience motivations, engagement and problem-solving capacities (McCallum, 2012). Five hospitality and tourism examples follow:

- The Australian Government's Office for Learning and Teaching funded the Online Business Simulations project (bizsims.edu.au), which evaluates and promotes pedagogies that enhance the learning outcomes of online simulations in business education. Hospitality and Tourism simulations include Hospitality Service Operation, Transport and Aviation Management as well as Hospitality Management.
- The World Heritage Awareness Campaign for Youth in Southern African Development Community (whacy.org) uses a game-like digital tool in order to train young people in Southern Africa on cultural and natural heritage and its potential use in the tourism sector.
- Workstar (workstar.com.au), a leading Australian eLearning company, worked with McDonald's Australia to develop the 'Welcome to our Team' course. This online simulation is integral to new employee orientation and induction.
- Marriott's 'My Marriott Hotel' online game helps the hotel chain identify and train potential employees through Facebook. The game gives users the possibility to adopt different hotel employee positions and helps the hotel chain demonstrate the responsibilities tied to each role.
- Floofl.com, an Oxford Tourism Business School-based social enterprise, offers a free *Rooms Management Simulation*.

MOOCs

MOOCs, which add **M**assive and **O**pen to the OC acronym, resemble OCs, with four major differences. MOOCs have massive scale, are open access, are offered at no cost and usually lack formal credit. To date, few hospitality and tourism MOOCs are available. Table 11.2 lists 25 MOOCs, 21 in hospitality/tourism and four in the related field of sustainability, just 0.6 percent of the existing 4121 MOOCs noted in this chapter's Introduction.

These 25 MOOCs give academia and industry educational resources, as well as continuing education opportunities and classroom supplements. Twenty-one of the 25 MOOCs are available in English (one of which has been translated into Arabic and Italian while another has Portuguese subtitles), two are in Spanish and one in French. Sixteen MOOCs have fixed dates and range from 5 to 13 weeks long. Nine MOOCs are self-paced, meaning the participants can start and continue as they wish. Two MOOCs were launched in 2013, with most starting in 2014. One hospitality/tourism MOOC, Tourism Industry Analysis, began its third iteration in April 2015.

Although Floofl.com offers six hospitality/tourism MOOCs, Table 11.2 omits these MOOCs due to log-in requirements to view the content. In addition, two providers in Table 11.2 list their MOOCs as self-paced, therefore with no fixed start date or time limit. And, at the time of writing this chapter, Università Telematica Internazionale and Alison's MOOCs' start dates are unavailable.

MOOC lecturers often rely on peer-to-peer, automated and self-assessment to deal with their thousands of students (Chauhan, 2014; Wilkowski et al., 2014a). Online courses and MOOCs have all three types of interaction, albeit with different emphasis. Given their massive size relative to online courses, MOOCs tend to have less S2T interaction and more S2S and S2C interaction. Furthermore, the amount of S2S interaction may depend on the MOOC pedagogy (Ferguson and Clow, 2015).

Table 11.2   Tourism, hospitality and sustainability MOOCs

Provider	Course	Debut	Latest Offer	Weeks	Languages
Tourism and Hospitality MOOCs (n = 21)					
Alison	Tourism – Marketing and Promotion		2015	Self-paced	English
Alison	English for Tourism – Restaurant Service		2015	Self-paced	English
Alison	English for Tourism – Tourist Information and Guided Tours		2015	Self-paced	English
Alison	Introduction to the Development of the Tourism Industry		2015	Self-paced	English
Alison	Tourism – Introduction to Retail Travel Sales		2015	Self-paced	English
Alison	Tourism – Introduction to Travel Patterns and Destinations		2015	Self-paced	English
Alison	Tourism Industry – Sectors and Career Development		2015	Self-paced	English
Alison	English for Tourism – Hotel Reception and Front Desk		2015	Self-paced	English
Cornell University	Introduction to Global Hospitality Management	2015	02/15	6	English
Escuela de Organización Industrial y l'juntament de Benissa	Innovación en Turismo Cultural	2014	2014	8	Spanish
Harvard	Science and Cooking: From Haute Cuisine to the Science of Soft Matter	2014	06/15	13	English
Taylor's University	Wonderful Styles of Food & Beverage around the World	2014	05/14	5	English
Taylor's University	Introduction to Wines 101	2014	09/14	14	English
The New School	Writing American Food	2015	05/15	6	English
Università Bocconi	Managing Food & Beverage Companies	2015	07/15	4	English
Università della Svizzera italiana	eTourism Communication Perspectives	2015	10/15	8	English
Università Telematica Internazionale	Statistics and Economic Statistics of Tourism		2015	Self-paced	Arabic, English, Italian
Universitat de Girona	Cambios en el Turismo Contemporaneo	2013	03/14	7	Spanish
Université de Jendouba et l'Université Toulouse – Jean Jaurès	L'écotourisme: Imaginons-le ensemble	2015	06/15	7	French

Table 11.2   (continued)

Provider	Course	Debut	Latest Offer	Weeks	Languages
University of Central Florida	Tourism Industry Analysis	2013	04/15	6	English
University of Central Florida	Hospitality Financial Management	2015	Forthcoming		English
Sustainability MOOCs (n = 4)					
Columbia University	The Age of Sustainable Development	2014	09/14	14	English
University of Illinois Urbana-Champaign	Introduction to Sustainability	2015	01/15	8	English, Portuguese subtitles
University of Bath	Make an Impact: Sustainability for Professionals	2014	03/14	6	English
University of Nottingham	Sustainability, Society and You	2014	01/14	6	English

3.   MOOC PEDAGOGY

3.1   Learning Theories

Online courses have existed for decades, but MOOCs' massive class size and intrinsic learner motivations complicate and complement online class delivery (Koller et al., 2013). Launched in 2008 with one type of pedagogy, MOOCs burst on the media scene in 2011 with a different pedagogy and hundreds of thousands of registrants in prestigious university – such as Stanford, Harvard and MIT – MOOCs (Pappano, 2012). Still evolving, MOOCs tend to be anchored by a dominant pedagogy complemented by other pedagogies. MOOC literature usually mentions two traditional and two recent pedagogies (Daniel, 2012; Klobas et al., 2014).

Cognitivism and behaviorism
Cognitivism and behaviorism evolved from divergent psychological learning theories and were the predominant educational pedagogies prior to the digital age (Anderson and Dron, 2011). Behaviorism stems from Pavlov's classical conditioning, Watson's stimulus-response and Skinner's operant conditioning theories. Behaviorism contends that learning is only observable and measurable by overt behaviors. Cognitive theories, a reaction to behaviorism, focus on the brain's ability to perceive experience, and retain and recall information (McGuire and Furniss, 2000). Extensive research coalesced the two divergent concepts in the mid-twentieth century (McGuire and Furniss, 2000).

Behaviorism dominated educational pedagogy up to the mid-1950s, until Piaget's field research of how children acquired problem-solving skills helped validate and promote cognitive research (McGuire and Furniss, 2000). Building on Piaget's work, subsequent independent and vast laboratory experiments delved into brain functions. This research formed the basis of contrasting and comparing the brain's processes to computers, how the brain inputs and assimilates data. In the 1970s, behavior therapies expanded due to extensive psychological research such as Bandura's social learning theory and Beck's cognitive theory (McGuire and Furniss, 2000).

The above cited theoretical expansions, based on psychological research, led to coupling cognitive behaviorism (CB) into a broad methodological approach to teaching and learning (McGuire and Furniss, 2000). Online educational CB models focus on an instructional system of clear, concise learning objectives with an emphasis on short-term memory inputs coded for long-term recall. The typical drill and grill approach to learning in most MOOCs relies upon CB pedagogy (Daniel, 2012).

Social constructivism

Social constructivism followed CB as a popular learning theory. This theory also emerged from psychological developmental theories such as those associated with Vygotsky, Bruner and Bandura's social cognitive theory (Kim, 2010). Two Vygotsky principles, the Zone of Proximal Development (ZPD) and the More Knowledgeable Other (MKO), complement each other and help explain learning (Galloway, 2010). A learner in the ZPD has almost mastered a task and can then master the task with the help of a MKO.

Social constructivism posits that learning is, basically, a socially mediated activity, a social process (Ferguson and Clow, 2015). Social constructivism views learning as constructed, not created, from individual cultural and social experiences that form an individual's knowledge base. Student to student interactions (S2S) in MOOCs, such as peer assessment, forums and wikis illustrate learning via social constructivism. FutureLearn, a platform and marketplace provider mentioned in Table 11.1, tends to use a constructivist pedagogy (Ferguson and Clow, 2015). Tellingly, a review of 266 proposals to the MOOC Research Initiative found that social learning had the greatest interest and highest success in attracting funding (Gašević et al., 2014).

Connectivism

Connectivism surfaced in 2005 and blossomed in 2008 due to Siemens and Downes launching the world's first MOOC, *Connectivism and Connective Knowledge* (Daniel, 2012; Klobas et al., 2014). Connectivism helps explain learning in the digital age; technology houses knowledge and links individuals to online communities with shared interests. 'It is more accurate – and pedagogically more useful – to treat learning as the formation of connections' (Downes, 2011).

Connectivist learning draws on the process of building and maintaining network connections across people and online resources and the ensuing connections among people and resources. Connectivism emphasizes that effective learning requires the individual to possess a specific skill set: the ability to pursue relevant information and the ability to parse irrelevant information (Kop and Hill, 2008). In a MOOC, the educator balances autonomy, social learning and chaos to cultivate knowledge creation and nurture connections among the learners (DeWaard et al., 2011; Siemens, 2012).

Community learning

Community learning extends social constructivism and connectivism to communities of practice (Murphy, 2012; Williams et al., 2011). With community learning, the process resembles an infinite game with flexible rules rather than a finite game with strict rules, set beginnings and set endings (Carse, 1986). A finite game's goal is to decide a winner or achieve an objective such as finishing a university course or degree. The goal of an infinite game, by definition, is to keep the game going (Carse, 1986). Community learning is ongoing learning rather than a class with given start and stop dates.

As a community learning exemplar, MOOCs may continue after the class finishes. Responding to student demand, for instance, MIT kept its initial MOOC website live after the class finished and students created an award-winning follow-up course (Watters, 2012). Students also wrote programs, such as an online text viewer for mobile devices, which MIT made available through the course wiki (Daniel, 2012). The two major MOOC types, extended (xMOOC) and connectivist (cMOOC), respectively lean towards finite and infinite games.

3.2   cMOOCs and xMOOCs

Two MOOC types, connectivist (cMOOC) and extended (xMOOC), anchor a range of MOOCs that are usually a hybrid of both types (Klobas et al., 2014). Most MOOCs tend towards xMOOCs (Chauhan, 2014; Daniel, 2012). xMOOCs garner most of the attention, thanks in part to their affiliation with popular elite universities and major MOOC providers such as Coursera, edX and Google (Murphy et al., 2014; Pappano, 2012; Wilkowski, 2013). In xMOOCs, instructors act as celebrities and content producers; cMOOC instructors tend to be guides and content facilitators (Chauhan, 2014; Ross et al., 2014).

Connectivist pedagogy in the inaugural MOOC, a cMOOC named *Connectivism and Connective Knowledge*, proposed that knowledge is across a network of connections; learning is the ability to construct and traverse those networks. The cMOOC delivery model includes 'daily newsletters, recommend readings, videos and recordings made by course facilitators, blog posts, tweets, discussion posts, bookmarks and whatever else we can think of' (Downes, 2011). A cMOOC should connect learners with a variety of online sources for watching, reading and playing (Downes, 2011).

xMOOCs, which emerged from the Stanford and MIT models, are an extension of the traditional cognitive behaviorist learning and knowledge duplication (Daniel, 2012; Siemens, 2012). xMOOCs use short videos to deliver content followed by quizzes that help drill and grill (Siemens, 2012). Similar to a traditional university class, xMOOCs follow a prescribed sequence of learning modules that the instructor has developed. Unlike a cMOOC, xMOOC students have a given curriculum with few options for deviating from that curriculum (Chauhan, 2014; Klobas et al., 2014; Ross et al., 2014). The xMOOC resemblance to traditional university OCs also extends to MOOC measures.

3.3   Measuring MOOCs

The tens of millions globally enrolled in Coursera, edX, Google and FutureLearn MOOCs illustrate the hunger for new learning content and methods (Lewin, 2013; Wilkowski, 2013). Yet the rapid growth of MOOCs did not occur because they were online or massive, but because they were open to all (Grimmelmann, 2014). MOOC completion rates, typically less than 10 percent (Jordan, 2014; Murphy et al., 2013), illustrate the conundrum of large enrolment free courses with certificates of participation rather than official university credit. Critics argue that MOOCs are a failure (Dolan, 2014). Others counter that the traditional academic notion of attendance and completion is an inappropriate MOOC comparison (DeBoer et al., 2013; Koller et al., 2013). And to date, there is no known correlation between course dropout rates and failure of the MOOC idea (Dolan, 2014).

Traditional course success measures – enrolment, participation, attendance, attrition and completion – applied to MOOCs typically describe a funnel of participation beginning with enrolment and then shrinking based on engagement. From one-half to two-thirds of MOOC registrants continue beyond registration, fewer participate in activities and eventually under one in ten earns a certificate of participation (Jordan, 2014; Murphy et al., 2013).

Completion rates are at best an incomplete MOOC measure, and at worst threaten the MOOC ideal of free, open access to education (Reich and Ho, 2014). MOOC enrolees have diverse motivations, such as gaining knowledge and skill, rather than completion (Breslow et al., 2013; DeBoer et al., 2013; Koller et al., 2013). For example, half the Mapping with Google registrants noted intrinsic motivations as their goal, not a certificate (Wilkowski et al., 2014b). Similarly, participants in the University of Central Florida's *Tourism Industry Analysis* wanted knowledge. Over three out of four participants (78 percent) were taking the course to learn about the subject and almost half (49 percent) wanted to gain skills for career opportunities (Hara et al., 2013). There is a need for appropriate measures of MOOC success.

MOOC measures
The original handful of cMOOCs, and MIT and Stanford xMOOCs, respectively tended to offer content related to online learning and science. A few years later, in September 2014, the six organizations mentioned in the Introduction collectively offered almost 1800 MOOCs in over a dozen languages. Supply, an intuitive MOOC measure, spans university, vocational training and secondary school content today. Notwithstanding this, MOOCs continue to reflect their English-speaking, male dominated elite university origins (Emanuel, 2013). MOOC supply challenges include overcoming inclusion barriers such as language, gender, education, techno-socio-economic inequalities and physical disabilities.

Enrolment, such as Alison's 200 000 monthly enrolments and Coursera's 12 million total enrolments, reflects demand for the MOOC ideal. Diversity, skewed toward English-speaking males in first world countries, seems equally or more important than enrolment numbers. A review of almost 100 MOOCs showed participants from over 100 countries, led by the US at about 30 percent (Murphy et al., 2013). Participants ranged in age from about 10 to 80, most over 25, with the largest age cohort from 25 to 34. Gender, predominantly male, ranged from 88 percent male in an MIT MOOC to 87 percent female in Edinburgh's Equine Nutrition.

Regarding education, the same study showed participants were roughly equal across no higher education, a bachelor's degree and a postgraduate degree (Murphy et al., 2013). This tendency towards educated males from developed countries taking MOOCs may exacerbate rather than reduce educational inequalites (Emanuel, 2013). Yet some of the 150 000+ registrants from 194 countries in MIT's initial MOOC reported no higher education but performed well (DeBoer et al., 2013). Furthermore, a study of engaged rather than registered MOOC users showed 83 percent with at least a two-year degree, and an even higher percentage in countries that should reflect the MOOC ideal of universal access: Brazil, Russia, India, China and South Africa (Emanuel, 2013).

Learning analytics and engagement

Access to massive numbers of learners – formal and informal – which for now only MOOCs can provide has created a burgeoning teaching and learning research field. Learning analytics draws on student-generated data such as their Internet Protocol (IP) addresses, clickstreams, platform interactions, assignment scores, exam scores, discussion forum posts and eye-tracking (Breslow et al., 2013; Daniel, 2012; Ferguson and Clow, 2015; Sharma et al., 2015). Researchers are scratching the surface of this rich data, developing participant profiles and correlating MOOC activities with learning (DeBoer et al., 2013; Kizilcec et al., 2013; Koller et al., 2013; Wilkowski, 2014b). Learning analytics, learner styles and motivations help highlight engagement, a promising MOOC measure (DeBoer et al., 2013).

A study of 97 MOOCs – six MOOCs from the University of Edinburgh, two Harvard, two Google, one Duke and 86 Coursera MOOCs – illustrates large enrolments and decreasing engagement (Murphy et al., 2013). Registrants in a single MOOC ranged from almost 13 000 to 155 000. At least one in three registrants were lookers, not bookers, who logged in or watched a video after registering. Those submitting the first assessment ranged from 2 percent to 29 percent. And those earning a certificate ranged from almost 1 percent for Computer Science at Harvard to 13 percent with Google. These traditional measures assume that students seek a certificate and launch the discussion on appropriate MOOC measures (Koller et al., 2013).

Three studies draw on learning analytics to divide the participants into learner sub-populations based on engagement and highlight the role of S2S interaction. Two studies of participants in one Google and three Stanford MOOCs using a cognitive/behaviorist pedagogy found four similar clusters (Kizilcec et al., 2013; Wilkowski et al., 2014b). The least engaged cluster registered for the MOOC and did little else. At the other extreme of engagement were the participants that earned a certificate. The cluster solutions differed, however, in a study using participants in a MOOC with a predominantly constructivist pedagogy (Ferguson and Clow, 2015). The authors concluded that the constructivist pedagogy necessitated a seven-cluster solution that accounted for the increased S2S interaction.

A final approach draws on S2S interaction to categorize participants into passive, active and community contributors (Koller et al., 2013). Two types of community contribution, forum participation and peer assessment, resemble Bandura's (1978) reciprocal interaction and associate positively with achievement in xMOOCs (Cisel, 2014). In the MIT xMOOC, *Circuits and Electronics*, only 3 percent of all students participated in the discussion forum (Breslow et al., 2013). Yet over half those earning a certificate, 52 percent, were active on the forum.

4.   CHALLENGES AND FUTURE DIRECTIONS

MOOCs offer many opportunities and challenges. MOOCs exemplify the intrinsic motivations of natural learning, that is, learning a topic simply for personal interest (Armstrong, 2012). Diverse learners, such as adults who might not otherwise undertake further studies and secondary school students seeking a challenge, could sample an institution through its MOOCs. Based on their MOOC experience, these participants may then formalize studies with the institution or other institutions.

Hospitality and tourism employers can turn to MOOCs for employee development, 'giving existing workers skills can be cheaper than hiring new workers' (Dellarocas and Van Alstyne, 2013, p. 27). A survey of 103 employers found that 59 percent were prepared to recognize MOOCs in recruiting and 83 percent saw their organization using MOOCs for professional development (Radford et al., 2014). MOOCs broaden the available learning opportunities without the need for staff members to travel, often at the employer's expense, to undertake training.

As alluded to in previous sections, major MOOC challenges relate to perceiving MOOCs as traditional OCs and using traditional measures such as completion rates. Andrew Ng, who built and taught Stanford's inaugural MOOC, estimated that to reach the 100 000+ students in his MOOC he would have to teach his traditional class for 250 years (Friedman, 2012). Enrolment numbers, enrolment diversity, new students, positive press and fulfilling the university's community outreach mission are a few of the opportunities that MOOCs offer.

As MOOCs are free to participants, another challenge is how institutions offering MOOCs can recover their costs (Dellarocas and Van Alstyne, 2013). MOOC development costs, for example through edX, can reach $250 000 per course, with an additional $50 000 fee each time the course is offered (Kolowich, 2013). There are also the associated human resource costs to familiarize educators with the MOOC environment/technologies and to manage both the course and team of facilitation staff. The challenge in overcoming adoption barriers with existing faculty is an opportunity for institutes to develop specialist MOOC facilitator programs.

Consumers might pay for services complementing the course, such as formal certification and credit. Coursera charges from US$ 30–90 for its 'Signature Track' option (coursera.org/signature/guidebook), affirming the learner's identity, and if the learner passes all course requirements, linking to a verified certificate on a secure Coursera web page. Institutions that develop successful MOOCs could license them through education partnerships, saving licensees the up-front MOOC development costs (De Freitas, 2013).

MOOC providers could also develop and monetize their large learner databases. Paid seminars, specialized conferences, podcasts, dedicated YouTube channels, collaborative research and community outreach projects all seem potential opportunities. These databases should prove useful to other entities. Textbook publishers, for instance, would relish being the recommended text for a MOOC with tens of thousands registrants (Howard, 2012).

5. SUMMARY AND CONCLUSIONS

Similar to pioneering websites in the 1990s that were slow to download, and made visitors endure music and animated introductions in their quest for useful information nuggets, individual MOOCs are often boring and frustrating, with completion rates under 10 percent. Few MOOCs are a roaring success and some fail. For example, a Cornell School of Hospitality Administration's three-week *New Media Marketing* MOOC appears no longer to exist; Georgia Tech cancelled their *Fundamentals of Online Learning* MOOC mid-term, and the lead professor for a University of California MOOC quit midway through the term (Murphy et al., 2014). Rather than sound planning, 'bandwagon' and 'me too' effects may have driven some early institutional MOOC adopters (Grimmelmann, 2014).

5.1 Industry and Academic Implications

MOOC business models, accreditation schemes and their impact on and integration with higher education are huge unknowns today. As organizations late to adopt an innovation, such as MOOCs, may succeed while the early adopters may fail (Rogers, 2003), organizations should define successful MOOC implementation prior to MOOC adoption. The flipped classroom is a cautious implementation strategy, a consortium-developed MOOC is an ambitious strategy and exploring MOOC alternatives is a third strategy. Importantly, clear and measurable objectives are incumbent to any MOOC strategies.

In the *flipped classroom*, lecturers incorporate an existing MOOC into their traditional university class (Martin, 2012; Murphy et al., 2014). Rather than for lectures, class time is for discussing the MOOC content and homework. Instructors supplement the MOOC with readings and assessments. Passing students earn regular university credits and students that pass the MOOC also earn a certificate of participation. Easy and inexpensive for the instructor to implement, the flipped classroom gives students an added learning experience and certificate, often from a prestigious university.

Instructors, however, have no control over when a MOOC will run. MOOCs with fixed start dates limit the window of opportunity for potential learners and the fact that most MOOCs run just annually trims the window even more. Some MOOCs, however, such as Google's Internet 101 (educourses.withgoogle.com/101), have no fixed dates. Lecturers could use this three-week MOOC or other short, asynchronous, introductory MOOCs as a class prerequisite or opening module (Murphy et al., 2014). Similarly, lecturers could explore Alison's wealth of skill-based MOOCs rather than the knowledge-based MOOCs with providers such as Courera, edX and NovoEd.

The small, annual MOOC window is one of several arguments for hospitality and tourism collaboration. A MOOC consortium could benefit learners, institutions and lecturers. Multiple start dates across partner schools open the MOOC window of opportunity. The universities could share financial, intellectual and staff resources, while customizing their MOOC with regional and cultural considerations. A MOOC with multiple schools should appeal to textbook publishers and non-government organizations interested in the MOOC space. These non-university partners could contribute financial, intellectual and staff resources and help explore MOOC iterations. For example, SPOCs, Small Private Online Courses (Chauhan, 2014; Fox, 2013), could appeal to chain operations, destination management organizations and universities.

Lecturers, universities, tourism destinations and non-governmental organizations will want to offer a MOOC for different altruistic, financial and branding objectives. Yet without clarifying the objectives and operationalizing success, it seems a waste of time, resources and effort to initiate any MOOC strategy. And for any MOOC strategy, all parties – lecturers, universities and other collaborative organizations – should set the metrics prior to launching the MOOC and draw on learning analytics to measure MOOC implementation results.

5.2   Limitations and Future Research

Limitations to this chapter, a conceptual review rather than an empirical study, stem from the nascence of MOOCs. Less than a decade old, MOOCs may take decades of evolution for effective educator, administrator, organizational and student use. Historically, communication innovations such as the telephone, radio and television take about three decades to come of age (Fidler, 1997). Similarly, MOOC research is in its early stages, particularly in hospitality and tourism. Research, exploratory and descriptive, is often case studies or focuses on xMOOCs; cMOOC research is just emerging (Daniel, 2012; Liyanagunawardena et al., 2013). In addition to these challenging caveats, this chapter reviewed literature published in English, yet MOOCs are a global phenomenon.

Given the dawning of MOOC research, future research opportunities abound across all disciplines, including hospitality and tourism. MOOC types and extensions – Big Open Online Courses (BOOCs), Distributed Open Collaborative Course (DOCCs), Little Open Online Courses (LOOCs), Massive Open Online Research (MOOR) and Small Private Online Courses (SPOCs) (Chauhan, 2014; Fox, 2013) – are one such avenue. Harvard, for example, is boldly going with SPOCS, selecting the students and charging for three classes that, successfully mastered, could trigger admission to a Harvard MBA (hbx.hbs.edu/hbx-core/core-faqs.html).

MOOC design (curriculum, assessment and pedagogy) is another promising research area. Different learner styles, abilities and motivations necessitate viewing MOOCs beyond the cMOOC versus xMOOC duality. Learners need participatory skills to navigate a MOOC successfully (Beaven et al., 2014). MOOCs and Internet technology alter the focus of education away from the traditional pedagogical instructor model towards heutagogy, also known as self-determined learning (Beaven et al., 2014; Liyanagunawardena et al., 2013). MOOC assessment, including defining achievement and self-and-peer assessment, is another emerging pedagogical research area (Admiraal et al., 2014; Wilkowski et al., 2014a). Finally, the use of learning analytics could compare and measure the results of different pedagogical approaches.

The flipped classroom is another promising pedagogical research area. A US Department of State initiative launched in 2013, MOOC Camp (eca.state.gov/programs-initiatives/mooc-camp) combines blended learning, a combination of online and offline learning (Garrison and Kanuka, 2004; Bernard et al., 2014), and the flipped classroom, whereby students review online material prior to discussing that material in a classroom (Martin, 2012; Forsey et al., 2013). Hosted at public spaces globally, volunteers facilitate and help interested learners navigate a MOOC. In its first year, MOOC Camp hosted 4000 students in over 200 MOOCs across 65 locations. Unlike the 5–10 percent completion rates, 40–60 percent of the MOOC Camp learners completed a MOOC at most locations and over 80 percent in some locations.

Pedagogy aside, MOOCs' inherent nature hinders traditional measures of course success. A key MOOC advantage is that participants can drop in and out, ignoring traditional course completion expectations. Moreover, MOOCs offer a natural open, free and asynchronous registration process. Future research could explore MOOCs' psychological, emotional and fulfillment aspects on learners' lives as perhaps the ultimate value of a MOOC.

Learning analytics mine participants' digital trails to understand online learning processes (Breslow et al., 2013; Daniel, 2012; DeBoer et al., 2013; Wilkowski, 2014b). MOOCs offer researchers access to massive data sets that could help uncover and discover patterns of learning behaviors and characteristics. In gaining access to these data sets, institutions, governments and organizations alike could develop research outcomes that go well beyond what we know about the nature of human beings' desire to learn new knowledge.

Finally, exploratory business models abound but none work that well! As referred to in the chapter, MOOCs as business units or revenue streams remain a big question on the minds of most innovators and early adopters. MOOCs eventually could offer commercial benefits to an institution, through direct and indirect revenue streams as well as reducing costs. Research in this area, miniscule for now, seems instrumental for the future of MOOCs and MOOC iterations.

ACKNOWLEDGEMENTS

This chapter contains some updated and revised content from APacCHRIE, ENTER, World Research Summit for Tourism and Hospitality and TEFI 8 conference papers, and a 2014 *Journal of Hospitality and Tourism Education* article. The authors thank Jingjing Lin, PhD candidate at the Università della Svizzera italiana, for her contribution to Table 11.2.

REFERENCES

Admiraal, W., Huisman, B. and Van de Ven, M. (2014), 'Self-and Peer Assessment in Massive Open Online Courses', *International Journal of Higher Education*, **3** (3), 119–28.

Anderson, T. (2003), 'Getting the Mix Right Again: An Updated and Theoretical Rationale for Interaction', *International Review of Research in Open and Distance Learning*, **4** (2), 1–14.

Anderson, T. and Dron, J. (2011), 'Three Generations of Distance Education Pedagogy', *The International Review of Research in Open and Distance Learning*, **12** (3), 80–97.

Armstrong, J.S. (2012), 'Natural Learning in Higher Education', in N.M. Seel (ed.), *Encyclopedia of the Sciences of Learning* (pp. 2426–33), New York: Springer.

Bandura, A. (1978), 'The Self System in Reciprocal Determinism', *American Psychologist*, **33** (4), 344–58.

Beaven, T., Hauck, M., Comas-Quinn, A., Lewis, T. and De los Arcos, B. (2014), 'MOOCs: Striking the Right Balance between Facilitation and Self-Determination', *MERLOT Journal of Online Learning and Teaching*, **10** (1), 31–43.

Bernard, R.M., Borokhovski, E., Schmid, R.F., Tamim, R.M. and Abrami, P.C. (2014), 'A Meta-analysis of Blended Learning and Technology Use in Higher Education: From the General to the Applied', *Journal of Computing in Higher Education*, **26** (1), 87–122.

Bernard, R.M., Abrami, P.C., Borokhovski, E., Wade, C.A., Tamim, R.M., Surkes, M.A. and Bethel, E.C. (2009), 'A Meta-Analysis of Three Types of Interaction Treatments in Distance Education', *Review of Educational Research*, **79** (3), 1243–89.

Breslow, L., Pritchard, D., DeBoer, J., Stump, G., Ho, A. and Seaton, D. (2013), 'Studying Learning in the Worldwide Classroom: Research into edX's First MOOC', *Research & Practice in Assessment*, **8** (Summer), 13–25.

Bull, G., Thompson, A., Searson, M., Garofalo, J., Park, J., Young, C. and Lee, J. (2008), 'Connecting Informal and Formal Learning Experiences in the Age of Participatory Media', *Contemporary Issues in Technology and Teacher Education*, **8** (2).

Cantoni, L. and Tardini, S. (2006), *Internet,* London and New York: Routledge.

Cantoni, L. (2006), 'Educational Communication and the Case for ICTs, A Two Ways Route', *Studies in Communication Sciences*, **6** (2), 9–22.

Cantoni, L., Kalbaska, N. and Inversini, A. (2009), 'E-learning in Tourism and Hospitality: A Map', *Journal of Hospitality, Leisure, Sport and Tourism Education*, **8** (2), 148–56.

Carse, J.P. (1986), *Finite and Infinite Games: A Vision of Life as Play and Possibility*, Toronto: Random House.

CEC (2001), *The eLearning Action Plan: Designing Tomorrow's Education*, Communication from the Commission to the Council and the European Parliament, COM(2000) 318 Final, Brussels: European Commission.

Chauhan, A. (2014), 'Massive Open Online Courses (MOOCS): Emerging Trends in Assessment and Accreditation', *Digital Education Review*, **25**, 7–17.

Cisel, M. (2014), 'Analyzing Completion Rates in the First French xMOOC', paper presented at the *European MOOCs Stakeholders Summit*, Lausanne, Switzerland.

Daniel, J. (2012), 'Making Sense of MOOCs: Musings in a Maze of Myth, Paradox and Possibility', *Journal of Interactive Media in Education*, **(2012)** 3.

Daniel, J., Kanwar, A. and Uvalić-Trumbić, S. (2009), 'Breaking Higher Education's Iron Triangle: Access, Cost, and Quality', *Change: The Magazine of Higher Learning*, **41** (2), 30–35.

De Freitas, S. (2013), 'MOOCs: The Final Frontier for Higher Education?', July, Coventry University.

DeBoer, J., Stump, G., Seaton, D. and Breslow, L. (2013), 'Diversity in MOOC Students' Backgrounds and Behaviors in Relationship to Performance in 6.002 x', in *Proceedings of the Sixth Learning International Networks Consortium Conference*, Boston, MA.

Dellarocas, C. and Van Alstyne, M. (2013), 'Money Models for MOOCs', *Communications of the ACM*, **56** (8), 25–8.

DeWaard, I., Abajian, S.C., Gallagher, M.S., Hogue, R., Keskin, N.Ö., Koutropoulos, A. and Rodriguez, O.C. (2011), 'Using mLearning and MOOCs to Understand Chaos, Emergence, and Complexity in Education', *The International Review of Research in Open and Distance Learning*, **12** (7), 94–115.

Dolan, V.L.B. (2014), 'Massive Online Obsessive Compulsion: What Are They Saying Out There about the Latest Phenomenon in Higher Education?', *The International Review of Research in Open and Distance Learning*, **15** (2), 268–80.

Donner, J. (2008), 'Research Approaches to Mobile Use in the Developing World: A Review of the Literature', *The Information Society*, **24** (3), 140–59.

Downes, S. (2011), 'Connectivism and Connective Knowledge', *Huffington Post*, 25 May, accessed 1 October 2014 at http://www.huffingtonpost.com/stephen-downes/connectivism-and-connecti_b_804653.html.

Emanuel, E.J. (2013), 'Online Education: MOOCs Taken by Educated Few', *Nature*, **503** (7476), 342.

Ferguson, R. and Clow, D. (2015), 'Examining Engagement: Analysing Learner Subpopulations in Massive Open Online Courses (MOOCs)', paper presented at the 5th International Learning Analytics and Knowledge Conference, Poughkeepsie, USA.

Fidler, R.F. (1997), *Mediamorphosis: Understanding New Media*, Thousand Oaks, CA: Pine Forge Press.

Forsey, M., Low, M. and Glance, D. (2013), 'Flipping the Sociology Classroom: Towards a Practice of Online Pedagogy', *Journal of Sociology*, **49** (4), 471–85.

Fox, A. (2013), 'From MOOCs to SPOCs', *Communications of the ACM*, **56** (12), 38–40.

Friedman, T.L. (2012), 'Come the Revolution', *The New York Times*, 15 May, accessed 1 October 2014 at http://www.nytimes.com/2012/05/16/opinion/friedman-come-the-revolution.html.

Galloway, C. (2010), 'Vygotsky's Constructivism', in M. Orey (ed.), *Emerging Perspectives on Learning, Teaching, and Technology* (pp. 48–9), Zurich: Jacobs Foundation.

Garrison, D.R. and Kanuka, H. (2004), 'Blended Learning: Uncovering its Transformative Potential in Higher Education', *The Internet and Higher Education*, **7** (2), 95–105.

Gašević, D., Kovanović, V., Joksimović, S. and Siemens, G. (2014), 'Where is Research on Massive Open Online Courses Headed? A Data Analysis of the MOOC Research Initiative', *The International Review of Research in Open and Distance Learning*, **15** (5), 134–76.

Gee, J.P. (2003), 'What videogames have to teach us about learning and literacy', *Computers in Entertainment*, **1** (1), 20.

Grimmelmann, J. (2014), 'The Merchants of MOOCs', *44 Seton Hall Law Review*, accessed 1 October 2014 at http://digitalcommons.law.umaryland.edu/cgi/viewcontent.cgi?article=2433&context=fac_pubs.

Gumport, P.J. and Chun, M. (1999), *Technology and Higher Education: Opportunities and Challenges for the New Era*, National Center for Postsecondary Improvement, Stanford University, School of Education.

Hager, P. and Halliday, J.S. (2006), *Recovering Informal Learning: Wisdom, Judgement and Community*, Dordrecht: Springer.

Hara, T., Moskal, P. and Saarinen, C. (2013), 'Preliminary Analyses of a Cutting-Edge Knowledge Distribution Method of MOOC (Massive, Open, Online Course) to Teach Tourism as an Industry', paper presented at the 3rd International Conference on the Measurement and Economic Analysis of Regional Tourism, Medellin, Columbia.

Holmberg, B. (1995), 'The Evolution of the Character and Practice of Distance Education', Considerations for Web-based Learning with Real Events 31, *Open Learning*, **10** (2), 44–7.

Howard, J. (2012), 'Publishers See Online Mega-Courses as Opportunity to Sell Textbooks', *The Chronicle of Higher Education*, accessed 1 October 2014 at http://chronicle.com/article/Can-MOOCs-Help-Sell/134446/.

Jordan, K. (2014), 'Initial Trends in Enrolment and Completion of Massive Open Online Courses', *The International Review of Research in Open and Distance Learning*, **15** (1), 133–59.

Kalbaska, N. (2012), 'Travel Agents and Destination Management Organizations: eLearning as a Strategy to Train Tourism Trade Partners', *Journal of Information Technology & Tourism*, **13** (1), 1–12.

Kapp, K.M. (2012), *The Gamification of Learning and Instruction: Game-based Methods and Strategies for Training and Education*, San Francisco: Pfeiffer.

Kim, B. (2010), 'Social Constructivism', in M. Orey (ed.), *Emerging Perspectives on Learning, Teaching, and Technology* (pp. 55–61), Zurich: Jacobs Foundation.

Kizilcec, R.F., Piech, C. and Schneider, E. (2013), 'Deconstructing Disengagement: Analyzing Learner Subpopulations in Massive Open Online Courses', paper presented at the *Third International Conference on Learning Analytics and Knowledge*, LAK 2013, Leuven, Belgium.

Klobas, J.E., Mackintosh, B. and Murphy, J. (2014), 'The Anatomy of MOOCs', in P. Kim (ed.), *Massive Open Online Courses: The MOOC Revolution* (Chapter 1), New York: Routledge.

Koller, D., Ng, A., Do, C. and Chen, Z. (2013), 'Retention and Intention in Massive Open Online Courses', *Educause Review*, **48** (3), 62–3.

Kolowich, S. (2013), 'Why Some Colleges are Saying No to MOOC Deals, at Least for Now', *The Chronicle of Higher Education*, 29 April, accessed 8 August 2014 at http://chronicle.com/article/Why-Some-Colleges-Are-Saying/138863/.

Kop, R. and Hill, A. (2008), 'Connectivism: Learning Theory of the Future or Vestige of the Past?', *The International Review of Research in Open and Distance Learning*, **9** (3), 1–13.

Kuttainen, C. and Lexhagen, M. (2012), 'Overcoming Barriers to SME E-Commerce Adoption using Blended Learning: A Swedish Action Research Case Study', *Journal of Information Technology & Tourism*, **13** (1), 13–26.

Lewin, T. (2013), 'Public Universities to Offer Free Online Classes for Credit', *The New York Times*, 23 January, accessed 1 October 2014 at http://www.nytimes.com/2013/01/23/education/public-universities-to-offer-free-online-classes-for-credit.html.

Liyanagunawardena, T.R., Adams, A.A. and Williams, S.A. (2013), 'MOOCs: A Systematic Study of the Published Literature 2008–2012', *The International Review of Research in Open and Distance Learning*, **14** (3), 202–27.

Martin, F.G. (2012), 'Will Massive Open Online Courses Change How We Teach?', *Communications of the ACM*, **55** (8), 26–8.

McCallum, S. (2012), 'Gamification and Serious Games for Personalized Health', *Proceedings of the 9th International Conference on Wearable Micro and Nano Technologies for Personalized Health*, pHealth.

McGuire, J. and Furniss, M.J. (2000), *Cognitive-behavioural Approaches: An Introduction to Theory and Research*, London: United Kingdom Home Office Communication Directorate.

Miralbell, O., Cantoni L. and Kalbaska, N. (2014), *The Role of e-learning Applications within the Tourism Sector*, ELC Research Paper Series, 1–68.

Murphy, J. (2012), 'LMS Teaching Versus Community Learning: A Call for the Latter', *Asia Pacific Journal of Marketing and Logistics*, **25** (5), 826–41.

Murphy, J., Brogan, P.J., Do, C., Williams, A. and Horton-Tognazzini, L. (2013), 'MOOCs and MOOC Measures', paper presented at the *World Research Summit for Tourism and Hospitality: Crossing the Bridge*, Orlando.

Murphy, J., Kalbaska, N., Williams, A., Ryan, P., Cantoni, L. and Horton-Tognazzini, L. (2014), 'Massive Open Online Courses: Strategies and Research Areas', *Journal of Hospitality and Tourism Education*, **26** (1), 39–43.

Negash, S. and Wilcox, M.V. (2008), 'E-learning Classifications: Differences and Similarities', in S. Negash, M. Whitman, A. Woszczynski, K. Hoganson and H. Mattord (eds), *Handbook of Distance Learning for Real-Time and Asynchronous Information Technology Education* (pp. 1–23), Hershey, PA: IGI Global.

Ong, W.J. (2012), *Orality and Literacy: The Technologizing of the Word*, New York: Routledge.

Pappano, L. (2012), 'Year of the MOOC', *The New York Times*, 2 November, accessed 1 October at http://www.nytimes.com/2012/11/04/education/edlife/massive-open-online-courses-are-multiplying-at-a-rapid-pace.html.

Peters, O. (2003), *Distance Education in Transition: New Trends and Challenges*, 3rd edn, Oldenburg: BIS.

Piccoli, G., Brohman, M.K., Watson, R.T. and Parasuraman, A. (2004), 'Net-Based Customer Service Systems: Evolution and Revolution in Web Site Functionalities', *Decision Sciences*, **35** (3), 423–55.

Prensky, M. (2006), *Don't Bother Me Mom – I'm Learning!* St Paul: Paragon House Publishers.

Radford, A.W., Robles, J., Cataylo, S., Horn, L., Thornton, J. and Whitfield, K.E. (2014), 'The Employer Potential of MOOCs: A Mixed-methods Study of Human Resource Professionals' Thinking on MOOCs', *The International Review of Research in Open and Distance Learning*, **15** (5), 1–25.

Reich, J. and Ho, A.D. (2014), 'The Tricky Task of Figuring Out What Makes a MOOC Successful', *The Atlantic*, 14 January, accessed 1 October 2014 at http://www.theatlantic.com/education/archive/2014/01/the-tricky-task-of-figuring-out-what-makes-a-mooc-successful/283274/.

Rogers, E.M. (2003), *Diffusion of Innovations* (5th edn), New York: Simon & Schuster.

Ross, J., Sinclair, C., Knox, J., Bayne, S. and Macleod, H. (2014), 'Teacher Experiences and Academic Identity: The Missing Components of MOOC Pedagogy', *MERLOT Journal of Online Learning and Teaching*, **10** (1), 56–68.

Sharma, K., Caballero, D., Verma, H., Jermann, P. and Dillenbourg, P. (2015), 'Looking AT versus Looking THROUGH: A Dual Eye-tracking study in MOOC Context', paper presented at Computer Supported Collaborative Learning, 7–11 June, Gothenburg, Sweden.

Siemens, G. (2012), 'MOOCs are Really a Platform', in G. Siemens (ed.), ELEARNSPACE.

Sigala, M. (2002), 'The Evolution of Internet Pedagogy: Benefits for Tourism and Hospitality Education', *Journal of Hospitality, Leisure, Sport & Tourism Education*, **1** (2), 29–45.

Traxler, J. (2009), 'Learning in a mobile age', *International Journal of Mobile and Blended Learning*, **1** (1), 1–12.

Watters, A. (2012), 'Top 10 Ed-Tech Startups of 2012', in A. Watters (ed.), *Hack Education*.

Wilkowski, J. (2013), 'A Comparison of Five Google Online Courses', 5 September, accessed 1 October 2014 at http://googleresearch.blogspot.ch/2013/09/a-comparison-of-five-google-online.html.

Wilkowski, J., Deutsch, A. and Russell, D.M. (2014b), 'Student Skill and Goal Achievement in the Mapping with Google MOOC', paper presented at the first ACM Conference on *Learning@ scale*, 4–5 March, Atlanta, GA.

Wilkowski, J., Russell, D.M. and Deutsch, A. (2014a), 'Self-evaluation in Advanced Power Searching and Mapping with Google MOOCs', paper presented at the first ACM Conference on *Learning@ scale*, 4–5 March, Atlanta, GA..

Williams, R., Karousou, R. and Mackness, J. (2011), 'Emergent Learning and Learning Ecologies in Web 2.0', *The International Review of Research in Open and Distance Learning*, **12** (3), 39–59.

12 ePortfolio task design: a high-impact tool for higher education teaching in tourism
Claudia Mössenlechner

1. INTRODUCTION AND BACKGROUND

Industry-wide benchmarking, establishing destination networks and relationships, online social networking and skills augmentation are vital drivers for the economic growth of the tourism industry (Braun and Hollick, 2006). Tourism is a sector of small and micro tourism enterprises (SME) which, in the European economy, contribute about 10 per cent of the annual GDP. In today's economy small and micro tourism enterprises are facing enormous challenges when it comes to their capability to compete with large tourism enterprises. On the one hand, consumers' planning and buying behaviour has profoundly changed, with the search for travel information and booking ranking amongst the most popular online activities worldwide. At the same time, tourism providers have changed the ways in which they design, promote, package and sell their products and services (European Commission, 2015).

This push towards the use of information and communication technologies (ICT) and Internet-based business environments put small businesses under severe pressure. Not only do these different settings change customer relations and benefits, but they also extend the needs for business and digital skills applied at both the strategic and operational levels to meet the expectations of an international tourism market.

Additionally, the multicultural tourism workplace and the inherently international nature of the tourism industry require a knowledgeable workforce that can collaborate irrespective of cultural–communicative differences (Sigala, 2002; Christou, 1999), make use of e-business applications and digital skills, and draw on the growing mergers and alliances among tourism companies and destinations. This can only be done by embracing ICT and the Internet. However, in the literature, there is consensus that industry preparedness in tourism is low in terms of skills and training for an ICT-driven sector (Evans et al., 2001; Braun and Hollick, 2006). This is especially true for small and micro enterprises that are usually restricted in resources and the number of skilled employees. For higher education this implies that students need to become versed in the use of technologies during their studies and that the purposeful use of technology for studying and teaching is at the same time a way to increase employability in the tourism sector. Integrating ePortfolio work in their teaching can help tourism educators to do exactly that.

The term 'ePortfolio' is most often defined as digitally documented collections of work (artefacts) including text-based, graphic or multi-media elements that are also available online (Lorenzo and Ittelson, 2005; Hornung-Praehauser et al., 2007; Barrett, 2010). The use of a web-based interface allows the user to make the ePortfolio available to a broad audience. The purpose of ePortfolios in higher education ranges from composing repositories of learning, to creating alternative assessment procedures, to designing a showcase of students' work for multiple audiences. Currently, more than 50 per cent of US colleges and universities are making use of ePortfolios of some form (Eynon et al., 2014). In comparison with North America, the history of the ePortfolio movement in Europe is relatively short and has taken a rather distinct focus on developing academic skills and generic, multi-disciplinary competencies. This is mainly due to the educational reform discourse in Europe, which focuses on stronger alignment of curricula and potential occupational areas. Strategies to achieve this include encouraging competency-oriented learning cultures and assessment procedures, as well as putting a strong emphasis on self-organized learning skills (Albert, 2008; Richter, 2008). In the literature, these developments are reflected in discussions on informal, formal and integrative learning and assessment and on the extent to which social software, educational technologies and ePortfolios do connect or, indeed, overlap (Eynon et al., 2014; Bryant and Chittum, 2013).

An increasingly growing motivator for European ePortfolio work in higher education is the Europortfolio project, which is funded with support from the European Commission as part of its Lifelong Learning Programme (Europäisches Parlament & Rat, 2006). This has to be seen in the context of the Europortfolio Initiative, which aims at becoming a single framework for European citizens to present their qualifications, skills and competencies (European Institute for E-Learning, 2014). Currently, many universities are in the stage of incorporating integrative, cross-curriculum ePortfolio programmes that intend to portray the competencies and skills a student has developed over the years (Bryant and Chittum, 2013). In Europe, this also becomes visible in the growing number of nation-specific chapters and universities joining the Europortfolio programme (European Network of ePortfolio Experts and Practitioners, 2014).

Currently, most research on *pedagogy* and ePortfolios focuses on the possible effects of ePortfolio work on the development of reflective skills in students and portfolio work as a means of (alternative) assessment. Although there has been considerable emphasis in research in defining and describing ePortfolio practice (Bryant and Chittum, 2013), it is noteworthy that relatively little attention has been given to the various possibilities of using ePortfolios as effective teaching tools, particularly in higher education. This also goes for higher education in tourism, where there has been a considerable emphasis on the discussion on developing a common body of knowledge, but very little has so far been said about teaching practice in the tourism sector (Stergiou, 2005).

In their literature review on ePortfolio effectiveness, Bryant and Chittum (2013) reveal that ePortfolio work can be a powerful tool for learning and can make great contributions to students' success when properly implemented. However, they also note a danger of looking at ePortfolio work as a 'cure-all' concept rooting in 'instances of enthusiasm overstepping what is known about a concept' (Bryant and Chittum, 2013: 196) and call for allowing ePortfolio projects to undergo a deeper maturation process. In the current context, this suggests that some preoccupation of researchers with what portfolio work can potentially trigger in terms of student learning seems to overwhelm issues related to ePortfolio pedagogy in terms of task design and learning goals. Or, in other words, the question of how to teach through ePortfolios has been overshadowed by a focus on the various functions of portfolio work as well as by the effects it can have on student learning. Moreover, although the number of tertiary tourism education institutions using technology and Internet tools is growing, only a few are looking at the possible value these tools can provide in terms of extending, or in fact developing, their pedagogical models

(Sigala, 2005) to further narrow the gap between the tourism industry and the education sector.

2.   EPORTFOLIO: CONCEPTS AND PRACTICE

The fact that the ePortfolio community is very diverse and includes students, faculty, researchers, instructional designers as well as external stakeholders might explain the lack of a consistent, common language used across the community (Rhodes et al., 2014). Different aims and diverse concepts of ownership make a common set of descriptors of ePortfolio work difficult at times. This becomes apparent when looking for a common definition of ePortfolios in higher education. By looking at ePortfolios as mere digital repositories of accomplishments, student learning as a core element of ePortfolio work is somewhat neglected because the ePortfolio is reduced to the visible end-product, rather than taking into account that ePortfolio work comprises the intentional goal of the student to make developmental steps of learning explicit and, mostly, by the element of choice, the student documents a personal reflection process throughout these learning stages. Although the research community has taken the product-process aspects of ePortfolio work into account, it is mostly the product- or evidence-based view that is emphasized in discussions on perceptions and attitudes towards ePortfolio work in higher education (Bryant and Chittum, 2013; Rhodes et al., 2014).

Gallagher and Poklop (2014: 12) identify four distinct types of ePortfolios that are 'distinguishable by purpose and audience' and include the type of evidence items and tasks involved:

1. *Process Portfolios*, including the evidence item (final product) as well as 'process artefacts' (Gallagher and Poklop, 2014: 12) like drafts taken and a final reflection.
2. *Showcase Portfolios* as semester-capstone projects, including edited texts, process artefacts and reflections.
3. *Reflective Portfolios* as semester-capstone projects, including in-depth, self-guided semester reflections and sometimes work samples.
4. *Project Portfolios* where the portfolio platform is the main workspace and where students develop a 'type of web-site' (Gallagher and Poklop, 2014: 12) rather than a single piece of evidence item.

Tasks involved in ePortfolio work are often linked to special software and digital tools with the purpose of enhancing the learning process. Evidence items can include samples of work that include tasks and activities like writing, doing research and reflections in form of text, photos, videos and so on. Increasingly ePortfolios also contain observations and feedback by student peers, instructors and, in fact, employers (Barrett, 2010; 2004–08). Sherman (2006) summarizes 11 different ways in which electronic portfolios can be used in education and that exemplify the added value in ePortfolio work, as outlined in Table 12.1.

It must not be overlooked that, in the course of the increasing use of ICTs and the growing development of university Learning Management Systems, the opportunities and potentials for broadening the audience for ePortfolios and, in fact, including feedback

Table 12.1   Uses of ePortfolios

Purpose	Added Value
Goal-setting as a way of instructional scaffolding.	By clearly outlining a task and articulating what is expected of students when fulfilling the task, instructors provide a clear sample of the single steps that are needed to reach a learning goal. This in itself gives learners a direction on comprehensive goal-setting and the processes involved in reaching a learning goal.
Artefact creation as meaningful context.	A focal point is on the creation of artefacts as a process that includes having to capture the essence of a task and communicate it by digitally creating something to be included in the ePortfolio. This becomes a concrete context for learning and applying a broad range of skills and competences.
Practice with a purpose.	ePortfolios give students the opportunity to work on their digital skills and literacy in a purposeful context.
Examples and non-examples.	ePortfolios provide easy access to relevant content for learning. Students can work on both knowledge and procedural skills by accessing content.
Assessment.	Through portfolio requirement criteria and examples (see above) students implicitly learn what quality assessment criteria are about. This will help learners to specifically relate to their own items, assess their own work and develop their own standards.
Reflection.	The student's review of the learning process and 'closure experience within the instructional element' enhances the student's knowledge on individual learning processes.
Communication.	Integrated communication features in ePortfolio management systems allow collaborative learning and immediate feedback.
Instructor planning and management tool.	ePortfolio management systems are at the same time management tools for learner-centred, instructional processes.
Learner organization tool.	The ePortfolio management system or platform allows students to see 'the big picture'. At the same time it represents a way to model organized ways to manage projects.
Interdisciplinary teaching and learning.	ePortfolios are often repositories of cross-curricular coursework, allowing students to integrate personal and field experience.
Historical records and stories as role models.	Through their ePortfolio work, students leave an official record of their work and learning experience and achievement behind. These records can help other, novice, students.

Source: Based on Sherman (2006).

other than from the instructor, can yet again change the very nature of ePortfolio work. By adding interactive communication tools and direct access to the Internet in ePortfolio systems or platforms, the ePortfolio becomes a 'workspace' (Barrett, 2010) including possibilities for digital conversation and interaction with multiple audiences. These additional capabilities imply a different kind of approach in terms of how to make full use of these features and their pedagogical potential.

According to Barrett, 'the real value of an e-portfolio is in the reflection and learning that is documented therein, not just the collection of work' (Barrett, 2010: 6). Barrett (2010) has suggested a broad typology of ePortfolios, that is, *Showcase* (with the primary purpose of accountability or showcase) and *Workspace* (with the primary purpose of immediate reflection on learning processes) Portfolios.

This becomes especially relevant when looking at the audiences of student ePortfolios. At first glance, one might only think of the educator who is also responsible for evaluating the students' work. However, a second glance reveals that ePortfolio audiences are usually much broader, including possible future employers, student peers, field experts and lecturers from other fields or educational institutes (Gallagher and Poklop, 2014). Gallagher and Poklop (2014) succinctly call the skill to address and negotiate needs of authentic, specific and/or multiple audiences' needs and expectations a vital skill for students. The skill includes, amongst other things, the ability to adapt, register and structure the use of visuals and contextualization and explanation of contents (Gallagher and Poklop, 2014: 13). Taking into account that information technologies in general and online social networking activities in particular will play a crucial role in commercial online interactions in tourism (Kasavana et al., 2010), the ability to address diverse audiences becomes highly relevant.

Depending on the main purpose and the audience of the ePortfolio, it can become a flexible tool to engage multiple audiences. Therefore, the use of web-based interfaces and open source tools and ICTs makes ePortfolios increasingly interactive and dynamic. ePortfolios are a *process, product and dynamic communication tool for multiple audiences* (see Figure 12.1). ePortfolio projects in higher education always include interactivity in terms of face-to-face communication in the form of coursework or course tutorials, and/or other forms of interactivity such as feedback from (multiple) audiences in the form of discussion forums, blogs or other forms of posts. Other forms of online interactivity include both synchronous and asynchronous communication with multiple audiences as well as some form of intercommunication with content in the form of text, sound, screencasts, visuals, games and simulations (cf. O'Donoghue, 2006: 72).

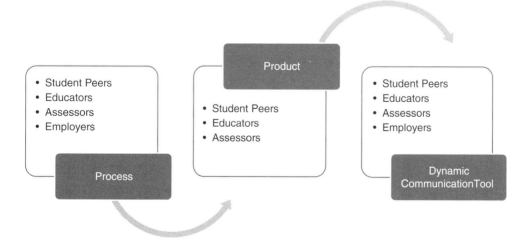

Figure 12.1   Typology of ePortfolios for multiple audiences

The differentiation between 'process', 'product' and 'dynamic communication tool' is important as it allows the educator to focus on each of the three determining elements when designing learning tasks, when deciding which audience to include, when choosing or creating digital environments and tools, both commercial and open source, and when assessing ePortfolio work. For the student, on the other hand, the question of which audience to address and the type of dynamic communication tool, does have far-reaching implications in the attempt to create evidence items for ePortfolio work.

3.   THE EPORTFOLIO TEACHING SPACE

The use of ICTs for teaching increasingly provides higher education with enhanced opportunities for knowledge construction, representation and communication. Essentially, technologies facilitate what Jonassen (1996) called 'turning computers into *mind tools*' when he analysed technology and the way it changes individual approaches to problem solving. Jonassen was quite succinct in stating that 'students cannot use mind tools as learning strategies without thinking deeply about what they are studying' (Jonassen, 1996: 1). In the literature on ePortfolios in higher education this view is somewhat reflected in a number of articles on the added value in ePortfolio work generated by building on students' reflective skills, creativity and self-study skills (Hamp-Lyons and Condon, 2000; Hartnell-Young and Morriss, 2007; O'Keeffe and Donnelly, 2013; Bryant and Chittum, 2013). Moreover, in an ePortfolio environment, students can individually work on developing digital skills as a set of '21st Century Skills' (Bryant and Chittum, 2013: 196), which students in higher education will need upon graduation. This is also especially relevant for students of tourism, as working with digital media and in online communities will also increase their employability and career readiness for the field.

When we define the use of mind tools as a way to design teaching and learning processes where the delineation of knowledge and learning for a specific audience is absolutely essential for the learning process itself, it becomes clear that ePortfolio work aims at triggering exactly these effects. It now becomes evident that, building on the three broad types of ePortfolios outlined earlier, educators in higher education are operating at the interface of various 'spaces' that influence them when designing frameworks and *tasks* for ePortfolios. This means that educators and instructional designers need to consider:

- the teaching and learning goals the ePortfolio work should address and which are part of the curriculum;
- the students' needs in terms of academic and professional skills and abilities that should be developed;
- the type of ePortfolio (Process/Product/Dynamic Communication Tool) and the audiences involved;
- the ePortfolio infrastructure.

The interface of these four factors determines the *ePortfolio Teaching Space*, as shown in Figure 12.2.

The ePortfolio Teaching Space is marked by an element of 'opportunity' as it describes vital components of the students' learning environment in which learning through

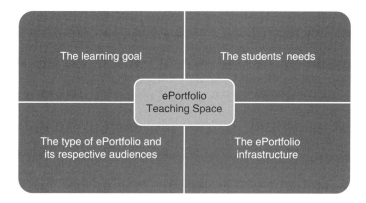

Source: Adapted from Mössenlechner (2012, p. 91).

Figure 12.2   The ePortfolio Teaching Space

engagement is intended to take place. Taking the complexity of the ePortfolio Teaching Space into account, it becomes apparent that ePortfolio task planning is not an easy task for educators.

4.   EPORTFOLIO AND PEDAGOGICAL TOOL

The literature describes numerous didactic procedures for planning, observing and using activities and tasks that promote learning. All didactic procedures, however, refer to three main criteria that are critical in the instructional setting: the mode of input, output and interaction. In the present context, the mode of *input* for ePortfolio work can take the form of in-course lectures, reading or, in abstract terms, by simply providing students with (digital) material and resources for self-study work. *Output* or production takes the abstract form of a (collaborative) task given to students. *Interaction* can be structured according to various patterns and involves the various audiences, that is, instructor/student(s); student(s)/student(s); student/external stakeholder; student/computer or material. It is important to understand, however, that in all of these procedures the instructor makes a (prior) decision about what the content or skills focus should be. Therefore, any teaching activity also reflects a syllabus (Mössenlechner, 2012). In this sense, all *teaching is an overt or covert way to intervene in the process of learning.*

In their essence, all pedagogic approaches suggest formative designs for teaching and learning that are based on a theory of learning. Pedagogic approaches become visible in the way knowledge is constructed, in how learners engage in learning processes through task design and discussion and in how the outcomes of learning are recorded and assessed. These pedagogic elements are also visible in ePortfolio work in higher education.

Following constructivist learning theories, where knowledge is acquired by meta-cognitive processes in which the learner is looking for and making connections to make meaning and integrate new knowledge in existing schemata, the active engagement of the learner is vital to reach a *state of knowing*, rather than static knowledge (Kafai and

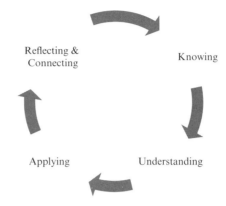

Source: Mössenlechner (2012, p. 84).

Figure 12.3   The learning loop

Resnick, 1996; Gagnon and Collay, 2006). This process can be compared with a continuous learning loop (see Figure 12.3) where the student is constantly going back and forth
from the state of knowing to understanding to applying to reflecting (Mössenlechner,
2012). The learning loop describes *goal states* in terms of pedagogical goals (cf. also
Bloom's taxonomy of educational goals, Bloom, 1956; Anderson et al., 2001) and, in
contrast to Bloom's educational goals, they are non-hierarchical and not static in nature.
In ePortfolio work that uses knowledge states in the learning loop as pedagogical *goal
states*, students are given the opportunity to acquire and apply knowledge and skills in
contexts relevant to their education. At the same time, they are required to actively engage
in personal understanding and experience.

Here, through tasks that are aligned to goal states, the ePortfolio as such becomes a
catalyst for learning in its entirety and serves as a learning hub *and* pedagogical tool. By
this, a shift can occur, where learning becomes a constructivist, self-managed process that
is fostered and supported by the teacher in an attempt to teach indirectly, that is, through
the ePortfolio task.

So far, the literature has looked at the process of learning and the planning thereof also in
the context of portfolio work (Korthagen, 2001; Barrett, 2004–08; Eynon et al., 2014). But
there appears to be a gap in research when it comes to the contextualization and task formation as an operative and *indirect teaching activity* in that a student task always reflects the
content and the skills that are being taught as well as the teaching and learning philosophy
applied. In other words, the representation of knowledge through a task becomes essential
for the construction of knowledge or skills-building that is targeted in a task.

4.1   Exploring the Link Between the Learning Loop and Portfolio Tasks

Although ePortfolio assignments offer a variety of possible pedagogical and (extra-)
curricular focuses, ePortfolio task design grounded in learning theory or on ePortfolio
work and learning outcomes (Bryant and Chittum, 2013) is under-researched. Sherman

(2006) also observes that 'discussion about the general instructional nature of ePortfolios only focuses on two distinct roles i.e. portfolios as a means of assessing specific student performance, and portfolios as a showcase for outstanding student accomplishments' (Sherman, 2006: 1).

However, ePortfolios are not only intended to display students' work and there is a need to re-focus on the dynamic process of learning that the tasks can trigger. It is not only about documenting the achievement of learning outcomes – it is the process the student engages in that adds value to Portfolio work. ePortfolios can provide a digital space for processing tasks that, ideally, lead to in-depth learning experiences which are evidenced in artefacts.

If we use the learning loop shown in Figure 12.3 as a main reference for developing an extended framework for task design within the ePortfolio Teaching Space (Figure 12.2) in which the use of ICTs is looked at as a way to provide mind tools (Jonassen, 1996) for learning to students, we can identify different ways in which ePortfolio tasks can be used as indirect teaching tools, as shown in Table 12.2.

This leads us to develop an integrative approach to using ePortfolio tasks as both *mind tools* to enhance student learning and teaching tools to indirectly teach and support students to achieve the desired goal state. By providing a concrete, goal-state-oriented and creation-oriented context and task, the instructor gives a clear direction with regard to the ePortfolio assignment and assessment.

Table 12.2   Learning loop and active engagement

Tasks that give student the opportunity to actively engage in the creation of a task to reach the knowledge state of:	Through task design, students may get the opportunity:
Knowing & Understanding	To use prior declarative knowledge or skills; to (re-) structure and organize declarative knowledge; to identify and read; to internalize; to respond and engage in a discussion; to negotiate meaning; to contextualize the understanding of the task; to compare abstract knowledge and reason for/against or comment on something critically; to construct explicit, new knowledge
Applying	To analyse and/or solve a problem in that they apply theories and schemes and abstract knowledge they have; to deduct or recognize connections and relationships with actual business practice in the field of tourism; to transfer knowledge; to infer and interpret from information; to discuss a business problem in a given context by building a clear line of argumentation; to communicate in a variety of contexts; to apply skills and abilities relevant to the tourism sector (e.g. intercultural skills, people skills, technological skills)
Reflecting & Connecting	To synthesize declarative and procedural knowledge and prior knowledge; to connect theory and tourism business; to reflect on learning by stating clear criteria, norms and knowledge; to critically reflect on the task using qualitative and quantitative criteria

4.2   The Impact of Task Design

As outlined earlier, ePortfolios are mainly used to support learner autonomy, organization, progress and professional skills development in that the ePortfolio provides evidence of these outcomes. It is often emphasized that ePortfolios are planned and designed by the student who, through choosing which elements to include in the ePortfolio, and by reflecting on the work that has been included, is taking full ownership of the work done. These notions are also heavily reflected in literature on ePortfolio research (Bryant and Chittum, 2013). However, literature and practice examples of ePortfolio work in higher education do not discuss the various ways in which learning outcomes are influenced or, in fact, *controlled* when single, explicitly formulated tasks for ePortfolio work are given to students. This is usually done in cases where students compile ePortfolios for an individual course and are often not given a choice about what to include. In contrast, students must provide evidence of a single task for course-based assessment and reflect on their evidence for presentation. It can be argued that in such cases, research outcomes related to pedagogy and the achievement of learning outcomes or task design as a means of indirect teaching would also apply in the case of explicit ePortfolio task design. However, given the dynamic nature of ePortfolios, the integration of professional skills development, and the various audiences the ePortfolio will target, a degree of complexity is added to such tasks that not only affects task assessment, but also influences the *task design*. Therefore, the conceptual framework for ePortfolio task design is complex in nature and includes the following dimensions (see Figure 12.4):

1. the goal-state targeting a specific knowledge state;
2. the opportunities the context of the task provides for (professional) skills development;
3. the opportunity the task provides in terms of creativity and digital skills development;
4. the feedback and assessment mode.

Figure 12.4   ePortfolio task design

Even when students are given the element of choice regarding what to include as evidence, the aforementioned dimensions of ePortfolio task design are relevant as they determine the success of teaching indirectly, that is, through the task. The dimensions of task design might also influence the choice the student makes in the selection process of evidence items. Therefore, the dimensions for ePortfolio task design are of paramount importance as they clearly delineate the content and skills focuses, as well as the opportunities for task fulfilment. Students will only learn meaningfully in so far as task design cultivates that.

4.3   ePortfolio Assessment

ePortfolio processes are not complete or may not lead to the desired learning outcome unless they are aligned with appropriate assessment strategies. In fact, the assessment processes and criteria can in themselves guide the learning processes of students. According to Gibbs (2004), students in schools are more likely to perceive a course as worthwhile when it includes grading and assessment. Additionally, carefully streamlining assessment strategies with future employability and learning can increase student engagement (Knight and Yorke, 2003).

In higher education, ePortfolios have always been used as a tool for self-reflection, assessment and evaluation. The artefacts students provide offer the possibility to measure what students have mastered and what it is they have to further work on, that is, where students have shortcomings when it comes to university standards and learning goals and overarching skills and abilities. ePortfolios are used for both formative (throughout a course of study) and summative (as a capstone project at the end of a programme) assessment tools. In any case, artefacts must relate to specified performance criteria, with each performance criterion described in a rubric which explains the degree to which the criterion is met. Providing students with a specific task as well as the assessment measure (rubric) beforehand will give the students directions in putting their work together, as well as providing them with standard (academic) criteria on which their work will be assessed. This does not exclude the possibility of giving students the freedom of choice when it comes to the format of their work.

In the context of ePortfolio work in higher tourism education, an alignment of university assessment strategies with the requirements of the industry seems to be indispensable. Some universities, especially in the UK (European Network of ePortfolio Experts and Practitioners, 2014), have already begun formative assessment of learning as opposed to single course assessment. This also points to an overarching approach to assess overall learning rather than merely assessing single learning outcomes, or, as Gibbs (2004) put it, moving from an 'assessment for grading' philosophy to 'assessment for learning'. However, commonly accepted rubrics to assess generic skills, abilities or competencies relevant for the tourism sector remain to be formulated. Given the nature of the tourism business fields, a distinct focus on communication and people skills, intercultural skills and interdisciplinary abilities will be valuable. Furthermore, links with the industry could be tightened by involving business professionals in the development of rubrics targeting key employability skills.

In Europe, this also affects assessment procedures for ePortfolio work as outcome-based assessment and employability skills are an overarching goal for the European

Lifelong Learning Programme. An example of how this affects assessment for ePortfolio work is the newly developed Europortfolio Maturity Matrix, which tries to combine the spaces of learning, working and social interaction. Recently (2014) a Competency Recognition Framework in the form of Open Badges (cf. European Network of ePortfolio Experts and Practitioners, 2014) was suggested and added to the matrix. Open Badges are 'badged credentials', a visual recognition of the professional and social skills and abilities that students are awarded in the course of their ePortfolio work. Open Badges include metadata such as, for example, the identity of the badge issuer, the criteria the badge holder met as well as the date of issue. In contrast, mere 'Digital Badges' are image files without any metadata available. Both types of badges are managed and hosted online. They are usually made visible on the site where they were earned, usually a third-party badge-issuing platform, but can easily be transferred to other platforms or repositories including social networking platforms, websites, job sites and more. To date, badging platforms are usually cloud-based and systems normally include tracking and metadata functions. Some European and Australian universities have recently started to create their own ePortfolio badges to recognize students' achievements (for example the University of Notre Dame, Curtin University, Deakin University). This is in itself a way to motivate students and give feedback for individual, outstanding work. Career pathways can easily be established as Open Badges can serve as indicators for students' achievement levels for the industry. Developing Open Badges and standards *together with* the tourism industry could be seen as an opportunity to promote industry links further and increase work placements and work-related learning for students. At the same time, the involvement of the industry will lead to what Barrett (2004–08) calls a 'culture of evidence' in academic institutions.

However, bearing in mind the multitude of badges that have already been developed by various universities (see above) and, for example, the Mozilla Foundation, there is a danger of creating an 'oversupply' of reference systems that are not easily understood and that can be a burden to existing application management systems the industry has in place. This becomes all the more relevant when we remind ourselves of the international character of the tourism industry. On the other hand an opportunity for both higher tourism education and the tourism industry may arise where, by means of a jointly developed reference system for open badges in tourism education, a clear reference system for the award of open badges in tourism education, or even an industry-related badge-issuing platform, could strengthen the ties between education and the industry and therefore also reduce part of the work involved in application processes or solve issues like badge verification and custodianship. In this way, Open Badges could become validated indicators of competencies and skills relevant for the tourism industry.

5.   EPORTFOLIOS: ADOPTION ISSUES AND CHALLENGES

For the higher education institution, the adoption of student ePortfolios as a teaching tool implies a number of issues and strategic challenges because the implementation of ePortfolios as teaching and learning tools can directly affect institutional structure and culture. As an initiative of some 24 campus ePortfolio leaders across North America, the Catalyst for Learning Project (Making Connections National Resource Center, 2015) provides a good overview of the different functions ePortfolio initiatives can have at universities.

When looking at the many uses of student ePortfolios in higher education (HE) institutions, three broad categories emerge that refer to the institutional function, the level and extent of institutional integration (course-level, programme-level, university-level) and the level and extent of integration of extra-curricular skills:

- academic and assessment-oriented (focus on monitoring academic achievement and single course or integrative assessment);
- career and industry-oriented (focus on tracking professional development and career skills; usually programme-integrated);
- reflective and cross-curricular (credential documentation of knowledge, competencies and skills and extra-curricular learning).

It is interesting to note, however, that with the growing use of ePortfolios as workspaces, the functions often merge, resulting in multi-purpose ePortfolios. Single course portfolios are very often a starting point for a larger ePortfolio initiatives in HE institutions.

Actively addressing the function the ePortfolio has for the HE institution is of significant importance and a demanding task as robust frameworks have to be established so that the ePortfolio initiative is sustainable and all relevant audiences and stakeholders are involved from the start. The pedagogical reasons to opt for student ePortfolios on a course- or subject-discipline level are easy to grasp and have been described here earlier. The implementation of ePortfolios at a programme or even institutional level is often triggered by strategic agendas like putting a focus on lifelong learning and employability, embedding a pedagogical approach across programmes and disciplines, making the HE institution more visible to external stakeholders or enhancing student engagement and alumni retention.

Once the decision to start an ePortfolio initiative on a course, programme or institutional level has been taken, the HE institution will have to: address questions concerning the pedagogical approach it is taking in its ePortfolio initiative and harmonize the assessment approach with learning outcomes; provide a framework for educators to coordinate learning outcomes and task design; decide upon a framework for the support it provides to students and faculty to learn about ePortfolio pedagogy and technology; choose the ways in which it involves all stakeholders and decide to what extent ePortfolio work is accessible to stakeholders outside the university; and look at questions concerning the scalability of the ePortfolio initiative, including decisions on portability and availability of ePortfolio workspace, a question that is directly linked to the choice of technology and systems to host the ePortfolios (Eynon et al., 2014). In Europe, the Europortfolio community is currently trying to support individuals and institutions in making these strategic decisions through the launch of a 'Self-Development Study MOOC' on the European Multiple MOOC Aggregator platform (cf. European Network of ePortfolio Experts and Practitioners, 2015).

5.1   Portability and ePortfolio Infrastructure

With the prevalent use of ePortfolio work in higher education there is also a wide variety of ePortfolio systems available. Many universities use home grown systems or systems that are part of their Learning Management System (LMS), which makes it easier for them to configure functions, options and the availability of ePortfolios to audiences outside their university. Through this they can provide structured online frameworks and workspaces for student ePortfolios. Home-grown systems are closed systems housed on university servers, which makes it easier to deal with questions of data security and protection as well as documentation, for example for the purpose of archiving ePortfolio work that is part of course assessment procedures. Copyright regulations, intellectual property rules and regulations can be monitored more easily and assessment management components like, for example, rubric libraries can be integrated. Nevertheless, home grown systems raise several issues including long-term support and maintenance and the question of storage quotas for large universities.

The question of storage (server) space can become a crucial issue when a university decides to make ePortfolio work an integrative part of a course programme or institution. Here, it can be wiser to use open source systems such as Mahara or freely available systems like Google Sites or commercial systems. Using open systems has a variety of other advantages:

- Students work with real-life tools that may be relevant for their careers and enhances the engagement of students in that they get their work in a digital space that is 'outside' their university.
- Some freely available systems like Google Sites offer accessible and ready-made multi-media tutorials for each of the tools available. These tutorials limit the time the university might have to dedicate to train and support students in acquiring digital skills for putting their ePortfolio together.
- Open systems are cost-effective in that they are available for free. Links to student portfolios can be 'hidden'.
- Open systems enable easy portability of ePortfolio work and easy accessibility for wider audiences.
- Open systems and freely available systems allow easy linkage to social media such as Google+, LinkedIn or Facebook.

In contrast, freely available systems (for example Google Sites) make it sometimes harder for universities to close ePortfolio sites that students have created as it is the student who has full ownership of the site. Some sites offer the possibility of shared, although limited, access. In terms of documenting students' work at a certain point in time (course deadlines) this can become an issue as students can access and change portfolio content at any time. Therefore, the university might have to download every single site and save it offline for documentation and assessment purposes, an activity that can only be applied to smaller groups. Open source ePortfolio systems that are fully interoperable with LMSs or commercial ePortfolio systems could be an alternative.

Currently, some universities are starting to combine ePortfolio initiatives with mobile technology. An example is Leeds University School of Medicine, which combines iPhone assessment and learning apps to support portfolio-based learning. In terms of portfolio infrastructure and systems used, this combination will become another challenge for HE ePortfolio infrastructure.

6. CONCLUSION AND FUTURE DIRECTIONS

The options available to educators in the area of ePortfolios are immense. There are many ways to use ICTs and web-based services and platforms to provide students with opportunities to work creatively on their ePortfolio tasks and at the same time enhance their professional skills in a meaningful way. ePortfolios can promote learning in higher levels of understanding and critical thinking such as, for example, critical thinking in relation to oneself and to subjective theories and practice, researching, solving problems and applying skills. In addition to this, ePortfolios can promote self-responsible learning and studying, planning goals and time management skills.

Despite the increasing adoption of ePortfolios in higher education, little has been said about ways to use ePortfolios as an integrative part of the (indirect) teaching process. This chapter aimed to fill this gap by reviewing the literature and by suggesting a way to use ePortfolios in higher education as a tool for teaching through task design. When looking at the concept of *task design* as an indirect way of teaching, ePortfolios are a tool for teaching in higher education in that they allow flexible and individualized workloads to be created for students, provide the opportunity to accommodate multiple audiences including the industry, enhance students' digital literacy, and actively monitor students' progress as well as skills development. The continuing transformation and development of ePortfolio task design will be paramount, especially when taking into account that ePortfolios are increasingly used as dynamic communication tools through which wider, authentic audiences can be included. The inclusion of Open Badge systems as a way to integrate evidenced assessment of transferable skills is an additional sign of a possibility to narrow the gap between education and the working world. At the same time, the line between what is known as eLearning and ePortfolio work in higher education will become blurred as many ePortfolio systems are starting to have similar, if not the same, features as those used in eLearning or, in fact, in blended learning in higher education.

In particular, an enhanced ePortfolio Teaching Space adds opportunities to make learning processes more flexible, collaborative and authentic. To make full use of these opportunities, however, educators need to carefully plan and reflect ePortfolio task design as it is from the task that the student derives a major learning experience. In the case of multi-purpose and campus-wide ePortfolios with large cohorts and multiple stakeholders, this will require educators, managers and administrators to work together to ensure a consistent pedagogical approach and meaningful evidence items as well as a purposeful ePortfolio system.

Tourism educators should continually try to critically apply and adapt task design for ePortfolio work and, in fact, include representatives of the industry in both assessment and task design. Therefore, ePortfolio work not only provides compelling opportunities to enhance knowledge and skills, but it can be a significant tool to narrow the gap between the tourism sector and its future workforce.

REFERENCES

Albert, U. (2008), 'Portfolio im Kontext von Evaluation', in Th. Bruestenmeister and K.D. Eubell (eds), *Evaluation, Wissen und Nichtwissen*, Wiesbaden: Verlag fuer Sozialwissenschaften, pp. 275–94.

Anderson, L.W., D.R. Krathwohl, P.W. Airasian, K.A. Cruikshank, R.E. Mayer, P.R. Pintrich, J. Raths and M.C. Wittrock (2001), *A Taxonomy for Learning, Teaching, and Assessing: A revision of Bloom's Taxonomy of Educational Objectives*, New York: Pearson, Allyn & Bacon.

Barrett, H. (2004–08), 'My online portfolio adventure', accessed 20 August 2014 at http://electronicportfolios.org/myportfolio/versions.html.

Barrett, H. (2010), 'Balancing the two faces of ePortfolios', *Educação, Formação &Tecnologias*, **3** (1).

Bloom, B.S. (1956), *Taxonomy of Educational Objectives, Handbook I: The Cognitive Domain*, New York: David McKay.

Braun, P. and M. Hollick (2006), 'Tourism skills delivery: sharing tourism knowledge online', *Education and Training*, **48** (8/9), 693–703.

Bryant, L.H. and J.R. Chittum (2013), 'ePortfolio effectiveness: A(n ill-fated) search for empirical evidence', *International Journal of ePortfolio*, **3** (2), 189–98.

Christou, E. (1999), 'Hospitality management education in Greece: An exploratory study', *Tourism Management*, **20** (6), 683–92.

Europäisches Parlament & Rat (2006), 'Empfehlung des Europäischen Parlaments und des Rates vom 18. Dezember 2006 zu Schlüsselkompetenzen für lebensbegleitendes Lernen', *Amtsblatt der Europäischen Union*, 2006/962/EG.

European Commission (2015), accessed 20 March 2015 at http://ec.europa.eu/enterprise/sectors/tourism/ict/index_en.htm.

European Institute for E-Learning (EIfEL) (2014), 'About EIfEL', accessed 20 September 2014 at http://www.eife-l.org/about.

European Network of ePortfolio Experts and Practitioners (2014), accessed 20 September 2014 at http://europortfolio.org.

Evans, G., J. Bohrer and G. Richards (2001), 'Small is beautiful? ICT and tourism SMEs – a comparative European study', *Information Technology and Tourism*, **3** (3/4), 139–53.

Eynon, B., L. Gambino and J. Török (2014), 'What difference can eportfolio make? A field report from the connect to learning project', *International Journal of ePortfolio*, **4** (1), 95–114.

Gagnon, G.W. and M. Collay (2006), *Constructivist Learning Design: Key Questions for Teaching to Standards*, New York: Corwin Press/Sage Publications.

Gallagher, C. and L. Poklop (2014), 'Portfolios and audience: Teaching a critical twenty-first century skill', *International Journal of ePortfolio*, **4** (1), 7–20.

Gibbs, G. (2004), 'Conditions under which assessment supports students' learning', *Learning and Teaching in Higher Education*, **1**, 3–31.

Hamp-Lyons, L. and W. Condon (2000), *Assessing the Portfolio: Principles for Practice, Theory and Research*, Cresskill, NJ: Hampton Press.

Hartnell-Young, E. and M. Morriss (2007), *Digital Portfolios: Powerful Tools for Promoting Professional Growth and Reflection*, Thousand Oaks, CA: Corwin Press.

Hornung-Praehauser, V., G. Geser, W. Hilzensauer and S. Schaffert (2007), *Didaktische, Organisatorische und Technologische Grundlagen von E-Portfolios und Analyse Internationaler Beispiele und Erfahrungeen mit E-Portfolio-Implementierung an Hochschulen*, Salzburg: Salzburg Research Forschungsgesellschaft im Auftrag der Forum Neue Medien in der Lehre Austria.

Jonassen, D.H. (1996), *Computers in the Classroom: Mindtools for Critical Thinking*, Columbus, OH: Merril/Prentice-Hall.

Kafai, Y. and M. Resnick (1996), *Constructionism in Practice: Designing, Thinking and Learning in a Digital World*, Hillsdale, NJ: Lawrence Erlbaum.

Kasavana, M.L., K. Nusair and K. Teodosic (2010), 'Online social networking: Redefining the human web', *Journal of Hospitality and Tourism Technology*, **1** (1), 68–82.

Knight, P. and M. Yorke (2003), 'Employability and good learning in higher education', *Teaching in Higher Education*, **8** (1), 3–16.

Korthagen, F.A.J. (2001), 'Reflection on reflection', in F.A.J. Korthagen et al. (eds), *Linking Practice and Theory: The Pedagogy of Realistic Teacher Education*, Mahwah, NJ: Lawrence Erlbaum, pp. 51–68.

Lorenzo, G. and J. Ittleson (2005), 'An overview of e-portfolios: EDUCAUSE Learning Initiative, Paper 1', accessed 20 August 2014 at net.educause.edu/ir/library/pdf/eli3001.pdf.

Making Connections National Resource Center (2015), retrieved 20 June 2015 at http://c2l.mcnrc.org/student-eportfolio-sample/.

Mössenlechner, C. (2012), *A Teacher's Roles: The Archetypes of Teaching*, Dissertation, English and American Studies, Klagenfurt: Alpen-Adria Universität Klagenfurt.

O'Donoghue, J. (ed.) (2006), *Technology Supported Learning and Teaching: A Staff Perspective*, Hershey, PA: Information Science Publishing.

O'Keeffe, M. and R. Donnelly (2013), 'Exploration of eportfolios for adding value and deepening student learning in contemporary higher education', *International Journal of ePortfolio*, **3** (1), 1–11.

Rhodes, T., H. Chen, E. Watson and W. Garrison (2014), 'Editorial: A call for more rigorous portfolio research', *International Journal of ePortfolio*, **4** (1), 1–5.

Richter, A. (2008), 'Portfolios im universitaeren Kontext: Wann, wo, wie? Eine andere Bewertungsgrundlage im Seminarraum', in I. Brunner, Th. Haecker and F. Winter (eds), *Das Handbuch der Porfolioarbeit: Konzepte, Anregungen, Erfahrungen aus Schule und Lehrerbildung*, Seelze-Velber: Klett/Kallmeyer, pp. 234–41.

Sherman, G. (2006), 'Instructional roles of electronic portfolios', in A. Jafari and C. Kaufman (eds), *Handbook of Research on ePortfolios*, Hersbey: Idea Group Reference, pp. 1–14.

Sigala, M. (2002), 'The evolution of internet pedagogy: Benefits for tourism and hospitality education', *Journal of Hospitality, Leisure, Sports and Tourism Education*, **1** (2), 29–45.

Sigala, M. (2005), 'e-Learning and e-Assessment', in D. Airey and J. Tribe (eds), *An International Handbook of Tourism Education*, Oxford: Elsevier, pp. 367–81.

Stergiou, D. (2005), 'Teaching', in D. Airey and J. Tribe (eds), *An International Handbook of Tourism Education*, Oxford: Elsevier, pp. 285–97.

13 Integrating Google Earth into the lecture: visual approaches in tourism pedagogy
Nicholas Wise

1. INTRODUCTION

Rose (2003) notes that visuals used in education are necessary, and decades ago Loya and Newhouse (1949) wrote about the importance of using visuals in the classroom. In disciplines such as geography and tourism, where maps are inherently important, knowledge of space and place define disciplinary approaches. The use of visual aids in the classroom has changed much over the years and the nascent technological paradigm and Web 2.0 have completely altered how (tourism-related) concepts such as regeneration, re-use or redevelopment are presented to learners. While it is important for learners to develop theoretical and conceptual understandings, putting theory into practice using visual learning techniques allows learners to obtain knowledge using technologies that bring the world into the classroom – relating to Morellato's chapter on technology-enhanced learning in tourism. This chapter will discuss the use of Google Earth in teaching. Particular examples presented below are framed around geography and tourism by discussing examples of urban regeneration used in existing lectures and seminars.

For learners studying tourism, one of the world's most far-reaching industries, it is becoming more essential that they have a strong command and knowledge of international destinations to assess and understand different planning/land use techniques and spatial practices. Geography is a field that has long informed scholars working in the field of tourism (Nelson 2013; Rickley-Boyd et al. 2014), and Google Earth technology brings the world into the classroom so learners can broaden their understandings of space, place and change. Moreover, by utilizing technologies, each lecture can potentially take learners beyond the classroom, grasping the wide availability of useful commands embedded in Google Earth. With an emphasis on internationalizing the curriculum and exposing learners to different places and ideas, Google Earth represents an inexpensive and effective teaching tool to bring the world into the classroom to look at wider regional issues and in-depth case studies. As this chapter will show, we can target and assess regenerated areas and visitor attractions in more detail using Google Street View and Google Photo Sphere (360 View), historical imagery settings and add notes/data to Placemarks and paths. This chapter will discuss the use of Google Earth as a classroom technology to contribute to learning and teaching in the area of tourism studies (by looking at regeneration examples). This chapter will start by framing visual learning and Google Earth before looking at lecturing and seminar task examples outlining several case studies from Great Britain and the United States.

2.   LITERATURE: VISUAL LEARNING AND GOOGLE EARTH

As noted, the learning environment is becoming increasingly visual, and educators are doing more to bring visuals into the classroom to reinforce understandings. When topics (and associated examples) are discussed in the classroom, integrating visuals give learners reference points and will allow them to maintain some particular aspect of knowledge through a particular association (see Rose 2003). Helmers (2006), drawing on discourse and semiotics, takes this further by discussing elements of visual analysis, focusing on how the world is becoming increasingly visual and how images and videos of people and places establish associations. Nevertheless, despite the visual being analyzed, space and place are inherent components of the equation, making it important to be critical by assessing notions of location, scene or landscape based upon critical concepts contributing to the wider picture (Cosgrove 1984; Helmers 2006; Patterson 2007; Rose 2011; 2014).

Visual interpretation, analyses and practices in the classroom are especially common in disciplines such as geography (Elwood 2010; Helmers 2006; Hsu and Song 2014; Rose 2011; 2014). Images and perceptions of places can be transformed through visual learning techniques and technologies. Google Earth represents a nascent approach to visual learning. According to Shellito (2012, p. 1):

> Google Earth is a virtual globe software program that allows you to utilize geospatial technology for a variety of very cool applications. You can zoom from Earth's orbit to see a satellite image or aerial photograph of your house, fly to any location on the globe, see cities and landscapes in 3D, and look at all sorts of geographic content from around the world.

Applications of Web 2.0 have been widely incorporated into the classroom to enhance the learning experience across a range of academic disciplines (Bodzin and Cirucci 2009; Guertin and Neville 2011; Hudson-Smith et al. 2009; Mering et al. 2010; Patterson 2007; Schultz et al. 2008; Sui 2004; Yu and Gong 2012). Such applications provide spatial insight utilized by geographers, but are easily adapted to lectures and seminars focusing on tourism and are found in the tourism workplace to better plan/manage destinations (Li and Hao 2010; Pandagale et al. 2014). Hudson-Smith et al. (2009) argue the benefits of using Web 2.0 applications as they have a very important spatial element to encourage learners to better understand other geographically informed notions of location and place. Work conducted by Stahley (2006) takes this emphasis on space and place further, suggesting that Google Earth allows learners to do the following: learn basic navigation skills to view images effectively; learn ways to determine distance measurements, elevations and coordinate locations; locate and analyze images based on personal research choices; share findings from their research with the class. These last two points highlighted by Stahley (2006) represent how Google Earth encourages learners to think critically about locations, pertinent to space, place, interrelationships and physical environments, each offering insight into how certain practices differ around the world.

Wider discussions of visual approaches relate to perception, and pertinent to this thought, behavioral geographers focus on imaginative perceptions as the production of new knowledge, regarded as 'ways of seeing' (Berger 1972), or interpreting images and places based upon someone's particular understanding (Lehtonen 2000). Part of the postmodernist paradigm of education, visual approaches are becoming increasingly important to encourage multiple understandings (Rose 2003). Maps are important in spatial understanding, whether engaging with more traditional cartography, mental maps, or engaging with technology. For behavioral theorists, much scholarly work has considered visual perception addressing people's social and cognitions of places (Madaleno 2010; Wise 2014). Sack (1997, p. 155) would argue that perspective guides geographical knowledge and perception, noting: 'awareness is the capacity to see things not only from our own partial and personal perspective but also from other points of view'. While inherently social and geographical, researchers must also engage with and become aware of social/cultural significances pertinent to geographical locales, and this is the same in the field of tourism. Images are not only insightful, but they allow learners to relate to the context and course materials being taught (Helmers 2006). In this respect, Google Earth as a visual learning technique can be used to reinforce understandings of particular tourism-related practices by virtually taking learners to actual locations to reinforce understandings, although it must be noted that the dates of aerial images differ by location and are not always recent images.

Beyond its uses in physical and geological sciences, geographers and urban/regional planners use remote sensing technologies and Google Earth in research to interpret cultural landscapes. Hong (2003), for example, incorporated aerial imaging with ethnographic research to display how this approach is advancing cultural landscapes interpretations. The use of Google Earth supports inductive social and cultural research relating to the area of qualitative GIS and remote sensing (Bender et al. 2005; Cope and Elwood 2009). Google Earth has become a tool to assist social science researchers with spatial observations and interpretations (for example Brunn and Wilson 2013; Kennedy and Bishop 2011; Lisle 2006; Wise 2015), and has even been referred to as 'desktop archaeology' (Kennedy 2009). In terms of storing data and referencing data, features imbedded in Google Earth allow researchers to look at historical images, measure distances and add data to Placemarks, lines and polygons – the latter is similar to storing data in GIS attribute tables (Wise 2015). According to Sui (2004), approaches utilizing nascent technologies encourage researchers to seek supplemental meanings (of places and landscapes). Google Earth allows researchers to conduct spatial analyses of landscapes, with the ability to zoom in on specific site locations and identify cultural and physical features based on the elements of recognition – such as shape, size, pattern, tone, texture, shadows, site, association, resolution – addressed by remote sensing (see Lillesand et al. 2008).

As implied, applying Google Earth technology to teaching represents an innovative learning experience for learners – and assists understandings of spaces and places, visually. Google Earth captures clear images of the urban landscape over time, and allows educators to show change (specifically relevant in modules focusing on regeneration) to identify meanings imprinted in the landscape, areas of change (regeneration) and what destinations offer. Some locations allow for three-dimensional viewing, which allows the educator to take learners into a place and look around through 360 degrees. There are books and resources available that offer tasks, assessment questions and step-by-step instructions on how to use Google Earth in the classroom (for example Shellito 2012).

3.   TEACHING APPROACHES

This section will acknowledge Google Earth as a visual learning tool to assess regeneration by presenting several examples of Google Earth lectures and seminar activities as examples used in the classroom to engage learners. By using this visual technology, we have another way to display lecture content visually using simulations or having learners add interpretations into the program for discussion, discussed below. To show how conceptualizations of space and place are understood alongside visual and practical concepts of regeneration and tourism, examples from lectures and activities from the United Kingdom and the United States are outlined. The Glasgow and Pittsburgh examples are teaching examples because of inherent similarities, given their industrial pasts and regenerative transformations, and they show how particular areas of a city change over time. Seminar activities and in-class tasks get learners to look at spaces critically to generate discussions based on a range of interpretations, planning activities and practices. Regeneration has a strong spatial element, and to understand how these places are in a state of change over time, it is useful to take learners directly to these areas. It is a good idea to start by selecting case studies that you and your learners are familiar with and can relate to. Working in Glasgow I have decided to incorporate examples from areas that I discuss in class and learners are aware of, and being from Pennsylvania I selected Pittsburgh. Moreover, starting with areas of familiarity then makes it possible to take learners out for ground-truthing. In subsequent lectures, by using international cases, this allows the educator to incorporate international perspectives/examples – to offer comparisons and/or contrasting insight.

3.1   Lectures: Glasgow and Pittsburgh

Looking at the case of Glasgow, the city hosted the 2014 Commonwealth Games in July. The event was part of a wider legacy initiative to continue improving the city's image to increase tourism. In 1990, the city was the European Capital of Culture. That year was seen as a transition period for cities hosting the European Capital of Culture where the focus shifted to regeneration (see Richards and Palmer 2010). Glasgow officials/planners have targeted specific areas in the city to regenerate, and the lecture looks at regenerated areas by assessing economic transitions, looking at conference/entertainment areas, the regeneration of Glasgow's East End and city center public spaces. Looking at the case of Glasgow, numerous screenshots from Google Earth are included and elaborated on, emphasizing how Google Earth is used to navigate us virtually through regenerated sections of the city (Figure 13.1). In Glasgow's case, much of the regeneration was linked to the 2014 Commonwealth Games (Smith 2012), but across the greater Glasgow region much has been done to promote regional tourism, and while images just show physical infrastructural regeneration, discussed content goes well beyond this. Figure 13.1 is a screenshot of a .kmz file prepared for a lecture looking at regenerated areas in Glasgow and the greater region. The lists of Placemarks on the left were strategically placed and can easily be navigated through by clicking on each one. The instructor can add them in succession in the order they wish to present.

   Figure 13.2a zooms into 'Placemark 1' in this particular .kmz file titled '1. Riverfront Regeneration'. This image gives an overview of the regenerated area here along the River

Source: Google Earth.

Figure 13.1   .kmz regeneration lecture of Glasgow and the wider region

(a)

(b)

Source: Google Earth.

Figure 13.2   (a) New venues and visitor attractions in Glasgow, former dockland area now hosts many of Glasgow's main conference/ entertainment venues; (b) regeneration of Glasgow's East End for the 2014 Commonwealth Games

Clyde, and there is also another prepared Placemark, 'Placemark 2', that moves down to Google Street View to navigate through this particular area and look at the pathways developed and the hotels built close to the Scottish Exhibition and Conference Centre (SECC), Clyde Auditorium and the SSE Hydro (which is still shown as a construction site in Figure 13.2a). Figure 13.2b focuses on an area in the East End of the city that was targeted specifically for the 2014 Commonwealth Games, regarded as the economically deprived area of Glasgow (see Smith 2012; Garcia 2005). Each Placemark in this case was strategically positioned to show construction sites (from the time of the imagery) and to show how regeneration in this area has been limited and fairly contained. To show how the landscape has changed over time where Placemarks were added, the time machine feature presents to learners change over time and space. Using such added features further emphasizes how regeneration is spatially contained and access is limited (Paton et al. 2012). When navigating around Glasgow's East End, educators can discuss the overall socio-economic make-up of this area of the city in relation to who has access to the newly built sporting venues (the Emirates Arena and Chris Hoy Velodrome). While this new venue will attract tourists and visitors during sporting events, and patrons to use the new facility, there has been little done in the immediately adjacent area to further attract and maintain visitors before and after events; this case differs from some of the examples presented later in this chapter (concerning the cases in North America). As noted above, Google Earth is good for showing similar and contrasting cases to compare planning agendas and look at how tourists and tourism is managed in different areas. Pertinent to Glasgow's case presented here, we see differences between the regenerated sites in the East End of the city and the area along the river in terms of the types of developments and facilities available to visitors. The Google Street View image brings learners right into the high traffic or visited areas in the city center to navigate through particular tourist paths. When in Google Street View, by clicking on the (yellow) paths it is possible to navigate down the street and rotate the view. To exit and move onto the next area in the interactive .kmz file you simply click on the next Placemark (shown on the left of Figure 13.1).

Moving on, the case of Pittsburgh was used in a particular lecture using Google Earth's timeline to look at past aerial images of the same frame to locate and discuss regeneration of the North Shore over time (Figures 13.3a, 13.3b, 13.3c and 13.3d). Looking at this particular area of Pittsburgh shows the North Shore regeneration: the timeline command allows you to scroll through a series of past aerial images and pause to elaborate on newly constructed venues and buildings with new visitor attractions. The change is apparent in the four images. In the 1990s there was one stadium housing two professional sports teams (Figure 13.3a), next we see two different venues (Figures 13.3b and 13.3c) and in Figure 13.3d supplemental visitor attractions built along the North Shore. We see a transition in an area that was primarily focused on sports in the 1990s to a range of visitor attractions built recently after the opening of the two new sporting venues in the early 2000s to generate visitor and tourism revenue year round as opposed to limiting income generation to the months of the year when baseball and American football are in season.

Referring back to the discussion above about Google Street View navigation, educators can take learners directly to the various visitor attractions built along the North Shore Trail in Pittsburgh. It is possible to navigate along the North Shore Trail along the (yellow) path in Google Street View to various visitor attractions along from the Three-Rivers Casino that connects to the Carnegie Science Center, Heinz Field and

Source: Google Earth.

Figure 13.3 (a) 7 April 1993; (b) 13 May 2003; (c) 27 September 2005; (d) 30 August 2012

PNC Park, before proceeding further to numerous establishments of restaurants and hotels built in the regenerated area. In lectures, these cases bring together several components of regeneration as outlined by Smith (2012) and Spirou (2010), linking aspects of physical, social and economic regeneration and land use/spatial planning agendas with the objective to improve targeted areas.

3.2   Seminar/Discussion Task

Seminar tasks using Google Earth can be completed in groups to encourage discussion among learners to critically examine particular areas of cities. In this case, Manchester (Figure 13.4) and Denver (Figure 13.5) are cases to consider when assessing inter-urban regeneration and spatial planning linked to tourism around professional sports stadiums. Stadiums are part of the regeneration process in many urban areas (Smith 2012), and act as catalysts to promote further economic development (for example Newsome and Comer 2000; Robertson 1995). Learners can also enter Google Street View to further assess an area to frame links between regenerated areas and place image. In many cases, areas will be revitalized but surrounding areas may be deprived and this could deter tourism outside of game days. In Pittsburg's case, much of the North Shore was developed to create new visitor attractions to sustain the economy in this area year round. In the case of Denver, the baseball stadium was located adjacent to the downtown. By assessing the surrounding areas and looking at surrounding places, we can understand spatial planning for locating venues for inter-urban tourism purposes. This will encourage learners to link the urban geography of the areas to understanding visitor/tourism-led change and how particular 'tourist paths' are created to maneuver people through particular areas of the city. Shown above in the case of Glasgow, much is oriented to Buchanan Street, or in Pittsburgh, the walkway along the North Shore connecting people to new visitor attractions.

In the cases outlined below in Figures 13.4 and 13.5, we see three similar cases of regeneration. While this particular regeneration is predominantly sport led, wider initiatives aim to attract more tourists to the area. By zooming in on the stadiums directly and moving to Google Street View, the learners can add Placemarks and input critical interpretations and reflections of what they see in a particular point or area. By consolidating interpretations, learners can open up further discussions on the topic or case study. Figure 13.5 presents an example of how learners can add content to Google Earth: this particular example looks at Denver. In this case we look at the privatization of space along Wynkoop Street and the re-use of buildings to bring visitors to the area adjacent to the baseball stadium.

The use of Google Earth in seminars encourages learners to think critically about space and place using images of areas that have been regenerated or that are currently regenerating to help with the tourism industry in the city. Not only is Google Earth a visual learning tool, it is an engaging interactive learning tool. As educators, we ensure learners have a strong commend of disciplinary-specific theory and content. Google Earth allows learners to apply this theory in a practical sense by looking at real 'on the ground examples' to link interpretations back to theoretical and critical understandings.

Figure 13.4 Manchester, England

Tourist/Consumer Path from 16th Street to Coors Field via Wynkoop Street

along Wynkoop Street many of the buildings have been converted into restaurants, gentrified area only a street visitors enter from the train station. Still much being built in the areas between the train station and stadium and the park, this is an area that has been in transition for many years. The redevelopments along these streets are targeted to appeal to visitor demands and to restore the image of this area of the city. Can link this to the work of Mitchell (2003) looking at the privatization of space and how this impacts visitor perceptions and experiences.

Source: Google Earth.

Figure 13.5 Denver, Colorado (the area being transformed near the baseball stadium), this is an example of a task where learners add their own interpretative content into Google Earth, linked to points and lines they identify

200

4. FUTURE DIRECTIONS

Using Google Earth to assess regeneration and explore and present conceptual practical concepts, it is important to look at tourism spaces, regeneration, land use and planning, as acknowledged in numerous cases displayed above. Educators continue to seek new technologies to complement and enhance the learning experience. Moreover, teaching content that is visual will further engage learners with class content. It is expected that as Google Earth expands and the capabilities of the program and the imagery in distant places are increasingly improved, it will be even easier to address regeneration, change and planning in remote places. By looking at current and ongoing areas going through transition, educators and learners can assess and manage the distribution of geospatial data linked to a particular location. In seminars, learners can also use Google Earth Fusion Tables (google.com/fusiontables) to link in data collected during fieldwork. This allows learners to collect original data through assessments of particular locations and then share data online as a method of collecting and sharing data to analyze multiple perspectives and understandings (of urban change and regeneration).

Google Earth presents a range of possibilities for educators beyond the uses discussed in this chapter addressing urban regeneration. For instance, it is possible to outline destination image and transportation infrastructure, which can help reinforce discussions of accessibility and mobility, which also impact tourism planning and competitiveness. In addition, Google Photo Sphere is a form of visual and interactive user-generated content that can be easily uploaded into Google platforms from a smartphone or tablet. Moreover, this allows Google Earth and Google Maps users to go beyond Google Street View, with the ability to go inside public spaces and navigate through internal settings such as hotels, shopping centers, visitor attractions and transportation terminals. While such content exists on official websites, such uploads now put the user in control to bring forward depictions of an area's entirety, to include scenes that may not be depicted on websites. These opportunities will allow for more in-depth virtual field studies to enhance learners' command of tourism planning in a wide range of settings.

Google has also prepared several Landsat Annual Timelapses from 1984 to 2012 of places around the world where rapid growth in residential areas and landscapes for leisure activity are having significant impacts. Dubai and Las Vegas are two examples that have been created and both link to the leisure industries. In the Dubai example we see the growth of coastal developments (focusing on the artificial Palm Islands on the coast), and in Las Vegas golf courses are becoming integral parts of the urban landscape to cater to this growing demand: both examples raise critical points of sustainability. Subsequently, Google Earth Pro allows educators to be even more interactive, and this technology 'can be used to aid planning, analysis and decision making' (Google, 2015) and allow learners to engage in computer-aided drafting and designing. Advances give learners more practical understandings through new visualization techniques, and assessments can be designed so that learners are able to share information with peers, educators and practitioners.

5.   CONCLUSION

This chapter outlined visual learning and the integration of Google Earth into lectures and seminars. Changes in the landscape and impacts of regeneration and tourism planning were outlined in several examples from cities in the United Kingdom and the United States. While I outline approaches used around cases that I am familiar with, it is useful to start with local examples and then take learners out to the field, and then navigate through destinations further afar. The ability to enter Google Street View and make use of Google Photo Sphere adds clarity to the understanding of planning and regeneration approaches from a range of places around the world.

Google Earth technologies and the ability to zoom in and out and see past imagery allow us as educators to navigate efficiently through time and space. Bringing examples from around the world allows learners to grasp understandings and challenges in other settings. To conclude, we are seeing a growing use of mobile technologies used in education. Google Earth is readily accessible on most available electronic devices and the capabilities of Google Street View and Google Photo Sphere and the ability to add content (in the form of text, images and videos) change the way we think and learn about space and place, and how we integrate visual approaches in the classroom.

REFERENCES

Bender, O., H. Boehmer, D. Jens and K. Schumacher (2005), 'Using GIS to analyze long-term cultural landscape change in southern Germany', *Landscape and Urban Planning*, **70** (1/2), 111–25.
Berger, John (1972), *Ways of Seeing*, London: British Broadcasting Association.
Bodzin, A. and L. Cirucci (2009), 'Integrating geospatial technologies to examine urban land use change: a design partnership', *Journal of Geography*, **108** (4/5), 186–97.
Brunn, S. and M. Wilson (2013), 'Cape Town's million plus black township to Khayelitsha: terrae incognitae and the geographies and cartographies of silence', *Habitat International*, **39**, 284–94.
Cope, Megan and Sarah Elwood (eds) (2009), *Qualitative GIS: A Mixed Methods Approach*, London: SAGE.
Cosgrove, Denis (1984), *Social Formation and Symbolic Landscape*, Madison, WI: University of Wisconsin Press.
Elwood, S. (2010), 'Geographic Information Science: visualization, visual methods and the geoweb', *Progress in Human Geography*, **35** (3), 401–408.
Garcia, B. (2005), 'Deconstructing the City of Culture: the long-term cultural legacies of Glasgow 1990', *Urban Studies*, **42** (5/6), 841–68.
Google (2015), 'Google Earth for Desktop', accessed 1 February 2015 at https://www.google.com/work/mapsea rch/products/earthpro.html.
Guertin, L. and S. Neville (2011), 'Utilizing Google Earth to teach students about global oil spill disasters', *Science Activities: Classroom Projects and Curriculum Ideas*, **48** (1), 1–8.
Helmers, Marguerite (2006), *The Elements of Visual Analysis*, New York: Pearson.
Hong, J. (2003), 'Stories remote sensing images can tell: integrating remote sensing analysis with ethnographic research in the study of cultural landscapes', *Human Ecology*, **31**, 215–31.
Hsu, C. and H. Song (2014), 'A visual analysis of destinations in travel magazines', *Journal of Travel & Tourism Marketing*, **31** (2), 162–77.
Hudson-Smith, A., A. Crooks, M. Gibin, R. Milton and M. Batty (2009), 'NeoGeography and Web 2.0: concepts, tools and applications', *Journal of Location Based Services*, **3** (2), 118–45.
Kennedy, D. (2009), 'Desktop archaeology', *Saudi Aramco World*, **60** (4), 3–9.
Kennedy, D. and M. Bishop (2011), 'Google Earth and the archaeology of Saudi Arabia: a case study from the Jeddah area', *Journal of Archeological Science*, **38**, 1284–93.
Lehtonen, Mikko (2000), *The Cultural Analysis of Texts*, London: SAGE.
Li, J. and Z-G. Hao (2010), 'Tourism planning based on Google Earth Virtual Earth Platform', *Remote Sensing for Land & Resources*, **22** (1), 130–33.

Lillesand, Thomas, Ralph Kiefer and Jonathan Chipman (2008), *Remote Sensing and Image Interpretation*, Hoboken, NJ: John Wiley and Sons.

Lisle, R. (2006), 'Google Earth: a new geological resource', *Geology Today*, **22** (1), 29–32.

Loya, J. and L. Newhouse (1949), 'The use of visual aids in the classroom', *Journal of Geography*, **48** (6), 257–9.

Madaleno, I. (2010), 'How do Southern Hemisphere residents perceive the world? Mental maps drawn by East Timorese and Mozambican islanders', *Scottish Geographical Journal*, **126** (2), 112–36.

Mering, C., J. Baro and E. Upegui (2010), 'Retrieving urban areas on Google Earth images: application to towns of West Africa', *International Journal of Remote Sensing*, **31** (22), 5867–77.

Nelson, Velvet (2013), *An Introduction to the Geography of Tourism*, New York: Roman & Littlefield.

Newsome, T. and J. Comer (2000), 'Changing intra-urban location patterns of major league sports facilities', *Professional Geographer*, **52** (1), 105–20.

Pandagale, P., M. Mundhe and A. Pathan (2014), 'Geospatial Information System for tourism management in Aurangabad City: a review', *International Journal of Research in Engineering and Technology*, **3** (5), 720–24.

Paton, K., G. Mooney and K. McKee (2012), 'Class citizenship and regeneration: Glasgow and the Commonwealth Games 2014', *Antipode*, **44** (4), 1470–89.

Patterson, T. (2007), 'Google Earth as a (not just) geography education tool', *Journal of Geography*, **106** (4), 145–52.

Richards, Greg and Robert Palmer (2010), *Eventful Cities: Cultural Management and Urban Revitalisation*, Amsterdam: Butterworth-Heinemann.

Rickley-Boyd, Jillian, Daniel Knudsen, Lisa Braverman and Michelle Metro-Roland (2014), *Tourism, Performance, and Place: A Geographical Perspective*, Farnham: Ashgate.

Robertson, K. (1995), 'Downtown redevelopment strategies in the United States: an end-of-the-century assessment', *Journal of the American Planning Association*, **61** (4), 429–37.

Rose, G. (2003), 'On the need to ask how, exactly, is geography "visual"?', *Antipode*, **3**, 212–21.

Rose, G. (2014), 'On the relation between "visual research methods" and contemporary visual culture', *The Sociological Review*, **62**, 24–46.

Rose, Gillian (2011), *Visual Methodologies*, London: SAGE.

Sack, Robert (1997), *Homo Geographicus: A Framework for Action, Awareness, and Moral Concern*, Baltimore, MD: The Johns Hopkins University Press.

Schultz, R., J. Kerski and T. Patterson (2008), 'The use of virtual globes as a spatial teaching tool with suggestions for metadata standards', *Journal of Geography*, **107** (1), 27–34.

Shellito, Bradley (2012), *Google Earth Exercises for World Regional Geography*, New York: W.H. Freeman.

Smith, Andrew (2012), *Events and Urban Regeneration*, London: Routledge.

Spirou, Costas (2010), *Urban Tourism and Urban Change: Cities in a Global Economy*, London: Routledge.

Stahley, T. (2006), 'Earth from above', *Science Teacher*, **73** (7), 44–8.

Sui, D. (2004), 'GIS, cartography, and the "third culture": geographic imaginations in the computer age', *The Professional Geographer*, **56** (1), 62–72.

Wise, N. (2014), 'Layers of the landscape: representations and perceptions of an ordinary (shared) sports landscape in a Haitian and Dominican community', *Geographical Research*, **52** (2), 212–22.

Wise, N. (2015), 'Placing sense of community', *Journal of Community Psychology*, **43** (7), 920–29.

Yu, L. and P. Gong (2012), 'Google Earth as a virtual globe tool for Earth science applications at the global scale: progress and perspectives', *International Journal of Remote Sensing*, **33** (12), 3966–86.

PART III

EXPERIENTIAL LEARNING

14 Experiential tourism and hospitality learning: principles and practice
Brian King and Hanqin Qiu Zhang

1. INTRODUCTION

According to Hoover and Whitehead (1975), experiential learning exists when a participant 'cognitively, affectively & behaviorally processes knowledge, skills, &/or attitudes in a learning situation characterized by a high level of active involvement'. It has been documented that such learning approaches are well suited to the preferences and competences of tourism and hospitality students. Various researchers in different discipline areas have documented how an experiential approach can contribute to deep learning. In his widely cited study of learning styles, Kolb (1984) proposed the notion, 'Tell me, and I will forget. Show me, and I may remember. Involve me, and I will understand'. This perspective supports the view that experiential learning should be prominent in the curriculum because it stimulates deep learning. A report by the National Training Laboratories Institute for Applied Behavioral Sciences (NTLIABS) noted that the medium of instruction influences student retention of their learning. The study observed that the poorest performing methods are lectures (5 percent retained) and reading (10 percent retained). At the other end of the spectrum 75 percent is retained through 'practice by doing' and 90 percent through 'teaching others' (Dale 1954). The concept of 'practice by doing' aligns closely with experiential learning. Another impetus for extending the reach of experiential learning is the need for tourism and hospitality staff to demonstrate well-developed 'soft skills' in handling complex intercultural service settings.

The widely used expression 'services economy' describes a well-established and dominant role for services in the developed world and their increasing presence in the developing countries. The service economy concept has, however, been progressively displaced by the so-called 'experience economy' which has acquired growing acceptance since it was first presented by Pine and Gilmore (1999). Critics have noted the prevalence of the model in free market capitalist economies such as the USA. Some services marketing and management researchers have argued that the value of goods and services is more attributable to 'co-creation' or to 'co-production' that involves interactions between consumers and producers. In noting this divergence of opinion, the present chapter explores examples of experiential learning across the curriculum and its capacity to increase active learner involvement.

Experiences occupy a central role and place in the contemporary world of consumption. The authors of this chapter argue that the advancing experience economy has accelerated the need for tourism and hospitality programs to incorporate a strong experiential learning component. They also note that currently predominant Millennial or Generation Y tourism and hospitality student cohorts possess a pre-existing familiarity with the world of experiences which awaits them on graduation. As they undertake their formal tourism and hospitality studies, these students continue to engage in consumer activities and experiences, including travel to and engagement with the accommodation sector. One example of experience provision which has resonated with many younger people is 'Voluntourism' (Wearing and McGehee 2013; Wearing 2001; Söderman and Snead 2008; McGehee and Andereck 2009). This manifestation suggests that formal learning cannot be divorced from the wider experience landscape that young people encounter. By volunteering overseas, many students from developed countries acquire extra-curricular experiences that have relevance to their field of study. This is a world of experiences where participants pay to engage in meaningful activities that will allow them to assist less well-resourced communities, particularly in developing countries. Engaging in voluntourism may form part of a student 'gap year', allowing participants to benefit from experiences which will inform their subsequent tourism studies. As discussed later in this chapter, many universities have introduced volunteering or 'service learning' as a credit-bearing subject, an indication that education leaders are aware of the merits of incorporating such elements within the curriculum. As mentioned later in this chapter, service learning is a strong feature of experiential learning at The Hong Kong Polytechnic University.

In this chapter the authors share experiences about learning and teaching in the School of Hotel and Tourism Management (SHTM) at The Hong Kong Polytechnic University (PolyU). PolyU is a large and research intensive public university which incorporates a 262-room university-owned training and research hotel: Hotel ICON. The context is both unusual and instructive. In exploring this setting, the researchers outline the role of experiential learning in the design of the four-year BSc in Hotel Management curriculum, including a compulsory six-month internship. The application of experiential learning is then explored in the context of individual subjects, both traditional classroom-based and service learning. Finally, the researchers document the introduction and implementation of learning outcome assessment plans (LOAPs). This inclusion provides the reader with insights into experiential learning at both the macro (program) and the micro (subject) levels and connects the overall learning philosophy with its implementation.

In their capacity as recipients of public funding and support, universities such as PolyU are increasingly assessed and ranked on the basis of whether students report favorably about their educational experience (Dill and Soo 2005). As an indication of the seriousness of institutions towards such assessment, many universities have established divisions with titles such as 'experience center' or 'office of experiential learning'. Universities also participate in international benchmarks of the student experience with counterpart institutions at both aggregate level (the overall university experience) and within specific fields of study (for example tourism and hospitality). Such benchmarking adopts a holistic view by acknowledging that the 'lived student experience' extends far beyond the classroom. Greater competition between institutions and associated data transparency has progressed the notion that learning has a strong experiential component (Mok 2005). When applied to international tourism and hospitality students, the 'student experience' concept encapsulates the various stages of acquiring an overseas qualification starting with the departure from the home environment to returning some years later (Brookes 2003). Whilst acknowledging this wider context for experiential learning, the present chapter focuses on dimensions of the study experience that are more directly influenced by tourism and hospitality schools.

Though some higher education providers approach tourism and hospitality as part of social sciences or of environmental studies, most provide students with a preparation for professional careers in business and incorporate a range of business oriented subjects. Whilst tourism and hospitality employment is loosely regulated and has few accreditation or certification requirements, students anticipate the acquisition of professional competencies during their studies. Students often demonstrate a desire to engage actively with 'real-world' facilities and situations. Such approaches have a lengthy history in tourism and hospitality education despite the relative youthfulness of the field. The long established Swiss hotel schools have addressed such concerns by combining craft-based and professional skills (for example culinary) with the desire for management and/or supervisory hospitality careers. In the Swiss hotel school learning model, students are accommodated on-site and acquire experiential learning by operating the establishments which house their fellow students. This approach is rare in campus-based university programs, where student experiences resemble those of their counterparts in other faculties and schools. This chapter presents a combination of these two approaches, namely a public university where students learn in the setting of a premium, boutique hotel where guests pay commercial rates.

The authors of the present chapter view experiential learning as integral for students enrolled in all credit-bearing programs offered by SHTM, ranging from higher diploma to bachelor's, master's and even doctoral level. Examples are provided of how the school incorporates experiential learning, particularly at undergraduate level. Internships (or cooperative education) are the archetypal experiential learning and are required for all students undertaking bachelor's degrees in tourism and/or hospitality. Zopiatis has defined an internship as a 'short-term practical work experience in which students receive training and gain experience in a specific field or career area of their interest' (Zopiatis, 2007, p. 65). Such opportunities may be offered in relevant outside enterprises or within a hotel or related operation that is either owned and/or operated by the institution (at PolyU this involves a 'hotel school' setting). At the time of writing, SHTM students undertake their internships at Hotel ICON or with an overseas tourism/ hospitality enterprise.

Having outlined the principles of tourism and hospitality experiential learning in the context of the experience economy, the chapter now explores its embedding in an undergraduate program – the Bachelor of Science in Hotel Management. Next, the authors explore experiential learning at the individual subject level, with particular reference to service learning. Finally, the chapter explores the respective learning outcomes at program and subject levels to show how experiential learning is implemented in practice. This explores the pursuit of consistency at the macro (program-wide) and micro (subject-specific) levels.

2.   EXPERIENTIAL LEARNING SUBJECTS AND METHODS

Researchers have proposed various methods of incorporating experiential learning within the curriculum generally and within tourism and hospitality in particular. As outlined in Table 14.1, these include apprenticeship and fellowship experiences, field work, practicums (for example active engagement in seminars or workshops), student teaching engagements and study abroad. It is evident that there are various ways of delivering experiential learning.

Table 14.1   Types of experiential learning

EL	Methods	Definitions
A	Apprenticeship experiences	'an opportunity to try out a job usually with an experienced professional in the field to act as a mentor' (NIU, p. 5)
B	Cooperative education experiences	'students alternate periods of paid work with campus study or split their time between the workplace and the campus' (Eyler, 2009, p. 1)
C	Fellowship experiences	'the training of students for a period of time, usually between 6 months to one year' (NIU, p. 6)
D	Fieldwork experiences	'to explore and apply content learned in the classroom in a specified field experience away from the classroom' (NIU, p. 6)
E	Internship experiences (externship)	'is viewed as a short-term practical work experience in which students receive training and gain experience in a specific field or career area of their interest' (Zopiatis, 2007, p. 65)
F	Practicum experiences (seminar, workshop)	'a required component of a course of study and placing students in a supervised and often paid situation' (NIU, p. 6)
G	Service learning experiences	'a form of experiential education that combines academic study with service in the community' (Eyler, 2009, p. 2)
H	Volunteer experiences	'service focused on benefiting the service recipient' (Cecil, 2012, p. 316)
I	Students' teaching experiences	'an opportunity to put into practice the knowledge and skills he or she has been developing in the preparation program' (NIU, p. 6)
J	Study abroad experience	'a unique opportunity to learn in another culture, within the security of a host family and a host institution carefully chosen to allow the transfer of credit to a student's degree program' (NIU, p. 7)
K	Field trip (field experience)	'enhance a student's understanding of the filed' (Cecil, 2012, p. 317)
L	Virtual environment	'defined as the use of a computer generated 3D environment – called a 'virtual environment'(VE) – that one can navigate and possibly interact with, resulting in real-time simulation of one or more of the user's five senses' (Guttentag, 2010, p. 638)
M	Laboratory (Clinical experiences)	(Easterly & Myers, 2009); (Loretto, 2011); (McCarthy & McCarthy, 2006)
N	Case study	'exposure to a setting where hospitality services are provided' (McCarthy & McCarthy, 2006)
O	Guest speaker	(McCarthy & McCarthy, 2006)
P	Job shadowing	'a work experience option where students learn about a job by walking through the work day as a shadow to a competent worker. The job showing work experience is a temporary, unpaid exposure to the workplace in an occupational area of interest to the student.' (Paris & Mason, 1995, p. 41)
Q	Video	(McCarthy & McCarthy, 2006)
R	Captive Hotel (Teaching hotel)	A place where 'students can actually study and work at the same time in the hotel' (Yan & Cheung, 2012, p. 22)

In the following section the authors highlight three subjects within the BSc in Hotel Management curriculum at the Hong Kong Polytechnic University. These are: (1) Convention Sales and Service; (2) Analysing and Interpreting Research; and (3) Tourism Planning and Policy. In the case of Convention Sales and Service, participating students are required to deliver an international conference to approximately 350 delegates. One example of implementation was the staging of the 9th annual APaC CHRIE Conference *Hospitality and Tourism Education: from a Vision to an Icon*. The conference was held at Hotel ICON, Hong Kong on 2–5 June, 2011. APaC CHRIE refers to the Asia Pacific division of the US-based the Council on Hotel, Restaurant and Institutional Education (CHRIE) scholarly network. The students were directed by an academic staff member to deliver this conference and assumed roles resembling professional conference organizers (PCO). Most commercially and profit oriented conferences are delivered by PCOs. The students engaged in the conference delivery from planning and conceptualization through to implementation. Consistent with the principle of 'knowledge through doing', the main student assignment is experiential in nature. Students are involved in inviting speakers and attracting sponsors followed by the design of a website and distribution of group emails. The students then prepare conference brochures, handle reception and registrations, engage in consultation and respond to enquiries. They are also responsible for the post-conference tour arrangements. Given the importance of preparing graduates for careers in conventions and events (degrees in events are increasingly popular globally), the opportunity to organize and deliver a conference helps to build their professional competences. Making use of student skills and talents rather than employing a PCO is also consistent with the mission of a tourism and hospitality school. It is also noteworthy that the conference was staged at Hotel ICON since the choice of an on-site teaching and research hotel ensures that the event is embedded within the school's operations. It also allows for synergies with student interns and with hotel and academic staff.

As mentioned previously, two other undergraduate subjects which embrace experiential learning are Analyzing and Interpreting Research and Tourism Planning and Policy. In the case of the former, the student project involves teams of three to four. Student groups initially discuss the formulation of an appropriate research topic. They then conduct a literature review, collect data via fieldwork, analyze the relevant data, make group presentations and finally engage in peer evaluation. As outlined in Table 14.2, students undertaking the subject acquire rich exposure by undertaking eight elements of experiential learning as outlined in the mapping of learning outcomes. In *Tourism Planning and Policy* students work in groups of three to four to design a regional tourism planning project. They participate in two field research trips, gather resources, undertake market research, prepare a report and finally engage in peer evaluation. Table 14.2 refers to Co-operative Education or Internships under the heading *Work Integrated Education*.

Five broad headings are used to illustrate how experiential learning methods have been deployed across the BSc in Hotel Management, consistent with undergraduate practices across the university. Column 1 outlines the applicable Program Outcomes. All PolyU undergraduate and postgraduate programs require such outcomes. It is notable that the service learning subjects incorporate a large number of experiential learning methods – nine. In Table 14.3, column 5 summarizes the range of student feedback, and examines the application of experiential learning at the individual subject level, specifically in the case of service learning.

Table 14.2   Curriculum of BSc (Hons) in Hotel Management at The Hong Kong Polytechnic University

No.	Subject Title	Credits	Experiential Learning Methods
A	*General University Requirement (GUR)*	*30*	
	Language & Communication Requirement (LCR) (3 subjects)	9	
	Cluster Area Requirement (CAR) (4 subjects)	12	
	Common Mandatory Subjects (3 subjects)	9	
	Freshman Seminar	3	
	Leadership and Intra-personal Development	3	
	Service Learning	3	D, F, G, I, M, N, O, Q, R
B	*Discipline Specific Requirement (DSR)*	*76*	
	Common Subjects (16 subjects)	46	
	Specialist Subjects (6 subjects)	18	
	Analysing and Interpreting Research	3	D, I, K, L, M, N, O, Q
	Career Track Option (2 subjects per option)	18	
	1. Hotel General Management	6	
	2. Restaurant & Hotel Foodservice Management	6	
	3. Hotel Administration	6	
	4. Convention Sales and Service	3	A, F, L, N, O, P, Q, R
	Honours Thesis OR Capstone Projects (2 subjects)	12	
C	*Minor (6 Subjects)*	*18*	
D	*Free Electives (5 Subjects)*	*15*	
	Total Academic Credits (A + B + C or D)	124 or 121	
E	*Work-Integrated Education & Professional Development*	Training credits	A, B, C, D, E, O, Q, R

All PolyU students undertaking four-year bachelor's degrees must successfully complete three credits (one subject) of service learning. Service learning has been described as 'service focused on benefiting the service recipient' (Cecil, 2012, p. 316). It has also been defined as 'a form of experiential education combining academic study with service in the community' (Eyler, 2009, p. 2). The service learning subject in Table 14.3 refers to Hospitality Management and Operation in Developing Regions. This unit is delivered *in situ* and aims to train local residents in developing countries with knowledge and skills that will enhance their ability to generate an income from hospitality. In the curriculum context the subject was delivered across two semesters and involved face-to-face contact during 9 of the 13 weeks during semester 2. This was followed by a 14-day trip to Cambodia during semester 3 (a shorter and more intense 'Summer Semester'). Students prepared the following activities during semester 2 as a foundation for service delivery in semester 3:

● understanding service learning by e-learning;
● meeting with the client (in this case Green Pasture Inn which is located in Phnom Penh, the capital of Cambodia) via teleconferencing;

Table 14.3   Sample of learning outcomes (service learning subject)

Program outcome	Student Learning Objectives	Experiential Learning Methods	Assessment	Student Feedback
A. Professional Competence	The role of Western restaurant or hospitality businesses; Transfer hospitality management and operations training; Apply hospitality management and operations training; Working effectively in teams to solve problems	F-practicum experience (workshop); Q-Video; G-Service learning experience; I-student teaching experience; M-laboratory	E-learning Module Project-specific seminars and workshops 20%; Performance in rendering service 40%; Plan/proposal for service 20%	'It allows students to perform the fullest extent for the professions, develop students' abilities and attributes, and build up social-mind so as to prepare to be a responsible global citizen' A12.
B. Critical Thinkers	Working effectively in teams to solve problems encountered in planning and delivering the service	G-Service learning experience; I-student teaching experience; M-laboratory; O-guest speaker; Q-video; R-captive hotel	Plan/proposal for service 20%; Performance in rendering service 40%	'it provides opportunities for critical reflection to enhance social responsibility, which cannot be learned from books in usual academic study' A3.
C. Effective Communicators	Communicate effectively with clients and /or other stakeholders	M-laboratory; O-guest speaker; Q-video; R-captive hotel	Plan/proposal for service 20%	'you need to be a good team player in the service-learning program as you cannot do all the things by yourself' A12.

Table 14.3 (continued)

Program outcome	Student Learning Objectives	Experiential Learning Methods	Assessment	Student Feedback
D. Innovative Problem Solvers	Apply/Transfer hospitality management and operations training	I-student teaching experience; M-laboratory; Q-Video; G-Service learning experience	Plan/proposal for service 20%; Performance in rendering service 40%	'I need to identify and define problems in professional and daily contexts, and produce creative and workable solutions to the problems' A3.
E. Lifelong Learners	Reflect on their role and responsibilities both as a professional in their chosen discipline and/or a responsible citizen	G-Service learning experience; I-student teaching experience	E-learning Module Project-specific seminars and workshops 20%; Reflective Journal 20%	'Service learning not only can benefit the targeted people, but also offering me to have a fruitful and enjoyable experience' A4.
F. Ethical Leaders	Reflect on their role and responsibilities both as a professional in their chosen discipline and/or a responsible citizen; Demonstrate empathy for people in need and a sense of civic responsibility	G-Service learning experience; I-student teaching experience; F-practicum experience (workshop)	Plan/proposal for service 20%; Reflective Journal 20%; E-learning Module Project-specific seminars and workshops 20%	'The most important thing about team work is that it enables individuals in the team to focus on one main objective. Since everyone contributes their unique abilities, which make the result of their objective more diverse' A4.
Specialism Outcomes	Link their service learning activities and experiences with the academic content of the subject	N.A.	Reflective Journal 20%	'this provides me a golden opportunity to try and get involved in hotel industry, becoming a hotel man, to experience the challenges of this industry in reality' A13.

- working on a business proposal and training manual within their team on one of the following topics: front office, housekeeping, food & beverage and marketing;
- on-site observation and hands-on experience in four departments of PolyU's Hotel ICON.

As indicated in Table 14.2, the instructors enhanced the student learning experiences by deploying 7 out of the total 18 experiential learning methods. These approaches included video, training hotel, laboratory, guest speaker, practicum experiences, fieldwork and student teaching. Table 14.3 connects the Program Learning Outcomes of the service learning subject to the subject level learning objectives and to the use of experiential learning methods, assessments, and student feedback on their learning (prior to, during, and after the field trip). In light of the earlier cited NTLIABS research findings, it is noteworthy that the subject delivery provides students with opportunities to engage in teaching, thereby enhancing the likelihood that they will retain their learning.

3.   CONCLUSIONS

Noting that future employees will need to acquire a strong service orientation, this chapter has demonstrated a potential role for experiential learning in tourism and hospitality within the context of the experience economy. The authors have drawn upon curriculum-related examples from Hong Kong PolyU including internships, service learning, conference organization and examples that occur within classroom-based subjects. The example of organizing a conference has demonstrated how student experiences can be aligned with wider institutional needs, allowing the cultivation of professional networks as well as professional and scholarly capabilities. Such experiential learning approaches provide a means of providing learners with positive attitudes, professional competence, communication skills and responsibility as prospective global citizens. These observations show the potential for integrating an experiential approach within university learning and pedagogical philosophies, in program design, delivery and assessment. In the Hong Kong PolyU case the delivery of experiential approaches to enhance learning and teaching has involved active roles for instructors and students and for the university and industry practitioners. The collaboration and involvement of various stakeholders suggests that experiential learning can play a role in tourism and hospitality education. It can build a shared understanding amongst academics, students and industry practitioners about achieving an appropriate balance between theory and application and accommodating the needs of the Generation Y and Millennial learners.

In this chapter the authors have shown that experiential learning provides a valuable medium for learners to acquire positive attitudes, professional competencies, communication skills and responsibility as citizens. It has been suggested that an experiential learning approach can be applied at all levels – as an institution-wide learning philosophy, in program design delivery and assessment at school level. The descriptions of hotel internships have shown how integration within a hotel operating alongside the school provides students with opportunities to acquire meaningful experiential learning. However, it is acknowledged that the mere provision of a hotel and/or training restaurant may not suffice to ensure an experiential learning base for the curriculum. It is concluded that the experiential aspects of student learning should consider all aspects of the curriculum. Whilst some subjects will be more self-evidently 'experiential' than others, the examples of regular classroom-based subjects in this chapter indicate that experiential learning can apply widely across the curriculum. To address student expectations, tourism and hospitality education providers must consider all of the touch points that connect the institution and the student both within and outside the classroom. It is anticipated that such comprehensive and integrative approaches will be increasingly important as cohorts of technologically savvy and experience-hungry students fill the lecture halls. As a post-script it is worth noting that the Hong Kong PolyU examples presented in this chapter cannot offer a template that is directly applicable to other providers. The circumstances encountered in Hong Kong are not readily found in other jurisdictions, notably the capacity to attract top academic students. In particular, the substantial initial investment in Hotel ICON (US$180 million) plus the requirement for ongoing resourcing requires strong and continuing support from the University Council. Nevertheless, it is evident that the positive encounters with experiential learning at Hong Kong PolyU are instructive and are a potential encouragement to those advocating an experiential approach in other settings.

REFERENCES

Brookes, M. (2003), 'Evaluating the "Student Experience": An Approach to Managing and Enhancing Quality in Higher Education', *Journal of Hospitality, Leisure, Sport & Tourism Education*, **2** (1), 17–26.
Cecil, A. (2012), 'A Framework for Service Learning in Hospitality and Tourism Management Education', *Journal of Travel and Tourism Teaching*, **12** (4), 313–31.
Dale, E. (1954), *Audio-visual Methods in Teaching*, New York: Dryden Press.
Dill, D.D. and Soo, M. (2005), 'Academic Quality, League Tables, and Public Policy: A Cross-National Analysis of University Ranking Systems', *Higher Education*, **49** (4), 495–533.
Easterly, T. and Myers, B. (2009), 'Using Experiential Learning to Integrate Field Trips and Laboratory Experiences', *American Association for Agricultural Education*, accessed 7 September 2010 at http://www.aaaeonline.org/files/national_09/posters/Using_Experimental_Learning.pdf.
Eyler, J. (2009), 'The Power of Experiential Education', *Liberal Education*, **95** (4), 24–31.
Guttentag, D. (2010), 'Virtual Reality: Applications and Implications for Tourism', *Tourism Management*, **31** (5), 637–51.
Hoover, J.D. and Whitehead, C.J. (1975), 'An Experiential-Cognitive Methodology in the first Course in Management: Some Preliminary Results', *Simulation Games and Experiential Learning in Action*, **2**, 25–30.
Kolb, D. (1984), *Experiential Learning: Experience as the Source of Learning and Development,* Englewood Cliffs, NJ: Prentice-Hall.
Loretto, P. (2011), 'Learning by Experience', accessed 31 August 2016 at http://internships.about.com/od/internships101/p/TypesExperEd.htm.
McCarthy, P.R. and McCarthy, H.M. (2006), 'When Case Studies Are Not Enough: Integrating Experiential Learning into Business Curricula', *Journal of Education for Business*, **81** (4), 201–204.
McGehee, N.G. and Andereck, K. (2009), 'Volunteer Tourism and the "Voluntoured": the Case of Tijuana, Mexico', *Journal of Sustainable Tourism*, **17** (1), 39–51.
Mok, K.H. (2005), 'The Quest for World Class University: Quality Assurance And International Benchmarking in Hong Kong', *Quality Assurance in Education*, **13** (4), 277–304.
NIU (n.d.), Northern Illinois University, Faculty Development and Instructional Design Center, accessed 31 August 2016 at http://www.niu.edu/facdev/.
Paris, K.A. and Mason, S.A. (1995), *Planning and Implementing Youth Apprenticeship & Work-Based Learning*, Madison, WI: Center on Education and Work.
Pine, J. and Gilmore, J. (1999), *The Experience Economy*, Boston, MA: Harvard Business School Press.
Söderman, N. and Snead, S.L. (2008), 'Opening the Gap: The Motivation of Gap Year Travellers to Volunteer in Latin America', in K. Lyons and S. Wearing (eds), *Journeys of Discovery in Volunteer Tourism*, Wallingford: CABI, pp. 118–29.

Wearing, S. (2001), *Volunteer Tourism: Experiences that Make a Difference*, Wallingford: CABI.

Wearing, S. and McGehee, N.G. (2013), 'Volunteer Tourism: A Review', *Tourism Management*, **38**, 120–30.

Yan, H. and Cheung, C. (2012), 'What Types of Experiential Learning Activities Can Engage Hospitality Students in China?', *Journal of Hospitality and Tourism Education*, **24** (2), 21–7.

Zopiatis, A. (2007), 'Hospitality Internships in Cyprus: a Genuine Academic Experience or a Continuing Frustration?', *International Journal of Contemporary Hospitality Management*, **19** (1), 65–77.

15 Learning from part-time employment: reflections from Australia
Anna Blackman and Pierre Benckendorff

1. INTRODUCTION

There is substantial evidence from the USA, UK and Australia that university students are increasingly mixing their studies with paid employment (Barron and Anastasiadou, 2009; Bradley, 2006; Greenbank et al., 2009; McInnis and Hartley, 2002; Moreau and Leathwood, 2006; Richardson et al., 2009). In Australia, many first year students are already in paid employment when they commence university and it is not unusual for some of these students to have a number of years of employment experience gained while studying at high school (Biddle, 2007). A recent Australian study of the first year experience reported that 53 percent of full-time students were engaged in paid work (Krause et al., 2005). This proportion appears to increase as students progress with their studies, with one Australian study reporting that over 80 percent of all full-time students were in paid employment (Bradley, 2006). However, Hall (2010) reports that Australian studies have found much higher levels of part-time work by full-time students than those found in UK studies.

The high rate of student participation in the labor market raises a number of interesting questions, particularly for those students enrolled in vocational areas such as business and tourism. While it has been claimed that the majority of student employment involves unskilled work where there is little or no connection with the student's course of study (Ford et al., 1995), business students are perhaps somewhat unique because they are not only studying business; they have an opportunity to work in and experience real businesses through their paid part-time employment. While many studies have focused on the negative impacts of work on time to study and academic achievement, some have reported positive effects, especially when the work is relevant to the course of study (Curtis and Shani, 2002; Hall, 2010; Sorensen and Winn, 1993). McKechnie et al. (1997) propose that students in more vocationally focused courses should be able to connect their experiences of working part time with their studies. This in turn should enhance academic knowledge and improve academic motivation and employment prospects. This makes business education quite different from many other disciplines (that is, nursing, medicine, psychology, education), where students have traditionally been placed in highly structured work environments in order to develop their practical skills.

This chapter reports on a survey conducted at two different Australian universities to evaluate what skills students develop through paid part-time employment and which considered how the perceived congruence between paid employment and academic study might affect the development of transferable skills.

2.   BACKGROUND LITERATURE

With more young people now going to university over the past decades we have seen more changes in youth employment (Broadbridge and Swanson, 2005). The reasons for increasing university student participation in the workforce are multi-faceted but have been well explored. Most authors have found that financial motives provide the greatest impetus for students entering the workforce (Curtis and Williams, 2002; Ford et al., 1995; Richardson et al., 2009). Watts and Pickering (2000) suggest that reduced government funding of means-tested grants in the UK was a major reason for students seeking paid employment while studying. The experience in Australia has been similar, with eligibility requirements for student grants and allowances becoming increasingly stringent. Even when students do qualify for government allowances, they do not appear to have kept up with the general cost of living and so are often insufficient as a sole source of income for students (Curtis and Williams, 2002). Besides financial necessity, supporting a lifestyle and gaining work experience to look good on a CV have been reported as other important reasons for undertaking part-time work while studying (Broadbridge and Swanson, 2005; Carney et al., 2005; Oi I and Morrison, 2005; Wang et al., 2010).

Hodgson and Spours (2001, p. 375) also argue that increased student participation in the labor force has been influenced by 'the rapid spread of 24-hour opening in the retail trade; changes to the Sunday trading legislation; continued economic growth, particularly in the service sector; the appearance of new expensive objects of youth consumption (for example, mobile phones) and the spectre of increased higher education debt.' Broadbridge and Swanson (2005) report that traditionally when people left school at 16 or earlier they entered low-level skilled manual work and service jobs. Due to the demise of the manufacturing industry and growth of service sectors this has meant that there is now a stronger demand for low-skilled labor in service sectors such as retail and hospitality. The trading hours for many of these service jobs are outside those of the traditional hours of a business day and therefore students are one of the groups that fill these types of jobs.

Anecdotal evidence suggests that students who work should be developing a range of practical skills and knowledge about the world of work and the operation of real businesses. However, previous studies have indicated that much of this work occurs in service industries such as retail and hospitality (Canny, 2002; Curtis and Shani, 2002; Curtis and Williams, 2002; Ford et al., 1995; Neill et al., 2004). Employers in these industries typically seek out cheap, flexible labor which can multi-task, make decisions and act responsibly, and university students appear well suited to these requirements (Curtis and Lucas, 2001). While work in these industries often requires the development of interpersonal skills such as communication, negotiation, problem solving and teamwork, some work tasks are described as marginal, less skilled, low-paid casual jobs that have been criticized for providing little understanding or experience of managerial business practices (Darmody and Smyth, 2008; Greenbank et al., 2009).

Some authors have argued that part-time work may detract from study, undermine motivation and require time that might otherwise contribute to better academic performance (Curtis and Shani, 2002; Humphrey, 2006; Manthei and Gilmore, 2005; Metcalf, 2003). Curtis and Williams (2002), in their study of undergraduate business students in the UK, found that 83 percent of students who had a part-time job indicated that their work detracted from their studies. This is despite the respondents being business students who were more likely to benefit from their employment by developing a better understanding of business. Bradley (2006) reported a similar finding but his study of 246 full-time university students also found that there were no significant differences in academic performance, academic motivation, perceptions of the difficulty of their university courses or satisfaction with university between students who worked and students who did not work. Furthermore, he found that Grade Point Averages (GPAs) were not significantly correlated with the number of hours students worked and that there was no evidence of poorer academic performance amongst students who were in paid employment for more than 20 hours per week. A more recent study conducted in Macau also found no negative relationship between doing part-time work and student academic performance (Wang et al., 2010). In fact, Wang et al. (2010) also reported that challenging or course-related part-time work increased Chinese students' GPAs, improved their learning attitudes and increased their social support network.

Although some studies have found that paid work impacts negatively on academic performance, it has also been claimed that students from working class backgrounds are more likely to engage in paid work (Hunt et al., 2004; Little, 2002). There is some evidence to suggest that working class students do not perform as well as more affluent students, irrespective of whether they are working (Hatcher, 1998; Moreau and Leathwood, 2006). The relationship between work and academic performance is therefore somewhat ambiguous and may be affected by social class. In summary, students who work while studying do exhibit higher levels of stress, and although many perceive that their work interferes with their study, the outcomes in terms of academic performance do not seem markedly different from those achieved by students who are not working. It has been suggested by Hall (2010) that actions to alleviate the problems created by part-time work could be overcome with better support from universities. In his study students suggested that providing better online resources, more flexibility around deadlines of assessment and more convenient class schedules could be areas of improvement for those that work while studying.

A contrary view is that part-time work may contribute to academic performance by developing business knowledge and skills that are transferable to university contexts and by providing students with a more grounded perspective which allows them to grasp abstract academic concepts more quickly and easily (Greenbank et al., 2009). According to this perspective, paid part-time work and academic studies can be viewed as complementary (Swanson et al., 2006). There is some support for this perspective from school teachers who have found students' work experience to be beneficial to in-class discussions and assignment work (Hodgson and Spours, 2001). Broader advantages include enhanced employability, increased confidence in the world of work, and the improvement of organizational and time management skills (Watts and Pickering, 2000). Rikowski (1992) also argues that paid work is often valued by employers over work experience because students carry it out in their own time, thereby demonstrating self-motivation, self-discipline and a preparedness to work. Taken together, the findings suggest that self-efficacy may be an important outcome of paid part-time work. On the other hand, higher education also needs to prepare students for entry into the labor market. According to the OECD Skills Strategy document this is one area of skills development that working age adults need 'to develop skills so that they can progress in their careers, meet the changing demands of the labor market, and don't lose the skills they have already acquired' (OECD, 2012, p. 9).

While a number of studies have examined the skills developed by students on placements and internships, surprisingly few studies have focused on the skills that students develop through paid part-time work (Martin and McCabe, 2007). One such study, conducted by Martin and McCabe (2007) in the UK, reported on the employability skills developed by postgraduate hospitality and tourism students through paid employment and how these might complement skills embedded within their curricula. Using Knight and Yorke's (2004) framework, they found that students were likely to develop a range of personal qualities such as interacting with people, adaptability, teamwork and feeling comfortable in a stressful environment. Similarly, Curtis and Shani's (2002) study of 359 undergraduate business students indicated that 38 percent of students thought that part-time work improved their ability to deal with people, 36 percent thought it improved skills such as communication, 34 percent thought it helped them understand how a business is run, and 31 percent thought it had helped their self-confidence. While these findings are consistent, there is clearly an opportunity to expand on this work by examining how paid-part time work in different sectors benefits students by facilitating the development of employability skills. The question that is of particular relevance to this chapter is whether students working part-time in different sectors develop different skill sets.

The discussion about paid part-time work and study extends beyond the development of skills and also highlights the need to consider the links between work and study. Swanson et al. (2006) propose that students who perceive greater congruence between paid part-time work and study should exhibit higher levels of satisfaction. However, there is little evidence that students appreciate the inter-relationships that exist between their work and study (Greenbank et al., 2009; Hodgson and Spours, 2001). A longitudinal study of part-time students reported that irrespective of whether graduates had changed job or employer, or if they had stayed in the same job, these individuals reported substantial work-related gains from their higher education studies (Callender and Little, 2015). Hodgson and Spours (2001) conclude that students appear more focused on balancing the separate worlds of study and work than on connecting them.

It has been argued that students' part-time employment experiences should be more closely linked with higher education (Richardson et al., 2009). Billett and Ovens (2007) propose that the educational value of students reflecting on their paid employment is a resource for developing informed and critical insights about work. They suggest that paid part-time work may be integrated effectively into the curriculum to provide a potentially viable and highly accessible alternative to structured work placement programs. Likewise, Richardson et al. (2009) argue that it will become increasingly important for universities to adapt courses in order to create credible connections between their studies and their work experience. Paid part-time work experiences which are integrated with the formal curriculum may provide a more effective means for developing the knowledge and commercial skills demanded by the business community. If part-time work does have useful integrative learning outcomes for students and if appropriately designed pedagogy can assist students to integrate their experiences in the workplace with the curriculum, then it stands to reason that costly work placement programs may not be required.

The purpose of this study is to explore the role of part-time work in helping business and tourism students understand the world of work and in allowing them to integrate theory and practice. The study has four aims. First, the chapter identifies and contrasts the skills learners felt they were developing as a result of the paid part-time work in different sectors. Secondly, the chapter evaluates whether part-time work in different industry sectors results in different benefits for learners. Thirdly, the chapter explores whether students working in different industry sectors experienced congruence between their paid part-time work and study. Finally, the chapter considers whether students working part-time in different sectors display different levels of self-efficacy.

3.   METHODS

Following the approach used by Billett and Ovens (2007), students were surveyed mid-semester following a one-hour workshop designed to sensitize them to the interface between work and study. The one-hour workshop was designed as an intervention to allow students to reflect on informal learning and tacit knowledge acquired in the workplace. The intervention and questionnaire were deliberately administered mid-semester to avoid exam periods when academic and employment demands may be atypical. The process required students to complete two worksheets. The first worksheet was completed individually and contained a number of open-ended questions requiring students to think about their paid part-time work. Students then used this information to complete the second worksheet in small groups. The second worksheet contained more focused questions, which allowed students to compare their paid part-time work experiences and outcomes of paid work with their peers. The small group discussions were followed by a full class discussion, which was designed to further illuminate the outcomes of paid work.

Once the class discussion had been concluded, students were asked to complete a questionnaire. The questionnaire was administered in the controlled environment of formal class time and under the supervision of the researcher in order to maximize the response rate and to address any questions students raised during the completion of the questionnaire.

The questionnaire was developed from a detailed review of the literature. The first section of the questionnaire asked respondents to provide a number of demographic details, including gender, age, living arrangements, and the number of hours per week typically spent on various activities (including work and study). The second section of the questionnaire required students to indicate their level of agreement with a number of statements related to work–study congruence using a five-point Likert scale. These scales were adapted from the work of Swanson et al. (2006). Following this, the questionnaire asked students to provide a range of details about their paid part-time employment, including hourly pay rate, length of time with their current employer, whether they were working prior to commencing university, the number of jobs they have had, the sector they are employed in and the size of the organization they worked for. The third section of the questionnaire focused on skills acquisition and included a list of 37 skills adapted from a study by Raybould and Wilkins (2005). Students were asked to use a five-point Likert scale to indicate their level of agreement about whether their paid work had helped them to develop each of the listed skills. The final section of the questionnaire contained a set of Likert scales to measure students' self-efficacy. The self-efficacy items were based on the eight-item unidimensional New General Self-Efficacy Scale developed and validated by Chen et al. (2001).

The sample for this study comprised 315 first and second year business and tourism students enrolled at a mid-sized regional Australian university and a large metropolitan

Table 15.1   Profile of respondents

Demographic Characteristics	No.	Percentage	Job Characteristics	No.	Percentage
Gender			*Hours worked/week (mean = 17.2)*		
Female	203	65.5%	Less than 10	36	17.6%
Male	107	34.5%	10 to 19	86	42.0%
			20 or more	83	40.5%
Age groups (mean = 20.6)					
18	105	34.4%	*Industry sector*		
19 to 20	104	34.1%	Shopping & retail	98	44.1%
21 to 25	70	23.0%	Tourism, hospitality &	63	28.4%
Over 25	26	8.5%	leisure	61	27.5%
			Other		
*Student Characteristics**			*Time with current employer (mean = 19.8)*		
FIF	129	49.8%	6 months or less	128	43.2%
NESB	36	13.9%	7 to 12 months	29	9.8%
Born overseas	60	23.3%	13 to 18 months	26	8.8%
ATSI	5	1.9%	19 to 24 months	14	4.7%
Rural/remote	72	27.8%	Over 24 months	99	33.4%
Caring for dependants	15	5.8%			
			Pre-tax hourly pay rate (mean = $17.63)		
Living arrangements			$12.00 or less	31	13.9%
On-campus	41	13.2%	$12.01 to $15.00	57	25.6%
Off campus shared	76	24.4%	$15.01 to $18.00	53	23.8%
accommodation			$18.01 to $21.00	48	21.5%
With parents	141	45.3%	$21.01 or more	34	15.2%
Single occupancy	14	4.5%			
Other	39	12.5%			
			Employer Size		
Prior work experience			Under 5 employees	37	15.0%
(number of jobs) (mean = 3.5)			5 to 20 employees	87	35.4%
One (i.e. current job)	35	14.2%	21 to 100 employees	60	24.4%
Two	63	25.5%	Over 100 employees	62	25.2%
Three	53	21.5%			
Four	33	13.4%			
Five or more	63	25.5%			

Note: * FIF = First in family to attend university; NESB = Non-English speaking background; ATSI = Aboriginal or Torres Strait Islander.

university. A profile of the sample is presented in Table 15.1. The gender split was biased toward female respondents, which is indicative of the general business student population at the two study sites. Most students had been employed before, with only 14.2 percent of students indicating that their current job was their first job. A majority of students had been in their current job for more than 18 months and, consistent with previous studies, students were more likely to be employed in retail, tourism and hospitality. As a result, students were grouped into three industry sectors (tourism, retail and other), which provide the basis for subsequent analysis. The 'other category' included part-time work in education and childcare and trade work but a majority of students in this category reported working in white-collar roles such as administration, accounting and clerical work. The students in this sample were working an average of 17.2 hours per week with average earnings of $17.63 per hour. Many students reported hourly earnings well below the Australian minimum wage of $17.29 per hour (before tax), which raises some concerns and questions beyond the scope of this chapter.

4.   FINDINGS

Before considering the findings in the context of the aims, it is necessary to establish whether there is a difference in the amount of time spent on different activities by students working across the three different industry sectors. This is important because it could be argued that different study and work activity patterns may confound the results presented later in this section. Work and study activity patterns were measured by asking students to indicate how many hours per week they spent on various activities. These values were then compared across the three industry sectors using One-way ANOVA analyses (Table 15.2).

The results in Table 15.2 indicate that more time was invested in paid part-time work than any other activity. On average, students spent almost as much time on social activities as they did in class. The ANOVA analysis highlighted that there were no significant differences between students working across different industry sectors.

The first aim of this chapter was to identify and contrast the skills learners felt they were developing as a result of their paid part-time work in different sectors. The 37 items used on the survey were grouped into eight broad skills categories to simplify interpretation. Table 15.3 presents the means and One-way ANOVA results for each of the eight categories.

Several observations can be made about skills development. First, the overall pattern of results highlights that students working across all three industry sectors felt that they were developing interpersonal, team work and adaptability skills. There were no significant

Table 15.2   Time spent on different tasks (hours per week)

Task	Tourism	Retail	Other	F	p
Class time	11.7	10.8	11.1	0.723	0.486
Using the web for study/research	6.4	6.4	6.4	0.001	0.999
Using the web for recreation	10.3	6.9	7.8	1.938	0.147
Group work	3.8	6.5	4.2	2.839	0.061
Private study	9.7	8.1	8.8	0.678	0.509
Course readings	4.0	3.2	3.6	0.591	0.555
Paid work	17.1	15.4	17.9	1.277	0.282
Volunteer work	4.6	3.9	5.4	0.280	0.758
Social activities	11.3	9.0	10.3	1.319	0.270
Extra-curricular activities	5.1	4.9	5.6	0.433	0.650
Using the library	6.4	4.1	5.6	1.975	0.143

Table 15.3   Student perceptions of skills developed from paid part-time work

Skills	Tourism	Retail	Other	F	p
Interpersonal and teamwork skills	4.02	3.87	3.91	0.725	0.485
Adaptability	3.72	3.71	3.81	0.265	0.767
Communication	3.53	3.59	3.90	3.688	0.027
Information technology	2.46	2.83	3.31	9.657	0.000
Management and leadership	3.17	3.28	3.31	0.389	0.678
Problem solving	3.25	3.53	3.51	2.262	0.107
Self management	3.55	3.54	3.71	1.098	0.335
Improved ability to work with numbers and money	3.66	3.93	3.55	2.265	0.106

Note: Mean based on 5 = Strongly agree . . . 1 = Strongly disagree.

differences between the three groups of students for these items. Second, students were least likely to indicate that they were developing information technology skills; however, those working in other sectors (that is, clerical and accounting) were significantly more likely to agree that they were developing these skills. Many frontline tourism and hospitality jobs do not involve intensive use of technology, so this finding is not surprising. Third, it is surprising to find significant differences in students' perceptions about communication skills. Many tourism and retail roles require interactions and communication with customers and other employees and yet students working in these two sectors were significantly less likely than students working in other sectors to agree that they had developed this skill area.

The second aim of this chapter was to explore other benefits that students might derive from paid part-time work across the three different industry sectors. Table 15.4 summarizes student responses to a range of broader benefits that might be associated with part-time employment.

Following the pattern observed in the earlier tables, the findings indicate that those working in other sectors were more likely to agree with the statements about benefits, while those in retail jobs were least likely to agree with these statements. A One-way ANOVA identified significant differences between students working in the three industry sectors. Post hoc testing indicated that most of these differences were explained by the disparity between the mean ratings provided by those in retail jobs and the high ratings provided by those working in other sectors (that is, clerical, accounting and administrative roles).

The third aim of the chapter was to explore whether students perceived some congruence between their paid part-time work and study. Table 15.5 presents the mean ratings and One-way ANOVA results for student responses to the items related to work–study congruence.

It is clear from the data presented in Table 15.5 that a majority of students agreed with most of the statements about work–study congruence. While business students were noticeably less likely to agree that their job had a positive effect on their academic studies or that their degree was related to their job, all of the other items received positive mean ratings, indicating a relatively high level of work–study congruence. There was good support for the argument that paid part-time work during study assisted

Table 15.4 Perceived benefits of paid part-time work

Benefits	Tourism	Retail	Other	F	*p*
My job helps me to understand how a business is run	3.78	3.46	3.78	2.027	0.134
My job has been good for my self-development[c]	3.73	3.45	3.90	3.228	0.042
My job helps me to understand the world of work	3.71	3.52	3.83	1.789	0.170
My job helps me to learn about the 'real world'	3.56	3.49	3.86	2.199	0.113
My job has helped me make better career decisions[c]	3.35	3.20	3.71	3.410	0.035
My job enables me to organize my time more effectively[b, c]	3.22	3.12	3.78	6.310	0.002
My job provides good networking opportunities[c]	3.11	2.76	3.40	4.379	0.014

Notes:
Mean based on 5 = Strongly agree . . . 1 = Strongly disagree.
Statistically significant differences (Sheffe post hoc test): a = tourism ⇔ retail; b = tourism ⇔ other; c = retail ⇔ other; d = tourism ⇔ retail ⇔ other.

Table 15.5 Perceived work–study congruence

	Tourism	Retail	Other	F	*p*
Working while studying helps my future job prospects[c]	3.32	3.01	3.61	4.271	0.015
Working helps me better understand concepts discussed in class[b, c]	3.17	2.96	3.63	6.066	0.003
I can apply my academic studies to my job	3.13	3.00	3.36	1.557	0.213
I can apply my job experience to my academic studies[c]	3.11	2.91	3.54	5.047	0.007
The degree I am studying is related to my job[d]	2.92	2.44	3.39	9.261	0.000
My job has a positive effect on my academic studies[a, c]	2.92	2.50	3.26	10.166	0.000

Notes:
Mean based on 5 = Strongly agree . . . 1 = Strongly disagree.
Statistically significant differences (Sheffe post hoc test): a = tourism ⇔ retail; b = tourism ⇔ other; c = retail ⇔ other; d = tourism ⇔ retail ⇔ other.

students with their future job prospects and most students agreed or strongly agreed that this work helped them to better understand concepts discussed in class. Many students also agreed that they were able to apply their academic studies to their job and vice versa. However, significant differences were evident between students working across the three sectors. Given unequal sample sizes across the three groups, the source of these differences was identified in the table using the Sheffe post hoc test. In most cases the differences between tourism and retail jobs were not significant and differences were the result of means reported by students working in other part-time jobs. Overall, those with jobs in other sectors were more likely to report a higher level of work–study congruence, while those in retail jobs consistently reported the lowest levels of work–study congruence.

The final aim was to examine whether there were any differences in the self-efficacy scores of students working in the each of three sectors. The links between self-efficacy,

Table 15.6 General self-efficacy of students employed across three industry sectors

Self Efficacy Items	Tourism	Retail	Other	F	p
I will be able to achieve most of the goals I have set for myself[b,c]	3.61	3.48	4.03	6.876	0.001
When facing difficult tasks, I am certain that I will accomplish them[c]	3.46	3.16	3.76	7.145	0.001
In general, I think I can obtain outcomes that are important to me	3.69	3.63	3.97	2.917	0.056
I believe I can succeed in almost any endeavor I set my mind to	3.67	3.67	3.98	2.471	0.087
I will be able to successfully overcome many challenges[c]	3.82	3.63	4.02	3.167	0.044
I am confident I can perform effectively on many different tasks[c]	3.80	3.68	4.12	4.354	0.014
Compared to other people, I can do most tasks very well	3.67	3.57	3.87	2.225	0.111
Even when things are tough, I can perform quite well[c]	3.64	3.45	3.95	5.590	0.004

Notes:
Mean based on 5 = Strongly agree . . . 1 = Strongly disagree.
Statistically significant differences (Sheffe post hoc test): a = tourism ⇔ retail; b = tourism ⇔ other; c = retail ⇔ other; d = tourism ⇔ retail ⇔ other.

work and learning are complex and the current study does not seek to model these linkages and relationships. Rather the intent is to explore whether a general pattern can be identified by comparing mean student scores across each of the eight self-efficacy items.

The findings in Table 15.6 indicate that students working in other industry sectors reported the highest levels of self-efficacy, while those working in retail reported the lowest levels of self-efficacy. This may be because students working in other sectors generally do not work in front line positions involving subservient or repetitive tasks that demand a high degree of emotional labor and affective regulation. A One-way ANOVA again identified a number of significant differences resulting primarily from the disparities between students employed in the retail sector and those employed in other sectors.

5.   DISCUSSION AND FUTURE DIRECTIONS

This chapter has made three key contributions. First, the chapter confirms that paid part-time work can play a role in developing career-relevant skills, particularly in the areas of interpersonal skills, teamwork, adaptation and communication. It is noteworthy that these same skills have been associated with traditional forms of work-integrated learning, such as placements and internships. It is useful for universities to reflect on whether these traditional WIL programs are necessary in settings where students can readily gain experience through paid part-time work. The sector that students are employed in does not appear to make a significant difference to the development of most of the skills examined in this study. Second, the findings indicate that paid part-time employment generates a number of non-skills-related benefits, such as understanding the world of work and how businesses are managed.

Third, the results confirm that students were able to make some links between their studies and their paid part-time work. This finding might explain why the literature reports that the performance of students in paid part-time employment does not differ significantly from those who do not work. The grounding and life experience that working students are able to bring to the classroom and to their assessment tasks may compensate for the fact that they have less time available to spend on their studies. Fourth, while the overall pattern of responses remains consistent, the results highlight some significant differences between students working across different industry sectors. It seems the sector and the job itself does matter and does impact on the extent to which students are able to link their work with their studies. The 'other' category in this study included many students working in clerical, administrative and accounting roles. Those students specializing in accounting within their business degree are therefore more likely to perceive benefits and links between their work and study. These findings raise further questions. If students derive more benefit from their paid part-time employment and if there is a high level of congruence between their work and study, does this lead to higher levels of self-efficacy? The findings certainly suggest that students working in tourism and hospitality roles are more likely to report benefits and linkages than students working in retail. Does this mean that universities should be advising students to search for part-time work in tourism rather than retail?

The findings highlight a number of potential future directions for the tourism industry as well as universities and educators. They provide an opportunity for the tourism industry to pause and reflect on the role they might play in supporting personal development. For universities, the results raise a series of questions. As already noted, one key question is whether internships and placements are necessary if students are easily able to find paid-part time employment in the tourism industry. How can educators bring the work experiences of students into the classroom? Innovative pedagogy and assessment could be designed to encourage student reflection on the links between paid part-time work and study. Further partnerships between educators and industry offer rich opportunities to harness and link the practical work experiences of students with the more abstract and theoretical world of university study.

6.   CONCLUSION

This chapter has reported on a number of the benefits of paid part-time work discussed by other researchers. It has identified that a majority of business students do perceive some congruence between their work and academic studies. In addition, the results have shown that from a student perspective, paid part-time work is perceived as a useful activity for developing a number of transferable skills, most notably interpersonal skills, teamwork and adaptability, numeracy skills, problem solving and communication. These skills are often challenging to develop through traditional, classroom-based instruction. By contrasting these variables across three industry sectors, the analysis has also highlighted the relative advantages of paid part-time work in the tourism sector.

At a more pragmatic level, the results provide some support for the notion that business students do develop skills that have been identified as being important in the business world through their paid part-time work. It would be interesting to explore more formally how the skills developed through paid part-time work contrast with other experiential learning approaches such as online business simulations and internships. Further research might also explore whether business students report higher levels of work–study congruence than students from other disciplines. Given the importance of work–study congruence, there is an opportunity for business schools to develop new pedagogic approaches, activities and assessment designed to increase work–study congruence for students. Such approaches might meaningfully help students to integrate their experiences from the world of work with their studies. It would also be useful to investigate ways to encourage students to articulate skills and work–study connections in interviews and job applications. Given sufficient time and resources, there is also some scope to work with employers to develop joint programs aimed at closing the gap between work and study.

REFERENCES

Barron, P. and Anastasiadou, C. (2009), 'Student part-time employment', *International Journal of Contemporary Hospitality Management*, **21** (2), 140–53.
Biddle, N. (2007), 'The labour market status of Australian students: who is unemployed, who is working and for how many hours?', *Journal of Education and Work*, **20** (3), 179–209.
Billett, S. and Ovens, C. (2007), 'Learning about work, working life and post-school options: guiding students' reflections on paid part-time work', *Journal of Education and Work*, **20** (2), 75–90.
Bradley, G. (2006), 'Work participation and academic performance: a test of alternative propositions', *Journal of Education and Work*, **19** (5), 481–501.
Broadbridge, A. and Swanson, V. (2005), 'Earning and learning: how term-time employment impacts on students' adjustment to university life', *Journal of Education and Work*, **18** (2), 235–49.
Callender, C. and Little, B. (2015), 'The hidden benefits of part-time higher education study to working practices: is there a case for making them more visible?', *Journal of Education and Work*, **28** (3), 250–72.
Canny, A. (2002), 'Flexible labour? The growth of student employment in the UK', *Journal of Education and Work*, **15** (3), 277–301.
Carney, C., McNeish, S. and McColl, J. (2005), 'The impact of part time employment on students' health and academic performance: a Scottish perspective', *Journal of Further and Higher Education*, **29** (4), 307–19.
Chen, G., Gully, S. and Eden, D. (2001), 'Validation of a new general self-efficacy scale', *Organizational Research Methods*, **4** (1), 62–83.
Curtis, S. and Lucas, R. (2001), 'A coincidence of needs?', *Employee Relations*, **23** (1), 38–54.
Curtis, S. and Shani, N. (2002), 'The effect of taking paid employment during term-time on students academic studies', *Journal of Further and Higher Education*, **26** (2), 129–38.
Curtis, S. and Williams, J. (2002), 'The reluctant workforce: undergraduates' part-time employment', *Education and Training*, **44** (1), 5–10.
Darmody, M. and Smyth, E. (2008), 'Full-time students? Term-time employment among higher education students in Ireland', *Journal of Education and Work*, **21** (4), 349–62.
Ford, J., Bosworth, D. and Wilson, R. (1995), 'Part-time work and full-time higher education', *Studies in Higher Education*, **20** (2), 187–202.
Greenbank, P., Hepworth, S. and Mercer, J. (2009), 'Term-time employment and the student experience', *Education + Training*, **51** (1), 43–55.
Hall, R. (2010), 'The work–study relationship: experiences of full-time university students undertaking part-time employment', *Journal of Education and Work*, **23** (5), 439–49.
Hatcher, R. (1998), 'Class differentiation in education: rational choices?', *British Journal of Sociology of Education*, **19** (1), 5–24.
Hodgson, A. and Spours, K. (2001), 'Part-time work and full-time education in the UK: the emergence of a curriculum and policy issue', *Journal of Education and Work*, **14** (3), 373–88.
Humphrey, R. (2006), 'Pulling structured inequality into higher education: the impact of part-time working on English university students', *Higher Education Quarterly*, **60** (3), 270–86.

Hunt, A., Lincoln, I. and Walker, A. (2004), 'Term-time employment and academic attainment: evidence from a large-scale survey of undergraduates at Northumbria University', *Journal of Further and Higher Education*, **28** (1), 3–18.

Knight, P. and Yorke, M. (2004), *Learning, Curriculum and Employability in Higher Education*, New York: Routledge.

Krause, K., Hartley, R., James, R. and McInnis, C. (2005), 'The first year experience in Australian universities: findings from a decade of national studies', Canberra: DEST.

Little, B. (2002), 'UK institutional responses to undergraduates' term-time working', *Higher Education*, **44** (3), 349–60.

Manthei, R. and Gilmore, A. (2005), 'The effect of paid employment on university students' lives', *Education+ Training*, **47** (3), 202–15.

Martin, E. and McCabe, S. (2007), 'Part-time work and postgraduate students: developing the skills for employment?', *Journal of Hospitality, Leisure, Sports and Tourism Education*, **6**.

McInnis, C. and Hartley, R. (2002), 'Managing study and work: the impact of full-time study and paid work on the undergraduate experience in Australian universities', Canberra: DEST.

McKechnie, J., Hobbs, S. and Lindsay, S. (1997), 'The nature and extent of student employment at the University of Paisley', in P. Kelly (ed.), *Working in Two Worlds: Students and Part-time Employment*, Glasgow: Scottish Low Pay Unit.

Metcalf, H. (2003), 'Increasing inequality in higher education: the role of term-time working', *Oxford Review of Education*, **29** (3), 315–29.

Moreau, M. and Leathwood, C. (2006), 'Balancing paid work and studies: working (-class) students in higher education', *Studies in Higher Education*, **31** (1), 23–42.

Neill, N., Mulholland, G., Ross, V. and Leckey, J. (2004), 'The influence of part-time work on student placement', *Journal of Further and Higher Education*, **28** (2), 123–37.

OECD (2012), *Better Skills, Better Jobs, Better Lives: A Strategic Approach to Skills Policies*, Paris: OECD.

Oi I, B.T. and Morrison, K. (2005), 'Undergraduate students in part-time employment in China', *Educational Studies*, **31** (2), 169–80.

Raybould, M. and Wilkins, H. (2005), 'Over qualified and under experienced', *Management*, **17** (3), 203–16.

Richardson, M., Evans, C. and Gbadamosi, G. (2009), 'Funding full-time study through part-time work', *Journal of Education and Work*, **22** (4), 319–34.

Rikowski, G. (1992), 'Work experience schemes and part-time jobs in a recruitment context', *Journal of Education and Work*, **5** (1), 19–46.

Sorensen, L. and Winn, S. (1993), 'Student loans: a case study', *Higher Education Review*, **25** (3), 48–65.

Swanson, V., Broadbridge, A. and Karatzias, A. (2006), 'Earning and learning: role congruence, state/trait factors and adjustment to university life', *British Journal of Educational Psychology*, **76** (4), 895–914.

Wang, H., Kong, M., Shan, W. and Vong, S.K. (2010), 'The effects of doing part-time jobs on college student academic performance and social life in a Chinese society', *Journal of Education and Work*, **23** (1), 79–94.

Watts, C. and Pickering, A. (2000), 'Pay as you learn: student employment and academic progress', *Education and Training*, **42** (3), 129–34.

16 Self-authorship development through tourism education: rethinking the outcomes of work-integrated learning
Julia Caldicott and Erica Wilson

1. INTRODUCTION

University education has the potential to significantly influence the learning and personal development of learners. It is widely acknowledged that the personal and work-related challenges of the twenty-first century are greater than in previous eras and that change is occurring at unprecedented rates (Barnett 2000; Jackson 2011; Staron 2011; Thomas and Brown 2011). One of the greatest challenges and responsibilities for universities is preparing students for living, working and learning in an unpredictable world (Jackson 2011). Educators ponder how best to develop graduates' skills, knowledge and competencies so that they become responsible global citizens.

For the past three decades there has been an explicit focus on the role of higher education in developing learners' skills and improving graduate employability (Barnett 2009; Barnett and Coate 2005; Peach and Matthews 2011). In many ways this is due to the higher education sector's response to questions regarding the cost, quality and value of education from a range of stakeholders, including students, their parents, the wider public, employers, and educational policy-makers (Hersh et al. 2009). Employers across Australia, the UK and the USA have expressed concern regarding gaps in graduate skills (BIHECC 2007; Jackson 2010; Smith and Worsfold 2013). Consequently, universities have faced growing pressure to ensure graduates have acquired the necessary range of capabilities to meet current social and industrial requirements (Hutcheson 1999; Yorke 2006). Universities responded by offering more programs with a specific occupational focus and incorporating authentic professional practice activities, such as work-integrated learning (WIL) (Billett 2011). WIL is commonly defined as 'an umbrella term for a range of approaches and strategies that integrate theory with the practice of work within a purposefully designed curriculum' (Patrick et al. 2008, p. iv). Such strategies are aimed at equipping learners with discipline-specific skills, but also at meeting the needs consistently reported by employers that university graduates should be confident communicators, good team players, critical thinkers, problem solvers and, in addition, be adaptive, adaptable and transformative people capable of initiating, as well as responding to change (Crebert et al. 2004; Harvey et al. 1997).

Tourism and hospitality university education often incorporates a workplace experiential component (Beggs et al. 2008; Gibson and Busby 2009; Solnet et al. 2007). This work-based component is variously referred to as work-integrated learning (WIL), an internship, an industrial placement, a work placement, cooperative education or a practicum. Commonly regarded as a strategy to equip learners with the required practical skills for the workplace, this opportunity is now recognized for providing learners the chance to interpret and integrate their workplace practice (and everyday experiences) with conceptualized ideas (Cooper et al. 2010). Consequently, work-integrated learning programs have the potential to bridge liberal and vocational education, overcoming the need for a trade-off between knowledge and skills, a challenge that is increasingly being discussed in relation to tourism higher education curriculum design (Busby 2003; Dredge et al. 2012).

In tourism higher education, there are calls for alternative models of education, capable of producing graduates who not only cope, but flourish in spite of the complexities of the twenty-first century. Tourism and hospitality have been recognized as world-making activities because they have a 'creative and transformative role in the making of people and places and in the production of meanings, values and understandings about the past, present and future' (Dredge et al. 2012, pp. 2159–60). Accordingly, there is growing recognition of the need for universities to provide tourism curricula that balance the needs and demands of industry, whilst equipping graduates with the knowledge, skills and practical wisdom to act ethically and responsibly in their world-making capacities (Dredge et al. 2012; Jamal 2004; Sheldon et al. 2011; Tribe 2002). This current chapter aims to explore the usefulness of self-authorship as a model of holistic development for tourism learners, as they prepare to be skilled practitioners facing the challenges of the tourism sector and the complexities of the future in general.

Originally coined by Kegan (1982), the term 'self-authoring' refers to a stage of self-evolution which is reached when an individual has progressed from relying on external others (for example educators, peers and parents) to taking responsibility for one's own meaning making. Kegan (1982) proposed that humans make meaning from their perceptions through three major dimensions, namely: cognitive (how we come to know); intrapersonal (how we view our identities) and interpersonal (how we construct our relationships). As humans develop, Kegan argues, they move through five stages of increasingly complex ways of knowing. The first two stages are experienced by children, with most individuals reaching the third stage in adolescence. The self-authoring mind is the fourth stage, which often is not reached until the late twenties, and the final stage in Kegan's (1994) stages of development is the self-transforming mind, which does not develop until mid-life, if at all.

Baxter Magolda (2001) is credited with substantially advancing the concept of self-authorship, (Kegan's fourth stage of meaning making) based on her twenty-five-year longitudinal study of college students' learning and development. Her findings reaffirmed Kegan's (1994) proposition that personal growth occurs as a developmental process from an external definition to an internal definition. Whilst individuals use unique and different ways of dealing with challenges, Baxter Magolda (2009) identified four common phases through which young adults (aged between 18 and 40 years) progress as they move towards, and into, self-authorship.

In the first phase, *following external formulas*, individuals rely on external others for what to believe in and how to succeed. Individuals tend to reach the *crossroads* phase when they encounter a situation which forces them to question the external formulas which they had previously relied on. *Becoming self-authored* occurs when individuals recognize that knowledge, self and relationships all develop and exist in the context of others and cultural norms lead to their construction of new answers that are internally defined. *Internal foundations*, the final phase of self-authorship (being the author of one's life), is reached when an individual develops an internal voice to guide their beliefs, identity and relationships (Baxter Magolda 2008). Developing self-authoring capacities in identity, relationships and knowledge during higher education reportedly provides young adults with a foundation for mature adult decision-making, interdependent relationships and effective citizenship (Baxter Magolda 2007). Such a foundation could be a significant asset for future tourism practitioners, and arguably one worth fostering during tourism higher education.

2.   LITERATURE

2.1   Tourism Higher Education

Tourism education has progressed substantially over the past 40 years (Airey 2008). With many tourism programs originating from on-the-job training in hotels (Airey and Tribe 2000), tourism university education has been traditionally regarded as vocational in nature, with the primary aim of providing graduates for tourism and hospitality industries (Beggs et al. 2008; Connolly and McGing 2006; Goeldner and Ritchie 2006; Harris and Zhao 2004; Kok 2000; Stuart 2002; Zopiatis and Constanti 2007). However, a significant challenge for tourism university education providers is the growing concern about finding the appropriate balance between a vocational and a liberal arts curriculum. Whilst the need for tourism graduates to possess significant practical skills to appeal to industry employers is well documented (Knowles et al. 2003; Wang et al. 2009), there is increasing support for such university degrees to provide a more liberal and reflective orientation in addition to the practical vocational curriculum (Airey and Tribe 2000; Belhassen and Caton 2011; King et al. 2003; Lashley 1999; Morrison and O'Mahony 2003; Pizam et al. 1982; Tribe 2000). Such a curriculum would aim to educate 'philosophic practitioners' (Tribe 2002), who could respond to the needs of the tourism industry, as well as be reflective individuals who are capable of questioning the social responsibilities of industry (Inui et al. 2006).

While there is growing concern about the over-emphasis on 'vocationalism' in tourism university education, and considerable interest in Tribe's philosophical practitioner model in the academic community (Belhassen and Caton 2011; Dredge et al. 2012; Ring et al. 2009), a recent study has highlighted a reluctance to incorporate a liberal social science component in university tourism programs. In a review of 64 undergraduate tourism programs, only 6 percent were found to feature a significant liberal component, suggesting that 'tourism programs adopt current issues and changing conditions too slowly' (Ring et al. 2009, p. 112).

Nevertheless, challenges to the dominant technical and vocational tourism curriculum continue to be advanced. The Tourism Education Futures Initiative (TEFI), for example, was established in 2007 and its members seek to 'provide vision, knowledge, and a framework for tourism education programs that promote global citizenship and optimism for a better world' (Sheldon et al. 2011, p. 2). The goal of TEFI is radical and transformational change in tourism education, to produce graduates that become responsible stewards guiding tourism development in the future. Additionally, the 'critical turn' in tourism inquiry, which challenges the dominant (post)positivist approaches and locates the phenomenon of tourism within its political, social, economic and cultural contexts

(Ateljevic et al. 2007), is exerting influence on tourism education. Curricula and pedagogy which provide diverse theoretical and applied knowledge to understand the complexities of tourism and hospitality experiences are required when educating future tourism leaders (Ayikoru et al. 2009; Cockburn-Wootten and Cockburn 2011; Dredge et al. 2010). Fullagar and Wilson (2012, p. 1) call for a critical pedagogy in tourism education that 'embraces reflexivity as a "practice" – a way of doing, thinking and transforming knowledge as we live it'. Such an approach would emphasize a more liberal and reflective curriculum, providing the opportunity for more complex learning outcomes.

2.2   Work-Integrated Learning (WIL) in Tourism Higher Education

Given the recent employability agenda being pursued by universities, most tourism higher education qualifications incorporate a work-integrated learning (WIL) component (Beggs et al. 2008; Gibson and Busby 2009; Solnet et al. 2007). The WIL component is frequently compulsory and includes an amount of time (which varies between institutions and programs) in which the learner experiences working life in a related industry sector (Solnet et al. 2007). Tourism and hospitality WIL programs can be paid or voluntary, and undertaken domestically or internationally. The amount of academic credit accrued during a WIL program varies among institutions, as does the level of institutional involvement in the management, administration and supervision of learners undertaking WIL placements. Yet rarely do tourism and hospitality WIL programs have the professional accreditation requirements of other disciplines such as nursing, engineering and education (Baker et al. 2011).

The tourism and hospitality industries are noted for difficulties in attracting and retaining well-suited employees (Dickerson 2009; Haven-Tang and Jones 2008; Richardson 2008; Solnet and Hood 2011). Tourism and hospitality careers are reportedly fast paced, exciting, dynamic, and provide the opportunity to travel and meet new people (Solnet and Hood 2011), yet the challenges that come with these careers are also well documented. Much of the literature regarding the negative aspects of a career in tourism and hospitality focus on the external dimensions of the industry such as low pay, irregular and anti-social hours, hostile workplace cultures, lack of training and development, unjust promotional systems and high emotional labor requirements (Chu et al. 2012; Cockburn-Wootten 2012; Solnet and Hood 2011). In a study of tourism students' perceptions of the industry, more than 50 percent reported that they were contemplating careers outside of the industry and most cited work experience in the industry as the main reason for this decision (Richardson 2008). Similarly, Raybould and Wilkins (2005) note that many hospitality graduates leave the industry because of unfulfilled expectations. Consequently, the dominant discourse in tourism and hospitality WIL literature is the need for higher education providers to work collaboratively with industry to manage learners' expectations, with the aim of increasing graduate employability and industry retention (Cho 2006; Lam and Ching 2007; Lee and Dickson 2010; Richardson 2009; Roberts 2009; Sigala and Baum 2003; Tse 2010; Zopiatis and Theocharous 2013).

Tourism and hospitality-specific research has identified a number of benefits of WIL programs for learners including stronger career intentions than learners who do not complete a WIL placement or have work experience (Busby 2003; Chuang and Dellmann-Jenkins 2010); increased employability in relevant positions after graduation (Purcell

1999 cited in Busby 2003); and faster advancement opportunities than their non-WIL counterparts (Harper et al. 2005). A key benefit to tourism and hospitality industries is the correlation between learners who have participated in highly structured WIL programs and increased industry retention (Dickerson and Kline 2008). However, as noted above, other studies have highlighted that familiarity with the hospitality industry was a major reason that individuals left the industry (Jiang and Tribe 2009; Richardson 2008; Teng 2008). Arguably, the success of the WIL placement is dependent on the curricula and pedagogic practices of the WIL program that influence learners' expectations and their subsequent clash with reality.

Many studies focus on the need to improve the work-integrated learning experience to retain graduates in industry (Lam and Ching 2007; Tse 2010). It is evident that learners report negative experiences during their tourism and hospitality internships (Tse 2010) or discrepancies between their expectations and satisfaction (Cho 2006; Lam and Ching 2007; Leslie and Richardson 2000; Raybould and Wilkins 2005; Tse 2010). Poor communication, unsatisfactory interpersonal relations and lack of knowledge to perform required tasks have been identified by learners following their tourism and hospitality internship (Lam and Ching 2007). Such negative perceptions of internships have been linked to psychological distress, frustration and depression (Lam and Ching 2007) and graduates leaving the industry (Richardson 2008). Research has identified that preparing learners for WIL is important so they know to expect difficulties and find their way to deal with these (Tse 2010).

While existing literature identifies the benefits and challenges of tourism and hospitality WIL placements from a learner perspective, there is limited knowledge about the developmental capacities of learners prior to and following their placement. Insights into the meaning-making structures of learners prior to their WIL placement may yield more comprehensive information about the curriculum and pedagogical requirements of the WIL preparation and placement stages. Additionally, there is a lack of information regarding the effect of dissatisfaction and disillusionment experienced during WIL placements on self-authorship development. Potentially, holistic and well-designed WIL programs may provide the opportunity for significant personal development in addition to the employability outcomes that they are often adopted for.

2.3   Self-authorship

Over the past decade it has 'become apparent that our educational institutions need to pay more attention to developing learners as whole people' (Jackson 2011, p. 2). Universities should foster a learner's will and spirit to *be* and *become* (Barnett 2007). In addition to the now widely recognized notion of lifelong learning, the complementary concept of lifewide learning is proposed as facilitating progression to complex learning (Jackson 2011). Advocates of lifewide learning propose that learning and development occurs in multiple and varied places and situations (Jackson 2011). A curriculum and pedagogical approach that fosters lifelong and lifewide learning is designed to increase learners' self-awareness of when and where learning occurs in their lives and to facilitate their progression to self-authorship. Self-authorship has been identified as central to a young adult's ability to succeed in complex work, educational and personal environments (Abes and Jones 2004; Baxter Magolda 2007; Torres 2010).

The expected core outcomes of most Western higher education programs include effective citizenship, critical thinking, complex problem-solving, interdependent relations with diverse others and mature decision-making (Baxter Magolda 2010a). Such overarching higher education outcomes require informational learning (that is, knowledge and skills) and transformational learning, where an individual acts on his/her own values, feelings and meanings rather than those that they have uncritically assimilated from others (Baxter Magolda 2010a; Kegan 2000; Mezirow 2000). Cognitive (knowing), intrapersonal (identity) and interpersonal (relationship) developmental capacities are required for transformational learning (Kegan 2000). The expectations on young adults in higher education and contemporary society in general, may therefore exceed their meaning-making capacities (Baxter Magolda 2010a; Kegan 1994).

In Baxter Magolda's longitudinal study, most of the participants became self-authoring in their late twenties, after leaving higher education and encountering their catalysts for change in work situations, personal relationships or health-related matters. Similarly, a number of studies in the United States have demonstrated that traditional-aged college students are not self-authoring at the end of their undergraduate studies (Kegan and Lahey 2009; King and Baxter Magolda 2011). However, following Baxter Magolda's initial findings in 1998 there has been a proliferation of studies exploring the applicability of self-authorship as a holistic framework of student development. The results indicate that self-authorship can be facilitated through pedagogical and curriculum changes in higher education (Baxter Magolda 2001; 2004; Baxter Magolda and King 2004; Hornak and Ortiz 2004; King and Baxter Magolda 2005; Pizzolato 2003). Although not offering prescriptive advice for curriculum design, Baxter Magolda's (2009) Learning Partnership Model outlines the challenges and support required to promote self-authorship. Similarly, engaged learning is an intentional educational philosophy designed to promote transformation from authority dependence to constructing one's own beliefs, values and vision, by balancing challenges with the necessary educational support (Hodge et al. 2009).

Human development has long been of interest to educators seeking to improve student learning processes and outcomes. As a relatively recent theory, self-authorship has its roots in the constructive-developmental research tradition, which asserts that humans actively construct their perspectives by interpreting their experiences (*constructivism*) and that these constructions form meaning-making structures that increase in complexity over time (*developmental*) (Kegan 1982). Developmental theory focuses on *how* we know rather than *what* we know (Boes et al. 2010). Constructive developmental theory, also known as the neo-Piagetian theory (Kegan 1982; McCauley et al. 2006), emerged from Piaget's (1954) seminal research into the cognitive developmental journey of children. Others such as Perry (1970), Belenky et al. (1986), Baxter Magolda (1992), and King and Kitchener (1994) extended Piaget's cognitive development theory in their research on higher education students.

As with cognitive developmental theories, constructive developmental theories explore the transformation in how people construct meaning (Schoper 2011). However, moving beyond the cognitive focus of Piaget's work, Kegan's (1982; 1994) constructive developmental theory of self-evolution proposed that human meaning-making occurs through the intersection of three dimensions, namely: cognitive; intrapersonal; and interpersonal. Meaning-making occurs simultaneously in all dimensions, and meaning making in one dimension mediates development in the other dimensions (Baxter Magolda 2012a).

The intertwining of these three dimensions of development undergirds an individual's thinking, feeling and social relating (Baxter Magolda 2009; Kegan 1994). Importantly, constructive development theories address the *structure* which humans use to construct meaning from their experience, not the *content* of their meaning-making (Boes et al. 2010). For example, two people may share the same ideas and views: one may have adopted these by relying uncritically on external sources, whereas the other, self-authoring individual will have used their internal voice to consider multiple perspectives to arrive at that decision (Baxter Magolda and King 2012).

Whilst Kegan's (1982) theory of human development spanned from birth to death and lacked empirical evidence at the time (Schoper 2011), Baxter Magolda's (2001) longitudinal study specifically focused on the self-authorship stage in Kegan's theory and gathered empirical evidence from her research on young adults in a college context. Baxter Magolda's twenty-five year study, initiated in 1986, has provided rich insight into how these undergraduate students decided what to believe in, how they perceived themselves and how they related to others during the college and post-college years (Baxter Magolda 2012a). Reaffirming Kegan's (1994) proposition that meaning making structures are multi-dimensional and interdependent, Baxter Magolda found that those participants who expressed complex ways of knowing often struggled to use them until they had also developed complex ways of seeing themselves and relating with others (Baxter Magolda 2010c). Self-authorship was found to develop in phases, with most study participants making little progress towards self-authorship during their university education (Baxter Magolda 2001).

Other studies have also identified that few traditional-age graduating students have developed self-authorship during their college years (Kegan and Lahey 2009; King and Baxter Magolda 2011). Reporting on the results of two large studies which focused predominantly on middle class, college educated professionals, Kegan and Lahey (2009) noted that 58 percent of respondents were not self-authoring. Similarly, King and Baxter Magolda (2011) report on numerous longitudinal studies of traditional-age college students not demonstrating the characteristics of self-authorship upon graduation. The few studies reporting contrary results have focused on populations who have experienced marginalization during their tertiary education, such as lesbian (Abes and Jones, 2004), high risk (Pizzolato 2003) and Latino (Torres 2010) college students.

Research into self-authorship has identified that it arises through an individual processing a disequilibrizing situation, and such dissonance acts as the primary catalyst in self-authorship development (Pizzolato 2005; Pizzolato et al. 2012). A situation which causes dissonance prompts an individual to question their previously uncritical dependence on external influences, and thus moves into the crossroads phase of self-authorship development (Baxter Magolda 2012a; Baxter Magolda 2010b). Baxter Magolda's (2001) longitudinal study indicated that many individuals spend most of their twenties navigating the crossroads phase of self-authorship development. Pizzolato's (2005) further work into the crossroads phase of self-authorship development identified that an individual may cycle through many instances of experiences of discontent with external ways of knowing, but not act in any purposeful way to relieve that dissatisfaction. A 'provocative moment' occurs when the individual moves beyond recognizing the dissonance, to actively committing to turn inward in their search for self-definition (Pizzolato 2005).

Benefits and importance of self-authorship

Given the complexities of the twenty-first century, self-authorship has been advanced as a developmental foundation for advanced learning outcomes (Baxter Magolda 2007). More complex meaning-making structures (associated with self-authorship) provide individuals with more options in decision making, more grounded reasons for their choices (tied to one's values rather than the expectations of others), and enhanced abilities to adapt in different contexts (Baxter Magolda 2012b). Introducing 'provocative moments' into higher education practices could act as a catalyst for learners' self-authorship development. A provocative moment has been described as similar to Mezirow's (2000) disorienting dilemma in that it is a situation in which usual expectations, assumptions and coping mechanisms do not provide an adequate solution to a problem (Meszaros and Duncan Lane 2010). Such a situation is believed to have the propensity to bring about transformative learning, a process 'by which adults learn how to think critically for themselves rather than take assumptions supporting a point of view for granted' (Mezirow 2009, p. 103). Transformational learning, not just informational learning, is believed to be required for learners to take personal responsibility for their beliefs and actions (Baxter Magolda 2012b). As argued by Baxter Magolda (2012b) and Kegan and Lahey (2009), cultivating these self-authoring capacities during higher education would be less risky than developing them in post-college work environments.

2.4   The Potential for Self-authorship Development through WIL in Tourism Higher Education

The authentic and contextualized learning environment afforded by WIL in tourism higher education presents opportunities to facilitate self-authorship development. As noted above, WIL in tourism higher education programs is known to present learners with challenges which, whilst potentially distressing at the time, can provide the provocative moment that prompts the evaluation of their previously unquestioned, externally derived beliefs and assumptions. Well-designed WIL programs incorporate opportunities for learners to reflect on their workplace experience. Such reflections could focus on learners' learning in the three dimensions of self-authorship, including cognitive (such as knowledge of destination marketing strategies or hotel staff induction programs); self (such as their values, strengths, decision-making preferences and learning styles); and interpersonal (such as how they work collaboratively in teams and interact with customers/guests). Tourism WIL programs that adequately prepare learners prior to their placement and provide the necessary support in order to benefit from the challenges inherent in WIL, could contribute to the evolution of future tourism leaders who will consciously and meaningfully self-author their lives.

3.   FUTURE DIRECTIONS

By rethinking, or expanding, the desired goals of a WIL program in tourism higher education, the opportunity to facilitate self-authorship development and the associated advanced learning outcomes could be realized. Such advanced learning outcomes are deemed necessary for future tourism leaders who will guide tourism development by responding to the needs of the tourism industry, whilst questioning the social responsibilities of the industry. Although a number of studies have found that the majority of traditional-aged higher education students are not self-authoring upon graduation, research does indicate that fostering self-authorship development during higher education is possible (Baxter Magolda and King 2004; Baxter Magolda 2012b). In addition to evoking a provocative moment, adequate support is deemed necessary when students are challenged out of their comfort zone (Baxter Magolda 2010b, Kegan 1994).

Fostering students' self-authorship development requires a customized approach, whereby each individual's current stage of cognitive, intrapersonal and interpersonal development is respected and used as a starting point to provide appropriate challenges to trigger more complex meaning making (Baxter Magolda and King 2007). This is similar to the concept of scaffolding, a common curriculum design strategy currently employed in higher education. Scaffolds (forms of support to help learners bridge the gap between their current abilities and intended goals) have been noted as particularly useful for teaching higher order cognitive strategies (Rosenshine and Meister 1992). Less common, however, are the other pedagogical and curriculum requirements thought to promote self-authorship development.

Whilst not prescriptive, Baxter Magolda's (2004; 2009; 2012b) Learning Partnership Model (LPM) outlines three supportive components and three challenges in the learning environment that educators can provide in order to promote self-authorship development. Support is provided through three principles:

- respecting learners' thoughts and feelings, thus affirming the value of their voices;
- helping them view those experiences as opportunities for learning and growth;
- collaborating with them to analyze their own problems, thereby engaging in mutual learning with them (Baxter Magolda 2009, p. 251).

Challenges are provided by:

- drawing attention to the complexity of their work and life decisions and discouraging simplistic solutions;
- encouraging them to develop personal authority by listening to their own voices in determining how to live their lives;
- encouraging them to share authority and expertise while working with others to solve mutual problems (Baxter Magolda 2009, p. 251).

A number of studies have demonstrated that using the principles of the LPM has resulted in undergraduate learners achieving complex learning outcomes, underpinned by progression towards self-authorship. Whilst not widespread, a number of studies have emerged following Baxter Magolda's (2004) learning partnerships model, detailing curricula and pedagogical examples of either designing innovative practices on the basis of the LPM, or applying the LPM framework to existing education practices. These include a two-year Earth Sustainability course (Bekken and Marie 2007), academic advising programs (Pizzolato and Ozaki 2007), a writing curriculum in an Honors program (Haynes 2004), a master of science program (Rogers et al. 2004), a semester-long cultural immersion experience (Yonkers-Talz 2004), a multicultural program in a business college curriculum

(Hornak and Ortiz 2004), and an urban leadership internship program (Egart and Healy 2004). There have been calls for future research into other education programs which are based on the LPM's principles, in order to understand the diversity of contexts that can foster self-authorship (Pizzolato and Ozaki 2007).

A well-designed and structured WIL program in tourism higher education could incorporate the three supports and challenges outlined in Baxter Magolda's Learning Partnerships Model and promote the development of self-authorship. For example, equipping learners with career development knowledge and job search skills to negotiate and secure their own WIL placements affirms the value of their voices and respects their thoughts and feelings. Further support for self-authorship development could be provided through reflective assessments which offer the opportunity for learners to view workplace successes and challenges as opportunities for learning and growth. Furthermore, an effective workplace supervisor who treats the learner as a peer during the WIL placement and seeks the learners' input, for example, can also provide support in terms of sharing the construction of knowledge.

Undoubtedly, WIL offers learners the opportunity to apply theoretical knowledge to practice and develop skills and professionalism, but additionally it can present a provocative moment – believed to be the catalyst for self-authorship development. The perceived complexities of the unfamiliar work environment in which WIL often occurs, creates opportunities for knowledge construction related to the learner's required tasks (cognitive dimension), evaluation of their performance (intrapersonal dimension) and how they relate to and are perceived by colleagues and customers (intrapersonal dimension). Whilst the unique characteristics of WIL offer significant potential for fostering self-authorship development, other aspects of a tourism higher education curriculum such as business ethics, sustainability, and organizational behavior modules may also be appropriate for incorporating the principles of the Learning Partnerships Model. Well-designed and delivered field trips, which expose learners to various stakeholders, may also offer potential for facilitating self-authorship development.

4.   SUMMARY AND CONCLUSION

As a stage of adult development, the concept of self-authorship has relevance for all adults, not only those engaged in higher education. However, there are a number of reasons why this concept has particular relevance for tourism higher education. Self-authorship is recognized as a necessary foundation for the advanced learning outcomes which are articulated as goals of most higher education institutions (Baxter Magolda 2007). Traditional-aged university students (that is, those aged between 18 and 30 years) still represent a significant proportion of all higher education students. Many students in this category are graduating without reaching the self-authorship stage during university (Kegan and Lahey 2009; King and Baxter Magolda 2011). Some existing research indicates that self-authorship development can be fostered by intentionally designed pedagogy during university. WIL, as a common component of tourism higher education, often presents learners with a period of discontent and provocative moments which are believed to foster self-authorship development. As we have attempted to illustrate here in this chapter, intentionally fostering self-authorship development may provide a number of benefits as we continue to equip our future tourism leaders to become responsible stewards of the twenty-first century.

REFERENCES

Abes, E.S. and S.R. Jones (2004), 'Meaning-making capacity and the dynamics of lesbian college students' multiple dimensions of identity', *Journal of College Student Development*, **45**, 612–32.
Airey, D. (2008), 'Tourism Education: Life begins at 40', *Teoros*, **27** (1), 27–32.
Airey, D. and J. Tribe (2000), 'Education for Hospitality', in C. Lashley and A. Morrison (eds), *In Search of Hospitality: Theoretical Perspectives and Debates*, Oxford: Butterworth Heinemann, pp. 276–92.
Ateljevic, I., A. Pritchard and N. Morgan (eds) (2007), *The Critical Turn in Tourism Studies: Innovative Research Methodologies*, Oxford: Elsevier.
Ayikoru, M., J. Tribe and D. Airey (2009), 'Reading tourism education: Neoliberalism unveiled', *Annals of Tourism Research*, **36** (2), 191–221.
Baker, L., J. Caldicott and J. Spowart (2011), 'Cooperative and work-integrated education in hospitality and tourism', in R.K. Coll and K.E. Zegwaard (eds), *International Handbook for Cooperative and Work-integrated Education: International Perspectives of Theory, Research and Practice*, Lowell, MA: World Association for Cooperative Education, pp. 219–27.
Barnett, R. (2000), 'Supercomplexity and the curriculum', in M. Tight (ed.), *Curriculum in Higher Education*, Buckingham: Open University Press.
Barnett, R. (2007), *A Will to Learn: Being a Student in the Age of Uncertainty*, Buckingham: Open University Press, McGraw Hill Education.
Barnett, R. (2009), 'Knowing and becoming in the higher education curriculum', *Studies in Higher Education*, **34** (4), 429–40.
Barnett, R. and K. Coate (2005), *Engaging the Curriculum in Higher Education*, Basingstoke: McGraw-Hill Education.
Baxter Magolda, M.B. (1992), *Knowing and Reasoning in College: Gender-related Patterns in Students' Intellectual Development*, San Francisco, CA: Jossey-Bass.
Baxter Magolda, M.B. (2001), *Making their Own Way: Narratives for Transforming Higher Education to Promote Self-development*, Sterling, VA: Stylus.
Baxter Magolda, M.B. (2004), 'Learning partnerships model: A framework for promoting self-authorship', in M.B. Baxter Magolda and P.M. King (eds), *Learning Partnerships: Theory and Models of Practice to Educate for Self-authorship*, Sterling, VA: Stylus, pp. 37–62.
Baxter Magolda, M.B. (2007), 'Self-authorship: The foundation for twenty-first-century education', *New Directions for Teaching and Learning*, **109**, 69–83.
Baxter Magolda, M.B. (2008), 'Three elements of self-authorship', *Journal of College Student Development*, **49**, 269–84.
Baxter Magolda, M.B. (2009), *Authoring your Life: Developing an Internal Voice to Navigate Life's Challenges*, Sterling, VA: Stylus.
Baxter Magolda, M.B. (2010a), Educating students for self-authorship: Learning partnerships to achieve complex outcomes', in C. Kreber (ed.), *The University and its Disciplines: Teaching and Learning Within and Beyond Disciplinary Boundaries*, London: Routledge, pp. 144–56.
Baxter Magolda, M.B. (2010b), 'Future directions: Pursuing theoretical and methodological issues in the evolution of self-authorship', in M.B. Baxter Magolda, E.G. Creamer and P.S. Meszaros (eds), *Development and Assessment of Self-authorship: Exploring the Concept Across Cultures*, Sterling, VA: Stylus, pp. 267–84.
Baxter Magolda, M.B. (2010c), 'The interweaving of epistemological, intrapersonal, and development in the evolution of self-authorship', in M.B. Baxter Magolda, E.G. Creamer and P.S. Meszaros (eds), *Development and Assessment of Self-authorship: Exploring the Concept Across Cultures*, Sterling, VA: Stylus, pp. 25–43.
Baxter Magolda, M.B. (2012a), 'Lifewide development: Authoring your life', *Lifewide Magazine*, **5**, 6–8.
Baxter Magolda, M.B. (2012b), 'Building learning partnerships', *Change*, **44** (1), 32–8.
Baxter Magolda, M.B. and P.M. King (eds) (2004), *Learning Partnerships: Theory and Models of Practice to Educate for Self-authorship*, Sterling, VA: Stylus.
Baxter Magolda, M.B. and P.M. King (2007), 'Constructing conversations to assess meaning- making: Self authorship interviews', *Journal of College Student Development*, **48** (5), 491–508.
Baxter Magolda, M.B. and P.M. King (2012), 'Assessing meaning making and self-authorship; theory, research and application', in K. Ward and L.E. Wolfe-Wendel (eds), *The ASHE Higher Education Research Report* (Vol. 38), San Francisco, CA: John Wiley & Sons.

Beggs, B., C.M. Ross and B. Goodwin (2008), 'A comparison of student and practitioner perspectives of the travel and tourism internship', *Journal of Hospitality, Leisure, Sport and Tourism Education*, **7** (1), 31–9.

Bekken, B.M. and J. Marie (2007), 'Making self-authorship a goal of core curricula: The Earth Sustainability Pilot Project', in P.S. Meszaros (ed.), *Self-authorship: Advancing Students' Intellectual Growth, New Directions for Teaching and Learning*, San Francisco, CA: Jossey-Bass, vol. 109, pp. 53–67.

Belenky, M., B.M. Clinchy, N. Goldberger and J. Tarule (1986), *Women's Ways of Knowing: The Development of Self, Voice, and Mind*, New York: Basic Books.

Belhassen, Y. and K. Caton (2011), 'On the need for critical pedagogy in tourism education', *Tourism Management*, **32**, 1389–96.

Billett, S. (2011), 'Curriculum and pedagogic bases for effectively integrating practice-based experiences', ALTC Project Final Report, accessed 30 March 2015 at http://www.acen.edu.au/resources/docs/Billett-S-Griffith-NTF-Final-report-2011.pdf.

Boes, L.M., M.B. Baxter Magolda and J.A. Buckley (2010), 'Foundational assumptions and constructive developmental theory: Self-authorship narratives', in M.B. Baxter Magolda, E.G. Creamer and P.S. Meszaros (eds), *Development and Assessment of Self-authorship: Exploring the Concept Across Cultures*, Sterling, VA: Stylus, pp. 1–23.

Busby, G. (2003), 'Tourism degree internships: A longitudinal study', *Journal of Vocational Education and Training*, **55** (3), 319–34.

Business, Industry and Higher Education Collaboration Council (BIHECC) (2007), *Graduate Employability Skills*, Canberra: BIHECC.

Cho, M. (2006), 'Student perspectives on the quality of hotel management internships', *Journal of Teaching in Travel & Tourism*, **6** (1), 61–76.

Chu, K.H., M.A. Baker and S.K. Murrmann (2012), 'When we are onstage, we smile: The effects of emotional labor on employee work outcomes', *International Journal of Hospitality Management*, **31**, 906–15.

Chuang, N. and M. Dellmann-Jenkins (2010), 'Career decision making and intention: A study of hospitality undergraduate students', *Journal of Hospitality & Tourism Research*, **34** (4), 512–30.

Cockburn-Wootten, C. (2012), 'Critically unpacking professionalism in hospitality: Knowledge, meaningful work and dignity', *Hospitality & Society*, **2** (2), 215–30.

Cockburn-Wootten, C. and T. Cockburn (2011), 'Unsettling assumptions and boundaries: Strategies for developing a critical perspective about business and management communication', *Business Communication Quarterly*, **74** (1), 45–59.

Connolly, P. and G. McGing (2006), 'Graduate education and hospitality management in Ireland', *International Journal of Contemporary Hospitality Management*, **18** (1), 50–59.

Cooper, L., J. Orrell and M. Bowden (2010), *Work Integrated Learning: A Guide to Effective Practice*, London: Routledge.

Crebert, G., M. Bates, B. Bell, C.J. Patrick and V. Cragnolini (2004), 'Developing generic skills at university, during work placement and in employment: Graduates' perceptions', *Higher Education Research & Development*, **23** (2), 147–65.

Dickerson, J.P. (2009), 'The realistic preview may not yield career satisfaction', *International Journal of Hospitality Management*, **28** (2), 297–99.

Dickerson, J.P. and S.F. Kline (2008), 'The early career impact of the co-op commitment in hospitality curricula', *Journal of Teaching in Travel & Tourism*, **8** (1), 1–22.

Dredge, D., P. Benckendorff, M. Day, M. Gross, M. Walo, P. Weeks and P. Whitelaw (2010), 'Conceptualising the perfect blend in the tourism and hospitality curriculum space', in M.J. Gross (ed.), *Proceedings of the CAUTHE Conference, 'Creating the Perfect Blend in Tourism and Hospitality Education'*, University of South Australia, Adelaide, 8–11 February, pp. 1–20.

Dredge, D., P. Benckendorff, M. Day, M. Gross, M. Walo, P. Weeks and P. Whitelaw (2012), 'The philosophic practitioner and the curriculum space', *Annals of Tourism Research*, **39** (4), 2154–76.

Egart, K. and M.P. Healy (2004), 'An urban leadership internship program: Implementing learning partnerships "unplugged" from campus structures', in M.B. Baxter Magolda and P.M. King (eds), *Learning Partnerships: Theory and Models of Practice to Educate for Self-authorship*, Sterling, VA: Stylus, pp. 125–50.

Fullagar, S. and E. Wilson (2012), 'Critical pedagogies: A reflexive approach to knowledge creation in tourism and hospitality studies', *Journal of Hospitality and Tourism Management*, **19** (1), 1–6.

Gibson, P. and G. Busby (2009), 'Experiencing work: Supporting the undergraduate hospitality, tourism and cruise management student on an overseas work placement', *Journal of Vocational Education and Training*, **61** (4), 467–80.

Goeldner, R. and J.R.B. Ritchie (2006), *Tourism: Principles, Practices, Philosophies*, 10th edn, Hoboken, NJ: John Wiley & Sons.

Harper, S., C. Brown and W. Irvine (2005), 'Qualifications: A fast-track to hotel general manager?', *International Journal of Contemporary Hospitality Management*, **17** (1), 51–64.

Harris, K.J. and F. Zhao (2004), 'Industry internships: Feedback from participating faculty and industry executives', *International Journal of Contemporary Hospitality Management*, **16** (7), 429–35.

Harvey, L., S. Moon and V. Geall (1997), 'Graduates' work: Implications of organisational change on the development of student attributes', *Industry and Higher Education*, **11** (5), October, 287–96.

Haven-Tang, C. and E. Jones (2008), 'Labour market and skills needs of the tourism and related sectors in Wales', *International Journal of Tourism Research*, **10** (4), 353–63.

Haynes, C. (2004), 'Promoting self-authorship through an interdisciplinary writing curriculum', in M.B. Baxter Magolda and P.M. King (eds), *Learning Partnerships: Theory and Models of Practice to Educate for Self-authorship*, Sterling, VA: Stylus, pp. 63–90.

Hersh, R.H., M. Bundick, R. Keeling, C. Keyes, A. Kurpius, R. Shavelson, D. Silverman and L. Swaner (2009), 'A well-rounded education for a flat world', *Educational Leadership*, **67** (1), 50–53.

Hodge, D.C., M.B. Baxter Magolda and C.A. Haynes (2009), 'Engaged learning: Enabling self-authorship and effective practice', *Liberal Education*, **95** (4), 16–23.

Hornak, A. and A. Ortiz (2004), 'Creating a context to promote diversity education and self- authorship among community college students', in M.B. Baxter Magolda and P. M. King (eds), *Learning Partnerships: Theory and Models of Practice to Educate for Self-authorship*, Sterling, VA: Stylus, pp. 91–124.

Hutcheson, P. (1999), *Educating a Globally Productive Citizenry: The Role of Higher Education in the Integration of Learning and Work: A Monograph for College Leader*, Boston, MA: National Commission for Cooperative Education.

Inui, Y., D. Wheeler and S. Lankford (2006), 'Rethinking tourism education', *Journal of Hospitality, Leisure, Sport and Tourism Education*, **5** (2), 25–35.

Jackson, D. (2010), 'An international profile of industry-relevant competencies and skill gaps in modern graduates', *International Journal of Management Education*, **8** (3), 29–58.

Jackson, N.J. (2011), *Learning for a Complex World: A Lifewide Concept of Learning, Education and Personal Development*, Bloomington, IN: Authorhouse.

Jamal, T.B. (2004), 'Virtue ethics and sustainable tourism pedagogy: Phronesis, principles and practice', *Journal of Sustainable Tourism*, **12** (6), 530–45.

Jiang, B. and J. Tribe (2009), 'Tourism jobs – short lived professions': Student attitudes towards tourism careers in China', *Journal of Hospitality, Leisure, Sport and Tourism Education*, **8** (1), 4–19.

Kegan, R. (1982), *The Evolving Self: Problem and Process in Human Development*, Cambridge, MA: Harvard University Press.

Kegan, R. (1994), *In Over our Heads: The Mental Demands of Modern Life*, Cambridge, MA: Harvard University Press.

Kegan, R. (2000), 'What "form" transforms? A constructive-developmental approach to transformative learning', in J. Mezirow and Associates (eds), *Learning as Transformation: Critical Perspectives on a Theory in Progress*, San Francisco, CA: Jossey-Bass, pp. 35–69.

Kegan, R. and L.L. Lahey (2009), *Immunity to Change: How to Overcome it and Unlock Potential in Yourself and Your Organization*, Boston, MA: Harvard Business Press.

King, B., B. McKercher and R. Waryszak (2003), 'A comparative study of hospitality and tourism graduates in Australia and Hong Kong', *International Journal of Tourism Research*, **5** (6), 409–20.

King, P.M. and M.B. Baxter Magolda (2005), 'A developmental model of intercultural maturity', *Journal of College Student Development*, **46** (6), 571–92.

King, P.M. and M.B. Baxter Magolda (2011), 'Student learning', in J.H. Schuh, S.R. Jones and S.R. Harper (eds), *Student Services: A Handbook for the Profession*, San Francisco, CA: Jossey-Bass, pp. 207–25.

King, P.M. and K.S. Kitchener (1994), *Developing Reflective Judgment: Understanding and Promoting Intellectual Growth and Critical Thinking in Adolescents and Adults*, San Francisco, CA: Jossey-Bass.

Knowles, T., R.M. Teixeira and D. Egan (2003), 'Tourism and hospitality education in Brazil and the United Kingdom: A comparison', *International Journal of Contemporary Hospitality Management*, **15** (1), 45–51.

Kok, R.M. (2000), 'Outside the box: Creating your own internship opportunities', *Journal of Travel and Tourism Education*, **12** (3), 21–3.

Lam, T. and L. Ching (2007), 'An exploratory study of an internship program: The case of Hong Kong students', *International Journal of Hospitality Management*, **26** (2), 336–51.

Lashley, C. (1999), 'On making silk purses: Developing reflective practitioners in hospitality management education', *International Journal of Contemporary Hospitality Management*, **11** (4), 180–85.

Lee, S. and D. Dickson (2010), 'Increasing student learning in the classroom through experiential learning programs outside the classroom', *Journal of Hospitality & Tourism Education*, **22** (3), 27–34.

Leslie, D. and A. Richardson (2000), 'Tourism and cooperative education in UK undergraduate courses: Are the benefits being realised?', *Tourism Management*, **21** (5), 489–98.

McCauley, C.D., W.H. Drath, C.J. Palus, P.M.G. O'Connor and B.A. Baker (2006), 'The use of constructive-developmental theory to advance the understanding of leadership', *The Leadership Quarterly*, **17** (6), 634–53.

Meszaros, P.S. and C. Duncan Lane (2010), 'An exploratory study of the relationship between adolescent risk and resilience and the early development of self-authorship', in M.B. Baxter Magolda, E.G. Creamer and P.S. Meszaros (eds), *Development and Assessment of Self-authorship: Exploring the Concept Across Cultures*, Sterling, VA: Stylus, pp. 85–99.

Mezirow, J. (ed.) (2000), *Learning as Transformation: Critical Perspectives on a Theory in Progress*, San Francisco, CA: Jossey-Bass.

Mezirow, J. (2009), 'An overview of transformative learning', in K. Illeris (ed.), *Contemporary Theories of Learning: Learning Theorists in their Own Words*, New York: Routledge, pp. 90–105.

Morrison, A. and G.B. O'Mahony (2003), 'The liberation of hospitality management education', *International Journal of Contemporary Hospitality Management*, **15** (1), 38–44.

Patrick, C-J., D. Peach, C. Pocknee, F. Webb, M. Fletcher and G. Pretto (2008), *The WIL (Work Integrated Learning) Report : A National Scoping Study*, Brisbane: Queensland University of Technology.

Peach, D. and J. Matthews (2011), 'Work integrated learning for life: Encouraging agentic engagement', in K. Krause, M. Buckridge, C. Grimmer and S. Purbrick-Illek (eds), *Research and Development in Higher Education: Reshaping Higher Education*, Gold Coast, Australia, 4–7 July 2011, pp. 227–37.

Perry, W.G. (1970), *Forms of Intellectual and Ethical Development*, New York: Holt, Rinehart and Winston.

Piaget, J. (1954), *The Construction of Reality in a Child*, New York: Basic Books.

Pizam, A., E. Lewis and P. Manning (1982), *The Practice of Hospitality Management*, Westport, CT: AVI Press.

Pizzolato, J.E. (2003), 'Developing self-authorship: Exploring the experiences of high-risk college students', *Journal of College Student Development*, **44**, 797–812.

Pizzolato, J.E. (2005), 'Creating crossroads for self-authorship: Investigating the provocative moment', *Journal of College Student Development*, **46** (6), 624–41.

Pizzolato, J.E. and C.C. Ozaki (2007), 'Moving toward self-authorship: Investigating outcomes of learning partnerships', *Journal of College Student Development*, **48** (2), 196–214.

Pizzolato, J.E., T.L.K. Nguyen, M.P. Johnston and S. Wang (2012), 'Understanding context: Cultural, relational, & psychological interactions in self-authorship development', *Journal of College Student Development*, **53** (5), 656–79.

Raybould, M. and H. Wilkins (2005), 'Over qualified and under experienced: Turning graduates into hospitality managers', *International Journal of Contemporary Hospitality Management*, **17** (3), 203–16.

Richardson, S.A. (2008), 'Undergraduate tourism and hospitality students attitude toward a career in the industry: A preliminary investigation', *Journal of Teaching in Travel & Tourism*, **8** (1), 23–46.

Richardson, S.A. (2009), 'Used and unappreciated: Exploring the role work experience plays in shaping undergraduate tourism and hospitality student's attitude towards a career in the industry', (Doctoral dissertation), Griffith University.

Ring, A., A. Dickinger and K. Wöber (2009), 'Designing the ideal undergraduate program in tourism: Expectations from industry and educators', *Journal of Travel Research*, **48** (1), 106–21.

Roberts, E. (2009), 'Mind the gap: Aligning learning and graduate outcomes through industry partnerships', *Journal of Hospitality and Tourism Management*, **16** (1), 130–38.

Rogers, J.L., P.M. Magolda, M.B. Baxter Magolda and K. Knight Abowitz (2004), 'A community of scholars: Enacting the learning partnerships models in graduate education', in M.B. Baxter Magolda and P.M. King (eds), *Learning Partnerships: Theory and Models of Practice to Educate for Self-authorship*, Sterling, VA: Stylus, pp. 213–44.

Rosenshine, B. and C. Meister (1992), 'The use of scaffolds for teaching higher-level cognitive strategies', *Educational Leadership*, **49** (7), 26–33.

Schoper, S.E. (2011), 'A narrative analysis of the process of self-authorship for student affairs graduate students', (Doctoral dissertation), accessed 12 June 2014 at: http://search.ebscohost.com/login.aspx?direct=true&db=psyh&AN=2012-99150-565&site=ehost-live.

Sheldon, P.J., D.R. Fesenmaier and J. Tribe (2011), 'The tourism education futures institute (TEFI): Activating change in tourism education', *Journal of Teaching in Travel & Tourism*, **11**, 2–23.

Sigala, M. and T. Baum (2003), 'Trends and issues in tourism and hospitality higher education: Visioning the future', *Tourism and Hospitality Research*, **4** (4), 367–76.

Smith, C. and K. Worsfold (2013), 'WIL curriculum design and student learning: A structural model of their effects on student satisfaction', *Studies in Higher Education*, **39** (6), 1–15.

Solnet, D. and A. Hood (2011), 'Generation Y as hospitality industry employees: An examination of work attitude differences', Hospitality Training Association, accessed on 15 June 2014 at http://www.hta.org.au/.

Solnet, D., R. Robinson and C. Cooper (2007), 'An industry partnerships approach in tourism education', *Journal of Hospitality, Leisure, Sport and Tourism Education*, **6** (1), 66–70.

Staron, M. (2011), 'Life-based learning model: A model for strength-based approaches to capability development and implications for personal development planning', paper presented at 'Student Lifewide Development Symposium', 1 March.

Stuart, M. (2002), 'Critical influences on tourism as a subject in UK higher education: Lecturer perspectives', *Journal of Hospitality, Leisure, Sport and Tourism Education*, **1** (1), 5–18.

Teng, C.C. (2008), 'The effects of personality traits and attitudes on student uptake in hospitality employment', *International Journal of Hospitality Management*, **27** (1), 76–86.

Thomas, D. and J.S. Brown (2011), *A New Culture of Learning: Cultivating the Imagination for a World of Constant Change*, Lexington, KY: CreateSpace.

Torres, V. (2010), 'Investigating Latino ethnic identity within the self-authorship framework', in M.B. Baxter Magolda, E.G. Creamer and P.S. Meszaros (eds), *Development and Assessment of Self-authorship: Exploring the Concept Across Cultures*, Sterling, VA: Stylus, pp. 67–84.

Tribe, J. (2000), 'Balancing the vocational: The theory and practice of liberal education in tourism', *Tourism and Hospitality Research*, **2** (1), 9–26.

Tribe, J. (2002), 'The philosophic practitioner', *Annals of Tourism Research*, **29** (2), 338–57.

Tse, T.S.M. (2010), 'What do hospitality students find important about internships?', *Journal of Teaching in Travel & Tourism*, **10** (3), 251–64.

Wang, J., H. Ayres and J. Huyton (2009), 'Job ready graduates: A tourism industry perspective', *Journal of Hospitality and Tourism Management*, **16**, 62–72.

Yonkers-Talz, K. (2004), 'A learning partnership: U.S. college students and the poor in El Salvador', in M.B. Baxter Magolda and P.M. King (eds), *Learning Partnerships: Theory and Models of Practice to Educate for Self-authorship*, Sterling, VA: Stylus, pp. 151–84.

Yorke, M. (2006), *Employability in Higher Education: What it is – What it is Not*, York: The Higher Education Academy.

Zopiatis, A. and P. Constanti (2007), '"And never the twain shall meet", Investigating the hospitality industry–education relationship in Cyprus', *Education and Training*, **49** (5), 391–407.

Zopiatis, A. and A.L. Theocharous (2013), 'Revisiting hospitality internship practices: A holistic investigation', *Journal of Hospitality, Leisure, Sport & Tourism Education*, **13**, 33–46.

17 The value of WIL in tourism and student perceptions of employability

Chris Fanning, Ceri Macleod and Lynn Vanzo

1. INTRODUCTION

Much work has been undertaken within Australian universities to define Work-Integrated Learning (WIL) to incorporate all of its guises and modes of implementation, from 'traditional' placements to on-campus 'virtual worlds'. At Flinders University, WIL is recognized as a strategic educational priority and a driver of student employability. WIL activities, in a variety of forms, are integrated across the majority of courses offered at the university, and there has been a significant increase in student placement activity in recent years due to the development and implementation of a number of strategic initiatives. The university aims to provide all undergraduates with the opportunity to access a WIL activity of some form during the course of their studies, with WIL being defined as an 'organized, supervised and assessed educational activity that integrates theoretical learning with its applications in the workplace' (Flinders University, 2010).

Whilst WIL can take a variety of forms in terms of its delivery, the nature of its inclusion in a degree course can vary considerably depending on whether or not there is a professional requirement to complete one or more WIL activities. WIL can be a mandatory element of a degree in order for the student to meet professional accreditation requirements, or, by virtue of an institutionally approved course structure offered to students as mandatory or elective activities (Macleod et al., 2010). By far the most significant form of placement with respect to numbers of students involved is in disciplines where the activity is mandated by the profession. Nursing, midwifery, education, law and social work are just some of the many disciplines where the profession has a significant involvement in the design and delivery of placements and where students are required to complete a compulsory WIL component for their degree before they are able to enter the profession. In these cases, universities and the profession work collaboratively, often within clearly defined frameworks and agreements. In other disciplines, WIL is either still a relatively new concept and/or is delivered as an optional activity, with students able to participate with varying input from the profession in terms of the nature and content of the WIL activity. In rare instances, students are also required to complete a compulsory WIL component without this being a specific requirement of the profession. An example of this approach can be found within the tourism degree at Flinders University.

The Bachelor of International Tourism began in the Flinders University School of Humanities in 1997, with WIL incorporated and embedded into the degree structure in the form of a number of compulsory activities, including placements and research projects. With strong support and collaboration from the tourism industry (including arts and events) substantial and continuing opportunities are provided for students. The objectives of the activities are to relate theory to practice, develop an empathy with, understanding of, and relevant experience in the day-to-day issues confronting operators in the tourism and events industry. This is not dissimilar to other fields such as hospitality where internships are used for the above purposes and to expose students to hospitality professionals (Downey and DeVeau, 1988). It is not specifically required by the profession, yet is offered by many universities offering a tourism degree. At Flinders University, WIL is a compulsory component of the tourism degree, despite the fact that fulfilling the Flinders University policy requirements in organizing, supervising, monitoring and assessing WIL activities is often complex and time-consuming, requiring a huge amount of time and personal commitment on the part of all stakeholders, yet all are committed to its delivery. Why, and to what gain?

2. LITERATURE

The significance of WIL as a tool with which to link theory and practice is well documented (Cooper et al., 2010; Patrick et al., 2008). With respect to the 'value' of WIL to stakeholders, there is also a significant body of research supporting the notion that WIL is a key driver of employability (Oliver, 2010), providing students with '. . . an authentic learning environment where they combine professional knowledge building and practice with workplace learning' (Patrick et al., 2008, p. 39). Exposure to workplace settings can provide students with the ability to 'make sense' of their studies, to bring them to life, and develop practical skills that will assist in their transition from academia to the workplace. Keeping in mind that no two experiences are the same, what affects one student may not affect another, so what individual students may learn from the same host organization can be highly individual (Dickerson and Kline, 2008). A comprehensive skills set is desirable to potential employers, who require work-ready graduates able to 'hit the ground running' (Coll et al., 2011). WIL provides a transition between university and employability in the field and can provide a substantial point of difference (Busby, 2003). According to Gibson and Busby (2009), students gain new skills including confidence, personal awareness, establishing networks and developing an ethical understanding. Many students tend to be involved with operational rather than managerial aspects of an organization, so these skills may take longer to develop and connecting the expectations of both stakeholders with this issue can be difficult (Baker et al., 2011; Beggs et al., 2008). Nevertheless, all of this new learning and these professional capabilities are important when students critically reflect on their industry experience in their assessments and further academic studies.

Research into graduate employability outcomes undertaken by Oliver et al. (2011) found that work-related knowledge and skills were recognized as significant drivers of employability by students, university staff and employers alike, particularly in the form of placements and authentic assessments. When the transferable skills meet the provider's needs, the likelihood of employment increases (Busby, 2003). Further, research in Australia, the United States and the United Kingdom illustrates that 'students who had undertaken a work-integrated learning experience or a skill-development component during their course of study were more likely than others to have reflected positively on their university experience' (Orrell, 2004, p. 1). Smith et al. (2009) argue that WIL has a significant role in acting as a vehicle to promote the broader notion of career development learning and in optimizing employability, whilst Koppi et al. (2010) argue that:

> Graduates with work experience appreciated the importance of communication, problem-solving and teamwork more so than graduates without work experience. In relation to these abilities, graduates with work experience observed that their readiness to engage in university learning was enhanced because they were aware of the relevance of these abilities in the workplace. (p. 114)

Additionally, from the host organization's point of view, placements raise the profile of potential employees (Kok, 2000).

Learning by doing reinforces classroom knowledge, especially when students can reflect on the experience and critically evaluate not just the host provider, but also the industry (Busby, 2003). As a university it is important to produce not just work-skilled graduates, but also individuals who are reflective and can critically question and aim to improve tourism practices (Inui et al., 2006; Ring et al., 2009).

3.   TEACHING APPROACH AND SURVEY

Incorporating WIL as a compulsory element by virtue of an institutionally approved course structure without it being mandated by the profession is unusual at Flinders University. WIL placements have, however, been a compulsory component of the University's tourism degree since its inception. Unlike some tourism WIL programs at other Australian universities (Solnet et al., 2007), the Flinders program, by virtue of being a core program, is inclusive and available to the full cohort of students. This all-encompassing focus allows each tourism student the opportunity to engage with industry at whatever level they are at.

Over time, the nature, scope and delivery of these activities has changed to reflect student and industry feedback, but has remained a consistently embedded and scaffolded part of the tourism degree program. The assessment (oral presentations and reflective journals) is based on the topic learning outcomes and connects strongly with the university's graduate qualities. The advantages of integrating career development learning (for example encouraging students to reflect on graduate qualities) within an assessable environment have been shown to enhance WIL activities and learning outcomes (Reddan and Rauchle, 2012). Whilst care is taken to match WIL assessment to learning outcomes, the learning outcomes themselves are flexible due to there not being any specific industry-mandated professional requirements (Toohey et al., 1996).

Designing, organizing, supervising and assessing the WIL activities undertaken by students is very time-consuming and relies heavily on the development of mutually beneficial partnerships between the university and the tourism industry. In undertaking a tourism degree at Flinders, students (generally at the end of the second year or at the beginning of the third year) are required to complete a 160-hour industry placement that is undertaken on-site with an industry provider. Postgraduate students are able to do placements as an elective. Industry placement providers range from major event organizations, local governments, heritage organizations and smaller tourism enterprises that are based in the city of Adelaide or the South Australian regions. Placement providers are also occasionally from interstate and overseas.

Degree students are also required to complete an industry-based research project (conducted in the student's final year) in addition to 'tourism projects'. Tourism projects can consist of a range of opportunities for students, for example assisting with Visitor Information Centers (VICs), a range of university events (open days, graduation dinners and conferences) and industry-based projects (ranging from managing an event to developing a marketing plan).

These WIL experiences are unpaid, assessable components of, and link directly back to, the requirements and outcomes of the tourism degree and provide a wide range of learning opportunities through hands-on, real-world experiences in the tourism industry (Van Gyn et al., 1997). Students are prepared for their placement through attendance at pre-placement seminars, undertaking online preparatory modules, and by preparing and submitting paperwork in accordance with the university's WIL policy.

The changing demography of today's university students and the increasing call from government and industry (Cooper et al., 2010; Patrick et al., 2008) to provide work-ready graduates is a challenge that needs to be met, most particularly within WIL programs. The tourism degree has long embraced and reflected the need to provide students with the opportunity to enter the tourism and events industry with relevant, appropriate knowledge, and as experienced, work-ready graduates. In providing such a wide variety of WIL opportunities, students are able to gain a true appreciation of the sector through meaningful and appropriate activities designed to reflect the nature of the tourism industry.

Accordingly, a study of past students was undertaken to measure the importance that students placed on WIL as a component of the tourism degree, in an attempt to measure the perceived 'value' and 'usefulness' of WIL activities offered, as a precursor to employment. The objectives of this survey were to determine:

- the value of WIL activities to students;
- whether the inclusion of WIL activities represented a determining factor in students choosing to undertake the Flinders University Tourism degree;
- whether the experiences gained by students upon completion of their WIL activities helped determine their profession;
- which aspects of their WIL activities were most beneficial to them;
- the ways in which the students believed their WIL activity had benefited the host organization.

The aim of this research was to determine whether WIL is considered by the students as an important and valued component of their degree, despite it not being a professional requirement of the industry.

3.1 Method

The study participants were Flinders University tourism alumni who had remained in contact with the Tourism Department via social media. The study took place in early 2014 via a questionnaire. The questionnaire consisted of four closed questions requiring a yes/no response, and six open-ended questions that allowed participants to expand on their answers to provide opinions. Participants completed the questionnaire anonymously via Survey Monkey, an online survey tool, with only one demographic-specific question (year of graduation) required. Descriptive data from the open-ended questions was manually coded into concepts as recommended by Braun and Clarke (2006). The response rate for completion of the questionnaire was 64 percent (n = 85). Whilst the sample size was small, each of the yes/no responses were more than 60 percent, indicating a +/−13.6 confidence variable (Veal, 2004).

This chapter primarily considers responses to the open-ended questions that were asked. Respondents were asked to identify the key personal outcomes resulting from the WIL activity they completed. A similar, but slightly varied question format asked what aspects were most beneficial to them. Respondents were also asked how they believed the host organization benefited from the industry placement (Braunstein et al., 2011). Eighty-six percent of respondents answered the open-ended questions. The yes/no response questions evaluated in this chapter included whether the opportunity to undertake a placement/project/research project (that is, a WIL activity) influenced their choice of degree or university and if the WIL activity had influenced the respondent's choice of career. The last question asked was what year the respondent graduated, to allow for a longitudinal study to identify possible trends. The open-ended questions were coded, and patterns identified and grouped accordingly (Miles and Huberman, 1994).

4.   FINDINGS AND DISCUSSION

Alumni were first asked whether the opportunity to undertake a placement influenced their choice of degree or university. An analysis of each of the comments received for the open-ended questions generated categories of comments (response themes). Respondents' comments were not forced to fit into a particular category and, in a number of cases, a comment was allocated to more than one category. The most cited response themes are shown in Table 17.1, in addition to selected comments against each theme.

Only 35 percent of respondents were influenced by the opportunity to undertake a WIL activity when choosing their degree, with the majority wanting to gain 'real world experience'. 'Real world experience' provides opportunities for external career-related benefits and internal benefits such as increased confidence (Van Gyn et al., 1997; Dressler and Keeling, 2011). Of the respondents who graduated in 2014, 55 percent were influenced by the opportunity to undertake a WIL activity. Anecdotal evidence from the 2014 first year tourism student cohort returned a much higher percentage (75 percent). It is possible this reflects growing awareness in recent years of changes to the global economic environment, that is, that future employability has become a more consciously significant factor

Table 17.1   Impact of placement opportunity on degree choice

Most cited response themes	Responses	Selected comments
Real world experience	9	It influenced me as I was interested to experience the 'real world' application of the degree.
Positively influenced my choice of degree	3	I undertook placements, a project as well as a research project whilst completing my degree. Having these options as part of the degree was definitely a big influence for choosing the Bachelor of International Tourism.

Table 17.2   Influence of placement on choice of career

Most cited response themes	Responses	Selected comments
Confirmed my career choice	32	Prior to my first placement I was undertaking the degree much more broadly. After my first placement I was pretty hooked on working in events. My second placement had me hooked on festivals and I've been working on festivals and events for the last 6 years now as a result.
Real world experience	21	Being actively involved in the nature-based tourism industry (during placement) allowed me to develop specific skills and understandings that gave me the confidence to apply for roles within the industry upon completion of uni.

in choosing a degree. This question needs further examination in a longitudinal study to identify any possible changes or trends occurring.

Alumni were asked whether their placement influenced their choice of career and the results are presented in Table 17.2. More than two-thirds (67 percent) of respondents were influenced in their choice of career by their placement opportunities. While their WIL experiences helped confirm career choices ('It confirmed what I wanted was right for me!'), the experiences also identified for students where they did not want to work ('Made me realize event management wasn't for me') (Bates, 2008; Dressler and Keeling, 2011; Chen and Shen, 2012). The range of work-integrated learning opportunities also provided respondents with opportunities they may not have initially thought of, but still gained from (Bates, 2008): 'They helped give me more experience in fields that I probably wouldn't have thought to choose for myself.'

Next, alumni were asked to identify the key outcomes of their placement/project. The outcomes in Table 17.3 identify that 'real-world' experiences are valued highly by respondents (43 percent). Alumni confirm that WIL had extended them beyond their normal comfort zone and exposed them to a wider range of professions. The

Table 17.3   Key outcomes of the placement/project

Most cited outcomes	Responses	Selected comments
Real world experience	25	From my placements I was able to learn a lot about Indigenous culture that I knew little about. . . All of these placements and projects helped me to grow in many ways from communication through to working within and managing a team.
Networking opportunities	18	It also introduced me to the industry and people within it. I made a lot of contacts but also a lot of friends.
Confirmed career/ further study path	15	My placement was completely interstate so I learnt that I could live outside of my comfort zone, I also learnt that I didn't want to be stuck in the office all day and that I needed variety in my work.

Table 17.4   Personal benefits of the placement/project

Most cited response themes	Responses	Selected comments
Networking/ contacts	39	Having the opportunity to talk about tourism with other people in the industry and gain insights on their opinions.
Confidence in my skills	15	Being thrown in at the deep end on my first placement helped me to grow quickly and to become independent and to rely on my abilities which I would not have done if I had been overly guided at the start.
Hands-on experience	14	Getting hands-on experience and applying my knowledge to 'real life situations', making what I studied relevant. Which gave me a new perspective when doing assignments
Identifying future employment opportunities	7	It was also really beneficial in helping me hone exactly what I wanted to do post-graduation.

opportunity to network and expand their contacts was also a significant response (31 percent).

Similarly, when asked about personal benefits, respondents saw networking contacts and engaging with industry professionals as the predominant benefit of the WIL activity (53 percent) (Table 17.4). Alumni also identified employment experience and employment opportunities as a benefit, and that they had gained dispositional knowledge such as confidence in their skills and abilities (Billett, 2009).

It was felt that making contact and getting to know people in the industry was a major benefit to them (60 percent). This benefit was followed by the opportunity to gain confidence in their own abilities (22 percent), a positive also recognized by Billett (2009). Respondents felt that being able to apply their university studies to a 'real life' situation made their studies more relevant (20 percent); equally it also showed where they may not want to work ('It was a great opportunity to find an area you would like to (or just as importantly, not like) to pursue').

Respondents confirmed what other researchers have highlighted in relation to the benefits of WIL to host organizations (Table 17.5). Having providers that value the knowledge, fresh ideas and approaches that students bring to placement is perceived by the respondents as important. Students can also add value to the organization, ease work-load pressures and complete tasks that the organization needs to do but has been unable to, due to being time and resource poor (Harvey, 2001). The provision of extra assistance to host organizations is perceived as the most positive outcome (62 percent), even though respondents received no monetary remuneration. One road block for providers in taking on WIL students can be a perception of the costs associated with resourcing a student placement (Leslie and Richardson, 2000), so for respondents to feel that they were easing a burden indicates that the industry providers they were attached to would value their input. This applies equally to respondents who felt that they were able to provide fresh ideas to a host organization (29 percent); to do so they must feel that the host is open to new ideas and values their input (Braunstein et al, 2011).

Respondents were also asked how many WIL placements and projects they undertook

Table 17.5   Benefits for the host organization

Most cited response themes	Responses	Selected comments
Extra assistance to ease the workload	37	My hosts were able to get some really useful information collated and reported to them. Furthermore, I was able to create some social media pages – they may not be able to afford a staff member to do this work.
Fresh ideas	17	Another pair of hands is always great and I brought in fresh ideas and ways of looking at things which were taken up by the host. They had access to a volunteer who had knowledge and suggestions to improve their organization. They could learn from some of the ideas or experiences that students had been exposed to.
Vetting future employees	5	I think it showcased Flinders Uni and the tourism students in a positive way, as students with good knowledge and employable skills. One of my hosts also employed me for nearly two years after my placement with their organization.

Table 17.6   WIL placements/projects completed during the degree

Number	Responses
One	2
Two	20
Three	16
Four or more	9

during their degree. Forty-seven responses were received to this question and are summarized in Table 17.6. The minimum number of WIL activities students could undertake in the tourism program was two;[1] a placement and a research project, which 40 percent of responders completed. However, 51 percent of respondents chose to do three or more WIL topics, with one alumnus undertaking six throughout their degree. This question could also be considered in a longitudinal study alongside question 1 in considering whether the opportunity to undertake WIL influences the choice of degree or university, and if so, how many activities do prospective students/alumni consider adequate. Equally, further research could also investigate whether completing more WIL activities provides even greater benefits towards employability, something that is not conclusive from this study.

When asked why they completed WIL projects and placements during their studies, most respondents (53 percent) stated that the WIL requirements were a core component of the course they were undertaking (see Table 17.7). However, other alumni recognized that they had the opportunity to improve their skills in a variety of settings (35 percent), which either supported or challenged their worldview and future career choices (Bates, 2008).

Table 17.7   Reasons for participating in WIL placements and projects

Most cited response themes	Responses	Selected comments
Requirements of the course	29	Undertaking one placement and research project were a core component of the degree, I chose to complete two to give me a wider variety, type of scale of events.
More than one placement improved my skills	19	I had the opportunity to do another placement that was very different to my first one and I took it so as to be exposed to a different part of the industry and I am so glad that I did.
Opportunity to apply university learning in the tourism sector	5	I enjoyed being able to apply my learning to a 'real' professional environment.
Clarified my future goals	2	Placements allow for interests and disinterests to be realized. Volunteering and hands-on learning is the best way to enter the real world.

5.   FUTURE DIRECTIONS

The necessity to network and meet tourism industry professionals to establish and further a career in the industry is discussed at length in the classroom, of course, but it is difficult to teach what 'networking' is until students are placed in an actual business setting and can experience it for themselves. The fact that alumni recognize this as a benefit needs further exploration. Is networking something that becomes identifiable as a benefit once students have graduated or were they aware of it whilst they were still a student? Certainly the idea of students building relationships with industry whilst still studying has been identified as a strong post-study employment strategy (Gardner and Perry, 2011).

Primarily respondents felt that the biggest benefit they provided to hosts was in easing the workload within a learning context, without feeling that they were being used as free labor. This finding is an extension of employer benefits noted by Braunstein et al. in 2011. It was important to alumni that they felt they were able to provide fresh ideas and felt of value overall to the host (Harvey, 2001; Tse, 2010). Further research on the host organization's perceptions of the benefits of WIL would confirm whether the alumni's perceptions are accurate. If, as suggested by Roberts (2009), the workplace managers themselves do not hold a degree or have never undertaken a placement then this may influence the experience they provide for a student and the value they place on them.

Whether WIL activities are a determining factor in students choosing to undertake a specific degree, in this case tourism, needs further investigation beyond this study. Whilst the results show that WIL was not a determining factor (35 percent) for selecting their academic program, the results for the most recent graduates identified the opposite (55 percent) and, anecdotally, 75 percent of the 2014 first year tourism cohort chose their degree because they could do a placement. In 2001 O'Mahony et al. noted that prospective students were influenced to choose the Hospitality Degree at Victoria University by the opportunity to undertake industry internships. A longitudinal study, with cross-tabulation of results, would clarify if the opportunity to undertake place-ments or internships influences the prospective student's choice of university program. What impacts do other factors, such as external economic pressures or internal combined degrees, articulated pathways, and so on (which do not offer placements) affect student choice of the program? The study could also be considered in light of hospitality educa-tion, which has traditionally expected students to undertake a WIL activity (Wood and Brotherton, 2008), compared to tourism, especially in Australia where compulsory WIL activities are less common (Day et al., 2012). As mentioned previously in this chapter, further research would be useful to identify whether completing more WIL activities provides even greater benefits towards employability, something that is not conclusive from this study.

The positive responses demonstrate that exposure to real world workplace set-tings allows students to clarify and confirm their future career and study path options (Dickerson and Kline, 2008). The personal benefits identified in the study correlate with past research by Orrell (2001) that confirms students are able to use WIL activities to put theory into practice and to gain a greater understanding that more than academic success is needed for successful employment and future careers. Equally the university needs to source and maintain strong industry relationships and strive to meet industry perceptions regarding the quality of its program and the reputation of the graduates who will become part of the future labor market (Roberts, 2009).

Oliver et al. (2011) found that work-related knowledge and skills were recognized as a significant driver of employability by students, university staff and employers alike, par-ticularly in the form of placements and authentic assessments. Whilst this study considers past students and their perceptions of employability, future research could consider the links between the assessments undertaken during their WIL activity in a non-mandated environment, and whether they concur with research such as that by Harvey (2001), that finds significant learning comes from reflective assessment of a work experience. Does the assessment allow students to clarify their ideas on possible career paths or was it purely the actual WIL experience that did this?

6. CONCLUSION

These findings provide insight into students' and consequently the alumni's perceptions of the benefits of WIL to themselves, the industry provider and the host organization. It is clear that WIL activities, by providing students with real world activities and extending their university education beyond the classroom, are perceived as offering significant benefits to, and that are highly valued by, alumni. Research conducted in Australia, the United States and the United Kingdom indicates that alumni who have undertaken a work-integrated learning experience during the course of their study are more likely to reflect positively on their university experience (Harvey and Knight, 1996; Fanning, 2010; Dressler and Keeling, 2011), results reflected in these findings. For the respondents of this study, WIL activities also enabled them (whilst still studying) to confirm their career choice. This is an essential step for educators endeavoring to create work-ready graduates (Daniel and Daniel, 2013).

Clearly WIL activities are desired by students and are seen as having a range of positive outcomes for both the student and the industry provider. More comprehensive research along the lines of this study will provide conclusive evidence that can be used by WIL coordinators (university) and industry to maximize the benefits of WIL activities to all, in a non-mandated environment. WIL also has the potential to be a marketable commodity to distinguish between university programs.

Whilst there are implications in terms of the impact of WIL on university staff, in terms of designing and managing appropriate WIL activities and assessments, developing and nurturing mutually collaborative partnerships within the tourism industry, and subsequent workload requirements, WIL is clearly a beneficial activity for Flinders University Tourism students, despite it not being a professional requirement.

NOTE

1. Two respondents cited one WIL activity undertaken. This is an unexplained anomaly in the responses of two students, possibly because they did not see their activity as a WIL activity, they may have gained alternative credit or possibly made an error in their response.

REFERENCES

Baker, L., Caldicott, J. and Spowart, J. (2011), 'Cooperative and work-integrated education in hospitality and tourism', in R.K. Coll and K.E. Zegwaard (eds), *International Handbook for Cooperative and Work-integrated Education: International Perspectives of Theory, Research and Practice* (pp. 219–27), Lowell, MA: World Association for Cooperative Education.

Bates, M. (2008), 'Work integrated curricula in university programs', *Higher Education Research & Development*, **27** (4), 305–317.

Beggs, B., Ross, C.M. and Goodwin, B. (2008), 'A comparison of student and practitioner perspectives of the travel and tourism internship', *Journal of Hospitality, Leisure, Sport and Tourism Education*, **7** (1), 31–9.

Billett, S. (2009), 'Realizing the educational worth of integrating work experiences in higher education', *Studies in Higher Education*, **34** (7), 827–43.

Braun, V. and Clarke, V. (2006), 'Using thematic analysis in psychology', *Qualitative Research in Psychology*, **3** (2), 77–101.

Braunstein, L.A., Takei, H., Wang, F. and Loken, M.K. (2011), 'Benefits of cooperative and work integrated education for employers', in R.K. Coll and C.W. Eames (eds), *International Handbook for Cooperative Education: An International Perspective of the Theory, Research and Practice of Work-integrated Learning*, Boston: World Association for Cooperative Education.

Busby, G. (2003), 'Tourism degree internships: a longitudinal study', *Journal of Vocational Education and Training*, **55** (3), 319–34.

Chen, T. and Shen, C. (2012), 'Today's intern, tomorrow's practitioner? The influence of internship programmes on students' career development in the hospitality industry', *Journal of Hospitality, Leisure, Sport & Tourism*, **11** (1), 29–40.

Coll, R.K., Eames, C.W., Paku, L.K., Lay, M.C., Hodges, D., Bhat, R., Ram, S., Ayling, D., Fleming, J., Ferkins, L., Wiersma, C. and Martin, A. (2011), 'An exploration of the pedagogies employed to integrate knowledge in work-integrated learning', *The Journal of Cooperative Education and Internships*, **43**, 14–35.

Cooper, L., Orrell, J. and Bowden, M. (2010), *Work Integrated Learning: A Guide to Effective Practice*, New York: Hoboken Taylor & Francis.

Daniel, R. and Daniel, L. (2013), 'Enhancing the transition from study to work: reflections on the value and impact of internships in the creative and performing arts', *Arts and Humanities in Higher Education*, **12** (2–3), 138–53.

Day, M., Walo, M., Weeks, P., Dredge, D., Benckendorff, P., Gross, M. and Whitelaw, P.A. (2012), *Analysis of Australian Tourism, Hospitality and Events Undergraduate Education Programs*, Sydney: Office of Teaching and Learning.

Dickerson, J.P. and Kline, S.F. (2008), 'The early career impact of the co-op commitment in hospitality curricula', *Journal of Teaching in Travel & Tourism*, **8** (1), 1–22.

Downey, J.F. and DeVeau, L.T. (1988), 'Hospitality internships: an industry view', *Cornell Hotel and Restaurant Administration Quarterly*, **29** (3), 18–20.

Dressler, S. and Keeling, A.E. (2011), 'Student benefits of cooperative education', in R.K. Coll and C.W. Eames (eds), *International Handbook for Cooperative Education: An International Perspective of the Theory, Research and Practice of Work-integrated Learning*, Boston: World Association for Cooperative Education.

Fanning, C. (2010), 'Flinders Tourism Work Integrated Learning Programmes: evaluating learning outcomes', *Proceedings of ACEN National Conference – Work Integrated Learning (WIL): Responding to Challenges*, Curtin University, Australia.

Flinders University (2010), 'Work-Integrated Learning Policy', accessed 16 September 2014 at htttp://www.flinders.edu.au/ppmanual/teaching-course-management/work-integrated-learning-policy.cfm.

Gardner, P. and Perry, A. (2011), 'The role of cooperative and work integrated education in graduate transition into the workforce', in R.K. Coll and C.W. Eames (eds), *International Handbook for Cooperative Education: An International Perspective of the Theory, Research and Practice of Work-integrated Learning*, Boston: World Association for Cooperative Education.

Gibson, P. and Busby, G. (2009), 'Experiencing work: supporting the undergraduate hospitality, tourism and cruise management student on an overseas work placement', *Journal of Vocational Education and Training*, **61** (4), 467–80.

Harvey, L. (2001), 'Defining and measuring employability', *Quality in Higher Education*, **7** (2), 97–109.

Harvey, L. and Knight, P.T. (1996), *Transforming Higher Education*, Buckingham: Society for Research into Higher Education & Open University Press (October).

Inui, Y., Wheeler, D. and Lankford, S. (2006), 'Rethinking tourism education', *Journal of Hospitality, Leisure, Sport and Tourism Education*, **5** (2), 25–35.

Kok, R.M. (2000), 'Outside the box: Creating your own internship opportunities', *Journal of Travel and Tourism Education*, **12** (3), 21–3.

Koppi, T., Edwards, S.L., Sheard, J., Naghdy, F. and Brookes, W. (2010), 'The case for ICT work-integrated learning from graduates in the workplace', in T. Clear and J. Hamer (eds), *ACE 2010 Proceedings of the Twelfth Australasian Conference on Computing Education*, **103**, 107–16.

Leslie, D. and Richardson, A. (2000), 'Tourism and cooperative education in UK undergraduate courses: are the benefits being realised?', *Tourism Management*, **21** (5), 489–98.

Macleod, C.A.L., Fanning, C.T., Cavaye, A.L.M., Mills, D.A., Oliphant, J. and Sweet, L.P. (2010), 'Learning and leading: an innovative approach towards maximizing the effectiveness of work integrated learning', in *5th ERGA conference: The Changing Face of Education*, Adelaide: Education Research Group of Adelaide.

Miles, M.B. and Huberman, A.M. (1994), *Qualitative Data Analysis: An Expanded Sourcebook*, London: Sage Publications.

Oliver, B. (2010), 'Benchmarking partnerships for graduate employability', LSN Teaching Development Unit, Curtin University, Australian Learning and Teaching Council.

Oliver, B., Whelan, B., Hunt, L. and Hammer, S. (2011), 'Accounting graduates and the capabilities that count: perceptions of graduates, employers and accounting academics in four Australian universities', *Journal of Teaching and Learning for Graduate Employability*, **2** (1), 2–27.

O'Mahony, G.B., McWilliams, A.M. and Whitelaw, P.A. (2001), 'Why students choose a hospitality-degree program: an Australian case study', *Cornell Hotel and Restaurant Administration Quarterly*, **42** (1), 92–6.

Orrell, J. (2001), 'Work-integrated learning in universities: Cottage industry or transformational partnerships?', paper presented at the GIHE/IPON Symposium on Work-Integrated Learning, Griffith University, Australia.

Orrell, J. (2004), 'Work-integrated learning programmes: management and educational quality', paper presented at the Australian Universities Quality Forum 2004.

Patrick, C-J., Peach, D., Pocknee, C., Webb, F., Fletcher, M. and Pretto, G. (2008), 'The WIL (Work Integrated Learning) report: a national scoping study', Brisbane: Queensland University of Technology.

Reddan, G. and Rauchle, M. (2012), 'Student perceptions of the value of career development learning to a work integrated learning course in exercise science', *Australian Journal of Career Development*, **21** (1), 38–47.

Ring, A., Dickinger, A. and Wöber, K. (2009), 'Designing the ideal undergraduate program in tourism: expectations from industry and educators', *Journal of Travel Research*, **48** (1), 106–21.

Roberts, E. (2009), 'Mind the gap: aligning learning and graduate outcomes through industry partnerships', *Journal of Hospitality and Tourism Management*, **16** (1), 130–38.

Smith, M., Brooks, S., Lichtenberg, A., McIlveen, P., Torjul, P. and Tyler, J. (2009), 'Career development learning: maximising the contribution of work-integrated learning to the student experience', Australian Learning & Teaching Council Final project report: University of Wollongong, Careers Central, Academic Services Division.

Solnet, D., Robinson, R. and Cooper, C. (2007), 'An industry partnerships approach to tourism education', *Journal of Hospitality, Leisure, Sport and Tourism Education*, **6** (1), 66–70.

Toohey, S., Ryan, G. and Hughes, C. (1996), 'Assessing the practicum', *Assessment and Evaluation in Higher Education*, **21** (3), 215–27.
Tse, T.S.M. (2010), 'What do hospitality students find important about internships', *Journal of Teaching in Travel and Tourism*, **10** (3), 241–64.
Van Gyn, G., Cutt, J., Loken, M. and Ricks, F. (1997), 'Investigating the educational benefits of cooperative education: a longitudinal study', *Journal of Cooperative Education*, **32** (2), 70–85.
Veal, A.J. (2004), *Business Research Methods: a Managerial Approach*, 2nd edn, Sydney: Pearson.
Wood, R.C. and Brotherton, B. (2008), *The SAGE Handbook of Hospitality Management*, London: Sage Publications

18 Students in action: a destination-based learning approach to student engagement

Ruth Craggs, Catherine Gorman, Kevin Griffin,
Ziene Mottiar, Bernadette Quinn and Theresa Ryan

1. INTRODUCTION

The question of how to engage students is at the centre of mainstream education discussion and debate (Zyngier, 2008). This is largely underpinned by the perception that engagement has declined (Barnett and Coate, 2005) despite the fact that it is 'a key factor for learning and personal development' (Salaber, 2014, p. 115). Knowing how students engage in learning practices plays a key role in managing and developing third-level education (Coates, 2007), and thus, engagement has been identified in the literature as a key area of research (Blasco-Arcas et al., 2013). This chapter responds to the need to develop such knowledge by documenting the development and application of a project undertaken to enhance student engagement through the 'Students in Action Project' in the Dublin Institute of Technology in Ireland. Cognisant of Kuh et al.'s (2007) claim that student engagement involves 'participation in educationally effective practices, both inside and outside the classroom', the project involved students across a number of programmes and modules in the School of Hospitality and Tourism working with the local community and businesses of Slane, Co. Meath and Drogheda, Co. Louth (in the 2012–13 and 2013–14 academic years respectively) in Ireland. The overall aim of the project was to involve students in an active collaborative learning environment with each destination, to identify ways in which tourism and hospitality could be enhanced. This would be achieved by engaging students in a multi-faceted project that would empower them to the benefit of the destination and of all members of the community.

This chapter outlines the motivation for undertaking the project, the process involved, the outcomes as well as benefits, in addition to the limitations and lessons learnt in undertaking such a project from the perspective of the academics involved. With specific regard to tourism destinations, it also challenges the current definitions of engagement to include the inseparable links that must be explored between industry, civic and wider community elements in order to develop a tourism experience within a destination. The project differs from many previous studies on student–community engagement, taking a more inclusive approach to 'community' by including local industry, industry groups as well as broader community members when identifying the key components of a destination. This is in keeping with the *National Strategy for Higher Education to 2030*, which includes business, the wider education system, and the community and voluntary sector in their definition of community (Hunt, 2011).

The publication in January 2011 of a *National Strategy for Higher Education to 2030* (Hunt, 2011) in the Republic of Ireland was greeted by many academics sceptically, with public commentators 'cherry-picking' their least favourite recommendation/issue or topic of conversation to vilify. Doran (2011) focuses on the possible reintroduction of third-level fees, while Education Matters (2011) raises a range of issues such as proposed mergers of educational institutions and a variety of finance-related sections of the report. The letters pages of the *Irish Times*, which is often viewed as a useful litmus test for intellectual debate in the country, focused on issues such as 'Shifting education costs onto students' and 'Getting more out of lecturers'. At the time of its publication, therefore, the media focus was firmly on the less palatable aspects of this report and, thus, many ignored the useful and interesting insights offered.

Hunt (2011, p. 21) identifies 'engagement with the wider society' as one of the report's 26 key recommendations for future college and university education in Ireland, stating, 'Engagement with the wider community must become more firmly embedded in the mission of higher education institutions'. To achieve this, higher education institutions will need to take the following actions:

- encourage greater inward and outward mobility of staff and students between higher education institutions, business, industry, the professions and wider community.
- respond positively to the continuing professional development needs of the wider community to develop and deliver appropriate modules and programmes in a flexible and responsive way.
- recognize civic engagement of their students through programme accreditation, where appropriate.
- put in place structures and procedures that welcome and encourage the involvement of the wider community in a range of activities, including programme design and revision. (Hunt, 2011, p. 21)

While the national strategy mentioned above raises a range of discussions and objectives for the future, the pedagogical focus of many institutions is on the simple challenge of attracting and retaining students, therefore much of the academic research being undertaken focuses on the areas of student experience and retention. In this context, a 2012 UK report on Student Engagement and Belonging (Thomas, 2012, p. 1) challenges institutions to reprioritize and consider looking at 'how the curriculum might be reorganised to provide for sustained engagement between teachers and students; how teaching can be organized to create student learning communities; and how to convey the message to students that they belong.'

This is based on the belief that a student's sense of belonging is central to their level of engagement in third level education, and, according to Thomas (2014), this sense of belonging is best cultivated, not by support services, campus facilities or student forums, but directly in the academic sphere. Thus, the challenge for academics is to develop a curriculum which develops staff–student–community engagement, not just for ethical and civic reasons, but also to provide a better educational experience and thereby ultimately to retain students.

Students today need to continually develop their capacity to communicate effectively with others, to support the learning of others, to work across cultures and institutions, and to operate in complex interconnected environments. Thus, building on this project each year using a different destination enables the authors to contribute to building an evidence-based framework that higher education institutions can use to inform decision-making during the development of such flexible experiential learning opportunities, involving co-creation in its many guises. In this regard, understanding the factors that drive successful student engagement and co-creation is currently an under-explored pedagogic field to which this project can make an important contribution.

At the outset it is important to define the term 'destination'. This is because experience to date has thrown up many complexities in engaging with people on the ground within specific destinations. Trying to apply a destination-based learning approach in tourism studies means endeavouring to engage with a wide array of very different actors in a way that challenges the singularity implied by the use of the term 'destination'. The supply side of a tourism destination comprises assets, amenities and accessibility (Burkart and Medlik, 1981, p. 45; Holloway 1994, pp. 6–9; Lohmann and Beer, 2013, p. 86). These elements include aspects such as history and culture, accommodation and services, and infrastructure and transportation. However, in order to provide an experience for the visitor, a destination is also about a series of interactions and inter- and intra-relationships between the place and stakeholders and between stakeholders themselves. It may exhibit a number of characteristics of industrial districts (Hjalager, 2000), territorial and social capital may be considered, or it may be considered as a Tourism Local Innovation System – TLIS (Prat et al., 2008). Destinations are made up of governments, businesses and communities embedded in varying degrees with the tangible place and intangibly with each other. However, despite this multitude of manifestations, the 'tourism destination' provides a learning space for students within which to apply, create, develop, challenge, explore and disseminate their knowledge.

2. LITERATURE REVIEW

Universities, since their foundation, have been inextricably linked to society and have played a key role within it (Boland, 2011). More recently, this role has come under scrutiny and the range of expectations which society has of higher education has expanded and diversified (Boland, 2011). Powell and Clark (2012) note that a 2011 report by the EU Committee on the Regions outlines that 'the gap between the latest research knowledge and real life practice is huge'. Thus, it is important that universities understand how the work they undertake can be turned into sustainable products and processes which are 'useful' to broader society. Indeed, developing an outward facing, dynamic and two-way exchange with the world beyond the academy is being encouraged by a host of external policy drivers but also by the values of many in the sector, both staff and students, who believe that universities are there to 'make a difference' and to transform individuals' lives (Owen and Hill, 2011, p. 3).

A greater emphasis, therefore, on engagement with wider society has for some years now been a key objective of many higher education institutes and authorities. This is evident in such reports as the Kellogg Commission's 'Returning to our roots: the engaged institution', published in 1999 in the US, which argued that 'it is time to go beyond outreach and service to . . . "engagement"' (1999, p. 9). Similarly, the 1997 Dearing Report in the UK argues that institutions need to 'turn to active and systematic engagement' (NCIHE, 1997). While students may have traditionally been seen as passive participants, the issue of student engagement is receiving increasing attention and has been linked to academic achievement, lower levels of student attrition, retention, motivation as well as overall institutional success (Beer et al., 2010). Defined by Coates (2007, p. 122) as 'active and collaborative learning; participation in challenging academic activities; formative communication with academic staff; involvement in enriching educational experiences; and feeling legitimated and supported by university learning communities', engagement is positively linked with student learning (Zyngier, 2008), as well as a host of desired outcomes, including high grades, student satisfaction and perseverance (Beer et al., 2010).

According to Mayer et al. (2009), students learn better when they engage in appropriate cognitive processes, so their engagement is in fact an important explanatory variable of their success. Ahlfeldt et al. (2005) highlight the importance of developing engagement not only for student motivation but also to increase the richness of the students' learning environment that leads to better student performance. Downes (2011) explains that students should have the opportunity to practise leadership, gain knowledge and be autonomous. Students should be provided with ways to get social attention and with opportunities to play and compete with each other. However, he claims, this is not enough; students should have the opportunity to make connections to deep philosophical issues, to obey moral codes, improve society and have connections to past and upcoming generations (Downes, 2011). Owen and Hill (2011, p. 3) claim that students are in fact seeking educational experiences that are socially engaged and prepare them for the challenges that they will encounter. However, they have also perceived a whole host of other outcomes, many of which might not be assessed as part of the course. These outcomes could include learning:

- how to extract meaning from experience;
- ways to apply academic knowledge to real world problems;
- about a specific community, population, geography;
- about expectations, quality, negotiation, client relationships;
- about self, society and context;
- about collaborative working (Owen and Hill, 2011, p. 5).

Salaber (2014) acknowledges that students can be engaged at different levels, for example, with the teacher, faculty or university, with other students, and with their own learning (active learning) and student engagement with others (collaboration). Similarly, Ruhanen et al. (2013) show how immersion as an intern in a destination can aid engagement and real life experience. In summary, engagement is the amalgamation of a number of distinct elements including active learning, collaborative learning, participation, communication among teachers and students and students feeling legitimated and supported. One of the most beneficial methods of active learning is collaborative learning, which occurs when students work together in small groups toward a common goal, creating meaning, exploring a topic or improving skills (Prince, 2004).

The Students in Action Initiative project explores many aspects of student engagement as discussed above, and applies these through collaboration with the stakeholders within a tourism destination. This engagement includes *both* the business and wider communities in a destination-based, active learning environment. The project exhibits collaboration on a number of levels: between lecturers (planning stage), between lecturers and the destination (planning stage), between students and the destination (process stage), between students themselves (process stage) and finally between all stakeholders involved (feedback and evaluation stages).

3.   CASE STUDY: STUDENTS IN ACTION

3.1   Objectives of the Project

In the context of the broad issues discussed above, this project was formulated as a means of tackling issues related to students and the sometimes perceived disconnect between them, academia, industry and community. The idea of the project therefore was to provide students with real life experiences as part of their studies, whereby they would be given the opportunity to contribute to a particular destination and community by developing ideas and engaging in assignment-based applied and academic research. In so doing it was hoped that they would be more engaged in modules, direct their own learning and create a lasting impression in terms of the experience. The project also aimed to develop both discipline-specific and transferable skills.

While heretofore, many individual lecturers, through their modules, had been engaging in field trips on an annual basis, the uniqueness of this project was focusing the attention of an entire department on a single destination each year. To date, this has generated positive impacts in terms of lecturer and student collaboration and it has also provided substantial benefit for the target community and destination. From the destination and its stakeholders' point of view the Students in Action project has provided them with an invaluable 'Generation Y' perspective of their area and product, offering ideas and comments on a variety of different aspects of tourism in the area.

From an educator's perspective, being involved in a particular destination has given staff and researchers a greater insight into current issues. It has provided access to and contact with key decision makers in the destination, and this in turn leads into research activity. Another advantage has been colleagues undertaking team teaching and project planning as they developed itineraries and resources to suit a wide variety of students and modules. Furthermore, this project has given very tangible opportunities for students and staff to contribute to development and planning in the destinations and thereby has facilitated new learning methods and levels of engagement for students.

The key objectives of the project are:

- Using a number of modules, to offer support to a tourism destination, its stakeholders and related organizations over the course of an academic year in the form of focused project work and research.
- To provide students with 'real life' experience to enhance their educational experience and skills development.
- To provide a more integrated approach to module assessment across programmes.
- To provide an opportunity for lecturing staff to enhance their knowledge and aid the development of new teaching materials and techniques.

3.2   Site Selection

At the time of writing, this project has been delivered twice: the first pilot version took place from September 2012 to June 2013, and the second iteration from September 2013 to June 2014. A further roll-out, building on this experience, has continued since then. In year one, personal connection between a lecturer and a key stakeholder provided the impetus for considering the commencement of a project in the pilot destination: Slane in County Meath. This is a small manorial village on the banks of the river Boyne, located 48 km north-west of Dublin City in County Meath. The town has an active community tourism forum and is often associated with the internationally renowned Slane Castle festival venue. The following year, building on the learning experiences from year one, Drogheda, in County Louth, 50 km north of Dublin, was chosen as the target destination. Drogheda, which has a population of 38 000 people, is located at the mouth of the River Boyne, was a significant port, and is the administrative centre for County Louth. A number of colleagues had personal contacts in Drogheda, which facilitated its selection as destination of choice.

Both destinations are located to the north of Dublin City (see Figure 18.1), and are situated at different points on the River Boyne in a very touristic area of Ireland. The sites were chosen due to their proximity to Dublin and the Dublin Institute of Technology and in both instances a wide range of issues relating to tourism and hospitality are

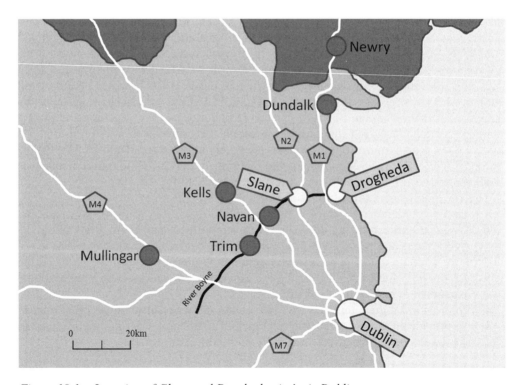

Figure 18.1   Location of Slane and Drogheda vis-à-vis Dublin

evident on the ground, thus providing a rich foundation for student assignments and experiences.

Reflecting on the site selection and with a view to identifying any future destination suitable to create the learning environment for the students, a number of considerations must be taken into account. These range from the logistics of transporting a large number of students and the related importance of proximity to DIT; the explicit and implicit touristic fabric of the destination; and, crucially, a willingness from the industry and community on the ground to work with both students and lecturers. These are all considered key to the successful implementation of the project. A further consideration, to simplify coordination between the student/staff and industry/community stakeholders, is the clear identification of a project coordinator (a position which should revolve annually) to act as a point of contact for everyone engaged in the project each year.

3.3   Managing the Project

The following section outlines the basic steps undertaken in managing this project, and draws on the experience of both project iterations. An initial set of meetings were undertaken including face-to-face, telephone, email and Skype communications with a variety of stakeholders in the chosen destination. This was an important element from the outset as it established key points of contact with the main players in order to facilitate a line of clear communication.

At school level the staff involved in planning the project sought expressions of interest from their fellow lecturers in line with the needs of the destination as expressed by the business and community contacts. Module content, expected student learning outcomes and relevancy were explored in light of the destination needs with a view to complementing all stakeholder requirements. This process was negotiated in a variety of ways, first, with the core team outlining the project at a school meeting and subsequently engaging with colleagues on a case-by-case basis when seen relevant for the project. An example of some of the modules that were connected to the project are presented in Figure 18.2.

Once a decision was made (by the core team and the destination stakeholders) regarding the inclusion of the most appropriate modules in the project, project refinement was undertaken with a view to developing a final proposal to be agreed by all involved, and ready to be actioned at the commencement of semester 1. At the outset, it was decided that one module each year would specifically address the needs of the community, and thus would explicitly be linked to the Institute's 'Students Learning with Communities' civic engagement initiative. While all other modules may implicitly involve civic and community engagement, their main focus would be to consider the overall tourism needs of the destination. A site visit was organized in each semester with a focus, programme and content pertinent to the different programme groups, the academic timetable and module needs.

As semester 1 commenced, students taking the modules associated with the programme were briefed on the assignment. The students came from a number of different programmes and so each module had a different cohort of students. Explanation regarding the programme of work, useful theoretical and industry material links relevant to both the module content and the destination were made available through various channels of communication, both web and non-web. The students were instructed on the importance

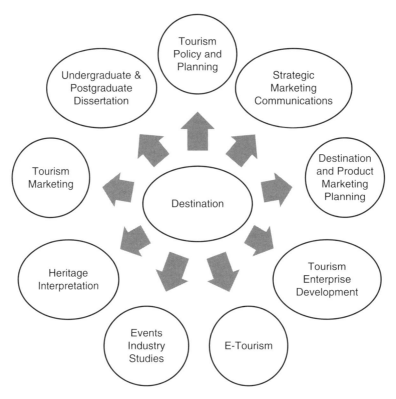

Figure 18.2   Sample of modules of relevance to the destinations under investigation

of gaining experience by applying their knowledge to a 'real-life 'situation where they would make a difference. Clear emphasis was placed on the importance of their individual and group input into the process of executing their assignment(s).

The site visit was developed through a collaborative approach employed by the lecturing staff, industry and the local community. Content varied according to knowledge requirements; however, the format generally involved the provision of short talks and presentations by a number of tourism and hospitality-related stakeholders followed by visits to sites relevant to the overall project and also tailored to the individual modules. These included visits/meetings with accommodation providers, tourist office staff, craft centres, galleries, heritage sites and food providers, to name but a few. To prepare for their visit, students undertook pre-visit activities in the classroom, such as discussion and question preparation relating to the site visit and their own particular assessment focus.

It is also considered important that during the site visit students were provided with free time during which they were encouraged to wander and explore the destination, to get a 'feel' for the place and to engage with local people. Figures 18.3 and 18.4 illustrate some of the local engagement undertaken as part of the programme itinerary during site visits.

On completion of the site visit, guided by lectures, students continued to reflect on and engage with the destination in a variety of ways (see Figure 18.5). For many, this simply involved submitting their assignments on the due date, others began their dissertations

Figure 18.3   Fieldtrip to Slane, discussing challenges such as traffic management with local tourism representative

using the destinations for data collection and so on, others undertook additional field-work, and a number of modules required visits to the class by individual destination stakeholders. Submission of materials/outputs usually took place towards the end of the first semester. A brief feedback to the destination took place post-marking whereby key points and recommendations arising from the student findings and outcomes of their work were presented.

The process was repeated in the second semester with further field trips taking place, relating to another set of modules being organized. On completion of the marking of semester 2 assessments, an event was organized at the destination, bringing together all those involved with a view to disseminating module outputs and provoking discussion.

3.4   Feedback and Evaluation

The key rationale for undertaking a closing event is three-fold. The primary reason is to present the students' findings to the destination using different types of media: poster presentations, executive reports, CDs and oral presentations (see Figure 18.6 for examples of posters). Ideally, the students should lead this process, though the scheduling of an event that does not clash with preparation for exams and year-end has proved to be challenging. While staff members presented the findings to the stakeholders in the first year, in year 2 of the project, a number of highly motivated students participated fully in the feedback event. The second reason for a feedback event is to gather the tourism,

*Figure 18.4   Fieldtrip to Drogheda, discussing heritage conservation and related issues
with local tourism representative*

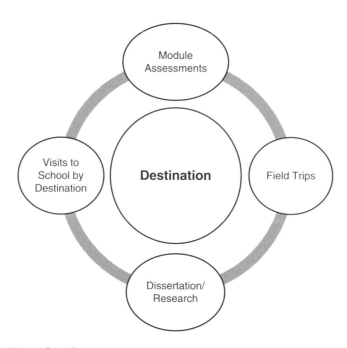

Figure 18.5   Examples of engagement

Figure 18.6   Examples of student posters illustrating findings

business and community stakeholders together at an event in order to highlight the project outcomes and bring the process to a conclusion. An interesting venue (a mill in year 1; an art gallery in year 2) and refreshments have proved to motivate interest and attendance. Finally, the event highlights participation in the project by DIT staff and students and disseminates project findings to wider audiences through the use of promotion in local media.

   An individual evaluation process takes place with the students on completion of each module through Institutional quality assurance measures. In all instances, more extensive feedback on this destination-centric approach to assessment has been sought from students in both verbal and written form at the end of the process. Evaluation, both face-to-face and written, was also sought from the destination stakeholders with a view to building on the experience and addressing challenges encountered along the way. Thirdly, in both iterations the various staff members involved in the project undertook a post-project group debrief session to identify the key learnings from the project, what should be changed and what worked really well.

4.   FINDINGS AND OUTCOMES

Whilst the literature acknowledges the benefits of student engagement projects, less is known about the challenges and impacts of such projects in terms of both operation and outcomes. Thus, this section explores the benefits and challenges experienced by staff, students and community who engaged with this DIT *Students in Action* project.

4.1   Benefits

Student engagement projects and research can help students to deepen their understanding of course content and enable them to integrate knowledge and theory with practice. Indeed, some DIT students reported that they remembered material better through the use of such an approach and that it aided their understanding of course content. Additionally, students expressed that they enjoyed applying what they learnt in class to a real issue/community problem. This is echoed in the literature where previous studies found that student–community engagement projects positively contributed to student learning, that is, increased understanding of course concepts and theory (Kuh, 1993; McKenna and Rizzo, 1999; Ward and Wolf-Wendal, 2000) and stimulated student interest in the subject content (Eyler and Giles, 1999). Other benefits for students include the development of transferable skills and the application of various types of skills, for example, critical thinking, reflective practice and problem solving. This is particularly pertinent for final year undergraduate students and postgraduate students, where the project or research may require higher level thinking. Alternatively, for first year undergraduate students, community engagement projects and research can provide a good introduction to a topic or issue, motivate students and enhance their skills in working collaboratively. Finally, engagement projects provide enjoyable experiences for students beyond the classroom and an alternative assessment to a typical essay, report or group project.

Community benefits include collaborative learning with students, improved relationships with the college, the opportunity to educate future professionals about community needs, knowledge exchange and a usable end-product for the community, that is, research reports, idea generation and problem solving. Community stakeholders have been found to value the enthusiasm, expertise and ideas of students and they explicitly identify the benefits they gain from the project outputs. Furthermore, community stakeholders can help throughout the project in a dynamic way, developing project and assessment ideas with academic staff to create a usable end-product for their community and gain increased access to college resources.

Finally, student–community engagement projects facilitate a process whereby lecturers and their institution can more easily partner with community organizations and build lasting ties between the college and communities. For example, this approach can be a catalyst for long-term research and scholarly work by dissertation students and staff. Projects also have the potential to engage students of all learning styles and levels (undergraduate and graduate), and thus can positively impact the curriculum, providing opportunities for renewing teaching and research and can increase access to community partners as co-teachers and guest lecturers. This can include subsequent access to the community for site visits and field trips. Additionally, the benefits for the school and institution can include an enhanced profile and public image due to positive media attention during and on completion of the project. Conclusively, projects can lead to new ideas and methods for programme and module design, and engagement between students and communities can lead to community development and ongoing research.

4.2   Challenges

Despite the benefits for students, communities and staff, there are limitations and challenges associated with engagement projects such as this. First, the destination stakeholders can have high or unrealistic expectations of student output, particularly in terms of the breadth and depth of what can be achieved within the timescale of the project (typically single semester modules, with the project running over one or two semesters). Linked to this, stakeholders may see the college or school as the elevated location where high-level knowledge lies and depending on the depth of knowledge required or requested, the reality of this will vary. For example, first year learning project outcomes will differ from those of graduate students. Therefore, it is imperative that these expectations are managed in the early stages of an engagement project. Agreement must be reached between the project team and the destination on issues such as realistic outputs and the fact that the quality of student work may vary between different year groups, modules and students.

A fundamental challenge for a project which requires this level of commitment is finding the ideal community partners and groups for collaboration. For example, for the Students in Action project, we needed to find suitable destinations and communities with a variety of different stakeholders who wanted to work with students and where there was scope for collaboration and engagement, that is, challenging questions, issues and problems for student projects.

The third main challenge is to match course content with the project. Students need to gain the skills and experiences necessary to fulfil their modular and programmatic learning outcomes while also addressing the issue that will satisfy the project objectives. Thus, course content may need to be expanded to support the students' projects. Related to this is the need for greater oversight by staff so that the quality of student work is sufficiently high and support is provided to students to think critically and solve problems. Finally, whilst student-engagement projects can develop student skills, some projects may require skills where students have limited proficiency or are not yet fully prepared to manage, and this can seriously impact on their ability to deliver outputs which will be useful for the destination.

Two final challenges involve funding and timetabling. First, projects of this nature may require funding, for example to facilitate student field trips to the community. Thus, applications for funding need to be made prior to, or in the early stages of, the process. Timescales regarding the integration of field trips, assessments and feedback sessions into the project need to be considered carefully, with considerable planning required from all staff members to facilitate full engagement in the project.

5.   LEARNING AND FUTURE DIRECTIONS

As stated at the outset, to date, the Students in Action project has been deployed in two different destinations; it is therefore still at an early stage in its development and the process has involved quite a steep learning curve for the lecturing team concerned. While key areas of learning are still emerging, three of the main factors of consideration are discussed below.

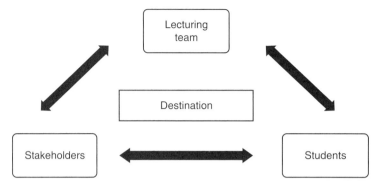

Figure 18.7   Reciprocal learning

5.1   Achieving Reciprocal Learning

This project began with the aim of producing mutually beneficial exchanges between each of the three partners involved: the lecturing team, students and industry/community (see Figure 18.7). While this seems to be self-evident in theory, in practice achieving reciprocity is quite difficult. The learning generated thus far has not been equal; in addition, not all of it was anticipated. The team soon came to realize that the potential for reciprocal learning lies not only between the three stakeholders – lecturers, students and communities – but that it also lies *within* all three groups. This stems from the fact that all three groups are heterogeneous in nature, something that had been insufficiently appreciated at the outset.

Reciprocity in engaged community learning is about differentiating between what is being done by students and lecturers 'in' or ' to' the community, and that which involves mutually beneficial collaboration and includes a degree of reflection by all participants (Saltmarsh et al., 2009). Taking the team of lecturers as an example, there was much to be learned from working collaboratively together. The team of lecturers involved had not worked as a team before and because of the project, communication has increased among the team. However, their involvement in the project stemmed from a variety of reasons, including a belief in the pedagogic value of fieldwork, an interest in strengthening the ties between teaching and research, a belief that tourism education should be more closely aligned to the tourism industry, a desire to develop a more integrated approach to module assessment across educational programmes and within particular student cohorts, as well as an interest in community learning. While negotiating a pathway through these different motivations, different teaching styles and different team-working skills was a challenge, there was much to be learned from each other.

5.2   A Framework for Learning

In both years of the project to date, the team was satisfied that the students involved acquired substantial learning in line with the benefits of student engagement discussed earlier. However, the student cohort involved was quite heterogeneous and the learning acquired was uneven. Students came to the project through different modules (for example

Tourism Enterprise Development, E-Tourism, Tourism Policy & Planning and Destination Marketing; see Figure 18.2). This worked very well in terms of delivering learning outcomes for the stakeholders at each destination. The students devised destination plans, generated ideas for new products, made suggestions to enhance marketing plans and so on, all of which complemented the holistic output being produced for the destination. However, the extent to which this holistic aspect has helped the students to develop their understanding of particular aspects and complexity of tourism is an issue that needs further investigation. The students involved in the project also differed in their programme level, ranging as they did from first year undergraduates to postgraduates. Undoubtedly all students acquired some learning but it was difficult to devise a learning format such that all levels of students benefited appropriately. This is an issue that needs more careful consideration in future.

A key aim from the outset was to devise a project that would bring students into close contact with the actuality of the 'real world'. However, learning how to negotiate those realities takes time. As already mentioned, one challenge was managing community expectations. In the first year, at the pilot stage of the project this task was particularly challenging because of a prior relationship that existed between some of the lecturing team and individual community members. This created a degree of familiarity, which resulted in some degree of difficulty at the outset when drawing boundaries. In the second year, the lecturing team worked though the local Chamber of Commerce. While this represented tourism interests (the specific focus of the project), it had a much broader remit and thus functioned as something of a mediator, filtering overly narrow perspectives and brokering an arrangement that accommodated a multitude of interests, though mainly from a business perspective. Working through a number of mediators, one of whom was a graduate of the college and therefore familiar with the educational requirements while also being attuned to the politics of local places proved to be very useful. This approach is being built into future projects.

5.3   Expression of Need

The team approached the project with a range of assumptions that turned out to be somewhat misguided. They failed to appreciate, in the first instance, the lack of unity of purpose among stakeholders at the chosen destination. For example, a starting premise was that people on the ground would inform the team (through dialogue) as to the issues and concerns that they would like students to address. This did occur within the context of some modules; however, overall the assumption that destination stakeholders can agree on a range of concerns proved not necessarily to be the case.

6.   CONCLUSION

Through the implementation of Students in Action, the project team learned that outcomes beyond those intended can arise from engaging with stakeholders outside the educational institution. The project provided useful networking opportunities for all parties concerned, resulting in a range of tangible and intangible outcomes. This in turn created opportunities to learn how to work with stakeholders in tourism destinations on matters such as negotiating and agreeing targets and objectives. The project presented opportunities to raise the profile of our students, programmes and institution in a very positive way, and in both Slane and Drogheda the project attracted media coverage. To date the project has been a steep learning curve for all involved. Planning, negotiation and reflection need to be key parts of the process, but all participants – staff, students and community stakeholders – agree unanimously that the rich project outputs justify the effort involved.

REFERENCES

Ahlfeldt, S., Mehta, S. and Sellnow, T. (2005), 'Measurement and analysis of student engagement in university classes where varying levels of PBL methods of instruction are in use', *Higher Education Research and Development*, **24** (1), 5–20.

Barnett, R. and Coate, K. (2005), *Engaging the Curriculum in Higher Education*, Maidenhead: SRHE/Open University Press.

Beer, C., Clark, K. and Jones, D. (2010), 'Indicators of engagement', in C.H. Steel, M.J. Keppell, P. Gerbic and S. Housego (eds), *Curriculum, Technology & Transformation for an Unknown Future*, Proceedings ASCILITE Sydney 2010 (pp. 75–86).

Blasco-Arcas, L., Buil, I., Hernández-Ortega, B. and Sese, F.J. (2013), 'Using clickers in class: The role of interactivity, active collaborative learning and engagement in learning performance', *Computers & Education*, **62**, 102–10.

Boland, J.A. (2011), 'Positioning civic engagement on the higher education landscape: Insights from a civically engaged pedagogy', *Tertiary Education and Management*, **17** (2), 101–15.

Burkart, A.J. and Medlik, S. (1981), *Tourism: Past, Present, and Future*, 2nd edn, London: Heinemann.

Coates, H. (2007), 'A model of online and general campus-based student engagement', *Assessment & Evaluation in Higher Education*, **32** (2), 121–41.

Doran, S. (2011), 'Hunt Report recommends reintroduction of third-level fees', accessed 30 March 2015 at http://www.universityobserver.ie/2011/01/18/hunt-report-recommends-reintroduction-of-third-level-fees/.

Downes, S. (2011), 'The wisdom of motivated crowds, Blog entry on Stephen's Web', accessed 30 March 2015 at http://www.downes.ca/post/56667.

Education Matters (2011), 'Hunt Report finally published', accessed 28 March 2015 at http://educationmatters.ie/em_news/hunt-report-finally-published/.

Eyler, J. and Giles, D. (1999), *Where's the Learning in Service-Learning?*, San Francisco: Jossey-Bass.

Hjalager, A.M. (2000), 'Tourism destinations and the concept of industrial districts', *Tourism and Hospitality Research*, **2** (3), 199–213.

Holloway, J.C. (1994), *The Business of Tourism*, London: Pitman.

Hunt, C. (2011), *National Strategy for Higher Education to 2030 – Report of the Strategy Group*, Dublin: Irish Department of Education and Skills.

Kellogg Commission (1999), 'Returning to our roots: The engaged institution', 3rd report of the Kellogg Commission on the Future of State and Land Grant Universities, accessed 17 September 2014 at http://www.aplu.org/NetCommunity/Document.Doc?id=187.

Kuh, D.H. (1993), 'In their own words: What students learn outside the classroom', *American Education Research Journal*, **30**, 277–304.

Kuh, G.D., Kinzie, J., Buckley, J.A., Bridges, B.K. and Hayek, J.C. (2007), *Piecing Together the Student Success Puzzle: Research, Propositions, and Recommendations*, ASHE Higher Education Report, **32** (5), San Francisco: Jossey-Bass.

Lohmann, M. and Beer, H. (2013), 'Fundamentals of tourism: What makes a person a potential tourist and a region a potential tourism destination?', *Poznan University of Economic Review*, **13** (4), 83.

Mayer, R.E., Stull, A., DeLeeuw, K., Almeroth, K., Bimber, B., Chun, D., Bulger, M., Campbell, J., Knight, A. and Zhang, H. (2009), 'Clickers in college classrooms: Fostering learning with questioning methods in large lecture classes', *Contemporary Educational Psychology*, **34** (1), 51–7.

McKenna, M. and Rizzo, E. (1999), 'Student perceptions of the learning in service-learning courses', in J.R. Ferrari and J.G. Chapman (eds), *Educating Students to Make a Difference: Community-based Service Learning*, New York: Haworth Press.

NCIHE (1997), 'Higher Education in the Learning Society, Report of the National Committee of Inquiry into Higher Education: The Dearing Report', London: HMSO, accessed 17 September 2014 at http://www.leeds.ac.uk/educol/ncihe/.

Owen, D. and Hill, S. (2011), 'Embedding public engagement in the curriculum: A framework for the assessment of student learning from public engagement', NCCCPE, accessed 12 September 2014 at http://www.publicengagement.ac.uk/sites/default/files/publication/assessing_student_learning_from_pe.pdf.

Powell, J. and Clark, A. (2012), 'Leadership for improved academic enterprise or university reach-out as it is more traditionally known', London: Leadership Foundation for Higher Education.

Prat, L., Guia, J. and Molina, F. (2008), 'How tourism destinations evolve: The notion of tourism local innovation system', *Tourism and Hospitality Research*, **8**, 178–91.

Prince, M. (2004), 'Does active learning work? A review of the research', *Journal of Engineering Education*, **93** (3), 8.

Ruhanen, L., Robinson, R. and Breakey, N. (2013), 'A tourism immersion internship: Student expectations, experiences and satisfaction', *Journal of Hospitality, Leisure, Sport & Tourism Education*, **13**, 60–69.

Salaber, J. (2014), 'Facilitating student engagement and collaboration in a large postgraduate course using wiki-based activities', *The International Journal of Management Education*, **12** (2), 115–26.

Saltmarsh, J., Giles, D.E., Ward, E. and Buglione, S.M. (2009), 'Rewarding community-engaged scholarship', *New Directions for Higher Education*, **2009**, 25–35.

Thomas, L. (2012), 'Building student engagement and belonging in Higher Education at a time of change: A summary of findings and recommendations from the What Works? Student Retention & Success programme', London: Paul Hamlyn Foundation.

Thomas, L. (2014), 'Improving student retention and success: Learning from experience in the UK', paper presented at *Improving Student Retention in Higher Education* Seminar 2014, Deloitte, Dublin.

Ward, K. and Wolf-Wendal, L. (2000), 'Community centred service learning: Moving from doing for to doing with', *American Behavioral Scientist*, **43** (5), 767–80.

Zyngier, D. (2008), '(Re)conceptualising student engagement: Doing education not doing time', *Teaching and Teacher Education*, **24**, 1765–76.

19 Student and practitioner experience from learning laboratories

Peter Wiltshier and Sarah Rawlinson

1. INTRODUCTION

This chapter explores the outcomes of experiential learning at the University of Derby in Buxton, Derbyshire, UK. The setting is the delightful spa market town of Buxton, elevation 300 metres, one hour south-east of Manchester, one hour north-west of Birmingham. The University of Derby has been delivering higher education in Hospitality, Resort, Spa, Tourism, Culinary and Events Management for two decades, and for nine years at Buxton in the heart of England's first National Park, the Peak District. We can attribute much of the success we discuss to the location of Buxton and the existence of England's important natural and built cultural heritage located within 20 minutes' drive of the university campus in Buxton. We also attribute the success to an academic approach to experiential learning and the presence of a team who have deliberately developed and delivered real-world learning to our students in this purpose-built heritage location. The chapter includes reflections on experiences obtained during degree studies by students and by the practitioners cooperating with the university. In addition to reflections we consider key stakeholders' expectations of students in reviewing partner organizations' management strategies, operations, projects implemented and interim outcomes.

2. LITERATURE

Experiential learning has its roots in Kolb and Kolb's experiential learning model (2005) explored through the lens of vocational higher education connecting the world of management to the students by a team of academics delivering real-world learning that is accessible, practical and easily understood by a range of stakeholders. This stakeholder approach is built around developing and reinforcing skills for employability that our industry advisory team has helped the University of Derby to construct in the last decade. Without the advisory group of stakeholders, we would struggle to differentiate the offer we make to students in Buxton from the offer of a range of competitors in close proximity.

Our second base for a strongly practitioner-focused delivery of management skills is the research focus of the university. This focus has at its core reflections of exemplary approaches to delivering vocationally relevant and adaptive courses and a body of knowledge developed in the university that observes, comments on and reviews the underpinning training of trainers, and the reflective capacity of staff and students in the body of evidence presented underpinning this real-world learning. Over the years that we have implemented experiential learning we have explored and included public policy initiatives underpinning the relevance of teaching, learning and assessment that is derived from contemporary perspectives (Mandelson, 2009; Leitch, 2006; Egan, 2004; Haskins, 2003, amongst others).

The philosophical approach to experiential learning adopted in this chapter is derived from the social constructivist approach used by Kolb and Kolb (2005). Primarily the learning laboratories used problem-based learning (PBL) through the engagement of students. Throughout and from the commencement of studies our students are encouraged and then directed to engage in participation in service sector-relevant management research and data collection. We have identified through extant projects at the university that skills needed by graduates for sustainable development are dependent on the learning acquired during experiential action. Our own holistic approach to the learning and knowledge shared mirrors UK initiatives to promote capacity development in ways to change knowledge applications across product and service boundaries (Dawe et al., 2005; Wals and Jickling, 2002; Haskins, 2003; Leitch, 2006; Taylor and Wilding, 2009; Hyslop, 2009).

UK government (central and local) policy encourages us to create graduates that can engage with the diversification and regeneration agenda. In addition, this experiential learning supported the University of Derby's agenda to promote experiential and entrepreneurial learning in students working at both undergraduate and postgraduate levels. This chapter accords with the current university initiatives to meet the student employability agenda through the application of PBL and knowledge management.

In the current higher education and market-led management environment, graduates need evidence of having successfully negotiated and achieved tasks in applied research. Our take on applied research includes partners from a range of public or private, profit and not-for-profit sector organizations. In addition to satisfying our stakeholders that the research and teaching is informed by relevant contemporary issues in society, we assure ourselves of the currency and relevance of teaching, learning and assessment in higher education through constructivist and problem-based learning (Hendry et al., 1999; Brown and King, 2000; Kolb and Kolb, 2005).

Our graduates are expected to have acquired and can demonstrate through their certification vocational, transferable, cognitive and intellectual skills to meet contemporary socio-cultural, political, economic and more importantly, educational, expectations. Moreover, the learning community now buys into the contract to provide students with learning opportunities within the workplace and in not-for-profit organizations as part of their social exchange with the university.

The approach is predicated on the value ascribed to experiential learning by non-academic partners (Reeve and Gallacher, 2005). It also relies on value developed by academics reflecting the contemporary skills needs of partners (Arpiainen et al., 2013). Our approach is also informed by learning styles needed to achieve partners' and students' expectations of work-based learning: what are the boundaries that must be crossed; and what are the preparations and mentoring for both students and academics (Raven, 2014; Dyke, 2009; Hovorka and Wolf, 2009; Greenbank, 2002; Gray, 2001). Finally the epistemological norms and frontiers need exploring and expanding for experiential learning to become a minimum approach and content of any award achieved in HE (Brundiers and Wiek, 2013; Elkington, 2013; Portwood, 2007).

Experiential learning theory emphasizes the role experience plays in the learning process. It requires the active involvement of the individual learner in a meaningful learning experience. Active engagement is essential, as is the link between action and thought that creates the experience, leading to one of the most powerful means of learning. According to Beard and Wilson (2006, p. 19), 'Experiential learning is the sense-making process of active engagement between the inner world of the person and the outer world of the environment.' Experiential learning requires meaningful engagement with the environment in which the learner will gain active knowledge and bring meaning to an interaction. The connection between action and reflection is central to Kolb's (1984) model of experiential learning, which involves a direct encounter with the phenomenon being studied and the opportunity to apply knowledge and skills within a relevant context.

Learning through experience is not a new phenomenon; however, as an educational approach within higher education, it is of growing significance, with students benefiting from knowledge acquisition opportunities that are not readily achievable within just classroom environments. There is a growing body of evidence identifying that graduates without experiential learning opportunities that are documented and evidenced independently are disadvantaged in their active pursuit of graduate-level jobs. Therefore, research at the University of Derby (Rawlinson, 2012) suggests there is a need to move towards a shared epistemology of work-based learning and learning that takes place in the university. Situations described by Portwood (2007) where the university uses the workplace to test subject-based knowledge through placements or where the university determines the validity of work-based knowledge through accreditation do not provide what Portwood (2007) terms a 'pragmatic philosophy'. Only by working together through a mutual partnership can both theory and practice be brought together to enable 'active knowledge' as described by Moore (1998) and Boreham (2004) and a shared epistemology. It is within this context that the University of Derby, Buxton has developed the concept of a University Learning Laboratory.

2.1   The Role of Knowledge Transfer in Learning Laboratories

The transfer of knowledge and skills is not easy in new situations and contexts and therefore the faculty's teaching and learning strategy is based on a model that advocates that students are taught to transfer knowledge and solve problems in 'real world learning' contexts. Universities profess to teach the transferability of generic skills, but Eraut (1997) suggests that there is a need to learn how to use conceptual knowledge (or propositional knowledge, the term Eraut uses) and skills in new contexts, particularly in the workplace. Eraut (1997) argues that conceptual knowledge and transferable skills are of little value in a knowledge-based economy unless the transfer of knowledge forms an important part of the learning process. The University of Derby therefore makes the transfer of conceptual knowledge and procedural knowledge central to its teaching and learning strategy using the Learning Laboratory concept and the university's commercial facilities. This approach provides a supportive environment in which students can learn to transfer their conceptual knowledge within the context of a workplace under supervision as part of their studies. Students who have had this opportunity have little difficulty in applying their conceptual knowledge in the workplace.

3.   TEACHING APPROACH

The experiential learning model used at the University of Derby proposes a shared epistemology of learning that takes place both in the classroom and in the commercial facilities operated by the university. Students learn the contextual supporting knowledge in the classroom and are taught to transfer that knowledge through appropriate teaching and learning strategies within realistic working environments such as the commercial spa, restaurant and outdoor leadership center. Students are trained in the context of the commercial facilities and spend time running the facilities, engaging in a number of roles from basic operation to duty management. We reflect on the feedback later in the chapter.

A critical consideration of the university approach to experiential learning is to provide evidence that knowledge rooted in the experience of work is a fundamental component of vocational degrees (Rawlinson and Dewhurst, 2013). Combining the different forms of knowledge is a powerful tool to vocational learning and provides employers with graduates that can demonstrate the skills and knowledge they require to make a difference to their businesses. We include three case studies from past employers detailing their satisfaction with students' innovation, communication skills, independent action and decision-making, contribution to management strategy and outcomes in building client relationships, flexibility, and adaptation to various technologies including numeracy and literacy.

Designing experiential learning programs can be complex and time consuming. It requires collaboration between industry practitioners and academics working together to blend the theoretical knowledge traditionally taught in university lecture theaters with the application of knowledge in an industry context. We found that applying the five key elements to designing project-based curricula advocated by Thacker (2002) was critical to the success of designing our experiential learning programs (see Table 19.1). Thacker (2002 p. 31) emphasizes the importance of:

- practitioner input;
- adoption of creative approaches to student learning;
- development of specific measureable outcomes;

Table 19.1   Preparing the learning laboratory

Thacker's five key elements	University of Derby approach
• Practitioner input • Adoption of creative approaches to student learning	• Project brief designed with industry partner • Designing and resourcing flexible teaching and learning plans to allow students to access the learning opportunity which is likely to be off campus
• Development of specific measurable outcomes • Observable demonstrations of the learning of those outcomes • Creation of projects grounded in real-world business problems	• Linking learning opportunities to programme and module intended learning objectives • Specifically designed assessments to include industry partners • Project outcomes are useful and valuable to the industry partner

- observable demonstrations of the learning of those outcomes;
- creation of projects grounded in real-world business problems.

The faculty established an advisory board and invited industry practitioners to review the curriculum content to provide advice on graduate skills and knowledge expected of graduates. Using industry advisers in this way gives credibility and legitimacy to the curriculum, ensures that graduates will have the skills required, and that the curriculum remains contemporary.

Designing good teaching and learning strategy using an experiential learning pedagogy requires academics with industry experience who can design projects and experiences that reflect the skills and knowledge identified by industry. We worked with our advisory panel to design learning opportunities in four ways:

- *Module content designed to provide an insight into authentic workplace activities:* the academic modules are aligned with the practical or practice-based components through teaching and learning activities that bring theory and practice together in meaningful ways. The modules align disciplinary demands with workplace relevance and are supported through the delivery of guest lectures by industry professionals and the use of authentic examples or case studies from the world of professional practice.
- *Assessment activities designed to simulate authentic workplace activities*: this form of experiential learning involves assessment activities that are designed to test the students' ability to apply knowledge and skills. The intended outcome is that students have experience in applying acquired knowledge and skills to the solution of real-world problems. These topics are designed to include standard assessment exercises to be undertaken by all students or they may be designed to permit individual negotiation and approval of assessment exercises between students and topic coordinators, depending on the students' needs and interests, provided that the topic objectives are met. One recommended approach is to use industry representatives as part of a panel assessing the students' work.
- *Real* world learning in the university's *commercial spaces:* this involves the faculty providing actual on-campus workplace environments in which students deliver a commercial service to real customers, with the students being assessed according to the quality of their performance. The students are closely monitored by members of both the university's academic and commercial teams.
- *Directed work experience in an industry or professional workplace:* this normally involves a supervised work placement, or professional development portfolio (PDP)-based internship, where the student is engaged in work and is located in a workplace typical of the profession for which their program of study is preparing them. The intended outcome is that, on completion of the course, students already have experience in the kind of workplace they anticipate entering. Such experience may be required for professional accreditation on course completion, and experiential learning topic design must be cognizant of professional accreditation requirements. A placement can include any educational work experience established by the faculty to integrate theoretical learning from a program of study with its practical application. The faculty's support must extend to organizing the student

placements, interacting with them, monitoring their work and progress, and assessing their performance throughout the period of the experiential learning activity.

The experiential learning activities are designed to integrate work-related practice with the students' academic studies. Within this environment they are closely monitored and receive high quality mentoring and supervision from the university. This in turn allows for effective assessment of their performance, whilst enabling the students to engage in effective self-reflection. A student (2) says: 'I have sufficient experience resolving situations in real-world context that has given me confidence. I am not anxious anymore.' We actively pursue good working relationships with prospective and current host organizations, positioning the university at the heart of a growing network of local agencies and organizations.

Adopting an experiential learning pedagogy is time consuming and resource intensive. Setting up the projects and facilitating student learning requires academics to have a good understanding of the context within which students are learning and to plan and manage students operating in different parts of the business. Academics need to be familiar with running commercial businesses and to have relevant and up-to-date knowledge of the issues and challenges facing organizations in their industry if they are to have any creditability with our industry partners and our students. A student (2) says: 'I had several job offers and it appears these offers were made as a result of the strength of my course. I was lucky'.

Using the workplace as a situation for learning to add value to a degree provides opportunities for applied subject knowledge, and requires universities to value the knowledge and learning that is taking place in work by employees in everyday work situations. The curriculum is not simply that of the university but of the workplace, and is designed for a particular work situation. This can be a challenge for some academics. Employing academics with the right skills, knowledge and commitment to this way of learning has been challenging for the faculty.

Identifying 'who does what' within the university and communicating this to the industry partner can be complex. Universities are notoriously complex organizations that can be confusing to the uninitiated. Where links are established between the university and the industry partner they often depend on interpersonal relationships that are vulnerable to staff turnover, making it difficult to maintain links.

A major challenge for this type of teaching and learning is management and organization. The teaching and learning strategy is complex. Students are scheduled into activities through rotas that change depending on student needs; activities are not always on campus; students participate in a high number of visits, which are costly to the university and are often challenged by the finance department. But the biggest challenge is the communication with students and industry providers. Our students tell us via the National Student Survey we don't always get this right and mark management and organization as an area for improvement.

The use of industry projects provides a more challenging and inspiring curriculum and gives students relevant experiences to refer to in job interviews. However, not all students make the connection. A student (1) asserts: 'I only realized after finishing my course that employers appreciated that I had done so much more.'

The development of a PDP portfolio is critical to the success of students recognizing the soft skills they are developing through their engagement with industry. A student (7) says: ' There's only so much we can do in a classroom; there's all the theory you want and it makes it easier to apply theoretical (positions) in practice. You can't be shielded.'

The key message in this type of learning and teaching strategy is one where everyone is clear about the need for students to have a good learning experience and not to be used as free labour. This approach is similar to that taken by HEIs in the southern hemisphere, especially those in Australia and South Africa where there has long been a tradition of Work Integrated Learning. Work Integrated Learning exposes students to the context and requirements of professional practice, providing them with an opportunity to:

- apply and refine their current knowledge and skills;
- develop new skills in areas such as communication and teamwork;
- develop an awareness of workplace culture and expectations;
- develop a practical appreciation of their chosen profession;
- develop practical skills to reflect upon in future studies.

4.   FINDINGS

The outcomes of the learning laboratory approach are further illustrated by a series of short case studies. The first case study explored how module content can be designed to provide an insight into authentic workplace activities. The academic team seek industry partners to assist them in delivering module content in the context of the workplace. For example, students are working on a project with the YHA to consider how the YHA might develop marketing strategies to engage a younger market segment. The project was designed to deliver the content of a marketing module that considered tourism marketing strategies targeted at generation Z. Through the engagement of a local company in delivering the content the students see the relevance and value of the topic. Students also realize the value of their knowledge as members of generation Z to finding solutions to business problems and the YHA also value the opportunity to engage with the students to learn more about the market segment with which they want to engage.

The second case study is concerned with the use of assessment activities designed to stimulate authentic workplace activities. The faculty designs projects with industry partners that allow students to apply theory in a work context. Using the principles of problem-based learning (PBL) the academic team encourages students to provide solutions to real world problems. This form of learning can be engaging and involves students in deep learning. For example, a local travel company has provided five projects that they are currently investigating in their business. One project is a competitor analysis and subsequent development of a new ski product. Assessments are designed so students can feed back their suggestions directly to the travel company.

The third case study involves real world learning in the university's commercial spaces. The University of Derby operates a commercial day spa, fine dining restaurant, an events management company and its campus is a regional tourist attraction. The university operates these businesses under the brand name of 'Dome'; Dome Spa, Dome restaurant, Dome events and the Dome itself is the tourist attraction. During the first year of their degree, students learn the practical skills to operate in these commercial businesses. As their skills and confidence develop, students take on supervisory roles in these facilities.

For some students this is during the first year of the degree program and for others it is in the second year of their degree program. Depending on skills and experience, students may be supervising on one occasion and being supervised on another, depending on the complexity of the activity. Final year students act as managers and run the facility and participate in business decisions. For the first time this year the university included experiential learning as part of its procurement process for the catering provision of the whole university. Providing experiential learning opportunities in the university catering facilities was a key component of the procurement selection process.

The final case study examines the role of directed work experience in an industry or professional workplace. Our directed work experience model engages students with a work placement opportunity as part of their program at all levels. Students can engage in a number of ways: at weekends, one day a week, and during holiday breaks from university such as Easter and summer. The benefits of participating in a work placement whilst still actively engaged in a degree program are that the students are able to transfer knowledge, and question and critically evaluate what they are learning in the classroom and how it applies in their placement. They can actively engage with their placement provider and bring together theory and action into active learning. Tourism students are spending a year with the Visit Peak District Destination Marketing Organization learning the complexities of engaging local businesses in a common marketing strategy for the area and considering dispersal activities to encourage visitors to visit some of the lesser known areas of the Peak District.

Traditionally universities have provided work-placement opportunities during the second and third year of a degree program. However, researchers have demonstrated that increasingly there are barriers to students participating in one-year placements (Busby, 2003; Ball et al., 2006; Morgan, 2006). For example, increasingly students study in their region to avoid accommodation costs; they have part-time jobs to support their studies and are keen to complete their studies as quickly as possible. A year-long placement is likely to incur additional costs such as accommodation and travel. The costs of participating in a placement away from home that may require students to give up part-time employment make embarking on a placement prohibitive for some. Providing a work placement alongside a degree program overcomes some of these barriers.

The advantage of one-year placements is that they allow students to immerse themselves in the workplace. However, a distinct disadvantage is that the student has minimal contact with their university and academic staff during their placement year. Students receive little or no guidance on how to transfer their conceptual knowledge in the context of the workplace and guidance on re-contextualizing their work-based knowledge takes place at short periods when students receive academic support during their placement year. A further disadvantage is that students do not make a distinction between the cognitive complexities of the curriculum and its application in the workplace. Sandwich degree programs allow students one opportunity to participate in placement. Whilst the placement is an extensive period of one year where students gain an insight into the operations and management of an organization and enhance their social and interpersonal skills, it does not provide opportunities for students to make a distinction between the application of knowledge at different levels and complexities.

We have measured the satisfaction of employers with these skills in our findings. The faculty's analysis of Work Integrated Learning led to its introduction of a suite of off-campus 'learning laboratories'. A University Learning Laboratory provides more than a work placement or internship opportunity. The concept allows local organizations to become a 'Real World Learning' venue for applied vocational learning supported by staff from the organization in on-the-job training. A learning laboratory also presents the opportunity for students to engage in live project work that can support an organization in delivering its strategic and operational goals. Key staff from the learning laboratories provide input into the design of the faculty degree programs, deliver master classes in the faculty, participate in the assessment process, often providing prizes for best student projects, and take a role in the Faculty Industry Advisory Board. Learning laboratories allow faculty staff to receive industrial updating via an annual series of secondment opportunities. A formal contract is made detailing the responsibilities of both university and partner practitioner to ensure that non-compliance, any reported under-performance or failure to complete tasks can be reported, agreed and reviewed to ensure that quality of experience, replicability of sample laboratory and advice to funding bodies in both organizations can be stored.

The partnerships and networks established through university learning laboratories are important in considering the resources used at both the university and workplaces. Without an excellent understanding of the cooperative nature of learning labs at all hierarchical levels in both organizations there is a chance that the purpose, outcomes and outputs are misunderstood, poorly articulated within workplaces and perceived as complex and unworkable by some partners. The resources required include an agreement that outlines the objectives and outcomes from the university learning laboratory. There must be preliminary meetings to establish the timeframe and resource expectations of both university and university learning laboratory and a review phase, most likely occurring annually.

Other practical considerations in operationalizing the university learning laboratory include contingency arrangements for students and industry employees, thorough and robust risk assessment procedures and a handbook detailing the structure, operational plans, risks, contact details and relevant insurance and indemnity information.

Our experience underpins the need to place emphasis on pragmatism in considering industry partners' needs. A learning lab agreement must include a plain English glossary, detail university and partner job roles and responsibilities and, more importantly, clear responsibilities for students to ensure coherence between expectations and perceptions (Hogarth et al., 2007) (see Table 19.2).

The formal adoption of a learning laboratory agreement forms the basis for reflection and further adaptation for following student cohorts working with an established partner in practice.

The university's teaching and learning model highlights the importance of the transferability of conceptual knowledge and makes it central to the framework for vocational curriculum design (Rawlinson, 2012). When revalidating or validating new programs we have immediate access to sector partners who reflect on core indicators of success in the learning laboratory such as communications, innovation, team working and client relationship building.

The model in Figure 19.1 highlights the need for the dominant logic of vocational curricula to focus on the workplace as a context for learning. The model advocates that vocational degree curriculum developers share the epistemology of work-based learning

Table 19.2   Mapping learning laboratory experiences

Skills	Example	Literature	Achieved by Students	Achieved by Practitioners
Problem solving	Evidence of consumer expectation/ satisfaction	Raven, 2014	Case Study 1 YHA	Y
Innovation		Brundiers and Wiek, 2013; Hovorka and Wolf, 2009	Case Study 4 Visit Peak District	Y
Networking	Ski Holidays	Greenbank, 2002	Case Study 2	Y
Partnership building	Co-branding	Reeve and Gallacher, 2005	Case Study 1	Y
Context Conceptual thinking	Spa	Chavan, 2011; Portwood, 2007	Case Study 3	Y
Reflective lifelong learning	Personal development portfolios on-line	Kolb and Kolb, 2005	Case Study 2	Y
Teamwork		Green and Sammons, 2014; Arpiainen et al., 2013	All case studies	Y

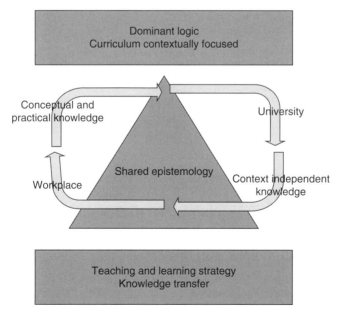

Source: Adapted from Rawlinson (2012).

Figure 19.1   Teaching and knowledge transfer

by bringing together the conceptual and procedural knowledge used in work with context-independent knowledge learnt within the university. This sharing of knowledge between the workplace and the university opens it up to scrutiny and review. It provides the student with the opportunity to analyse their workplace learning (context-dependent learning) outside its context in classes with academic staff and to re-contextualize their context-independent learning (learning that takes place in the university) back in its context of the workplace. This shared epistemology approach will provide students with the opportunity to engage in active learning (Moore, 1998; Boreham 2004) and what Portwood (2007, p. 16) refers to as 'pragmatic philosophy', and develops a culture of learning that values knowledge gained from active engagement in the workplace (Teare, 1998).

Research at the University of Derby (Rawlinson, 2012) found that students on spa management programs, where the dominant logic of their program focuses on the context of the workplace, have the skills and knowledge required by industry. The research conducted with spa graduates and employers sought to refine the understanding of the concepts and historical evolution of knowledge acquisition within higher education and particularly within vocational and work-based learning. It found that spa graduates have the necessary commercial awareness and business acumen for a successful career in the spa industry and that they have a combination of good practical skills and management and leadership qualities. The spa management degree made effective use of the commercial spa as a learning resource to allow students to immerse themselves in a professional learning environment and to share that experience both with industry professionals and academic staff. The commercial spa and work-placement opportunities provided the context for the students to learn how to transfer their conceptual and procedural knowledge to industry. Students were able to demonstrate skills and competencies as part of knowledge rather than separate from it and were able to demonstrate to employers what they could do. The failure of graduates to demonstrate to employers what they can do leads employers to question the credibility of vocational degrees and the quality of graduates. This research concluded that when vocational degrees develop the concepts of the discipline within the context where these concepts are applied then graduates are better prepared to make judgments in the workplace. The research also concluded that, where vocational degrees provide opportunities for students to learn how to transfer conceptual knowledge in context, they provide better prepared graduates for industry.

5.   FUTURE DIRECTIONS

In this chapter we explored student perspectives and practitioner reflections on learning laboratories. We have identified how learning laboratories reinforce teaching and the relationships between real-world learning and traditional classroom-based activity. We have used models established in learning laboratories for critical reflection in classroom settings. Students have built research activity around tasks at the laboratory and may review findings against contemporary practices in market research, building audience participation and satisfaction indicators for the sector and for specific sites to use as benchmarks. Problem-based learning works in tandem with the emerging opportunities to reinforce the university learning laboratory. The four case studies used form the basis for exploration in future learning laboratories. We also mirror the university learning laboratory with student placements. Successful employment has been derived from using work-based learning experiences at the Visit Peak District and Derbyshire Destination Management Partnership. We still perceive there is academic and practice work to coordinate and co-create field work and university learning laboratories. Academics must reflect more on practices used and their perceived value to the stakeholders. Our students are delivering exceptional customer service in ways in which students should use practical experiences in their personal development portfolios. Messages around communicating the outcomes of project work (Reeve and Gallacher, 2005) will prove relevance and sustain the practices with partners. We can already observe that partners engage with universities for consultancy work that the partner struggles to conduct without employing a consultant at regular fees and charges. We also acknowledge that practitioners struggle with creating realistic expectations and occasionally a project is mismanaged or the time-frame is unworkable (Raven, 2014; O'Bannon and McFadden, 2008). We occasionally observe what happens when students engaged in experiential learning activity during the course cannot complete the task assigned.

These highlight the continuing need for synergies of classroom with practice. Public relations and promotion or marketing activity must work for the partners (Lee and Dickson, 2010). Some partners promulgate and distribute outcomes of successful partnership projects undertaken by students during their experiential learning.

Finally we ponder the capacity to innovate and capacity to explore and experiment (Green and Sammons, 2014). Occasionally students apply theoretical approaches from the classroom to real-world issues yet cannot resolve problems from the partners' perspective. This can lead to incomplete tasks due to students' inability to analyze and synthesize the key issues.

6. CONCLUSION

The future demands that we develop partnerships with stakeholders that reinforce learning laboratories. Our networks of real-world learning experiences mirror stakeholders' expectations and enable resources to be used for the future.

We have identified ways in which a low-cost opportunity for partner organizations can be embedded in university and industry relationships. Our showcase projects that students have completed have been delivered to partners' satisfaction. Consultancy and special projects are key high-ticket budget items for all organizations. The university indemnifies organizations and students against misadventure and insures the parties against any possible financial or reputation loss.

We value visiting fellows from industry as they have the ability to cross the divide between praxis and academia. We are continuously identifying ways in which partners' staff can become adjunct or associate teaching staff for the university. In the context of strategic and operational roles and relevant contexts from theory we have found that we can incorporate industry teaching days without additional charges accruing to the partners or stretching resources that are needed for day-to-day operations.

The university now has an evidence base of consultancy work conducted for visiting industry fellows and practices that embeds knowledge in the courses offered; more importantly it provides a legacy of experiences and knowledge that partners can use as the basis for ongoing development work.

REFERENCES

Arpiainen, R.L., Täks, M., Tynjälä, P. and Lackéus, M. (2013), 'The sources and dynamics of emotions in entrepreneurship education learning process', *Trames*, **17** (4), 331–46.

Ball, C., Collier, H., Mok, P. and Wilson, J. (2006), 'Research into barriers to work placements in the retail sector in the south East', Higher Education Careers Service Unit and the National Council for Work Experience.

Beard, C.M. and Wilson, J.P. (2006), *Experiential Learning: A Best Practice Handbook for Educators and Trainers*, London: Kogan Page Publishers.

Boreham, N. (2004), 'Orienting the work-based curriculum towards work process knowledge: A rationale and a German case study', *Studies in Continuing Education*, **26** (2), 209–27.

Brown, S.W. and King, F.B. (2000), 'Constructivist pedagogy and how we learn: Educational psychology meets international studies', *International Studies Perspectives*, **1**, 245–54.

Brundiers, K. and Wiek, A. (2013), 'Do we teach what we preach? An international comparison of problem-and project-based learning courses in sustainability', *Sustainability*, **5** (4), 1725–46.

Busby, G. (2003), 'Tourism degree internships: A longitudinal study', *Journal of Vocational Education and Training*, **55** (3), 319–34.

Chavan, M. (2011), 'Higher education students' attitudes towards experiential learning in international business', *Journal of Teaching in International Business*, **22** (2), 126–43.

Dawe, G., Jucker, R. and Martin, S. (2005), 'Sustainable development in higher education: current practice and future developments', York: Higher Education Academy.

Dyke, M. (2009), 'An enabling framework for reflexive learning: Experiential learning and reflexivity in contemporary modernity', *International Journal of Lifelong Education*, **28** (3), 289–310.

Egan, J. (2004), 'Skills for sustainable communities', London: Office of the Deputy Prime Minister.

Elkington, S. (2013), 'Ways of seeing degrees of leisure: From practice to pedagogy', *Leisure Studies*, **32** (4), 447–61.

Eraut, M. (1997), 'Perspectives on defining "The Learning Society"', *Journal of Education Policy*, **12** (6), 551–8.

Gray, D. (2001), 'Work-based learning, action learning and the virtual paradigm', *Journal of Further and Higher Education*, **25** (3), 315–24.

Green, A.J. and Sammons, G.E. (2014), 'Student learning styles: assessing active learning in the hospitality learners model', *Journal of Hospitality & Tourism Education*, **26** (1), 29–38.

Greenbank, P. (2002), 'Undergraduate work experience: An alternative approach using micro businesses', *Education + Training*, **44** (6), 261–70.

Haskins, C. (2003), *Rural Delivery Review*, London: Defra.

Hendry, G., Frommer, M. and Walker, R. (1999), 'Constructivism and problem based learning', *Journal of Further and Higher Education*, **23** (3), 369–71.

Hogarth, T., Winterbotham, M., Hasluck, C., Carter, K., Daniel., W.W., Green, W.W. and Morrison, J. (2007), 'Employer and university engagement in the use and development of graduate level skills', Institute for Employment Research, University of Warwick.

Hovorka, A.J. and Wolf, P.A. (2009), 'Activating the classroom: Geographical fieldwork as pedagogical practice', *Journal of Geography in Higher Education*, **33** (1), 89–102.

Hyslop, A. (2009), 'CTE's role in energy and environmental sustainability', *Techniques: Connecting Education and Careers (J1)*, **84** (3), 22–5.

Kolb, D.A. (1984), *Experiential Learning: Experience as the Source of Learning and Development* (Vol. 1), Englewood Cliffs, NJ: Prentice-Hall.

Kolb, A.Y. and Kolb, D.A. (2005), 'Learning styles and learning spaces: Enhancing experiential learning', *Higher Education Academy of Management Learning & Education*, **4** (2), 193–212.

Lee, S. and Dickson, D. (2010), 'Increasing student learning in the classroom through experiential learning programs outside the classroom', *Journal of Hospitality & Tourism Education*, **22** (3), 27–34.

Leitch, L. (2006), 'Prosperity for all in the global economy – world class skills: final report', London: H.M. Stationery Office.

Mandelson, P. (2009), *Skills For Growth: The National Skills Strategy*, London: H.M. Stationery Office.

Moore, C. (1998), 'Process knowledge', in Fischer, L. (ed.), *Excellence in Practice Volume II*, Lighthouse Point, FL: WARIA.

Morgan, R. (2006), 'Using clinical skills laboratories to promote theory–practice integration during first practice placement: An Irish perspective', *Journal of Clinical Nursing*, **15** (2), 155–61.

O'Bannon, T. and McFadden, C. (2008), 'Model of experiential andragogy: Development of a non-traditional experiential learning program model', *Journal of Unconventional Parks, Tourism & Recreation Research (JUPTRR)*, **1** (1), 23–8.

Portwood, D. (2007), 'Can work-based learning add to the research inventory of higher education? The case of collaborative research', *Research in Post-Compulsory Education*, **12** (3), 279–90.

Raven, N. (2014), 'Assessing an approach to the capturing and sharing of work-based learning with a focus on improving practice and provision', *Research in Post-Compulsory Education*, **19** (2), 119–31.

Rawlinson, S. (2012), 'Exploring a new model for vocational degrees: A case study in spa management', unpublished doctoral thesis, University of Derby.

Rawlinson, S. and Dewhurst, P. (2013), 'How can effective university–industry partnerships be developed?', *Worldwide Hospitality and Tourism Themes*, **5** (3), 255–67.

Reeve, F. and Gallacher, J. (2005), 'Employer–university "partnerships": A key problem for work-based learning programmes?', *Journal of Education and Work*, **18** (2), 219–33.

Taylor, P. and Wilding, D. (2009), 'Rethinking the values of higher education: The student as collaborator and producer? Undergraduate research as a case study', Quality Assurance Agency for Higher Education (QAA).

Teare, R. (1998), 'Supporting managerial learning in the workplace', in Teare, R., Bowen, J.T. and Hing, N. (eds), *New Directions in Hospitality and Tourism: A Worldwide Review*, London: Cassell.

Thacker, R (2002), 'Revising the HR curriculum: An academic/practitioner partnership', *Education + Training*, **44** (1), 31–9.

Wals, A.E. and Jickling, B. (2002), 'Sustainability in higher education: From doublethink and newspeak to critical thinking and meaningful learning', *International Journal of Sustainability in Higher Education*, **3** (3), 221–32.

20 Investigating fieldtrips
Kevin Griffin

1. INTRODUCTION

With increased workloads and larger class sizes, academics and institutions are increasingly familiar with terminology such as rationalization and increased efficiencies. This leads program planning groups to identify areas where non-essential and 'extra' activities can be cut back or even eliminated. As a researcher/lecturer I come from a geographical background, whereby fieldwork is an integral component of teaching, and I have continued to utilize geography-influenced pedagogical approaches in the delivery of tourism-related modules. However, with increased external influences such as concern over 'health and safety', insurance and liability, not to mention the time element of organizing and running fieldwork-related activities, I have begun to question the benefits to be gained from utilizing this pedagogical tool.

Therefore, the purpose of this chapter is twofold, first to provide an overview of current international practice in relation to fieldtrips, and secondly to draw inspiration from the expertise of international colleagues regarding the value of undertaking fieldwork activity.

2. FIELDTRIP PEDAGOGY

Ironically, the first academic paper I consulted when commencing this project was Kelner and Sanders's 2009 work entitled 'Beyond the field trip: teaching tourism through tours', in which the authors categorically state that they 'found almost no reference to the pedagogical use of field trips in the literature on the teaching of tourism studies' (2009: 137). They then qualify this statement somewhat, indicating that the literature does recognize the importance of the fieldtrip as a tool for engaging students as 'active learners', which is typically embedded in Dewey's 1938 notion of experiential education. However, they would like to move beyond this and build on the concept of tourism as 'a configuration of spatial and cultural knowledge practices centered on movement, semiotics, interaction, ritual and consumption' (Kelner and Sanders, 2009: 137), with fieldtrips acting as exemplars of tourism experience, to be used for educational development.

While derided somewhat by Kelner and Sanders, the focus on fieldtrips as opportunities for experiential-based observation of society resonates throughout the literature. For example, Arcodia and Dickson (2013), in framing their field study work as an integration of experience, activity and technique, lean heavily on Kolb's theory of experiential education. They suggest that 'field studies' can satisfy Kolb's first step in experiential learning – that is, the provision of relevant experience, from which reflective learning arises – thus resulting in more meaningful learning experiences. A plethora of papers exist wherein the authors present the 'meaningful learning' they have achieved for their students via their field studies to 'exotic' landscapes such as the Antarctic (Johnston et al., 2014), on cruise ships (Lohmann, 2014; Weeden et al., 2011), to the Gambia (Wright and Hind, 2011), Malawi (Whitfield, 2008) and even virtual/online field trips (Patiar et al., 2014). While not specifying any particular destination, Caruana and Ploner (2011) make a cogent argument in highlighting the importance of these field-based practices for enhancing students' international experience, and in so doing they cite the work of Goh and Ritchie (2011), Gretzel et al. (2009), Weeden et al. (2011) and Wright and Hind (2011). Xie (2004, discussed extensively by Goh, 2011) also focuses on experiential learning, albeit from a slightly different perspective – the expectation and experience of the students themselves.

Research by the likes of Janette Griffin (dealing with second-level museum visits) broadens beyond the focus on experiential learning, in suggesting three important aspects of trips: 'the overall educational value of the trips; the impact of preparing for field trips; and . . . studies into the complexity of elements that influenced student learning' (Griffin, 2004: S59). The author ultimately claims that student groups who visit museums clearly demonstrate cognitive gain.

Other authors considering pedagogical questions beyond student engagement and experiential learning include Lovell and Weeks (2011), who propose an exploratory pedagogy for evaluating shallow and deep learning styles, while considering the element of 'gaze' as a tool for fostering cognitive and affective learning. The aforementioned paper by Kelner and Sanders (2009) addresses similar themes, in evaluating issues such as gaze, group and culture in field-based courses. Mains (2014) also takes a more challenging pedagogical stance, discussing the importance of evaluating cognitive gain via creative and appropriate assessments. While presented in a much simpler manner, this is also discussed briefly by Myers and Jones (2004) as part of their basic advice on the planning of fieldtrips (see also Wong and Wong, 2008). Related to planning is the need to consider student motivation, and thus how this can be understood to leverage involvement (Arcodia et al., 2014). A final paper worth mentioning here is the challenging in-depth reflection provided by Morrissey et al. (2013), who seek to engage their students in higher order field-based learning, which engages critical participatory education, comprising both academic and civic engagement. While this focuses primarily on Master's-level students and their involvement with advanced geographical themes, much could be learned by tourism educators from such reflections.

From this review of tourism-related fieldtrip literature, it becomes clear that the main emphasis in the extant body of work is on the opportunities for experiential learning, with much of the published material focusing on single events and their post-activity evaluation. However, some authors are expanding the pedagogical boundaries beyond singular descriptive overviews of personal experience. In an effort to add to the understanding of fieldtrips, the current study draws together the expertise and knowledge of a broad range of academics, with an expansive experience of fieldtrip planning and execution.

3.   METHODOLOGY

The data in the chapter derive from a survey which was undertaken at the end of the 2013–14 academic year, facilitated by a College Teaching Fellowship Award at the Dublin Institute of Technology, Dublin, Ireland. The survey was administered using the web-based Bristol Online Surveys platform, and participants were contacted via a range of professional networks on LinkedIn and Facebook, in addition to more traditional academic groups. While a response rate of approximately 15 percent (152 valid responses from individuals who undertake fieldtrips) was achieved, this is better than it appears, since the target population (approximately 1000 individuals were contacted) would have included many academics who do not engage in fieldtrip activity.

The aim of the overall project was to commence a dialogue with colleagues in tourism, geography and other related disciplines, to explore this experiential, socializing-educational tool, and begin to develop guidelines and frameworks for more efficient and more effective fieldwork activities. To that end, this chapter synthesizes the main findings of the research, and presents an international, interdisciplinary overview of current practice in fieldtrip activity.

4.   FINDINGS

The findings presented in the following sections are a summary of the main survey responses, interspersed with interpretations and illustrations drawn from interviews with practitioners over the course of the research. This begins with an overview of the respondents, who are highly experienced lecturers from over thirty countries, mainly in the areas of tourism, business, hospitality and geography. The next section outlines the type of fieldtrips that participants organize, which range from off-campus trips which last a couple of hours, to travel of extended duration, with the majority being overnight, 2–3 night or week-long trips. In the main, fieldtrips are obligatory, but a variety of selection processes exist, and while educational motives dominate, fun and socialization are not absent. A complex pattern exists regarding the relationship between educational issues, logistics and entertainment, with respondents, students and institutions placing different importance on the various elements of planning. The findings then elucidate issues of management and financing, in addition to exploring how the academics prepare their students for trips. Individual variance in these topics is evident, but the majority of lecturers exclusively manage fieldtrips on their own, and undertake detailed academic and behavior-related preparation in advance of the trips. As the next section illustrates, many academics are concerned about the pressures they are under regarding personal responsibility and bureaucratic procedures; therefore, while they are deeply interested in attaining educational outcomes, much energy is focused on logistics and liability issues. The next sections of the findings outline a range of educational, evaluation and assessment elements which the participants utilize, and the findings conclude with examples of best practice identified by the respondents.

4.1   Respondents

As the researcher is based in Ireland, and was seeking to undertake both a domestic and international investigation, 45 percent of respondents were Irish, the next largest groups were academics based in the UK (15 percent), USA (9 percent), and Italy (4 percent). Other countries where more than one respondent answered the survey included Australia, Canada, Germany, Japan, Nigeria, Portugal, Greece, New Zealand and United Arab Emirates. Responses were also received from Argentina, Austria,

Table 20.1   Schools and departments

Respondents' School/Department	% of Respondents
Tourism	32.2
Hospitality/Hotel	12.5
Geography	11.2
Leisure	5.3
Culinary	3.9
Events	2.0
Business	17.8
Management	8.6

Belgium, the Czech Republic, India, Iran, Israel, Kazakhstan, Kenya, Lebanon, Macau, Malta, the Netherlands, Poland, South Africa, Sweden and Taiwan. By far the largest portion of respondents are based in a tourism school/department, but a variety of other areas are represented in the findings (see Table 20.1).

The respondents themselves are highly qualified, with 98 percent holding an undergraduate degree, 90 percent a Master's and 78 percent a Doctorate degree. In addition, 56 percent have a professional qualification and 44 percent hold some 'other' form of qualification. When asked about the main subjects that they teach, 43 percent teach tourism-related subjects, 18 percent geography, 9 percent marketing, and others focus on areas such as culinary arts, planning, events, hospitality, environment, culture and heritage.

An important consideration which gives credibility to this chapter is the level of expertise that the respondents possess. The average length of service for those who responded to the survey (see Figure 20.1) is just over 12 years, with one respondent serving 38 years in their current job. While it is somewhat tongue-in-cheek to point out, the views represented

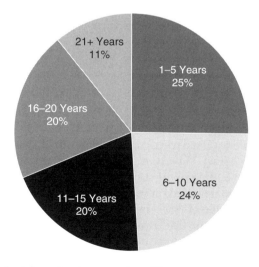

Figure 20.1   Respondents' service in current position

in this chapter represent an aggregated 1795 years of experience by the 147 respondents who answered this question.

4.2   Type of Fieldtrip

Frequency and duration
Only seven of the respondents do not currently undertake fieldtrips but still felt able to answer the full survey. Seven others undertake fieldwork on a weekly basis, 34 percent run trips a number of times per semester, 35 percent once per semester and 22 percent once per year. Thus, this is an experienced population of academics who undertake regular trips for educational purposes. The length of trip varies: the majority of respondents undertake a variety of trips ranging from almost two-thirds spending a couple of hours off campus (62 percent); half undertaking day-long fieldtrips (52 percent); and approximately a quarter each undertaking overnight (23 percent), 2 to 3 night (24 percent) or week-long trips (27 percent). A small number of respondents undertake trips ranging from 10 days to a fortnight, and some even extend to a month of more. This latter group is in the minority, but demonstrates the range of learning experiences.

Accommodation and transport
In general, the academics use a range of accommodation types. The most popular forms used by those who stay overnight are either budget (48 percent) or mid-price hotels (22 percent) and hostels (36 percent). From their comments, the selection of accommodation is primarily cost driven, but some academics base their choice on the experiential value of the stay. For example, one person stays in indigenous villages, another uses a mix of premises to 'enrich the experience' for those on the trip. Another uses university seminar facilities, and another stays at home during fieldtrips and commutes to the destination on a daily basis. The other main forms of accommodation are student accommodation (16 percent), camping (7 percent), rented houses (3 percent) and family stays (2 percent).

   In total, 86 percent of respondents use either coach hire (68 percent) and/or public transport (40 percent) for their travel, but a range of other modes (walking: 37 percent; flight: 26 percent; personal car: 24 percent; boat: 5 percent; or college transport: 4 percent) are also employed to undertake the fieldwork.

Location
The duration of trip and selection of transport mode strongly reflect the distance traveled. Only five individuals always remain in their local area but, in total, 30 percent of respondents remain within their local or regional area. The remaining participants undertake national or international trips, with the majority of this group also undertaking additional trips close to home; 35 percent undertake international trips. Because of the range of nationalities responding to the survey, it is difficult to see a pattern, and while it would be wrong to extrapolate based on such a small sample, 17 of the 24 UK respondents travel internationally. One of these individuals, who undertakes a lot of fieldwork, outlined their activity as '3 hour fieldtrips twice a month to tourism attractions in the city, one overnight fieldtrip to a tourist destination in the UK and a five night stay in Nice (France)'. International destinations for trips from the UK include Mediterranean countries such as Malta and Southern France, the Swiss Alps, the Scottish Highlands,

Barcelona, Dublin, the Netherlands and other European countries, with one UK colleague travelling to Kenya.

In contrast, only two of the 18 respondents from the USA undertake international trips, but unfortunately did not identify their destinations. An Irish respondent stated that they have been on 'numerous local day and half day trips, 3 day trips to other counties, 4 day trip to Wales, and 7 day trip to Spain'. The most popular international destination for Irish organizers is the UK, but a number of groups travel to Germany, Spain, France and further afield. One respondent reminds us that the local or international nature of trips is not always due to the desires of the organizer, but may be due to economic or other reasons: 'I ceased undertaking international trips a number of years ago due to the cost element'.

4.3   Participation

For 68 percent of practitioners, participation in fieldtrips is an integral part of a module/program so all students must attend; for 27 percent, participation is optional. In addition, 10 percent operate a first come, first served system, where places are limited, and 5 percent operate a system where getting a place on a trip is competitive. One respondent stated that students are 'selected' for the fieldtrip, but gave no indication of how this process works. Another pointed out the reason for the 'optional' nature of their fieldtrips: 'The University is afraid of being sued if there were an accident during a field trip. Students can't be required to attend due to fear of lawsuits'. A very different system operates in another institution, whereby participation is simply based on ability to pay, whereas in Australia it is not possible to make a field trip a compulsory part of a program if the students are required to pay for the trip.

While socialization (32 percent) and fun (13 percent) are identified as motivating factors in the organizing of fieldtrips (see Table 20.2), not a single respondent identified either of these without also identifying pedagogical motives. A total of 86 percent identified general educational motivations, 51 percent identified discipline-specific motives while 48 percent cited module and/or program specific motivations. Other respondents have aims when undertaking fieldwork, ranging from a number who run research-based programs where the fieldwork is part of the teaching, to others who use fieldwork to 'enrich the curriculum' or 'reinforce classroom teaching'. One respondent finds it 'very difficult to conceive of teaching practical subjects without doing practical things – and fieldwork is

Table 20.2   Main aims of fieldtrips

Reason	%
Educational motivations	86.0
Discipline-specific motives	51.0
To satisfy module requirements	38.5
To satisfy program requirements	36.4
Socialization	31.5
Fun	13.3
Other	16.1

one of the best places to do such practical things!' Others use these activities to develop cultural awareness and linguistic skills, networking, team building or to 'learn more about the "real world" of business from practitioners.' One passionate respondent states that their aim is to:

> expose the students to the subject matter, learning from literature is not always conducive to all students of different levels. I have found field trips are an integral part of teaching as students do not participate in reading as in previous decades. View, engage and learn is my main objective.

4.4   The Logistics of Fieldtrips

Prior to undertaking the survey, the researcher undertook a number of discussions with active fieldtrip practitioners and, inevitably, these conversations turned to topics of liability and responsibility linked to issues of risk, health and safety. In order to assess how this 'preoccupation' with health and safety influences academics, the survey asked respondents to rate the importance of a range of issues including insurance, health and safety, logistics, learning and education, educational alignment and fun. In each instance, they were asked to identify what was important and what was unimportant for them as well as their perceptions of what was important for their students and for their institution. All rankings were on a five-point Likert scale, and the findings are summarized in Table 20.3.

For staff members, the two most important issues are 'learning and education' (ranked as important – that is, very important or important – by 98.6 percent) and 'health and safety' (93.8 percent importance). Interestingly, while the most important issue for students is 'fun' (93.2 percent importance) the second most important is 'learning and education' (86.3 percent). While a range of issues are seen to be important for institutions, their

Table 20.3   The important fieldtrip considerations

Issues	Perceived Importance	(% of Respondents)		
		Staff	Students	Institution
Learning/Educational issues	Important	98.6	86.3	76.7
	Unimportant	1.4	3.4	5.5
Logistic issues	Important	90.4	69.9	65.8
	Unimportant	4.8	13.0	8.2
Insurance	Important	78.8	44.5	85.6
	Unimportant	9.6	24.7	4.1
Health and safety	Important	93.8	58.2	89.7
	Unimportant	2.7	17.1	2.1
Fun	Important	80.8	93.2	20.5
	Unimportant	14.4	1.4	44.5
Educational alignment	Important	92.5	63.7	74.0
	Unimportant	1.4	11.0	4.1

Note: Totals do not equal 100% as 'don't know' answers have been omitted from this table.

main emphasis appears to be on 'health and safety' (89.7 percent importance), followed closely by 'insurance' (85.6 percent importance). The only factor with a high unimportance rating for institutions (unimportant or very unimportant) is 'fun' (44.5 percent unimportance). In total 14.4 percent of staff see 'fun' as unimportant and 9.6 percent see 'insurance' as unimportant, whereas students see 'insurance' (24.7 percent), 'health and safety' (17.1 percent) and 'educational alignment' (11.0 percent) as unimportant.

4.5 Initiating, Managing and Financing Fieldtrips

To a great extent, fieldtrips are initiated by individual lecturers on a random basis (64 percent). While they are also initiated by program teams (35 percent) or tutors (34 percent), over half of the respondents who initiate trips do so entirely on their own, apparently without the support of colleagues or institutions. This dependence on the individual academic is even more accentuated when one considers management. Seventy-eight percent of trips involve lecturers managing their planning, booking and administration. In some cases, this is with the support of school administration (23 percent of fieldtrips) or students themselves (10 percent). External agencies are used by some (7 percent); however, in the vast majority of these various cases, the lecturer is also involved. In fact, 57 percent of all fieldtrips are exclusively managed by the academic.

The funding of fieldtrips varies considerably. To avoid financial limitations and to allow fuller participation, 30 percent of individuals undertake trips which have zero cost, 6 percent undertake trips funded by external agencies, and the vast majority of the remainder are funded from multiple sources, with 36 percent receiving institute funding, 23 percent funded exclusively by students themselves, a further 13 percent are paid for by students' own fundraising efforts, and 45 percent are paid for by a combination of student/institute/agency funding. Further variations range from using college transport to avoid costs, to schools sponsoring buses with students paying entry to attractions. Government grants are sought in some instances, while tourism bodies support other institutions. For many institutions/organizers, the type of trip dictates the funding model. One respondent stated: 'For international fieldtrips students pay, but the trip is substantially subsidized from department funds. Day trips are free to students'. For a local trip one lecturer states: 'I usually get some petty cash for coffees and try to use college transport'.

4.6 Preparation

In many cases (68 percent) students and staff agree on a code of behavior in advance of traveling, with a further 17 percent sometimes setting such an agenda. Only 15 percent do not do this before their fieldtrip.

The level of formality regarding these arrangements ranges from academics who have 'informal discussions' or believe that good behavior is 'implicit', where 'Informally we pass along the idea that they are representing the program, the university, and us as individuals'. In these cases, students are 'given a briefing before the fieldtrip regarding their conduct'. At the other end of the scale, a more formal process based on a risk assessment is completed by the organizer, followed by students being 'issued with a set of rules to be adhered to while on a trip'. In a number of cases an 'agreement' or 'code of practice' is signed by students. The formulation of this agreement varies from ones based on risk: 'A code of conduct was agreed on the basis of our completed risk assessment form – conduct in terms of students' interaction with field sites, not necessarily inter-personal conduct'; to measures which seem to cover every possibility: 'Students sign a medical form and health & safety form relating to contact persons, insurance, crossing roads, safe drinking, responsible behavior, permission to use their image in subsequent promotional material etc.'

The sanctions in the event of misbehavior are clear for a number of individuals: 'it has become more formal . . . I "threaten them"!!!! bad behavior = possible expulsion . . . this is only an issue on overnight trips where drink tends to play a role. . .'. For another participant: 'students are informed of what constitutes inappropriate behavior and are informed that should they participate in inappropriate behavior they will be sent home'. Others focus less on the negative and stress positive issues to their students in advance, such as timekeeping, a uniform or formal/semi-formal dress policy whereby 'the rules are laid down and it is hoped students will comply', with the main motivation coming from the individual. In some instances, behavior is governed by the institution, where there are: 'university rules with regards to discipline and that they are institutional ambassadors'.

4.7   Biggest Challenges

When asked to identify the biggest challenges when organizing a fieldtrip, a curious feature of the responses received is that only 10 percent of respondents identified educational issues. However, 30 percent stated that bureaucratic challenges were the biggest issue, while 53 percent found the logistical/operational issues to be a challenge (see Figure 20.2).

Looking at these in more detail, an overall comment from one respondent relates to the poor recognition of fieldwork by institutions which seem to overload organizers with red tape: 'there are difficulties fitting what we want to do within institutional structural constraints'. This is echoed by many others who make statements such as: 'There are several bureaucratic problems in our institution about fieldwork'. These problems range in nature from 'a lot of paperwork to get permission, for insurance and financial reasons',

Figure 20.2   Most challenging aspects of organizing field trips

to enormous pressure from institutions, colleagues and the students themselves 'to catch up with classes later'. In fact, 'getting the time out of a busy timetable to take students away on a field trip is always an issue as it impacts on other lecturers' classes'. This suggests that this form of activity is misunderstood and not valued.

Complaints abound about 'paperwork associated with being out of the office and risk assessments', in addition to ethics and logistical form filling. All of these bureaucratic challenges are brought together by one respondent who stated bluntly: 'There is a lack of support for the undertaking of such trips from a university perspective'. This is accentuated when one considers the issues that academics are concerned about: 'Logistics of extra paper work relating to health, safety, risk etc. I have had several accidents on trips which I have dealt with (with no repercussions); however, I am a little concerned due to litigious society of how long this will last.' This suggests that the individual academic fears that they will be held personally responsible if something goes wrong.

An issue of concern for a number of interviewees is the logistics of dealing with large numbers of students and the related difficulties of finance and attaining student buy-in. One experienced organizer suggests that poor engagement and increasing difficulty to attract students may be linked to the 'over-organization' and control of trips by institutions, which acts as a disincentive for students to take ownership or responsibility. Thus, it is difficult to 'get students to understand the educational importance of trips' and inevitably, they lose focus. This isn't helped on residential fieldtrips when students lack enthusiasm 'after a late night out socializing'.

A further issue which was mentioned by a number of respondents is the lack of institutional funding, which results in inequality of access: 'only the wealthy students are attending the trips'. The gloomy challenges of poor student enthusiasm as faced by many have brought one practitioner to a halt:

> Usually, I leave transportation to the students. They may choose to use busses or car share. This past term is the first in which students refused to car share for a day trip to a location about 100 km away from campus. They also refused to contribute to the cost of hired transportation. I cancelled the fieldtrip as a result.

4.8 Educational Elements

The importance of educational considerations is evident from the respondents. Ninety-four percent align their fieldtrip activity to module/program objectives; this is made up of 63 percent whose trips are always very closely aligned, a further 25 percent where some trips are closely aligned and 6 percent who try to satisfy some learning outcomes. Only 4 percent of respondents feel their fieldtrip activity is not as well aligned as it should be.

As illustrated in Table 20.4, a broad range of fieldtrip elements are undertaken, and in many cases, the elements depend on the subject matter and location of the fieldtrip. Ninety-two percent of academics utilize observation, with talks by professionals on-site being the second most important (83 percent). Other important elements include walking tours (58 percent), recording and photography (55 percent), survey work and interviewing (44 percent each). Socializing, while not as important as some of the more formal educational activities, is seen by 37 percent as being important, with bus tours being important for 25 percent of interviewees. Nightlife is only ranked as an element

Table 20.4   Important activities/elements of fieldtrips

Element	No. of Respondents
Observation	134
Recording – photography	78
Survey work of landscape/facilities etc.	63
Interviewing locals/tourists	63
Talks by professionals on-site	118
Walking tour	83
Bus tour	36
Socializing	53
Nightlife	12
Other	12

by 8 percent of the academics, with one clearly stating that it is 'not seen by me as part of the trip'. The range of elements utilized by an individual depends on the type of fieldtrip, with considerable overlap and the use of multiple elements. One respondent clearly articulated their view: 'Most of my field experiences are relate to specific projects. However, my colleagues often take students to industry and academic conferences, for example. These experiences emphasize networking, tours, and socializing much more than mine do.'

4.9   Meeting with Professionals

Of the respondents who meet professionals during their fieldtrips, 87 percent visit professionals, administrators or managers, while 64 percent meet with company owners and managers. Forty-nine percent of organizers meet with local academics and/or visit local colleges and educational institutions. Thirty-five percent pay for local guides and 47 percent visit sites as tourists. Twenty-six percent of organizers utilize their own alumni, visiting graduates of their own programs. This is seen as a particularly valuable tool, whereby students not only see the job opportunities in the sector, but specifically the possibilities from the program they are studying.

4.10   Evaluation and Assessment

An impressive array of evaluation processes are utilized by the respondents and these comprise both formative and summative activity. Seventy-four percent undertake either formative feedback sessions (61 percent) or on-trip feedback sessions (51 percent). Written project work in the form of essay style reports (47 percent) and reflective journals (4 percent) is utilized. Fifty-six percent of evaluation processes feed into the organizer's own module assessments or those of another lecturer. Unstructured feedback from participants is also regarded as important for 40 percent of participants, with word-of-mouth feedback also playing a part (18 percent). A small number of individuals undertake presentations, discussions and focus groups on returning to their classroom. The selection of assessment 'varies depending on the trip and the group' but most practitioners utilize multiple approaches. One individual for example stated: 'The trip I currently lead involves

Figure 20.3   Best practice advice

a group oral presentation in the field (40 percent) and an individual essay due around 6 weeks after we return (60 percent)', while others have utilized the entire set of assessment forms discussed here.

4.11   Best Practice

In talking about the single best thing either the respondent or colleagues do in managing fieldtrips (that is, tips for others; see Figure 20.3), a number of respondents went to lengths in their comments to point out that fieldtrips are in fact an extension of the classroom, and that similar learnings take place: 'A field trip is similar to a classroom lecture in that the students engage and participate in activities. Learning from the experience is vital for their progression. It helps to marry academia and practical function.'

   However, others emphasize that there are learning opportunities in this pedagogical process that go beyond that which is possible in the classroom. Fieldtrips involve what one respondent labeled 'back of the bus time', that is, 'informal chatting about what's been seen or done. This generates high quality reflection'.

   As would be expected, a number of practitioners advocate the importance of 'advance organization'. This covers a variety of approaches to overall 'planning' of the event such as 'a very well planned itinerary', undertaking a pre-trip reconnaissance of the site, having sufficient time for administration and providing a 'Fieldtrip Handbook'. While it is important to select 'relevant sites', to 'know your area' and to 'have alternatives in case of bad weather', such planning has to be balanced by 'flexibility', since 'nothing ever goes to plan'. The planning process needs to extend beyond the logistic elements and encompass the sites/individuals who are visited: it is important to carefully select industry speakers who are 'informed and also effective communicators', who are well briefed and prepared in advance, and who represent different stakeholder groups. Selecting the correct site can 'provide an opportunity to explore/experience . . . the issues dealt with in class', provide 'real life examples' and in certain scenarios 'showcase our graduates'.

   In order to ensure student buy-in, the aims and objectives of the fieldtrip must be 'aligned to an ongoing module or topic of study' and thereby linked to class-based activity and assessments. Thus, an important planning element is 'preparation of students – getting them to think critically about the sites and different stakeholders'.

A further key element of fieldwork is the involvement of colleagues, and while it is important to have support 'for insurance and Health and Safety purposes', that is, 'in case something goes wrong', it is important to also realize that 'it is great to get to chat with a colleague off-site in unusual surroundings' as the benefits of this collegiality last long into the future.

There appears to be some disagreement between the practitioners in the area of scheduling and structure. Some advocate that the organizer should 'never pack in too much', whereas others comment that 'idle time in the past has created some difficulties, they are students after all!', and thus it is important not to have too much 'free time'. Irrespective of the level of free time, there is general agreement regarding the need for 'really intelligent scheduling', and it appears that this means different things in different situations. Thus, a fieldtrip must 'keep the students busy' while also creating 'a relaxed atmosphere for students [with] an interesting, challenging but fun program'.

There is a general consensus that since fieldtrips 'cannot be organized by only one person' (despite earlier evidence that they usually are!), it is very useful to engage the students and to facilitate them to take ownership. This can range from students as partners in the planning, implementation and evaluation of the trips, to the use of second year students as mentors on first year trips. For this delegation/devolution to the students 'the key to success is structure', whereby the fieldtrip leader 'explains the aims of activities to students', being 'clear about the schedule and expectations'. When this clarity is present students can become more involved or even feel they 'own' the fieldtrip. One tutor goes so far as to say, 'Know your students and empower them with your trust . . . they rarely let you down':

> Having the majority of the trip student led. This is very challenging for both staff and students (the level of assistance provided to the students in preparation means it is just as time consuming for staff as if they were leading the trip) but also enables the students to learn much more (in terms of core subject knowledge and knowledge of the location, as well as more generic transferable skills) than they would through a more traditional staff led trip . . . Also if at all possible have three members of academic staff lead the trip as this makes managing unexpected challenges . . . much easier.

5.   CONCLUSIONS

A number of conclusions can be drawn from the data presented in this chapter. First, the importance of individual academics' 'experience' when organizing fieldtrips is clearly emphasized. However, when asked to share their thoughts, the participants in this research have been extremely generous, with all of them giving words of advice and support. Despite this, the operational and logistical know-how possessed by individual fieldtrip 'experts' seems to be poorly recorded, and thus the success of this tool is highly dependent on individual staff members. An absence of logistical guidelines and pedagogical discussion on the logistical aspects of fieldtrips (as alluded to by Kelner and Sanders, 2009) emphasizes how dependent this tool is on the individual, and how pedagogical discussions are limited in their breadth and depth.

One of the main limitations regarding trips is funding – and it is particularly upsetting for staff when they see experiential opportunities (Arcodia and Dickson, 2013) being determined by the financial ability or inability of an individual student to participate. The emphasis in the literature on reporting the outputs of extravagant international fieldtrips (see section 2) overlooks this basic concern of many practitioners. Academics should be encouraged to report on low-cost fieldwork, while institutions should consider the integral importance of fieldtrip elements for their individual programs. Where it is deemed appropriate, administrations should consider embedding fieldtrips into their modules, while ensuring that they are financially accessible to all students, not just the privileged and wealthy.

It appears that individual passion drives this form of academic activity; however, organizing and running fieldtrips is time consuming and stressful and is usually undertaken over and above an academic's timetabled workload, often with little recognition accruing from the institution. Going forward, institutions should be encouraged to support and assist staff in the planning and implementation of this important pedagogical tool, making it a recognized academic activity (see Griffin, 2004, discussed earlier), rather than a goodwill gesture by an individual practitioner. Furthermore, academic reflection on the pedagogical merits and advancement of fieldwork should be encouraged at every level of academia.

Institutions should consider formally supporting communities of best practice in this area. This is particularly important if the pedagogical benefits of fieldwork (as identified by the likes of Lovell and Weeks, 2011; Mains, 2014 and Myers and Jones, 2004, all mentioned above) are considered to be worthwhile; institutes should explore creative ways of administratively, logistically and financially supporting colleagues who undertake fieldwork. Thus, formal provision should be made to reward the efforts of staff that organize and manage fieldtrip activity, with administrative systems supporting rather than policing the efforts of passionate individuals.

The closing comments of this chapter should really be left to the respondents:

> Despite the work involved in preparing foreign trips, they are invaluable for the learning and life experience students gain from the trip. They are often the aspects of a program of study the students will recall years later and students always request more rather than fewer field trips.

> I think the benefits of undertaking a period of fieldwork for students can be huge and I believe that, particularly given the level of fees students now pay, that these should be compulsory to tourism students and should be funded by institutions to ensure that everyone benefits from these opportunities and not just those with the highest level of disposable income.

> Due to my own college experience, fieldtrips have always been part of learning, and many still remain in my own memory. Students, and especially as they are tourism focused, almost expect field/site work. The UK and further afield provide excellent models. However we have limited resources and have to try and work within these.

> Management should show some appreciation for staff who do field trips.

> Field trips are the practical classes for tourism studies. Students really enjoy them and they learn loads without even realizing it, which is the best form of learning. I believe that (if logistically possible) nearly all classes should contain a trip.

REFERENCES

Arcodia, C. and Dickson, C. (2013), 'Tourism field studies: Experiencing the carnival of Venice', *Journal of Hospitality and Tourism Education*, **25** (3), 146–55.

Arcodia, C., Cavlek, N. and Abreu-Novais, M. (2014), 'Factors influencing motivations and expectations of field trip attendance', *Current Issues in Tourism*, **17** (10), 856–61.

Caruana, V. and Ploner, J. (2011), *A Critical Review of Contemporary Practice in Internationalisation in the Hospitality, Leisure, Sport and Tourism (HLST) Subject Communities*, Project Report, Higher Education Academy, UK.

Goh, E. (2011), 'The value and benefits of fieldtrips in tourism and hospitality education', *Higher Learning Research Communications*, **1** (1), 60–70.

Goh, E. and Ritchie, B. (2011), 'Using the theory of planned behaviour to understand student attitudes and constraints toward attending field trips', *Journal of Teaching in Travel & Tourism*, **11** (2), 179–94.

Gretzel, U., Jamal, T., Stronza, A. and Nepal, S. (2009), 'Teaching international tourism: An interdisciplinary, field-based course', *Journal of Teaching in Travel & Tourism*, **8** (2–3), 261–81.

Griffin, J. (2004), 'Research on students and museums: Looking more closely at the students in school groups', *Science Education*, **88** (Supplement 1), S59–S70.

Johnston, M.E., Dawson, J.P., Childs, J. and Maher, P.T. (2014), 'Exploring post-course outcomes of an undergraduate tourism field trip to the Antarctic Peninsula', *Polar Record*, **50**, 147–55.

Kelner, S. and Sanders, G. (2009), 'Beyond the field trip: Teaching tourism through tours', *Teaching Sociology*, **37** (April), 136–50.

Lohmann, G. (2014), 'Learn while cruising: Experiential learning opportunities for teaching cruise tourism courses', *Tourism in Marine Environments*, **10** (1–2), 115–20.

Lovell, G. and Weeks, P. (2011), 'An exploratory pedagogy "gaze" and tourism hospitality fieldwork . . . a brilliant blend!', in Gross, M.J. (ed.), *Tourism Creating a Brilliant Blend*, Proceedings of the 21st Annual CAUTHE Conference, 8–11 February, pp. 1195–9.

Mains, S. (2014), 'Fieldwork, heritage and engaging landscape texts', *Journal of Geography in Higher Education*, **38** (4), 525–45.

Morrissey, J., Clavin, A. and Reilly, K. (2013), 'Field-based learning: The challenge of practicing participatory knowledge', *Journal of Geography in Higher Education*, **37** (4), 619–27.

Myers, B. and Jones, L. (2004), 'Effective use of field trips in educational programming: A three stage approach', Florida Cooperative Extension Electronic Data Information Source, Document AEC 373, accessed 30 March 2015 at http://edis.ifas.ufl.edu/WC054.

Patiar, A., Ma, E. and Cox, R. (2014), 'Undergraduate hotel management students' perceptions of a virtual field trip website', in Chien, P.M. (ed.), *CAUTHE 2014: Tourism and Hospitality in the Contemporary World: Trends, Changes and Complexity*, Brisbane: School of Tourism, The University of Queensland.

Weeden, C., Woolley, J. and Lester, J. (2011), 'Cruise and learn: Reflections on a cruise field trip', *Journal of Teaching in Travel & Tourism*, **11** (4), 349–66.

Whitfield, S. (2008), 'The educational and continuous professional development value of a study visit to Malawi', *Hospitality, Leisure, Sport and Tourism Network*, September, accessed 20 March 2015 at http://scotland.heacademy.ac.uk/assets/hlst/documents/case_studies/whitfield_long_case_study08.pdf.

Wong, A. and Wong, S. (2008), 'Useful practices for organizing a field trip that enhances learning', *Journal of Teaching in Travel and Tourism*, **8** (2/3), 241–59.

Wright, R. and Hind, D. (2011), 'International field trips: The tourism & entertainment management field trip to the Gambia, West Africa', *Assessment, Teaching and Learning Journal* (Leeds Met), **11** (Summer), 83–92.

Xie, P.F. (2004), 'Tourism field trip: Students' view of experiential learning', *Tourism Review International*, **8** (2), 101–11.

21 Learning by doing: intercultural competence and fieldtrips

Nicolai Scherle and Dirk Reiser

1. INTRODUCTION

Fieldtrips that provide students with intercultural experiential learning outside the lecture theatre can be very effective educational tools, especially for courses in tourism and hospitality. On the one hand, they facilitate the acquisition of knowledge from hands-on field experience, for example through conversations with experts or by visiting tourism and hospitality businesses. On the other hand, fieldtrips promote so-called soft skills, such as team building and conflict resolution. The following chapter focuses on the development of intercultural competence (in the context of an international fieldtrip of German students to Morocco), a concept that is often under-valued but increasingly important due to the internationalization of tourism courses.

In recent decades, the increasing influence of internationalization in the workplace has necessitated changes in the skillsets of those working in a wide variety of business and service sectors. This new paradigm requires the capability to analyze the multi-layered consequences of this internationalization process and to act accordingly. For example, improved intercultural competence allows businesses to better address cross-border cooperation issues that are often not just related to the use of different strategies, but may also be associated with different business cultures (Casmir and Asuncion-Lande, 1989; Scherle, 2004; Browaeys and Price, 2011). Hence, there is now an increased demand for so-called 'Euromanagers' or 'Globalpreneurs' who are not only recognized experts in their field, but also have the capacity to solve complex problems that arise from the collaboration of people with different cultural backgrounds and therefore different communication patterns and value structures (Kramer, 1999; Hilb, 2009; Rothlauf, 2012).

The following section provides a conceptual understanding of educational fieldtrips with a focus on the link between education and travel. Second, the relatively new research areas of 'intercultural communication' and 'intercultural competence' are discussed. In this context, the personal pre-conditions for successful management across cultures are identified and analyzed. Finally, a qualitative case study involving German tourism students visiting Morocco is examined in order to demonstrate the utility of fieldtrips for developing intercultural competence.

2. FIELDTRIPS

Education and travel have been linked for centuries. Examples include the Grand Tour, the voyages of the naturalists, or the more general phenomenon of modern cultural tourism. Education is 'a constant unveiling of reality' that invites students to develop a critical awareness of their social worlds. Central to the learning process should be involvement in activities that link classroom and community to establish a relevant context for student engagement (Jakubowski, 2003). Fieldtrips can achieve contextual engagement by bringing students into social or cultural settings that they might not otherwise experience (Hondagneu-Sotelo and Raskoff, 1994). This fosters a new understanding of the social world as it can motivate students to question their social environment including the dominant culture both within and outside their home countries (Shor, 1992). However, universities often follow the model of classroom-based education as the most suitable model without recognizing the potential of learning outside the classroom through events such as fieldtrips. This perspective has been reinforced by research (for example Stone and Petrick, 2013, p. 740) that suggests 'further study is needed to determine in which way travel is educational'. Our study addresses this gap in knowledge by contributing to our understanding of the learning outcomes of fieldtrips, especially with regard to intercultural competence.

Education invites students to develop a critical awareness of their social worlds (Jakubowski, 2003) and to look at them from differing viewpoints (Shor, 1992). Traditionally, educational institutions, such as universities, have relied upon lecture-based learning as the primary vehicle for transmitting knowledge to society. It is generally accepted that this approach is an effective method for transferring knowledge to students. However, lecture-based learning affords limited opportunities for practicing active learning and can objectify students and marginalize knowledge that stems from personal life experience (student-as-sponge model by Waldstein and Reiher, 2001; banking by Freire, 1970). As early as 1938, Dewey suggested that participatory, active learning is essential for individuals to grow and develop as citizens and consequently should be an integral component of 'progressive education'. Similar thinking is also reflected in Freire's (1970) idea of education which views students as active rather than passive participants in learning. It follows that learning in a less formal and less structured way, which is characteristic of the learning that occurs on fieldtrips, should therefore be an important element of university teaching and learning.

Broomhall et al. (2010), for example, argue that learning that occurs in a less structured context than formal education can make an equally important contribution to the development of individuals. A recent study that involved 100 higher education students and 50 teachers (Shakil et al., 2011) supports these findings. A large number of the respondents agreed that fieldtrips stimulate interest in learning and provide a practical approach for the curriculum. Shakil et al. (2011) argue that if education is the process of acquiring knowledge, then it should not be restricted to universities and textbooks, but should include the types of experiences and observations that can be gained from fieldtrips. Additionally, students often find fieldtrips enjoyable, regardless of their age or upbringing (Bitgood, 1989; Orion and Hofstein, 1991; Boud et al., 1993; Knapp, 2000; Chieffo and Griffiths, 2004). Further, a study by Wright and Hind (2011, p. 88) that focused on the experiences of English students on a fieldtrip to Gambia reveals that 'the most popular reason for participating in the fieldtrip was the fact that they [students] wanted to do something that they thought they would never have the opportunity to do again . . . The second reason . . . is their desire to engage with a completely different culture.' These findings clearly support Falk's (1983) conclusions regarding the importance of the perceived novelty value of taking students out of the classroom and placing them into less structured learning environments. Personal experiences of this nature have the potential to bring theory into real-world settings (Wright and Hind, 2011), a finding that supports the research of the last three decades and explains why fieldtrips are so popular with students.

Experiential learning methods, in particular those that incorporate interactive components such as fieldtrips, can help to compensate for the shortcomings of traditional lecture-based learning (Goh, 2011). Experiential learning is one model that can provide insights into how people learn while traveling (Stone and Petrick, 2013). As noted above, Dewey (1938) was an early adopter of the value of experiential learning. He argued that the skills and knowledge that students acquire in practical circumstances can be valuable for understanding and reacting to subsequent life experiences (Stone and Petrick, 2013). This form of experiential learning can occur through, for example, seminars, internships, volunteering and fieldtrips. Kolb (1984) proposed a four-stage experiential learning model in which individuals acquire knowledge through the transformation of experience. Even though this model was subject to much criticism (for example Kayes, 2002; Bergsteiner et al., 2010), its intuitive appeal makes it one of the most cited models on experiential learning. Its four stages are concrete experience (stage 1), reflective observation (stage 2), abstract conceptualization (stage 3), and active experimentation (stage 4). Travel provides opportunities for this model of transformative, experiential learning (Morgan, 2010).

With regard to tourism education, Goh (2011, p. 60) argues that fieldtrips are 'a useful educational tool for transforming learning experience beyond the traditional classroom', because they enhance students' learning and increase practical knowledge and non-vocational skills (that is, interpersonal skills, analysis and reflection). Both teaching and learning can become more meaningful through experiential education. Cultivating 'a pedagogy of experience can be facilitated through the use of a critically responsive approach to teaching and learning that is grounded in experience, critical thinking, reflection and action . . .' (Jakubowski, 2003, p. 568).

The fieldtrip experience is a three-stage learning process consisting of the pre-trip, the on-trip and the post-trip stages (Porth, 1997). It could be argued that tourism and hospitality education is particularly well suited for fieldtrip learning, which provides students with different perspectives for understanding the complexities of tourism (Xie, 2004). In general, there is a need for further research that focuses on the values and validity of academic fieldtrips within the context of higher education. Considering the growing internationalization of universities, research should focus on the implications of international excursions on students' ability to relate theory to practice. It is therefore argued that universities should explore the value of offering international fieldtrips in order to distinguish their products from other institutions of higher education (Wright and Hind, 2011). This includes further research into students' perception and experiential learning opportunities on international fieldtrips (Xie, 2004).

3.　BRIDGING THE GAP: INTERCULTURAL COMPETENCE

Although research that addresses intercultural competence, especially from an applied perspective, has developed into one of the core areas of intercultural communication, its conceptualization is still in its infancy. Most approaches focus primarily on the development of behavioral characteristics and skills, such as the recognition and appreciation of unique cultural traits, tolerance, mutual understanding, sensitization to shared core values and norms, and the development of intercultural experiential and practical knowledge. In this context, both intercultural learning and intercultural interaction can be effective in reducing shortfalls in knowledge and awareness of other cultures, perceptions of dominance and superiority, fear of potential threats, destructive stereotyping and prejudices, as well as latent fear of unfamiliar cultures (Spitzberg and Changnon, 2009; Lane, 2010; Lustig and Koester, 2013).

According to Ruben (1989), Koester et al. (1993) and Moosmüller (1996), intercultural competence encompasses all abilities and skills that enable an individual to interact with a member of a different culture in an efficient and appropriate manner. Efficiency, in this context, implies that the respective goals of the actors involved are achieved. Actions are considered appropriate if they do not compromise the needs of interacting individuals or overstep the boundaries of what is considered customary for the culture in question. This view of intercultural competence requires that actors progressively develop, at least in a rudimentary fashion, relational competence (the ability to develop and maintain positive social relationships), information-transfer competence (the ability to transmit information with minimum loss and distortion), and goal attainment competence (the ability to secure a certain level of cooperation and consent). Intercultural competence is seen as a continuous learning process that is primarily achieved through concrete experiences, reflective observations, abstract conceptualizations, and active experimentation. Learning in the intercultural context thus requires that the actors involved not only possess the ability to constructively engage with other cultures, but also have a cultural awareness that includes insights into the relativity of their own cultural reality and the ability to step back and objectively re-evaluate the perceptions and value systems of their own culture (Byram, 1997; Stüdlein, 1997; Byram et al., 2001).

The acquisition of intercultural competence is an ongoing process that requires a significant amount of self-initiative. Ultimately, intercultural competence can at best facilitate a gradual convergence of cultures but cannot be expected to achieve a universal understanding of unfamiliar behavioral patterns. It is self-evident that intercultural competence cannot be equated with the leveling of cultural differences in favor of cultural universalities but rather represents a pragmatic approach to 'bridging the gap' between cultures (Apfelthaler, 1998) or 'managing across cultures' (Schneider et al., 2014), which in the ideal case, helps to overcome monocultural or ethnocentric perspectives. The way in which cultural differences are addressed plays a key role, especially in the context of communication:

> Cultural differences will have a negative effect if they impede the flow of communication between participants. They will have a positive effect if they motivate two individuals to work harder at understanding each other. Thus the crux of the whole process is HOW *cultural* differences are managed by the participants in any act of communication. It is this phenomenon that is used to further distinguish intercultural communication from other forms or contexts of communication. (Casmir and Asuncion-Lande, 1989, p. 284, emphasis in original)

Intercultural interactions always occur at the intersections between the familiar patterns of behavior, thought and emotion of one's own culture and the unfamiliar patterns of behavior, thought and emotion of foreign cultures. Intercultural interactions are influenced by the interplay between 'cultural differences' (related to different systems of cultural orientation), 'individual differences' (related to personal characteristics and life histories), and existing 'intercultural knowledge and experiences' (Thomas et al., 2003). A factor that should not be underestimated in its effect on intercultural interaction is ethnocentrism. In the worst case, it can impede or even prevent the development of intercultural competence. Ethnocentrism primarily develops in circumstances where people with different cultural identities work or live together. It is generally associated with legitimizing or concealing the limits of one's own thoughts and actions.

The question of which personal preconditions for success will motivate an individual to interact efficiently and appropriately in situations of intercultural overlap has stimulated lively research activities in recent decades (Stahl, 1995; Schneider et al., 2014). From the perspective of trait theory, the prototype of an interculturally competent actor can be defined as follows:

> The resulting profile is of an individual who is truly *open to* and *interested in* other people and their ideas, capable of building relationships of trust among people. He or she is *sensitive to the feelings and thoughts of another*, expresses *respect* and positive regard for others, and is *nonjudgmental*. Finally, he or she tends to be *self-confident*, is able to take *initiative*, is *calm* in situations of frustration or ambiguity, and is *not rigid*. The individual also is a *technically* or *professionally competent* person. (Kealey and Ruben, 1983, p. 165, emphasis in original)

Based on this characterization, Kühlmann and Stahl (1998) identified several criteria of intercultural competence, which are essential preconditions for intercultural effectiveness (see Table 21.1).

These ideal-typical criteria outline crucial, but not necessarily sufficient conditions for successful intercultural interactions. Although the construct of intercultural competence may be complex, there is no question that the necessary skillsets that foster productive management of cultural differences can be learned, at least at a basic level. Intercultural

Table 21.1   Personal preconditions for success in the context of managing across cultures

Precondition	Description
Ambiguity tolerance	The predisposition to react appropriately in complex situations – especially those characterized by insecurity and ambiguity – or to at least not feel impaired.
Behavioral flexibility	The ability to quickly adapt to changing situations and to draw from a broad behavioral repertoire.
Determination	The ability to work towards the achievement of given tasks in a goal-oriented manner, even under difficult circumstances.
Sociability	The predisposition to actively establish and develop social contacts and to maintain existing relationships.
Empathy	The ability to recognize the needs and intentions of interacting partners and to react in a manner that is appropriate to the situation.
Polycentrism	The ability to be unbiased towards divergent opinions, attitudes and behavior patterns, especially in relation to different cultures.
Metacommunicative competence	The ability to intervene in difficult conversations by steering the discourse in a positive direction and to resolve communication issues.

Source: Based on Kühlmann and Stahl (1998, p. 216).

training can establish the basis on which intercultural competence can progressively develop. This type of education creates the opportunity to engage in the general and specific aspects of cultural differences in a cognitive and affective manner and to be prepared for the challenges that accompany intercultural relations (Cushner and Brislin, 1996; Moosmüller, 1996; Deardorff, 2006).

In summary, it is clear that a definitive answer to the question of how cultural differences can be managed successfully cannot be provided. Against this backdrop, we advocate for an open-minded change of perspective in the approach to one's own as well as foreign cultures, which transcends a mere delineation, or assimilation and accommodation (see Aderhold and Heideloff, 2001). This management of cultural boundaries could also be defined as oscillation. This new cultural awareness is best described as fluid, rather than static, and enhances the ability to oscillate between different cultural perspectives. Existing cultural differences are clearly delineated, and thus are also negotiable, whereby a pragmatic 'bridging the gap' or 'managing across cultures' should, by no means, be an abandonment of cultural differences in favor of cultural universalities. Difference as difference (and not as identity) always remains, which is the paradox of intercultural communication in general and intercultural competence in particular.

4.   METHODOLOGY

The empirical results introduced in the following paragraphs refer to a research project in which the relevance of fieldtrips for the development of intercultural competence was investigated. A primarily qualitative approach was adopted, in which four university students were interviewed prior to a fieldtrip to Morocco that was led by the two authors. Qualitative approaches are especially well suited to a sensitive in-depth analysis of intercultural issues (Koester et al., 1993; Kopp, 2003; Scherle and Nonnenmann, 2008). The original interview comprised ten questions and provided ample opportunity for student narratives. Three of these questions are listed below and the results are discussed in greater detail:

- Which aspects are associated with the term 'intercultural competence'?
- What is expected of an interculturally well-versed fieldtrip leader?
- What characterizes a 'good' fieldtrip?

In addition, the interview investigated students' mental images of the fieldtrip destinations against the background of the often very one-sided media reports on the Arab region. In this context, the following two questions (amongst others) were posed:

- Which mental images are associated with the term 'Morocco'?
- To what extent does the present political situation (such as the implications of the Arab Spring; Islamic State) influence the students' expectations of the fieldtrip?

5.   FINDINGS

Because of the complexity of the subject matter and the multi-faceted nature of the student narratives, only a small segment of the empirical results can be introduced in this chapter. First, we present the mental images that the four student interviewees connect with the fieldtrip region. One of the female students answered the 'icebreaker' question of what mental pictures she associates with Morocco, or the Orient, as follows:

> When I think of the Orient, first of all a lot of things from my childhood come to my mind. When you, for example, in the past watched the film Aladdin, then you somehow have to think of flying carpet, camels or, for instance, also these typical magic lamps in the shape of a teapot. Yeah, I would also associate it with bright and warm colors. Somehow also the desert – these are the images that stay in your head from childhood.

For this student, the fieldtrip region primarily evokes a journey into her own childhood, which is associated with positive connotations. The following quote reflects numerous exoticisms – also with positive associations – which have affinities with imaginative geographies and strategic destination marketing (Gregory, 1995; Pott, 2007; Scherle and Jonasson, 2014):

> Also, with the term Orient, for me personally, pictures of these souks immediately come to my mind and the towers of spices, these bright colors, these warm colors. Then these sand colors, these sand-colored houses, the soil out of sand. Then the people with sun-beaten and darker complexion, the darker hair and eyes. . . . Camels, great fabrics . . . That's very enchanting for me, in some way also romantic. You really feel like in a picture book . . . It seems like a film set. Yeah, I feel as if I were in a movie, because it simply is so beautiful in a surreal way . . . .

Common to both citations is a media-oriented perception of the fieldtrip region, which is reflected, in an almost paradigmatic manner, in the comparison with a picture book or a film set. It is noteworthy that potentially controversial subjects (such as the implications of the so-called Arab Spring or Islamic terror) were initially not addressed by the students.

Subsequently, the fieldtrip participants were asked to elaborate on what they associate with the term 'intercultural competence'. This question is of particular interest, considering that it has been repeatedly hypothesized – at least implicitly – that fieldtrips can make a valuable contribution to the development of intercultural competence. The first quote comes from a female student, who not only addresses the closely interconnected aspects of social categorizations (in particular: prejudices) and tolerance, but also establishes an explicit connection with the fieldtrip region by means of an example:

> Well, for me 'intercultural competence' means that each human being has the competence to engage with other cultures and generally with people that believe in something different or have different ways of life. . . . That you just have this competence; that you are not prejudiced. That you tolerate, for example, when Muslims want to pray several times a day or something. That is, that you are simply tolerant and have the competence to deal with it [a different culture] and get involved in it.

In the ideal case, fieldtrips facilitate more tangible intercultural understanding and acceptance than can be achieved through abstract tolerance alone. Further, intercultural fieldtrips involve sensitization to both cultural differences and cultural commonalities, which can make it easier to settle into an unfamiliar culture. In particular, a clear understanding of the different systems of values and norms that have shaped people from unfamiliar cultures facilitates a more culturally sensitive introduction to a foreign country. In addition, intercultural knowledge that enhances cultural understanding can be valuable for raising awareness of one's own culture and for minimizing possible misinterpretations of other cultures. The following quote from a fieldtrip participant reveals no less exciting perspectives on the subject of intercultural competence:

> For me, it means that you are a cosmopolitan! That is, that you move interculturally and naturally, no matter in which culture, in which country, in which religion you happen to be. When you aren't shy of other people, other countries, or other customs, but are open, eager to learn, and enthusiastic for what's different. That is, that you see the differences as an opportunity and added value and not as something bad or as a burden. That you don't think: 'Oh God, now I will have problems, because . . . my colleague is from China – she sees things very differently from me.' But that you think: 'Her perspective is different, but because of this I can also see much more, because my radius is extended.'

This quote is particularly valuable with regard to two aspects: on the one hand, the subject of intercultural competence is viewed in close connection with cosmopolitism, a concept that has distinct transcultural aspects and promotes a worldview beyond the dichotomies of 'one's own' and the 'unfamiliar' (Hannerz, 1996; Beck, 2000; Scherle, 2014). On the other hand, a connection is established – at least implicitly – with diversity or diversity management, a management concept that, from a strategic perspective, strongly emphasizes the added value of heterogeneity (Thomas and Ely, 1996; Page, 2008; Herring and Henderson, 2015).

Against the backdrop of a political situation that has been exceedingly difficult for some time, as well as the frequent presence of the Arab region in the Western media, the interviews sought to understand to what extent the present political situation may have impacted the students' expectations of the fieldtrip. In this context, one of the interviewed students made the following – particularly nuanced – statement:

> I am interested in the whole topic of Islam anyway. Especially because it is always in the media and because it makes me so sad, that Islam gets directly associated with terror – because it isn't like that. And people that do not just skim over that [negative news] and always see in the BILD [a German boulevard paper], 'Ah, Islamic terrorists, they blew up a bomb there or there.' They immediately think that all Muslims are bad. I read up on it; I am personally very interested in it. And I read different media from different countries, not only German ones.

Such a nuanced statement is by no means the rule. The intrinsic motivation to prepare oneself for fieldtrip-relevant topics – in this case a general knowledge of Islam – seems particularly remarkable. While reading represents a comparatively abstract process, fieldtrips – at least the ones that are planned and executed in a culturally sensitive fashion – offer the clear advantage of immersing oneself into the everyday life of residents. The students explicitly stressed the importance of providing opportunities for cultural immersion, as one of their expectations of an interculturally well-versed fieldtrip leader, as is illustrated by the following two citations:

> For us Europeans it's always easy to say: 'God, this poor guy works twenty hours and earns two Euros an hour.' But when you aren't on the spot and know what the circumstances are and can

compare: Two Euros are so and so many Dirham [Moroccan currency]. So that one has an idea on how the work life is here for employees in the factories or in the supply and production chains.

I hope that we will have a lot of contact with Moroccan people so that you can see how 'normal' Moroccans live. What essentially is different between Germany and Morocco? How do people think, what does the everyday life look like? . . . What I also really hope for is to go to a mosque, because I have never been in one!

It is precisely these immediate intercultural changes in perspective that make a fieldtrip so valuable in comparison to other tools for the development of intercultural competence. The objective is not only to recognize the differences in the other culture in the passive role of a spectator but to gain proactive cultural comprehension in order to advance intercultural understanding, which is linked to the dialectics of understanding both one's own and a foreign culture. As important as an intercultural change in perspective may be, a fieldtrip should not be reduced solely to the role of bridging the gap. With the above in mind, we conclude with the following citation, in which one of the student interviewees aptly states:

I think, it should be a good mix of information and fun. I can't think of the keywords right now, but that you see a lot, learn a lot, discover a lot of new things, but also have time to explore the city by yourself a little. But also that you have fun as a group, maybe go out for a nice meal, sit around the table for a long time, chat with one another and have time. And not that it is so stressed, like 'The main thing is that we have to see ten mosques a day' – so, the mix, I think, makes it in the end.

6.   SUMMARY AND CONCLUSIONS

This chapter analyzes the importance of fieldtrips from an intercultural perspective using the example of an excursion of German tourism and hospitality students to Morocco. It exemplifies the importance of fieldtrips as an educational tool for experiential learning that links theoretical concepts learned in the classroom with practical experiences 'in the field'. Unlike most educational activities, fieldtrips not only facilitate student independence through 'learning by doing', but also enable a largely holistic way of learning that involves all senses (in accordance with the famous Swiss pedagogue Pestalozzi). In addition, fieldtrips that are designed in a culturally sensitive manner can make a significant contribution to the development of intercultural competence, for instance when they result in immediate changes of perspective between one's own culture and a foreign culture. These skills are essential in an increasingly internationalized workplace, especially for tourism and hospitality students (Jordan, 2008; Egron-Polak and Hudson, 2010; 2014; Sulkowski and Deakin, 2010).

Nevertheless, the connection between fieldtrips and the development of intercultural competence has received little attention in the scientific literature. In light of the progressive internationalization of the workplace that tourism graduates will enter, general management competence will likely no longer be sufficient to meet the increasingly more complex operational and strategic demands of the tourism sector (Freyer and Pompl, 2000; Knowles et al., 2004; Scherle, 2007).

Of the various reasons why intercultural issues have not been more thoroughly researched in recent decades, two are particularly noteworthy. First, the fundamental question regarding whether business structures and processes are culturally bound or culturally free has not been resolved. In this context, research focused on intercultural issues can be viewed in light of two diverging theoretical perspectives that may directly influence research strategies: those who adhere to the culture-bound hypothesis, the so-called culturalists, advocate the position that the respective cultural context of a region may significantly influence economic structures and processes. In contrast, advocates of the culture-free hypothesis, the so-called universalists, argue that management techniques are universal and are therefore ultimately independent of culture-specific influences (Braun and Warner, 2002; Holzmüller, 2009; Schmid and Kotulla, 2010). Second, the question remains whether or not (or to what extent) intercultural differences – as well as communalities – can be conceptualized, let alone measured adequately. Further, in an increasingly transnational hybrid world that is characterized by migration, the research community has for the most part abandoned the concepts of homogeneous cultural regions *à la* Huntington (1993) (Appiah, 2007; Berndt and Pütz, 2007; Ludwig and Röseberg, 2010).

The academic education of prospective tourism and hospitality employees would be markedly improved by further inclusion and integration of international fieldtrips in future curricula (as is the case with many other disciplines). Unfortunately, in many countries, university education in tourism and hospitality still has a strong focus on national aspects, and does not adequately consider the international or transnational character of the sector. In addition, the conveyance of intercultural competence in curricula has in many cases not progressed beyond teaching regional geography and foreign languages, whereas the immediate, reflexive and – in the ideal case – productive integration of cultural differences and communalities continues to be a secondary consideration. Fieldtrips that are designed using a culturally sensitive approach can, due to their action-oriented and holistic character, counteract these shortcomings and generate very positive experiences for (and feedback from) students. These findings are consistent with the empirical results presented in this contribution. Finally, it is important to consider that graduates who have gained intercultural skills are an important precondition for improving the overall quality of the tourism and hospitality sector. Also, tourism programs that focus on integrating intercultural competence are ultimately an excellent asset that allows universities to gain an advantage in the intensified competition for future students.

REFERENCES

Aderhold, Jens and Frank Heideloff (2001), *Kultur als Problem der Weltgesellschaft? Ein Diskurs über Globalität, Grenzbildung und kulturelle Konfliktpotenziale*, Stuttgart: Lucis & Lucius.
Apfelthaler, Gerhard (1998), *Interkulturelles Management als Soziales Handeln*, Vienna: Service Fachverlag.
Appiah, Anthony (2007), *Cosmopolitanism: Ethics in a World of Strangers*, London: Penguin Books.
Beck, U. (2000), 'The cosmopolitan perspective: sociology of the second age of modernity', *British Journal of Sociology*, **51**, 79–105.
Bergsteiner, H., G.C. Avery and R. Neumann (2010), 'Kolb's experiential learning model: critique from a modelling perspective', *Studies in Continuing Education*, **32** (1), 29–46.
Berndt, Christian and Robert Pütz (eds) (2007), *Kulturelle Geographien: Zur Beschäftigung mit Raum und Ort nach dem Cultural Turn*, Bielefeld: Transcript.
Bitgood, S. (1989), 'School Field Trips: an Overview', *Visitor Behaviour*, **IV** (2), 3–6.
Boud, David, Ruth Cohen and David Walker (eds) (1993), *Using Experience for Learning*, Buckingham: Open University Press.
Braun, Werner and Malcolm Warner (2002), 'The "culture-free" versus "culture-specific" management debate',

in Malcolm Warner and Pat Joynt (eds), *Managing Across Cultures: Issues and Perspectives*, London: Thomson, pp. 13–25.

Broomhall, Sue et al. (2010), *Articulating Lifelong Learning in Tourism: Dialogue Between Humanities Scholars and Travel Providers*, Canberra: Australian Learning and Teaching Council.

Browaeys, Marie-Joëlle and Roger Price (2011), *Understanding Cross-Cultural Management*, Harlow: Prentice Hall.

Byram, Michael (1997), *Teaching and Assessing Intercultural Communication Competence*, New York: Multilingual Matters.

Byram, Michael, Adam Nichols and David Stevens (eds) (2001), *Developing Intercultural Competence in Practice*, New York: Multilingual Matters.

Casmir, Fred L. and Nobleza C. Asuncion-Lande (1989), 'Intercultural communication revisited: conceptualization, paradigm building, and methodological approaches', in James A. Anderson (ed.), *Communication Yearbook 12*, Newbury Park: Routledge, pp. 278–309.

Chieffo, L. and L. Griffiths (2004), 'Large-scale assessment of student attitudes after a short-term study abroad program', *Frontiers: The Interdisciplinary Journal of Study Abroad*, **10**, 165–77.

Cushner, Kenneth and Richard W. Brislin (1996), *Intercultural Interactions: A Practical Guide*, Thousand Oaks: Sage.

Deardorff, D.K. (2006), 'Identification and assessment of intercultural competence as a student outcome of internationalization', *Journal of Studies in Intercultural Education*, **10**, 241–66.

Dewey, John (1938), *Experience and Education*, New York: Macmillan.

Egron-Polak, Eva and Ross Hudson (2010), *Internationalization of Higher Education: Global Trends, Regional Perspectives*, IAU 3rd Global Survey Report, Paris: International Association of Universities.

Egron-Polak, Eva and Ross Hudson (2014), *Internationalization of Higher Education: Growing Expectations, Fundamental Values*, IAU 4th Global Survey Report, Paris: International Association of Universities.

Falk, J.H. (1983), 'Field trips: a look at environmental effects on learning', *Journal of Biological Education*, **17** (2), 137–42.

Freire, Paulo (1970), *Pedagogy of the Oppressed*, New York: Herder and Herder.

Freyer, Walter and Wilhelm Pompl (2000), 'Schlüsselkompetenzen für das internationale Tourismusmanagement', in Silke Landgrebe (ed.), *Internationaler Tourismus*, Munich: Oldenbourg, pp. 114–30.

Goh, E. (2011), 'The value and benefits of fieldtrips in tourism and hospitality education', *Higher Learning Research Communication*, **1** (1), 60–70.

Gregory, D. (1995), 'Imaginative geographies', *Progress in Human Geography*, **19**, 447–85.

Hannerz, Ulf (1996), *Transnational Connections: Culture, People, Places*, London: Routledge.

Herring, Cedric and Loren Henderson (2015), *Diversity in Organizations: A Critical Examination*, New York: Routledge.

Hilb, Martin (2009), *Glocal Management of Human Resources*, Vienna: Lit-Verlag.

Holzmüller, Hartmut H. (2009), 'Prozedurale Herausforderungen in der Forschung zum Interkulturellen Management und Ansätze zu deren Handhabung', in Michael-Jörg Oesterle and Stefan Schmid (eds), *Internationales Management: Forschung, Lehre, Praxis*, Stuttgart: Schäffer-Poeschel, pp. 251–82.

Hondagneu-Sotelo, P. and S. Raskoff (1994), 'Community service-learning: promises and problems', *Teaching Sociology*, **22** (3), 248–54.

Huntington, S.P. (1993), 'The clash of civilizations', *Foreign Affairs*, **72** (3), 22–49.

Jakubowski, L.M. (2003), 'Beyond book learning: cultivating the pedagogy of experience through field trips', *Journal of Experiential Education*, **26** (1), 24–33.

Jordan, F. (2008), 'Internationalization in hospitality, leisure, sport and tourism higher education: a call for further reflexivity in curriculum development', *Journal of Hospitality, Leisure, Sport and Tourism Higher Education*, **7** (1), 99–103.

Kayes, D.C. (2002), 'Experiential learning and its critics: preserving the role of experience in management learning and education', *Academy of Management Learning and Education*, **1** (2), 137–49.

Kealey, Daniel J. and Brent D. Ruben (1983), 'Cross-cultural personnel selection criteria, issues and methods', in Dan Landis and Richard W. Brislin (eds), *Handbook of Intercultural Training: Issues in Theory and Design (Vol. 1)*, New York: Pergamon Press, pp. 155–75.

Knapp, D. (2000), 'Memorable experiences of a science field trip', *School Science and Mathematics*, **100** (2), 65–72.

Knowles, Tim, Dimitrios Diamantis and Joudallah Bey El-Mourhabi (2004), *The Globalization of Tourism and Hospitality: A Strategic Perspective*, London: Continuum.

Koester, Jolene, Richard L. Wiseman and Judith A. Sanders (1993), 'Multiple perspectives of intercultural communication competence', in Richard L. Wiseman and Jolene Koester (eds), *Intercultural Communication Competence*, Newbury Park: Sage, pp. 3–15.

Kolb, David A. (1984), *Experiential Learning: Experience as the Source of Learning and Development*, Englewood Cliffs: Prentice-Hall.

Kopp, Horst (ed.) (2003), *Area Studies, Business and Culture: Results of the Bavarian Research Network for area*, Münster: LIT.

Kramer, W. (1999), 'Zum Profil des Euro-Managers: Aufgabe und Anforderungen', in Jürgen Bolten (ed.), *Cross Culture – Interkulturelles Handeln in der Wirtschaft*, Sternenfels: Verlag für Wissenschaft und Praxis, pp. 83–98.

Kühlmann, Torsten M. and Günter K. Stahl (1998), 'Diagnose interkultureller Kompetenz: Entwicklung und Evaluierung eines Assessment Centers', in Christoph I. Barmeyer and Jürgen Bolten (eds), *Interkulturelle Personalorganisation*, Sternenfels: Verlag Wissenschaft und Praxis, pp. 213–24.

Lane, Shelley D. (2010), *Interpersonal Communication: Competence and Contexts*, Boston: Allyn & Bacon.

Ludwig, Ralph and Dorothee Röseberg (eds) (2010), *Tout-Monde: Interkulturalität, Hybridisierung, Kreolisierung: Kommunikations- und gesellschaftstheoretische Modelle zwischen 'alten' und 'neuen' Räumen*, Frankfurt am Main: Lang.

Lustig, Myron W. and Jolene Koester (2013), *Intercultural Competence: Interpersonal Communication Across Cultures*, Boston: Pearson.

Moosmüller, Alois (1996), 'Interkulturelle Kompetenz und interkulturelle Kenntnisse: Überlegungen zu Ziel und Inhalt im auslandsvorbereitenden Training', in Klaus Roth (ed.), *Mit der Differenz Leben: Europäische Ethnologie und Interkulturelle Kommunikation*, Münster: Waxmann, pp. 271–90.

Morgan, A. (2010), 'Journeys into transformation: travel to an "other" place as a vehicle for transformative learning', *Journal of Transformative Education*, **8** (4), 246–68.

Orion, N. and A. Hofstein (1991), 'The measurement of students' attitudes towards scientific fieldtrips', *Science Education*, **75** (3), 513–23.

Page, Scott E. (2008), *The Difference: How the Power of Diversity Creates Better Groups, Firms, Schools, and Societies*, Princeton: Princeton University Press.

Porth, S.J. (1997), 'Management education goes international: a model for designing and teaching a study tour course', *Journal of Management Education*, **21**, 190–99.

Pott, Andreas (2007), *Orte des Tourismus: Eine raum- und gesellschaftstheoretische Untersuchung*, Bielefeld: Transcript.

Rothlauf, Jürgen (2012), *Interkulturelles Management: mit Beispielen aus Vietnam, China, Japan, Russland und den Golfstaaten*, München: Oldenbourg.

Ruben, B.D. (1989), 'The study of cross-cultural competence: traditions and contemporary issues', *International Journal of Intercultural Relations*, **13**, 229–40.

Scherle, N. (2004), 'International bilateral business in the tourism industry: perspectives from German–Moroccan co-operations', *Tourism Geographies*, **6** (2), 229–56.

Scherle, Nicolai (2007), 'Managing across cultures, Reflexionen zur interkulturellen Kompetenz im Tourismusmanagement', in Armin Günther et al. (eds), *Tourismusforschung in Bayern: Aktuelle Sozialwissenschaftliche Beiträge*, München: Profil, pp. 336–40.

Scherle, Nicolai (2014), 'The incarnation of personalized mobility in the global age? Reflections on the concept of the cosmopolitan', in Eric Sucky et al. (eds), *Mobility in a Globalized World*, Bamberg: Bamberg University Press, pp. 117–32.

Scherle, Nicolai and Mikael Jonasson (2014), '"1001 Places to See Before You Die": constructing oriental holiday worlds in European guide books', in Steffen Wippel et al. (eds), *Under Construction: Logics of Urbanism in the Gulf Region*, Farnham: Ashgate, pp. 147–58.

Scherle, N. and A. Nonnenmann (2008), 'Swimming in cultural flows: conceptualizing tour guides as intercultural mediators and cosmopolitans', *Journal of Tourism and Cultural Change*, **6** (2), 120–37.

Schmid, S. and T. Kotulla (2010), 'Die GLOBE-Studie: Kultur und erfolgreiches Leadership in Zeiten der Globalisierung', *Wirtschaftswissenschaftliches Studium*, **39** (2), 61–7.

Schneider, Susan C., Jean-Louis Barsoux and Günter K. Stahl (2014), *Managing Across Cultures*, Harlow: Pearson.

Shakil, A.F., F. Waqar-un-Nisa and S. Hafeez (2011), 'The need and importance of field trips at higher level in Karachi, Pakistan', *International Journal of Academic Research in Business and Social Sciences*, **2** (1), 1–16.

Shor, Ira (1992), *Empowering Education: Critical Teaching for Social Change*, Chicago: The University of Chicago Press.

Spitzberg, Brian H. and Gabrielle Changnon (2009), 'Conceptualizing intercultural competence', in Darla K. Deardorff (ed.), *The Sage Handbook of Intercultural Competence*, Los Angeles: Sage, pp. 2–52.

Stahl, Günter K. (1995), 'Die Auswahl von Mitarbeitern für den Auslandseinsatz: Wissenschaftliche Grundlagen', in Torsten M. Kühlmann (ed.), *Mitarbeiterentsendung ins Ausland: Auswahl, Vorbereitung, Betreuung und Wiedereingliederung*, Göttingen: Verlag für angewandte Psychologie, pp. 31–72.

Stone, Matthew J. and J.J. Petrick (2013), 'The educational benefits of travel experiences: a literature review', *Journal of Travel Research*, **52** (6), 731–44.

Stüdlein, Yvonne (1997), *Management von Kulturunterschieden: Phasenkonzept für internationale strategische Allianzen*, Wiesbaden: Gabler.

Sulkowski, N. and M.K. Deakin (2010), 'Implications of internationalization on learning and teaching: listening to the winds of change?', *Journal of Hospitality, Leisure, Sport and Tourism Education*, **9** (1), 110–16.

Thomas, Alexander, Katja Hagemann and Siegfried Stumpf (2003), 'Training interkultureller Kompetenz', in Niels Bergemann and Andreas L.J. Sourisseaux (eds), *Interkulturelles Management*, Heidelberg: Springer, pp. 237–72.

Thomas, David A. and R.J. Ely (1996), 'Making differences matter: a new paradigm for managing diversity', *Harvard Business Review*, **74** (5), 79–90.

Waldstein, F.A. and T.C. Reiher (2001), 'Service-learning and students' personal and civic development', *The Journal of Experiential Education*, **24** (1), 7–13.

Wright, R.K. and D. Hind (2011), 'International field trips: the tourism & entertainment management fieldtrip to the Gambia, West Africa', *Assessment, Teaching and Learning Journal (Leeds Met)*, **11** (Summer), 83–92.

Xie, P.F. (2004), 'Tourism field trip: students' view of experiential learning', *Tourism Review*, 8 (2), 101–11.

PART IV

INTERNATIONALIZATION

22 Internationalization of tourism education
Cathy H.C. Hsu

1.   INTRODUCTION

The globalization of the tourism and hospitality industry will increasingly require gradu-ates who are able to work with a culturally diverse workforce either in their home country (due to increased mobility of labor and an increase in cultural diversity of community) or in foreign locations due to their overseas assignments. Thus, preparing graduates to participate in a global economy and understand diverse cultures, developing sensitivity to different perspectives, being capable of working and communicating with people from around the world, and fostering global citizenship are at the heart of higher educa-tion today (Stoner et al., 2014). Institutions have an obligation to prepare graduates to compete in the global marketplace with global competency, which means 'having an open mind while actively seeking to understand the cultural norms and expectations of others, leveraging this gained knowledge to interact, communicate and work effectively outside one's environment' (Hunter, as cited in Hunter et al., 2006, p. 270). Therefore, internation-alization has become a key strategic element for universities around the world (Maringe, 2009). However, Lunn (2006) reported that hospitality graduates have only developed a moderate level of global perspectives and the need exists for further development of cultural diversity awareness within hospitality education (Hearns et al., 2007).

Some countries have national policies and mechanisms designed to encourage interna-tionalization. For example, the growing impacts of globalization have continued to press the South Korean government to transform its higher education system (Byun and Kim, 2011). Singapore, Malaysia and Hong Kong have also introduced government policies on higher education development. Australia is actively working in this area as well, due to its diverse international student cohort. Internationalization has been a priority area for a number of national grant programs administered by the Australian Learning and Teaching Council (ALTC) as well as its predecessor, the Australian Government Office for Learning and Teaching (OLT). Australia's New Colombo Plan (Australian Government, 2014) and efforts to increase student mobility between Australia and Asia are additional examples. At the heart of these national and regional policies is the encouragement of internationalization of their tertiary education as a way to increase the quality of edu-cation and skills of graduates (Hsu, 2014). The most commonly adopted definition of internationalization of higher education is 'the process of integrating an international, intercultural or global dimension to the purpose, function or delivery of post-secondary education' (Knight, 2003, p. 2). As a process, it requires ongoing effort and continuing support from multiple stakeholders, including the government, institution, program administrators, the industry and faculty members, to name a few.

Even with the emphasis placed on internationalization by higher educational insti-tutions, the tourism literature has only paid scant attention to this topic. According to Tribe (2005), of the publications on tourism education until 2001, 86 percent were related to curriculum issues and only 3 percent addressed globalization. The early literature treated globalization both as a development that tourism education has to adapt to and as a threat to local autonomy and culture. Of the recent journal articles published on the internationalization of tourism education, focuses included reviews of internationalization of Thailand's hospitality and tourism education (Wisansing, 2008; Sangpikul, 2009); a case study of internationalization of tourism education in Austria (Zehrer and Lichtmannegger, 2008); an investigation of the internationalization of UK hospitality management degrees (Brookes and Becket, 2009); and a comparative study of US and non-US internationalization practices (Ayoun et al., 2010). Further, Black (2004) reviewed factors that contribute to the internationalization of a program of study, and McCabe et al. (2009) reported the development of a postgraduate international hospitality management program curriculum based on considerations for best practice. A welcomed addition to the tourism education community is the Tourism Education Futures Initiative, which presented five values-based principles (that is, stewardship, knowledge, professionalism, ethics and mutuality) to be embodied in tourism education programs (Sheldon et al., 2011). The mutuality dimension embraces diversity, inclusion, equity, humility and collaboration, all of which might be developed through internationalization efforts.

In terms of students' learning experiences, Williams and Best (2014) examined students' motivation and satisfaction of short study tours abroad and the effectiveness of short study tours on students' knowledge acquisition and learning. Stoner et al.'s (2014) analysis of previous empirical studies also concluded that short-term experiential educational travel programs nurture global perspectives when coupled with sound pedagogy. Lai and Wang (2013) demonstrated the effectiveness of an international cooperative learning activity that involved students from two tourism geography courses in two different countries. Gretzel et al. (2011) reported the use of Facebook as a platform to engage students from Finland and the US in an international learning experience.

A search of the general education literature, however, is more fruitful, with numerous publications discussing the issue from various perspectives, including approaches to internationalization, motivations for and barriers to internationalization, and mechanisms required to ensure effective student learning (for example, Altbach and Knight, 2006; Hovland, 2009; Kehm and Teichler, 2007; McKeown, 2009; Peterson and Helms, 2013). These publications guide the following discourse on aspects of internationalization efforts, barriers to internationalization, and impacts on student learning. Implications for and examples from tourism programs are observed throughout the discussion.

2.   APPROACHES TO INTERNATIONALIZATION

The literature has generally categorized internationalization activities into the following aspects: strategies, students, faculty, curriculum, research, organizational support and international networking (Ayoun et al., 2010; Peterson and Helms, 2013; Brookes and Becket, 2009; Sangpikul, 2009). Specific activities under each category can be used as indicators of the progress toward internationalization. Although hospitality and tourism programs' internationalization efforts are supported and guided by the institutional environment, initiatives can be taken at the program level. Thus, the discussion here covers topics both at the institutional and program/discipline levels, with attention given to the issues of strategies, curriculum, faculty, students and international collaboration.

2.1   Strategies

Institutions seeking to internationalize often focus on a few initiatives, such as offering instruction in foreign languages or engaging in study-abroad programs. Many universities around the world do not have a coherent, strategic direction that connects across the different activities. An exception can be found in Australia, where many universities have well-developed internationalization strategies or plans, with a dedicated international office headed by a member of each university's senior management team to enact the plans. The University of Queensland is an example of having such a plan and organization structure (University of Queensland, 2013).

Efforts at department or program level are often also on an ad hoc basis; and there is still a great deal of debate on how to internationalize higher education, particularly at the program level (Kehm and Teichler, 2007). The American Council on Education used the term 'comprehensive internationalization', which is a strategic, coordinated process that aligns and integrates international policies, programs and initiatives and that positions colleges and universities to be more globally oriented and internationally connected (Peterson and Helms, 2013). Such a process requires a clear commitment from the leadership, affects the curriculum and institutional policies and programs, and involves a broad range of people. The International Association of Universities (IAU, 2000) further clarified that the meaning of internationalization is to integrate an international and intercultural dimension into teaching, research and service functions.

Motivations of universities to internationalize include financial benefits, increased access and demand absorption, improved cultural composition of the student and staff population, competitiveness, prestige and enhanced strategic alliances with other institutions (Altbach and Knight, 2006). The charge of fostering a global awareness is incorporated into the mission statement and included in university-wide learning outcomes of an increasing number of US institutions (Stearns, 2009). Having international/global education or other aspects of internationalization as part of the mission statement would provide a clear direction and articulate the value placed on international activities. Once it is clearly stated in the mission statement, strategies, policies and implementation plans for the development of internationalization and engagement need to be developed.

With strategies and plans in place, the receipt of organizational support, such as resources and agenda priority, would be better justified. Some programs may form an international taskforce to develop and implement plans or evaluate opportunities presented; others may rely on the program administrators (for example, Dean, Director, Department Head) to spearhead such actions. A comprehensive plan would encompass strategies related to curriculum, faculty, students and networking.

2.2   Curriculum

An internationalized curriculum ensures that all students, including those who do not study abroad, are exposed to international perspectives and have opportunities to build global competence (Peterson and Helms, 2013). An 'internationalized curriculum' can be reflected in different ways. At the program level, program aims and learning outcomes could include global outlook and foreign language proficiency. Some programs prominently position themselves by including the scope of the curriculum as part of the program title, such as International Tourism Management. However, programs need to develop tourism curricula that both adapt to the globalization phenomenon and retain local culture and values to make each program unique. In some non-Western countries, nevertheless, government education policies and indicators are oriented toward the US system, and thus lose their institutional and national identity (Cho and Palmer, 2013).

International learning outcomes could be addressed by having international perspective credit requirements, such as language and culture courses, or infusing international perspectives in various tourism and hospitality courses (Leask, 2001). For example, courses could focus on global environments, use international case studies and learning materials, incorporate an international perspective in various topics of discussion and assign projects involving international/multicultural contexts (Lai and Wang, 2013).

Educational travel can foster a transformative experience that can lead to a shift in perspective, awareness and worldview (Stoner et al., 2014). These programs provide a first-hand experience of cultural immersion and exposure to values and beliefs different from students' own (Gmelch, 1997). Learning opportunities, such as study tours, student exchanges and internships, outside of the home jurisdiction are often offered to increase students' awareness of international activities and trends and expose students to the global environment (Jarvis and Peel, 2008).

2.3 Educators

Educators drive teaching and research activities and are the front line personnel who establish and deliver the curriculum, thus playing a pivotal role in creating and sustaining campus internationalization. By employing educators from different countries of origin, the program offers a multinational, multicultural working environment reflecting the global business situation. Besides recruitment, it is important to have strategies to retain overseas faculty members by providing necessary support, such as maintaining a multilingual environment and friendly atmosphere. Hosting visiting professors who are on sabbatical could also be a win–win situation for the host and guest.

To provide an overview of the extent of internationalization among tourism faculty, stocktaking was conducted of the top hospitality and tourism programs worldwide based on a list of faculty members obtained from the programs' websites. Various sources of information, including faculty members' LinkedIn and Facebook as well as personal contacts, were used to identify their country of origin. The faculty profile, as of 21 September 2016, is summarized in Table 22.1. The University of Surrey is the most internationalized based on the percentage of international faculty composition, and The Hong Kong Polytechnic University (PolyU) is the most internationalized according to the number of countries represented.

For local and long-serving faculty members, continued staff development activities in an international context are imperative. A variety of approaches are available to provide support for faculty to gain the background and skills needed to internationalize the curriculum and their courses. Staff development activities could include provision of foreign language courses or international experience. Support could be provided to staff

Table 22.1   Faculty origin of top hospitality and tourism programs

Institution[a]	No. of faculty members[b]	Origin		No. of countries represented
		Local[c] (%)	International (%)	
Cornell University	68	79	21	10
The Hong Kong Polytechnic University	61	39	61	15
University of Central Florida	59	51	49	14
University of Nevada, Las Vegas	43	72	28	8
Pennsylvania State University[d]	42	81	19	8
Griffith University	37	54	46	13
University of Surrey	35	37	63	13
Texas A&M University	26	73	27	8
The University of Queensland	24	50	50	11
Temple University	24	54	46	8
Purdue University	21	57	43	8
University of Illinois at Urbana-Champaign	18	72	28	6
Washington State University	14	57	43	7
Virginia Polytechnic Institute and State University	13	62	38	5
Ben-Gurion University of the Negev	6	100	0	1

Notes:
[a]   Top ranked hospitality and tourism programs based on Park et al. (2011), listed in descending order of faculty size.
[b]   The number excludes visiting/adjunct faculty, professor of practice and honorable/emeritus members.
[c]   Locals are those who were born in the same country where the university is located. For Hong Kong, locals refer to those who were born in the city (Hong Kong) and 'International' includes those who were born in Mainland China.
[d]   The numbers represent both School of Hospitality Management and Department of Recreation, Park, and Tourism Management. Specifically, the School of Hospitality Management has 24 faculty members, with 79% local and 21% international, from 6 countries; while the Department of Recreation, Park, and Tourism Management has 18 faculty members, with 83% local and 17% international, from 4 countries.

to engage in professional development, graduate study overseas, international events and organizations, industry engagement, exchanges and sabbatical opportunities for teaching, consultancy and research. Faculty members could also be involved in contract training programs overseas or offer online education to international audiences. They can, through these experiences abroad, build relationships with peers in other countries. Such relationships can form the basis for broader, institution-level global engagement (strategic partnership). Educators who are location bound can gain or refresh international perspectives by engaging in research and publication with an international focus or joint research and publication with overseas scholars using online media as a platform of communication. Some countries also actively recruit their nationals who obtained their education overseas to return home.

2.4   Students

Opportunities could be provided to local students traveling overseas for educational purposes. For example, overseas study tours, exchange programs, internships and study abroad could be designed as an integral part of the curriculum. The NHTV Breda University of Applied Sciences' Master in Tourism Destination Management (NHTV Breda University, n.d.) requires students to complete a semester conducting fieldwork abroad. Students could also be encouraged to attend international conferences or competitions. Another model to encourage student mobility is the inclusion of a 'grand tour' in students' learning experience, where students study at an institution's offshore campuses or partner universities in different countries to gain exposure of various cultures. The Stenden University (2014) in the Netherlands is an example of such a model. Students from the Netherlands can spend various periods of time in South Africa, Qatar, Thailand and/or Indonesia during their study.

Students can also gain international exposure while staying home through curricular or extracurricular activities, including taking courses with international perspectives or a foreign language component; taking courses taught in English in non-English-speaking countries; interaction with students from other countries through projects or social, informal exchanges; and attending international activities, workshops, training or conferences on campus. Student development could also occur in their involvement in global organizations or student chapters of international organizations. Examples include Eta Sigma Delta Honor Society (ESD Honor Society, n.d.), which is an international hospitality management society under the umbrella of I-CHRIE, Hospitality Financial and Technology Professionals (HFTP) student chapter and Pacific Asia Travel Association (PATA) Young Tourism Professionals (YTP).

There are also opportunities for international internships and Work Integrated Learning experiences. Many universities work with hospitality and tourism businesses overseas for student internship placement. Often these arrangements are on an ad hoc basis and negotiated at the property or business unit level. An example of a more systematic model is the Disney International Programs, which offer opportunities to college students from all parts of the world to participate in the company's various program offerings at different locations.

At The Hong Kong Polytechnic University's School of Hotel and Tourism Management (SHTM), a two-semester course is offered to students who assume the role of the organizing committee of an international conference. Students are in charge of program planning, venue coordination, conference sponsorship and marketing, and the actual execution of the conference. In 2014, for example, the conference attracted more than 300 delegates from 30 countries and regions around the world. Students have to regularly communicate with international sponsors, speakers and conference attendees, which enriches students' learning experience with an international dimension.

Recruiting international students (sometimes with scholarships) is a commonly used strategy to diversify the student population. However, institutions tend to focus more on student numbers than on the experience of international students once they arrive, not to mention their role in advancing internationalization (Peterson and Helms, 2013). It is important for international students to be integrated into the campus life so that domestic and international students can interact in ways to enhance international competence for all. By creating programs and policies that focus on what students are learning and interactions with peers from other countries, institutions can maximize the impact of the resources they invest in student mobility and ensure that student learning (rather than quantitative measures such as the number of international students) remains the focus of such activities.

2.5   International Partnerships

Globalization has created a new interconnected landscape of higher education worldwide (Peterson and Helms, 2013). Institutions' relationships with international partners are seen as being critical to the development of sustainable competitive advantage. There are endless approaches to collaboration among institutions, including faculty exchange, student exchange/study abroad, co-organizing international conferences, collaborative research and jointly designed and taught courses. For a deeper level of collaboration, branch campuses overseas with a local partner, dual/multiple degree programs or joint degree programs with international partners (achieving part of the qualification in each institution) could be launched.

Examples of offshore programs with a local partner include Edinburgh Napier University in Hong Kong and University of Nevada Las Vegas in Singapore. Students of these programs will be able to take courses from foreign universities' professors without leaving their place of origin. These programs also offer educators the opportunity to teach in a different culture. Dual/multiple degree programs allow students to obtain two/multiple degrees, one from each partner institution. An example is the Florida International University (FIU) Tianjin Center (China), where students receive one degree from FIU and another from Tianjin University of Commerce upon completion of degree requirements (Florida International University, n.d.). Joint degree programs could take the form of a '2+2' arrangement where students can study the first two years in their home country, and the second two years overseas to complete their undergraduate degree. The collaboration between Edith Cowan University in Australia and Arellano University in the Philippines as well as between The University of Queensland in Australia and Sun Yat-Sen University in China are two such examples.

Another example of a joint degree program is the planned Master's program to be launched in late 2015 by The Hong Kong Polytechnic University (2014), University of Houston (2014) and Ecole hôtelière de Lausanne (2014). The three institutions will develop a common curriculum for the degree and students from Europe, Asia and North America will spend one semester in each of the three continents. Such an arrangement will enable participants to think global and act local, and thus effectively lead organizations in a connected world. Upon graduation, students will receive a Master of Science in Global Hospitality Business degree from their home institution and a Certification of Completion from the other two partners. Another example of a multinational joint program is the *European Master in Tourism Management,* designed for students to spend three semesters in three different countries (Denmark, Slovenia and Spain) before completing the thesis during the fourth semester in any of the three countries or at other partner universities in other countries (University of Girona, 2014).

3.   BARRIERS TO INTERNATIONALIZATION

Although options and good reasons for internationalization abound, numerous barriers exist. Jiang and Carpenter (2013) identified critical issues that impede international strategy implementation, including resource allocation, communication, operational process, cooperation and coordination, organizational culture, resistance to change, student support and external environment. Three prominent sources of barriers are discussed in this section.

3.1   Institutional Barriers

While many universities or departments include internationalization in their strategic plan, the various policies and procedures are not always in alignment with the strategic direction. For example, bureaucratic procedures and administrative red tape (for example, complicated activity approval and expense reimbursement processes) could disincentivize the participation in international initiatives. Kehm and Teichler (2007) also suggested a general lack of coordination and information available regarding engagement in international initiatives.

Other obstacles include limited staff funding available for international work and lack of support staff and personnel to facilitate international initiatives. Because the successful launch of any international activities, such as study abroad programs, is time intensive, the workload credit given to staff may not reflect the actual hours involved, thus discouraging many from attempting to launch new programs (Dewey and Duff, 2009). Although more institutions are considering international background, experience and interests in the hiring process, staff promotion and tenure decisions usually do not take systematic consideration of international work or experience. To facilitate faculty members' participation, incentives are required, which could include funding for international travel and research, grants to bring international educators as visitors, course release to offer time for international curricular development, recognition of international work and staff support such as by hiring part-time student helpers. Policies and procedures related to international activities should be simplified so as not to create a barrier (real or psychological) to participation.

Another barrier that needs to be addressed at the institutional level is the campus hardware and software, which are not always ready to accommodate international students or staff. For example, attitudes and cross-cultural competencies of local students and staff (both teaching and non-teaching) have a significant impact on the cultural ambience of the institution as a whole. The unfriendliness of the campus environment could be a result of mindlessness or oversight from the host population. Simple examples include campus signs and the various forms of communication which present challenges for non-local language speakers functionally and psychologically and yet are not recognized by the locals as being problematic. Other examples include the provision of spiritual guidance, prayer facilities, and appropriate food choices. Institutions with internationalization strategies should have plans and resources in place to get the campus ready for the global community. Faculty and student champions of intercultural awareness could be nominated to cultivate the organizational culture.

3.2   Staff and Educator Barriers

Black (2004) concluded that internationalization for students, the curriculum and the establishment of international alliances depends on the internationalization of faculty and that there is an underlying need for educators to be developed to fulfill their role in enabling higher education institutions to become internationalized. Green (2007) contends that staff must develop an internationalized mindset to create learning that is comparative, integrative, interdisciplinary, contextual and global.

Faculty members' importance is evidenced in their interaction with both local and international students. For study abroad programs to facilitate local students' learning effectively, staff must often intervene before, during and after these experiences (Vande Berg, 2007). When international students are recruited to the campus, educators need to understand their learning needs and styles, have the cross-cultural skills to implement pedagogies that encourage international students to share their experiences and views and bring out their contribution to the learning community, interpret them appropriately to other members of the community, and facilitate them working together as members of multinational work groups on coursework and extracurricular projects (Black, 2004).

Due to the importance of staff in internationalization of higher education, continued professional development is of utmost importance. However, funding from the institution may be limited. Thus, faculty members must think outside the box and actively pursue research or other funding that supports collaboration among international partners or engagement in cross-cultural activities. For example, The Japan Foundation (2014) offers an annual call for application for activities related to arts and culture, language education, cultural exchange, or Japanese studies and intellectual exchange. The Fulbright Scholar Program (2015) offers US educators the opportunity to lecture and research overseas and invite non-US scholars for advanced research and university lecturing in the US. Some countries also have joint research funding programs. For example, The Research Grants Council (RGC) and the Consulate General of France (CGF) in Hong Kong annually invite applications for research collaboration between Hong Kong and France by providing researchers in the two places with one-year and two-year travel grants. The scheme also offers conference/workshop grants to sponsor conference/workshop in Hong Kong and in France.

Faculty members could also initiate international collaboration in course offerings that provide students with international learning opportunities. For example, through the use of technology, students can learn from and work with members of the international tourism community. An example is the use of Second Life for students to have borderless learning experience and have the opportunity to interact with industry practitioners from overseas who participate in the virtual discussion (Penfold, 2009). Other examples illustrate the use of social media and online learning platforms involving students from different countries to work on joint projects and build a collaborative knowledge base (Gretzel et al., 2011; Lai and Wang, 2013).

3.3   Student Barriers

Difficulties involved in overseas learning experiences include international exchange partners running on different academic calendars or offering different curricula, financial constraints of families and parents' over-protective parenting style. Program administrators could facilitate exchange by identifying partners with similar curriculum structures and academic calendars, and be accommodating as much as practical in accepting credit transfer or exemption. Costs involved in overseas study tours, exchange programs, internships and study abroad vary greatly, depending on the locations of the home and host institutions. While traveling outside of the students' home country could be quite easy for European students, traveling overseas for students from Australia or New Zealand would be costly. Study abroad scholarships and other forms of financial assistance could help reduce financial difficulties so as to increase the number of students who can participate in overseas experiences.

Today's undergraduate students who belong to the Generation (Gen) Y cohort are by far the most protected generation (Howe and Strauss, 2000). Many parents of Gen Yers have resorted to a new child-rearing style named 'helicopter parents' because of the tendency to hover around and attempt to get involved in every aspect of their children's lives. Some parents are hesitant to 'let go' of children who might benefit from overseas experiences. Thus, parents need to be informed of the benefits of an internationalized campus and sending their children overseas for various learning activities. Public universities with limited physical capacity could face the challenge of taxpayers who question the need to admit students from overseas who could be seen as 'competitors' to their children for various resources. With the high level of parents' involvement in students' lives, they need to be convinced of the value of an internationalized education.

4.   IMPACT ON STUDENT LEARNING

Student learning is among the most critical focus areas for internationalization. To ensure that institutional efforts are relevant to student learning or for the purpose of enhancing student experience, mindful planning is required. Beyond the obvious pedagogical planning, provision of support services and the inclusion of an assessment component of the internationalization efforts should also be incorporated.

4.1   Pedagogical Planning

Engle and Engle (2003) suggested that well thought-out instructional design, learning outcomes and specific characteristics of the program are essential for academic and student development to occur. Using study abroad as an example, without intentional, comprehensive instructional design, study and other learning abroad experiences do not always produce the kind of learning, development and transformation that is intended (Green, 2007). Learning outcomes may include personal development (Harrison, 2006), functional knowledge/learning (McKeown, 2009) and the development of intercultural competencies (Hovland, 2009). These programs can also promote an awareness of global issues (Dolby, 2007) and nurture global citizenship (Tarrant et al., 2011). Focused and reflexive interaction with the host country and culture, and time to process the experience are paramount in providing meaningful learning outcomes (Spencer et al., 2005). Education travel programs need to be grounded by a sound pedagogical framework that ensures academic rigor, establishes and measures resultant learning outcomes, and ascertains whether proposed goals are achieved (Stoner et al., 2014). Otherwise, this would be just an extended holiday.

Study abroad programs may also include a service component and be offered within one or more fields of study to further expand the intended learning outcomes. At Hong Kong PolyU, all undergraduate students need to take a service learning course before graduation. Most of these service learning courses take the students away from Hong Kong to less developed countries and communities where they can apply their professional knowledge in a meaningful context. As more learning takes place when engaging in holistic education with a blend of emotional, intellectual and social learning, students on these service learning trips reported increased cultural awareness, sensitivity and competence, as well as communication skills, and returned home with transformed worldviews and value systems. Service learning courses have been designed with specific intended learning outcomes, which are aligned with teaching methods, learning activities and assessments. For other study tours offered at SHTM, PolyU, the instructors have to provide pedagogical reasons for the tours to demonstrate that the intended learning outcomes can only be or best achieved through overseas field trips and the study tour activities must constitute a minimum of 30 percent of the course's overall assessment.

4.2 Support Services

Internationalization of the student population can create 'win–win–win' situations for foreign students, local students and the institution. Many programs use internationalized student body in recruitment materials, including students' testimonials on their enjoyment of the multi-cultural learning environment. However, the presence of international students alone does not constitute the internationalization of degree programs (Wright and Lander, 2003). The reality on many campuses is that students are segregated in silos due to the natural tendency of gathering among people with similar background and language.

Support services are needed to facilitate the active engagement of local and overseas students so that they work together as part of multinational and multicultural teams and to solve problems together. Such integration provides students with learning opportunities and experiences in multicultural competence and prepares them to work in the global marketplace. Arrangements could be made in the classroom to encourage various forms of interaction, and extracurricular activities could be planned at the program or campus level. Individual lecturers could draw on international students' experiences in class and facilitate peer learning on content and culture/global views. All members of the community should take advantage of the fact that international students provide elements of a culturally diverse environment and contribute to the exchange of knowledge and understanding (Black, 2004).

Support services are also required for faculty members in various areas. While hiring foreign faculty members can bring cultural diversity to a campus and the student learning experience, they need cultural awareness training themselves so as to understand the background and characteristics of the students. Such awareness will enable them to use culturally appropriate and effective techniques in motivating and interacting with students. Similar support services are needed for faculty members assigned to teach at offshore campus locations or partner institutions overseas. In addition to having cultural competencies, they need to understand the specific location's tourism industry and trade practices so that students' learning will take place in a meaningful context.

4.3   Evaluation

According to Dewey and Duff (2009), a systematic approach to internationalization must comprise concurrent assessment of institutional rationales, activities, outcomes and processes. To evaluate any activities effectively, a systematic assessment mechanism needs to be in place with properly selected performance indicators. Coryell et al. (2012) stressed the need to underpin the implementation of higher education internationalization processes with: (1) a shared understanding of what internationalization is and the way it should ultimately impact student learning, and (2) a collection of assessment methods for evaluating internationalization efforts and learning outcomes. In a rush to compete in a global economy, many post-secondary educational efforts toward internationalized curricula have been compartmentalized, with little assessment done to determine the success of the results (Deardorff, 2006). Coryell et al.'s (2012) study also showed the need for enhanced, systematic ways to evaluate internationalization efforts. Institutions under their study did not have ways to assess how their work actually impacts student learning and university development. Thus, they concluded that it may be more complex to measure the outcomes of these processes and initiatives than it is to measure the inputs. Such a phenomenon further stresses the need to have strategies and plans in place, because once formalized, assessment of the impact and progress of internationalization efforts is likely to be an integral part of the implementation plan.

Ideally, performance indicators of internationalization should include both qualitative and quantitative achievements. Nevertheless, based on an assessment of the South Korean higher education internationalization policy, quality and quantity have collided and the internationalization policy has surrendered the quality of university in favor of the number of foreigners, English medium of instruction courses, and publications in English (Cho and Palmer, 2013). At the student learning level, Brookes and Becket (2009) found that international aspects are not always explicitly stated in aims and outcomes of UK hospitality management degree programs; and there was no evidence of the provision of internationalization of student experience in documentation reviewed. They observed very limited mention of any indicators under internationalization of student experience. Thus, much more work needs to be done in assessing the impact of internationalization efforts on student learning.

The assessment of the effect of internationalization on student learning could be performed through direct or indirect means. Direct measures could include course-embedded activities and outcome assessment, entry and exit tests of student competencies and the achievement of preset performance indicators (for example, performance on foreign language tests). Indirect measures could include benchmarking in faculty and student international experience, internationalization of curriculum design, results of student feedback mechanisms such as the International Student Barometer survey, and student placement location after graduation.

In addition to the various forms of assessment, an often-overlooked important task is the use of outcome assessment data for continuous improvement. Once feedback is obtained from the various stakeholders, how institutions and individual faculty use the information to close the quality assurance loop is often poorly documented, even when follow-up actions have been taken. It is important for institutions or individual projects to go through and document the full plan–act–evaluate–improve cycle to demonstrate the effectiveness of internationalization activities and the accountability of the project owner.

5.   CONCLUSION

Based on a review of tourism and general education literature, several approaches to internationalization and barriers to such efforts have been identified. Anecdotal evidence suggests that compared to other disciplines tourism education is often at the forefront of internationalization on university campuses. However, much of the tourism education research has focused on curriculum issues; and efforts and effectiveness of international-related activities are not well documented. Continued scholarship on the effectiveness of these activities and their impact on student learning and experience are desperately needed. The tourism academic community should embrace tourism education as a legitimate subject of research and value its role in solidifying tourism as a field of study. Such a view will encourage more tourism education research in the various areas in need of investigation.

To further enhance students' learning experience and expand their worldviews, tourism programs are suggested to more explicitly include internationalization in their mission and strategic plan so that efforts are more coherent and better managed. The implementation plan of the internationalization strategies should include specific components such as aims and objectives, action plans, responsible personnel, resources available, evaluation measures, and the feedback loop to develop follow-up actions for continuous improvement.

REFERENCES

Altbach, P.G. and J.K. Knight (2006), 'The internationalization of higher education: Motivations and realities', *The NEA 2006 Almanac of Higher Education*, accessed 15 December 2014 at http://www.nea.org/assets/img/PubAlmanac/ALM_06_03.pdf.
Australian Government (2014), 'New Colombo Plan', accessed 16 June 2015 at http://dfat.gov.au/people-to-people/new-colombo-plan/pages/new-colombo-plan.aspx.
Ayoun, B., M.K. Johnson, M.K. Vanhyfte and M. O'Neill (2010), 'A comparison study of US and non-US education internationalization practices of hospitality and tourism programs', *Journal of Teaching in Travel & Tourism*, **10** (4), 335–61.
Black, K. (2004), 'A review of factors which contribute to the internationalization of a programme of study', *Journal of Hospitality, Leisure, Sport & Tourism Education*, **3** (1), 5–18.
Brookes, M. and N. Becket (2009), 'An investigation of the internationalisation of UK hospitality management degrees', *Journal of Hospitality & Tourism Education*, **21** (3), 17–24.
Byun, K. and M. Kim (2011), 'Shifting patterns of the government's policies for the internationalization of Korean higher education', *Journal of Studies in International Education*, **15** (5), 467–86.
Cho, Y.H. and J.D. Palmer (2013), 'Stakeholders' view of South Korea's higher education internationalization policy', *Higher Education*, **65** (3), 291–308.
Coryell, J.E., B.A. Durodoye, R.R. Wright, P.E. Pate and S. Nguyen (2012), 'Case studies of internationalization in adult and higher education: Inside the processes of four universities in the United States and the United Kingdom', *Journal of Studies in International Education*, **16** (1), 75–98.
Deardorff, D.K. (2006), 'Identification and assessment of intercultural competence as a student outcome of internationalization', *Journal of Studies in International Education*, **10** (3), 241–66.

Dewey, P. and S. Duff (2009), 'Reason before passion: Faculty views on internationalization in higher education', *Higher Education*, **58** (4), 491–504.

Dolby, N. (2007), 'Reflections on nation: American undergraduates and education abroad', *Journal of Studies in International Education*, **11** (2), 141–56.

Ecole Hôtelière de Lausanne (2014), 'Master of Science HES-SO in global hospitality business', accessed 16 June 2015 at http://www.ehl.edu/en/study/master-global-hospitality-business.

Engle, L. and J. Engle (2003), 'Study abroad levels: Toward a classification of program types', *Frontiers: The Interdisciplinary Journal of Study Abroad*, **9**, 1–20.

ESD Honor Society (n.d.), 'ESD honor society', accessed 16 June 2015 at http://www.chrie.org/esd-honor-society/index.aspx.

Florida International University (n.d.), 'Marriott Tianjin China program overview', accessed 16 June 2015 at http://hospitality.fiu.edu/undergraduate/hospitality-management/marriott-tianjin-china-program-overview/.

Fulbright Scholar Program (2015), 'Fulbright Scholar Program', accessed 16 June 2015 at http://www.cies.org/.

Gmelch, G. (1997), 'Crossing cultures: Student travel and personal development', *Journal of Intercultural Relations*, **21** (4), 475–90.

Green, M.F. (2007), 'Internationalizing community colleges: Barriers and strategies', *New Directions for Community Colleges*, **138**, 15–24.

Gretzel, U., A. Isacsson, D. Matarrita and E. Wainio (2011), 'Teaching based on TEFI values: A case study', *Journal of Teaching in Travel and Tourism*, **11** (1), 94–106.

Harrison, J.K. (2006), 'The relationship between international study tour effects and the personality variables of self-monitoring and core self-evaluations', *Frontiers: The Interdisciplinary Journal Study Abroad*, **13**, 1–22.

Hearns, N., F. Devine and T. Baum (2007), 'The implications of contemporary cultural diversity for the hospitality curriculum', *Education + Training*, **49** (5), 350–63.

Hong Kong Polytechnic University (2014), 'Master of Science (MSc) in global hospitality business', accessed 16 June 2015 at http://hotelschool.shtm.polyu.edu.hk/eng/academic/programs_overview.jsp?ID=42&Tag=1&Program=pgd&SubProg=msc&SA=posthk.

Hovland, K. (2009), 'Global learning: What is it? Who is responsible for it?', *Association of American Colleges and Universities Peer Review*, **11** (4), 4–7.

Howe, N. and W. Strauss (2000), *Millennials Rising: The Next Great Generation*, New York: Random House.

Hsu, C.H.C. (2014), 'Tourism and hospitality education in Asia', in D. Dredge, D. Airey and M.J. Gross (eds), *The Routledge Handbook of Tourism and Hospitality Education*, Abingdon: Routledge, pp. 197–209.

Hunter, B., G.P. White and G.C. Godbey (2006), 'What does it mean to be globally competent?', *Journal of Studies in International Education*, **10** (3), 267–85.

International Association of Universities (2000), 'Towards a century of co-operation: Internationalization of higher education – IAU statement', accessed 20 December 2014 at http://www.unesco.org.iau/tfi_statement.html.

Japan Foundation (2014), 'What's new', accessed 15 January 2015 at http://www.jpf.go.jp/e/.

Jarvis, J. and V. Peel (2008), 'Study backpackers: Australia's short-stay international student travelers', in K. Hannam and I. Ateljevic (eds), *Backpacker Tourism: Concepts and Profiles*, Clevedon: Channel View, pp. 157–73.

Jiang, N. and V. Carpenter (2013), 'A case study of issues of strategy implementation in internationalization of higher education', *International Journal of Educational Management*, **27** (1), 4–18.

Kehm, B.M. and U. Teichler (2007), 'Research on internationalization in higher education', *Journal of Studies in International Education*, **11** (3/4), 260–73.

Knight, J. (2003), 'Updated internationalization definition', *International Higher Education*, **33**, 2–3.

Lai, K. and S. Wang (2013), 'International cooperative learning and its applicability to teaching tourism geography: A comparative study of Chinese and American undergraduates', *Journal of Teaching in Travel & Tourism*, **13** (1), 75–99.

Leask, B. (2001), 'Bridging the gap: Internationalizing university curricula', *Journal of Studies in International Education*, **5** (2), 100–15.

Lunn, J. (2006), *Global Perspectives in Higher Education Subject Analysis: Tourism and Hospitality*, London: Royal Geographic Society with IBG.

Maringe, F. (2009), 'Strategies and challenges of internationalization in HE: An exploratory study of UK universities', *International Journal of Educational Management*, **23** (7), 553–63.

McCabe, V.S., M.J. Gross and P. Reynolds (2009), 'Toward the development of best practice in a postgraduate international hospitality management program', *Journal of Teaching in Travel & Tourism*, **8** (2/3), 283–304.

McKeown, J.S. (2009), *The First Time Effect: The Impact of Study Abroad On College Student Intellectual Development*, Albany, NY: State University of New York Press.

NHTV Breda University (n.d.), 'Master in tourism destination management', accessed 16 June 2015 at http://www.nhtv.nl/ENG/masters-courses/masters-cursussen/masters/master-in-tourism-destination-management/introduction.html.

Park, K., W.J. Phillips, D.D. Canter and J. Abbott (2011), 'Hospitality and tourism research rankings by author, university, and country using six major journals: The first decade of the new millennium', *Journal of Hospitality & Tourism Research*, **35** (3), 381–416.

Penfold, P. (2009), 'Learning through the world of second life: A hospitality and tourism experience', *Journal of Teaching in Travel & Tourism*, **8** (2/3), 139–60.

Peterson, P.M. and R.M. Helms (2013), 'Internationalization revisited', *Change: The Magazine of Higher Learning*, **45** (2), 28–34.

Sangpikul, Aswin (2009), 'Internationalization of hospitality and tourism higher education: A perspective from Thailand', *Journal of Teaching in Travel and Tourism*, **9** (1–2), 2–20.

Sheldon, P.J., D. Fesenmaier and J. Tribe (2011), 'The Tourism Education Futures Initiative (TEFI): Activating change in tourism education', *Journal of Teaching in Travel & Tourism*, **11** (1), 2–23.

Spencer, S., T. Murray and K. Tuma (2005), 'Short-term programs abroad', in J. Brockington, W. Hoffa and P. Martin (eds), *NAFSA's Guide to Education Abroad for Advisers and Administrators* (3rd edn), Washington, DC: NAFSA – Association of International Educators, pp. 373–87.

Stearns, P.N. (2009), *Educating Global Citizens in Colleges and Universities: Challenges and Opportunities*, New York: Routledge.

Stenden University (2014), 'Grand tour', accessed 15 January 2015 at http://www.stenden.com/en/studies/study-abroad/grandtour/Pages/default.aspx/.

Stoner, K.R., M.A. Tarrant, L. Perry, L. Stoner, S. Wearing and K. Lyons (2014), 'Global citizenship as a learning outcome of educational travel', *Journal of Teaching in Travel & Tourism*, **14** (2), 149–63.

Tarrant, M.A., L. Stoner, W.T. Borrie, G. Kyle, R.L. Moore and A. Moore (2011), 'Educational travel and global citizenship', *Journal of Leisure Research*, **43** (3), 403–26.Tribe, J. (2005), 'Overview of research', in D. Airey and J. Tribe (eds), *An International Handbook of Tourism Education*, Oxford: Elsevier, pp. 24–43.

University of Girona (2014), 'Structure & curriculum', accessed 15 January 2015 at http://www.udg.edu/emtm master/WhatisEMTM/StructureCurriculum/tabid/20240/Default.aspx.

University of Houston (2014), 'Global hospitality master's program', accessed 16 June 2015 at http://www.uh.edu/hilton-college/About/Global-Hospitality-Masters/.

University of Queensland (2013), 'Global strategy and internationalization plan 2013–2017', accessed 16 June 2015 at http://www.uq.edu.au/international/docs/global_strategy_and_internationalisation_at_UQ.pdf.

Vande Berg, M. (2007), 'Intervening in the learning of US students abroad', *Journal of Studies in International Education*, **11** (3–4), 392–99.

Williams, K.M. and G. Best (2014), 'Short study tours abroad: Internationalizing business curricula', *Journal of Teaching in Travel & Tourism*, **14** (3), 240–59.

Wisansing, J. (2008), 'The three waves of internationalization sweeping Thailand's tourism and hospitality education: Current progress and future prospects', *Journal of Hospitality & Tourism Education*, **20** (1), 13–19.

Wright, S. and D. Lander (2003), 'Collaborative group interactions of students from two ethnic backgrounds', *Higher Education Research and Development*, **22** (3), 237–52.

Zehrer, A and S. Lichtmannegger (2008), 'The internationalization of tourism education: The case of MCI', *Journal of Hospitality & Tourism Education*, **20** (1), 45–51.

23 Internationalizing the tourism curriculum via study abroad
Ara Pachmayer, Kathleen Andereck and
Rebekka Goodman

1. INTRODUCTION

Study abroad has been cited as a way to internationalize the curriculum. While some studies suggest that study abroad is not more effective in internationalizing curricula than other options (Soria and Troisi, 2013; Vance et al., 2011), much past research shows that study abroad can be used as a tool to successfully internationalize the curriculum and help to produce globally aware graduates (Coelho, 1962; Domask, 2007; Douglas and Jones-Rikkers, 2001; Kitsantas, 2004; Kitsantis and Meyers, 2002; McCabe, 2001; Praetzel et al., 1996; Williams and Best, 2014). Specifically, this chapter proposes that study abroad is an effective, efficient way to internationalize curricula, identifies teaching approaches to designing study abroad programs and coursework, identifies ways to assess if goals were met, and lastly discusses future directions on this topic.

2. LITERATURE

2.1 Theories and Frameworks

Contact theory, the process models of intercultural competence, and experiential education theory are critical to advance understanding of the topic at hand, internationalizing the tourism curriculum through study abroad. They help to both explain the significance of the topic and provide a lens through which to view the issue.

Contact theory was initially proposed by Allport (1954) to further understand the interactions and relationships between groups of people different from one another. The framework for contact theory included several criteria that Allport considered imperative for positive interactions and effective communication between these differing groups. In his original work, *The Nature of Prejudice*, Allport outlined these factors: (1) contact between groups must be prolonged and go deeper than one-time surface interactions; (2) groups must be of equal status; (3) groups must cooperate and have common goals; and (4) there must be institutional support for this contact (Allport, 1954). Allport proposed that when these factors were present in interactions there would be a resulting decrease in prejudices. Since the presentation of contact theory in Allport's work, some scholars have criticized the necessity of these factors (Pettigrew and Tropp, 2008) and others expanded on the theory (Koschate and Van Dick, 2011). Allport developed contact theory primarily in the context of interactions between minority and non-minority groups. However, the theory has been applied in research across many disciplines and settings including education, ethnic relations, tourism and study abroad. In researching study abroad programs, contact theory, for example, provides a framework for both general academic research on the outcomes of study abroad participation and in the design and delivery of study abroad programs, which give participants opportunities to realize a variety of cross-cultural goals.

Intercultural competence theory and specifically the works of Deardorff (2006) and Fantini (2000) in the field of international education are clearly related to contact theory, though their writings only indirectly point to Allport's work. Where contact theory is concerned with positive communication between differing groups which may result in the reduction of prejudices, intercultural competence theory details the attitudes, skills and traits necessary for an individual to achieve the desired outcome of intercultural competency.

Deardorff (2006) sought to achieve consensus on defining intercultural competency and designing a way to accurately assess the development of intercultural competency in an individual. Her research, involving a dialogue with international education administrators and intercultural scholars, resulted in the development of two process models for intercultural competency. A few elements from the research deemed necessary to achieve intercultural competency included cultural awareness and an in-depth understanding of culture, respect for and openness to others, adaptability and flexibility.

In his work, Fantini (2000) developed three 'domains of ability' (p. 27) to describe intercultural competence specifically for the setting of a study abroad program. They are:

* the ability to develop and maintain relationships;
* the ability to communicate effectively and appropriately with minimal loss or distortion;
* the ability to attain compliance and obtain cooperation with others.

Similar to Deardorff's (2006) work, Fantini suggested his 'domains of ability' were attainable in individuals who possessed certain traits such as respect, flexibility, openness and adaptability.

Often study abroad programs have stated goals to develop cultural awareness and intercultural competency in participants. When developing a study abroad program with these aims it is important to consider both the framework of contact theory and intercultural competence theory, as contact theory provides the path and intercultural competence theory can provide the details to follow the path successfully. Based on Deardorff (2006) and Fantini (2000) we can say that some desirable goals of a study abroad program could be the ability to communicate effectively in another culture, ability to adapt and be flexible in another culture and ability to understand another culture without ethnocentrism, all elements important for an individual to be successful in the global economy. In the case of the current chapter, contact theory provides the set of circumstances necessary for successful interactions between differing groups, while intercultural competence theory provides both the path needed for attaining intercultural competency and a way to assess cultural competency in an individual.

The modern concept of experiential education theory derives from the early works of Dewey (2007) who expressed a system of education 'that linked knowing to doing' (Katula and Threnhauser, 1999, p. 241) where students were a part of the learning process and encouraged to understand their own experiences as they apply to learning. The Association for Experiential Education defines experiential education as: 'a philosophy that informs many methodologies in which educators purposefully engage with learners in direct experience and focused reflection in order to increase knowledge, develop skills, clarify values, and develop people's capacity to contribute to their communities' (Association for Experiential Education, n.d.). Experiential education involves students being more than simply the passive receivers of information. It is thought that when students are engaged in applying topics they have learned about to real world scenarios, learning and understanding will be more in-depth (Katula and Threnhauser, 1999; Warren, 1995).

The National Society of Experiential Education (NSEE) further contributed to better understanding of the concept of experiential education by developing a set of guidelines for both the learner and the facilitator to follow for experiential learning activities. The guidelines include: (1) intention; (2) preparedness and planning; (3) authenticity; (4) reflection; (5) orientation and training; (6) monitoring and continuous improvement; (7) assessment and evaluation; and (8) acknowledgment (National Society for Experiential Education, n.d.).

Many scholars put much weight on the role of experiential education theory in our society today. Itin (1999) stated, 'the philosophy of experiential education is what is needed to help develop a community which actively involves all in cooperatively solving problems and contributing to the greater good of society' (p. 98). Itin also makes what he feels is an important distinction between experiential education theory and the related teaching approaches. According to Itin, whereas experiential education is a philosophy of education, study abroad programs and other methods are teaching approaches to experiential education. However, studies suggest that study abroad or other methods involving field studies accelerate the learning process for the student (Henthorne et al., 2001; Praetzel et al., 1996).

2.2   What is a Study Abroad Program?

While known by other names such as international education or exchange programs, study abroad programs are essentially academic experiences where the student is away from the home country to study in another country for a specified period of time. A study abroad student is not attempting to receive a degree from the foreign country in which they study but instead will return to their home country and home institution once the study abroad program has ended. Students opt to study abroad for multiple reasons including the opportunity to be both immersed in another culture, if even for a brief period, and to attempt to develop intercultural competency and cross-cultural skills. The ability to communicate across cultures with little distortion is an extremely important skill to have, considering the interconnectedness of the world today. Many consider participation in study abroad programs to be a major national goal. In a report delivered to the President and Congress of the USA in 2005, the Commission on the Abraham Lincoln Study Abroad Fellowship Program addressed the significance of study abroad participation. The report stated, 'What nations don't know can hurt them. The stakes involved in study abroad are that simple, that straightforward, and that important. For their own future and that of the nation, college graduates today must be internationally competent' (Lincoln Commission, 2005).

2.3   Study Abroad Program Types

While participating in study abroad programs, cross-cultural interactions are often a daily occurrence for most study abroad programs. In order for students to both learn and grow from the experience in the host country, many study abroad programs intentionally include these types of interactions with the host culture. Programs may include interactions intentionally integrated into the program such as: home stays; organized events with locals; or coursework, or in less formalized ways such as becoming friends with or simply interacting with locals.

   There are multiple different formats for a study abroad program including: short-term study tours, which may offer courses along with a tour of several different destinations; programs where a group of students from the home country live and go to school together; or immersive independent experience where students are integrated fully into school and everyday life of the host country. The Forum on Education Abroad (n.d.), a non-profit organization dedicated to developing standards for the field of education abroad, established a set of study abroad program types in an effort to create consistency in naming conventions used in education abroad. While programs can vary in duration and educational experience, the study abroad program models that the Forum advanced included field study programs, integrated university studies, overseas branch campuses, study abroad centers, and travel seminars.

   Other researchers have called for further defining study abroad programs in relation to opportunities for cross-cultural encounters and more specifically on the quality of the study abroad program (Engle and Engle, 2003). In this example, the researchers do not imagine that short-term programs can result in development of cross-cultural skills. However, according to the most recent Open Doors Report (Institute of International Education, 2014), 60 percent of US students are studying abroad on short-term programs defined as summer programs or programs of eight weeks or less. If planned appropriately, all models of study abroad programs may offer participants the opportunity to deepen both their cultural understanding and intercultural competence. Research has shown that experiences students have while participating in study abroad can result in long-term changes in attitudes and behaviors, which will be discussed later in this chapter (Coelho, 1962; Douglas and Jones-Rikkers, 2001; Kitsantas, 2004; Kitsantis and Meyers, 2002; McCabe, 2001).

2.4   Internationalizing the Curriculum

The desire to internationalize university curricula has been an ongoing pursuit for the last couple of decades in the higher education system of the United States and elsewhere around the world. Multiple motives for internationalizing the curriculum have been cited including: enriching both curriculum and research; developing student and faculty knowledge in the realms of cultural understanding and cultural competency; preparing graduates for a globally inter-dependent professional environment; raising the global profile of a university to recruit students and staff; and ultimately improve university profit margins, among other reasons (Altbach and Knight, 2007; Ayoun et al., 2010; Knight, 2004). A simple Internet search for internationalizing the campus reveals that a multitude of universities have stated goals to internationalize their curriculum but often cite different definitions of what that means. Knight (2004) introduced a more general definition of internationalization of higher education so that it could be utilized across multiple cultures, countries and higher education structures. Knight stated that internationalization is 'the process of integrating an international, intercultural or global dimension into the purpose, functions or delivery of post-secondary education' (p. 2). For additional details, see Hsu's chapter in this book.

In addition to varying definitions, the strategies followed by universities to internationalize the curriculum can differ depending on goals and resources. The list might include employing international faculty or guest lecturers in courses; establishing international partnerships; introducing global content to existing courses; creating new courses with a global focus; requiring students take a foreign language or offering international internships, service learning, volunteering or study abroad programs to students (Ayoun et al., 2010; Hobson and Josiam, 1996; Sangpikul, 2009).

When considering the field of tourism, much research suggests that we are behind in terms of internationalizing the curriculum (Ayoun et al., 2010; Brookes and Becket, 2011; Ring et al., 2009; Smith and Cooper, 2000). In addition, tourism study programs are often considered to be overly vocational (Ring et al., 2009; Wattanacharoensil, 2013) and focused mainly on providing graduates with a less than comprehensive education about the role of tourism in our society. Even so, researchers and other academics involved in the study of tourism realize the important role tourism has to play in helping to improve global problems (Ring et al., 2009; Tribe, 2002). Recognizing the potential power of tourism to transform, the World Tourism Organization (WTO) identified four of the United Nations Millennium Development Goals (MDG) upon which the tourism sector can focus: (1) eradication of poverty; (2) gender equality; (3) environmental sustainability; and (4) global partnerships for development. The WTO believes that 'responsible and sustainable tourism allows destinations and companies to minimize the negative impacts of tourism on the environment and on cultural heritage while maximizing its economic and social benefits' (UNWTO, 2010, p. 5).

A vocational education is required to ensure students can be effective workers after graduation. However, an internationalized curriculum may give students a global viewpoint and elucidate the connection they will have to make between the local and the global in their careers by instilling in them both intercultural competence and cultural awareness. Tourism students must have an understanding of international issues and the ways in which tourism can help alleviate global problems. An internationalized tourism curriculum can result in graduates who are culturally competent, have in-depth understanding of global problems and the circumstances which created these problems, and ultimately are better prepared to be change makers at the forefront of the industry.

Often cited as not simply a goal but a responsibility for universities is the importance of preparing students who will graduate and succeed in the global economy (Brustein, 2007; Deardorff and Hunter, 2006; Fantini, 2000). Today, in most careers, cross-cultural communication will likely be a daily occurrence in the workplace, whether with colleagues, clients or other professionals. The tourism industry is no different, and is possibly even more impacted than other sectors by the demands of our globally connected society simply due to the nature of tourism where tourists frequently cross borders and land in a culturally unfamiliar environment.

One approach to achieve the desired goals of cultural understanding and cultural competency through internationalizing the curriculum is through the delivery of study abroad programs. In the literature, study abroad, whether short or long term, has been shown to be an effective method to internationalize the curriculum (Praetzel et al., 1996; Williams and Best, 2014) and enhance cultural understanding, intercultural competency and global awareness of participants (Carlson and Widaman, 1988; Coelho, 1962; Kitsantas, 2004; Kitsantas and Meyers, 2002; Kuh and Kauffmann, 1984; McCabe, 1994; Sindt and Pachmayer, 2006).

The outcomes of study abroad participation have been a topic of research for over five decades, with an early study conducted by Coelho (1962). Writing well before Deardorff (2006) suggested a definition of intercultural competency, Coelho used the term 'international understanding' to refer to the improvements in study abroad participants' understanding of international relations and their development of connections with different people while studying abroad. Similar to contact theory (Allport, 1954), Coelho stated 'familiarity breeds good will, or at least that the knowledge gained is a necessary . . . condition of friendliness' (p. 56). He found that when people interact more with one another relations improve.

Multiple studies have been conducted since Coelho (1962) to explore how participation in study abroad can impact students' development of cultural understanding and intercultural competency in a positive way. Ultimately, these changes can lead study abroad participants to an awareness of global problems and a desire to translate that awareness into action. In a study involving both students who studied abroad and those who did not during junior college, Carlson and Widaman (1988) tested their hypothesis that studying abroad would result in greater changes in student attitudes in the realms of what they also referred to as international understanding. In the study students were asked to specify how they felt about a variety of statements designed to assess international understanding. Students responded to this section before and after their junior year. Statements included, for example:

- awareness of problems common to many nations;
- concern of problems in Third World Countries;
- desire for international peace;
- wish to help find solutions to global problems such as hunger, disease, etc.;
- respect for historical and cultural traditions and achievement of nations other than your own;
- need for closer cooperation among nations (p. 5).

After their junior year, both groups of respondents were then asked to determine how their views on a certain number of issues had changed over the course of the year. The statements tested included:

- your negative feelings about foreigners;
- your critical views of your own country;
- your views that values of your own society are not universal and that values of other societies are just as valid;
- your belief that problems of developing nations should be of no concern to the developed ones (p. 5).

After performing a factor analysis of the results, they found the students who studied abroad had significant changes in the areas of cross-cultural interest and cultural cosmopolitanism, which they define as 'an interest in peoples, language, and traditions from other cultures' (p. 11). Carlson and Widaman (1988) concluded, 'study abroad can be an important contributor to international awareness and potentially contribute to attitudes and behaviors that help foster international understanding' (p. 15).

McCabe (1994) explored the development of what he called a global perspective in students participating in a Semester at Sea program. Using qualitative research methods, including participant observation and student journaling, the researcher considered changes in global perspectives along five dimensions including: '(1) fear versus openness; (2) people as the same or different versus people as the same and different; (3) naivety versus cross-cultural knowledge and understanding' (p. 278). The results showed that as a result of participation in the study abroad program, students became more open in terms of openness to experiencing cultures new to them, their cross-cultural understanding improved, and they became more interested in and aware of world events.

In a study designed similarly to Carlson and Widaman (1988) involving a pre- and post-test of students who participated in study abroad and those who did not, Kitsantas and Meyers (2002) employed a questionnaire which assesses adaptability in other cultures. The Cross Cultural Adaptability Inventory (CCAI) has been used in a variety of scenarios to understand the criteria necessary to succeed when studying, working or living in another culture. In their study Kitsantas and Meyers found that participation in a study abroad program did improve students' cross-cultural adaptability and further confirmed that scores on the CCAI could predict success in a cross-cultural environment.

Later, Kitsantas (2004) completed a study related to Kitsantas and Meyers (2002) where students again completed the Cross Cultural Adaptability Inventory (CCAI) in a pre- and post-test. Additionally, student motives to study abroad were assessed to explore the link between motives and the development of cross-cultural skills and global understanding and post-test participants completed supplementary questions related to their understanding of global perspectives. Cross-cultural skills and global understanding improved after students completed the study abroad program. Kitsantas concluded the results of the study 'demonstrated that study abroad programs significantly contribute to the preparation of students to function in a multicultural world and promote international understanding.' (p. 447).

Internationalizing the curriculum and developing cultural competencies and cultural awareness in students are closely connected. The development of cultural competencies which will allow students to function effectively in the multi-cultural environments they are likely to experience in the workplace must be taken into account when considering internationalizing any curriculum.

3.   TEACHING APPROACHES/CASE STUDIES

3.1   Developing a Study Abroad Program

Research has shown that all the various models of study abroad may offer learning opportunities for students and indeed study abroad has the potential to help tourism students understand how they might contribute to the goals of positive global change. It is easy to assume that study abroad programs can naturally provide an experiential education opportunity for students simply due to their structure whereby students are in a different environment and have the opportunity to learn from that new environment. However, study abroad programs do not always achieve this experiential goal because they are often not designed to use the context of the international location as a part of the coursework. Among other challenges, frequently the pressure to maintain a familiar academic structure leads to teaching and learning simply being transplanted from one locale to another without consideration for how the students might learn from the host country or the issues experienced in the host country. However, by following the approach of experiential education while constructing a program which emphasizes location as a learning laboratory, reflection and critical analysis we suggest we can use study abroad as a means to internationalize the tourism curriculum. At the same time, we can help our students acquire a greater sense of global citizenship and in turn an understanding of the role tourism can play in addressing global problems.

The development of a study abroad program must be approached by considering preparation and onsite activities. Preparation and activities should consider Allport's (1954) positive factors: (1) contact between groups must be prolonged and go deeper than one-time surface interactions; (2) groups must be perceived and valued as having equal status; (3) groups must cooperate and have common goals; and (4) there must be institutional support for this contact. In addition, achieving the cross-cultural goals of study abroad must be at the forefront of program development: the ability to communicate effectively in another culture, ability to adapt and be flexible in another culture, and ability to understand another culture without ethnocentrism.

In the best manifestation, study abroad students have general knowledge of the host culture before arriving, are typically in the country for a longer period than a tourist and therefore have the opportunity to develop a familiarity and relationships with the hosts and their culture. Therefore, these students have at least the potential to be more than just a tourist in their host culture. Participants should be well informed about their host country prior to departure. This should include information on standards of behavior, dress, cultural norms (gender, communication, power roles for example), customs, differences between the host and home culture, and local language. This can be accomplished with several orientation sessions prior to departure and assigned readings on the host country. In addition, online resources exist to explain general cultural differences and how to apply understanding of these differences in real world situations such as the Safety Abroad First – Educational Travel Information (SAFETI) Clearinghouse Project (Center for Global Education, 2015) and 'What's up with Culture?' (2014). Aspects of these resources have been successfully adapted by organizations like the Peace Corps to train volunteers effectively to live and work in another culture. Preparation can continue onsite with cultural exercises in the community or region (mapping exercises, excursions, cultural tours) where the program is taking place.

Taking advantage of the location as a laboratory for learning can involve students in the cultural learning process and help them to 'understand the evolution, tensions and cultural significance of the city life . . .', which has shown to impact 'behavioral skills needed for negotiating the cultural differences they encounter' (Blair, 2011, p. 53). Once onsite, the program can best facilitate achievement of cross-cultural goals by integrating the student into the local community as much as possible through activities with residents (that is, volunteering, home stays, coursework with local students). Home stays in particular are a natural place where cross-cultural goals can be met while still staying within Allport's framework. However, home stays have been shown to be ineffective and have negative results if the student does not understand what to expect (Engle and Engle, 2003), which is where we can return to the in-depth preparation which should happen prior to departure and throughout the program.

Daily activities can be turned into learning experiences where a student is developing the skills and knowledge for cultural competencies (Deardorff, 2006; Fantini, 2000). For example, scavenger hunts for everyday items (shampoo, groceries and so on) could be developed where students will be sent out into the local community individually to find these items. While seemingly an inconsequential activity, depending on the location, students may use skills they are not used to being in tune with on a daily basis such as observation or simple listening. Development (or re-development) of these skills in a different cultural context can lead to intercultural competency (Deardorff, 2006).

With respect to equality between groups, this is potentially difficult to manage for students in activities that may not be monitored by the institution, particularly for students venturing to developing countries. Given that much of a student's time abroad is spent doing normal tourist activities, there needs to be a realization and understanding on the part of the student that 'in many of the places you travel, your relationship to the local population is primarily economic and is broadly influenced by dramatic differences in wealth' (Chambers, 2005, p. 32). In an article considering how anthropology might make people better travelers, Chambers explores this issue of inequality. There are probably no solutions to this problem. We can recommend that students pay reasonable prices for tourist goods and services for example. Perhaps just the realization of the vast differences which exist between typical college students from more developed nations and the majority of the world will be eye-opening enough as to encourage cultural empathy, which is related to Allport's factor of cooperation and common goals. Educating students on the concepts of authenticity in tourism (MacCannell, 1973) and the difference between staged authenticity or cultural performances and real experiences could also aid them in awareness of the unique host–guest situation they are experiencing.

3.2   Case Study: Study Abroad in the School of Community Resources and Development

The School of Community Resources and Development at Arizona State University in the USA currently offers two study abroad opportunities to students, one in Guatemala and the other in Fiji/Australia. The primary goal of these programs is to strengthen and enhance the curriculum and to serve as the bridge between what students learn about global problems in the classroom and what they can see on the ground in the field. Both programs were created with specific aims and objectives to encourage experiential learning about tourism and sustainable development, and in the case of the Guatemala program, how tourism can contribute to achieving the Millennium Development Goals (MDGs). This section of the chapter focuses on a program entitled 'Sustainable Community Development and Tourism in Guatemala' as a case study. This study abroad program began by following the eight principles of good practice provided by the National Society for Experiential Education as described earlier.

The Guatemala study abroad program met all eight principles while focusing on specific learning objectives aimed at helping students see the connections between the MDGs (as a platform for achieving sustainable development) and tourism. This meant carefully choosing partnerships with NGOs whose focus is on achieving the MDGs and who use tourism as one of the avenues through which to do so. The program began with five all-day sessions prior to leaving for Guatemala that focused heavily on readings and discussions. This was to ensure students had a strong foundation of the key concepts of sustainable development (focusing on cascading effects, unintended consequences, trade-offs, scale and long-term development), the complexities of the MDGs and their relationship to sustainable development, and how tourism development plays a role. This was followed by 20 days on the ground in Guatemala. Students earned three credit hours for their time and work. The program was broken into three parts in three different locations in Guatemala. The first segment worked closely with an NGO called SHARE Guatemala in the department of Chimaltenango (a department in Guatemala is an administrative sub-division of the federal government). SHARE describes itself as follows:

> Our work is based on a participative methodology working in close relation with organized groups and local partners in rural communities of Guatemala. We develop instruction programs in health and nutrition, education, agriculture and food production, administration and finance, as well as developing sustainable projects. We also assist and implement risk mitigation programs in localities that have been affected by natural disasters. (Share Tours, 2014b)

SHARE works on achieving the MDGs through improved food security, which includes education on nutrition and health, organic food production, capacity building, improved community infrastructure, and improved access to primary education. SHARE also encourages small and medium sized business development (with a strong focus on women) through micro-credit lending. SHARE includes tourism in their development strategy as well. They work with tourists in three ways:

- Development Support: in which tourists participate in infrastructure development and education projects as volunteers in different rural communities of the country.
- Cultural Exchange: local cultural immersion through coexistence and participation in cultural activities and visits to families in the community.
- Tours: guided tours to see highlights throughout the most popular regions.

According to SHARE, their tourism program is a way to seek support for development in a 'humane and sincere way where the participating groups are able to take away a part of the local culture' (Share Tours, 2014a). This portion of the study abroad experience allows students to see local community empowerment, poverty alleviation through micro-credit lending and education (with a focus on gender equality), environmental sustainability through organic farming initiatives and maternal and infant health care through all of the aforementioned activities. During the most recent program, each day began with a review of the day's activities, what the students would be doing, and what they could expect. This allowed the students some time to prepare themselves cognitively as well as emotionally for what they were going to experience. Activities included visits to different communities that SHARE works with as well as question and answer sessions with local community members, school children, and SHARE employees. Students did not have to speak Spanish to attend this study abroad, but were encouraged to try and speak with community members as best they could or through the several Spanish speakers present. Each afternoon, students were given time to rest and reflect personally on the day's experiences, and each evening was spent reflecting as a group and relating what had been learned during the day to the coursework and readings that had been completed prior to the study abroad experience. The role of the instructor was to guide the students through discussions and reflections, and assessment was based on the students' ability to connect what they experienced to the theoretical knowledge they accumulated while in the classroom prior to the international experience. SHARE's isolated location and the level of development meant very little tourism in the area. Students were encouraged to discuss the tradeoffs, unintended consequences, and cascading effects of tourism development in the area, both positive and negative, in relation to achieving the MDGs.

Students had several opportunities to experience the different ways in which food and gardening play a role in SHARE's agenda. SHARE allowed students to walk through several completed gardens that they had helped build from the ground up. SHARE's contributions came in the form of seeds, nutritional classes, and information on organic farming methods and composting. In some cases, farmers had received micro-credit loans to purchase goats and/or chickens and received information on ways to care and keep the animals. Students received 'lectures' from the locals who allowed us to tour their gardens, explaining the type of assistance they had received from SHARE as well as how it had affected them and their families. Families offered up fresh fruit from their gardens and even offered students unique local vegetables (that were prepared traditionally and eaten at the hotel), serving as a rare cultural exchange not often offered to tourists.

As a part of SHARE's development support goals and by far the most connecting and interactive activity that students were able to participate in was the building of an educational garden with local primary school children. Prior to ASU's arrival, the local students had submitted designs for a garden that would serve to educate about the basics of botany and organic farming methods. With ASU students present, the children voted on the winning design, and a SHARE member quickly laid down chalk to designate where to dig trenches. ASU students then got busy along with locals. School children had also collected empty 2-liter soda bottles that were cut in half and filled with dirt. These were placed spout down to manage growth of the plants and keep the design. Once all digging and placement of bottles was complete, ALL students, local and ASU, were given seeds to plant. It was an engaging, functional and entertaining experience for both parties, and represented how tourism, non-profits and local communities can work together.

After working with SHARE, the program moved on to its second segment, in Antigua. Antigua is a UNESCO World Heritage Site due to its cobblestone streets, colonial architecture, and ruins scattered throughout the small city of approximately 35 000 people. The town of Antigua depends primarily on tourism and language schools as its industries and provides an excellent 'classroom' to demonstrate the imbalance in which tourism development can result. The safety and excellent tourism infrastructure of the area allowed more student independence. Each morning students were given a prompt that would guide them through the day, forcing them to explore the city and speak with tourists and locals. Afternoons were spent in discussion again, reflecting on the relationships between communities in rural Guatemala and this tourism hub, their unique challenges and creative ways to spread the benefits of tourism.

The third segment of the trip included two trips to famous Guatemalan tourist sites. The first was Lago de Atitlan and the second was the great Mayan ruins of Tikal. Both locations have important historical and cultural significance and both locations suffer from environmental degradation as a consequence of tourism development, making them perfect field sites to again apply important sustainability concepts to issues of development. In these locations students stayed at eco-lodges where available. The objective was to focus on the trade-offs of increased economic gains from tourism in environmentally sensitive areas and the ways local community members are attempting to minimize any negative trade-offs. This program ran successfully for the first time in June 2012 with an amended and shortened program running in March 2014. It is hoped that a version of this trip will run each year.

In program evaluations students indicated their cross-cultural understanding was improved as a result of participation in the Guatemala program. For example, when participants were asked what they would say to other students considering participating in the program, one participant stated 'A trip abroad causes you to reconsider parts of your life that you had taken for granted and gives you perspective on aspects of life and culture even outside of the specific subject you are studying.' Additionally, one participant in the June 2012 program took part in a photo elicitation interview about her experiences in Guatemala. For the study she submitted a photo from a local market in San Martín Jilotepeque. Even though her time in Guatemala was short, she had started to feel a part of the communities she was visiting. She stated, 'It was just cool that I could be a part of that community because this wasn't a typical tourist destination so looking back at it, it's just cool to think that I was involved in their daily activity'. This theme of identifying with the host culture came up frequently as part of the overall study and relates to the development of intercultural competency. Openness to others, adaptability and flexibility are traits which contribute to an individual's capacity to succeed in cross-cultural situations (Deardorff, 2006; Fantini, 2000; Hannigan, 1990; Kitsantas and Meyers, 2002). This participant also talked about communicating with locals while in Guatemala. While she spoke 'zero Spanish', she was able to form good relationships with children she worked with when they were planting a garden with a community and in other projects.

4.   FUTURE DIRECTION AND CONCLUSIONS

While it seems clear that study abroad programs result in benefits for students via the development of an improved understanding of other cultures, there is still much to be learned about the effectiveness of these kinds of programs and how that effectiveness can be enhanced. Assuming the goal is to internationalize the curriculum, it is important that study abroad programs are evaluated with this goal in mind. Because research has been mixed with respect to the effectiveness of study abroad programs as a vehicle for curricular internationalization, a systematic and comprehensive effort to investigate the characteristics of international study programs that relate to student development of intercultural competence and other outcomes is desirable.

One way to develop programs that meet internationalization outcomes is to consider the theoretical frameworks and other research-based findings that can guide program development. Often, theory is used to guide research, but it can also be helpful when designing curricula. Using either the theoretical frameworks discussed in this chapter, or others that have been useful with other studies, curricula can be developed to optimize intercultural competence and other objectives of international programs. The theory can then be used to guide program assessment.

Experiential education holds promise for furthering the ability of programs to have a lasting impact on students. There are several class designs of study abroad programs. The 'old' design has been one where a faculty-led program is simply one or more classes taught in another country with minimal use of the country's resources and people to augment the curriculum. It is becoming increasingly common, however, to use the country as a living laboratory, making the most of the location to enrich the program. In addition, more programs are incorporating internships, service learning and/or community service projects into the curriculum. Further investigation is needed to determine the extent to which these kinds of experiences enhance the outcomes a student receives from their experience abroad.

There are still questions as to the most effective types and characteristics of programs. For example, program length and format, the extent of student–host cross-cultural interaction and ways to optimize this, community engagement activities, and other programmatic features require further investigation. However, as described in this chapter, there are a number of aspects of the structure of an international study program that clearly result in better and more impactful effects on students. Another area not yet fully understood is the importance future employers place on the outcomes achieved via international study. While intuitively it seems that in tourism such experiences would be valued, this has not been documented in a systematic way.

A continuing challenge as educators strive to internationalize university curricula is, fundamentally, how is 'internationalization' defined? What is meant by 'internationalization' and what strategies should be used to achieve this? What experiences can be provided to students that are truly transformational in nature? While the focus of this chapter has been study abroad programs, this is not an option that is available to all students due to financial, time or other constraints. While questions remain, the weight of the evidence suggests that study abroad programs do result in increased levels of cross-cultural understanding and intercultural competence, important outcomes as we strive to facilitate development of global citizens.

REFERENCES

Allport, G.W. (1954), *The Nature of Prejudice*, Cambridge, MA: Addison-Wesley Publishing Company.

Altbach, P.G. and Knight, J. (2007), 'The internationalization of higher education: Motivations and realities', *Journal of Studies in International Education*, **11** (3–4), 290–305.

Association for Experiential Education (n.d.), 'What is experiential education?', accessed 10 September 2014 at http://www.aee.org/what-is-ee.

Ayoun, B., Johnson, M.K., Vanhyfte, M. and O'Neill, M. (2010), 'A comparison study of US and non-US education internationalization practices of hospitality and tourism programs', *Journal of Teaching in Travel & Tourism*, **10** (4), 335–61.

Blair, S. (2011), 'Study abroad and the city: Mapping urban identity', *Frontiers: The Interdisciplinary Journal of Study Abroad*, **20**, 37–54.

Brookes, M. and Becket, N. (2011), 'Internationalising hospitality management degree programmes', *International Journal of Contemporary Hospitality Management*, **23** (2), 241–60.

Brustein, W.I. (2007), 'The global campus: Challenges and opportunities for higher education in North America', *Journal of Studies in International Education*, **11** (3–4), 382–91.

Carlson, J.S. and Widaman, K.F. (1988), 'The effects of study abroad during college on attitudes toward other cultures', *International Journal of Intercultural Relations*, **12** (1), 1–17.

Center for Global Education (2015), 'SAFETI Program Audit Checklist', accessed 19 March 2015 at http://globaled.us/safeti/program_audit_checklist.asp.

Chambers, E. (2005), 'Can the anthropology of tourism make us better travelers?, *NAPA Bulletin*, **23** (1), 27–44.

Coelho, G.V. (1962), 'Personal growth and educational development through working and studying abroad', *Journal of Social Issues*, **18** (1), 55–67.

Deardorff, D.K. (2006), 'Identification and assessment of intercultural competence as a student outcome of internationalization', *Journal of Studies in International Education*, **10** (3), 241–66.

Deardorff, D.K. and Hunter, W. (2006), 'Educating global-ready graduates', *International Educator*, **15** (3), 72–83.

Dewey, J. (2007), *Experience and Education*, New York: Simon and Schuster.

Domask, J.J. (2007), 'Achieving goals in higher education: An experiential approach to sustainability studies', *International Journal of Sustainability in Higher Education*, **8** (1), 53–68.

Douglas, C. and Jones-Rikkers, C.G. (2001), 'Study abroad programs and American student worldmindedness: An empirical analysis', *Journal of Teaching in International Business*, **13** (1), 55–66.

Engle, L. and Engle, J. (2003), 'Study abroad levels: Toward a classification of program types', *Frontiers: The Interdisciplinary Journal of Study Abroad*, **9** (1), 1–20.

Fantini, A. (2000), '*A central concern: Developing intercultural competence*', *SIT Occasional Papers Series*, inaugural issue, 'Notes about our institution', Brattleboro, VT: World Learning.

Forum on Education Abroad (n.d.), 'Education Abroad program features and types', accessed 10 September 2014 at http://www.forumea.org/EducationAbroadProgramFeaturesandTypes.cfm#StudyAbroadProgramTypes.

Hannigan, T.P. (1990), 'Traits, attitudes, and skills that are related to intercultural effectiveness and their implications for cross-cultural training: A review of the literature', *International Journal of Intercultural Relations*, **14** (1), 89–111.

Henthorne, T.L., Miller, M.M. and Hudson, T.W. (2001), 'Building and positioning successful study-abroad programs: A "hands-on" approach', *Journal of Teaching in International Business*, **12** (4), 49–62.

Hobson, J, and Josiam, B.M. (1996), 'An integrated approach to internationalizing the hospitality and tourism curriculum in the USA', *Journal of Transnational Management Development*, **2** (1), 13–34.

Institute of International Education (2014), 'Open Doors Data', accessed 10 September 2014 at http://www.iie.org/Research-and-Publications/Open-Doors/Data.

Itin, C.M. (1999), 'Reasserting the philosophy of experiential education as a vehicle for change in the 21st century', *Journal of Experiential Education*, **22** (2), 91–8.

Katula, R.A. and Threnhauser, E. (1999), 'Experiential education in the undergraduate curriculum', *Communication Education*, **48** (3), 238–55.

Kitsantas, A. (2004), 'Studying abroad: The role of college students' goals on the development of cross-cultural skills and global understanding', *College Student Journal*, **38** (3), 441–52.

Kitsantas, A. and Meyers, J. (2002), *Studying Abroad: Does it Enhance College Students' Cross-cultural Awareness?'*, ERIC Report No. ED 456 648, Educational Resources Information Center.

Knight, J. (2004), 'Internationalization remodeled: Definition, approaches, and rationales', *Journal of Studies in International Education*, **8** (1), 5–31.

Koschate, M. and Van Dick, R. (2011), 'A multilevel test of Allport's contact conditions', *Group Processes & Intergroup Relations*, **14** (6), 769–87.

Kuh, G.K. and Kauffman, N.F. (1984), *The Impact of Study Abroad on Personal Development of College Students*, ED 245 591, Bloomington, IN: Indiana University School of Education.

Lincoln Commission (2005), 'Global competence and national needs: One million Americans studying abroad', *Final Report from the Commission on the Abraham Lincoln Fellowship Program*, Washington, DC.

MacCannell, D. (1973), 'Staged authenticity: Arrangements of social space in tourist settings', *American Journal of Sociology*, **79** (3), 589–603.

McCabe, L.T. (1994), 'The development of a global perspective during participation in semester at sea: A comparative global education program', *Educational Review*, **46** (3), 275.

McCabe, L.T. (2001), 'Globalization and internationalization: The impact on education abroad programs', *Journal of Studies in International Education*, **5** (2), 138–45.

National Society for Experiential Education (n.d.), 'Eight principles of good practice for all experiential learning activities', accessed 14 September 2014 at http://www.nsee.org/8-principles.

Pettigrew, T.F. and Tropp, L.R. (2008), 'How does intergroup contact reduce prejudice? Meta-analytic tests of three mediators', *European Journal of Social Psychology*, **38** (6), 922–34.

Praetzel, G.D., Curcio, J. and Dilorenzo, J. (1996), 'Making study abroad a reality for all students', *International Advances in Economic Research*, **2** (2), 174–82.

Ring, A., Dickinger, A. and Wöber, K. (2009), 'Designing the ideal undergraduate program in tourism: Expectations from industry and educators', *Journal of Travel Research*, **48**, 106–21.

Sangpikul, A. (2009), 'Internationalization of hospitality and tourism higher education: A perspective from Thailand', *Journal of Teaching in Travel & Tourism*, **9** (1–2), 2–20.

Share Tours (2014a), 'Strategic Areas – Share Tours', accessed 5 March 2015 at http://www.shareguatemala.org/index.php?option=com_content&view=article&id=77&Itemid=122&lang=en.

Share Tours (2014b), 'Who we are', accessed 5 March 2015 at http://www.shareguatemala.org.

Sindt, P. and Pachmayer, A. (2006), 'Identifying the outcomes of short term study abroad', *IIE Networker Online Journal*.

Smith, G. and Cooper, C. (2000), 'Competitive approaches to tourism and hospitality curriculum design', *Journal of Travel Research*, **39** (1), 90–95.

Soria, K.M. and Troisi, J. (2013), 'Internationalization at home alternatives to study abroad: Implications for students' development of global, international, and intercultural competencies', *Journal of Studies in International Education*, **8** (3), 261–80.

Tribe, J. (2002), 'The philosophic practitioner', *Annals of Tourism Research*, **29** (2), 338–57.

Vance, C.M., Sibeck, G., McNulty, Y. and Hogenauer, A. (2011), 'Building global competencies through experiential coursework in international travel and tourism', *Journal of International Education in Business*, **4** (1), 30–41.

Warren, K. (1995), *The Theory of Experiential Education: A Collection of Articles Addressing the Historical, Philosophical, Social, and Psychological Foundations of Experiential Education*, Dubuque, IA: Kendall/Hunt Publishing.

Wattanacharoensil, W. (2013), 'Tourism curriculum in a global perspective: Past, present, and future', *International Education Studies*, **7** (1), 9–20.

What's up with Culture? (2014), accessed 14 September 2014 at http://www2.pacific.edu/sis/culture/.

Williams, K.M. and Best, G. (2014), 'Short study tours abroad: Internationalizing business curricula', *Journal of Teaching in Travel & Tourism*, **14** (3), 240–59.

UNWTO (2010), 'Tourism and the Millennium Development Goals', accessed 10 September 2014 at http://www.unwto.org/tourism&mdgsezine/.

24 Building high-impact mobility programs for increased student internationalization

Catherine Vertesi

1. INTERNATIONALIZING TOURISM STUDENTS THROUGH HIGH-IMPACT MOBILITY PROGRAMS

Over the last 25–30 years the commitment to graduate students who are more globally aware, cross-culturally competent, multilingual and internationally networked has reached across universities and colleges, disciplines and continents. Student exchange and short-term visit programs have proliferated, as evidenced by the extraordinary growth in attendance at NAFSA: Association of International Educators, the EAIE (European Association for International Education) and other annual international conferences where the leading reason to attend is 'networking' and 'meeting with partners' (NAFSA, 2012). According to Open Doors 2013 (Institute of International Education, 2013), the number of students studying abroad from the USA continues to grow as do the numbers reported by *Erasmus Facts, Figures and Trends* (European Commission, 2014).

As post-secondary educators we hope that our education has provided all our graduates with a transformative and broadening experience, one that in addition to their discipline studies has prepared them to operate with greater knowledge, sophistication and sensitivity as citizens and professionals in an increasingly globalized world. International mobility programs are one of the mechanisms supporting these outcomes. Through mobility programs students become 'the other', confront obstacles not faced in their domestic environment and are forced to cope with different paradigms and habits of daily living as a citizen rather than a hotel-dwelling tourist looking out from a window in a tour bus. These experiences can, with educational guidance, provoke insights to inform their personal ethos as well as future professional conduct (Van Hoof, 1999, 2000, 2001; Van Hoof and Verbeeten, 2005).

In most institutions participation in an international experience is not universal; nevertheless, those who stay home can still benefit greatly from mobility programs offered in their departments without ever traveling themselves. In fact, at a time of diminishing resources, mobility programs should always be designed to serve students beyond the traveling few. Classmates who have travelled abroad for study, when encouraged, can play an important role in internationalizing the local classroom, thus offering the benefits of their insights more broadly.

Mobility programs in tourism education are more complex than those for most other students. While we expect study abroad to precipitate similar personal changes, tourism students must observe and later master the mechanisms involved in their transformation so that they may become skilled at not only reacting appropriately in a multicultural environment but at designing and providing excellent experiences that may elicit some of the same responses in their clients and guests. Tourism graduates spend their professional lives in the company of other cultures, languages, experiences and behaviors and must plan for and enter into these interactions with dexterity.

Although the focus in the past decade has been on increasing the numbers of students leaving their home university for an international study experience, newer research has shown that merely going abroad is not enough to transform participants into global citizens (Vande Berg et al., 2012). It is increasingly clear that in planning exchange and other study abroad opportunities for students, the teaching, the orientation activities and the mentoring surrounding the travel are key to maximizing the impact of the foreign immersion and achieving the global citizen goals we wish for them (Brewer and Cunningham, 2009). This chapter will focus on the practical aspects of developing a portfolio of offerings, the selection of partners and participants, the cultural orientation, itinerary development, values examination and reflection, and reintegration. Initially the focus will be on affecting the transformation of the individual student. Later in the chapter we will revisit the need for returning students to assist in meeting the internationalization needs of the department. Educators need to assist students to deconstruct aspects of their international experience to better inform the experiences they will engage in for themselves and to contribute to the internationalization of those who stay home.

2.   ORGANIZATIONAL STRUCTURES

Most universities and colleges have some established partnerships and centralized services (Van de Water, 2002). It is critical, however, that some program/faculty level control be established. As in all of the educational programming we do, it is necessary to define the set of outcomes for the educational experience and these should be specific to the tourism department. Institutional commitment to internationalization as reflected in mission statements, yearly goals and the investment in central services are all very important but they cannot take the place of the department's commitment to internationalization goals and strategy specific to the explicit learning outcomes the tourism faculty desire for their students. Whenever possible the majority of services like orientation, visas and accommodation can be performed by the professional staff of an international office but the selection of partners, length of stay away, location of short-term programs, selection of student participants, pre-departure context preparation, academic performance tracking, course selection and credit transfer must be controlled by a well informed academic department.

Beyond providing some individual students with a life-changing experience, the needs of the entire tourism student body for an internationalized educational experience must be central to the procedures established for exchange program management. The identification of institutional partners, selection criteria for student participants, integration programs for visiting students and the expectations placed on returning students should all reflect the internationalization goals for the department. For example, a goal of academic travel for the *majority* of students in a department affects not only the number and variety of opportunities being developed but the selection criteria and academic record required from the participants.

Beyond the outcomes related to intercultural competencies, increased global awareness and language skills, tourism partnerships can also present industry-specific learning enrichment. The student from a winter destination may benefit significantly from a partnership in Florida or Australia, a New World adventure tourism school from an Old World cultural opportunity, a Westerner from an Eastern experience.

There is an additional benefit to the development of semester exchange programs: the introduction to your classrooms of students from foreign cultures who would not normally attend your institution. Universities of renown may attract students from everywhere but smaller, less well-known programs have much greater difficulty in attracting students from other jurisdictions. In addition, schools that have tuition fees are challenged to attract those from locations that are tuition free. Deliberately seeking exchange partners whose students will add a new cultural dimension to the home classroom benefits all students, and can provide a needed stimulus for long-term faculty members. One professor in the business school at my university reported his delight in adding European students to his Canadian classroom. I assumed he was speaking about the students themselves. He said, 'Oh yes, yes. They are very nice – but it's their presentations. When I ask Canadians to report on innovative companies they all pick the same ones. It is so refreshing to learn about Nokia, or what Mercedes is doing to stay competitive or some company in Denmark with amazing recycling!' The incoming students offer different perspectives in classroom discussion as well, thus enriching the international content in the home institution. Although these incoming students require some special services and support, the resulting curricular enrichment is worth the investment.

3.   A PORTFOLIO APPROACH TO MOBILITY OFFERINGS

Currently full semester or year-long exchange students make up only a modest proportion of the student body. According to Open Doors in 2013, less than 10 percent of US students have either a long-term or short-term international experience for credit. In Canada the numbers for full semester academic exchange are around 4 percent (CBIE, 2012). In Germany the numbers are as high as 33 percent (CBIE, 2012) but even with this excellent record a full two-thirds of the students in Germany are not leaving home for study even though geography and distance are not significant barriers.

There are also other shifts in the student populations in OECD countries. More than a quarter of the students choose to study part-time and almost a third continue to participate in the labor force while studying. In the United States the number rises to 42 percent of full-time students and 72 percent of part-time students are employed, with a surprising 25 percent of full-time students working more than 25 hours per week (IES, 2014). In addition, we can no longer assume that students begin an undergraduate program directly upon completing their secondary education. Therefore, a considerable proportion of our students cannot leave for three months or more due to ongoing employment, financial or family obligations, so other international study opportunities must be developed for them. For the purposes of this discussion short-term programming refers to credit-bearing study abroad activities lasting for one to eight weeks, thus meeting the constrained mobility needs of many of our students.

Short-term programming may also better fit learners in shorter programs, for example two year diplomas. Unless a joint or dual diploma is offered, faculty may be reluctant to give over a large proportion of a student's time to another institution. Even when the partner is a well-known school there is a reluctance to award a credential to a graduate who has spent too little time in the home institution.

Further, short-term programming can allow for visits to places where language and cultural challenges pose significant barriers or there is no parallel institution with duly respected credit for transfer in the location. There may be great value in these regional visits, especially for tourism students who may have an interest in travel into areas with few amenities, community development through tourism or those involved in service learning projects.

Short programs are also less expensive, require less commitment from risk-averse students, may be more supported by the families of students who are reluctant to allow their son or daughter to travel, allow departments to take advantage of 'one time' events in a target country, can provide an opportunity for faculty leaders to explore the desirability of committing to a deeper relationship with the region or institution, and can serve as a confidence builder for students who are eligible for a full semester program later in their studies (Mullens and Cuper, 2012).

However, because the contact with the host culture is time-limited, even greater care in preparation and reflection is necessary for transformative learning to take place (Mullens and Cuper, 2012). Many aspects of short-term and full-term programming are identical but the specialized approaches needed in each case will be examined separately.

4.   STUDENT EXCHANGE PROGRAMS

Exchange programs are those arrangements where students spend a semester abroad at a partner institution and the home institution in turn receives students from these partners in equal numbers. Generally, tuition and international fees are waived and numbers are monitored to ensure reciprocity. In the main, students are integrated into the regular programming of the host institution although there are some institutions where, primarily because of language constraints, some of their classes are segregated.

Besides student exchange there are so-called 'island programs' that are also a semester or one year in length. These are programs that are situated away from the student's own country but the attendees are usually fellow citizens rather than those from the host country. This avoids language, academic culture and structural differences, while allowing students to gain an international exposure. These island programs are common offerings for American students and often include being taught by their own faculty members in a foreign environment. Short-term study abroad programs are also generally 'island' programs with students either traveling around or staying in one particular place with their class-mates or country-mates. The degree of attitude change and intercultural knowledge gained from these programs is mixed and seem to be connected to the degree of engagement with the host culture (Paige and Vande Berg, 2012).

4.1   Departmental Decisions

There are several decisions that should be made at the departmental level of the home institution:

- How many students should be involved in full semesters abroad?
- Will the home institution limit the number of students coming from a partner institution?
- In which semester(s) should student exchanges take place?
- What is the 'wish list' of countries and institutions with which the home institution would like to exchange?

An inventory is necessary of what the home institution offers and what makes it a desirable study destination (remember exchange is a two-way proposition) and a realistic attempt to identify peer institutions. The home institution should carefully articulate its teaching philosophy, its relationship with the local tourism industry, research commitments and interests and then begin to look for good matches. You may be from an institution with a myriad of agreements meeting many needs from your campus. However, as a department you want to activate linkages where there are good tourism learning opportunities for your students, you are comfortable in granting transfer credit, are attractive enough to make student recruitment relatively straightforward and where deeper relations may be a possibility.

Always consult with student administration and finance personnel before proceeding. In US universities this often involves the registrar but in other countries consultation with a wide range of institutional stakeholders, including academic advisors or international/study abroad/exchange offices may be required. There may be established policies and procedure, but if not, you want to work with them to establish processes that work for the institution as well as the department and students.

4.2 Establishing Partnerships for Student Exchange

After establishing a list of countries/regions/institutions, the first place to look for exchange partners is from the established partnership list within your institution. These will already have jumped the hurdles of credibility, credit transfer and paperwork that arise in every new institutional partnership. You will have information from the student services staff as to the support provided there for incoming and outgoing students and other details, such as cost of living, library facilities, housing and so on.

The annual meetings of international education professionals like NAFSA: Association of International Educators, European Association for International Education (EAIE), Asia Pacific Association for International Education (APAIE), Canadian Bureau for International Education (CBIE), International Education Association of Australia (IEAA) and others are excellent places to find partners for student exchange. The first two are very large conferences and provide sessions and meeting space to facilitate the 'one-stop' chance to meet with existing partners and find additional ones. For existing partnerships, they allow for face-to-face discussion and updating in a cost-effective way. Even the smaller conferences listed here and others provide opportunities to locate potential partners, initiate discussions and plan for further information exchange that may lead to a formal agreement.

In assessing the suitability of a potential partner there are several attributes that should be considered in addition to academic match. Appendix 24A.1 provides a checklist for mobility that is a helpful prompt in setting up an exchange program. The first questions are linked to your own department's realistic assessment of what you offer a partner. They include:

- What type of institution is it and what programs do they offer?
- Are there parallel credentials awarded?
- Are their semester dates compatible?
- Is their location desirable to students?
- Is there potential for additional work together (for example research, short programs, executive training)?
- How does this institution fit into your overall portfolio of offerings?
- Are there other partners you can contact about their experiences?

Most of the subtle differences between institutions will not create barriers, but if discussed and understood before initiating the agreement a multitude of misunderstandings and annoyances will be avoided and time saved. Details surrounding credit transfer, language levels, workload, evaluation methodologies, admission and registration procedures, deadline dates, transcript exchange, privacy waivers, fees, insurance needs and so on require clarification and agreement. For example, in the case of privacy waivers, many countries have strict privacy laws that require that the student give permission for anyone other than themselves to receive their grades. Therefore, release forms must be signed by all exchange participants in order that you receive their grades for tracking and other academic management purposes. If possible identify some links in your community that you can count on, for example, friendship and immigrant clubs, religious facilities, potential employers and so on. These contacts can assist the incoming students and take some of the pressure off you and your staff. Centralized international services know the answers to many of the issues and can assist in preparing the exchange contract. Most institutions have a standardized format.

Selecting partners that are a match and where you have exercised due diligence should permit you to worry only minimally about course-by-course transfer. If your partner is a reputable institution, then you must assume your colleagues abroad must have something useful to teach your students. Do not be concerned if courses are not identical. My rule of thumb is if two-thirds of the course is the same as my home course I give the student transfer credit and do not allow him/her to repeat the course at home when only a third of the material will be new.

4.3   Motivations for Study Abroad: Faculty vs. Student Drivers

Faculty and students share goals for an international experience but there are significant differences. Understanding the salient factors for your target audience (for example, the student) helps determine not only where they go but all the other tactics you will employ that will lead them to the adoption of this 'product'. There is very little research into faculty motivation for developing international programs for their students. However, experience and a perusal of websites from around the world emphasize cultural and curricular benefits, geo-political knowledge acquisition, linguistic benefits and some exposure to academic knowledge not available at home. It is also clear that faculty assume these programs will be an adventure and a maturing experience for their students and contribute to their general education. Both students and faculty value the opportunity to learn first-hand about another location and to do it without losing credit or time to completion. Faculty members also anticipate future professional and societal returns from those graduates who are more multiculturally literate.

Students, on the other hand, tend to be more focused on their discipline and choose programs abroad based on their majors rather than their general education needs. When asked, they rate future prospects and career needs highly (Van Hoof and Verbeeten, 2005). Further exploration reveals the appeal of adventure, relief of boredom, a change in their social environment and some notions of personal development. North American students are often seeking their cultural roots and those who live with their families use study abroad as a socially acceptable way to leave home (Nyaupane et al., 2011; Jarvis and Peel, 2008).

In my view, these are partial answers. Cubillo et al. (2006) described a process used by students from a variety of disciplines when choosing an international destination that was affected by five factors that included the effects of country image and of city image. In other research this is referred to as a 'pull' factor. Generally, it is these two location images that form the strongest first attraction for exploring study abroad options. They are not evident in most of the literature because the interactional frame of questionnaires led students to play the role of 'keen student' and give what their researchers would consider socially acceptable answers. No student will tell an interviewer that they want to go to Paris because it is 'so cool'. And yet, high profile or 'cool' places will catch their attention and encourage them to consider the study abroad possibility. In my career, dozens of students have entered my office with the notion they are going to Paris or New York and have subsequently attended an institution in Helsinki or Atlanta more suited to their academic goals, interests and temperament, but the glamour of Paris brings them into the office to enquire in the first place. It is therefore important to ensure that your list of exchange opportunities includes a couple of highly desirable 'bling-like' locations. A variety of price points are also important. Outside of the major cities there are some excellent lower cost alternatives that give options to less affluent students.

Of course none of these motives matter if an international experience is a required element in the program. Then the choice is where to go and for how long, not whether to go at all. But if your student's international experience is optional, then understanding how their motives as individuals are different from yours as an educator helps you to design information sessions and materials that are an inducement to participate.

5. SHORT-TERM PROGRAMMING (1–8 WEEKS)

Generally, to build high rates of international study experiences in a student population it is necessary to add short-term programming to capture those students with barriers to full semester participation. Short programs allow a different group of students to gain an international experience and can yield significant gains in global-mindedness, despite a more limited exposure (Mullens and Cuper, 2012). There are obvious financial benefits to traveling for a shorter time period, thus increasing access to less affluent students. But perhaps most important is the opportunity for a faculty-led experience, integrated into the home tourism curriculum goals such as visits to less developed regions, visits to areas without institutions focused on tourism studies, visits that take advantage of some faculty member's connections or expertise or travel to a series of sites connected by a course of study designed by the department.

Research on the impacts of mobility programs tends to focus on outcomes such as global mindedness, cultural curiosity, interest in an international career, stress management and self-confidence. Using instruments like Bennett and Hammer's Intercultural Development Inventory (Bennett and Hammer, 2002), the Intercultural Sensitivity Scale (Chen and Starosta, 2000) and an older test called the Cross-Cultural Adaptability Inventory (CCAI) (Kelley and Myers, 1995), researchers, mainly in the USA, have attempted to judge the impact of study abroad on the measured transformation of student attitudes relative to their stay-at-home peers as well as the length of study. Most report significant changes in the traveling student group relative to those who remained at home. However, many researchers report positive gains in intercultural competence even in short programs provided the experience was accompanied by significant preparation, mentoring and reflection (Mullens and Cuper, 2012).

5.1   Faculty Decisions

What kind of programs and how many would you like to have? Again, starting with the learning outcomes desired for the various credentials and interests offered in your department coupled with available faculty expertise, departments can examine ideas for what should be on offer. It is advisable to develop a standardized proposal process, format and time line in order to deal fairly should you receive competing suggestions. The offerings should be used to broaden the learning opportunities for students. The range of short-term offerings and approaches used by institutions is wide. In some institutions short-term programs are required of all students, so everyone travels in the same period to a variety of locations and classes are suspended to accommodate travel for all. In others, offerings are spread across the school year and are of differing lengths and credit value, thus offering several price points and a choice of travel times. In some, the students travel from place to place while others establish a single residence point and develop site visits from there. Service learning opportunities are frequently built into short-term courses in a single location. Remember the diverse travel backgrounds of your students as well. There are those intrepid ones who will go to the deepest jungle with delight and still others who will come only because a favorite teacher is leading them. Both will benefit but the greater impact is with the latter group. Departments need 'safe' choices for less intrepid students.

Some basic planning principles apply regardless of the detail of your program. These are generally developed through the administrative framework in your institution but should be clarified.

1. *Financing:* Are there fees associated with the program? Generally, the participants cover their own costs and the costs associated with the institution's employees accompanying them. Most commonly, faculty salaries come from the departmental budget and form part of the departmental offerings. In some places there is a servicing charge from the central administration to cover administrative costs of the program. This may also need to be passed on to the students. Payment timetables, including deposits and policies on withdrawals and refunds must be defined.
2. *Budgeting:* There are some excellent detailed budget planning tools available including NAFSA's Abroad by Design CD, which includes excellent templates for the novice budget builder. Still, in developing your budget there are several issues

that need to be considered. Are you including transportation costs to and from the destination? With the proliferation of airline points systems, it may be advisable to separate the airfare from the rest of the costs. Are meals included? If so, how many? Are you expected to generate a surplus? Break even? Cover overheads? And after including the costs as indicated above, how many students do you need to break even? Is the number reasonable? In my experience in leading many graduate and undergraduate groups, two employees are required to support about 25 participants. Add staff if your numbers are higher – about one for every 15 additional students. When the group gets too large, even counting heads becomes a challenge.

3. *Building sufficient participant numbers:* Although you are building programs for the tourism students in your department there may be others who would benefit from the program you are offering. Consider which other students from your institution would gain from attending. As a small institution you might look for a partner among other small programs in your country or region and offer a joint program drawing on both student populations.

4. *Risk mitigation:* Many guidelines are needed to mitigate risk in traveling with your students and to protect faculty and the institution. For example, there should be two employees on all trips and one must have formal first aid training. Student attendance at an orientation program designed for the trip should be mandatory. A designated chain of command in the home institution must be established, with one individual available 24/7 in case of emergency. Detailed contact information for next of kin, passport copies and health records should be kept by the key emergency contact at home as well as carried by the group leader. A cellphone should be provided for the group leader and a regular 'reporting in' protocol should be established before departure. Political unrest, natural disasters and dangerous criminal activity can all be reasons for canceling programs. In my institution we use the government travel advisories to monitor our actions (for example, http://travel.gc.ca/; http://www.smart raveller.gov.au/). When riots erupted in Thailand we were able to move a planned trip to a safer location in the region but we canceled a planned trip to Northern Mexico when, due to the high level of criminal activity, the Canadian government issued a travel warning. In general, when programs are canceled for this reason full refunds are provided. Be sure to build this provision into your airline arrangements and warn those buying their own tickets to do so too.

   Faculty members who lead groups require training and orientation as well. It may be a reflection of my North American experience but I advise keeping a written record of the training received. If a serious incident with a student occurred while traveling, your institution may be asked to show your emergency guidelines as well as evidence of the leader's preparedness for shouldering the responsibility.

5. *Faculty commitment:* Leading a study program is both exhilarating and exhausting. On the plus side, you have the chance to share what excites you about where you are, inspire curiosity and enthusiasm in your students and participate with them in what is reported by them as one of the highest-impact learning experiences in their educational career (NSSE, 2013). But faculty leaders need to be aware that it is a 24/7 kind of commitment when abroad. Students break bones, have their wallets stolen, get food poisoning from eating street food, break up with their girl/boyfriend and come

to you for help, often in tears and frightened. One is not expected to be a 'parent' to the participants but if a problem arises, the leader must take charge.

6. *Itinerary planning:* Once locations have been established and the academic goals clarified, the itinerary is planned. The length of the program may be determined by term times at home as well as travel time to the location. For example, in traveling to Vietnam from Europe or the Americas, travel days must be added to either end of the educational itinerary you have in mind. It is also wise to remember that the longer one is away, the more expensive the trip will be. If students are self-financing this may limit your recruits to the program.

    Included in the visits should be activities not available to the individual. For example, a 'behind the scenes' visit to a museum or factory, a meeting with a leading political figure or an opportunity to speak with your government representatives in the region. Plan with any local holidays in mind. Sometimes there are activities you can join in with. Sometimes a local holiday means that there is no one available to meet with you or travel schedules are different on that particular day.

    Always try to find some way for your students to meet peers. Every post-return evaluation has identified meeting peers as the highlight of the experience. Vande Berg, Paige and Lou, in their co-edited book, *Student Learning Abroad: What our Students are Learning, What They're Not, and What We Can Do About it* (2012), emphasize that for deeper learning to take place one must 'Engage with the culture being visited'. Most universities have clubs or language classes that can give students a chance to meet face to face. If you are from a smaller country with a less universal language such as Danish or Thai, then this is more challenging. If you cannot find a common language, then use interpreters. Otherwise, ask your embassy officials or target country Chambers of Commerce for suggestions and contacts. However, deeper interaction does not happen by chance. If left alone, the students will revert to the universal language of American movies and MTV. Therefore, structure the interactions with assigned questions. First interactions can trade information on social customs: how people get married, celebrate birthdays, welcome new babies and recognize death. The discussions can move to the education system: how old are you starting school, what are class hours and holidays, how do you choose a post-secondary school and who gets to go? Finally, how do you get a job after graduation, what happens if you are laid off, injured, get sick, become disabled? These discussions expose societal differences and lay a foundation for later dialogue with your students on what the cultural practices they learned about reveal about underlying values. Coupled with their pre-departure preparation on culture, these interactions help students unpack their own assumptions and begin to see themselves relative to others, an important starting point for becoming a global citizen.

7. *Enrichment:* Remember to take advantage of the full range of learning opportunities available in the locations you visit. Too often itineraries focus entirely on activities related to the academic course being studied. For example, you may be taking your students to a destination like Las Vegas and examining their branding, positioning and pricing strategies. Take the opportunity to visit one of the canyon parks nearby to learn about the geological history of the North American continent. One of my colleagues, in leading a group to London as part of a course on hosting major international events like the Olympic Games, built in a visit to the National Gallery, the

Royal Observatory at Greenwich and a football match. Take every opportunity to stimulate the curiosity and broaden the perspectives of your participants. Build in time for discussions and reflection within the group. Add themed discussion at meal-times, while waiting for your bus, in the evening. Consider that everyone needs alone time too. Being with 20 others all of the time is daunting even for the most gregarious of attendees.

6.   STUDENT SELECTION

6.1   Attracting Participants

Student recruitment, when carried on through an academic department/faculty will connect the student to study abroad as an educational endeavor, not a vacation. Central offices recruit focused on the fun and adventure of the destination. Departmental members focus on what the student will gain academically and professionally.

For those of us who embrace travel it is sometimes difficult to understand why our students would not jump at the chance that exchange and study abroad offers them. While a higher proportion of tourism students are ready to travel, there are still those who are reluctant, especially to strike out on their own as would be required for an exchange program. The intrepid students will always show up; it is the ones who need encouragement that we should focus on.

Endorsement by a faculty member and the department is the most powerful tool in recruiting students to international programs (BaileyShea, 2010). Therefore, use faculty members to make announcements regarding information sessions in class time. Try to hold information sessions in the same places the students have classes and encourage faculty supporters to refer to the programs when they teach. Work with instructors to identify their best students and those who are active in class and invite them to apply. This encouragement by a professor is evidence that study abroad is a valued endeavor and may be all that is needed to convince a student to apply.

BaileyShea (2010) also identified other key factors: worry over credit transfer, finances and the perspective of friends and family. So in promoting the opportunities, be sure to identify the credit that students will receive and that in exchange programs, students continue to pay their fees at home at whatever rate they currently pay. Opportunities for financial aid should also be indicated. Use photos and social media tools featuring current students from your program. Prospective participants should recognize themselves in the images. Well-publicized blogs from current students who are abroad will also encourage the next year of applicants. In short programs assign each participant a day to blog about their activities and provide the address to parents. It is helpful to parents whose sons or daughters don't think to write home and saves worried phone calls to the international office staff. Also provide it to faculty and senior administrators to showcase the internationalization initiatives from your department.

BaileyShea (2010) added the opportunity to travel during college, learn about oneself and enhanced career opportunities as the last positive drivers in student decisions. These can also be reflected in visuals as well as in the information sessions. Be sure to hold many information sessions at different times of day but in the same location if possible.

Utilize returning students as spokespersons whenever possible as they are convincing to their peers and know what issues are salient for applicants as they make a decision to go abroad.

6.2   Selection Criteria

If your international program is a credential requirement, then the emphasis of your effort will be in student pre-departure orientation. However, for optional semester and short programs, student selection processes are important elements contributing to program success. As a department member your commitment is to a serious international study experience; you are not merely their tour guide. All selected students will not only represent your department, your institution and often your country but they will also have an important role in bringing a broader perspective into the classroom when they return. As such, all programs should have a formal application process. The actual application process itself will set the tone for the programs you offer and help to eliminate the 'party animal' or highly immature student from the selectees.

If you are just beginning student exchange programs, then there are two elements to consider in making selections: the impact that students can have on both your reputation in the partner institution and on their peers when they return home. For the first few years of an exchange partnership the reputation of your school is shaped by that school's experience with your students. Additionally, you need returning students who will not only share their insights but inspire their classmates to apply to go the following year.

The most obvious starting point is with a student's academic record. An above-average (B-level) academic record is a fairly standard minimum requirement in selecting full semester exchange students. Because my educational philosophy incorporates an international opportunity for as many students as possible I have used short-term faculty-led programming to include students with weaker academic records who cannot meet a higher standard. The requirement for a short-term program at my university is only 'average'. My rationale is that they will be led and fairly closely supervised by a faculty member from our home institution.

Students should submit a résumé and covering letter indicating where they wish to go and their rationale. The student should also provide faculty references. However, make this a very easy task for faculty by using a simple form (see Appendix 24A.2). Faculty can alert the selectors of exceptionally good students as well as those who are chronically underprepared or attend rarely. It is important to identify those who participate actively in class and in extracurricular activities as these gregarious students will inevitably have a higher impact on the non-traveling students and overall program internationalization.

I believe strongly that all outgoing students should be interviewed, usually by two people. This allows you to assess maturity levels and the seriousness with which the student is approaching the opportunity, and to answer questions. It is during this appointment that students can be directed to partners that they may be particularly well suited for. For short-term programs it is generally the faculty leader along with a staff member who interviews. Interviews should be standardized and include questions on financing, family support and course planning. Once your students are selected, begin creating opportunities for them to get together. It will reduce your drop-out rate considerably.

7. PRE-DEPARTURE ORIENTATION

'Some students learn effectively when enrolled in programs abroad that provide little or no support for their learning, but many don't. Many more succeed when they participate in programs that intervene strategically – throughout the program – in student learning and development' (Vande Berg, 2009). 'As institutions prepare to send even more students abroad, it is imperative that as much attention be paid to preparing them to learn from their study abroad experience as is paid to crafting the experience itself' (Anderson and Cunningham, 2009).

Pre-departure orientations are the beginning of the journey for all study abroad programs. Not only are they necessary for student safety and well-being, they are instrumental in moving the student towards the global mindedness and intercultural fluency we desire. General orientation and preparation can be carried out by a central office. The academic department needs to lead sessions offering specific contextual knowledge about the country to be visited as well as laying the ground work for reflection and critical thinking necessary to make the best use of what the international learning opportunity affords. The curricula of many tourism degrees and diplomas around the world include some coursework in intercultural studies so your students may have been exposed to some cultural assessment tools. Expertise in intercultural communication training may already reside in your department. If not, seek it externally. There are excellent intercultural training programs available from the various international professional organizations and consultants who can help.

In addition to these important self-awareness and observational skills, students are expecting to acquire country-specific knowledge: history, economy, climate, geography, culture, traditions and current issues. For exchange students, the department should provide materials and links for the partnership countries for self-study. Reporting out pre-departure is necessary to make sure that the student has completed this homework through essays, questionnaires or group sharing. Some programs ask the student to suggest some element of society in which they have an interest and require that they write a comparative analysis to the parallel element at home. Summative evaluations of these types of assignments can be shared by faculty and staff and require only a Satisfactory/ Unsatisfactory grade.

In short group programs the faculty member leading the group should organize an orientation that will provide the student with the context through which to experience and understand the target country. Background materials from a variety of sources should be made available. However, using guest speakers with direct in-country experience greatly enriches the pre-departure sessions and can stimulate enthusiasm and deeper curiosity in your students. For example, I live in a port city and as part of the itinerary on a China Study Tour our students were visiting the port of Tianjin. Most of my participants knew very little about ports so we arranged a local speaker and tour before leaving Vancouver. In Tianjin, the students were awestruck by the vastness of the facility because they had a tangible comparison with Canada. Many report that the visit was a turning point in their understanding of the enormous power of the Chinese economy.

There are a variety of approaches currently in use to prepare students for exchange and many sources with detailed descriptions of what should be included. Some schools have one or more credit courses offered before travel. Some have an online course running concurrently with the exchange experience. Most common are non-credit pre-departure orientations run by international office staff and ongoing assignments during the away time. Whatever method your department chooses, consider that more frequent interaction with you as a faculty member leads to greater academic and cultural learning (Brewer and Cunningham, 2009).

Orientation should not only give students an understanding of appropriate behavior in the country being visited but also clearly define acceptable behavior and consequences as a member of your university's group. Samples of various code of conduct forms are widely available. Define zero tolerance behaviors clearly in writing and orally and then follow through should they occur while abroad.

8.   WHILE ABROAD

Interaction while abroad is essential regardless of whether it is credit or non-credit bearing. The institution has an obligation to monitor the student's academic and psychological progress while away. I have used a structure with four email reports over a semester, the last of which is submitted within four weeks of returning home. Have the students report in shortly after arrival. Start with fairly superficial questions surrounding arrival activities, their host's orientation program, their impression of their courses and the physical plant of the institution and so on. At the end of the first month the questions move to observing cultural differences such as: What are some of the major differences you have noted between your home and the host city? Climate? Geography? Transportation? People? What communication difficulties have you experienced? Tell us about a local special occasion you have experienced – holiday, birthday, festival. Report on a visit to a local attraction: art gallery, museum, performance, hiking destination.

The third report becomes deeper and more personal, including personal definitions of democracy, justice, freedom, art, relaxation, spirituality and so on, asking for comparative observations. It also asks them to consider what they have learned about how members of their host community perceive their home society. Any key moments of insight are explored and they are asked what additional goals they have for learning in their final weeks away.

The final questionnaire is in the form of a report that is then made available to future students considering choosing their location. Questions move back to the less personal and are more information intensive. However, returnees now show insight, enthusiasm and sensitivity to the strengths as well as the challenges in the location and can provide a clear indication of the growth and maturity attained by each of them from the experience.

There are many methods of staying in touch. Dedicated blogs, Facebook and Dropbox locations, group Skype calls and emails reinforce that their home department has not forgotten them. However, at least some of the interaction should try to drive deeper thinking about what they are seeing and learning, some of which should be conducted on an individual basis.

8.1   Incoming Exchange Students

Your department needs to augment any incoming student orientation offered by your institution because we expect these visitors to contribute to the internationalization of all of your students. They need to learn about the local academic culture; in Canada it is one of meaningful deadlines, frequent assessments, group work and fairly casual interactions with faculty members. It is also helpful to identify courses that may suit the incoming student or ones they should avoid because of emphasis on local knowledge, such as national practices in taxation or law.

It has also been my practice to notify instructors of the exchange students in their classes with encouragement to seek out contributions from them during class discussions. A fairly straightforward database program can generate notifications automatically and manage this information even when large numbers of students are involved.

8.2   The Returning Student

Tourism students have some additional needs from their international study. They need to reflect at a more macro level: what was planned, what happened, how did I feel at different stages of the experience? What interventions would have helped? As tourism professionals they may be called upon to design experiences for others. Just as going abroad brings intercultural theories to life, the experiences also enliven coursework focusing on tourism product design and itinerary development. Post return, students can be asked to either design or correct itineraries to various locations around the world. With guidance they can discover principles that are useful for many different types of offerings and re-examine their own learning while away. This is also a useful post-return exercise as students have a very strong need to talk about their experience in some depth, reordering their learning and sorting through their changed values.

Although interaction with incoming exchange students and listening to their input during class discussions provides an excellent experience for the stay-at-home student, the best input comes from their classmates who return from abroad. The returnees intuitively know how to describe other countries and describe their practices relative to their home culture. The benefits of selecting students who are outgoing and good classroom contributors now become clear. These are the students who will speak up in discussions, presenting newly discovered insights to the class. In debriefing, these returnees should be encouraged to speak out. Your returning students can be instrumental in raising international perspectives in classroom when appropriate, initiate international activities on campus for the incoming students and raise overall participation rates in your programs. Returnees are your best promoters of future programs. Use them in information sessions, debates, and with the senior officials of your institution.

Is all this necessary? Won't returning students talk to their friends? Students report that their non-traveling friends are only interested in the social aspect of their travel – the beer, the girls, the guys, and so on. Therefore, the classroom and special sessions are essential in order to spread a more global perspective to the non-travelers. Planned re-entry activities where returnees can discuss their experiences are welcomed, mitigate the effects of reverse culture shock and reinforce the learning and attitude changes that they have experienced.

Most international education professionals will encourage you to find special ways to recognize the students who have elected to go abroad. For the majority of students, it is a step outside of their comfort zone and takes some courage to face the challenge. All students are excited but nervous when they leave their familiar classrooms and culture, yet virtually all would recommend the experience to everyone they know. Many travel a second time if the first is early in their program (Mullens and Cuper, 2012).

9.   EVALUATION

Research into the impacts of mobility programs on their participants using various measurement tools has consistently indicated that there is greater progress towards intercultural competency and global mindedness in those who travel than in the cohorts who do not leave their home campus. These findings make the need for mobility program development in tourism even more compelling, given the roles that will be assumed by graduates and their future careers. Almost all students return excited by their experience but we know that their degree of learning and attitude shifting is directly related to the integration of the experience into their pre-departure and post-return programming and less to the length of time they were away (Vande Berg, Paige and Lou, 2012). Listening to students immediately upon returning and again in a year or more can assist in adjusting your programs and curriculum as well as providing reassurance that you are providing a valuable experience for them. You may want to use the intercultural tools like the IDI if you are interested in more detailed tracking.

Because it is essential to broaden the benefit derived from mobility programs beyond the individual to the entire department, it has been my practice to only select those students for exchange placements who have coursework to complete back at our campus after their experience abroad. I encourage returnees to offer some of their newly acquired knowledge in discussions in their classes and then survey them to see who has had an opportunity to do so. In one semester 31 returning students enrolled in 160 courses reported that they shared extensively in 141 class discussions.

10.   CONCLUSION

There is a great need for tourism students to gain significant intercultural sophistication, and increasingly research tells us that real progress on this dimension comes to students who have studied abroad. It will be necessary for faculty members to engage in better pre-departure preparation and develop new ways to integrate the international experience into the regular curricular offerings. There are four things that are critical in creating a successful set of offerings that contribute to the internationalization of your students and your program overall. Firstly, select appropriate partners so you can trust them to deliver sound educational programming and you do not get tied up in the minutiae of transfer credit detail. Secondly, take the time to hand-pick your students. Send those who will represent you well, contribute to your classes and generate enthusiasm in their classmates when they return. Thirdly, prepare them not only with the context of the place they will visit but with the skill to observe, listen, describe, interpret and reflect.

This is the essence of experiential learning. Lastly, take advantage of your travelers as a resource for your entire department. Make them explicit in the classroom, by name, by photo, by inviting them to present at faculty meetings and to their fellow students. Internationalization and global perspectives do not happen by chance or some form of social osmosis. They happen through careful planning, nurturing, never losing sight of the departmental investment in the process and by refusing to become merely a student travel service!

BIBLIOGRAPHY

Anderson, C.S. and Cunningham, K. (2009), 'Developing ethnographic skills and reflective practices connected to study abroad', in E. Brewer and K. Cunningham (eds), *Integrating Study Abroad into the Curriculum: Theory and Practice Across the Disciplines*, Sterling, VA: Stylus, pp. 63–84.

BaileyShea, Chelsea (2009), *Factors that Affect American College Students' Participation in Study Abroad*, Thesis for Doctor of Philosophy, Margaret Warner Graduate School of Education and Human Development, University of Rochester, NY, accessed 24 February 2015 at hdl.handle.net/1802/10264.

Bathurst, L. and La Brack, B. (2012), 'Shifting the locus of intercultural learning: Intervening prior to and after student experiences abroad', in M. Vande Berg, R.M. Paige and K.H. Lou (eds), *Student Learning Abroad: What our Students are Learning, What They're Not, and What We Can Do About it*, Sterling, VA: Stylus Publishing, pp. 261–83.

Bennett, M.J. and Hammer, M.R. (2002), *The Intercultural Development Inventory*, Portland, OR: Intercultural Communications Institute.

Berardo, K. and Deardorff, D.K. (eds) (2012), *Building Cultural Competence: Innovative Activities and Models*, Sterling, VA: Stylus Publishing.

Brewer, Elizabeth and Cunningham, Kiran (2009), *Integrating Study Abroad into the Curriculum: Theory and Practice Across the Disciplines*, Sterling, VA: Stylus Publishing.

Canadian Bureau for International Education (2012), 'Facts and figures', accessed 24 February 2015 at www.cbie.ca/about-ie/facts-and-figures/.

Chen, G.M. and Starosta, W.J. (2000), 'The development and validation of the intercultural sensitivity scale', *Human Communications*, **3**, 1–15.

Council on Standard for International Education Travel (2013), 'International and youth exchange statistics 2012–2013', accessed 24 February 2015 at www.csiet.org/documents/CSIETStatsReport2012-13-FINAL.pdf.

Cubillo, J.M., Sanchez, J. and Cervino, J. (2006), 'International students' decision-making process', *International Journal of Educational Management*, **20** (2), 101–15.

European Commission (2014), 'Erasmus facts, figures and trends: The European Union support for student and staff exchanges and university cooperation in 2012–2013', accessed 24 February 2015 at ec.europa.eu/education/library/statistics/ay-12-13/facts-figures_en.pdf.

Filson, Cory (2010), *Abroad by Design: Key Strategies (CD)*, Washington, DC: NAFSA: Association of International Educators.

Gore, J.E. (2005), *Dominant Beliefs and Alternative Voices: Discourse, Belief and Gender in American Study Abroad*, New York: Routledge.

Hill, Barbara and Green, Madeline (2008), *A Guide to Internationalization for Chief Academic Officers*, Washington, DC: American Council on Education.

Hovland, Kevin (2010), 'Global learning: Aligning student learning outcomes with study abroad', accessed 24 February 2015 at www.nafsa.org/uploadedFiles/NAFSA_Home/Resource_Library_Assets/Networks/CCB/AligningLearningOutcomes.pdf.

IES: National Centre for Education Statistics (2014), 'The condition of education', accessed 24 February 2015 at nces.ed.gov/pubsearchpubsinfo.asp?pubid=2012083.

Institute of International Education (2013), 'Opendoorsreportoninternationalexchange', accessed 24 February 2015 at www.iie.org/Who-We-Are/News-and-Events/Press-Center/Press-releases/2013/2013-11-11-Open-Doors-Data.

Jarvis, J. and Peel, V. (2008), 'Study backpackers: Australia's short-stay international student travellers', in K. Hannam and I. Ateljevic (eds), *Backpacker Tourism: Concepts and Profiles*, Clevedon: Channel View Publications, pp. 157–73.

Kelley, C. and Meyers, J. (1995), *Cross-Cultural Adaptability Inventory* (rev. edn), Minneapolis: National Computer Systems.

Khanna, Tarun (2014), 'Contextual Intelligence', accessed 24 February 2015 at hbr.org/2014/09/contextual-intelligence/ar/1.

Lutterman-Aguilar, Ann and Gingerich, Orval (2002), 'Experiential pedagogy for study abroad: Educating for global citizenship', *Frontiers: The Interdisciplinary Journal of Study Abroad*, **8** (2), 41–82.

Mullens, Jo Beth and Cuper, Pru (2012), *Fostering Global Citizenship through Faculty-Led International Programs*, Charlotte, NC: Information Age Publishing.

NAFSA Association of International Educators (2012), 'NAFSA 2013: Annual Conference and Expo Registration Brochure', distributed at the George R. Brown Convention Center, Houston, p. 12.

NSSE (National Survey of Student Engagement) (2013), *Promoting High-Impact Practices: Pushing Boundaries, Raising the Bar*, Bloomington, IN: Indiana University Center for Postsecondary Research.

Nyaupane, Gian, Paris, Cody Morris and Teye, Victor (2011), 'Study abroad motivations, destination selection and pre-trip attitude formation', *International Journal of Tourism Research*, **13** (3), 205–17.

Paige, R.M. and Vande Berg, M. (2012), 'Why students are and are not learning abroad: A review of recent research', in M. Vande Berg, R.M. Paige and K.H. Lou (eds), *Student Learning Abroad: What our Students are Learning, What They're Not, and What We Can Do About it* (pp. 29–58), Sterling, VA: Stylus Publishing.

Shaftel, J. and Shaftel, T.L. (2011), 'Running ahead: Evaluation of study abroad outcomes', accessed 12 October 2014 at cete.ku.edu/sites/cete.drupal.ku.edu/files/docs/Presentations/2011/Evaluation%20of%20Study%20Abroad%20Outcomes.pdf.

Van de Water, J. (2002), 'Moving from international vision to institutional reality: Administrative and financial models for education abroad at Liberal Arts Colleges', accessed 18 March 2015 at www.jmu.edu/international/docs/AdminChallenges.pdf.

Van Hoof, H.B. (1999), 'The international student experience: A US industry perspective', *Journal of Studies in International Education*, **3** (2), 57–71.

Van Hoof, H.B. (2000), 'The international internship as part of the hospitality management curriculum: Combining work experience with international exposure', *Journal of Hospitality & Tourism Education*, **12** (1), 6–15.

Van Hoof, H.B. (2001), 'International internship exchange: Using existing resources', *NAFSA International Educator*, **10** (1), 7–9.

Van Hoof, Herbert B. and Verbeeten, Marja (2005), 'Wine is for drinking, water is for washing: Student opinions about international exchange programs', *Journal of Studies in International Education*, **9** (1), 42–61.

Vande Berg, M. (2009), 'Intervening in student learning abroad: A research-based inquiry', *Intercultural Education*, **20** (sup1), S15–S27.

Vande Berg, M., Paige, R.M. and Lou, K.H. (eds) (2012), *Student Learning Abroad: What our Students are Learning, What They're Not, and What We Can Do About it*, Sterling, VA: Stylus Publishing.

Vande Berg, M., Quinn, M. and Menyhart, C. (2012), 'An experiment in developmental teaching and learning: The council on international educational exchange's seminar of living and learning abroad', in M. Vande Berg, R.M. Paige and K.H. Lou (eds), *Student Learning Abroad: What our Students are Learning, What They're Not, and What We Can Do About it*, Sterling, VA: Stylus Publishing.

Vertesi, Catherine (1999), 'Students as agents of change', in Cheryl Bond and Jean-Pierre Lemasson (eds), *A New World of Knowledge: Canadian Universities and Globalization*, Ottawa: International Development Research Centre.

Williamson, W. (2010), '7 signs of successful study-abroad programs', accessed 4 October 2014 at chronicle/article/7-Signs-of-Sucessful/123657.

APPENDIX 24A.1

Checklist for Student Exchange Compatibility

International Cooperation Agreements June 2014
This list is meant as a guide to the issues that need to be clearly understood and recorded by all partners developing joint academic programming.

Choosing Potential Partners
General type of institution and the programming they offer
What parallel credentials do they offer?
What is the general desirability of their location?
Who are their other partners?
Are their term dates compatible?
Is there more than one thing you can do together?

Developing the academic program:
What are the objectives of the partnerships? Special opportunities?
What is the duration and structure of the academic study period?
Compare the student contact hour pattern and measurement?
Is there an understanding of the credit transfer system (for example, ECTS)?
Have the regulations concerning the different national grading systems been set up?
Has the language skill level been determined?
Has the curriculum been set up?
Has it been determined what workload students will undertake?
Has course evaluation methodology been discussed?
Have you clarified exam supplemental/rewrite policy?

Student processing:
Have the attributes for student selection been clarified?
Have the regulations concerning tuition and other fees been set up?
Have the admission and registration procedures and timetable been set up?
Have you explored the grading systems?
Have you arranged for samples of your forms and transcripts to be exchanges between institutions?

Organizational issues:
Have you clarified housing arrangements, cost of living information?
Is there an international office to give students services?
Do they have a planned orientation?
Who is the contact for you as the administrator and for the students?
Have the questions concerning insurance coverage and risk been settled?
Have you notified immigration in countries where visas are needed?
Have you clarified issues around students' ability to work?
Have you clarified who is responsible for supervising the students?
Have you exchanged emergency contact numbers?

APPENDIX 24A.2

SAMPLE   Student Name: _____

The Study Abroad Office at XXX University has exchange opportunities throughout Europe, the United States, Australia, Mexico, Japan and China. In addition to your comments, all students will be asked to submit academic records, a résumé and a letter of intent. They will all be interviewed before the selection is made.

Please complete the following form. Be frank, and do not hesitate to indicate if you do not know the student well enough to provide this information. Your comments will be confidential and will be seen only by the selection committee. Part of the strategy in 'internationalizing' education is to encourage students who have been abroad to return and share their experiences in their XXX University classes. Therefore, active class participation is a must. Also, we wish to screen out students who are not serious about his/her studies and those who lack maturity. These students represent us abroad and affect our reputation. Our concern is that we send students with good academic and interpersonal skills.

Please seal the form in an envelope, sign over the seal and give it to the student or use campus mail to the Study Abroad Office. Students interested in an exchange experience will NOT be considered without this reference form. Thank you.

Class Participation:		Attends all classes and actively participates.
		Attends all classes and participates occasionally.
		Conscientious but quiet.
		None of the above.
Academics:		This student is serious about his/her studies (A or B performance).
		This student is average.
		This student is weak.
Character:		I know the student, and believe her/him to be mature and expect she/he will both benefit personally from this exchange program and be an excellent ambassador of XXX University.
		This student might not have the maturity required for a program like this.
		I do not know this student well enough to comment on his/her maturity and conduct.

Comments:_____

_____

_____ (continue on back if necessary)

_____   _____   _____
Signature of Faculty Member   Please Print Surname   Date

PART V

CRITICAL PERSPECTIVES AND EDUCATION FOR SUSTAINABILITY

25 Teaching for strong sustainability in university tourism courses
Debbie Cotterell, Charles Arcodia and Jo-Anne Ferreira

1. INTRODUCTION

With growing pressure on the tourism industry to reduce its ecological footprint (Dolnicar et al., 2008), improve its economic performance and earn greater community acceptance (Yu et al., 2011), increasing attention is being given to the education of university students and their capacities to think holistically about sustainability issues (Bush-Gibson and Rinfret, 2010; McKercher and Prideaux, 2011). It seems that it is no longer enough to simply increase awareness of the myriad of environmental, economic and social problems but rather what is required is cultivating a sustainable mindset and a capability to think in complex, critical, systematic, holistic and interdisciplinary ways (Gretzel et al., 2014; Rieckmann, 2011). According to UNESCO (2005), it is important that universities prepare individuals who are capable of running tourism businesses that deliver economically profitable, socially responsible and ecologically viable services.

Despite a decade of support for sustainability education by the United Nations (UNESCO, 2005) and strong evidence that universities have taken sustainability issues on board (for example campus greening), the extent to which sustainability has been embedded into the curriculum and teaching and learning activities is still limited (Boyle, 2012; Ferreira and Tilbury, 2012). Graduates continue to display weak sustainability ideals and studies indicate that they have a narrow view of sustainability (Reid et al., 2009). Alternatively, learners develop an unbalanced view of sustainability by focusing only on one dimension, such as the environment (Kagawa, 2007; Zeegers and Clark, 2014). McKercher and Prideaux's (2011) global survey of 2968 hospitality and tourism students also revealed that they had a limited knowledge of critical tourism issues and subsequently showed little evidence of holistic and systemic thinking. This is concerning given that a key sustainability capability is the ability to think holistically. The question then is whether this stems from tourism courses being framed on weaker conceptualizations of sustainability or from a lack of substantial focus on developing learners' capabilities to think holistically about sustainability.

With increasing pressure on the tourism industry to reduce its ecological footprint in order to protect natural resources and loss of biodiversity (Chambers et al., 2000), the industry is being forced to make continuous changes to the way in which destinations manage and plan for sustainable tourism (Dwyer et al., 2010, p. 739). An important outcome of a university business education is to shape individuals who are capable of managing sustainable businesses that are not only profitable but have positive social and environmental benefits (Innui et al., 2006). In preparing future sustainable tourism workers, universities also need to design curricula that develop the learners' capabilities to think with foresight and empathy towards all surrounding stakeholders. The aim of this chapter, therefore, is to discuss the ways in which sustainability is currently conceptualized within tourism undergraduate courses, and current and effective teaching and learning approaches to sustainability. The chapter also discusses education for sustainability as a means to encourage deeper and more complex understandings of sustainability for the future leaders of an increasingly complex and dynamic industry.

2.   SUSTAINABLE TOURISM EDUCATION

As the Decade of Education for Sustainable Development (UNDESD) comes to a close, many universities have recognized and embraced the importance of developing socially responsible citizens. Many governments have developed plans of action for this important task, including the Australian Government, who devised the National Action Plan for Education for Sustainability (Department of the Environment, Water, Heritage and the Arts, 2009). This section provides an overview of Education for Sustainability (EfS) pedagogy in higher education generally, and within tourism education.

2.1   Education for Sustainability

According to UNESCO (2005), a variety of pedagogical techniques are needed if EfS is to be effective in developing the sorts of higher-order thinking skills that are necessary to transition to a sustainable society. According to Wals and Blewitt (2010), this is not occurring in higher education because 'most universities are too often still advancing the kind of thinking, teaching and research that leads to unsustainability and ignoring alternate ways of knowing and being, that are not rooted in Western (scientific) traditions' (p. 70).

Traditional forms of learning, which are often behaviorist, need to be complemented by alternative learning theories (Wals and Dillon, 2013) if learners are going to be equipped with the skills and capacities necessary for their future careers in the sustainable tourism industry. The field of education for sustainability offers a range of alternative teaching and learning approaches, including transformative learning, transdisciplinary learning, anticipatory learning, collaborative learning, and social learning (Wals, 2011), all of which have 'emancipatory' characteristics. Other commonalities in these approaches include the socially interactive nature of learning, its transdisciplinary nature, and a view that learning is more than knowledge acquisition (Wals, 2011). Indeed, the capacity to think in more complex ways is recognized as a key competence for managing sustainability effectively. As a consequence, further insights are needed to determine to what extent such complex ways of thinking about sustainability are underpinning tourism curriculum and pedagogy. As the context of this book is tourism education, the next section of this chapter explores the range of approaches already in use in sustainable tourism education.

2.2   Tourism Education

University tourism education has placed an emphasis on developing employability skills and attributes (Innui et al., 2006). Preparing graduates to enter an industry that has the potential to influence and change the surrounding social and cultural environment suggests that universities should place equal emphasis on developing a curriculum that educates the learners to develop skills in critical thinking and their capacity to influence and effect social and cultural change (Dredge et al., 2012). Innui et al. (2006) further suggest that it is equally important to educate learners about the philosophical and vocational foundations of tourism to enable learners to deal effectively with the social aspects of the phenomenon. The task of creating a curriculum that develops university students' vocational and philosophical skills requires, however, a curriculum that addresses vocational skills while at the same time teaching the learners to be critical and reflective thinkers who are able and willing to act ethically. It is only in this way, Tribe (2002) argues, that graduates will become 'philosophical practitioners'. A curriculum aimed at developing philosophical practitioners consists of two dimensions: the educational journey and the end result of employability (Tribe, 2002). According to Tribe (2002), if the purpose of education is intrinsic and the stance is reflective, educators can develop individuals who are capable of creating and critiquing tourism management actions. Although this acts as a framework for designing curricula, Tribe's (2002) work does not seem to include specific pedagogical strategies for developing learners' understandings in order to shape tourism managers capable of driving sustainable tourism.

The Tourism Education Futures Initiative (TEFI), created in 2007 by a group of concerned educators, provides some tools to address the future challenges of the tourism industry. As part of the initiative, educators devised a framework for a new curriculum to promote global citizenship. The TEFI framework consists of five pillars representing key values that include: mutuality, ethics, professionalism, knowledge and stewardship. One of the core values, 'stewardship', is underpinned by the ability to manage sustainability and complex adaptive systems by acting in responsible ways (Sheldon et al., 2008). This framework provides a more holistic way of thinking about sustainability although some researchers have found these values impractical to incorporate into curriculum design (Farber Canziani et al., 2012). It is the ongoing commitment of communities of educators, such as that of TEFI, concerned with sharing best practice and improving the space of learning, who do well to increase and promote collaboration between individuals and universities.

Finally, a review of university web pages suggests many universities are attempting to address the notion of developing socially responsible citizens by ensuring alignment between the curriculum and strategic plans. For example, the Griffith University Business School, as part of their *Business Group Strategic Plan 2013–2017*, revised its mission statement to include 'Developing tomorrow's globally responsible leaders', with one of the core values: 'supporting staff and students to become responsible leaders who demonstrate the highest levels of integrity and ethical behavior' (Griffith Business School, 2013, p. 1). If these ideals are to be realized, however, universities must ensure that these core values are embedded into all courses but especially sustainability-specific courses. Some tourism courses have already made substantial changes to their curriculum design, for example by incorporating an action research approach to develop learners' critical thinking skills and reflection regarding sustainability (Jennings et al., 2010). There is still, however, limited research on the extent to which universities are fostering these skills, particularly in tourism courses. It is evident that curriculum design needs to focus more on developing the learners' ability to see the complex interconnections of sustainability (Kagawa, 2007, p. 335). It seems essential that curriculum change occurs if universities' strategies to enable graduates to become responsible leaders are to be successful. Part of the challenge lies in current conceptualizations of sustainability held by not only educators, but also those that learners initially bring to the classroom. These two factors are important considerations when designing tourism curricula.

2.3   Conceptualizing Sustainability in Tourism Education

One of the challenges of educating for sustainability through tourism education lies in the complexities surrounding definitions of sustainable tourism. Sustainable tourism is defined as 'tourism that takes full account of its current and future economic, social and environmental impacts, addressing the needs of visitors, the industry, the environment and host communities' (United Nations World Tourism Organization, 2013, para. 1). A quadruple bottom line with the addition of 'culture' (Hawkes, 2001) and later 'climate' has also been suggested, thereby encouraging destinations to incorporate actions to address climate change into their decision-making for more sustainable forms of tourism (United Nations World Tourism Organization, 2007). More recently, geopolitical sustainability – the positive influence that travel can have on political relationships between regions or countries – has been suggested as an important component of the quadruple bottom line (Weaver and Lawton, 2014).

Variations in what constitutes sustainable tourism, sustainability and sustainable development are also complex. It is evident, however, that the success of tourism destinations depends largely on planning strategies and educating staff in order to help sustain local economies, host communities and the environment (The International Centre of Excellence in Tourism and Hospitality, cited in Richardson and Fluker, 2008). This requires considerable change on the part of tourism managers and destinations, including learning to continuously adapt to change, and to take a proactive role in educating staff and customers. This means managers need to undertake continuous interventions in the form of policy and management, as well as educational interventions. Universities have a significant role to play in educating future tourism workers by preparing and fostering graduates who can deal with complex issues, think holistically, and who are committed to participating in and managing ethical and strongly sustainable tourism practices.

The Implementation Plan for the UN DESD refers to three realms of sustainability, environmental, social and economic, as the core issues or overlapping spheres (UNESCO, 2005) that need to be taken into account in education efforts. This is also commonly referred to as the triple bottom line (Hall, 2008), with sustainable tourism indicators often referring to these three key elements. Although the model has undergone numerous iterations to include political, cultural, socio-cultural and even spiritual factors, the core 3 Ps (people, planet and profit) remain. It has been argued that this model emphasizes financial outcomes at the expense of social or environmental consequences (Springett, 2003). For this reason, the triple bottom line model of sustainability can therefore be interpreted as a weak form of sustainability due to the anthropocentric focus on profit/economics. An anthropocentric focus is seeing the environment in terms of what it can provide for humans either as a product or as a service provider to maintain or enhance human existence (Carew and Mitchell, 2008). Sustainable tourism is sometimes referred to as 'product-focused' in so much as only minimal maintenance of the environment is undertaken to ensure the product continues to make a profit (sustainable growth) (Hunter, 2002). There have also been criticisms of the term 'sustainable development' as this too implies sustainable 'growth' that is anthropocentric and, therefore, also points to a weaker form of sustainability (Hunter, 1997).

Early understandings of sustainable tourism located sustainable tourism at the opposite end of a continuum to mass tourism, given that negative economic, social and environmental impacts were often attributed to destinations associated with mass tourism (Lu and Nepal, 2009). Since the 1990s, however, researchers have acknowledged that it is possible for ecotourism to be unsustainable and for mass tourism to be sustainable (Weaver, 2012; 2013). This has led to the current view that the main objective of any type of tourism should be moving towards sustainability by adapting management strategies and practices (Clarke, 1997; Lu and Nepal, 2009).

Strong forms of sustainability, in contrast, place emphasis on social and environmental justice (Springett, 2010), or activity that is ecocentric in nature. This is similar to the 'ecological ethos' whereby conservation is at the heart of living, and society aims to find ways of reducing waste, conserving resources and living in harmony with nature (Fien and Ferreira, 1997). According to Dovers (2005), categorizations of strong forms of sustainability tend to be ecological in nature, whereas government and business sectors tend to display predominantly weak forms of sustainability. By making clear the conceptualizations of sustainability underpinning course design, universities can then look at approaches to teaching and learning that encourage deeper learning to take place. Deep learning involves empowering learners to look for connections between new information and past experience; think critically; and be actively involved in the learning process (Marton and Saljo, 1997). Such an approach to learning will enable university students to graduate with the capability to think holistically and critically about the complex situations they will face in the tourism industry.

3. TEACHING AND LEARNING ABOUT SUSTAINABILITY

While it is vitally important that educators examine their own personal understandings of the concept of sustainability and understand how these influence and frame their course designs, it is also vitally important that educators reflect on how learners learn about sustainability. An understanding of these two influences will allow for a deep reflection on the different approaches available for teaching about sustainability.

Epistemology, that is, the nature of knowledge and ways of acquiring knowledge, is central to understanding the learners' conceptualizations of sustainability, and how learners gain these understandings of sustainability. From a philosophical point of view, some would argue that knowledge is simply a recall of information or knowledge that already exists within the mind, such as the rationalist tradition of Plato (cited in Watkins, 2000). The empiricist tradition, in contrast, argues that knowledge lies outside of the learner. The following subsection aims to review the literature concerning how individuals might gain knowledge about sustainability and the ways in which the phenomenon can be taught and learnt. Particular focus is given to alternative methods of achieving more complex ways of thinking about sustainability in order for tourism students to graduate with sustainability mindsets.

3.1   Conceptions of Teaching and Learning

Learning differs from person to person, context to context, and country to country. For example, there are numerous external and internal factors that a learner brings into the classroom that impact on the learners' learning (for example parenting, community, motivation). Broadly speaking, there are two contrasting conceptions of teaching and learning. At one end of the spectrum, the educator is seen as a transmitter of information (Biggs, 1991). The argument here is that as long as the educator is knowledgeable in the content area and can communicate this content in a clear manner, the content will then be absorbed by the learner. The learner is therefore understood as an 'empty vessel' who memorizes facts and figures, which are then tested at a later date. This is a teacher-focused or teacher-centered approach to teaching and learning, and is sometimes referred to as the 'banking concept of education' (Freire, 2014). The motivation to learn here is not intrinsic and the outcome is that minimal information is retained beyond memorization for examination. Such approaches rely on extrinsic motivations such as the fear of failure to motivate learners to learn (Biggs, 1991).

In stark contrast to this approach to teaching and learning is a view that places the learner at the center of the educational exchange. While the educator prepares activities that enable the learner to construct meanings, they also have an interest in understanding phenomena from the learner's perspective. In this approach, the learner is interested and motivated to learn in order to satisfy a curiosity as well to as develop new understandings of the world around him/her (Killen, 2009). This approach is also known as a student-centered approach to teaching and learning (Entwistle, 1997).

These two very different approaches result in different sorts of learning. Teacher-centered approaches will generally result in what is referred to as surface learning, that is, a low-level understanding of concepts and topics (Entwistle cited in Marton and Saljo, 1997). In contrast, a more student-centered approach to teaching will result in a much deeper level of understanding of concepts and topics (Biggs, 1991).

In order to encourage deeper learning to take place, however, educators must not only foster intrinsic motivations; they must also teach the procedural knowledge needed to perform the main tasks (Biggs, 1991). If educators want to enable learners to become effective problem-solvers, for example, then educators must explicitly teach problem-solving skills. In other words, it is necessary to explicitly teach the skills needed rather than expecting that deep learning will happen naturally (Biggs, 1991).

Jickling and Wals (2008) also outline the differences between 'transmissive education', which is similar to a teacher-led approach, and 'transformative education', which is more student-focused, where knowledge is co-created and allows learners the freedom to critically reflect and transform their knowledge of sustainability, 'enabling thought and action'. The argument here is that by constantly challenging learners to be critical, reflective and systematic as well as active in the learning process, their learning can be improved (Biggs, 1991). This can be achieved, for example, by promoting activities that require higher-order thinking such as problem solving, researching and being creative. Such activities have been found to encourage learners to engage in more complex ways of thinking (Killen, 2009). This is in line with Bloom's Taxonomy (Bloom, 1956), which shows that the learners' cognitive processes range from remembering and understanding through to applying, analyzing, evaluating and creating. As this chapter is concerned with developing more complex understandings and knowledge, the following subsections will explore key learning theories in more detail.

3.2   Learning Theories

Three broad theoretical explanations to explain learning are behaviorism, cognitivism and humanism. This chapter is concerned with cognitive theories of learning since the interest lies in how learners construct meaning and develop critical thinking skills and deeper understandings of a phenomenon. Cognitive learning theory is concerned with internal mental processes and how people derive meanings from new information and experiences they receive (Glasersfeld, 2005). Constructivism is one of the major cognitive learning theories because it combines the roles of the individual and social interaction in constructing knowledge (Wals and Dillon, 2013). The two versions of constructivism are: individual constructivism, which stems from Piaget's work on cognitive development, which states that individuals move through a series of progressive stages or schemas in order to construct knowledge; and social constructivism, which argues that knowledge does not lie within the individual but is dependent on social interaction, which is predominantly the work of Vygotsky (Krause et al., 2010).

Often referred to as constructivist education, knowledge here is understood to be actively constructed by the learner rather than imparted by the educator (Marton and Saljo, 1997). Constructivism in the classroom requires learner-centered activities that focus on the background knowledge and experiences of the individuals as well as opportunities for individuals to work in groups (for example collaborative learning and peer-assisted learning) (Killen, 2009); it also requires a certain amount of reflection by both the learner and the educator. Some critics of constructivist education argue that an educator will still influence the teaching and learning activities based on what they 'already know, think and feel about a topic' (Prosser and Trigwell, 1999, cited in Carew and Mitchell 2008, p. 106). Furthermore, Tobias and Duffy (2009) claim that there is no obvious evidence to show effective learning as an outcome from the learning principles derived from constructivism. They suggest that constructivism is more of a philosophical framework rather than a theory as it does not accurately describe instruction or prescribe design strategies.

3.3   Transformative Learning

Wals and Dillon (2013) believe that these traditional theories of learning need to be complemented with alternative learning theories that better capture the complexity of sustainability. They suggest that what is required for learning about sustainability is transformative learning. Transformative learning is learning that transforms the learner by enabling the learner to shift to a new way of being and seeing (O'Sullivan, 2001). Mezirow (1978) identified a number of phases to the transformative learning process, which range from feeling disorientated and feeling shameful, angry or guilty after self-examination to challenges to one's assumptions, which lead to acquiring new knowledge and skills, to eventually creating new relationships and behaviors (Mezirow and Taylor, 2009). Sipos et al. (2007) used Mezirow's work to develop a framework for 'transformative sustainability learning' (TSL) using the synergies of head, heart and hand to enable engagement in sustainability. While transformative learning is generally seen as a positive way to approach learning for sustainability, it can, however, be challenging for educators to deliver. This is due to the transformative nature that is designed to shift learners' consciousness and forever change the way in which they see the world (Sterling, 2010). One strategy often used is to encourage learners to understand the different ways in which situations can be understood and analyzed, using a technique such as de Bono's Six Thinking Hats (De Bono, 2008).

3.4   Other Forms of Learning

Other forms of learning useful for developing the capabilities needed to deal with high risk and complex scenarios such as sustainability are transdisciplinary learning, collaborative learning and social learning (Wals, 2011). Similarities in these types of learning are that they are transdisciplinary, cross-boundary in nature and flexible, encouraging a responsiveness to shifting learning objectives as learning develops (Wals, 2011). Social learning, although not a new form of learning, has become popular in education for sustainability because it can be powerful in terms of the transformation that can take place in heterogeneous settings (O'Sullivan, 2001). Exploring one's ideas and values in a group setting that is cohesive is said to encourage better listening skills as well as the qualities needed for switching to varying sustainability mindsets (otherwise known as 'Gestaltswitching') (Wals and Blewitt, 2010). Gestaltswitching is the ability to switch back and forth between temporal, spatial, disciplinary and cultural dimensions of sustainability, which can lead to transformative learning as well as more ecocentric approaches to sustainability (Wals, 2011).

3.5   Systems Thinking

Another way in which to learn about a phenomenon such as sustainability is a process known as 'Systems Thinking'. Systems thinking is a key goal of and strategy for educating about sustainability (ARIES, 2009). Systems thinking enables learners to identify connections and relationships in order to better understand complex situations (ARIES, 2009) and complex concepts such as sustainability. The theory was developed in the 1930s by Bertalanffy, a biologist, who realized that multi-disciplinary ways of looking at living organisms could help to better understand a phenomenon of interest. Bertalanffy (1972) claims general systems theory is 'a way of seeing things that were previously overlooked or by-passed' (p. 424). Since the 1970s, systems theory has been applied to tourism research as it helps to explain the elements and interrelationships between the elements, as well as their relationship with the surrounding environment within which a system is located (Leiper, 1995). General systems theory is concerned with any complex system comprising interrelated systems and subsystems arranged in a relationship of hierarchy and subsidiarity (Leiper, 1995).

   Systems thinking is particularly useful for teaching and learning about sustainability given the complexity of sustainability particularly within tourist destinations. A 2009 survey of professionals in the field showed, for example, that 'systems thinking' as a skill was rated amongst the top capabilities needed in the workplace (Williard et al., cited in Sterling and Thomas, 2006, p. 215). Notably, two of the five key principles of Education for Sustainable Development (ESD) are critical thinking and systemic thinking (Tilbury and Mulà, 2009, p. 11). Despite this, research undertaken to analyze sustainability capabilities evident in Australian university graduate attribute statements showed that although many capabilities were present in two-thirds of Australian university statements, 'systems/holistic thinking' was not represented (Thomas and Day, 2014). This study, however, did not examine the extent to which sustainability capabilities are being implemented into curriculum design and pedagogy; and according to Boyle (2012) more emphasis needs to be placed on curriculum development, and teaching and learning. Senge (2006) argues that systems thinking is a skill that has to be taught and learned over time, while others see it as a pattern of thinking that can be easily learned and once acquired can be applied to differing situations and contexts with ease (Cabrera et al., 2008). Mind maps are a useful technique that can enable learners to learn how to think systemically (Senge, 2006).

Systems thinking, however, needs to be explicitly taught as a skill if learners are to develop a deep understanding of systems and concepts such as interconnectedness (Booth Sweeney and Sterman, 2000). Various systems models exist to explain the tourism destination (for example Leiper, Gunn, Hall) and to illustrate various subsystems in a systematic and holistic way. Systems thinking, however, does not seem to take into account the learners' previous experiences or the understandings that they bring to the classroom. According to Tribe (2001), such understandings are necessary for developing an interpretivist curriculum, which contrasts with the more common positivist approach used by many tourism curriculum designers.

3.6   Phenomenography as an Approach to Explaining Learning

Despite the many different approaches to teaching and learning theories, Marton and Booth (1997) believe that educators need to focus on the learner's experience of what is to be learnt. They believe it is necessary for educators to have an awareness of the learners' past experience and knowledge of the object of study (Marton and Booth, 1997). Marton and Booth (1997) argue that from a phenomenographic perspective, knowledge is created through an internal relation between us and the world around us.

As previously discussed, individual constructivists explain that knowledge about the external world comes from within the learner, whereas social constructivists believe that knowledge comes from outside the learner. That is, they believe that individuals create meaning through social interactions and therefore our internal world is explained by use of the external world around us (Lo, 2012). Therefore, phenomenography posits that learning is relational in that 'it takes place through an interaction between the student, the content of learning material, and the overall learning environment' (Entwistle, 1997, p. 129).

Phenomenography was developed in the 1970s as an interpretivist approach to research whereby the researchers' aim is to understand the qualitatively different ways in which people experience a phenomenon. It is this interest in seeking to understand the way in which individuals experience a phenomenon that leads to identification of the variations in ways of experiencing a phenomenon. These different ways of experiencing are often hierarchical in that they are represented in a logical manner of increasing complexity; a less developed understanding of the phenomenon will always include a partial knowledge or experience of the more developed way of understanding in the hierarchy. This is useful in an educational setting when seeking to develop more complex understandings in the learners (Marton and Booth, 1997).

As a research approach, phenomenography is well suited to answering learning and teaching research questions. It must also be noted here that phenomenography itself is purely an approach rather than a theory or a method. There are various criticisms of the use of phenomenography in terms of the subjectivity in constructing categories of descriptions, preferences for other methodologies and questions over phenomenography as a methodology (Entwistle, 1997). Despite these criticisms, numerous studies have still posited its usefulness as a tool for educators (for example Stamouli and Huggard, 2007) including its usefulness in industry settings of leisure and tourism education (for example Watkins and Bell, 2002; Watkins and Bond, 2007). Novais et al. (2014), however, point out that limited studies have been conducted to investigate the effect of using the phenomenographic approach on understanding tourism experiences.

In addition to the benefits of a phenomenographic approach in uncovering a person's understanding of how they experience a phenomenon, and using phenomenographic interview techniques and analysis to inform categories of descriptions that form the hierarchal variations, phenomenography has various sub-methods, including variation theory and the learning study. Variation theory will now be discussed as a possible effective teaching and learning strategy in EfS.

3.7   Using Variation Theory to Inform Teaching and Learning

Based on the previous discussion that learners will experience phenomena in qualitatively different ways, it is necessary to 'develop a pedagogy that caters for [those] individual differences' (Lo and Pang, 2006, p. 11). As described by Lo (2012), variation theory employs the findings from phenomenographic research to build 'a theoretical framework of concepts aimed at helping educators to structure learning experiences in ways that cater for individual ways of seeing things'. Therefore, rather than a learning theory, variation theory can be seen as a pedagogical strategy (Lo, 2012).

Most teaching and learning deals with learning objectives as the driving force behind the way in which subject matter is taught and learnt. The principles of variation theory, however, rather than focus on the end result (learning objectives or outcomes), focus on the 'how' to get there. In order for a learner to understand a concept, they must come to understand that concept from the external world in which it exists. The way in which a learner 'sees' (or experiences) and therefore understands a phenomenon is based on the aspects that the learner focuses on at one time, meaning two people can simultaneously experience the same phenomena in varying ways (Marton and Tsui, 2004). Varying aspects – called 'critical aspects' – must be discerned simultaneously in order for the learners to change their way of seeing (Pang and Ling, 2012). The argument here is that if the learners can experience variation in a critical aspect of the phenomena, then they will be able to discern the variations that exist, and in turn, their understanding will improve and deep learning will take place (Pang and Ling, 2012).

The learners also bring with them preconceived ideas of the concept to be learnt based on prior experience. If an educator has a more nuanced knowledge of the subject matter to be taught, it makes sense for the educator to first understand the way in which the learner experiences the concept in order to design learning activities that guide the learners towards a more complex understanding that matches the educators or the learning outcome/objective (Lo, 2012). In this way, variation theory deals with the relationship between the learner and the learning outcome (or object of learning) rather than only focusing on the objective of learning, and thus the process involves a high degree of iteration and reflection on the part of the educator (Marton and Booth, 1997).

This is where the notion of 'categories of description' plays a role in aiding the learner to experience the concept in varying degrees of complexity from less to more developed. This is not to say that a more complex understanding is superior to a less developed category of understanding but rather a set of interrelated ways of understanding that can be developed over time and through experience. Furthermore, the most complex approach to understanding a phenomenon often includes and draws upon all previous less complex experiences and knowledge of the phenomena in order to discern variation to the point of acquiring the most complex understanding (Marton and Trigwell, 2000).

Variation theory proposes that learners gain knowledge by: (1) developing the ability to discern the critical dimensions of a phenomenon; (2) appreciating variation in the values of the dimensions; and (3) being simultaneously aware of two or more dimensions (Marton and Booth, 1997). Thus, variation theory proposes that educators design activities that help generate the skill of discernment needed for the learners to learn.

An example of how one could use variation theory in sustainable tourism courses is to focus on presenting the learners with teaching and learning activities that expose them to variations in a concept. For example, using two case studies that demonstrate different approaches to the phenomena of sustainability enables the learners to discern and identify differences, helping them to move to more complex ways of understanding a phenomenon. Another strategy might be a field trip where the learners engage with a range of stakeholders including indigenous groups, developers, community leaders, politicians, business owners and conservationists. Exposing learners to the different perspectives on a phenomenon such as sustainability can help the learners to discern variation and therefore develop more complex understandings. Various studies have explored the usefulness of variation theory in the classroom with promising results. A principal benefit is that it allows educators to discern the different ways in which learners experience and learn about phenomena (Davies and Dunnill, 2006; Runesson, 2006; Tong, 2012), and can serve as a tool to strengthen the 'space of learning'.

3.8   Summary

As previously discussed, research suggests that not only is learning in sustainable tourism courses generally based on potentially 'weak' conceptualizations of sustainability, but it also shows that university students are still graduating with a limited or surface level understanding of sustainability (McKercher and Prideaux, 2011) and without the capability to think in more complex ways about this phenomenon. Further research is therefore needed on how university educators can foster capabilities of more complex ways of thinking about sustainability by designing courses, as well as teaching and learning strategies, that encourage and enable the learners to conceptualize strong sustainability (Connell et al., 2012). It is also necessary to conduct ongoing research on ways to educate for sustainability, as well as within a sustainable tourism context (Ballantyne and Packer, 2005), in particular alternative approaches to teaching and learning (Wals and Dillon,

2013) and alternative ways of knowing (Wals and Blewitt, 2010). The research has identified that a phenomenographic approach may be a viable alternative to develop more complex understandings of sustainable tourism and may address many of these issues.

4.   FUTURE DIRECTIONS

Analysis of existing research clearly identifies limited evidence that university courses are being underpinned by more complex ways of thinking, such as critical, holistic and systems thinking (Thomas and Day, 2014). Evidence suggests instead that many tourism courses are based on the triple bottom line approach and/or sustainable growth, which may not represent the most effective approach for understanding sustainability (Springett, 2003). Strong sustainability, on the other hand, is striving to conserve (or enhance) our natural capital and maintain constant stocks regardless of human-made capital (Wackernagel and Rees, 1998). If learning is based on potentially 'weak' conceptualizations of sustainability, then it is no surprise that university students are graduating with a limited or surface level understanding of sustainability (McKercher and Prideaux, 2011) and without the skills needed to think in more complex ways about this phenomenon. Therefore, ongoing research is needed into how university educators can foster their learners' capabilities to develop more complex ways of thinking about sustainability. A starting point could be by designing courses, as well as utilizing teaching and learning strategies, to better represent strong conceptualizations of sustainability (Connell et al., 2012).

From the review of the literature, it is apparent that part of the challenge is defining the phenomenon of sustainability. There are challenges in the way in which the phenomenon is conceptualized and subsequently the way in which it is underpinning curriculum, and therefore teaching and learning. It is apparent that further research is needed on ways to educate for sustainability, as well as within a sustainable tourism context (Ballantyne and Packer, 2005).

Furthermore, many tourism curricula tend to use a positivist approach to curriculum design as opposed to an interpretivist approach (Tribe, 2001). There is a need for an interpretive approach to curriculum design including understanding and meaning from all stakeholders, including the learners themselves (Tribe, 2001). This is something that all tourism educators can build into courses by using the learners' knowledge at the outset of a course to guide curriculum design.

Further research into alternative approaches to teaching and learning about sustainability (Wals and Dillon, 2013) as well as alternative ways of knowing (Wals and Blewitt, 2010) is also required. There is no one-size-fits-all approach to teaching and learning about sustainability. However, if educators remain curious about incorporating and trialing different approaches to teaching and learning within courses and continuously reflecting on the outcomes, they then have a better chance of shaping their learners as individuals who are capable of working in and operating businesses that deliver economically profitable, socially responsible and ecologically viable services.

5.   CONCLUSION

This chapter has explored current conceptualizations of sustainability underpinning tourism course design and identified the possibility that some courses may be designed using a 'weak' conceptualization of sustainability. Several approaches to teaching and learning about sustainability within tourism education were discussed. Tourism educators have the potential to shape the learners' worldviews and ultimately contribute to their ability to act ethically and responsibly. This requires educators to lead by example and share and demonstrate strong ethics and morals. To lead by example, it is necessary to address our own motives and desires to be sustainable and to continuously reflect on our practices (Ferreira et al., 2013), committing to ongoing professional development and lifelong learning by, for example, engaging with like-minded sustainability educators. Sustainability is often seen as a philosophy of continuously committing to a long-term goal of becoming the most sustainable that we can possibly be. Educators should therefore continuously strive to achieve sustainable mindsets in our learners as they are potentially the future generation of change-makers that may lead to a more sustainable tourism industry.

REFERENCES

Australian Research Institute for Environment and Sustainability (ARIES) (2009), 'Education for sustainability: The role of education in engaging and equipping people for change', accessed 10 February 2015 at aries. mq.edu.au/publications/aries/efs_brochure/pdf/efs_brochure.pdf.

Ballantyne, R. and J. Packer (2005), 'Promoting environmentally sustainable attitudes and behaviour through free-choice learning experiences: What is the state of the game?', *Environmental Education Research*, **11** (3), 281–95.

Bertalanffy, L.V. (1972), 'The history and status of general systems theory', *The Academy of Management Journal*, **15** (4), 407–26.

Biggs, John B. (1991), *Teaching for Learning: The View from Cognitive Psychology*, Hawthorne, Victoria: ACER.

Bloom, Benjamin S. (1956), *Taxonomy of Educational Objectives, Handbook I: The Cognitive Domain*, New York: David McKay.

Booth, Susan (1992), *Learning to Program: A Phenomenographic Perspective*, Gothenburg: Vasastadens Bokbinderi.

Booth Sweeney, L. and J. Sterman (2000), 'Bathtub dynamics: Initial results of a systems thinking inventory', *Systems Dynamics Review*, **16** (4), 249–86.

Boyle, A.R. (2012), 'Teaching sustainability: A pathway forward for tourism education', *Proceedings of the 12th Annual Australasian Campuses Towards Sustainability Conference*, Brisbane, Australia, accessed 10 February 2015 at www.acts.asn.au/wp-content/uploads/2012/09/12th-ACTS-Conference-Proceedings-Boyle.pdf.

Bush-Gibson, B. and S.R. Rinfret (2010), 'Environmental adult learning and transformation in formal and nonformal settings', *Journal of Transformative Education*, **8** (2), 71–88.

Cabrera, D., L. Colosi and C. Lobdell (2008), 'Systems thinking', *Evaluation and Program Planning*, **31**, 299–310.

Carew, A.L. and C.A. Mitchell (2008), 'Teaching sustainability as a contested concept: Capitalizing on variation in engineering educators' conceptions of environmental, social and economic sustainability', *Journal of Cleaner Production*, **16**, 105–15.

Chambers, Nicky, Craig Simmons and Mathis Wackernagel (2000), *Sharing Nature's Interest: Ecological Footprints as an Indicator of Sustainability*, London: Earthscan.

Clarke, J. (1997), 'A framework of approaches to sustainable tourism', *Journal of Sustainable Tourism*, **5** (3), 224–33.

Connell, K., S. Remington and C. Armstrong (2012), 'Assessing systems thinking skills in two undergraduate sustainability courses: A comparison of teaching strategies', *Journal of Sustainability Studies*, **3**, March.

Davies, P. and R. Dunnill (2006), 'Improving learning by focusing on variation', *Teaching Business & Economics*, **10** (2), 25–31.

De Bono, Edward (2008), *Six Thinking Hats*, London: Penguin Books.

Department of the Environment, Water, Heritage and the Arts (2009), 'Living sustainably: The Australian government's national action plan for education for sustainability', accessed 10 February 2015 at www.environment.gov.au/system/files/resources/13887ab8-7e03-4b3e-82bb-139b2205a0af/files/national-action-plan.pdf.

Dolnicar, S., G.I. Crouch and P. Long (2008), 'Environment-friendly tourists: What do we really know about them?', *Journal of Sustainable Tourism*, **16** (2), 197–214.

Dovers, Stephen (2005), *Environmental and Sustainability Policy: Creation, Implementation, Evaluation*, Sydney: Federation Press.

Dredge, D., P. Benckendorff, M. Day, M. Gross and M. Walo (2012), 'The philosophic practitioner and the curriculum space', *Annals of Tourism Research*, **39** (4), 2154–76.

Dwyer, Larry, Peter Forsyth and Wayne Dwyer (2010), *Tourism Economics and Policy*, Tonawanda, NY: Channel View Publications.

Entwistle, N. (1997), 'Introduction: Phenomenography in higher education', *Higher Education Research & Development'*, **16** (2), 127–34.

Farber Canziani, B, S. Sönmez, Y. Hsieh and E.T. Byrd (2012), 'A learning theory framework for sustainability education in tourism', *Journal of Teaching in Travel & Tourism*, **12** (1), 3–20.

Ferreira, Jo-Anne and Daniella Tilbury (2012), 'Higher education and sustainability in Australia: Transforming experiences', in *Higher Education's Commitment to Sustainability: From Understanding to Action, Higher Education in the World 4. Barcelona: Global University Network for Innovation*, Basingstoke: Palgrave MacMillan, pp. 96–9.

Ferreira, J., V. Keliher and J. Blomfield (2013), 'Becoming a reflective environmental educator: Students' insights on the benefits of reflective practice', *Reflective Practice*, **14** (3), 368–80.

Fien, J. and J. Ferreira (1997), 'Environmental education in Australia: A review', *International Research in Geographical and Environmental Education*, **6** (3), 234–9.

Freire, Paulo (2014), *Pedagogy of the Oppressed* (30th edn), New York: Bloomsbury Publishing.

Glasersfeld, E. von (2005), 'Thirty years of radical constructivism', *Constructivist Foundations*, **1** (1), 9–12.

Gretzel, U., E.B. Davis, G. Bowser, J. Jiang and M. Brown (2014), 'Creating global leaders with sustainability mindsets: Insights from the RMSSN Summer Academy', *Journal of Teaching in Travel & Tourism*, **14** (2), 164–83.

Griffith Business School (2013), 'Business Group Strategic Plan: 2013–2017', accessed 10 February 2015 at www.griffith.edu.au/business-government/griffith-business-school.

Hall, Michael C. (2008), *Tourism Planning: Policies, Processes and Relationships* (2nd edn), Frenchs Forest: Pearson Australia.

Hawkes, John (2001), *The Fourth Pillar of Sustainability: Culture's Essential Role in Public Planning*, Melbourne: Common Ground.

Hunter, C. (1997), 'Sustainable tourism as an adaptive paradigm', *Annals of Tourism Research*, **24**, 850–67.

Hunter, C. (2002), 'Sustainable tourism and the touristic ecological footprint', *Journal of Environment, Development and Sustainability*, **4**, 7–20.

Innui, Y., D. Wheeler and S. Lankford (2006), 'Rethinking tourism education: What should schools teach?', *Journal of Hospitality, Leisure, Sport and Tourism Education*, **5** (2), 25–35.

Jennings, G., S. Kensbock and U. Kachel (2010), 'Enhancing "education about and for sustainability" in a tourism studies enterprise management course: An action research approach', *Journal of Teaching in Travel & Tourism*, **10** (2), 163–91.

Jickling, B. and A.E.J. Wals (2008), 'Globalization and environmental education: Looking beyond sustainable development', *Journal of Curriculum Studies*, **40** (1), 1–21.

Kagawa, F. (2007), 'Dissonance in students' perceptions of sustainable development and sustainability: Implications for curriculum change', *International Journal of Sustainability in Higher Education*, **8** (3), 317–38.

Killen, Roy (2009), *Effective Teaching Strategies: Lessons from Research and Practice* (5th edn), South Melbourne: Cengage Learning.

Krause, Kerri Lee, Sandra Bochner, Sue Duchesne and Anne McMaugh (2010), *Educational Psychology for Learning and Teaching* (3rd edn), South Melbourne: Cengage Learning.

Leiper, Neil (1995), *Tourism Management*, Abbotsford, VIC: RMIT Press.

Lo, M.L. (2012), 'Variation theory and the improvement of teaching and learning. Volume 323 of Gothenburg studies in educational sciences', accessed 10 February 2015 at gupea.ub.gu.se/bitstream/2077/29645/5/gupea_2077_29645_5.pdf.

Lo, Mun Ling and Wing Yan Pang (2006), 'Catering for individual differences: Building on variation', in Mun Ling Lo, Wing Yan Pong and C.P.M. Pakey (eds), *For Each and Everyone: Catering for Individual Differences Through Learning Studies*, Hong Kong: Hong Kong University Press, pp. 9–26.

Lu, J. and S.K. Nepal (2009), 'Sustainable tourism research: An analysis of papers published in the journal of sustainable tourism', *Journal of Sustainable Tourism*, **17** (1), 5–16.

Marton, Ference and Susan Booth (1997), *Learning and Awareness*, Mahwah, NJ: Lawrence Erlbaum Associates.

Marton, F. and R. Saljo (1997), 'Approaches to learning', in F. Marton, D.J. Hounsell and N.J. Entwistle (eds), *The Experience of Learning*, Edinburgh: Scottish Academic Press, pp. 39–58.

Marton, F. and K. Trigwell (2000), 'Variatio Est Mater Studiorum', *Higher Education Research & Development*, **19** (3), 381–95.

Marton, Ference and Amy B.M. Tsui (2004), *Classroom Discourse and the Space of Learning*, Abingdon: Routledge.

McKercher, B. and B. Prideaux (2011), 'Are tourism impacts low on personal environmental agendas', *Journal of Sustainable Tourism*, **19** (3), 325–45.

Mezirow, John (1978), *Education for Perspective Transformation: Women's Re-entry Programs in Community Colleges*, New York: Teacher's College, Columbia University.

Mezirow, Jack and Edward W. Taylor (eds) (2009), *Transformative Learning in Practice: Insights From Community, Workplace, and Higher Education*, San Francisco, CA: Jossey-Bass.

Novais, Margarida Abreu, Cavlek Nevenka and Charles Arcodia (2014), 'Using phenomenography as a research approach to investigate the tourism experience', in Monica P. Chien (ed.), *CAUTHE 2014: Tourism and Hospitality in the Contemporary World: Trends, Changes and Complexity*, Brisbane: School of Tourism, The University of Queensland, accessed 10 February 2015 at search.informit.com.au/documentSummary;dn=4 08481812528126;res=IELBUS.

O'Sullivan, Edmund (2001), *Transformational Learning*, London: Zed Books.

Pang, M.F. and L.M. Ling (2012), 'Learning study: Helping teachers to use theory, develop professionally, and produce new knowledge to be shared', *Instructional Science*, **40**, 589–606.

Reid, A., P. Petocz and P. Taylor (2009), 'Business students' conceptions of sustainability', *Sustainability*, **1** (3), 662–73.

Richardson, John I. and Martin Fluker (2008), *Understanding and Managing Tourism*, Frenchs Forest, Australia: Pearson.

Rieckmann, M. (2011), 'Future-oriented higher education: Which key competencies should be fostered through university teaching and learning?', *Futures*, **44**, 127–35.

Runesson, U. (2006), 'What is it possible to learn? On variation as a necessary condition for learning', *Scandinavian Journal of Educational Research*, **50** (4), 397–410.

Senge, Peter M. (2006), *The Fifth Discipline: The Art & Practice of the Learning Organisation*, London: Random House Business Books.

Sheldon, P., D. Fesenmaier, K. Woeber, C. Cooper and M. Antonioli (2008), 'Tourism education futures 2010–2030: Building the capacity to lead', *Journal of Teaching in Tourism and Travel*, **7** (3), 61–8.

Sipos, Y., B. Battisti and K. Grimm (2007), 'Achieving transformative sustainability learning: Engaging head, hands and heart', *International Journal of Sustainability in Higher Education*, **9** (1), 68–86.

Springett, D.V. (2003), 'Corporate conceptions of sustainable tourism in New Zealand: A critical analysis', PhD Thesis, Durham University, accessed 10 February 2015 at etheses.dur.ac.uk/3147/1/3147_1172.pdf?UkUDh:CyT.

Springett, Delyse (2010), 'Education for sustainability in the business studies curriculum: Ideological struggle', in Paula Jones, David Selby and Stephen Sterling (eds), *Sustainability Education: Perspectives and Practice Across Higher Education*, Abingdon: Earthscan, pp. 75–92.

Stamouli, I. and M. Huggard (2007), 'Phenomenography as a tool for understanding our students: International Symposium for Engineering Education', accessed 10 February 2015 at doras.dcu.ie/447/1/Stamouli-huggard_ISEE07.pdf.

Sterling, S. (2010), 'Transformative learning and sustainability: Sketching the conceptual ground', *Learning and Teaching in Higher Education*, **5**, 17–33.

Sterling, S. and I. Thomas (2006), 'Education for sustainability: The role of capabilities in guiding university curricula', *International Journal of Innovation and Sustainable Development*, **1** (4), 349–70.

Thomas, I. and T. Day (2014), 'Sustainability capabilities, graduate capabilities, and Australian universities', *International Journal of Sustainability in Higher Education*, **15** (2), 208–27.

Tilbury, D. and I. Mulà (2009), 'Review of education for sustainable development policies from a cultural diversity and intercultural dialogue: Gaps and opportunities for future action', Paris: UNESCO, accessed 10 February 2015 at unesdoc.unesco.org/images/0021/002117/211750e.pdf.

Tobias, Sigmund and Thomas M. Duffy (2009), *Constructivist Instruction: Success or Failure?*, Abingdon: Routledge.

Tong, S.Y.A. (2012), 'Applying the theory of variation in teaching reading', *Australian Journal of Teacher Education*, **37** (10), 1–19.

Tribe, J. (2001), 'Research paradigms and the tourism curriculum', *Journal of Travel Research*, **39**, 442–8.

Tribe, J. (2002), 'The philosophic practitioner', *Annals of Tourism Research*, **29** (2), 338–57.

United Nations Educational, Scientific and Cultural Organization (UNESCO) (2005), 'The UN Decade of Education for Sustainable Development (2005–2014): International Implementation Scheme', Paris: UNESCO, accessed 10 February 2015 at unesdoc.unesco.org/images/0014/001486/148654e.pdf.

United Nations World Tourism Organisation (UNWTO) (2007), 'From Davos to Bali: A tourism contribution to the challenge of climate change', paper presented at the second international conference on tourism and climate change, accessed 10 February 2015 at sdt.unwto.org/sites/all/files/docpdf/ccbrochdavbalmembbg.pdf.

United Nations World Tourism Organisation (UNWTO) (2013), 'Sustainable development of tourism: definitions', accessed 10 February 2015 at sdt.unwto.org/en/content/about-us-5.

Wackernagel, Mathis and William Rees (1998), *Our Ecological Footprint: Reducing Human Impact on the Earth*, Gabriola Island, BC: New Society Publishers.

Wals, A.E.J. (2011), 'Learning our way to sustainability', *Journal of Education for Sustainable Development*, **5** (2), 177–86.

Wals, Arien E.J. and John Blewitt (2010), 'Third-wave sustainability in higher education: Some (inter)national trends and developments', in Paula Jones, David Selby and Stephen Sterling (eds), *Sustainability Education: Perspectives and Practice Across Higher Education*, Abingdon: Earthscan, pp. 55–74.

Wals, Arien E.J. and John Dillon (2013), 'Conventional and emerging learning theories: Implications and choices for educational researchers with a planetary consciousness', in Robert Stevenson, Michael Brody, Justin Dillon and Arien E.J. Wals (eds), *International Handbook of Research on Environmental Education*, New York: Routledge, pp. 253–61.

Watkins, M. (2000), 'Ways of learning about leisure meanings', *Leisure Sciences*, **22**, 93–107.

Watkins, M. and B. Bell (2002), 'The experience of forming business relationships in tourism', *International Journal of Tourism Research*, **4**, 15–28.

Watkins, M. and C. Bond (2007), 'Ways of experiencing leisure', *Leisure Sciences*, **29** (3), 287–307.

Weaver, D. (2012), 'Organic, incremental and induced paths to sustainable mass tourism convergence', *Tourism Management*, **33** (5), 1038–41.

Weaver, D. (2013), 'Asymmetrical dialectics of sustainable tourism: Towards enlightened mass tourism', *Journal of Travel Research*, **53** (2), 131–40.

Weaver, David B. and Laura Lawton (2014), *Tourism Management* (5th edn), Milton, Australia: John Wiley & Sons.

Yu, C.H.S., H.C. Chancellor and S.T. Cole (2011), 'Measuring residents' attitudes toward sustainable tourism: A re-examination of the sustainable tourism attitude scale', *Journal of Travel Research*, **50**, 57–63.

Zeegers, Y. and I. Clark (2014), 'Students' perceptions of education for sustainable development', *International Journal of Sustainability in Higher Education*, **15** (2), 242–53.

26 Integrating sustainability in the tourism curriculum: dilemmas and directions
Andrea Boyle

1. INTRODUCTION

1.1 Defining Sustainability

Sustainability can be viewed as an ideological debate with multiple meanings (Davidson, 2014). It appears difficult to reconcile as it is dependent on the paradigmatic vantage point of whoever defines it. Conceptualizations range from a 'strong' perspective, concerned with the natural environment and its biophysical systems (biocentric, deep or dark green), towards a 'weak' viewpoint (anthropocentric, pale green), emphasizing sociocultural sustainability and where the overriding aim concerns economic imperatives (Turner, 1993). The idea of 'sustainable development', enshrined in *Our Common Future* in 1987 (the Brundtland Report), generates conflicted opinions about the association of 'sustainability' with 'development' (Landorf et al., 2008). Some contend sustainable development is an 'inherently paradoxical policy slogan' (Stables, 2013, p. 17), while commentators in the field of tourism denounce 'sustainable tourism development' as an ambiguous and problematic concept (Sharpley, 2009).

1.2 The Role of Education

Education has an important role to play in addressing pressing and critical challenges facing the future of humankind (UNESCO, 2006). Sustainable education researchers believe the planet can no longer afford a 'wait and see' attitude and requires action at every level and in a way that brings about a new kind of thinking about what and how we learn (Orr, 2004; Sterling, 2010b; Wals, 2011). This involves a paradigm shift in education, where principles of sustainability are embedded in all practices and learning (Sterling, 2010a). Building on previous educational declarations, the United Nations Decade for Education for Sustainable Development (UNDESD), 2005–14, clearly outlined the need to implement sustainability learning throughout all education (UNESCO, 2006). One approach gaining momentum is the concept of education for sustainability (EfS), which has come to denote the presence of sustainability ideals in education.

1.3 Defining Education for Sustainability

With its roots in environmental education, the concept of EfS, known globally as education for sustainable development (ESD) and sometimes 'sustainability education', plays a central role in tackling issues that effect societal change. EfS represents education that requires a paradigm shift from traditional ways of thinking and acting upon environmental problems towards an approach that demands future-orientated thinking and acting (Tilbury and Cooke, 2005). It symbolizes a move beyond education that is 'in and about' the environment to one that is 'for' the environment, an approach that promotes critical reflection with an overt agenda for proactive and systemic social change (Tilbury and Cooke, 2005). EfS aims to develop 'capacity building' skills of critical thinking, reflection, creativity, innovation and problem solving, which enable students to tackle future challenges and harness opportunities (Tilbury et al., 2005).

Promoters of EfS claim curricula require several important features to assist students' critical assessment of information with regard to the global environmental problem and issues of sustainability (Sterling, 2010b). Rather than an approach that treats sustainability as a vague and abstract concept, an explicit engagement with values in real-life environmental contexts is recommended (Lewis et al., 2008). To achieve greater awareness of social and moral responsibilities (Sibbel, 2009), EfS involves tapping into the affective domain of students' learning (Shephard, 2008; Sipos et al., 2008). Moreover, since a transformative goal of EfS involves systemic change, interdisciplinary participation is deemed beneficial to holistically embed sustainability in the curriculum (Savelyeva and McKenna, 2011).

However, the concept of EfS is multifaceted, disputed and continually evolving (Landorf et al., 2008). EfS action appears dependent on how academics interpret sustainability through the 'lens of personal beliefs' (Cotton et al., 2009, p. 725). Indeed, one of the challenges raised by Scott and Gough (2006, p. 90, emphasis in original), is that academics 'don't *have* to take sustainable development seriously, except to the extent that there is accreditation pressure, or that they are interested, or that students demand it'. The dilemma posed, therefore, is how the lessons learnt from EfS research can inform a meaningful, holistic tourism higher education curriculum (the term 'tourism' in this chapter includes hospitality and events).

The voice of the higher education academic is one that is rarely captured in the EfS discourse (Christie et al., 2015; Reid and Petocz, 2006). This chapter presents findings from a qualitative study which explored the tourism educational practitioner's perspective, that is, the academic inspired by the role of teaching sustainability principles in a tourism higher education context. The study aimed to explore how sustainable tourism lecturers understand 'sustainability' and how they interpret the concept in teaching. It sought to uncover challenges tourism academics face when integrating EfS-related aspects into curricula and pedagogy. Additionally, it searched for future directions that may help embed EfS in tourism education.

2.   LITERATURE

2.1   Higher Education's Response to Sustainability

In response to the call for sustainable action, many universities have implemented 'campus greening practices', such as, dedicated sustainability offices, solar panel installations, recycling programs and carbon footprint mapping (Koester et al., 2006). Changes in environmental management practices are easier to achieve though; institutions operate within a regulatory environmental framework and are keen to respond to financial incentives (Scott and Gough, 2006). Consequently, while environmental management practices appear well developed in most Australian universities and worldwide, the embedding of sustainability principles into higher education teaching and learning practices has lagged behind (Fisher and Bonn, 2011; Shephard, 2010). The need to develop graduate capabilities to tackle the challenges of sustainability is clear; however, some universities are challenged with how to turn the abstract concept of sustainability into the practice of EfS (Lang et al., 2006). Moreover, universities contend with well documented challenges, pointing to numerous logistical, pedagogical and political issues (Holmberg and Samuelsson, 2006; Leihy and Salazar, 2011; Scott et al., 2012).

A university's approach to sustainability can be located within a 'weak to strong' spectrum (Krizek et al., 2012). At the weaker end, sustainability is a tokenistic add-on in the curriculum, resulting in superficial understanding and focus on learning about isolated tasks, such as paper recycling (Cotton and Winter, 2010; Krizek et al., 2012). A weaker view tends to favor a 'bolt-on' approach, where sustainability is treated as a stand-alone or separated topic/subject within a program (Sterling and Thomas, 2006). It is contended that this approach represents a 'business-as-usual attitude', where action towards change tends to be rhetorical (Moore, 2005).

A strong sustainability approach, on the other hand, involves diffusion of EfS throughout the entire curriculum (Fisher and Bonn, 2011; Sterling, 2004). The EfS literature advocates the ultimate goal to be a 'whole-of-university' approach towards sustainability (Koester et al., 2006; McMillin and Dyball, 2009). In spite of the aspiration for systemic curricula transformation, most programs have simply added a unit on sustainability because it is far easier to implement such a change (MacVaugh and Norton, 2012). Other studies have shown that systematic change towards the implementation of sustainable principles in teaching and learning is predicated on receiving support from senior university decision makers (McNamara, 2010; Scott et al., 2012; Wright and Horst, 2013). Nonetheless, although being hard to achieve and regardless of discipline, a move towards a stronger sustainable focus in curricula continues to be recommended (Sterling, 2004; Krizek et al., 2012).

2.2 Tourism Education's Response to Sustainability

Tourism is an excellent phenomenon through which to critically examine issues such as unsustainable development; for example, ensuing issues of social justice and equity for 'host' societies (Higgins-Desbiolles, 2006). Scholars acknowledge the importance of future-oriented tourism curricula that enable students to think deeply and creatively about their vision of tourism (Ring et al., 2009; Sheldon et al., 2011). Critical scholarly thought about sustainable tourism is growing, reflected by the growth of journals such as the *Journal of Sustainable Tourism* (established in 1993) and the *Journal of Ecotourism* (established in 2002).

Yet, despite highlighting the need to embed principles of sustainability into the tourism curriculum (Jurowski and Liburd, 2001), research indicates that the integration of sustainability concepts has been slow and limited in both business and tourism degrees. While many now advocate for a critical *research* agenda, some question whether the 'critical turn' has extended its reach into tourism *education* (Wilson and Von der Heidt, 2013). Worldwide generally there is little evidence of a holistic or integrated sustainability approach in tourism curricula (Fáilte Ireland, 2008; Boley, 2011; Von der Heidt et al., 2012; Fisher and Bonn, 2011; Naeem and Neal, 2012; Deale and Barber, 2012). In Australian tourism higher education, the inclusion of sustainability concepts in the curriculum has been found to be relatively piecemeal (Boyle et al., 2015). To proceed with the paradigm change deemed necessary in education (Sterling, 2001), the challenge for some is where and how to incorporate EfS in tourism curricula.

3.   METHOD

An interpretive study investigated Australian tourism academics' understanding of sustainability and its place in the curriculum. Previous research which had surveyed educational institutes for their response to EfS recommended a deeper understanding was required (Fisher and Bonn, 2011; Sherren, 2008; Von der Heidt and Lamberton, 2011). A qualitative in-depth interview method was utilized to seek a richer and more nuanced understanding of how academics make meaning of sustainability in their teaching practices. Participant selection was aided by an initial desktop scoping study of curriculum documents publicly available on 25 Australian university websites, and also informed by the recent comprehensive mapping of Australian tourism curricula undertaken by Dredge et al. (2012). A purposive sampling technique identified potential interview participants. The selection criteria required participants to work at one of the 25 institutions, identify themselves as tourism academics and have some experience in teaching sustainability. Assisted by a snowball technique, 31 tourism academics from universities around Australia were interviewed over a six-month period either face-to-face or via Skype.

   Thematic content analysis was employed to identify emerging themes from the interviews (Attride-Stirling, 2001; Braun and Clarke, 2006). The results were analyzed within the context of the EfS academic literature to seek commonalities and anomalies in theoretical knowledge about EfS in general and EfS in tourism higher education in particular. This chapter describes the major dilemmas tourism academics experience with EfS and suggests possible directions to integrate sustainability in tourism curricula.

4.   FINDINGS

The interviewed academics raised a number of dilemmas that impacted negatively on their teaching of sustainability. Although some concurred with previously recognized barriers in the EfS literature, several dilemmas appeared especially heightened in the Australian tourism higher educational context. Two major categories of dilemma affecting the incorporation of sustainability in the tourism curriculum were apparent: dilemmas of a more personal nature and dilemmas arising from the institutional context.

4.1   Personal Dilemmas

Educators' comments revealed several personal dilemmas had a detrimental effect on EfS. These included: lack of staff proficiency and/or interest in the topic; reliance on one or two individuals to 'carry the sustainability message'; private conflict with the school's

Table 26.1 Personal dilemmas when integrating sustainability into tourism curricula

Dilemma	Excerpts from academic interviews
Lack of proficiency	'A lot of my colleagues are enthusiastic about the ideas but lack skills themselves. . .some of it is very badly taught'.
Insufficient staff interest	'You need staff in all subjects committed to these concepts and not all the staff are'.
Private conflict with faculty/ school paradigm	'Business schools are very much in that mainstream model of business I don't like. Very much profit orientated'.
Lack of student interest	'It's always reduced to recycling, light bulbs and water saving, not beyond that. They think why they need to know what all the other things are about, it doesn't really matter'.

dominant paradigm; and grappling with students' disinterest in sustainability matters. Table 26.1 summarizes the dilemmas, accompanied by a sample of interview comments.

Integration of EfS in curricula was often impeded, as explained by one educator, when: 'staff are either not interested or too overworked to make changes'. Several others found that despite staff interest and enthusiasm, a general lack of experience, skills, confidence or knowledge contributed to a weak incorporation of sustainability in the curriculum. Another impediment was confusion over sustainability-related tourism terminology: 'If you don't know the difference between sustainable tourism and ecotourism you can't very well design an effective curriculum'. The question of how to address limited staff expertise was raised, with one lecturer commenting: 'Finding some resources and space in the current circumstances to help staff develop their skills to do this is another constraint'. Some lecturers felt there was reliance on a few individuals to 'carry the weight' of sustainability throughout an entire program. One educator reflected: 'If I move, leave one day, I think the [sustainable] subject might easily be replaced'.

A number of academics found the dominant paradigm of growth and profit, associated with business-focused tourism curricula, rather confronting. Due to differing and sometimes conflicting value systems and worldviews, they felt isolated from the perceived values of the business-focused majority in their school. One disclosed: 'I don't fit in. The business faculty is profit focused and hard business'. Another felt: 'there are people in business who have sets of values I find really interesting, but as an overall group and where it is headed, no'. One educator indicated concern about the 'business-as-usual' approach, saying: 'even the way we teach sustainability is still very much a pro-growth model of sustainability. So there are triple bottom line impacts, but tourism is still good'. Another believed a move away from a business dominated paradigm would enable 'a softer approach, looking at people and social justice'. Obtaining whole school/faculty commitment towards sustainability-related ideals was commonly viewed as an essential factor for embedding EfS across the entire curriculum.

Diversity of student engagement and enthusiasm appeared to make EfS challenging for many lecturers. As one observed: 'a large bulk of students appear far less motivated and are not coming to lectures'. Another commented: 'lots are just passive. There's not much passion'. Some lecturers thought business-focused tourism students were preoccupied with work and employability skills, and beyond sustaining the economic bottom line of business, appeared generally less interested in broader sustainable principles. This raised a dilemma about the purpose of tourism education for some teachers: do they educate for a tourism vocation or do they educate to develop broader awareness of what it means to participate sustainably as a global citizen? Furthermore, some believed increasing numbers of Asian students had added another layer of challenge. According to one lecturer, 'Chinese students don't seem as convinced about the whole sustainability argument. They come from an education system where the focus is just on productivity, efficiency and growth'. The dilemma for some, therefore, was how to tackle a lack of interest about environmental and social issues amongst sections of the tourism business student cohort.

4.2   Institutional Dilemmas

Tourism academics faced a range of dilemmas arising from the institutional context in which they were located. The factors which appeared to impede EfS stemmed from: tokenistic attitudes to sustainability by the overall institution and/or faculty; finding space in a crowded curriculum; limitations of a narrow vocational focus; standardization of education; and loss of experiential learning opportunities. A summary of the institutional dilemmas is provided in Table 26.2, accompanied by excerpts from academics' interviews.

A general absence of interest and commitment for sustainability by the university and school/faculty at large was seen to hamper interest and support for EfS. As seen in Table 26.2, some academics felt cynical about the response taken by their university or school/faculty. One believed sustainability was 'a decoration; they'll put it on as they need to and then they'll dump it as soon as they see the opportunity'.

When the academics were asked where sustainability fitted in the degree, a lack of space

Table 26.2   Institutional dilemmas when integrating sustainability into tourism curricula

Dilemma	Excerpts from academic interviews
Tokenistic commitment	'In a business school environment it's mostly superficial sustainability or superficial environmentalism. A lot of it is tokenism and ties into green washing'.
Crowded curriculum	'Trying to fit everything into a degree program everybody thinks they should have continues to be the ongoing challenge'.
Limitations of narrow vocational focus	'Increasingly we are asked to produce work-ready graduates. There is this huge gap between producing technically adequate graduates who can do coalface jobs and producing mindful graduates who can take a position and be global citizens in the future'.
Standardized delivery	'The massification of higher education and all these incredibly complex teaching arrangements promote the standardized delivery across different institutions that operate in different cultures; that's very problematic for the teaching of meaningful exchanges around sustainability'.
Loss of experiential learning opportunities	'Everything is so administrative, much more risk management and scared of being sued and it really does inhibit creativity and innovation, particularly in the way we deliver content. So the safest way to do it, the easiest and the least bureaucratic is just show up in the classroom and lecture the same two-hour block every week for 13 weeks. Instinctively I think it's completely wrong'.

in the curriculum was the main reason given, and why one thought sustainability was 'usually left to one subject'. Another lecturer acknowledged their subject was probably 'the only exposure students have to practical sustainability in their whole degree'. Some perceived themselves to be one of a small number, or in some cases the only one, interested in incorporating sustainability-related concepts in the curriculum. Moreover, rather than being a compulsory subject in the degree program, the one or two stand-alone sustainability subjects were often an optional subject.

Many of the academics interviewed believed the prevailing business-dominated paradigm restricted tourism studies to a narrow business-focused curriculum. They thought the vocational perspective underpinning their programs constrained students' engagement with broader liberal education, which was considered more conducive to EfS. Many indicated little room remained in the curriculum for non-business subjects. One lecturer felt: 'the way universities are designed now you lose a lot of that inter/multi-disciplinary focus. Our tourism students just go along and have their business degree'. Overall the consensus amongst the educators was that the limited number of alternative subjects had impeded opportunities to integrate sustainability concepts in the degree's curriculum.

In Australia, the majority of tourism university courses are located in business or management schools and/or faculties (Boyle et al., 2015). Many tourism programs adopt a vocational focus driven by a highly competitive consumer orientated market (Dredge et al., 2012). Research shows that students just want to 'get a job' and industry wants graduates who are skilled for work (Benckendorff et al., 2012b; Wang and Ryan, 2007; Zehrer and Mössenlechner, 2009). These factors may account in part for some student and staff disinterest with alternative narratives that are not focused on industry growth and employability. Tension appears to exist, therefore, between the educators, who are intent on preparing students to be work-ready for the tourism industry, and those with an aim to equip students with broader life skills and wider sustainability capabilities.

4.3 Broader Systemic Issues

The findings of this study indicate that some broader systemic issues are at play which impact EfS. One issue raised was the challenge of integrating EfS into expanding online education. One lecturer remarked: 'It's about students really learning from that personal level of interaction and there is less and less of that, more and more is that separation. My question is what are they really learning?' Mounting administrative bureaucracy, as well as issues of student equity with multi-campus delivery and increasing numbers of distance (external) students, had resulted in the demise of experiential learning outside the classroom. Many of the educators interviewed believed this was detrimental to EfS; immersive experiences presented a chance for students to explore sustainable/unsustainable concepts first-hand and they lamented the loss of field trips.

Academic comments suggested that a pervasive neoliberal economic management philosophy impeded their capacity to integrate EfS into curricula. With its capitalist pro-growth agenda, one ramification of neoliberal ideology is that technocratic managerialism dominates (Manteaw, 2008). The standardization of the Australian university sector is known to have generated a range of challenges for teachers. One outcome discussed is the 'massification' of education, resulting in rapidly changing modes of delivery away from face-to-face contact with students to converged, or education by distance, modes of delivery (Dredge et al., 2013). Other scholars argue that neoliberal principles in the higher education sector, noted to prevail in tourism higher education (Ayikoru et al., 2009), conflict with ideals of sustainability (Manteaw, 2008; Sherren, 2008).

Within the current compressed economic climate, it is probably inevitable that pressures have been exerted on the curriculum, as expressed by the interviewed tourism academics. Problems arising from the standardization of education are considered elsewhere; setting of standards has resulted in reduced space in education (Wals and Jickling, 2002). Other scholars agree that the reality of mass higher education and tight budgets makes progress towards EfS challenging (Cotton et al., 2009; Kemmis, 2012). The incorporation of sustainability is a long-term commitment and there are challenges fitting it into university time frames and annual budget targets (Bacon et al., 2011). It appears that unless broad systemic issues are addressed, they risk stifling academic creativity and innovation, which, according to sustainability educator Sterling (2004), are essential to foster EfS.

5.   FUTURE DIRECTIONS

Integrating sustainability concepts into tourism higher education is not only required because it is a UNDESD goal and deemed important for higher education generally, but also because it is particularly crucial to this area of study. However, analysis of tourism academics' experiences shows more needs to be done generally for EfS in tourism education. When asked what opportunities could be harnessed in the future, several themes emerged from lecturers' comments. Taking advantage of existing expertise and interest was seen as a way to propagate a wider engagement with sustainability amongst staff who are less sustainably inclined. Furthermore, actively engaging students with the university's local community and organizations were avenues that many schools/faculties could exploit further.

Many lecturers saw opportunities within existing school/faculty procedures which could be harnessed to stimulate an environment conducive to change. Some of the cited occasions where curriculum planners and lecturers could work towards integrating sustainability across tourism programs included: program reviews; systematic curriculum mapping; or compliance audit processes for teaching and learning. A first step suggested by several teachers was allowing greater flexibility with programming so students could select subjects from other disciplines as part of their tourism business degree. A few lecturers went further and recommended a more radical transformative approach necessitating a total rethink and redesign of tourism education where sustainability was holistically integrated across the entire curriculum.

Positioning tourism studies within a business paradigm appears to compound the problem of lack of alternative theoretical engagement to 'business-as-usual' (Pritchard et al., 2011). To counter this, making space in curricula for dialectic conversation about sustainability appears essential. Moreover, inclusion of critical perspectives in curricula would allow the critique of the hegemonic power of 'business-as-usual' attitudes which perpetuate unsustainability in society (Springett, 2010). Since critical thinking lies at the core of liberal education (Sherren, 2006), a holistic understanding of tourism's relationship with social, cultural, environmental, economic and political perspectives is warranted. Allocating time in the tourism curriculum for students to question and reflect critically about industry responsibilities (Inui et al., 2006) appears an effective way to begin fostering EfS.

Interest in sustainability issues can be roused by pedagogy which engages students in active-learning techniques (Springett, 2005; MacVaugh and Norton, 2012; Jamal et al., 2011). Evidence is pointing to the benefit of values-based education to encourage students' reflection on their own beliefs, values and attitudes and stimulate learning about sustainability (Nowak et al., 2008; Shephard, 2008; Sipos et al., 2008). Younger students have been found to be concerned about environmental issues and sustainability (Benckendorff et al., 2012a). By adopting innovative teaching and learning activities, the link between critical values thinking and sustainable life skills can tap into students' interest in these matters (Sibbel, 2009). Consequently, dialectic interactions amongst students and teacher are encouraged to reveal different perspectives (Sund and Öhman, 2014). Tourism teachers are thus encouraged to take every opportunity to shift from a passive, non-critical culture of education that is value-free, to one that challenges current students' way of thinking, is value-laden and emancipatory (Springett, 2005; 2010).

Educators have an important role to play in helping to trigger sustainability learning (Barth and Rieckmann, 2012; Hegarty, 2008). To encourage a grassroots momentum of commitment by academics, several studies have highlighted the need for staff development where awareness and expertise of EfS was lacking (Barth and Rieckmann, 2012; Holdsworth et al., 2008; Thomas and Benn, 2009). Investment in resource support for staff to follow through with capacity building is recommended as an important first step (Martin et al., 2006).

Few academics interviewed in this study appeared to take an inter/trans-disciplinary approach with the curriculum or pedagogy, suggesting this concept is yet to be fully understood in the Australian tourism higher education context. Also, the use of evolving virtual technology as an educational tool for EfS was rarely mentioned. Nevertheless, proponents of EfS claim inter/trans-disciplinary styles of education stimulate forward thinking and new ways of doing education (Brown, 2010). Similarly, opportunities for EfS are possible with the emergence of 'virtual reality' in the field of tourism (Guttentag, 2010), coupled with advancement of simulated learning technology in teaching and learning (Singh and Lee, 2009). These emerging approaches could provide promising pathways for tourism education and are worthy of further examination in the context of EfS.

6. CONCLUSION

Academics interviewed for this research were motivated to pursue EfS in some form or other. The focus of this chapter, however, was to highlight the dilemmas tourism academics faced when integrating sustainability principles into the tourism curriculum. This group of tourism academics revealed a number of personal and institutional dilemmas were present. Dilemmas of a personal nature included coping with staff lack of interest and expertise, and conflict with the prevailing paradigm of the faculty/school. A number of dilemmas were grouped around the institutional context in which academics were located. It appeared that an integration of sustainability into tourism business degrees was particularly impeded by a narrow business curriculum and vocational focus.

To proceed towards a paradigm change, it seems that a radical rethink of what a futures-orientated tourism education looks like appears necessary (Sheldon et al., 2011). This study has shown that from the academic perspective, many tourism programs require a review and reallocation of priority and space for sustainability-related concepts. An important first step would be an overview of current curricula using existing curriculum or program development opportunities. Key to this process is the provision of supported opportunities for staff to gain skills and expertise with how to integrate sustainability education into teaching.

The ramifications of Australian higher education operating within a neoliberal environment were discussed. Issues associated with increasing technocratic managerialism were seen as challenges for EfS. An overarching premise appears to be genuine institutional top-down commitment and bottom-up support for sustainability (Scott et al., 2012). Although top-level leadership governs the long-term success of EfS across the institution, some initiatives at the school/faculty and individual academic level can stimulate sustainability education. Tourism educators are encouraged to lean their programs away from a 'business-as-usual' approach towards more critical tenets. What this entails from a values-based perspective is important to establish and embed into all tourism curricula.

Finally, sustainability is context-dependent and often regarded as a journey rather than a set goal (Milne et al., 2006); there is no 'right way'. Nonetheless, a pedagogical shift that is critical, transformative and experiential is recommended. Wherever an institution, school/faculty or individual academic is positioned within a 'weak to strong' spectrum of sustainability, ongoing genuine support for EfS progress and space in tourism higher education appear essential.

REFERENCES

Attride-Stirling, J. (2001), 'Thematic networks: An analytic tool for qualitative research', *Qualitative Research*, **1** (3), 385–405.

Ayikoru, M., J. Tribe and D. Airey (2009), 'Reading tourism education: Neoliberalism unveiled', *Annals of Tourism Research*, **36** (2), 191–221.

Bacon, C.M., D. Mulvaney, T.B. Ball, E.M. DuPuis, S.R. Gliessman, R.D. Lipschutz and A. Shakouri (2011), 'The creation of an integrated sustainability curriculum and student praxis projects', *International Journal of Sustainability in Higher Education*, **12** (2), 193–208.

Barth, M. and M. Rieckmann (2012), 'Academic staff development as a catalyst for curriculum change towards education for sustainable development: An output perspective', *Journal of Cleaner Production*, **26** (0), 28–36.

Benckendorff, P., G. Moscardo and L. Murphy (2012a), 'Environmental attitudes of generation Y students: Foundations for sustainability education in tourism', *Journal of Teaching in Travel & Tourism*, **12** (1), 44–69.

Benckendorff, P., P. Whitelaw, D. Dredge, M. Day, M. Gross, M. Walo and P. Weeks (2012b), 'A stakeholder approach to curriculum development in tourism, hospitality and events (TH&E) education: Issues Paper No. 3', accessed 20 March 2015 at www.tourismhospitalityeducation.info.

Boley, B (2011), 'Sustainability in hospitality and tourism education: Towards an integrated curriculum', *Journal of Hospitality & Tourism Education*, **23** (4), 22–31.

Boyle, A., E. Wilson and K. Dimmock (2015), 'Space for sustainability? Sustainable education in the tourism curriculum space', in D. Dredge, D. Airey and M. Gross (eds), *The Routledge Handbook of Tourism and Hospitality Education*, Abingdon: Routledge, pp. 519–31.

Braun, V. and V. Clarke (2006), 'Using thematic analysis in psychology', *Qualitative Research in Psychology*, **3** (2), 77–101.

Brown, V.A. (2010), 'Collective inquiry and its wicked problems', in V.A. Brown, J.A. Harris and J.Y. Russell (eds), *Tackling Wicked Problems Through the Transdisciplinary Imagination*, London: Earthscan, pp. 61–81.

Christie, B.A., K.K. Miller, R. Cooke and J.G. White (2015), 'Environmental sustainability in higher education: What do academics think?', *Environmental Education Research*, **21** (5), 655–86.

Cotton, D. and J. Winter (2010), 'It's not just bits of paper and light bulbs: A review of sustainability pedagogies and their potential for use in higher education', in P. Jones, D. Selby and S. Sterling (eds), *Sustainability Education: Perspectives and Practice Across Higher Education*, London: Earthscan, pp. 39–54.

Cotton, D., I. Bailey, M. Warren and S. Bissell (2009), 'Revolutions and second-best solutions: Education for sustainable development in higher education', *Studies in Higher Education*, **34** (7), 719–33.

Davidson, K. (2014), 'A typology to categorize the ideologies of actors in the sustainable development debate', *Sustainable Development*, **22** (1), 1–14.

Deale, C. and N. Barber (2012), 'How important is sustainability education to hospitality programs?', *Journal of Teaching in Travel & Tourism*, **12** (2), 165–87.

Deale, C., J. Nichols and P. Jacques (2009), 'A descriptive study of sustainability education in the hospitality curriculum', *Journal of Hospitality & Tourism Education*, **21** (4), 34–42.

Dredge, D., P. Benckendorff, M. Day, M. Gross, M. Walo, P. Weeks and P. Whitelaw (2012), 'Building a stronger future: Balancing professional and liberal education ideals in undergraduate tourism and hospitality education: Final report', accessed 20 March 2015 at www.tourismhospitalityeducation.info.

Dredge, D., P. Benckendorff, M. Day, M. Gross, M. Walo, P. Weeks and P. Whitelaw (2013), 'Drivers of change in tourism, hospitality, and event management education: An Australian perspective', *Journal of Hospitality & Tourism Education*, **25**, 1–14.

Fáilte Ireland (2008), 'Educating for sustainability: Creating a comprehensive, coherent and compelling approach – Guidelines for sustainability standards and resource materials', Ireland: Tourism Research Centre at Dublin Institute of Technology, National Tourism Development Authority, accessed 20 March 2015 at arrow.dit.ie/tfschhmtrep/12/.

Fisher, J. and I. Bonn (2011), 'Business sustainability and undergraduate management education: An Australian study', *Higher Education*, **62** (5), 563–71.

Guttentag, D.A. (2010), 'Virtual reality: Applications and implications for tourism', *Tourism Management*, **31** (5), 637–51.

Hegarty, K. (2008), 'Shaping the self to sustain the other: Mapping impacts of academic identity in education for sustainability', *Environmental Education Research*, **14**, 681–92.

Higgins-Desbiolles, F. (2006), 'More than an industry: Tourism as a social force', *Tourism Management*, **27** (6), 1192–208.

Holdsworth, S., C. Wyborn, S. Bekessy and I. Thomas (2008), 'Professional development for education for sustainability: How advanced are Australian universities?', *International Journal of Sustainability in Higher Education*, **9** (2), 131–46.

Holmberg, J. and B.E. Samuelsson (eds), (2006), 'Drivers and barriers for implementing sustainable development in higher education: Education for sustainable development in action', Technical Paper (Vol. 3), Paris: UNESCO.

Inui, Y., D. Wheeler and S. Lankford (2006), 'Rethinking tourism education: What should schools teach?', *Journal of Hospitality, Leisure, Sport & Tourism Education*, **5** (2), 25–35.

Jamal, T., J. Taillon and D. Dredge (2011), 'Sustainable tourism pedagogy and academic–community collaboration: A progressive service-learning approach', *Tourism and Hospitality Research*, **11** (2).

Jurowski, C. and J.J. Liburd (2001), 'A multi-cultural and multi-disciplinary approach to integrating the principles of sustainable development into human resource management curriculums in hospitality and tourism', *Journal of Hospitality & Tourism Education*, **13** (5), 36–51.

Kemmis, S. (2012), 'Pedagogy, praxis and practice-based higher education', in J. Higgs, R. Barnett, S. Billett and M. Hutchings (eds), *Practice-Based Education: Perspectives and Strategies*, Dordrecht: Springer, pp. 81–100.

Koester, R.J., J. Eflin and J. Vann (2006), 'Greening of the campus: A whole-systems approach', *Journal of Cleaner Production*, **14** (9–11).

Krizek, K.J., D. Newport, J. White and A.R. Townsend (2012), 'Higher education's sustainability imperative: How to practically respond?', *International Journal of Sustainability in Higher Education*, **13** (1), 19–33.

Landorf, H., S. Doscher and T. Rocco (2008), 'Education for sustainable human development: Towards a definition', *Theory and Research in Education*, **6** (2), 221–36.

Lang, J., I. Thomas and A. Wilson (2006), 'Education for sustainability in Australian universities: Where is the action?', *Australian Journal of Environmental Education*, **22** (2), 45–58.

Leihy, P. and J. Salazar (2011), 'Education for sustainability in university curricula: Policies and practice in Victoria', Melbourne: Centre for the Study of Higher Education, University of Melbourne.

Lewis, E., C. Mansfield and C. Baudains (2008), 'Getting down and dirty: Values in education for sustainability', *Issues in Educational Research*, **18** (2), 138–55.

MacVaugh, J. and M. Norton (2012), 'Introducing sustainability into business education contexts using active learning', *International Journal of Sustainability in Higher Education*, **13** (1), 72–87.

Manteaw, B.O. (2008), 'When businesses go to school: Neoliberalism and education for sustainable development', *Journal of Education for Sustainable Development*, **2** (2), 119–26.

Martin, S., G. Dawe and R. Jucker (2006), 'Embedding education for sustainable development in higher education in the UK', in J. Holmberg and B.E. Samuelsson (eds), *Drivers and Barriers for Implementing Sustainable*

Development in Higher Education, Education for Sustainable Development in Action, vol. 3, Paris: UNESCO, pp. 61–7.

McMillin, J. and R. Dyball (2009), 'Developing a whole-of-university approach to educating for sustainability: Linking curriculum, research and sustainable campus operations', *Journal of Education for Sustainable Development*, **3** (1), 55–64.

McNamara, K.H. (2010), 'Fostering sustainability in higher education: A mixed-methods study of transformative leadership and change strategies', *Environmental Practice*, **12** (1).

Milne, M.J., K. Kearins and S. Walton (2006), 'Creating adventures in wonderland: The journey metaphor and environmental sustainability', *Organization*, **13** (6), 801–39.

Moore, J. (2005), 'Barriers and pathways to creating sustainability education programs: Policy, rhetoric and reality', *Environmental Education Research*, **11** (5), 537–55.

Naeem, M. and M. Neal (2012), 'Sustainability in business education in the Asia Pacific region: A snapshot of the situation', *International Journal of Sustainability in Higher Education*, **13** (1), 60–71.

Nowak, M., A. Rowe, G. Thomas and D. Klass (2008), 'Weaving sustainability into business education', *Journal of the Asia-Pacific Centre for Environmental Accountability*, **14** (2), 19–34.

Orr, D.W. (2004), *Earth in Mind: On Education, Environment and the Human Prospect*, Washington: Island Press.

Pritchard, A., N. Morgan and I. Ateljevic (2011), 'Hopeful tourism: A new transformative perspective', *Annals of Tourism Research*, **38** (3), 941–63.

Reid, A. and P. Petocz (2006), 'University lecturers' understanding of sustainability', *Higher Education*, **51** (1), 105–23.

Ring, A., A. Dickinger and K. Wöber (2009), 'Designing the ideal undergraduate program in tourism: Expectations from industry and educators', *Journal of Travel Research*, **48** (1), 106–21.

Savelyeva, T. and J.R. McKenna (2011), 'Campus sustainability: Emerging curricula models in higher education', *International Journal of Sustainability in Higher Education*, **12** (1), 55–66.

Scott, G., D. Tilbury, L. Sharp and E. Deane (2012), 'Turnaround leadership for sustainability in higher education', Sydney: Office for Learning & Teaching, accessed 20 March 2015 at www.sustainability.edu.au.

Scott, W. and S. Gough (2006), 'Universities and sustainable development in a liberal democracy: A reflection on the necessity for barriers to change', in J. Holmberg and B.E. Samuelsson (eds), *Drivers and Barriers for Implementing Sustainable Development in Higher Education: Education for Sustainable Development in Action*, vol. 3, Paris: UNESCO, pp. 89–95.

Sharpley, R. (2009), *Tourism Development and the Environment: Beyond Sustainability?*, London: Earthscan.

Sheldon, P., D.R. Fesenmaier and J. Tribe (2011), 'The Tourism Education Futures Initiative (TEFI): Activating change in tourism education', *Journal of Teaching in Travel & Tourism*, **11** (1), 2–23.

Shephard, K. (2008), 'Higher education for sustainability: Seeking affective learning outcomes', *International Journal of Sustainability in Higher Education*, **9** (1), 87–98.

Shephard, K. (2010), 'Higher education's role in "education for sustainability"', *Australian Universities' Review*, **52** (1), 13–22.

Sherren, K. (2006), 'Core issues: Reflections on sustainability in Australian university coursework programs', *International Journal of Sustainability in Higher Education*, **7** (4), 400–13.

Sherren, K. (2008), 'Higher environmental education: Core disciplines and the transition to sustainability', *Australasian Journal of Environmental Management*, **15** (3), 189–96.

Sibbel, A. (2009), 'Pathways towards sustainability through higher education', *International Journal of Sustainability in Higher Education*, **10** (1), 68–82.

Singh, N. and M.J. Lee (2009), 'Exploring perceptions toward education in 3-D virtual environments: An introduction to "Second Life"', *Journal of Teaching in Travel & Tourism*, **8** (4), 315–27.

Sipos, Y., B. Battisti and K. Grimm (2008), 'Achieving transformative sustainability learning: Engaging head, hands and heart', *International Journal of Sustainability in Higher Education*, **9** (1), 68–86.

Springett, D. (2005), 'Education for sustainability' in the business studies curriculum: A call for a critical agenda', *Business Strategy and the Environment*, **14**, 146–59.

Springett, D. (2010), 'Education for sustainability in business studies curriculum: Ideological struggle', in P. Jones, D. Selby and S. Sterling (eds), *Sustainability Education: Perspectives and Practice Across Higher Education*, London: Earthscan, pp. 75–92.

Stables, A. (2013), 'The unsustainability imperative? Problems with "sustainability" and "sustainable development" as regulative ideals', *Environmental Education Research*, **19** (2), 177–86.

Sterling, S. (2001), *Sustainable Education: Re-visioning Learning and Change*, Totnes: Green Books.

Sterling, S. (2004), 'Higher education, sustainability, and the role of systemic learning', in P.B. Corcoran and A.E.J. Wals (eds), *Higher Education and the Challenge of Sustainability: Problematics, Promise, and Practice*, Dordrecht: Kluwer Academic Publishers, pp. 47–70.

Sterling, S. (2010a), 'Learning for resilience, or the resilient learner? Towards a necessary reconciliation in a paradigm of sustainable education', *Environmental Education Research*, **16** (5–6), 511–28.

Sterling, S. (2010b), 'Living "in" the earth: Towards an education for our times', *Journal of Education for Sustainable Development*, **4** (2), 213–18.

Sterling, S. and I. Thomas (2006), 'Education for sustainability: The role of capabilities in guiding university curricula', *International Journal of Innovation and Sustainable Development*, **1** (4), 349–70.

Sund, L. and J. Öhman (2014), 'On the need to repoliticise environmental and sustainability education: Rethinking the postpolitical consensus', *Environmental Education Research*, **20** (5), 639–59.

Thomas, J. and S. Benn (2009), 'Education *about* and *for* sustainability in Australian business schools – Stage 3: An action research program', Canberra, accessed 20 March 2015 at www.aries.com.au.

Tilbury, D. and K. Cooke (2005), *A National Review of Environmental Education and its Contribution to Sustainability in Australia: Frameworks for Sustainability*, Canberra, accessed 20 March 2015 at www.aries.mq.edu.au.

Tilbury, D., A. Keogh, A. Leighton and J. Kent (2005), *A National Review of Environmental Education and its Contribution to Sustainability in Australia: Further and Higher Education – Key Findings Vol. 5*, Canberra: Australian Government Department of the Environment and Heritage, accessed 20 March 2015 at www.aries.mq.edu.au.

Tribe, J. (2002), 'The philosophic practitioner', *Annals of Tourism Research*, **29** (2), 338–57.

Turner, R.K. (1993), 'Sustainability: Principles and practice', in R.K. Turner (ed.), *Sustainable Environmental Economics and Management: Principles and Practice*, New York and London: Belhaven Press, pp. 3–36.

UNESCO (2006), *Framework for the UN DESD International Implementation Scheme (Section for Education for Sustainable Development*, (ED/PEQ/ESD) Division for the Promotion of Quality Education), Paris: UNESCO.

Von der Heidt, T. and G. Lamberton (2011), 'Sustainability in the undergraduate and postgraduate business curriculum of a regional university: A critical perspective', *Journal of Management and Organisation*, **17** (5), 670–90.

Von der Heidt, T,. G. Lamberton, E. Wilson and D. Morrison (2012), 'To what extent does the Bachelor of Business curriculum reflect the sustainability paradigm? An audit and evaluation of current sustainability embeddedness in curriculum and assessment in the first-year Bachelor of Business in Southern Cross Business School and School of Tourism and Hospitality Management', unpublished Final Report, Lismore: Southern Cross University.

Wals, A.E.J. (2011), 'Learning our way to sustainability', *Journal of Education for Sustainable Development*, **5** (2), 177–86.

Wals, A.E.J. and B. Jickling (2002), '"Sustainability" in higher education: From doublethink and newspeak to critical thinking and meaningful learning', *Higher Education Policy*, **15** (2), 121–31.

Wang, Z. and C. Ryan (2007), 'Tourism curriculum in the university sector: Does it meet future requirements? Evidence from Australia', *Tourism Recreation Research*, **32** (2), 29–40.

Wilson, E. and T. von der Heidt (2013), 'Business as usual? Barriers to education for sustainability in the tourism curriculum', *Journal of Teaching in Travel & Tourism*, **13** (2), 130–47.

Wright, T. and N. Horst (2013), 'Exploring the ambiguity: What faculty leaders really think of sustainability in higher education', *International Journal of Sustainability in Higher Education*, **14** (2), 209–27.

Zehrer, A. and C. Mössenlechner (2009), 'Key competencies of tourism graduates: The employers' point of view', *Journal of Teaching in Travel & Tourism*, **9** (3/4), 266–87.

27 Cultural and environmental awareness through sustainable tourism education: exploring the role of onsite community tourism-based Work-Integrated Learning projects

Stephen Wearing, Michael A. Tarrant,
Stephen Schweinsberg and Kevin Lyons

1. INTRODUCTION

This chapter explores the potential of Work-Integrated Learning (WIL) in promoting cultural and environmental awareness through sustainable tourism education. WIL is a form of experiential learning and education that integrates academic learning in workplace environments (Buabeng Assan, 2014; Edgar and Connaughton, 2014; Smith and Worsfold, 2014; Xia et al., 2014; Zegwaard and McCurdy, 2014). While the term 'WIL' is commonly used throughout Australia, in other parts of the world it may be known as Learning Content Management Systems, Integrated Learning Systems, or Learning Management Systems. For the purpose of this chapter, however, we will consider WIL as synonymous with the aforementioned terms.

WIL experiences such as internships, placements, cooperative programs, industry projects and service learning are a common feature of many tourism programs (Dorasamy and Balkaran, 2011; Keating, 2012). Its application here is considered using the context of onsite community-based tourism projects that provide learners with the opportunity to actively engage with communities and to 'apply knowledge, skills and feelings in an immediate and relevant setting' (Smith, 2001). Such placements have the potential to promote what Orrell (2007, in Peach et al., 2013) has described as the 'transformative stakeholder ethos'; a holistic approach to learning where students may develop new ideas and innovations through the blending of class-based education with first-hand workplace experiences.

In this chapter we consider the ecological paradigm shift that underpinned the rise of environmental education, and marry it with an experiential framework as a conceptual foundation for community-based Work-Integrated Learning projects. We argue that such an approach exposes learners to a concrete experience, but also has the capacity to introduce them to authentic practices through interaction with industry and community leaders and players. We briefly describe a couple of examples of how such an approach has been successfully applied in diverse settings, drawing on two tertiary case studies from the University of Georgia and the University of Technology (Sydney). We conclude by considering less formal learning contexts such as the gap year, in which knowing and learning are co-constructed through ongoing and reciprocal processes (Billet, 2001) that may benefit from the framework discussed in this chapter.

2.   LITERATURE

Much has been written about paradigm shifts. In 1970 the renowned scientific historian Thomas Kuhn wrote that paradigms are 'a constellation of beliefs, values and techniques, and so on shared by the members of a given community' (Kuhn, 1996, p. 175). Since the publication of Kuhn's work, *The Structure of Scientific Revolutions*, there has been a profound evolution in green philosophies as they relate to management practice. In the late 1970s Dunlap and Catton introduced the notion of green paradigms as the antithesis of the dominant social paradigms of the day (Dunlap, 2008). By questioning the almost universally held beliefs in the merits of zero limits to growth and the primacy of economic growth over environmental protection (see Hay, 2002), early proponents of environmental thought were able to question the basis of the dominant anthropocentric philosophies that had defined the nature of humankind's relationship to the world since the industrial revolution. Such thinking gave birth to environmental education.

Proponents of environmental education have long recognized that ecological understanding involved more than learning concepts. At its heart it is a process of enacting a shift to a green paradigm by fundamentally changing the way individuals view the world (Lyle, 1996). The process whereby human beings develop the skills to prioritize the often competing social, economic and biological aspects of sustainability starts with environmental education (Global Development Resource Centre, n.d.). Environmental education was defined at the 1977 Tbilisi Conference as encompassing three broad goals:

- to foster clear awareness of, and concern about, economic, social, political and ecological interdependence in urban and rural areas;
- to provide every person with opportunities to acquire the knowledge, values, attitudes, commitment and skills needed to protect and improve the environment;
- to create new patterns of behavior of individuals, groups and society as a whole, towards the environment (Global Development Research Centre, n.d.).

Within each of these goals lies the universal charter of environmental education, which is to broaden the consciousness of the need to apply sustainability principles collectively and in our everyday lives (Haigh, 1995 in Scott and Van Etten, 2013). Over the last thirty years a number of international conventions and agreements have taken up the cause of environmental education. Kyburz-Graber (2013, p. 23) notes that it was political strategizing at the United Nations Conference on the Human Environment in Stockholm in 1972 that took environmental education from being a niche concern of 'engaged biology and geography teachers' and developed it into a political force. The report *Our Common Future* subsequently identified education as one of the primary facilitators of the process whereby human beings may develop 'new values that would stress individual and joint responsibility towards the environment and towards nurturing harmony between humanity and environment' (Brundtland, 1987, p. 111).

Tilbury (1995) notes that it was in the 1990s that sustainability became a stated objective of environmental education. Reflective of evolving human understanding of sustainability itself; environmental educators have increasingly realized the need for a holistic approach to environmental education for sustainability. In doing so, a range of theoretical interpretations of environmental education have come into vogue.

One that is particularly relevant in the present chapter is the socio-ecological approach. The essential premise of socio-ecological environmental education is that positive learning outcomes are best achieved by 'promoting competencies for critically analysing and reflecting on situations, living conditions and values, and for developing a multiperspective understanding of the complexity of these issues' (Kyburz-Graber et al., 2006, p. 111). To achieve such constructivist outcomes requires that practitioners ponder the multilayered demands of a diverse range of stakeholder groups and actively consider the ways in which the personal and critical reflection of their own value positions can be combined with participatory approaches to learning (Kyburz- Graber, 2013). In short, such an approach blends environmental and experiential forms of education through what is now known as Work-Integrated Learning (WIL).

3. TEACHING APPROACHES

It has been well argued that WIL is a form of experiential learning and education that integrates academic learning in workplace environments (Buabeng Assan, 2014; Edgar and Connaughton, 2014; Smith and Worsfold, 2014; Xia et al., 2014; Zegwaard and McCurdy, 2014). Our approach to Work-Integrated Learning (WIL) is contextualized in an experiential learning framework, that is, it is project-based community engagement which provides learners with the opportunity to gain and 'apply knowledge, skills and feelings in an immediate and relevant setting' (Smith, 2001). WIL exposes learners to a concrete experience; it may also introduce learners to authentic practices through interaction with industry and community where through a project-based approach there can be an opportunity for conceptual change which can be advanced through collaborative social interaction in the culture of the domain (Resnick, 1988). 'Social situations – such as workplaces – are not just one-off sources of learning and knowing. Instead, they constitute environments in which knowing and learning are co-constructed through ongoing and reciprocal processes' (Billett, 2001, p. 434).

We propose that experiential learning is an ideal educational paradigm upon which to build WIL experiences because of its relationship with many sustainable traditional learning styles. Experience-based learning, in which the learner is directly in touch with the realities being studied, contrasts with learning in which the learner only reads about, hears about, and talks or writes about these realities (Keeton and Tate, 1978, p. 2). Joplin claims that the emphasis and goal within experiential education is 'toward monitoring the individual's growth and the development of self awareness' (Joplin, 1990, p. 158). As such, the major characteristics of experiential education proposed by Joplin (adapted, p. 159) are (1) learner based, rather than teacher based; (2) personal, not impersonal; (3) process and product oriented (i.e., how a learner arrives at an answer, as well as how correct that answer may be); (4) evaluative – for both internal and external reasons (i.e., a focus on learner skill development and on external agent monitoring of the learner learning experience); (5) holistic (including an understanding and component analysis, representing the complexity of situations stressed over the simple summation); (6) that learning is organized around (and begins with) an experience; (7) based on both real/perceived and theoretical foundations; and (8) individual rather than group based (and thereby stress the 'individuals' development in a self-referenced fashion'). The

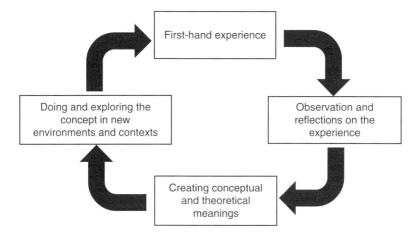

Source: Adapted from Kolb (1984).

Figure 27.1   Experiential learning framework

theoretical framework of experiential education is best conceptualized by Kolb (1984) in Figure 27.1.

An examination of Figure 27.1 suggests some methods that can be used for sustainable tourism education contexts. First, the First-hand Experience relies heavily on emotive-based judgments and specific learning situations and, as such, forms an integral basis of teaching and learning in many indigenous communities. This education, for example, enables the participant to focus on specific, but familiar, natural environments within their local area that is part of their culture or community experience. In contrast, conceptualization (the polar opposite of First-hand Experience) suggests a more rational and conceptual approach to education, one in which participants adopt (or prefer) symbolic interactions over personal learning interactions (see, for example, Shuttenberg and Poppenlagen, 1980, p. 30). This style of approach relates strongly to the way we learn about sustainability, so exposure introduces learners to learning patterns that reinforce sustainable tourism approaches based on one's personal beliefs.

The final two categories in Figure 27.1 allow the integration of components of sustainability and sustainable tourism that is desired through the WIL process. Observation and refection is a pre-requisite to learning in a WIL project, often with the learning dimension being based on 'being'. This involves careful observation rather than involvement, as well as thinking about and comparing ideas. Indeed, this may be considered as the preferred way to learn about sustainability (Rickinson, 2001). The polar opposite, however, represents active testing and experimentation. This approach is oriented towards 'doing' by facilitating learning, and is therefore an approach that invites trying things out and then modifying behavior in the light of success or failure. This is why WIL is an essential component in the learning process for sustainable tourism.

Overall Figure 27.1 represents an approach that is based on the integration of a number of different learning styles, thus facilitating bi-cultural learning opportunities and applications for learners (as well as local people) involved in WIL sustainable tourism projects.

Additionally, it allows for the integration of culturally distinctive approaches to learning. Historically the teaching techniques of advanced industrial nations, which concentrate on objectivity and rationality, have been criticized for their insensitivity to sustainable tourism education on the basis that, 'different styles of interpersonal communication are manifestations of underlying differences in world view and there is clear potential for conflict' (Harris, 1990, p. 39). One outcome of this conflict is likely to be ineffective learning. However, Mascarenhas et al. (1991, p. 11) maintain that where attitudes of outsiders are right and rapport is good, it has been repeatedly shown that villagers know a great deal, and this knowledge itself helps to drive innovations.

Locals involved in sustainable tourism projects are themselves often the main innovators of change. As such, a WIL framework of sustainable tourism seeks to incorporate biological adversity and social development within the traditional economic, market-driven paradigm; thus turning the cliché 'Think globally, act locally' into a form of practical politics. One extension is that learners can be educated on the effects their lifestyle has on the physical and cultural environment of other regions. Thus education and training in this way offer the opportunity to educate both learners and local stakeholders.

Effective sustainable tourism education requires that responsibility must be given to those people nearest the core of the issue (Shiva et al., 1991). This places it within the hands of those communities who have the greatest stake in project ownership and success, and who possess the greatest store of historical, social and cultural knowledge of the local area. By promoting local–learner relations, learners directly receive the benefit of this knowledge.

> If you want to rehabilitate the environment, you must rely on villagers and not on government officers to do the job. But people will care for their environment only if they have legal rights to manage it and to use its products. People already have the knowledge, what they must get are rights over their local environments. (Shiva et al., 1991, p. 118)

Local communities must have a major role in WIL for sustainable tourism education projects and be empowered to take major roles in the education and training that is at the heart of these projects. As a result, local communities can teach learners how to manage the resources on which their livelihood and culture depend. However, this education must attempt to address a range of criteria suggested by Shiva et al. (1991) before it is undertaken. Such criteria include: protecting and promoting local knowledge and innovations; the support of conservation and utilization of local biological resources; strengthening local-based research and development; and support for community institutions and improved security.

The Convention for Biodiversity (Shiva et al., 1991) outlines the need for research, training and education by incorporating training specialists in: ecosystem functioning; research in natural resources; formal and non-formal education of the general public and the local population; development of research institutions in developing countries; and strengthening information exchange between government and non-government agencies. Stapp (1972, p. 32) further outlines a number of requirements for environmental education that are applicable to the Sustainable Tourism Education Process (STEP). These should enable the learner and other stakeholders to develop a critical perspective and understanding of our natural resources (their characteristics, status, distribution and values), an ecological awareness (a blend of previous experiences that will develop interest and respect towards the environment), and an economic and political awareness (an understanding of the factors – political and economic – which interfere with conservationist policies).

Essential to successful WIL sustainable tourism project education is understanding and managing community dynamics, especially community stakeholders that are internal and external to the local environment. It is necessary to ensure these stakeholders (and their respective organizations, if appropriate) are involved in establishing any project educational program. This is because they will provide invaluable information and interaction in the learning process.

The following text provides two case studies of how this experiential approach to WIL has been applied in the context of community-based projects in two diverse settings operated by two different higher educational institutions.

4.   CASE STUDY 1: HOMESTAY EXPERIENCE WIL IN FIJI: SUSTAINABILITY IN ACTION

Over a four-week period in June/July 2014, 10 university learners (mostly undergraduate) from the University of Georgia in the United States traveled to the South Pacific island nation of Fiji where they partnered with a local community (Waitabu) to establish a commercially viable international tourism business venture in the village. The goal of the Fiji WIL is for learners to work collaboratively (as a cohort) with village elders and local community members to create a village homestay opportunity for international tourists that, once developed, would be maintained and marketed by the community. Learners registered for six semester credits at the university, for which they undertook coursework both prior to, and upon completion of, their month-long overseas village experience.

Waitabu, a traditional Fijian village, is located on the north-east coast of Fiji's third largest island, Taveuni. Taveuni (a population of around 15 000 mainly indigenous Fijians), known as the Garden Island, lies on the 180-degree meridian and its remoteness has meant it has been much less impacted by tourism than Viti Levu and its adjacent off-shore islands. It contains some of the world's best soft coral, has unique wildlife and natural resources not found elsewhere, and a rich cultural history. Approximately one-third of the island is protected as a World Heritage Area. The 130 residents of Waitabu live in a collectively owned village unit of 25 houses. The cash economy is dependent on crop farming (especially taro and kava) and subsistence fishing, with average salaries of USD70/month. The village receives some limited income from cruise ship tourists, but the elders and residents are keen to expand on their tourism opportunities by creating a homestay for visitors wishing to stay one or more nights to learn and experience the culture and natural ecology of the area.

Waitabu represents an ideal location for the Fiji WIL for at least the following reasons: (1) a locally managed marine protected area (LMMPA), the Waitabu Marine Park, was established in 1998 to provide a tourism attraction (besides the proposed homestay experience itself); (2) the Fiji WIL has the full support of the Waitabu village chief and elders (meetings were held on at least three separate occasions prior to the WIL project inception); (3) Waitabu village has, or is in close proximity to, critical resources such as a local

24/7 field nurse and first aid clinic, radio phone and generator; and (4) all 22 family homes in Waitabu had previously been evaluated (as part of a comprehensive family homestay assessment conducted for a prior study abroad program).

The WIL project consisted of learners developing a series of plans for the village. (1) A business and leadership plan consisting of a viable accounting and financial system, and green business model for administering and managing the homestay, along with appropriate business ethics to operate in a global and sustainable environment. (2) A tourism needs assessment plan identifying the range of tourism services demanded and opportunities available, and the potential tourism market that exists (that is, for whom, when, and how should the opportunities be delivered). (3) A stewardship and community engagement plan including a process for collaboration and decision-making; specifically, how does the business operate sustainably at local, regional, national and international levels, who are the key stakeholders and how are they involved? (4) A marketing plan with publicity and promotional materials, and a market information system to recruit tourists. (5) A health and safety plan addressing health, safety and risk assessment objectives for operating a homestay experience. (6) An infrastructure plan to identify facility needs such as buildings (interpretive center/classroom/library, upgrades to homes such as toilets) and creation of an online booking system. (7) An educational plan, with specific learning objectives, for homestay visitors. At Waitabu this included, for example, tourists being involved with the following types of activities:

- impact mapping of the LMMPA (for example, documentation and mapping of coastal erosion, benthic categories, reef surveys, LMMA boundaries – which remain highly contentious – and fish species);
- land use mapping outside of the LMMA (for example, documentation and mapping of cultural and ecological resources including artifacts, plantations, medicinal plants);
- cultural interpretation (for example, oral history and timeline of the village based on historic occurrences such as hurricanes and deaths of a chief that can be then grounded on the Western calendar; art interpretation of the village history);
- tourism impacts and education (for example, reef restoration efforts, snorkel guide training, development of new interpretive materials, educational activities for cruise ship tourists and backpackers);
- primary school education and teaching at the local school.

(8) Finally, an ongoing maintenance plan (including training system) to enable Waitabu residents to cooperatively manage the homestay as an ongoing, financially viable, project in all aspects of business, marketing, education, health/safety, and infrastructure.

At the time of writing, it is too early to determine whether the village homestay will be a successful and long-term viable business endeavor for the village. A second cohort will participate in the Fiji WIL (this time at a different village in Fiji, Soso in the Yasawas) in 2015 and will include a follow-up with Waitabu. However, Waitabu program evaluations clearly show that the success of the Fiji WIL rests on several key principles. First, establishing a strong relationship with the village prior to WIL inception, in order to gain an intimate knowledge of the community and political structure and to garner support of the project from village elders. Second, ensuring that learners understood the social, business and ecological dynamics of the WIL project and the promises and pitfalls of creating a sustainable and viable tourism venture in a developing nation. Third, and perhaps most importantly, creating an environment in which learners engaged in levels of cross-cultural communication as they recognized the importance of operating within the local community's cultural framework, rather than with a purely Western mindset.

5.   CASE STUDY 2: COMMUNITY ENGAGEMENT WIL IN THE NORTHERN TERRITORY, AUSTRALIA AND OVERSEAS

A long-running innovative WIL initiative at the University of Technology, Sydney in conjunction with the Youth Challenge Australia Program (YCA) embeds experiential learning in a dedicated subject on Community Engagement (see Figure 27.2).

In this case project-based community engagement provides learners with the opportunity to gain and 'apply knowledge, skills and feelings in an immediate and relevant setting' (Smith, 2001). This approach to WIL exposes learners to a concrete experience and has introduced learners to authentic practices through interaction with industry and community where through a project-based approach there can be an opportunity for conceptual change. Such an experiential, learner-centered learning approach is shown in Figure 27.3 (University of Technology, Sydney's Youth Challenge Australia program), which was recognized with the Tourism Transport Forum's *Corporate Leadership Award* for innovation. The project encourages tourism learner volunteers to work on grassroots development projects in regional and remote towns in indigenous communities in the Northern Territory.

Over 200 learners have participated in the WIL projects, with many going on to higher degree studies, and it has furthered UTS's sustainable tourism management area for having a strong reputation for having a practical and 'real-world' focus and twice being used by the University in National Tertiary Education submissions to demonstrate its community contribution. The work that these WIL participants have carried out over this period includes:

- construction of important community buildings such as school houses, health clinics and community centers;
- participation in a variety of environmental projects which secure the natural flora and fauna of the regions, that may otherwise be under threat from development or subsistence lifestyles;
- participation in the Surgical Eye Expeditions projects, where volunteer medical staff provide surgical expertise to remove cataracts and prevent other forms of eye disease that, left untreated, may lead to blindness;
- numerous health and environmental awareness projects, where interaction with the local community has meant that awareness is spread effectively at a grassroots level.

In addition to the benefits provided through these projects to local communities, the impact on participants has been remarkable. Many of those involved have been dramatically affected by their experiences and now seek to create a greater positive influence through their careers and even day-to-day lives. Past participants are involved in aid relief,

Figure 27.2   WIL subject at UTS community engagement

YOUTH CHALLENGE AUSTRALIA

International Volunteer Positions:

Earn Academic Credit

Undergraduate or Postgraduate

Elective Subject, Internship or Research

Vanuatu, Guyana, Costa Rica, Guatemala, India and Central Australia

Community Engagement

Community Development, International Development, Project Management, Education, Health, Social Work, Tourism, Environmental Studies, Youth Work, Community Welfare, Human Rights, Cultural Studies, Outdoor Education, Indigenous Studies, Humanities, Political Studies

UNIVERSITY OF TECHNOLOGY SYDNEY

School Of Leisure, Sport and Tourism
Faculty of Business
University Of Technology, Sydney
PO Box 222, Lindfield, NSW 2070
Phone: 02 9514 5497   Fax 02 9514 5195
www.business.uts.edu.au/leisure/index.html

For information on topics and study:
Associate Professor Stephen Wearing
Email: S.Wearing@uts.edu.au

For eligibility criteria, enrolment applications and general course information:
Sue Upton, Admin Assistant
Phone 02 9514 5497   Fax 02 9514 5195
Email s.upton@uts.edu.au

UNIVERSITY OF TECHNOLOGY SYDNEY

Youth Challenge Australia
c/o University of Technology, Sydney
PO Box 222, Eton Road, Lindfield
NSW 2070
Ph. 02 9514 5512
Fax. 02 9514 5130
Email: yca@uts.edu.au
www.youthchallenge.org.au
ABN. 55 053 902 840

YOUTH CHALLENGE AUSTRALIA

FAQS

If I am a student at UTS who is enrolled in a school other than the School of Sport, Leisure & Tourism, can I still get uni credit for my participation in a YCA field program?
Yes. This class is available as an elective to all UTS students.

Will I need to pay a HECS fee over and above the cost of my YCA fees?
Yes. As this is a unit elective, you will be required to pay the usual uni HECS fee that is mandatory for all classes.

Will I get uni credit if I participate in a YCA field program during my summer holidays?
Yes. YCA programs run at various times throughout the year depending on the host country, so the timing of fieldwork may not always coincide with the uni calendar year.

I don't attend uni at UTS. Can this subject be transferred and applied to my studies at another university in Australia?
Yes, this is generally fine; however, this will vary depending on the transfer policies of the university in question. You will need to check with your own uni about credit transfer criteria and processes. Some unis recognise YCA placements as a matter of course.

For more information about earning academic credit or to apply for the Youth Challenge Australia volunteer program, please contact the office:

yca@uts.edu.au
(02) 9514 5512
www.youthchallenge.org.au

Figure 27.3   Outline of WIL subject community engagement

working with children and refugees from devastated areas, in experiential education, politics, social justice issues and environmental concerns, to name just a few of the important areas that have benefited from the experience of these learners.

The use of Work-Integrated Learning (WIL) through onsite, community-based tourism projects to provide cultural and environmental awareness in sustainable tourism education has been a critical step, leading the way forward for many other professional areas. This chapter has provided a framework for those interested in developing WIL for sustainable tourism education projects, specifically based at a community level. It has focused particularly on the theory and practice in order to demonstrate how this can provide projects that seek to provide the opportunity of a learning approach to the benefit of learners in an environment where they offer the opportunity to work with the local people (and their natural and cultural environments) to be environmentally and culturally sustainable. However, further developments of WIL need to reach outside of the framework of dedicated university courses where there is a likelihood that some 'preaching to the converted' may be occurring. In the remainder of this chapter we look at two contexts for such expansion. The first focuses upon informal learning experiences as contexts for WIL and the second concludes this chapter by challenging how sustainable education in higher education needs to provide access to WIL opportunities that lead students to a critical knowing about themselves and others.

6.   FUTURE DIRECTIONS: INFORMAL LEARNING CONTEXTS

For sustainable tourism education both the formal and informal learning that derives from volunteering, living and working overseas have been positively linked to greater employability for young adults (Powell et al., 2006; Canadian Council on Learning, 2008). O'Reilly (2006), Martin (2010) and Heath (2007, 2009) claim that travel experiences contribute to travelers' 'soft skills', such as communication skills, open mindedness, adaptability, motivation and resourcefulness, making travelers more attractive to potential employers when they seek to re-enter the job market. It has been identified in Sustainable Tourism education as a valuable factor when contextualized in a WIL context, as being able to provide the skills and qualities gained during lengthy sojourns are transferable and 'particularly suited to the current context of flexible employment conditions' (O'Reilly, 2006, p. 1012).

Future application of this framework may also be suitable for more informal experiential contexts that reach beyond formal WIL initiatives. One area that offers an opportunity for more informal sustainable tourism education is that provided by the gap year. A gap year has been defined as a nominal period during which a person delays further education or employment in order to travel (Lyons et al., 2012). Although this interlude may be experienced at any point across the lifespan, it is within the period of early adulthood that the gap year phenomenon has become most popular and commonly it involves a year off after completing secondary school or tertiary studies. A gap year is increasingly recognized as a *rite of passage* for many young people in developed nations (Lyons et al., 2012), yet as a means for WIL it remains in its infancy. In the past a gap year has been used and offered for tourism learners as many in the area of sustainable tourism education saw it as the opportunity to elicit *desirable* learning outcomes and that these should be formally recognized by, and integrated into, institutions of higher education (Lyons et al., 2012; Lyons and Wearing, 2011). While a gap year may be experienced at any point across the lifespan it is undertaken predominantly by university-aged learners for non-credit (Abidi, 2004; Jones, 2004). Given recent government initiatives to expand university participation from 25 percent to 40 percent by 2025 (Universities Australia, 2013), institutions of higher education have a perfect opportunity to target the gap year as an opportunity for WIL. Integrating these informal learning contexts into higher education environments through credit arrangements and recognition of prior learning presents challenges that are yet to be addressed.

7.   CONCLUSION: TOWARD A CRITICAL KNOWING THROUGH WIL

Schweinsberg et al. (2013) have recently argued that sustainability education is predicated on students, teachers and universities embracing notions of 'criticality' in curriculum design. In the wake of the global financial crisis, many universities have been suitably lambasted for a historically dominant focus on profit generation as the key deliverable from a neoliberal-based tertiary education (see Quigley, 2011). Responding to such concerns, in 2010 the BEST Education Network identified five value sets that tourism 'students must imbibe to be successful leaders of a fragile industry in uncertain times. They are ethics, stewardship, professionalism, knowledge and mutual respect' (Sheldon, in Liburd and Edwards, 2010, p. viii). All of these value sets are, we would argue, characterized as 'occupational values' (see Evetts, 2011), which define the perceived position of business in society.

The rapid globalization of business interests after the Second World War has sparked considerable academic interest into notions of business ethics and corporate social responsibility (Carroll, 1999; Donaldson and Dunfee, 1994; Ferrell and Fraedrich, 2014; Goodpaster, 1991). Business does not exist in isolation from its environmental context and as such there is a necessity to explore how best to communicate environmental and social values to future business leaders. Jurowski and Liburd (2001) argued that sustainability is best taught not as distinct subjects, but as a philosophy, which impacts on all mainstream tourism business subjects. The present authors agree with such an approach in as much as it helps ensure that sustainability education cannot be parked as a niche concern of an elective unit, but instead centralizes a doctrine of sustainability into all facets of business education. Where such approaches can run into problems, however, lies in the notion of the 'journey metaphor' and the possibility that by focusing too much on their own constructions and journeys towards sustainability, businesses may inadvertently (or perhaps deliberately) side-step important questions and miss opportunities for actual required changes to organizational practice (Milne et al., 2004). One mechanism whereby this can be addressed is through the development of what Tribe (2002) describes as 'critically knowing' graduates. Critical knowing, Tribe (2002) notes, is not just related to the development of 'narrow professional competence that may be characterized as vocational'. Instead, he notes, there is a need to develop broader ethical competence. One mechanism for achieving such competences is through the enhancement of opportunities for experiential learning. By offering opportunities for students to engage in workplaces with the full spectrum of tourism stakeholder groups as evident in the case studies discussed earlier in this chapter (including mainstream commercial tourism providers, NGOs such as Tourism Concern, WWF and so on), graduates will gain a greater appreciation of the roles of tourism in society.

REFERENCES

Abidi, Z.J. (2004), *Taking a Gap Year? Report for Rank Foundation Youth Work Schemes*, London: YMCA George William Collage.
Billett, S. (2001), 'Knowing in practice: Re-conceptualising vocational expertise', *Learning and Instruction*, **11** (6), 431–52.
Brundtland, G. (1987), *Report of the World Commission on Environment and Development: Our Common Future*, Brussels: United Nations.
Buabeng Assan, T.E. (2014), 'Work integrated learning (WIL): A phenomenographic study of student teachers' experiences', *Mediterranean Journal of Social Sciences*, **5** (7), 300–306.
Canadian Council on Learning (2008), 'Health literacy in Canada: A healthy understanding', accessed 1 September 2014 at www.ccl-cca.ca.
Carroll, A.B. (1999), 'Corporate social responsibility evolution of a definitional construct', *Business and Society*, **38** (3), 268–95.
Donaldson, T. and Dunfee, T.W. (1994), 'Toward a unified conception of business ethics: Integrative social contracts theory', *Academy of Management Review*, **19** (2), 252–84.
Dorasamy, N. and Balkaran, R. (2011), 'Inculcating a service culture among hospitality management learners through work integrated learning (WIL): A case study of Durban University of Technology', *Corporate Ownership and Control*, **8** (3), 479–86.
Dunlap, R.E. (2008), 'The new environmental paradigm scale: From marginality to worldwide use', *The Journal of Environmental Education*, **40** (1), 3–18.
Edgar, S. and Connaughton, J. (2014), 'Exploring the role and skill set of physiotherapy clinical educators in work-integrated learning', *Asia-Pacific Journal of Cooperative Education*, **15** (1), 29–36.
Evetts, J. (2011), 'A new professionalism? Challenges and opportunities', *Current Sociology*, **59**, 406–22.
Ferrell, O.C. and Fraedrich, J. (2014), *Business Ethics: Ethical Decision Making and Cases*, Boston: Cengage Learning.
Global Development Research Centre (ND), 'Tbilisi Declaration 1977', accessed 10 March 2015 at www.gdrc.org/uem/ee/tbilisi.html.
Goodpaster, K.E. (1991), 'Business ethics and stakeholder analysis', *Business Ethics Quarterly*, **1** (1), 53–73.
Harris, S. (1990), *Two-Way Aboriginal Schooling: Education and Cultural Survival*, Canberra: Aboriginal Studies Press.
Hay, P.R. (2002), *Main Currents in Western Environmental Thought*, Bloomington: Indiana University Press.
Heath, S. (2007), 'Widening the gap: Pre-university gap years and the "economy of experience"', *British Journal of Sociology of Education*, **28** (1), 89–103.
Heath, S. (2009), 'Full time UK based volunteering and the gap year', *Youth and Policy*, **101** Winter, 33–41.
Jones, A. (2004), 'Review of gap year provision', Research Report No. 555, Department of Education and Skills, University of London.
Joplin, L. (1990), 'On defining experiential education', in Kraft, R. and Sakofs, M. (eds), *The Theory of Experiential Education*, 2nd edn, Colorado: Association for Experiential Education.
Jurowski, C. and Liburd, J. (2001), 'A multi-cultural and multi-disciplinary approach to integrating the principles of sustainable development into human resource management curricula in hospitality and tourism', *Journal of Hospitality and Tourism Education*, **13** (5), 36–50.
Keating, K. (2012), 'Mentorship of hospitality management learners during work-integrated learning', *Asia-Pacific Journal of Cooperative Education*, **13** (2), 89–102.
Keeton, M. and Tate, P. (1978), 'A boom in experiential learning', in Keeton, M. and Tate, P. (eds), *Learning by Experience: What, Why, How?*, San Francisco: Jossey-Bass.
Kolb, D.A. (1984), *Experiential Learning: Experience as the Source of Learning and Development*, Englewood Cliffs, NJ: Prentice-Hall.
Kuhn, T.S. (1996), *The Structure of Scientific Revolutions*, 3rd edn, Chicago: University of Chicago Press.
Kyburz-Graber, R. (2013), 'Socio-ecological approaches to environmental education and research: A paradigmatic response to behavioral change orientations', in R.B. Stevenson, M. Brody, J. Dillon and

A.E.J. Wals (eds), *International Handbook of Research on Environmental Education*, New York: Routledge, pp. 23–32.

Kyburz-Graber, R., Hofer, K. and Wolfensberger, B. (2006), 'Studies on a socio-ecological approach to environmental education: A contribution to a critical position in the education for sustainable development discourse', *Environmental Education Research*, **12** (1), 101–14.

Liburd, J. and Edwards, D. (eds) (2010), *Understanding the Sustainable Development of Tourism*, Oxford: Woodeaton.

Lyle, J.T. (1996), *Regenerative Design for Sustainable Development*, New York: John Wiley and Sons.

Lyons, K. and Wearing, S.L. (2011), 'Gap year travel alternatives: Gen-Y, volunteer tourism and global citizenship', in K.A. Smith, I. Yeoman, C. Hsu and S. Watson (eds), *Tourism and Demography*, London: Goodfellow Publishers, pp. 101–16.

Lyons, K., Hanley, J., Wearing, S. and Neil, J. (2012), 'Gap year volunteer tourism: Myths of global citizenship?', *Annals of Tourism Research*, **39** (1), 361–78.

Martin, A.J. (2010), 'Should students have a gap year? Motivation and performance factors relevant to time out after completing school', *Journal of Educational Psychology*, **102** (3), 561–76.

Mascarenhas, J. et al. (eds) (1991), *Participatory Rural Appraisal: Proceedings of the February 1991 Bangalore PRA Trainers Workshop*, Bangalore: MYRADA and London: IIED.

Milne, M.J., Kearins, K. and Walton, S. (2004), 'Business makes a "journey" out of "sustainability": creating adventures in wonderland?', paper presented at the 4th APIRA conference, Singapore.

O'Reilly, C.C. (2006), 'From drifter to gap year tourist: Mainstreaming backpacker travel', *Annals of Tourism Research*, **33** (4), 998–1017.

Peach, D., Gomez, R. and Ruinard, E. (2013), 'Reconstructing places and spaces in blended work integrated learning', in S. Frielick, N. Buissink-Smith, P. Wyse, J. Billot, J. Hallas and E. Whitehead (eds), *Research and Development in Higher Education: The Place of Learning and Teaching (Volume 36)*, refereed papers from the 36th HERDSA Annual International Conference, Higher Education Research and Development Society of Australasia, Inc, AUT University, Auckland, pp. 336–45.

Powell, S., Bratovic, E. and Dolic, A. (2006), *Pro-social Value/Behaviour and Employability Amongst Young People in SEE and the Impact of Volunteer Work Camps*, Sarajevo: South-East Europe Youth Network.

Quigley, R. (2011), 'Sustaining momentum', *U*, **6**, pp. 10–11).

Resnick, L. (1988), 'Learning in school and out', *Educational Researcher*, **16** (9), 13–20.

Rickinson, M. (2001), 'Learners and learning in environmental education: A critical review of evidence', *Environmental Education Research*, **7** (3), 207–320.

Schweinsberg, S., Wearing, S.L. and McManus, P. (2013), 'Exploring sustainable tourism education in business schools: The Honours program', *Journal of Hospitality and Tourism Management*, 20 (1), 53–60.

Scott, R.H. and Van Etten, E. (2013), 'Environmental and conservation volunteering as workplace integrated learning for university learners', *Issues in Educational Research*, **23** (2), 242–57.

Shiva, V., Anderson, P., Schücking, H., Gray, A., Lohmann, L. and Cooper, D. (1991), *Biodiversity: Social and Ecological Perspectives*, London: Zed Books.

Shuttenberg, E. and Poppenhagen, B. (1980), 'Current theory and research in experiential learning for adults', *Journal of Experiential Education*, **3** (1), 27–32.

Smith, C. and Worsfold, K. (2014), 'WIL curriculum design and student learning: A structural model of their effects on student satisfaction', *Studies in Higher Education*, **39** (6), 1070–84.

Smith, M.K. (2001), 'David A. Kolb on experiential learning', *The Encyclopaedia of Informal Education*, accessed 24 August 2014 at www.infed.org/b-explrn.htm.

Stapp, W.B. (1972), 'Inservice teacher training in environmental education', in W.B. Stapp (ed.), *Environmental Education Resource Book*, Newtown, PA: McGraw Hill, pp. 254–60.

Tilbury, D. (1995), 'Environmental education for sustainability: Defining the new focus of environmental education in the 1990s', *Environmental Education Research*, **1** (2), 195–212.

Tribe, J. (2002), 'Education for ethical tourism action', *Journal of Sustainable Tourism*, **10** (4), 309–24.

Universities Australia (2013), *An Agenda for Higher Education Australia*, Canberra: Universities Australia.

Wearing, S., Lyons, K.D. and Snead, S. (2010), 'Volunteer tourism', in J. Liburd and D. Edwards (eds), *Understanding the Sustainable Development of Tourism*, London: Goodfellow Publishers, pp. 188–204.

Xia, J., Caulfield, C. and Ferns, S. (2014), 'Work-integrated learning: Linking research and teaching for a win–win situation', *Studies in Higher Education*, **40** (9), 1560–72.

Zegwaard, K.E. and McCurdy, S. (2014), 'The influence of work-integrated learning on motivation to undertake graduate studies', *Asia-Pacific Journal of Cooperative Education*, **15** (1), 13–28.

28 Ecotourism and interdisciplinary skills
Vivina Almeida Carreira and Pedro Bingre do Amaral

1. INTRODUCTION

The tourism sector generates more than 12 percent of the Portuguese GDP and provides employment to 11 percent of the workforce (PENT 2007). Nature tourism, defined as eco-tourism practiced within protected nature areas, is the product demanded by 6 percent of those who visit the country to spend their leisure time. This demand has been growing at 7 percent a year at least since 1996 (THR 2006), has not shown signs of abating in recent years, and is expected to continue into the future (PENT 2013). Such is the favorable context in which the only Portuguese Ecotourism degree in existence was born in 1998 at Coimbra Higher School of Agriculture (Escola Superior Agrária de Coimbra, ESAC) and has been taught ever since. However, this rapid pace of development has pushed for the provision both of more segmented product offerings and more extensive proficiency of Ecotourism professionals.

Confronted with a great demand for ecotourism education, a scientific area still in its infancy and with very few other academic institutions providing a benchmark on the subject, ESAC had to innovate and learn from the feedback it received from several sources whose topics should be emphasized both in research and in lectures. The results seem to be worth sharing.

The purpose of this chapter is therefore to give an insight into the history of a higher education program in ecotourism, unique in Portugal and the Iberian peninsula, and into the way its objectives were in line with the mission of the school that launched it. At the same time, it is important to document how both the curriculum and the teaching and learning methodologies have been adapted to respond to external changes, in particular the need to meet the guidelines emerging from the Bologna Process (Bologna Declaration 1999). And more than that, this chapter also examines the implementation of interdisciplinary approaches taking advantage of the wide range of knowledge operating in other degree courses, offering a concept of teaching and learning based on values of respect for nature and the environment as well as for the symbolic and cultural values of the Portuguese society and the global society.

2. LITERATURE REVIEW ON ECOTOURISM HIGHER EDUCATION

The interdisciplinary scope of ecotourism poses some wide-ranging questions about which skills should be taught to both undergraduate and graduate students of this subject. Such a problem affects also the broader field of tourism research (McKercher and Prideaux 2014). After analyzing 85 explanations of the term 'ecotourism' used in academic literature, Fennel (2007) opted to define it as: 'a sustainable, non-invasive form of nature-based tourism that focuses primarily on learning about nature first-hand, and which is ethically managed to be low impact, non-consumptive, and locally oriented (control, benefits and scale). It typically occurs in natural areas, and should contribute to the conservation of such areas' (p. 24).

This definition implies the curricula most appropriate to obtain a degree in such areas should include disciplines focused on applied ecology, applied environmental ethics, environmental science education, and tourism marketing. Nevertheless, there are as yet only three named degrees in ecotourism on offer in European universities, each presenting a different curriculum. The same observation applies to tourism degrees, where the diversity of curricula requires a general integration and consolidation of sub-disciplines (Fidgeon 2010, Busby and Huang 2012). In addition, it is also useful to reflect both upon the framing of internships so as to provide more meaningful learning through immersion experiences in ecotourism destinations (Ruhanen et al. 2013) and the provision of lifelong learning for ecotourism professionals (Cuffy et al. 2012).

The previous considerations need also to take into account the impact the European-wide adoption of the 'Bologna model' for higher education has made both in the demand for academic programs in Portugal (Cardoso 2008) and in their recognition in a European-wide context (Huisman et al. 2012): prospective students prefer to study a syllabus that is easily integrated with equivalent ones within the European Higher Education Area. The fact that there are only three academic programs on ecotourism in Europe, each one still with its own peculiar scope, makes it clear that a standard curriculum is still a work in progress. However, it is not yet clear whether these diverse pedagogical offerings will coalesce into one standard, or diversify in order to provide more choices for the market place.

Caldwell and Spinks (1998) had already foreseen an extension of the foundations of teaching and learning enabling the inclusion of problem-solving methodologies, encouraging creativity, innovation and student preparation for lifelong learning education. Miller et al. (2008) present an overview of the educational scene in 2020, in which the traditional school will be transformed into an area of intensive, experimental, creative, reflective, inclusive, motivating and emotional learning. It is important that the traditional school model fits the new student profile which has substantially changed in recent decades due to the democratization of education and the diversification as well as the changing needs of an inclusive and multicultural society. The survival of higher education institutions concurrently depends on this adaptation, confronted, in the current socio-economic context, with the need to present ever higher performance rates. *The World Declaration on Higher Education in the Twenty-First Century: Vision and Action* (UNESCO 1998) contained in its Foreword reference to the unprecedented demand for higher education, permeated by diversification. Institutions of higher education are expected to suffer directly the consequences of the resulting diversification, being, however, the task of higher education to overcome them:

> A renewal of higher education is essential for the whole of society to be able to face up to the challenges of the twenty-first century, to ensure its intellectual independence, to create and advance knowledge, and to educate and train responsible, enlightened citizens and qualified specialists, without whom no nation can progress economically, socially, culturally or politically so that our society, which is currently undergoing a profound crisis of values, can transcend mere economic considerations and incorporate deeper dimensions of morality and spirituality. (p. 8)

It is in this context that the use of active teaching and learning methods can help to increase the effectiveness of teaching and learning, promoting inter- and multidisciplinary knowledge through the creation of learning environments directly linked to the reality of the student, placing him/her as a subject responsible for his/her learning process. The active methods are educational tools that pave the way for the development of the students' autonomy, critical awareness and ethics.

Project work, in particular, provides a learning process in which the student is encouraged to seek and process information, making use of his/her mental faculties – observing, thinking, questioning, associating, reflecting, interpreting, inferring – actively building knowledge rather than passively receiving it from the teacher. The lecturers guide the process of teaching and learning, not resigning from their role of advisors and facilitators, and have at their disposal numerous techniques and motivational strategies (Labegalini and Marçolla 2009).

Ecotourism education should also foster global awareness and promote 'global citizenship'. Global citizenship has been defined as a 'meritorious viewpoint that suggests that global forms of belonging, responsibility, and political action counter the intolerance and ignorance that more provincial and parochial forms of citizenship encourage' (Lyons et al., 2012, p. 361). It is generally accepted that within these notions of global citizenship exist three key dimensions (Morais and Ogden 2011; Schattle 2009; Tarrant et al. 2011; Stoner et al. 2014): social responsibility (a concern for humanity and the environment); global awareness (alertness and responsiveness to issues that are global in nature); and civic engagement (active, informed participation in local, national and global affairs).

From preparing graduates to participate in a global economy and understand diverse cultures to developing a sensitivity to different perspectives and being capable of working with people from around the world, fostering global citizenship among students is arguably at the heart of higher education's twenty-first-century purpose. For example, the American Academy of Arts and Sciences (2013) focuses specifically on promoting language learning, expanding education in international affairs and transnational studies.

Another learning technique should be critical reflection, the mechanism by which students begin to make meaning out of their experiences and adjust their frames of reference (Moore 2005). Critical reflection, as a process, engages students in deeper thought, in 'scratching below the surface' where they begin to reconceptualize and reframe the perspective that defines their worldview.

This state of affairs points to the need for a new conceptualization of identity and relationality with others: namely, global citizenship, or the attitude and behavior of holding a commitment to the whole of planet earth and the human family, not in place of, but in addition to and indeed even in priority over one's more localized self-understandings and loyalties. Fortunately, global citizenship is becoming a matter of increasing concern across the higher education landscape (Lewin 2009).

Tourism education, its institutions, academics and students, need to be at the heart of this change by virtue of their contribution to the tourism-related private, public and third sectors' pool of human and intellectual capital. Tourism's critical role in the context of global citizenship is undeniable, as a global phenomenon, where the pleasure-seeking of guests from one part of the world has impacts on the social, cultural and economic well-being of hosts in the locales (often in other corners of the world) they visit (Wall and Mathieson 2006). The environmental impacts of tourism activity affect the entire planet and its complex climate system, including communities that neither travel widely nor benefit from tourism (Schott et al. 2010). More positively, however, tourism is also a global force that has powerful potential to encourage cross-cultural communication and peace-building (Higgins-Desbiolles 2006).

There is a conviction that global citizenship is a crucial orientation in today's 'experience economy' (Pine and Gilmore 2011): consumer values are changing in such a way that people no longer seek primarily 'stuff and status', but rather prefer to look for 'more meaning, more deeply felt connections, more substance, more control and a greater sense of purpose' (Pollock 2013). Ethical concerns have been increasingly conditioning consumerism, including in tourism (Weeden and Boluk 2014). Organizations are recognizing that approaches which are not in step with this changing consumer ethos and not sustainable for the planet and the people on it are not going to be conducive to their own long-term survival (KPMG International 2012). The future success of tourism rides not only on our ability to harness and channel its positive impacts, but also to come to terms with tourism's negative impacts by taking responsibility for positive change. Both hosts and guests will increasingly demand this (Pollock 2013; Reisinger 2013; Weeden and Boluk 2014).

But there are also more profound reasons for grounding tourism education in an ethic of global citizenship. As Higgins-Desbiolles (2006) argues, we often focus so much on tourism as an economic powerhouse – and hence on training students to work within tourism as an economic sphere – that we tend to forget that it also has a serious social function: tourism is no less than a world-making force (Hollinshead 2008). At its best, it can bring people together across lines of difference to encounter one another, and one another's cultures and spaces, and can therefore potentially foster understanding and peace. Far from being the mere fancy of idealists and romantics, this social function of tourism as a promoter of peace has been highlighted by global organizations such as the United Nations and is receiving increasing scholarly attention (Moufakkir and Kelly 2014). These developments point to the establishment of a set of values-based principles that tourism students need to embrace to become responsible future leaders in the tourism industry and in their communities. The five value sets, which have been recently proposed as part of the Tourism Education Futures Initiative (TEFI), can be identified as ethics, stewardship, knowledge, mutuality and professionalism (Sheldon et al. 2011).

3.   ECOTOURISM DEGREES IN PORTUGAL AND OTHER EUROPEAN HIGHER EDUCATION SCHOOLS

Ecotourism has been taught as a BSc (Hons) degree at Escola Superior Agrária de Coimbra (ESAC) since 1998. This course offers a curriculum with a wide range of scientific areas, for which the ESAC, being a center for agriculture, forestry and environmental studies, has a very wide-ranging and qualified teaching staff. This diversity of academic areas fosters synergies with other courses offered on the same premises. Examples are the use and conservation of natural resources, the processing of agro-food products in rural contexts, the integration of tourist routes, enotourism, equine sports and management, organic agriculture, bird watching, among others.

The first formal agricultural studies programs to be offered in Portugal were inaugurated in 1887, when ESAC was founded. The school's facilities occupy several buildings in a surrounding area of about 140 ha. Its buildings are surrounded by contemporary gardens where recent topiary coexists with monumental trees and ancient groves. The National Agriculture Museum is sited at the campus of ESAC, occupying four rooms of a classified building which was once the summer residence of the Bishop of Coimbra. From 2007 onwards, the Bologna Process strategic guidelines were applied to ESAC's syllabus, thereby reinforcing the polytechnic characteristics of this school as far as the nature of lectures was concerned, putting an emphasis on the practical nature of the teaching/learning process so as to ensure learning by doing.

The Bologna Process has also provoked comparisons between the syllabuses of similarly named degrees within the European continent. According to The International Ecotourism Society (TIES), a non-profit worldwide organization that brings together universities, environmental NGOs, businesses and individual professionals, there are in the European space of Higher Education two other programs, besides ESAC, offering a degree in Ecotourism: BSc in Natural and Cultural Heritage Management at University College of Northern Denmark, and BSc (Hons) Ecotourism at the University of Derby (UK). The latter facility also offers three programs of 'combined degrees': BA (Hons) in Ecotourism and Adventure Tourism, BSc (Hons) in Ecotourism and Countryside Management, and BA / BSc (Hons) in Ecotourism and Outdoor Recreation.

The Danish BSc in Natural and Cultural Heritage Management aims to provide students with the understanding of 'cultural heritage, natural heritage, and the economy of [tourism] experience'. To this end, students are taught three groups of curricular units: management of natural heritage (ecology, conservation and management of nature, nature tourism activities), management of cultural heritage (culture and forms of expression, art and aesthetics, history of culture, foreign languages and cultures), economics and innovation in tourism (creative entrepreneurship, innovation processes, methodologies for the management of tourist experiences production). Whether in regard to the objectives or methods of achieving them – particularly the combination of curricular units offered – there is a remarkable similarity between the cycle BSc in Natural and Cultural Heritage Management and the cycle BSc in Ecotourism proposed by the ESAC/ Polytechnic Institute of Coimbra.

The British BSc (Hons) Ecotourism aims to train professionals capable of mitigating the impacts suffered by the environment due to tourism activities. In this sense, it offers its students a curriculum consisting of 17 courses, six in pure or applied ecology, seven in management and entrepreneurship, two within geography, plus one unit of seminar and another of autonomous research. This range of subjects is comparable to that offered in the degree in Ecotourism at the ESAC, though the latter contemplates several curricular units in the Humanities – including foreign languages, cultural history, heritage interpretation, and others.

A joint honours BSc (Hons) in Countryside Management and Ecotourism is combined with the aforementioned program, and includes nine modules, among which are such curricular units as Introduction to Environment, Ecology, Nature Conservation, Management and Legislation of Rural Areas, Environmental and Outdoor Education. The emphasis placed on issues related to Agro-Environmental Sciences and Forestry makes it remarkably similar to the one that is offered by the degree program in Ecotourism at ESAC.

4.   FINDINGS AND OUTCOMES: ESCOLA SUPERIOR AGRÁRIA (ESAC) AS A CASE STUDY ON ECOTOURISM

4.1   Rationale for the 2008 Ecotourism Study Program

The economic sectors of agriculture and forests, the original scope of the educational, scientific and cultural project of the ESAC, have been in the last three decades increasingly conditioned by two new realities: the emergence of environmental concerns and the birth of rural and nature-based tourism markets. The agricultural and forestry landscapes are increasingly being seen in many areas as tourism products whose operation must meet standards of environmental sustainability. At the same time, management policies of protected areas for nature conservation – par excellence territories for the practice of ecotourism – have been increasingly integrating expenses related to the protection of natural values as part of general economic activities. It is expected that ecotourism markets will succeed in increasing revenue, which would not only benefit the producers but would also finance the conservation and protection of rural landscapes, biodiversity and geological heritage. The objective of the ESAC program in ecotourism was to train professionals able to implement all of these new and interdependent aspirations of society and markets. The ESAC is capable of offering a wide range of curricular units which cover all of these subject areas, because ecotourism takes place precisely in natural and rural contexts to which this school has dedicated its attention, analyzing them under the perspectives of the life and environmental sciences, agricultural sciences, the humanities and the provision of services. The Ecotourism Program underwent a number of changes defined by the Bologna Process guidelines. This was a very timely opportunity to make a revision of the study plan after ten years of existence.

As a result, the 2008 Ecotourism Program of Studies (see Table 28.1) was implemented over three main axes:

- Economical Management, imparting tools for the management of businesses in this activity sector;
- Logistical Management, covering technical and material aspects of the organization of ecotourism activities, environmental and quality legislation and rules, the creation of adequate conditions to provide services in this sector;
- Content Production, imparting tools for the production of interpretation contents for Ecotourism programs.

4.2   Results Appraisal: Evaluating the Professional Outcomes of Former Students

Since the Ecotourism diploma offered by ESAC has been the sole degree in this subject area in Portugal, and one of the relatively few available in Europe, its program has had to face the problems many pioneers encounter: namely, to evaluate its success without the benefit of a comparable alternative, or the means to benchmark its results against a possible competitor in the academic arena. The only realistic appraisal of the diploma's merit is, then, is the evaluation of its usefulness to those who have graduated and subsequently had professional involvement in this field of expertise.

Table 28.1   Structure and content of the ESAC Ecotourism Program (2008)

1st Semester	ECTS	3rd Semester	ECTS	5th Semester	ECTS
Biology	6	Environment and Society	5	Enterprise Management and Entrepreneurship	6
Geography	5	Social Sciences	6	Nature Conservation	5
Mathematics and Computer Science	6	English for Specific Purposes	4	Rural Development	4
English language and Communication Skills	3	French I/Spanish I	4	Wild Fauna	4
Introduction to Tourism	5	Ecology I	5	Tourism Products	5
Agricultural Productions	5	Agricultural Systems	6	Sustainable products	6
2nd Semester		**4th Semester**		**6th Semester**	
Biology	6	Economics	4	Tourism Management	6
Geography	5	French II/Spanish II	4	Interpretation of Cultural and natural heritage	6
Mathematics and Computer Science	6	Tourism Recreational Activities	5	Training Placement	18
English language and Communication Skills	3	Ecology II	5		
Introduction to Tourism	5	Ethno-botany	5		
Agricultural Productions	5	History and Cultural heritage	7		

Therefore, in order to evaluate whether the syllabus offered to students actually matched their subsequent professional career, an enquiry was made via email and social networks. A list of every graduate student who obtained their diploma in Ecotourism at Escola Superior Agrária between the course's inception in 1998 and the year 2012 was compiled, totaling a universe of 140 BSc (Hons) titleholders. Then a short questionnaire was sent either by email or social networks (LinkedIn, Facebook), according to the available contacts. The questions posed were as follows:

1. Are you currently employed or unemployed? (y/n)
2. Did you find any job, either in the tourism sector or any other, less than 12 months after finishing your degree? (y/n)
3. Have you been employed specifically in the ecotourism or tourism industry since obtaining your diploma? (y/n)
4. Have you been working in Portugal or abroad? If the latter, in which country?
5. Considering your working experience, which topics do you think should be added to, or reinforced in, the ecotourism syllabus?

To these questions only 48 former students gave answers – a sample representing 34 percent of the universe under analysis. The results were:

1. Among graduates, 44 individuals (92 percent of the sample) were currently employed.
2. A year after finishing their degree, 33 former students (69 percent of the sample) had already found a job.

3. Among those employed, 41 (75 percent) were working in the tourism industry.
4. Currently 9 graduates (18 percent of the sample) are working abroad: 3 in Spain, 2 in England, 1 in Germany, 1 in Brazil, 1 in Iceland, 1 in São Tomé e Príncipe.
5. Only 9 graduates answered the last question, each one stressing the need to reinforce the syllabus in a specific topic, namely: Cartography, Orientation and GIS; Computer Applications in Tourism; Statistic Methods; Equestrian Activities; Regional Products and Local Traditions; Tourism Marketing; Active Tourism and Outdoor Sports; Gastronomy and Wine; Public Relations and Event Organization.

These outcomes suggest that the Ecotourism degree has been a valuable asset in the curriculum vitae of graduates: at 8 percent, the unemployment rate among those holding this diploma is half that of the Portuguese active population. Furthermore, a very high percentage (75 percent) of those who had concluded their studies were working in ecotourism-related fields. However, this optimism may be offset by the fact that almost one fifth of former graduates chose to leave Portugal, either to work in ecotourism companies in countries where many ecotourists depart from (Germany, England) or in countries to which these same clients head (Spain, Brazil, São Tomé e Príncipe, Iceland).

The suggestions provided by answers to the final question could be accommodated without changing the syllabus dramatically by providing deeper and more market-oriented approach to practical issues. The major exception to these recommendations concerns active tourism and outdoor sports, subject areas to which the degree's curriculum does not yet devote much attention.

5.   FUTURE DIRECTIONS

In 2014, the Ecotourism Program underwent a few more changes motivated by three main issues: an admission on the part of students and lecturers that the program was lacking new approaches; suggestions on the part of graduates in the labor market; and a recommendation on the part of the national Agency for the Quality of Higher Education. The revised program in Ecotourism distributes its focus between three major scientific fields, allocating 25 percent of its total ECTS to each: life sciences, humanities, and tourism/services – the latter with a strong component of applied business sciences. The remaining ECTS are distributed in areas such as agriculture, forestry, social sciences and business, among others. These study areas are integrated into the final year's internship program.

The teaching of life sciences aims to make students competent in identifying, analyzing and sustainably handling natural assets with tourist attractiveness. The study of humanities aims to enable the students to perform good oral and written communication of information contents in multiple languages. It also aims to make them aware of cultural heritage, in particular that associated with rural and natural areas. Learning in the scientific area of personal services, in turn, provides the student with the ability to integrate the interdisciplinary skills acquired in the management of tourism facilities and assets in rural areas. This new program (see Table 28.2) took into account the suggestions made by former students now working as full-time ecotourism professionals.

The training placement, an internship of no less than six weeks carried out in local companies or organizations operating in the tourism sector, was not awarded a higher

Table 28.2   Revised structure and content of the ESAC Ecotourism Program (2012)

1st Semester	ECTS	3rd Semester	ECTS	5th Semester	ECTS
Biology	6	Products of the Land and Local products	3	Tourism Management	5
Statistical Methods	6	Terrestrial and Aquatic Ecology and Landscape	6	Interpretation of Cultural and Natural Heritage	5
Communication Skills	3	Ethno-botany	5	Business Creation and Entrepreneurship	5
English I	4	English III	5	Biodiversity and Conservation	6
Introduction to Tourism	5	French I	4	Active Tourism	4
Agrarian Systems	6	History and Cultural Heritage	4	Gastronomy and Wine	4
		Computer Applications in Tourism	3		
2nd Semester		**4th Semester**		**6th Semester**	
English II	4	Tourism Economics	5	Cultural Tourism Products	6
Geography	4	Rural Areas and Tourism	6	Local Development	5
Tourism and Sustainability	5	French II	5	Public Relations and Event Organization	4
Cartography, Orientation and GIS	3	Tourism Marketing	4	Training Placement	15
Environment and Society	5	English IV	5		
General Ecology	6	Wildlife and Tourism	5		
Equestrian Activities	3				

ECTS but was given a longer period of time. Throughout this internship the student is expected to deliver some intellectual product that provides added value to the hosting company's portfolio, applying as much as appropriate to the full range of interdisciplinary knowledge he or she has acquired during the learning program; this product should also be feasible enough to reflect first-hand acquaintance with the company's needs and potentialities. Examples are to prepare a business plan and an operational plan for a new product, a research study about undeveloped market niches and the technical solutions needed to exploit them, an optimization agenda for environmental, economic and social sustainability of already existing operations, and so on.

6.   CONCLUSION

Ecotourism as a higher education degree is still a novelty both in Portuguese and European universities: there are only three such diplomas on offer across the European continent, the oldest of them originating in 1998. An international consensus as to the contents of its syllabus has not yet been reached. Nevertheless, there is a high demand for this study course in Portugal, and the labor market for its graduates is enticing. Feedback from former students now working in this sector has enabled ESAC to fine-tune its syllabus, all the while seeking to strengthen its affinities with comparable courses in countries that had signed the Bologna Accord. This frontal approach to the demands of the labor market, conjugated with a decidedly multidisciplinary curriculum focusing on natural sciences, social sciences and humanities, provides a fruitful program that may be advantageously reproduced in other higher education institutions.

REFERENCES

American Academy of Arts and Sciences (2013), *The Heart of the Matter: The Humanities and Social Sciences for a Vibrant, Competitive, and Secure Nation*, Cambridge, MA: American Academy of Arts and Sciences.

Bologna Declaration (1999), Joint declaration of the European Ministers of Education convened in Bologna on 19 June 1999, Bologna.

Busby, G. and Huang, R. (2012), 'Integration, intermediation and tourism higher education: conceptual understanding in the curriculum', *Tourism Management*, **33** (1), 108–15.

Caldwell, B. and Spinks, J.M. (1998), *Beyond the Self-Managing School*, New York: Routledge.

Cardoso, A.R. (2008), 'Demand for higher education programs: The impact of the Bologna Process', *CESifo Economic Studies*, **54** (2), 229–47.

Cuffy, V., Tribe, J. and Airey, D. (2012), 'Lifelong learning for tourism', *Annals of Tourism Research*, **39** (3), 1402–24.

Fennel, D. (2007), *Ecotourism* (3rd edn), New York: Routledge.

Fidgeon, P.R. (2010), 'Tourism education and curriculum design: A time for consolidation and review?', *Tourism Management*, **31** (6), 699–723.

Higgins-Desbiolles, F. (2006), 'More than an "industry": The forgotten power of tourism as a social force', *Tourism Management*, **27** (6), 1192–208.

Hollinshead, K. (2008), 'Imagining the many worlds of tourism: The rise of postdisciplinary research outlooks', *Proceedings of the Conference 'Where the "Bloody Hell" Are We?'* Gold Coast, Australia, 11–14 February. Melbourne: Council for Australian University Tourism and Hospitality Education.

Huisman, J., Adelman, C., Hsieh, C.C., Shams, F. and Wilkins, S. (2012), 'Europe's Bologna process and its impact on global higher education', in D.K. Deardorff, H. de Wit, J.D. Heyl and T. Adams (eds), *The SAGE Handbook of International Higher Education*, Thousand Oaks: Sage Publications, pp. 81–100.

KPMG (2012), 'Expect the unexpected: Building business value in a changing world', accessed 18 March 2015 at www.kpmg.com/Global/en/IssuesAndInsights/ArticlesPublications/Documents/building-business-value.pdf

Labegalini, A. and Marçolla, R. (2009), *Comunicação e Educação: A Didática a Serviço do Ensino Superior*, São Paulo: Editora Arte and Ciência.

Lewin, R. (2009), 'The quest for global citizenship through study abroad', in Lewin, R. (ed.), *The Handbook of Practice and Research in Study Abroad: Higher Education and the Quest for Global Citizenship*, New York: Routledge, pp. xiii–xxii.

Lyons, K., Hanley, J., Wearing, S. and Neil, J. (2012), 'Gap year volunteer tourism: Myths of global citizenship?', *Annals of Tourism Research*, **39** (1), 361–78.

McKercher, B. and B. Prideaux (2014), 'Academic myths of tourism', *Annals of Tourism Research*, **46**, 16–28.

Miller, R., Shapiro, H. and Hilding-Hamann, K. (2008), *School's Over: Learning Spaces in Europe in 2020: An Imagining Exercise on the Future of Learning*, Luxembourg: Office for Official Publications of the European Communities, accessed 29 August 2014 at ftp.jrc.es/EURdoc/JRC47412.pdf.

Moore, J. (2005), 'Is higher education ready for transformative learning? A question explored in the study of sustainability', *Journal of Transformative Education*, **3** (1), 76–91.

Morais, D.B. and Ogden, A.C. (2011), 'Initial development and validation of the global citizenship scale', *Journal of Studies in International Education*, **15** (5), 445–66.

Moufakkir, O. and Kelly, I. (2014), 'Tourism as peace education: A role for interpretation', in Wohlmuther, C. and Wintersteiner, W. (eds), *International Handbook on Tourism and Peace*, UNWTO-AVARA.

PENT (2007), *Plano Estratégico Nacional do Turismo*, Lisbon: Turismo de Portugal.

PENT (2013), *Plano Estratégico Nacional para o Turismo: Revisão e Objectivos 2013–2015*, Lisbon: Turismo de Portugal.

Pine, J.B. and Gilmore, J.H. (2011), *The Experience Economy*, Boston, MA: Harvard Business Press.

Pollock, A. (2013), 'Waking tourism up to an uncertain future', paper presented at Tourism Education Futures Initiative 7th Conference, Oxford: Oxford Brookes University, 13–16 April.

Reisinger, Y. (ed.) (2013), *Transformational Tourism: Tourist Perspectives*, Wallingford: CABI.

Ruhanen, L., Robinson, R. and Breakey, N. (2013), 'A tourism immersion internship: Student expectations, experiences and satisfaction', *Journal of Hospitality, Leisure, Sport and Tourism Education*, **13**, 60–69.

Schattle, H. (2009), 'Global citizenship in theory and practice', in Lewin, R. (ed.), *The Handbook of Practice and Research in Study Abroad: Higher Education and the Quest for Global Citizenship*, New York: Routledge, pp. 3–20.

Schott, C., Reisinger, A. and Milfont, T.L. (2010), 'Tourism and climate change: Interrelations and implications', in Schott, C. (ed.), *Tourism and the Implications of Climate Change: Issues and Actions*, Bingley: Emerald Group Publishing.

Sheldon, P.J., Fesenmaier, D.R. and Tribe, J. (2011), 'The Tourism Education Futures Initiative (TEFI): Activating change in tourism education', *Journal of Teaching in Travel and Tourism*, **11** (1), 2–23.

Stoner, K., Tarrant, M., Perry, L., Stoner, L., Wearing, S. and Lyons, K. (2014), 'Global citizenship as a learning outcome of educational travel', *Journal of Teaching in Travel and Tourism*, **14** (2), 149–63.

Tarrant, M.A., Stoner, L., Borrie, W.T., Kyle, G., Moore, R.L. and Moore, A. (2011), 'Educational travel and global citizenship', *Journal of Leisure Research*, **43** (3), 403–26.

THR (2006), *Turismo de Natureza*, Lisbon: Turismo de Portugal.

UNESCO (1998), *Declaration Mondiale sur l'Enseignement Superieur pour le XXIe Siècle: Vision et Actions*, Paris: UNESCO.

Wall, G. and Mathieson, A. (2006), *Tourism: Change, Impacts, and Opportunities*, Harlow: Pearson Education.

Weeden, C. and Boluk, K. (eds) (2014), *Managing Ethical Consumption in Tourism*, London: Routledge.

29 Criticality in tourism education
Émilie Crossley

1. INTRODUCTION

The notion of criticality in tourism studies has gained prominence in recent years through what has come to be known as the field's 'critical turn' (Ateljevic et al., 2005; Ateljevic et al., 2013; Bianchi, 2009). The critical turn has generated forums for productive dialogue and debate between researchers of varied theoretical proclivities and has centered largely on revelations of tourism studies' epistemological underpinnings (Franklin and Crang, 2001; Ren et al., 2010; Pritchard et al., 2011), a drive towards methodological innovation, particularly in terms of qualitative methods (Ateljevic et al., 2007; Hollinshead and Jamal, 2007; Phillimore and Goodson, 2004; Riley and Love, 2000), and strong advocacy for research informed by a social justice agenda (Pritchard et al., 2011; Higgins-Desbiolles, 2006; Higgins-Desbiolles et al., 2012). Tribe (2005a) characterizes the move towards criticality in tourism studies as part of a wave of 'new tourism research', which has seen a transition from the rather narrow perception of tourism as an applied business field to a research environment that draws on the full gamut of philosophical, theoretical and methodological resources available within the social sciences and humanities. This development has opened up tourism studies to research topics as diverse and intriguing as embodiment, post-colonialism, gender, race, sexuality, subjectivity, affect and narrative (for example Aitchison, 2001; Fullagar, 2002; Hall and Tucker, 2004; Hollinshead, 1999; Johnston, 2001; Picard and Robinson, 2012; Pritchard, 2004; Veijola and Jokinen, 1994).

The critical turn has taken on an increasingly established character through a number of major published works and events such as the biennial Critical Tourism Studies Conference, which is now in its tenth year. While these activities have taken place mainly in the UK and Europe, nascent groups in other parts of the world, such as the Council for Australasian University Tourism and Hospitality Educators' (CAUTHE) Critical Approaches in Tourism and Hospitality (CATH) special interest group in Australia and New Zealand, point to the legitimation of critical voices across the globe (Wilson et al., 2008). While clearly still not accepted as 'mainstream' thought within tourism studies as a whole – if, indeed, it is possible to think of the field/discipline as such (Tribe, 1997; Echtner and Jamal, 1997) – critical tourism studies has cohered in many crucial respects. It now faces the challenge of remaining unified for the sake of its strength as an alternative research orientation while maintaining an ethos of theoretical and methodological pluralism in order to preserve 'a vital intellectual space for reflexive debate' (Fullagar and Wilson, 2012, p. 2). Furthermore, Fullagar and Wilson (2012) have argued that radical intellectual positions can become unreflexively polemic and entrenched in binary thinking, such as margin/center or critical/mainstream, to the extent that differences between perspectives become exaggerated. The potential for such distortions serves as a reminder that a critical engagement with the production of knowledge needs to encompass not only challenges to the perceived mainstream but also criticality itself.

Despite this growth and revitalization of critical approaches within tourism research, there is a general consensus that tourism education has remained largely insulated from these radical and potentially transformative academic currents. University tourism programs, located predominantly in business and management schools, have conventionally focused on the development of specific managerial competencies and skills in their learners in a bid to produce employable graduates (Ayikoru et al., 2009; Cooper and Shepherd, 1997; Fidgeon, 2010; Inui et al., 2006; Ryan, 1995). Critical perspectives have been dismissed as irrelevant by many universities that 'assign value to more pragmatic outcomes that are framed in terms of industry relevance or hierarchical research values' (Fullagar and Wilson, 2012). However, the dominance of vocationally oriented courses, which foreground *training* as opposed to *education*, has been critiqued for constituting a production line of tourism managers who will go into the industry ready to run efficient yet potentially exploitative businesses (Inui et al., 2006). The lack of educational components addressing issues of environmental sustainability, ethical decision-making and social justice has led to further accusations that tourism education perpetuates an ideological commitment to managerialism, market values and neoliberalism (Tribe, 2008; Walmsley, 2009; McLaren and Jaramillo, 2013).

In a remedial move, Tribe (2001; 2002; 2008) has advocated a model of education that fosters what he calls 'philosophic practitioners', who are able to achieve both vocational and ethical competence within the tourism industry. Tribe suggests that this can be achieved by introducing a component of liberal reflection into conventional tourism business courses in order to allow learners to reflect critically on their future role as tourism managers. Belhassen and Caton (2011) liken this approach to critical management studies, which they draw on to suggest changes to tourism curricula in order to include issues of sustainability together with a more reflexive understanding of management as a social force (see also Cockburn-Wootten and Cockburn, 2011; Fulop, 2000; Sinclair, 2007a; 2007b). These pedagogical movements converge around a perceived need to do more to foreground salient issues of ethics, politics and sustainability within tourism education. Building on these emergent models of progressive tourism education, this chapter explores the plural and contested meanings of criticality as both a theoretical orientation and pedagogical practice, and makes an attempt to understand how a renewed focus on criticality might impact tourism education.

2.   CRITICALITY: THINKING, PEDAGOGY, REFLEXIVITY

As Brookfield (2005) notes, criticality is a plural, contested term that has historically been enlisted by different social groups to serve their own ideological ends. As such, it is not my intention to attempt to pin down and define the term but rather to explore 'what critical practices mean in the embodied space of teaching and within the discursive parameters of the curriculum' (Fullagar and Wilson, 2012, p. 3). While these two educational dimensions that Fullagar and Wilson identify are inevitably intertwined, it is my contention that insufficient attention has been paid to the ways in which aspirations for a reformed tourism curriculum might be affected by the embodied and subjective practices that occur within the classroom, including, for example, learners' receptivity to more critical material and power dynamics between educators and learners (cf. Ellsworth, 1989; Belhassen and

Caton, 2011; Leopold, 2013). The predominant focus of tourism educators on curriculum development has previously been noted by Tribe (2005b, p. 28; 2005c), who estimated at the time that as much as 86 percent of relevant research might be related to curriculum compared to only 3 percent on teaching and learning. As Schwarzin (2013) emphasizes, critical content needs to be accompanied by an equally important creative and dialogical pedagogical context in order to engage and nurture learners. The following discussion will show that criticality presents an invitation to reevaluate not only the content of tourism courses with a greater focus on political, ethical, ecological and epistemological issues, but also the ways in which these are delivered and how educators and learners each play their part in the reproduction and interrogation of tourism knowledge.

In this section, I discuss three pedagogical moments along a continuum of criticality, which moves progressively towards uncertainty and reflexivity, and evaluate the potential of each for enriching teaching and learning in tourism. The first moment takes critical thinking as a relatively straightforward deployment of criticality, which introduces learners to ways of interrogating knowledge creation and embracing complexity. These skills are advanced and politicized in the second pedagogical moment, critical pedagogy, in which more formalized theoretical resources are drawn upon to unveil naturalized ideologies and forms of structural oppression operating through tourism. The third moment adopts a post-structural, reflexive stance that critiques the modernist discourses that inform critical pedagogy, including claims of rationality, human emancipation and progress. While the first two positions provide learners with the skills and theoretical resources to be able to critically interrogate the knowledge and power relations intrinsic to tourism as an industry and field of study, I believe that this final pedagogical moment moves a step closer towards more fully exploring important issues of positionality, investments and unconscious barriers to learning. By placing these various conceptualizations of criticality in juxtaposition, I hope to provoke debate regarding potential forms of change within educational institutions and the type of 'literacies' with which we feel tourism graduates need to be equipped to deal with the rapidly changing landscape of tourism practice (Jamal et al., 2011).

2.1   Critical Thinking and Critical Pedagogy

The first pedagogical application of criticality that I want to examine comes from the 'critical thinking' literature (Fisher, 2001; Moon, 2008). Put simply, critical thinking is about developing the capacity to think more thoroughly, systematically and with greater scrutiny regarding what is commonly accepted as 'knowledge' or 'truth'. Developing this, Burbules and Beck (1999, p. 46) identify critical thinking as concerned 'primarily with criteria of epistemic adequacy'; that is to say, the 'critical' element of critical thinking involves developing rigorous skills of logical reflection in order to distinguish between sound and unsound arguments. Over time, the critical thinker thus develops the ability to recognize 'faulty arguments, hasty generalizations, assertions lacking evidence, truth claims based on unreliable authority, ambiguous or obscure concepts, and so forth' (p. 46). In addition to developing the capacity to analyze truth claims external to the individual thinker, Fisher (2001, p. 5) also notes critical thinking's reflexive, or 'metacognitive' dimension, through which learners are encouraged to 'think about their thinking' in order to become more discerning and to recognize their own potential for fallibility. So while critical thinking can be distinguished from critical pedagogy, which I will come to in a moment, on the basis of its concern with epistemic adequacy rather than with a political agenda, there is still 'an implicit hope that enhanced critical thinking could have a *general* humanizing effect, across all social groups and classes' (Burbules and Beck, 1999, p. 46, original emphasis).

Critical thinking would appear to be the most readily assimilable form of criticality into existing models of teaching and learning, given its focus on equipping learners with transferable skills, and it has already received strong backing from tourism educators (Cho and Schmelzer, 2000; Cho et al., 2002; Jamal, 2004; Jamal et al., 2011; Leopold, 2013; Sheldon et al., 2011). For example, critical thinking contributes to the 'knowledge' component of seven values advanced by the Tourism Education Futures Initiative (TEFI) – a progressive education movement that aims to enable 'students [to] become responsible leaders and stewards for the destinations where they work or live' (Sheldon et al., 2011, p. 79). Sheldon et al. (2011, p. 83) identify critical thinking as an essential cognitive process that 'calls for an unrelenting examination of any form of knowledge and the knowledge creation process' in order to contextualize information, make explicit the implicit, and unveil bias and unfounded assumptions. Furthermore, within the TEFI framework, critical thinking is linked to both ethics and creativity, implying that the goal of criticality is not simply to achieve epistemic accuracy but to build a more just society, and that there may be a variety of creative ways of enacting such critique. Similarly, Jamal et al. (2011) advocate critical thinking as a crucial analytical skill that forms part of seven core 'literacies' required in order to advance a sustainable tourism pedagogy.

The goals of critical thinking might appear beneficial to tourism education, yet the approach has been subject to criticism for being too vague and potentially exclusionary to some learners due to its cultural specificity (Atkinson, 1997; Vandermensbrugghe, 2004). In a notable rebuttal of these claims, Gieve (1998, p. 123; see also Benesch, 1999) commends Atkinson (1997) for his observation that critical thinking is a social practice rather than a 'decontextualised cognitive skill', but argues against his claims that the practice is culturally hegemonic in terms of transmitting Western modes of thinking to learners. Rather, Gieve distinguishes between two forms of critical thinking: *monological* critical thinking, which is founded upon principles of abstract, logical reasoning, and *dialogical* critical thinking, which entails rational debate and dialogical exploration of arguments as social practices. While both approaches rest on assumptions regarding what constitutes 'rational' argumentation, the key distinction is between monological critical thinking's judgment of the validity of an argument using a universalizing logic and a singular, predetermined cognitive process compared to dialogical critical thinking's more fluid approach, encouraging the evaluation of different viewpoints and epistemologies. While the former approach is endogenous to Western culture, Gieve argues that the dialogical approach presents a more inclusive method for debating and contesting truth-claims. It seems, therefore, that interpretations of critical thinking can vary from a cognitive skill to a dialogical method of argumentation, and from an approach concerned primarily with epistemic accuracy to one that seeks to examine relations of power. This distinction is relevant to the changing nature of tourism classrooms in which we see increasingly diverse and internationalized cohorts of learners, challenging educators to reflect on the ways in which learners can become positioned through culturally embedded bodies of knowledge.

While the aim of critical thinking is to accurately describe and understand the world through sound, rational argumentation, critical pedagogy aims to transform what is seen as an inherently unequal, unjust and oppressive society. This liberatory philosophy is expressed candidly in McLaren and Jaramillo's (2013, p. xxxiii) appeal for critical pedagogy within tourism: 'A transformative pedagogy for critical tourism studies must attempt to create an explicit connection with a philosophy of liberation that projects the path to a totally new society'. Embedded in the tradition of critical theory, critical pedagogy aims to instill in learners a political and ethical consciousness, an understanding of power dynamics both at the societal level and as manifest in the classroom itself, and the ability to turn these radical ideas into constructive, emancipatory action (Freire, 2014; 1998; Giroux, 2007). So, to compare these two pedagogical moments along the spectrum that I am demarcating, while critical thinking is primarily concerned with establishing that knowledge is founded on robust epistemological foundations, critical pedagogy questions the ideological nature of such knowledge: '[Critical pedagogy] regards specific belief claims, not primarily as propositions to be assessed for their truth content, but as parts of systems of belief and action that have aggregate effects within the power structures of society' (Burbules and Beck, 1999, p. 47).

   Again, while critical thinking generally posits a disembodied cognitive process that can be adopted by any thinker, critical pedagogy frames the learner as an empowered social actor who is always socially embedded. As Giroux puts it, 'critical pedagogy opens up a space where students should be able to come to terms with their own power as critical agents' (2007, p. 1). In other words, the learner's capacity to reflect and act on their agentive potential will be affected by their social positioning and identity. Commenting on the application of critical pedagogy within the burgeoning field of critical management studies, Belhassen and Caton (2011, p. 1394) suggest that a curriculum that challenges learners to reflect on their own position of privilege within an unfair society can 'cultivate a productive form of cognitive dissonance' that is likely to induce in the learner a realignment of their ideological commitments. In a tourism context, this might entail learner engagement with the tourism industry's role in global economic development, exploitative business practices, issues of classed and privileged mobilities, and the dominance of neoliberal economic and social practices. However, Belhassen and Caton (2011, p. 1393) are keen to underscore their belief that any change in a learner's worldview or political beliefs should be 'a matter of free and reasoned choice, not of coercion by any institution or individual', drawing attention to the complex terrain that critical, politicized explorations of power, privilege and values traverse.

   In addition to the conceptual, curricular aim of introducing learners to issues of power and oppression, critical pedagogy presents a more fundamental challenge to conventional classroom practices and to the desired outcome of students' learning. After all, within this pedagogical perspective, schools and universities exist as state apparatus designed essentially to indoctrinate learners and to maintain the political status quo. Thus, the usually accepted dichotomy between educator and learner, and the conventional spatial and temporal structure of schools and classrooms, become themselves sites to be critiqued and reconfigured. In line with Giroux's comments about learners' discovery of their own agency, there is an expectation that students should attempt to transcend their subjugation and passivity, and instead become actively involved in their own learning. As Freire (2014, p. 76) explains, within the traditional classroom, the educator's role is to '"fill" the students by making deposits of information which he or she considers to constitute true knowledge', thereby rendering the learner a passive, empty vessel upon which ideologically driven information can be imprinted. Therefore, within the classroom of the critical pedagogue, the dynamic between active lecturer, who transmits their privileged knowledge to a group of passive, ignorant learners, is reversed; learners are encouraged to question, to critique, to draw on their own experience and understandings, and the educator becomes a more passive facilitator of this process of discovery and exploration.

Regarding the desired outcome of students' learning, critical pedagogy proposes not only an expanded political consciousness but also the conversion of this new awareness into action. This sentiment resonates with Jamal et al.'s (2011, p. 136) argument for a move beyond the 'self-oriented liberal education model towards a progressive learner who is oriented towards social action', which they believe is essential in order to tackle important social and environmental issues arising through tourism. The authors advocate a form of critical pedagogy that is tailored specifically to the needs of future tourism practitioners – sustainable tourism pedagogy – which posits six core literacies: technical, analytical, ecological, multicultural, ethical, policy and political. In its scope, sustainable tourism pedagogy appears to exceed the strictly political aims of critical pedagogy, yet both approaches share a commitment to enacting meaningful social change. Jamal et al. discuss a collaborative, community based service-learning project, which they link to two concepts: *phronesis* (practical wisdom) and *praxis* (social change). They thereby draw a distinction between orthodox academic knowledge and applied, practical wisdom, which acts as a path towards enacting social change. This example of experiential, practical learning invites us to question the extent to which conventional classroom learning needs to be supplemented by community service-learning (Cone and Harris, 1996; Speck and Hoppe, 2004).

2.2　Critical Reflexivity

So far, I have attempted to trace some of the points of convergence and difference between two forms of criticality: critical thinking and critical pedagogy. While both of these peda-gogical approaches present more progressive, innovative alternatives to the conventional, uncritical curriculum and teaching style deployed within many tourism courses, they have themselves been subject to criticism. The final pedagogical moment that I want to examine along our spectrum of criticality foregrounds discourse, positionality and reflex-ivity in a post-structural critique of the previous two perspectives. By drawing attention to the discursive and ideological construction of pedagogical discourses themselves, post-structuralism provides a critical perspective on pedagogies claiming to be critical – a form of meta-criticality, if you like. One of the central tenets of post-structuralism is its critique of universal propositions and the regular disavowal of their historical, social and cultural situatedness (Peters and Burbules, 2004; Peters, 1998). Instead, knowledge is posited as situated, partial and constantly in flux. So in the context of the present dis-cussion, post-structural critique might target critical thinking's appeal to an immutable, transcultural logic, or critical pedagogy's appeal to universal values of human progress and emancipation.

I want to consider Elizabeth Ellsworth's (1989) influential critique of critical pedagogy, which she claims operates within a highly unreflexive, rationalist discourse. The first part of her critique targets critical pedagogy's core proclamation of emancipation and empow-erment as its guiding principles, with Ellsworth taking issue with the seemingly abstract, ahistorical, universal nature of such propositions. She poses the question of, 'empowerment for what?', citing likely answers from critical pedagogues as, 'empowerment for "human betterment", for expanding "the range of possible social identities people may become", and "making one's self present as part of a moral and political project that links production of meaning to the possibility for human agency, democratic community, and transformative social action"' (1989, p. 307). Ellsworth argues that these statements reflect priorities and values associated with Western society that, while seemingly well intentioned, carry with them an implicit symbolic violence. In particular, she links such universalizing statements to a pervasive rationalism that governs both the form of argument against oppression that is endorsed by critical pedagogy and its desired social outcome:

> These rationalist assumptions have led to the following goals: the teaching of analytic and critical skills for judging the truth and merit of propositions, and the interrogation and selective appropriation of potentially transformative moments in the dominant culture. As long as educators define pedagogy against oppressive formations in these ways the role of the critical pedagogue will be to guarantee that the foundation for classroom interaction is reason. (Ellsworth, 1989, p. 303)

Ellsworth goes on to say that educators can 'no longer regard the enforcement of rationalism as a self-evident political act against relations of domination' (p. 304), arguing that claims to the universality of rational statements can themselves function in dominating and oppressive ways. This is because notions of rationality, progress and emancipation have emerged within a particular socio-historical context, bringing an imperial dimension to the suggestion that these epistemologies and political aims are shared by all people. Furthermore, from a feminist perspective, Ellsworth (1989, p. 304) argues that the figure of the ideal rational person – embodied in the astute learner of critical pedagogy – has been socially constructed in implicit opposition to an irrational 'Other', which has denigrated 'those who are not European, White, male, middle class, Christian, able-bodied, thin, and heterosexual'.

This critique invites us to reflect on how differently positioned learners and educators will respond to various pedagogical contexts. As Leopold (2013, p. 115) points out, one's ability to think critically will be influenced by epistemological issues of educators' and learners' socio-cultural and personal background. This ties in with Belhassen and Caton's (2011) observation that not all learners exposed to the radical ideas of critical pedagogy will concur with its political objectives or undergo a transformation in their ideological leanings. Indeed, as I have suggested, it may be possible for learners to find the framing of critical pedagogy alienating not solely on the basis of its transformative socio-political vision, but on other grounds such as a perception of cultural bias and the erasure of social differences. Ellsworth (1989, p. 310) suggests that as educators it is imperative that we reflect not only on our learners' positioning and subjective experience, but also on our own gendered, raced and classed position in order to avoid reproducing 'the category of generic "critical teacher" – a specific form of the generic human that underlies classical liberal thought'.

In addition to this reflexive dimension of pedagogical practice, Ellsworth also draws attention to the embodied nature of the classroom and the diversity of learners' identities and allegiances that are brought into play in every class. More specifically, she argues that the formula for dialogue presented by critical pedagogy, and in particular by Giroux, 'assumes a classroom of participants unified on the side of the subordinated against the subordinators, sharing and trusting in an "us-ness" against "them-ness"' (Ellsworth, 1989, p. 315). Depending on the issue under discussion, learners identifying with an elite or oppressive social group might feel as if they are being personally attacked, given the power of identificational investments in one's social group. Ellsworth therefore argues that critical pedagogy, when put into practice using simplistic binary understandings, 'fails to confront dynamics of subordination present among classroom participants and within classroom participants in the form of multiple and contradictory subject positions' (1989, p. 315). While critical pedagogy certainly does appeal to universal emancipatory values, this second dimension of Ellsworth's critique is more contestable as the management of classroom dynamics is likely to reflect the style and interpretations of each pedagogue. However, her argument draws attention to the relevance of exploring teaching and learning practices alongside alterations to the tourism curriculum.

Against the certainty of critical thinking's logic and critical pedagogy's rational, liberatory discourse, what I refer to here as 'critical reflexivity' draws on post-structural theory to interrogate the modernist discourses that construct these pedagogical approaches. As I have already mentioned, reflexivity encompasses critical reflection on educators' positionality within the classroom and in relation to the material being explored, but it is also a term that reaches far beyond the individual pedagogue or learner's capacity for self-reflection (Fullagar and Wilson, 2012; Ateljevic et al., 2005). Ateljevic et al. (2005) discuss 'positionality' as just one element of reflexivity, which also includes 'ideologies and legitimacies', 'research accountability' and 'intersectionality with the researched'. The authors stress that the aim of reflexive practice in tourism studies should be to reveal the epistemological foundations of knowledge, as determined through the role of disciplinary discourses, institutions, and individuals engaged in teaching and research. Similarly, Fullagar and Wilson (2012) argue that a reflexive academic identity should exist across individual, institutional and disciplinary levels (cf. Caldicott and Wilson, Chapter 16, this volume). Therefore, my suggestion that a move towards uncertainty may be productive for critical tourism pedagogies is not an attempt to endorse complete epistemological relativity, but rather to introduce important reflexive mechanisms in order to maintain the ethical and intellectual integrity of the understandings produced in tourism classrooms.

3.   FUTURE DIRECTIONS

In this chapter, I have presented three pedagogical moments in dialogue with one another in an attempt to show a variety of interpretations of 'criticality' and the concept's implications for curriculum and for teaching and learning in tourism education. I have explored how criticality can be conceptualized as a mechanism of logical reflection, a tool for debating the validity of arguments, a theoretical resource for revealing hidden power relations, and an epistemological orientation towards the very discourses that construct tourism pedagogies. It is my belief that these pedagogies are not mutually exclusive and that it may be possible to construct a pedagogical approach that implements multiple forms of criticality in a complementary fashion. Indeed, when we look beyond their differences, these approaches appear to cohere around a central concern with ensuring that future tourism practitioners or managers are discerning, aware of the outcomes of their actions and, ultimately, socially and environmentally responsible. As I have argued, this comes in a climate in which tourism education has been accused of holding a sustained ideological commitment to managerialism, market values and neoliberalism (Tribe, 2008; Walmsley, 2009; McLaren and Jaramillo, 2013). Engaging with criticality as an important facet of tourism pedagogy may provide a productive avenue for addressing these value-laden aspects of our teaching in the hope of nurturing both vocationally and ethically competent 'philosophic practitioners' (Tribe, 2001; 2002; 2008).

It should be clear from the preceding discussion that the implementation of criticality in tourism education could take a number of forms, depending on how the concept is interpreted. Criticality presents an invitation to reevaluate not only the content of tourism courses in terms of a greater focus on political, ethical, ecological and epistemological issues, but also the ways in which these are delivered and how educators and learners each play their part in the reproduction and interrogation of tourism knowledge. The extent to which curriculum adaptation is a requirement of criticality depends on the school of thought to which one subscribes. For proponents of critical thinking, the content of a tourism curriculum may be less important than the accuracy of the facts and arguments presented to learners. Critical pedagogy, in contrast, would advocate a curriculum shift in line with its agenda of social justice and political change while at the same time challenging learners to reflect on their own position of privilege. It could be argued that some areas of study within tourism invoke criticality more than others, such as the inherent focus on tourism's environmental and social impacts in the study of sustainable or eco-tourism. The challenge for tourism educators lies in applying the principles of criticality across the board and not just to those areas of the curriculum that seem to lend themselves to more unconventional or politicized thinking.

Similarly, the forms of criticality that I have explored seem to suggest that learners should be assessed not only on their knowledge of tourism issues but should also be capable of demonstrating critical thinking skills, analytic abilities and core competencies that will enable them to enact meaningful change in their future roles as tourism practitioners and managers. This point connects with critical pedagogy's emphasis on learner empowerment and potential transitions from conventional classroom learning to projects that facilitate participatory, community-based learning. In terms of pedagogic practice more generally, criticality problematizes the relationships between educators, learners and knowledge in increasingly complex ways. While critical thinking encourages a more skeptical, astute stance from the learner towards knowledge, conventional distinctions between teacher and learner remain more or less intact. This is in contrast to the approaches of critical pedagogy and critical reflexivity, which both propose, to varying degrees, a reconceptualization of the knowledgeable/ignorant, active/passive binaries embodied in the distinction between educator and learner. Beyond these summarizing reflections, it is not my desire to develop prescriptive methods of implementing criticality within tourism education, as to do so would strip the concept of its multiplicity, complexity and invitation to reflect.

Moving forward, I want to support Fullagar and Wilson's insistence that critical scholars and pedagogues within tourism and hospitality should maintain a 'relational dialogue' with those identified as being located in the 'mainstream': 'One of the key challenges that we face in tourism and hospitality is working with more diverse understandings of criticality to move beyond assumptions that "critical thinking" is primarily negative, polemic or totally incompatible with industry or government concerns' (2012, p. 2).

As Fullagar and Wilson argue, while there can be a certain satisfaction derived from occupying the radical periphery of academic discourse, this may not always be the most productive or progressive stance to take. Rather, engaging with those in positions of influence within the tourism industry, government or within the academy is likely to be the surest route to ensuring that critical perspectives are given greater credence in the long run.

4.   CONCLUSION

Building on emergent debates within the field of tourism education, this chapter has explored the plural and contested meanings of criticality as a theoretical orientation and pedagogical practice. I identified three pedagogical moments along a continuum of criticality, which moves progressively towards uncertainty and reflexivity, and evaluated the potential of each for enriching teaching and learning in tourism. Critical thinking, critical pedagogy and critical reflexivity each provide different lenses through which existing practices in tourism education can be explored. Collectively, they foreground academic rigor, independent thinking skills, learner empowerment, social transformation, and reflexivity regarding the production and consumption of knowledge in tourism studies. In a climate in which educational programs overwhelmingly focus on producing graduates with pragmatic management competencies rather than the ability to engage critically with the social and environmental challenges faced by tourism practitioners, an emphasis on criticality has the potential to dramatically alter the scope and vision of contemporary tourism education.

REFERENCES

Aitchison, C. (2001), 'Theorizing other discourses of tourism, gender and culture: can the subaltern speak (in tourism)?', *Tourist Studies*, **1**, 133–47.

Ateljevic, I., N. Morgan and A. Pritchard (eds) (2013), *The Critical Turn in Tourism Studies: Creating an Academy of Hope*, London: Routledge.

Ateljevic, I., A. Pritchard and N. Morgan (eds) (2007), *The Critical Turn in Tourism Studies: Innovative Research Methodologies*, Oxford: Elsevier.

Ateljevic, I., C. Harris, E. Wilson and F.L. Collins (2005), 'Getting "entangled": reflexivity and the "critical turn" in tourism studies', *Tourism Recreation Research*, **30** (2), 9–21.

Atkinson, D. (1997), 'A critical approach to critical thinking in TESOL', *TESOL Quarterly*, **31** (1), 71–94.

Ayikoru , M., J. Tribe and D. Airey (2009), 'Reading tourism education: neoliberalism unveiled', *Annals of Tourism Research*, **36** (2), 191–221.

Belhassen, Y. and K. Caton (2011), 'On the need for critical pedagogy in tourism education', *Tourism Management*, **32** (6), 1389–96.

Benesch, S. (1999), 'Thinking critically, thinking dialogically', *TESOL Quarterly*, **33** (3), 573–80.

Bianchi, R.V. (2009), 'The "critical turn" in tourism studies: a radical critique', *Tourism Geographies*, **11** (4), 484–504.

Brookfield, S. (2005), *The Power of Critical Theory for Adult Learning and Teaching*, Maidenhead: Open University Press.

Burbules, N.C. and R. Beck (1999), 'Critical thinking and critical pedagogy: relations, differences, and limits', in T.S. Popkewitz and L. Fendler (eds), *Critical Theories in Education: Changing Terrains of Knowledge and Politics*, London: Routledge, pp. 45–65.

Cho, W. and C.D. Schmelzer (2000), 'Just-in-time education: tools for hospitality managers of the future?', *International Journal of Contemporary Hospitality Management*, **12** (1), 31–7.

Cho, W., C.D. Schmelze and P.S. McMahon (2002), 'Preparing hospitality managers for the 21st century: the merging of just-in-time education, critical thinking, and collaborative learning', *Journal of Hospitality and Tourism Research*, **26** (1), 23–37.

Cockburn-Wootten, C. and T. Cockburn (2011), 'Unsettling assumptions and boundaries: strategies for developing a critical perspective about business and management communication', *Business Communication Quarterly*, **74** (1), 45–59.

Cone, D. and S. Harris (1996), 'Service-learning practice: developing a theoretical framework', *Michigan Journal of Community Service Learning*, **3**, 31–43.

Cooper, C. and R. Shepherd (1997), 'The relationship between tourism education and the tourism industry: implications for tourism education', *Tourism Recreation Research*, **22** (1), 34–47.

Echtner, C.M. and T.B. Jamal (1997), 'The disciplinary dilemma of tourism studies', *Annals of Tourism Research*, **24** (4), 868–83.

Ellsworth, E. (1989), 'Why doesn't this feel empowering? Working through the repressive myths of critical pedagogy', *Harvard Educational Review*, **59** (3), 297–324.

Fidgeon, P.R. (2010), 'Tourism education and curriculum design: a time for consolidation and review?', *Tourism Management*, **31** (6), 699–723.

Fisher, A. (2001), *Critical Thinking: An Introduction*, Cambridge: Cambridge University Press.

Franklin, A. and M. Crang (2001), 'The trouble with tourism and travel theory?', *Tourist Studies*, **1** (1), 5–22.

Freire, P. (1998), *Pedagogy of Freedom: Ethics, Democracy, and Civil Courage*, trans. P. Clarke, Lanham, MD: Rowman and Littlefield.

Freire, P. (2014), *Pedagogy of the Oppressed*, 30th Anniversary edn, London: Bloomsbury.

Fullagar, S. (2002), 'Narratives of travel: desire and the movement of feminine subjectivity', *Leisure Studies*, **21** (1), 57–74.

Fullagar, S. and E. Wilson (2012), 'Critical pedagogies: a reflexive approach to knowledge creation in tourism and hospitality studies', *Journal of Hospitality and Tourism Management*, **19** (1), 1–6.

Fulop, L. (2000), 'Practicing what you preach: critical management studies', *Organization*, **9** (3), 428–36.

Gieve, S. (1998), 'A reader reacts . . .', *TESOL Quarterly*, **32** (1), 123–9.

Giroux, H.A. (2007), 'Introduction: democracy, education, and the politics of critical pedagogy', in P. McLaren and J.L. Kincheloe (eds), *Critical Pedagogy: Where Are We Now?*, New York: Peter Lang, pp. 1–7.

Hall, C.M. and H. Tucker (eds) (2004), *Tourism and Postcolonialism: Contested Discourses, Identities and Representations*, London: Routledge.

Higgins-Desbiolles, F. (2006), 'More than an "industry": the forgotten power of tourism as a social force', *Tourism Management*, **27** (6), 1192–208.

Higgins-Desbiolles, F., K. Powys Whyte and A. Mian (2012), 'Abandon hope: the importance of remaining critical', paper presented at the 22nd Annual CAUTHE conference, Melbourne, 6–9 February.

Hollinshead, K. (1999), 'Surveillance of the worlds of tourism: Foucault and the eye-of-power', *Tourism Management*, **20** (1), 7 –23.

Hollinshead, K. and J. Jamal (2007), 'Tourism and the "third ear": further prospects for qualitative inquiry', *Tourism Analysis*, **12**, 85–129.

Inui, Y., D. Wheeler and S. Lankford (2006), 'Rethinking tourism education: what should schools teach', *Journal of Hospitality, Leisure, Sport and Tourism Education*, **5** (2), 25–35.

Jamal, T.B. (2004), 'Virtue ethics and sustainable tourism pedagogy: phronesis, principles and practice', *Journal of Sustainable Tourism*, **12** (6), 530–45.

Jamal, T., J. Taillon and D. Dredge (2011), 'Sustainable tourism pedagogy and academic–community collaboration: a progressive service-learning approach', *Tourism and Hospitality Research*, **11** (2), 133–47.

Johnston, L. (2001), '(Other) bodies and tourism studies', *Annals of Tourism Research*, **28** (1), 180–201.

Leopold, T. (2013), 'Critical thinking in the tourism curriculum', in I. Ateljevic, N. Morgan and A. Pritchard (eds), *The Critical Turn in Tourism Studies: Creating an Academy of Hope*, London: Routledge, pp. 110–20.

McLaren, P. and N.E. Jaramillo (2013), 'Foreword: dialectical thinking and critical pedagogy – towards a critical tourism studies', in I. Ateljevic, N. Morgan and A. Pritchard (eds), *The Critical Turn in Tourism Studies: Creating an Academy of Hope*, London: Routledge, pp. xvii–xl.

Moon, J. (2008), *Critical Thinking: An Exploration of Theory and Practice*, London: Routledge.

Peters, M.A. (1998), *Naming the Multiple: Poststructuralism and Education*, Westport, CT: Bergin and Garvey.

Peters, M.A. and N.C. Burbules (2004), *Poststructuralism and Educational Research*, Oxford: Rowman and Littlefield.

Phillimore, J. and L. Goodson (2004), *Qualitative Research in Tourism: Ontologies, Epistemologies and Methodologies*, London: Routledge.

Picard, D. and M. Robinson (eds) (2012), *Emotion in Motion: Tourism, Affect and Transformation*, London: Ashgate.

Pritchard, A. (2004), 'Gender and sexuality in tourism research', in A.A. Lew, C.M. Hall and A.M. Williams (eds), *A Companion to Tourism*, Malden, MA: Blackwell, pp. 316–26.

Pritchard, A., N. Morgan and I. Ateljevic (2011), 'Hopeful tourism: a new transformative perspective', *Annals of Tourism Research*, **38** (3), 941–63.

Ren, C., A. Pritchard and N. Morgan (2010), 'Constructing tourism research: a critical inquiry', *Annals of Tourism Research*, **37** (4), 885–904.

Riley, R.W. and L.L. Love (2000), 'The state of qualitative tourism research', *Annals of Tourism Research*, **27** (1), 164–87.

Ryan, C. (1995), 'Tourism courses: new concerns for new times?', *Tourism Management*, **16** (2), 97–100.

Schwarzin, L. (2013), 'To act as though the future mattered: a framework for hopeful tourism education', in I. Ateljevic, N. Morgan and A. Pritchard (eds), *The Critical Turn in Tourism Studies: Creating an Academy of Hope*, London: Routledge, pp. 135–48.

Sheldon, P.J., D.R. Fesenmaier and J. Tribe (2011), 'The tourism education futures initiative (TEFI): activating change in tourism education', *Journal of Teaching in Travel and Tourism*, **11** (1), 2–23.

Sinclair, A. (2007a), *Leadership For the Disillusioned: Moving Beyond Myths and Heroes to Leading That Liberate*, Sydney: Allen and Unwin.

Sinclair, A. (2007b), 'Teaching leadership critically to MBAs: experiences from heaven and hell', *Management Learning*, **38** (4), 458–72.

Speck, B.W. and S. Hoppe (2004), *Service-Learning: History, Theory, and Issues*, Westport, CT: Praeger.

Tribe, J. (1997), 'The indiscipline of tourism', *Annals of Tourism Research*, **24** (3), 638–57.

Tribe, J. (2001), 'Research paradigms and the tourism curriculum', *Journal of Travel Research*, **39** (4), 442–8.

Tribe, J. (2002), 'The philosophic practitioner', *Annals of Tourism Research*, **29** (2), 338–57.

Tribe, J. (2005a), 'Editorial: new tourism research', *Tourism Recreation Research*, **30** (2), 5–8.

Tribe, J. (2005b), 'Overview of research', in D. Airey and J. Tribe (eds), *An International Handbook of Tourism Education*, Oxford: Elsevier, pp. 25–43.

Tribe, J. (2005c), 'Tourism knowledge and the curriculum', in D. Airey and J. Tribe (eds), *An International Handbook of Tourism Education*, Oxford: Elsevier, pp. 47–60.

Tribe, J. (2008), 'Tourism: a critical business', *Journal of Travel Research*, **46** (3), 245–55.

Vandermensbrugghe, J. (2004), 'The unbearable vagueness of critical thinking in the context of the Anglo-Saxonisation of education', *International Education Journal*, **5** (3), 417–22.

Veijola, S. and E. Jokinen (1994), 'The body in tourism', *Theory, Culture and Society*, **11** (3), 125–51.

Walmsley, A. (2009), 'Tourism education: beyond ideology', *ICRT Occasional Paper*, (OP16), 1–14.

Wilson, E., C. Harris and J. Small (2008), 'Furthering critical approaches in tourism and hospitality studies: perspectives from Australia and New Zealand', *Journal of Hospitality and Tourism Management*, **15** (1), 15–18.

30 A pedagogy of tourism informed by Indigenous approaches
Freya Higgins-Desbiolles

1. INTRODUCTION

The teaching of tourism and hospitality has become a staple of universities around the world. Programs are often located in business departments, attracting large numbers of enrolments as tourism becomes a key engine of prosperity in numerous economies around the globe. Additionally, the tertiary sector has been transformed in the era of neoliberalism and universities are increasingly being directed to the certification of professionals to practice in their disciplines; as Tribe described it: 'the underlying dominant commonsense view (ideology) that permeates most literature and research on the tourism curriculum is a vocationalist one' (2001, p. 446). In such a context, the business and industrial capacities of tourism have assumed predominance and this has over-shadowed the contributions of tourism as a significant social force (Higgins-Desbiolles, 2006). This is unfortunate because we have lost sight of the capacities for tourism and hospitality to contribute to more than just the need for economic growth, including its capacities for personal well-being, cross-cultural understanding and perhaps even fostering greater peace and harmony. Certain niches still offer us opportunities for insights into these social capacities of tourism, including the one under discussion here, the tourism and Indigenous interface.

This interface where tourism engages with Indigenous peoples is a complex and fraught space due to the history of colonization, exploitation and denigration that many Indigenous peoples have suffered in the global community. Following on from the wave of decolonization that occurred in the 1960s and 1970s, concerted efforts to achieve and defend Indigenous rights have started to change centuries of abuse. This has impacted on the academy as Indigenous scholars and scholarship have challenged Western-centric knowledges and practices (Smith, 2003). Additionally, as many nations have embarked on recognizing the civil rights of minority and marginalized communities and also accepted multiculturalism as a pathway to shared futures, concern with how the curriculum might be transformed to prepare learners for a multicultural future has been a significant goal (Torres, 1998). In terms of Indigenous engagement, efforts to embed Indigenous content and perspectives in the curriculum and even 'Indigenizing' the curriculum have created an innovative space with multiple and multifold benefits and challenges (Kincheloe and Steinberg, 2008). This chapter will use the experience of teaching a topic on 'Tourism and Indigenous Peoples' as a case study to explore what Indigenous approaches offer to the pedagogy and practice of tourism.

The course is an undergraduate elective offered in the tourism degree of the School of Management at the University of South Australia. The course has been offered in both internal, face-to-face mode as well as external, off-campus mode since 2004. It was developed through a process of extensive consultations with Indigenous Australian academics, community leaders and experts, based on a philosophy of Indigenous rights and featuring Indigenous voices as the key pillar of the curriculum. This was done by a non-Indigenous academic who has held a long-term commitment to principles of solidarity, reciprocity and empowerment in relationships between Indigenous and non-Indigenous Australians. This experience serves as a possible model of pedagogy both within Indigenous interfaces with tourism and beyond. The course has been the subject of an earlier journal article, focusing on appropriate practice as a non-Indigenous educator; see Higgins-Desbiolles (2007).

2.   LITERATURE REVIEW

The interface of academia, Indigenous communities and tourism is not a 'smooth' space. There are tensions that are evident from both the perspectives of the Indigenous in resistance and from the privileged in power. As Martin Nakata has noted, negotiating the requirements and procedures of the academy and 'Indigenous knowledge, standpoints or perspectives' is profoundly challenging (2004, p. 14).

Universities are implicated in the imperial project and this tarnished history must be addressed and overcome for Indigenous content to be successfully engaged with in tourism curriculum. As Maori Professor Linda Tuhiwai Smith has demonstrated in her pioneering work *Decolonizing Methodologies* (2003), the Western-centric dominance of research theory and praxis makes the university an inhospitable environment for Indigenous students and staff. Additionally, Smith argues, 'scientific research is implicated in the worst excesses of colonialism . . . the word itself, "research", is probably one of the dirtiest words in the indigenous world's vocabulary' (2003, p. 1).

The place of Indigenous content in the curriculum is contested due in part to the political disputes that underpin considerations of Indigenous and non-Indigenous relations in a post-colonizing context. Termed the 'history wars', disputes have raged about the shameful episodes in national histories and how current generations should address these. In Australia, during the tenure of the conservative government from the mid-1990s these history wars were fought with the conservatives calling revisionist history a 'black arm band view' (Macintyre, 2003). As a result, the education sector has become an important site in the battle because the colonial history of Australia with its legacies from invasion, dispossession and attempted cultural genocide has never been fully faced and so teaching Indigenous issues in Australian classrooms is often problematic.

Critical voices have drawn attention to the inadequacy of current practice based on a civil rights view of Indigenous curriculum that fails to confront the structural and ongoing injustices that are clear from the point of view of Indigenous scholars. As Foley and Muldoon (2014, para. 22) have argued, 'we need many voices to demand greater attention to Indigenous perspectives and some much-needed academic rigour'. It is important to remember that in Australia, a key moment of change was the Royal Commission into Aboriginal Deaths in Custody of 1991, which 'stressed the urgent need for the wider community to get to know Indigenous Australians, to learn about the shared history and to plan an inclusive future that respects and values Indigenous culture and heritage' (Universities Australia, 2011, p. 18). However, this does not have to be seen as only an exercise in exploring a negative history as a vital component of this curriculum interface is the exploration of what Indigenous knowledges can offer to enhance the wider society. As former Social Justice Commissioner Tom Calma stated: 'we need to respect and promote Indigenous knowledges and perspectives. They have much to offer all Australians. Tertiary education institutions exercise cultural leadership when they offer courses that are enriched by Indigenous knowledges and perspectives. This is reconciliation in action' (2009).

As with Indigenist research, Indigenizing pedagogy is radical practice that profoundly challenges and potentially transforms the academy. Therefore, it is useful to be attentive to changing thought in Indigenist research and consider how this might inform Indigenizing the tourism curriculum. This scrutiny of contemporary research practices on, or about, Indigenous peoples, their lives and cultures, has been led by Indigenous academics themselves, who, in so doing, are actively claiming a research space which is transformative and overtly seeks to create change (Rigney, 1996; 1999; 2001). Central to this developing Indigenous research agenda is the requirement for researchers, both Indigenous and non-Indigenous, to incorporate Indigenous ways of 'Knowing, Being and Doing' into research methodologies (Martin, 2001b). Moving beyond collaboration, privileging Indigenous voices and integrating their diverse cultural practices and social mores into all aspects of research is now seen as essential to ethical and just research (Atkinson, 2002; Martin, 2001a; 2001b; 2002; Smith, 2003).

2.1   Indigenous Peoples, Indigenous Knowledges and the Western Academy

Since the 1980s Indigenous peoples around the world have asserted their rights to self-determination, resisted colonial domination and called for reparations and solutions to the history of exploitation, marginalization and dispossession, culminating in the 2007 United Nations Declaration on the Rights of Indigenous Peoples. Institutions such as universities have had to engage with the implications of these changing social relations and work to rectify their roles in perpetuating disadvantage and injustice. Universities have introduced a number of strategies for fostering what has been called 'Indigenous cultural competency'. For instance, Australia has set these as guiding principles:

- Indigenous people should be actively involved in university governance and management;
- all graduates of Australian universities should be culturally competent;
- university research should be conducted in a culturally competent way that empowers Indigenous participants and encourages collaborations with Indigenous communities;
- Indigenous staffing will be increased at all appointment levels and, for academic staff, across a wider variety of academic fields;
- universities will operate in partnership with their Indigenous communities and will help disseminate culturally competent practices to the wider community (Universities Australia, 2011, p. 8).

These principles represent a broad range of possibilities of what universities can do to address Indigenous disadvantage and their historical roles contributing to the abuse of Indigenous rights and peoples.

A great deal of scholarship and analysis has been devoted to best practice inclusion of Indigenous content in the curriculum or even 'indigenizing the curriculum' (for example Marshall, 1997; Williamson and Dalal, 2007; Nakata, 2004; Universities Australia, 2011). The learning from these endeavors has been significant and points to a number of valuable approaches. For instance, Williamson and Dalal (2007, p. 52) report on efforts to embed Indigenous perspectives in the humanities and human services curricula of the Queensland University of Technology and from their review of approaches undertaken so far, they found:

- the need to problematize the endeavor of embedding Indigenous perspectives;
- the requirement that students deconstruct their own cultural situatedness in order to appreciate the ways in which the 'Other' is framed;
- the hegemonic and appropriating capacities of 'Western' disciplines and the dissonance between Indigenous and 'Western' ways of knowing;
- the complexities of interactions at the cultural interface and the difficulties of achieving cross-cultural understandings and acquiring cultural competencies;
- the need to reorient curricula by engaging with alternative ways of knowing and alternative skill sets.

2.2   The Indigenous View of Tourism: A Context of Exploitation Resulting in Suspicion

In the context of tourism studies, all educators must be aware that the Indigenous view of, experience of and engagement with the forces of tourism may be entirely different from those of Western peoples. In many countries such as Australia, New Zealand, the USA and Canada, tourism was often imposed on Indigenous communities as a part of the process of conquest and colonization. Non-Indigenous peoples came to triumphantly gawk at Indigenous people as remnants of primitive and dying cultures of interest in effectively a human zoo situation; for instance, Indigenous peoples were presented at world fairs as tokens of the wars of conquest in the imperial age (for example Welch, 2011). Frequently, creation of national parks for the enjoyment and recreation of mobile middle classes resulted in the dispossession of Indigenous peoples and their exile from their country in the interest of conservation of the last 'wilderness' areas (Mowforth and Munt, 2003). Tourism has also been used as a cover for bio-piracy of Indigenous traditional ecological knowledge on plant use for medicines and incorporated into the commercial pharmaceutical industry with no recognition of or returns to Indigenous custodians (McLaren, 2003). These are only a few of the experiences that have resulted in many Indigenous peoples having a strong antipathy to tourism.

Ha'aheo Guanson of the Hawai'i Ecumenical Coalition stated, 'tourism is not an Indigenous issue. It is really not a way of life for Indigenous people. They have been thrown into tourism for the profits of those who are in business' (International Forum on Indigenous Tourism film, 2002). De Chavez has characterized the impacts of tourism and globalization on Indigenous peoples as 'deadly' and argues that 'tourism's impact on indigenous peoples' way of life and on their control and access to their resources and environment has been more pronounced with globalization of the world economy' (1999). Seton (1999) stated that, in the contemporary era of economic globalization, the lands, cultures and peoples of the Indigenous world are now seen 'in economic terms' as unutilized natural resources that can be harnessed as a national and global resource for greater economic growth and 'development'. Specifically focusing on tourism, Pera and McLaren (1999) argued that tourism delivers little of the promised 'sustainable' development opportunities to Indigenous communities, and instead has some significant negative impacts such as environmental damage, human rights abuses, displacement and cultural damage. Pera and McLaren (1999, para. 2) stated that tourism, in the context of capitalist globalization, 'threatens indigenous knowledge and intellectual property rights, our technologies, religions, sacred sites, social structures and relationships, wildlife, ecosystems, economies and basic rights to informed understanding; reducing indigenous peoples to simply another consumer product that is quickly becoming exhaustible'.

Elsewhere, McLaren (2003, p. 5) has also criticized tourism for being 'a pre-eminent salesperson for western development' and in the process undermining Indigenous economies and Indigenous self-reliance, and making Indigenous peoples dependent on a precarious globalized economy.

This context of exploitation and abuse cannot be ignored by the tourism academy and is an essential context for studies of tourism and Indigenous peoples. Such experiences invite tourism scholars to re-examine tourism with a critical lens, as the tourism phenomenon looks entirely different when viewed through the lens of Indigenous experience. Such critical approaches to tourism encourage efforts to historicize, contextualize and politicize, which is quite a challenging approach for more conventional analysts in tourism studies. This Indigenous tourism niche demands such approaches and thereby opens up possibilities to transform our wider understanding of the discipline, its priorities and its operations.

It is also important to understand that principles of Indigenous rights and self-determination have permeated into tourism and are changing the interface at this time. This may be best exemplified in 'the Oaxaca Declaration of the International Forum on Indigenous Tourism (IFIT)' of 2002, which resulted from a gathering of Indigenous peoples of the Americas who came together to challenge the United Nations' International Year of Ecotourism. This declaration stated 'tourism is only beneficial for Indigenous communities when it is based on and enhances our self-determination' (IFIT, 2002). More recently, the Pacific Asia Travel Association convened a conference on Indigenous tourism in Darwin, Australia, which resulted in 'the Larrakia Declaration on the Development of Indigenous Tourism' (Pacific Asia Indigenous Tourism Conference, 2012). In its preamble, this document points to the profound possibilities of Indigenous tourism when done from an approach of respect for Indigenous rights and self-determination:

- Recognizing that for Indigenous tourism to be successful and sustainable, Indigenous tourism needs to be based on traditional knowledge, cultures and practices and it must contribute to the well-being of Indigenous communities and the environment;
- Recognizing that Indigenous tourism provides a strong vehicle for cultural understanding, social interaction and peace;
- Recognizing that universal Indigenous values underpin intergenerational stewardship of cultural resources and understanding, social interaction and peace.

This preamble outlining the norms and values that should underpin Indigenous tourism suggests that Indigenous peoples are demanding their rights in tourism, have much to offer tourism and its practice through Indigenous knowledges and are open to working towards more harmonious relations with non-Indigenous peoples using tourism as a tool for building understanding.

3.   TEACHING APPROACH

My teaching philosophy is based on the emancipatory capacity of critical pedagogy, inspired by bell hooks. hooks advocates teaching which: confronts power; encourages learners to challenge privilege in order to inspire more engaged and equitable communities; and fosters pedagogies of hope (2003). According to Tribe (2001), critical pedagogy is vital to tourism as it provides our students with the ability to engage with all tourism stakeholders, not just the powerful. As a critical educator, my teaching goal is to inspire students to recognize their capacity to contribute to building a better world as professionals, citizens and people. In my teaching of the course 'Tourism and Indigenous Peoples', I have been inspired by the vision set by Kincheloe and Steinberg's (2008, p. 135) work as they explore:

> the education and epistemological value of indigenous knowledge in the larger effort to expand a form of critical multilogicality – an effort to act educationally and politically on the calls for diversity and justice that have echoed through the halls of academia over the past several decades. Such an effort seeks an intercultural/interracial effort to question the hegemonic and oppressive aspects of Western education and to work for justice and self-direction for indigenous peoples around the world. In this critical multilogical context, the purpose of indigenous education and the production of indigenous knowledge does not involve 'saving' indigenous people but helping construct the conditions that allow for indigenous self-sufficiency while learning from the vast storehouse of indigenous knowledge that provides compelling insights into all domains of human endeavor.

A key facet of success in the teaching of this course has been a conducive academic context. The university where this work has taken place has held a long commitment to Indigenous engagement, employment and education. This is derived from its Act of Establishment: section 5.1 c of The University of South Australia Act states that one of the university's core functions is to 'provide such tertiary education programmes as the University thinks appropriate to meet the needs of the Aboriginal people'. Even before it was amalgamated in the University of South Australia, its predecessor organization, the South Australian Institute for Technology, was a pioneer in creating the Aboriginal Taskforce in the 1970s, which was described by Stanley Nangala as 'the epicentre, attracting people from all over Australia to join in a passion and drive for education and for social change' (UniSA, 2014, para. 5). Since that time, UniSA has fulfilled this commitment in tangible ways, including: the establishment of the David Unaipon College of Indigenous Education and Research (DUCIER), an Indigenous Employment Strategy managed by a dedicated officer, a Reconciliation statement and memorials on all campuses, a Reconciliation Action Plan and a policy of Incorporating Indigenous Content in Undergraduate Programmes.

As universities such as my own have responded to the changing recognition of Indigenous peoples' status, particularly since the passage of the United Nations Declaration on the Rights of Indigenous Peoples, many universities have focused on indigenizing the staff employed to teach Indigenous content. This term refers to a policy to recruit, employ and retain the appropriate Indigenous staff for the delivery of academic content, particularly that pertaining to Indigenous peoples, cultures and knowledges, whenever possible. Such efforts to Indigenize the academy through employment of Indigenous staff to deliver relevant Indigenous content in the curriculum is essential for many reasons, but not the least of which is appropriate presentation of Indigenous knowledges and attaining equity in employment as so few Indigenous people are represented in academic jobs. This raises the question of whether it is appropriate for non-Indigenous staff to teach Indigenous content, and if so, under what conditions.

This is a critical issue but one that is not easily broached. As Indigenous rights advance, the pressures to indigenize scholarship, pedagogy and all practices associated with the academy increases. This is a positive development but it does not necessarily mean that there is then no role for non-Indigenous educators to engage in the efforts to embed Indigenous content in the curriculum. Even with sufficient Indigenous educators to offer all Indigenous content in the curriculum, it would not be desirable for non-Indigenous educators to withdraw from this space. Non-Indigenous educators offer the capacities to serve as a bridge between confronting Indigenous perspectives and what is mainly a non-Indigenous student body in most cases; to help students confront their white privilege; to support Indigenous colleagues in the work and assume some of the emotional labor that can feature in this educational space; and, finally, to model collaborative and appropriate practice. But the work of the non-Indigenous educator should be based on critical reflexivity and sensitive approaches that seek to work in collaboration with Indigenous colleagues and experts. Williamson and Dalal (2007, p. 55) provide useful advice on this when they recommend:

- recognition and implementation of levels of engagement beyond the 'intellectual';
- a consistent unsettling of 'Western' authority;
- acknowledgement of Indigenous positions/positioning;
- ongoing critical self-reflection.

Their discussion of each of these is recommended, but for the field of tourism and Indigenous engagement, it is their elucidation of the last point that is perhaps most essential. In terms of the need for critical self-reflection, Williamson and Dalal (2007, p. 57) observe: 'this implies a shift in motivation from a "helping" ethos, which engages with Indigenous perspectives in terms of the "ideological, political and intellectual", to a focus on "personal work" and the dilemmas of white, academic positionality'. Here the educator confronts their power and positionality and recognizes that having the capacity to call Indigenous experts into the class to perform their narratives is highly problematic and requires collaborative, emancipatory practices to ensure that white power and privilege are not inadvertently reinforced rather than overturned.

In early work on 'Aboriginal education' in Australia, Keefe and Schmider (1988) outlined the essentials of curriculum development to ensure best practice engagement with Indigenous perspectives. These included that the curriculum must be rational, coherent, fundamental, contemporary, socially relevant, action-oriented, broad and balanced, learnable and teachable, intrinsically interesting and meaningful, developed with Aboriginal participation, have a clearly defined rationale and aims and sit within a well thought-out curriculum framework. The course 'Tourism and Indigenous Peoples' was developed with these essentials in mind. Key was its development in consultation with the staff of the Indigenous Australian studies program of the university and key leaders in the Indigenous communities of South Australia, particularly in the tourism and cultural education sectors. This work was undertaken a year in advance of the course being offered and has been continuous and ongoing. Additionally, the course curriculum is underpinned by a theme of Indigenous rights in tourism and therefore looks at tourism from an angle of Indigenous benefits and control rather than the focus in other niches which tends to be on tourist demand, destination marketing and product development (hence the name of the course, 'Tourism and Indigenous Peoples' rather than 'Indigenous Tourism'). All elements of the curriculum and teaching pedagogy prioritize Indigenous voices, including Indigenous scholars, Indigenous tourism operators and Indigenous community leaders, which are evident in the required course readings, the extensive guest lecture program, the audio-visual resources shown and in the field experiences offered. Recognizing the need to ensure that content engages with contemporary Indigenous contexts and addresses complex issues of social relevance is vital but not easy to do in tourism courses because the indicators of disadvantage can be overwhelming and also because some would see these as not relevant to tourism studies. However, such a view can be challenged by con-sidered arguments on how things like pervasive societal racism play out in both the wider contemporary society and are also manifested in and through tourism.

In terms of the course curriculum, careful attention is given to materials that do not essentialize Indigenous people, particularly stereotyping them into certain categories, nor fail to engage with the social and political contexts which often are the causes of Indigenous disadvantage (see more on this below). The assessments are largely designed to be action-oriented, setting learners on learning experiences that engage them in prac-tical tasks tackling realistic problems and requiring the practice of key competencies. Such work focuses learners on developing personal, interpersonal and social skills with an unashamed goal of social transformation. Figure 30.1 provides insight into the peda-gogy underpinning the practice in this course, showing the layers forming a pedagogy of tourism informed by Indigenous approaches.

As a result of analysis of the literature on Indigenous experiences with tourism, engage-ment with cutting edge thinking of the emerging Indigenist paradigm and experience in running the course in collaboration, I would present the following as a preliminary list of the potential benefits of embedding Indigenous studies in the tourism curriculum:

- respect for different cultural values and beliefs;
- analyzing tourism through a different paradigm;
- appreciation of the value of Indigenous culture and heritage to tourism;
- appropriate engagement with Indigenous knowledges and application of these insights for a more sustainable form of tourism;
- development of awareness, empathy, compassion and critical skills;
- understanding how tourism may be viewed from an Indigenous perspective as exploitative, imperialistic and oppressive;
- understanding of the impacts of invasion and settlement on Indigenous peoples pro-vides a context for students to historicize, contextualize and politicize tourism studies;
- development of a critical, multilogical approach to tourism studies.

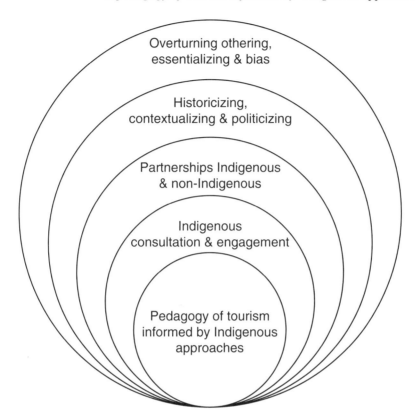

Figure 30.1   *Conceptual model: a pedagogy of tourism informed by Indigenous*
approaches

It will not be possible to offer detailed, specific information and data from the running of the course 'Tourism and Indigenous Peoples' in this brief chapter. However, I will offer one example which will be used to illustrate how the pedagogy employed in the offering of this course works in a practical example. In the course content, I have tried to demonstrate the inappropriateness of casting Indigenous people as an essentialized 'Other' at key points in the curriculum. In the introductory seminar, when introducing the various ways that Indigenous people have been defined, I introduce the key concept that self-identification is an essential criterion for Indigenous rights; as the Working Group on Indigenous Peoples stated: 'Indigenous peoples have a collective and individual right to maintain and develop their distinct identities and characteristics, including the right to identify themselves as indigenous and to be recognized as such' (United Nations, 2004). This has led to a confrontation of stereotypes such as students' prior learnings that particular skin color, exotic clothing or geographic location are the defining markers of Indigeneity. In this discussion, I draw attention to Indigenous peoples of which they may not be aware, such as the Sami peoples of Northern Europe and to urban Indigenous Australians who they may pass every day but not identify as Indigenous due to light skin color and urban residency.

Following on from this discussion I move to defining Indigenous tourism, during which I highlight two often forgotten facets of Indigenous tourism: Indigenous people as tourists (Peters and Higgins-Desbiolles, 2012) and Indigenous product on offer in the mainstream (non-cultural) tourism sector (for example the Novotel Hamilton Tainui hotel in New Zealand owned by the local Maori iwi or tribe called Tainui). The invisibility of these two important phenomena is arguably a clear symptom of the pathological focus on the Indigenous performing of culture that is an outcome of the prevailing practice of 'Othering' that the tourism industry and tourists often inflict on Indigenous people. Table 30.1 is offered to provide some brief additional insights into key learning opportunities offered in the course, which may be helpful in providing pragmatic tips and insights into ways to embed Indigenous content in tourism curriculum.

4.   FINDINGS

The inclusion of Indigenous issues in the tourism curriculum challenges the conventions of tourism studies and introduces multifocal, multifaceted and 'multilogical' approaches to the field (as per Kincheloe and Steinberg, 2008). As the material here has suggested, inclusion of Indigenous content in the tourism curriculum needs to be done in a critical and reflexive manner and necessitates adherence to certain practices and protocols. In the following paragraphs, I will outline key recommendations that result from the experiences of teaching this course in a collaborative, critically multilogical manner with a dedication to Indigenous rights in tourism as a foundational ethos.

Indigenous content presented by Indigenous experts: A key principle of incorporation of Indigenous content in the tourism curriculum is that appropriate Indigenous experts, representatives and community leaders should be involved in the development, presentation and evaluation of all Indigenous content included in tourism programs. This is essential to ensure that Indigenous views and voices are accurately, fairly and effectively presented to tourism learners. This is not to suggest that there is no role for non-Indigenous academics in these endeavors; however, their roles must always be based on partnerships and collaborations. Finally, it is imperative to ensure the cultural safety of these guest presenters as well as the learners who may find some discussions challenging (Universities Australia, 2011, p. 76). The technique of panel presentations may assist in terms of the former and preparing the students in advance for the topics may help in terms of the latter.

Payment of Indigenous speakers: When the expertise of Indigenous people from outside of the university is called on in the classroom, the Indigenous person is utilized as an expert guest lecturer and should be paid accordingly. The only exceptions occur when the Indigenous person is a paid public servant or conducts their presentation as part of their job duties; it is best to consult with the individual to ask them about the suitability of payment and any gifts that may be given. It is also highly recommended that university departments, divisions and/or administrative bodies develop dedicated funds for such purposes in an effort to enable proper engagement with Indigenous expertise in the classroom and demonstrate a commitment to such practices.

Acknowledgement of Indigenous intellectual property and adherence to Indigenous protocols: The source and ownership of all Indigenous studies input should be acknowledged in order to respect ownership of knowledge and material items. Indigenous intellectual

Table 30.1 Sample learning activities in course 'Tourism and Indigenous Peoples'

Type of Activity:	*Indigenous welcome* Lecture/reflective journal
Aim/s:	1. To encourage students to try to understand issues from an Indigenous perspective 2. To provide students with an experience of intercultural dissonance 3. To demonstrate protocols of recognition that the tourism industry should apply.
Description of Activity:	The first lecture of an Indigenous tourism course is a Welcome to Country followed by a 50-minute talk by a Kaurna Aboriginal Elder. According to their reflective journal entries, students often find the talk confronting because this Elder does not conform to their expectations of Indigenous Australians and raises many issues about power and perspectives. This is intentional: the experience of dissonance is a normal part of the intercultural learning experience. The effectiveness of this exercise is demonstrated by the fact that a few weeks into the course, journal comments indicate that students are starting to make sense of the talk.
Benefits of Activity:	The activity allows a genuine intercultural experience within the confines of the traditional lecture format. The reflective journal means students can track the progress of their own intercultural learning.
Issues for consideration:	Students may need to be reassured that their initial reaction to the talk is a natural for an intercultural experience.
Type of Activity:	*Group discussion on stereotyping* Tutorial discussion
Aim/s:	1. To raise awareness of the effects of stereotyping and how it is perpetuated 2. To analyze the impact of the tourism industry's use of stereotypical imagery in marketing campaigns on Indigenous communities and individuals.
Description of Activity:	Tourism marketers are often accused of perpetuating stereotypes. In small groups, students are asked to recall instances of when they may have stereotyped others, or been stereotyped themselves, and to discuss the implications of this. Students need to be challenged to speak about their own experiences, rather than just stereotypical experiences they have had of others, particularly Indigenous others.
Benefits of Activity:	Making the stereotyping experience personal highlights the implications of stereotyping at the individual level as well as engaging the emotional aspects of learning.
Issues for consideration:	Stereotypes can often be offensive, e.g. Thai students are usually shocked to discover the stereotyping of their culture relating to the sex industry. The activity needs to be prefaced appropriately, and revelations of negative stereotypes can be balanced to some extent by first-person descriptions of being stereotyped. Care must be taken to ensure learners' emotional safety in this exercise.
Type of Activity:	*Kaurna Walking Trail* Field Trip/Learning on Country
Aim/s:	1. To provide tourism students with an accessible, urban example of Indigenous tourism 2. To raise students' awareness of places of significance to Indigenous Australians in their local environment

Table 30.1   (continued)

Type of Activity:	*Kaurna Walking Trail* Field Trip/Learning on Country 3. To emphasize that Indigenous Australians maintain traditional attachments to urban environments and that Indigenous Australians are not only found in remote communities.
Description of Activity:	Tourism students receive a guided tour of the City of Adelaide's Kaurna Walking Trail in the heart of the CBD. The guide is a noted cultural educator and trained tour guide who is able to speak to students about professional experiences and concerns.
Benefits of Activity:	Learners experience learning on country, a key requirement for Indigenous ways of learning.
Issues for consideration:	Initially the Kaurna tour guide was uncomfortable with guiding a group of university tourism students; this was overcome through building relationships. Learners may need to be instructed in Indigenous learning styles which feature deep listening; distractions of technology and the city environment need to be proactively addressed for the experience to be fully effective.

property rights must be respected in full. Misappropriation and misinterpretation of Indigenous cultures, arts, practices and knowledges has occurred far too often in the past and has frequently been a feature in the tourism encounter. Malpractices of this nature may result in sacred/secret information being shared with inappropriate audiences, perpetuations of false and damaging stereotypes and falsehoods and continuing mistrust between Indigenous and non-Indigenous peoples. Such actions may have serious repercussions for Indigenous individuals and communities and must be avoided. Universities and their staff should consult with the relevant Indigenous community, their own Indigenous studies staff and experts, appropriate organizations, and committees such as the Australian Institute of Aboriginal and Torres Strait Islander Studies in the case of Australia. Particularly helpful in following appropriate practice are protocols and guidelines such as Australia's National Best Practice Framework for Indigenous Cultural Competency in Australian Universities (Universities Australia, 2011). Of course, using appropriate Indigenous guest experts to teach all content on Indigenous cultures and knowledges may be helpful in the effort to avoid misrepresentation.

Training and professional development of academic staff: Inclusion of Indigenous content in the tourism curriculum should be done by culturally competent staff. To achieve this, a well-planned, well-supported and well-funded program of professional development is essential. University Indigenous studies departments and Indigenous community experts should be involved in the development, implementation and evaluation of these programs. This is essential for numerous reasons but not least because this provides experience of Indigenous community contact, consultation and negotiation, which will be needed to follow sound practice in the classroom.

Learning on country essential in Indigenous tourism: Many indigenous peoples are characterized by their relationships to their total environment (termed 'country' in Australia). Much greater learning can be achieved when learners are hosted and guided on country by an Indigenous expert or community. As Universities Australia has noted, 'while relatively short visits are unlikely to lead to long-term relationships, they can provide culturally safe environments for initial experiences for non-Indigenous students, most of whom have probably never spent time with Indigenous people' (2011, p. 76). Such 'field experiences' may act as vital 'third spaces' for learning, where power shifts and creative possibilities open as a result.

Indigenous tourism as an introductory subject and not as an end in itself: Inclusion of Indigenous tourism issues in the tourism curriculum is an important outcome of a rich and full tourism program. However, it should not be viewed as sufficient on its own. It is recommended that it be seen as a pathway to further Indigenous studies so that the learner can gain greater depth in knowledge and understanding; it may also be seen as one among many cross-cultural curriculum focuses that should be pursued to open up the minds of tourism learners.

While these recommendations arise from a dedicated and long-term practice of embedding Indigenous content in the tourism curriculum in a critical and collaborative manner, it does not provide a checklist that frees the educator from embarking on their own journeys of critical, reflexive practice. As Williamson and Dalal warn, there is a danger in working to include Indigenous knowledges in the curriculum that perhaps 'once again, their [Indigenous peoples'] knowledges will be appropriated and corrupted' (2007, p. 57). We must be sure to keep such a risk in mind and militate against it by continual reflexivity, engagement with Indigenous experts and culturally appropriate evaluations of progress.

5.   FUTURE DIRECTIONS

Tourism studies lags behind other fields in giving considered thought to the embedding of Indigenous content in the curriculum. But this is clearly set to change as there are increasing pressures for change from such forces as: university-wide efforts to embed Indigenous content in all programs, evidence of growing interest by scholars in this topic area, pressures from a diverse range of actors to engage with the emerging Indigenous rights regime and the emergence of Indigenous scholars contributing to tourism studies. There is much work to be done in this area and much to be gained by such efforts.

Recently, Edmonds of the World Indigenous Tourism Alliance (WINTA) made a presentation to the Tourism Education Futures Initiative (TEFI) Conference of 2014 held at the University of Guelph in Canada entitled 'Tourism Education a Catalyst for Indigenous Human Rights'. Here he 'invited universities providing tourism courses to review the respective readiness of their institutions to engage with Indigenous communities in order to give practical effect to the United Nations Declaration on the Rights of Indigenous Peoples 2007, through tourism' (email from Marion Joppe to TRINet 6 December 2014).

As a direct result, TEFI and WINTA have agreed to collaborate on a new pilot project that promises to advance efforts in promoting the embedding of Indigenous content in tourism curriculum. The project announcement stated:

> [the pilot project] seeks to understand the current state and nature of relationships between universities (which provide tourism-related programs) and Indigenous Peoples, with an intention to devise strategies that will:

- define best practice for deployment by Universities for engagement with Indigenous Peoples;
- recognize those Universities deploying best practice;
- assist Universities seeking to develop their engagement practices with Indigenous peoples. (Email from Marion Joppe to TRINet, 6 December 2014)

This is an important indication of the prioritization that this work will receive in the future and heralds much further insight to be gained when the results of this pilot study are presented. It is likely to reveal some stellar examples in particular pockets and some significant gaps that will need to be addressed. As this chapter has attempted to argue, the dedication to this curriculum development task will pay off in multiple ways and may even contribute to transformative practice in the discipline.

However, we clearly need more than this. It is recommended that the tertiary sector involved in tourism, hospitality and events studies should:

- establish a network to advance this work building on the example set by WINTA and TEFI;
- identify a way to further attract the contributions of Indigenous scholars to tourism studies;
- establish scholarships and pathways to secure academic opportunities for Indigenous people in tourism academia;
- develop models of collaborative engagement with Indigenous communities that universities can follow; these must be fully reciprocal and long-term commitments.

Obviously practical questions arise about who should fund and implement this and clear obstacles arise in a time of neoliberal budget tightening in universities across the globe. It is beyond the remit of this chapter to argue the trends in the narrowing of university (and tourism studies) missions as a result of the neoliberalization of the university. It will have to stand as an idealistic assertion of what 'should be' based on the multiple benefits to be gained by such efforts as argued in this chapter. However, in these inopportune times, such restrictions may force us to become more creative in our responses; clearly some Indigenous communities are securing great wealth for themselves through the economic initiatives they have been fortunate and clever enough to take advantage of (for example Native American casinos and Treaty of Waitangi investments in New Zealand). Creative coalitions may be auspicious in these times and educators should seek to go beyond the structures of the university at this moment. The collaboration modeled by TEFI and WINTA and described above may be just the beginning of many such creative coalitions.

6.   CONCLUSION

This chapter has made the case for embedding Indigenous content in the tourism curriculum. It has reviewed literature to show the context in which such efforts are made in order to argue that respect for the emerging Indigenist paradigm provides clear guidance on how such work should be undertaken. It has argued that this interface of academic studies with

Indigenous knowledges offers an opportunity to develop a multilogicality that goes beyond the limits of the Western academy and opens up multiple ways of Knowing, Being and Doing, which offers profound possibilities in our engagement with the world and with each other. In terms of tourism, it has shown that Indigenous approaches offer us the chance to engage with the tourism phenomenon on an entirely different basis; it shifts the focus of the curriculum from conventional tourism concerns of tourist demand and product development, to rights of host communities, social capacities of tourism and alternative paradigms.

The approach described in this chapter is based on the experience of teaching in the particular context of Australia and its Indigenous peoples. The learning here could be adapted and adopted in similar settler-colonial contexts such as found in New Zealand/ Aotearoa and North America. It is hoped that researchers with expertise in teaching in other contexts where multiculturalism and diverse nations co-exist in the same nation-state will explore the relevance of this example to their own teaching contexts. It is likely that the experience of the European Indigenous peoples known as the Sami may be similar and therefore directly comparable, while other groups like the Welsh, the Roma and Occitan speakers, for instance, may yield equally valuable insights into these issues. I recommend Inayatullah (1995) for an Islamic perspective on tourism, which suggests the rich possibilities of applying diverse cultural lenses to the study (and teaching) of tourism.

At a time when multicultural understanding is under strain and our world faces profound challenges, this pedagogy of tourism informed by Indigenous approaches is a transformative approach, which offers exciting possibilities for the critical and concerned educator. However, it is also important to acknowledge that Indigenous perspectives suggest that learning comes from the embedded relationships between people, place and culture and therefore each Indigenous people's approach is unique to that people. In fact, an Indigenous perspective suggests that we should not be looking for universal applicability of principles. This sets the challenge to engage with multiple cultural interfaces in our classrooms and to be open to the rich learnings that each might offer us in our efforts to create transformative learning opportunities for ourselves and our students.

REFERENCES

Atkinson, J. (2002), *Trauma Trails, Recreating Song Lines: The Transgenerational Effects of Trauma in Indigenous Australia*, North Melbourne: Spinifex Press.

Calma, T. (2009), 'Enriching tertiary education with Indigenous voices', accessed 14 December 2014 at www.humanrights.gov.au/news/speeches/enriching-tertiary-education-indigenous-voices.

De Chavez, R. (1999), 'Globalisation and tourism: Deadly mix for Indigenous peoples', accessed 6 June 2002 at www.twnside.org.sg/title/chavez-cn.htm.

Foley, G. and Muldoon, E. (2014), 'Pyning for Indigenous rights in the Australian curriculum', accessed 14 December 2014 at www.theconversation.com/pyning-for-indigenous-rights-in-the-australian-curriculum-30422.

Higgins-Desbiolles, F. (2006), 'More than an industry: Tourism as a social force', *Tourism Management*, **27** (6), 1192–208.

Higgins-Desbiolles, F. (2007), 'Touring the Indigenous or transforming consciousness? Reflections on teaching Indigenous tourism at university', *Australian Journal of Indigenous Education*, **36** (1), 108–16.

hooks, b. (2003), *Teaching Community: A Pedagogy of Hope*, New York: Routledge.

Inayatullah, S. (1995), 'Rethinking tourism: Unfamiliar histories and alternative futures', *Tourism Management*, **16** (6), 411–15.

International Forum on Indigenous Tourism (IFIT) (2002), Oaxaca Declaration, Oaxaca, Mexico.

International Forum on Indigenous Tourism film (2002), Directed by Juan José Garcia, Oaxaca: Indigenous Tourism Rights International.

Keefe, K. and Schmider, J. (1988), 'Aboriginal Australian studies bicentennial Australian studies schools project', Canberra: Department of Employment, Education and Training.

Kincheloe, J.L. and Steinberg, S.R. (2008), 'Indigenous knowledges in education: Complexities, dangers and profound benefits', in N.K. Denzin, Y.S. Lincoln and L. T. Smith (eds), *Handbook of Critical and Indigenous Methodologies*, Thousand Oaks, CA: Sage, pp. 135–66.

Macintyre, S. (2003), 'The history wars', accessed 10 December 2014 at www.kooriweb.org/foley/resources/pdfs/198.pdf.

Marshall, M. (1997), 'Developing and teaching Indigenous perspectives in management', accessed 30 June 2006 at www.carrickinstitute.edu.au/carrick/webdav/site/carricksite/users/siteadmin/public/dissemination%20strategies%20project%20brief.doc/Marshall%20M.cutsd.ped.

Martin, K. (2001a), 'Aboriginal people, aboriginal lands and indigenist research: A discussion of re-search pasts and neo-colonial research futures', Master's thesis, James Cook University, Townsville.

Martin, K. (2001b), 'Ways of knowing, ways of being and ways of doing: Developing a theoretical framework and methods for indigenous re-search and indigenist research', accessed 18 September 2004 at www.aiatsis.gov.au/rsrch/conf2001/papers/martin.pdf.

Martin, K. (2002), 'Ways of knowing, being and doing: A theoretical framework and methods for indigenous and indigenist re-search', *Journal of Australian Studies*, **27** (76), 203–14.

McLaren, D.R. (2003), 'Indigenous peoples and ecotourism', in M. Honey and S. Thullen (eds), *Rights and Responsibilities: A Compilation of Codes of Conduct for Tourism and Indigenous and Local Communities*, Center for Ecotourism and Sustainable Development and International Ecotourism Society, accessed 11 November 2003 at ecotourism.org/rights_responsibilities.html.

Mowforth, M. and Munt, I. (2003), *Tourism and Sustainability: Development and New Tourism in the Third World* (2nd edn), London: Routledge.

Nakata, M. (2004), 'Indigenous Australian studies and higher education', accessed 12 December 2014 at www.aiatsis.gov.au/events/wentworth.html.

Pacific Asia Indigenous Tourism Conference (2012), 'The Larrakia Declaration on the Development of Indigenous Tourism', accessed 12 August 2014 at www.winta.org/the-larrakia-declaration/.

Pera, L. and McLaren, D. (1999), 'Globalization, tourism and Indigenous peoples: What you should know about the world's largest "industry"', accessed 21 May 2003 at www.planeta.com/ecotravel/resources/rtp/globalization.html.

Peters, A. and Higgins-Desbiolles, F. (2012), 'De-marginalising tourism research: Indigenous Australians as tourists', *Journal of Hospitality and Tourism Management*, **19** (1), 76–84.

Rigney, L-I. (1996), 'Tools for an Indigenist research methodology: A Narungga perspective', paper presented at the World Indigenous Peoples Conference: Education, Albuquerque, New Mexico, 15–23 June.

Rigney, L-I. (1999), 'The first perspective: Culturally safe research practices on or with Indigenous peoples', in Proceedings of 1999 Chacmool Conference, Calgary, Canada.

Rigney, L-I. (2001), 'A first perspective of Indigenous Australian participation in science: Framing Indigenous research towards Indigenous Australian intellectual sovereignty', *Kaurna Higher Education Journal*, **7**, 1–13.

Seton, K. (1999), 'Fourth World nations in the era of globalisation', accessed 27 March 2001 at www.cwis.org/fwj/41/fworld.html.

Smith, L. T. (2003), *Decolonizing Methodologies: Research and Indigenous Peoples*, London: Zed Books.

Torres, C.A. (1998), *Democracy, Education and Multiculturalism: Dilemmas of Citizenship in a Globalized World*, Lanham, MD: Rowman and Littlefield.

Tribe, J. (2001), 'Research paradigms and the tourism curriculum', *Journal of Travel Research*, **39** (4), 442–8.

United Nations (2004), 'The concept of Indigenous peoples', accessed 4 January 2015 at www.un.org/esa/socdev/unpfii/documents/workshop_data_background.doc.

Universities Australia (2011), *National Best Practice Framework for Indigenous Cultural Competency in Australian Universities*, Canberra: Universities Australia.

University of South Australia (UniSA) (2014), 'Exhibition marks UniSA as a heartland for Indigenous Education', accessed 22 May 2015 at www.unisa.edu.au/Media-Centre/Releases/Exhibition-marks-UniSA-as-a-heartland-for-Indigenous-Education/#.VJoUGdU-AA.

Welch, C. (2011), 'Savagery on show: The popular visual representation of Native American peoples and their lifeways at the World's Fairs (1851–1904) and in Buffalo Bill's Wild West (1884–1904)', *Early Popular Visual Culture*, **9** (4), 337–52.

Williamson, J. and Dalal, P. (2007), 'Indigenising the curriculum or negotiating the tensions at the cultural interface? Embedding Indigenous perspectives and pedagogies in a university curriculum', *The Australian Journal of Indigenous Education*, **36** (1), 51–8.

31 Indigenization of curricula: trends and issues in tourism education
Tamara Young and Amy Maguire

1. INTRODUCTION

The tourism curriculum space is diverse and complex. The maturity of academic enquiry in tourism research, where reflexive and critical knowledge has surpassed the traditional applied business research base (Pritchard et al. 2011), is mirrored in tourism education. This increasingly provides a space through which critical pedagogies and alternative disciplinary perspectives can enhance the learning experiences and outcomes for students. There are, however, challenges inherent in developing curricula that bridge critical tourism theory and tourism industry needs. On a global scale, tensions exist between the market model of higher education and liberal model of higher education. Tourism courses are increasingly being taught only within business and management schools (Airey 2008). A business-oriented curriculum is often directed towards 'skills training' for employment within the tourism, hospitality and events industries, with a focus on competencies transferable to the workplace (Wells 1996; Belhassen and Caton 2011). However, there is a need for tourism education to move beyond the limits of an economic perspective – for the business orientation of tourism curricula to be balanced by a liberal component (Tribe 2000; 2001; 2002a; 2002b; 2008) – as a narrow industry focus belies the significance of tourism as a social force and cultural phenomenon (Higgins-Desboilles 2006; Belhassen and Caton 2011).

As much as tourism experiences can expose individuals to places, people and cultures and provide a space for cultural learning and identity formation (Wearing et al. 2010), the tourism curriculum can likewise expose students to ideas outside of their natural discourses. Caton (2014, p. 26) argues that the 'growing recognition of tourism as a worldmaking force is indeed the driver behind calls for curriculum development beyond the narrow confines of a vocationalistic, or even a mangerialistic, model'. Tourism educators require the tools to enable a better understanding of such a critical space, particularly the worldmaking power of tourism (Hollinshead 2007). Arguably, a key component of that sense of critical knowing is an understanding of Indigenous perspectives in tourism. As Hollinshead (2007, p. 283) states, a new Indigenous critical space is opening up within tourism research, generating new ways of seeing and projecting Indigenous Australian history, culture, identity and knowledge.

In this chapter, we are concerned with the ways in which tourism educators can implement Indigenized curricula to educate students with a strong and developed sense of knowing about social responsibility, equity and justice in relation to Indigenous rights and self-determination. Such objectives are central to the Indigenization of curricula within tertiary institutions. The incorporation of these outcomes into tourism education – and, indeed, business education more generally (Rhea 2009) – can provide students with the critical knowledge to 'act in the tourism world – whether as tourists, or tourism professionals or political activists' (Tribe 2002a, p. 309).

The Indigenization of curricula ought to be a priority in global tertiary education. Yet the necessary forms of curriculum renewal and the literature considering it are limited. The purpose of this chapter is to explore the Indigenization of curricula and to elucidate its benefits to tourism education. We outline the emergence of a debate regarding the Indigenization of university curricula, and examine key trends and issues in the teaching of Indigenous related content, including the incorporation of Indigenous knowledges and perspectives. We argue that interdisciplinarity and cultural competency are essential to the tourism teaching agenda. Whilst this chapter focuses on an Indigenized curriculum in the Australian context, this dialogue is relevant to tourism education internationally, particularly given the global prevalence of Indigenous tourism and the representation of Indigenous cultures in tourism promotion (Higgins-Desboilles 2007; Young et al. 2011).

2.   INDIGENIZING CURRICULA: THE AUSTRALIAN CONTEXT

The tertiary education sector in Australia is repositioning in line with changes in global and national social, political and institutional developments. Over the past decade, Indigenous collaboration and education initiatives have emerged as significant priorities for universities across Australia. Such initiatives aim, in part, to address the disadvantages experienced by Aboriginal and Torres Strait Islander peoples and to assist in the process of Aboriginal reconciliation.[1] Aboriginal and Torres Strait Islander peoples in Australia are notably disadvantaged in the higher education context, with participation rates and success outcomes significantly below the population as a whole (Behrendt et al. 2012; Commonwealth of Australia 2015). In response to this, universities across Australia are prioritizing Indigenous cultural competency and the Indigenization of curricula, and this direction is reflected in the strategic plans of a number of institutions, including The University of Sydney (2010), The University of Melbourne (2011), The Australian National University (2011) and The University of Queensland (2012). At the University of Newcastle, the institution where the authors of this chapter are based, the *New Directions 2013–2015 Strategic Plan* (The University of Newcastle, 2012) identifies a commitment to developing pathways for academic attainment for Indigenous students, increasing the numbers of Indigenous staff, embedding Indigenous knowledge systems into programs, fostering commitment to social justice in our students, and developing the cultural competence of all staff and students.

The Indigenization of curricula, a process that has been positioned as a 'whole-of-university-responsibility' (Butler and Young 2009), is central to Indigenous collaboration and education initiatives, and essential in signaling to students that Indigenous-related content and perspectives are important. By embedding Indigenous knowledges through-out the curriculum, rather than focusing only on discrete courses (or avoiding inclusion entirely), academics can shift the expectations of students and teachers regarding the intellectual boundaries of their fields of study, and challenge them to critique the relationship between Indigenous and non-Indigenous knowledge systems. A group of academics from settler-colonial states found this to be true when they taught a comparative Indigenous rights course via videoconferencing between students in Australia, Canada, New Zealand and the United States (Stephenson et al. 2006). These actions can ensure that all students are taught in culturally appropriate ways to meet the wider responsibility of educating all students for equity, social justice and anti-racism.

The Indigenization of curricula requires the sensitive and appropriate incorporation of Indigenous-related content and perspectives in university courses and programs. Butler and Young (2009) offer an open-ended definition of Indigenization, stating that Indigenized curricula should encompass two key objectives. First, a curricular justice goal that aims to provide educational opportunities and outcomes to address the disadvantages faced by Indigenous students seeking tertiary education; and second, a wider responsibility goal that focuses on educating all students for social justice through programs of anti-racism education. The broad nature of this definition supports commitment to a diverse and responsive approach to Indigenization, rather than a homogenizing and ultimately essentialist position. Such an approach allows both staff and students to reflect on the nature, scope and relevance of Indigenization for their discipline's philosophy and practice (Young et al. 2011).

Carey (2008) notes that the inclusion of Indigenous studies value-adds to other disciplines because it diversifies the knowledges and skills with which students will leave university. Maori legal academic Carwyn Jones (2009) finds that Indigenous perspectives can assist in developing students' understanding of the social role and effect of law, by reflecting on law in action and providing a critical framework for analyzing laws and legal systems. However, an Indigenized curriculum is not only concerned with educating students to understand historical and cultural Indigenous perspectives, it also involves the inclusion of Indigenous students (in areas such as recruitment, retention and support), and the inclusion of non-Western knowledge in general. Indeed, teaching and learning that is relevant to, and reflective of, Indigenous cultures is seen as important in increasing the participation of Indigenous students (Gair 2007). These central tenets of Indigenization of curricula are explored, below, to examine the trends and issues in the teaching of Indigenous-related content.

3. INDIGENIZING CURRICULA: TRENDS AND ISSUES

Whilst there is a call for tertiary education to construct pedagogical practices that have relevance and meaning to the social and cultural realities of all students (Howard 2003), research concerned with the Indigenization of curricula is limited. Definitions of Indigenization are often ambiguous, and attempts to Indigenize curricula run the risk of promoting corrupted understandings of Indigenous knowledge (Nakata 2007). Here we consider the Indigenization of curricula from various disciplinary perspectives in an effort to unpack definitions of Indigenization and to examine the overarching trends and issues.

The inclusion of Indigenous content and the embedding of Indigenous perspectives into the curricula are examined by Hart and Moore (2005) through the concept of the 'third space'. Following Bhabha (1994), they contend that hybrid understandings occur through the interaction of the colonizer with the colonized, with a 'cutting edge' or 'third space' of negotiation resulting. Thus, in their approach to curriculum design for Australian Studies courses, they focused on challenging the existing beliefs of students to encourage them to arrive at new and individualistic understandings. They suggest that within a negotiated interpretative 'third space', students can consider alternative views that disrupt their 'common sense' understandings of Australian culture and history and Australian Aboriginality (Hart and Moore 2005).

Carey (2008), in a study on the dialogical space between Indigenous studies and other disciplines, discusses the process of Indigenizing curricula and critiques her institution's early attempts to 'Aboriginalize' the curriculum. She engages an alternative conceptualization of the third space as advocated by Aboriginal scholar Langton (1993). In doing so, Carey (2008) argues that Indigenized curricula must emerge out of an anti-colonial dialogue as distinct from a post-colonial paradigm. Such an approach places Indigenous standpoints at the center of Indigenized curriculum and serves to protect the unique methodological, epistemological and pedagogical features of Indigenous studies.

An approach that embeds Indigenous knowledge provides a new way to conceptualize the transformative effects of Indigenous studies for students and works to support an anti-colonial dialogue between Indigenous studies and other disciplines (Carey 2008). Hence, debates over the appropriate place of Indigenous knowledges within curricula can be understood as a broad process encompassing the iterative de-privileging of dominant colonial discourses.

Maori scholar Durie (2005) describes such an approach as 'the third way' that provides an interface between Indigenous knowledge and other knowledge systems, to generate new insights, built from two systems:

> While it is often valued because of its traditional qualities, the perception of Indigenous knowledge and culture as applicable only to the distant past ignores the thrust for development that is part of the Indigenous journey. Arising from the creative potential of Indigenous knowledge is the prospect that it can be applied to modern times in parallel with other knowledge systems. (Durie 2005, p. 304)

The interface approach recognizes the distinctiveness of different knowledge systems, but sees opportunities for employing aspects of both so that dual benefits can be realized and Indigenous worldviews can be matched with contemporary realities. The intercultural dialogue between two knowledge systems is thus recognized as a powerful transformative space (Durie 2005; Carey 2008).

There are, however, challenges associated with the implementation of two knowledge systems – of Indigenous knowledges and Western knowledges – in higher education, particularly at the 'cultural interface' where the bridging of, or moving between, the two knowledge systems takes place (Nakata 2007). The issue of potentially incompatible ways of knowing or, more precisely, what ways of knowing are seen as legitimate, emerges. Nakata (2007, p. 8) argues that these challenges are no less than an incompatibility 'on cosmological, epistemological and ontological grounds . . . [such that] it is not possible to bring in Indigenous knowledge and plonk it in the curriculum unproblematically as if it is another data set for Western knowledge to discipline and test'. For Nikora (2008), Maori knowledge in academia has struggled to be recognized for this reason as it has been presented from the perspective of being 'acted on' rather than 'acted with'.

In a humanities context, Williamson and Dalal (2007) have argued that some pedagogical approaches can translate cultural interface complexities into curriculum outcomes, which then link to graduate capabilities. These approaches require an unsettling of

Western authority and hence critical self-reflection (Williamson and Dalal 2007). This is done by engaging on levels other than the 'intellectual', using holistic teaching methods that connect with students on emotional, spiritual and intellectual levels, and acknowledging the limits of Western knowledge (Williamson and Dalal 2007) and, we would argue, the shortcomings of traditional Western teaching methods and curriculum design. Through challenging students' existing beliefs, and opening up a space for students to consider alternative views to their common sense understandings, an opportunity arises for the consideration of Martin/Mirraboopa's (2003) three main constructs of a theoretical framework for Indigenist research: ways of knowing, ways of being and ways of doing.

Yet the mobilization of Indigenous knowledge in education can be problematic. A key issue is the dominance of non-Indigenous educators (Gair 2007). Indeed, this mobilization requires a cultural shift within academia itself:

> The challenge we as educators are facing today is how to rupture the 'taken-for-granted' positions, to bring about change and counter the years of Eurocentric discourse that has pervaded our society. We need to look to different epistemological paradigms and act from both within and outside the academy. We need to look to other forms of experience and knowledge. This can be done most successfully, we would argue, by Indigenous and non-Indigenous scholars alike to find ways to make more explicit the colonial structures and frames of mind that pervade our thoughts and actions. (Edwards and Hewitson 2008, p. 3)

Edwards and Hewitson (2008, p. 98) argue that to create a counter-hegemonic education system, we need to create 'tertiary educational programmes based on Indigenous epistemologies and worldviews as well as adopting systems that normalize . . . [Indigenous] epistemologies'. As the decolonization of curricula requires a 'centering' of Indigenous knowledge (McLaughlin and Whatman 2011) and an 'unsettling of "Western" authority' (Williamson and Dalal 2007, p. 52), efforts to embed Indigenous knowledge in curricula often face resistance from staff who are uncomfortable with the prospect of change at both the professional and subjective level (Williamson and Dalal 2007, p. 52). Any attempts to embed Indigenous knowledge in curricula will, and should by their very nature, require unsettling aspects such as decolonizing methodologies to disturb the hegemonic Western knowledge project (Tuhiwai Smith 2012).

Martin/Mirraboopa (2003) offers a paradigm for implementing what she terms an 'Indigenist research' perspective that incorporates her subjectivities as an Aboriginal researcher as well as a Western-educated researcher. The principles she espouses are:

- Recognition of our worldviews, our knowledges and our realities as distinctive and vital to our existence and survival;
- Honoring our social mores as essential processes through which we live, learn and situate ourselves as Aboriginal people in our own lands and when in the lands of other Aboriginal people;
- Emphasis of social, historical and political contexts which shape our experiences, lives, positions and futures;
- Privileging the voices, experiences and lives of Aboriginal people and Aboriginal lands. (Martin/Mirraboopa 2003, p. 205)

By implementing these principles, Martin/Mirraboopa (2003) outlines a framework to synthesize the Western practice of research with Indigenous ways of knowing and, as such, points to possible ways in which the Indigenization of curricula might occur.

4.   TOWARDS AN INDIGENIZED TOURISM CURRICULUM

The importance of incorporating multiple ways of knowing into tourism curriculum design has been identified as the key to providing students with the opportunity to 'critically engage with the big questions around the role of tourism in society (and their own role in it)' (Dredge et al. 2013, p. 91). Engaging alternative paradigms in curriculum content avoids domination by any one interest and offers the prospect of an educational environment where a wider ethical and cultural framework is valued (Tribe 2002b). A curriculum comprised of multiple ways of knowing can lead tourism students on different educational journeys. Tribe (2002b) suggests a curriculum framework that includes the dimensions of 'ends' and 'stance'. Ends can include, for example, vocational employability, as well as more liberal ends, such as freedom of thought about tourism. Where the ends of the curriculum are liberal, Tribe (2002b) argues that they are unconstrained, and knowledge and actions are judged appropriate for different reasons. In the context of an Indigenized curriculum, knowledge which helps establish truths, or assists in an ethical argument of good or just tourism (see Tribe 2002b), is relevant and useful.

Young et al. (2011) argue that the tourism education community needs to rigorously debate its approach to Indigenous inclusion in the curriculum. This is particularly necessary given the tendency for Indigenous academics to be based in fields of research other than tourism (Higgins-Desboilles 2007). Thus, one of the challenges for non-Indigenous academics teaching tourism is to acknowledge the creative potential of Indigenous knowledge and to incorporate that knowledge into course content. Certainly, the Indigenous standpoint needs to be at the center of any Indigenized curriculum (Carey 2008). Indigenous issues should not merely be taught as an add-on; Indigenous materials should ideally be integrated into a course rather than only representing stand-alone topics (Graham 2009). One way of introducing relevant material and incorporating multiple knowledges into the curriculum is to engage with local Indigenous communities in course development and delivery. One of the most significant contributions to an Indigenized tourism curriculum is evident in the work of Higgins-Desboilles (2007). In the development of her Indigenous Tourism course, Higgins-Desboilles carried out extensive consultations with Indigenous staff and communities, and created partnerships with Indigenous academics in the teaching of Indigenous tourism. Higgins-Desboilles (2007) argues for the privileging of Indigenous voices throughout the curriculum and achieves this in her course in various ways:

- the incorporation of case studies of the experiences of Indigenous people in relation to Indigenous rights and self-determination;
- the inclusion of writings of Indigenous authors to provide knowledge of what Indigenous people hope to achieve through tourism;
- the inclusion of Indigenous documents, declarations and statements;
- the use of audio-visual materials to reinforce case studies and readings;
- engagement with Indigenous academics and community members who deliver guest lectures and tutorial content;
- field trips to local Indigenous communities.

Thus, there are a number of clear ways forward by which tourism educators can design Indigenized curricula. The development of networks with Indigenous academics and communities is key, but not the only way to include counter-discourses to Western knowledge. Indeed, the capacity of a curriculum to incorporate Indigenous knowledges requires the self-reflexivity of the non-Indigenous academic. Whilst the process of critical self-reflection may be uncomfortable for educators (McLaughlin and Whatman 2011), particularly for non-Indigenous academics who have never had to question their own white privilege (Higgins-Desboilles 2007), a decolonized curriculum embedded with Indigenous perspectives can only be accomplished with: '[T]he recognition of Indigenous knowledge in disciplines and the preparedness of non-Indigenous academics to investigate their own subjectivities and cultural positioning, in order to fully engage with embedding Indigenous perspectives into the content, teaching methodologies and assessments' (McLaughlin and Whatman 2011, p. 368).

The need for critical self-reflection is further evident when non-Indigenous educators are teaching non-Indigenous students about Indigenous issues and perspectives in the context of tourism (Gair 2007; Higgins-Desboilles 2007). This racial and cultural incongruence between teachers and students merits ongoing discussion and reflection (Howard, 2003). The analysis of racial identities on behalf of teachers is critical to the development of a culturally relevant pedagogy that ensures that non-Indigenous educators are not 'speaking for' Indigenous people (Nikora 2008). Thus, we need to be advocating tourism curriculum design that promotes the sensitive and appropriate inclusion of Indigenous content through engagement with Indigenous people and perspectives.

5. CONCLUSION: FUTURE DIRECTIONS

At an institutional level, universities in Australia and other countries with Indigenous populations can do much to improve educational outcomes for both Indigenous and non-Indigenous students. Educators should consider building their courses with a view to the sensitive and appropriate inclusion of Indigenous content and perspectives. Understanding the existence of multiple Indigenous perspectives is vital, as the process would be invalidated by any presentation of Indigenous experiences and perspectives as singular or monocultural. Furthermore, Indigenized curricula should seek to educate all students with a sense of knowing about social responsibility, equity and social justice in relation to Indigenous rights and self-determination. This chapter has considered the central tenets of the Indigenization of curricula in the context of tourism education in Australia, and argued that the case for embedding Indigenous perspectives into the tourism curriculum is very convincing.

Tourism is widely viewed as having the potential to contribute to economic self-sufficiency for Indigenous communities. At the same time, the tourism industry and tourism studies 'have been instrumental for casting Indigenous people as the exotic "Other" for profit and exploitation' (Higgins-Desboilles 2007, p. 110). Our ongoing research seeks to explore the development of Indigenized curricula that academics, both Indigenous and non-Indigenous, will feel empowered to deliver. Further, we aim to consider how Indigenous and non-Indigenous students can best gain from the Indigenization imperative. We aspire to meet these aims by developing models for the application of embedding Indigenous perspectives into curricula. We urge tourism educators to reflect upon their teaching, particularly the ways in which areas of interdisciplinarity and intercultural dialogue can be applied to the tourism teaching agenda. In this way, the gap between content inclusion *about* Indigenous people and cultures, and a broader engagement *with* Indigenous peoples and perspectives, will be narrowed effectively.

NOTE

1. Reconciliation, in this context, is a term used to refer to the bringing together of Indigenous and non-Indigenous Australians in an attempt to overcome underlying divisions and inequalities, which have arisen from Australia's colonialist roots. See Burridge (2006) for a more comprehensive discussion of the meaning of the term 'reconciliation'.

REFERENCES

Airey, D. (2008), 'In search of a mature subject?', *Journal of Hospitality, Leisure, Sport and Tourism Education*, **7** (2), 101.
Australian National University (2011), 'ANU by 2020', accessed 20 March 2015 at unistats.anu.edu.au/strategic-framework/strat-plan.pdf.
Behrendt, L., Larkin, S., Griew, R. and Kelly, P. (2012), *Review of Higher Education Access and Outcomes for Aboriginal and Torres Strait Islander People: Final Report*, Canberra: Department of Industry, Innovation, Science, Research and Tertiary Education.
Belhassen, Y. and Caton, K. (2011), 'On the need for critical pedagogy in tourism education', *Tourism Management*, **32** (6), 1389–96.
Bhabha, H. (1994), *The Location of Culture*, London: Routledge.
Burridge, N. (2006), 'Meanings of reconciliation in the school context', *Australian Journal of Indigenous Education*, **35**, 68–77.
Butler, K. and Young, A. (2009), 'Indigenization of curricula: Intent, initiatives and implementation', *Proceedings of AUQF2009 – International and External Quality Assurance: Tensions and Synergies*, Alice Springs, Northern Territory.
Carey, M. (2008), 'Indigenization, interdisciplinary and cultural competency: Working the dialogic space between Indigenous studies and other disciplines at Curtin University', paper presented at the Psychology and Indigenous Australians: Teaching Practice and Theory Conference, 14 July.
Caton, K. (2014), 'Underdisciplinarity: Where are the humanities in tourism education?', *Journal of Hospitality, Leisure, Sport and Tourism Education*, **15**, 24–33.
Commonwealth of Australia (2015), 'Closing the gap: Prime Minister's report 2015', accessed 18 March 2015 at www.dpmc.gov.au/sites/default/files/publications/Closing_the_Gap_2015_Report_0.pdf.
Dredge, D., Benckendorff, P., Day, M., Gross, M.J., Walo, M., Weeks, P. and Whitelaw, P. (2013), 'Drivers of change in tourism, hospitality, and event management education: An Australian perspective', *Journal of Hospitality and Tourism Education*, **25** (2), 89–102.
Durie, M. (2005), 'Indigenous knowledge within a global knowledge system', *Higher Education Policy*, **18** (3), 301–12.
Edwards, S. and Hewitson, K. (2008), 'Indigenous epistemologies in tertiary education', *The Australian Journal of Indigenous Education*, **37**, 96–102.
Gair, S. (2007), 'Pursuing Indigenous-inclusive curriculum in social work tertiary education: Feeling my way as a non-Indigenous educator', *The Australian Journal of Indigenous Education*, **36**, 49–55.
Graham, N. (2009), 'Indigenous property matters in real property courses at Australian universities', *Legal Education Review*, **19** (1/2), 289–304.
Hart, V. and Moore, K. (2005), '"To see through the eyes of another": The third space – An alternative view of Australian studies', paper presented at the Social Change in the 21st Century Conference, Queensland.
Higgins-Desboilles, F. (2006), 'More than an "industry": The forgotten power of tourism as a social force', *Tourism Management*, **27** (6), 1192–208.
Higgins-Desboilles, F. (2007), 'Touring the Indigenous or transforming consciousness? Reflections on teaching Indigenous tourism at university', *The Australian Journal of Indigenous Education*, **36**, 108–16.
Hollinshead, K. (2007), 'Indigenous Australia in the bittersweet world: The power of tourism in the projection of the "old" and "fresh" visions of Aboriginality', in R. Butler and T. Hinch (eds), *Tourism and Indigenous People: Issues and Implications*, Oxford: Butterworth-Heinemann, pp. 282–304.

Howard, T. (2003), 'Culturally relevant pedagogy: Ingredients for critical teacher reflection', *Theory into Practice*, **42** (3), 196–202.

Jones, C. (2009), 'Indigenous legal issues, indigenous perspectives and indigenous law in the New Zealand law curriculum', *Legal Education Review*, **19**, 257–70.

Langton, M. (1993), *Well I Heard it on the Radio and Saw it on the Television . . .*, Woolloomooloo: Australian Film Commission.

Martin, K. [Booran Mirraboopa] (2003), 'Ways of knowing, being and doing: A theoretical framework and methods for Indigenous and Indigenist re-search', *Journal of Australian Studies*, **27** (76), 203–14.

McLaughlin, J. and Whatman, S. (2011), 'The potential of critical race theory in decolonizing university curricula', *Asia Pacific Journal of Education*, **31** (4), 365–77.

Nakata, M. (2007), 'The cultural interface', *The Australian Journal of Indigenous Education*, **37**, 7–14.

Nikora, L. (2008), 'Indigenizing psychology: The Maori way', keynote presentation at the Psychology and Indigenous Australians Conference, University of South Australia.

Pritchard, A., Morgan, N. and Ateljevic, I. (2011), 'Hopeful tourism: A new transformative perspective', *Annals of Tourism Research*, **38** (3), 941–63.

Rhea, Z. (2009), 'Indigenizing international education in business', *Journal of International Education in Business*, **2** (2), 15–27.

Stephenson, M., Morse, B., Robertson, L., Castan, M., Yarrow, D. and Thompson, R. (2006), 'International and comparative Indigenous rights via videoconferencing', *Legal Education Review*, **19**, 237–56.

Tribe, J. (2000), 'Balancing the vocational: The theory and practice of liberal education in tourism', *The International Journal of Tourism and Hospitality Research*, **2** (1), 9–26.

Tribe, J. (2001), 'Research paradigms and the tourism curriculum', *Journal of Travel Research*, **39** (4), 442–8.

Tribe, J. (2002a), 'Education for ethical tourism action', *Journal of Sustainable Tourism*, **10** (4), 309–24.

Tribe, J. (2002b), 'The philosophical practitioner', *Annals of Tourism Research*, **29** (2), 338–57.

Tribe, J. (2008), 'Tourism: A critical business', *Journal of Travel Research*, **46** (3), 245–55.

Tuhiwai Smith, L. (2012), *Decolonizing Methodologies: Research and Indigenous People* (2nd edn), London: Zed Books.

University of Melbourne (2011), 'The University Plan 2011–2014', accessed 20 March 2015 at http://www.unimelb.edu.au/publications/docs/universityplan2011–2014.pdf.

University of Newcastle (2012), 'New Directions Strategic Plan: 2013–2015', accessed 20 March 2015 at www.newcastle.edu.au/__data/assets/pdf_file/0004/33538/NeW-Directions-StrategicPlan.pdf.

University of Queensland (2012), 'Strategic Plan 2013–2017: Learning, discovery, engagement', accessed 20 March 2015 at www.uq.edu.au/about/docs/strategicplan/StrategicPlan2013.pdf.

University of Sydney (2010), 'The University of Sydney 2011–2015 Strategic Plan', accessed 20 March 2015 at sydney.edu.au/strategy/docs/strategic_plan_2011–2015.pdf.

Wearing, S., Stevenson, D. and Young, T. (2010), *Tourist Cultures: Identity, Place and The Traveller*, London: Sage.

Wells, J. (1996), 'The tourism curriculum in higher education in Australia: 1989–1995', *The Journal of Tourism Studies*, **7** (1), 20–30.

Williamson, J. and Dalal, P. (2007), 'Indigenizing the curriculum or negotiating the tensions at the cultural interface? Embedding Indigenous perspectives and pedagogies in a university curriculum', *The Australian Journal of Indigenous Education*, **36**, 51–8.

Young, T., Pearse, A. and Butler, K. (2011), 'Indigenizing curricula: Lessons from tourism studies', in M.J. Gross (ed.), *Tourism: Creating a Brilliant Blend, CAUTHE2011 National Conference Proceedings*, School of Management, University of South Australia: Adelaide.

PART VI

TEACHING, LEARNING AND RESEARCH

32 Teaching–research nexus in tourism, hospitality and event studies
Johan R. Edelheim

1. INTRODUCTION

I was happy to accept the task when I was asked to write a chapter on the teaching–research nexus in tourism studies. Through my career as a teacher in the fields of tourism, hospitality and events (which I will hereafter refer to as TH&E studies as I consider them to be an integral whole) I have been reflecting on that nexus. I have pondered upon what it means for myself, how I collect material for courses, how I use my own research to back up syllabi, and how I reflect and publish on teaching and learning practices. My current work, as director for an institute constituted of three TH&E departments in three organizations, where I coordinate the departments' strategies and operations, is very much related to this same nexus. The institute's stated aim is to carry out teaching, research and services in the field of TH&E. Whilst this on the surface sounds like a straightforward aim, the reality is far from it, because those words mean different things to the stakeholders in the different organizations. Here I am not simply talking about organizational cultures or differences in opinion, but I am talking about crucial differences in what it means 'to teach', 'to research' and 'to provide services', depending on what type of TH&E organization is in question. I will therefore analyze what these concepts can mean, and how these meanings alter people's practices.

The empirical case, and the context this chapter acts within, will take you to northern Finland, to Lapland – the region of the European Union that is mostly north of the Arctic Circle. The case study is an institute based in Lapland, and the legislation and organizational context will be Finnish – but the implications I highlight are global in their reach, and I will show why this subjective case is a good proxy for the larger context. The 'teaching–research nexus – TRN' (Angelo and Asmar, 2005) carries within it assumptions about teaching and learning that takes place as an outcome of research conducted, but also much more than that. A nexus is a theoretical concept which presumes that there are two separate entities that relate to one another through 'a complex series of connections' (Crowther, 1995, p. 782). How they relate to one another, and what sort of implications this has on curricula created, and on teaching practices, is what I will focus on.

If you are a reader accustomed to management texts then you might at times be dissatisfied with the freedoms I am taking in addressing you in person, and in talking about myself in the first person – but let us immediately clarify that epistemologically the 'truth', the data, and the new knowledge this chapter will provide in no way differ from ones that would be written in a pseudo-scientific third-person tense – I would still be writing it, and you would still be reading it, regardless of whether it is stated openly or not.

1.1   Teaching – What Does it Actually Mean?

I know that it is the philosopher in me that comes to the surface each time when I am asked to discuss a particular matter, because analyzing TRN could be done in a very different manner: by simply accepting the concept for what it is defined as in the literature, a discussion of the literature, and an application of it in an empirical context. What I instead start thinking of is what the words mean, and why they carry those specific meanings for us. Teaching is naturally a noun, and to be precise a reified noun. A reified noun differs from other nouns in the sense that it is not a thing – it is only the abstract understanding of an action; in a phenomenological sense, the only reality is the verb – the action that takes place when somebody is teaching.

The verb 'to teach' carries a range of meanings, from practical senses of showing somebody how to do things, to more abstract meanings of relating information to another person. It can also be more negatively perceived as encouraging people to accept a principle, or even to punish them so they do not do something again; 'this will teach you' (Crowther, 1995, p. 1225). The meaning of teaching in the concept 'TRN' would be most closely related to the two first interpretations, that is, vocationally to teach skills by showing how to do something, or more abstractly to teach data which is intended to give learners knowledge that allows them to understand causes and effects, relationships between matters, and larger wholes. I am in this chapter referring to the people doing the teaching as teachers, even though I am fully aware of the fact that university staff engaged in teaching seldom see themselves as teachers, and instead are careful to point out that they are 'lecturers' or 'educators'.

The reason why we are all teachers is that also the other professional names are by their etymological root tied back to the same practice (Scott, 2005): a lecturer lectures, and professor professes – only the level of abstraction increases. By comparing the verbs related to teaching to one another, one can see that 'coach' is a hands-on practice, often related to sports, 'train' and 'instruct' are also often related to skills and competences (Crowther, 1995, p. 1225). 'Lecture' comes from written work and 'reading out loud', whereas 'profess' comes from declaring something openly, avowing, or acknowledging, often in a religious sense – this later led to the understanding of a person professing 'to be expert in some art or science' (Barnhart, 2003, p. 585 and p. 844f). I am not trying to be funny in explaining these meanings; my aim is to lead our understanding of meanings ascribed to words to the practice those meanings lead to. Teaching, and its related terms, refers to the transfer of information from one person to others; this can be done in person, or by proxy – such as written work. To do research and to publish it, is therefore also teaching, which leads us to the second word of interest in TRN, namely: research.

1.2   Research – What Does it Actually Mean?

In a workshop some months ago, for the staff at work, the discussion turned to what research means to us. It was a revealing moment when a colleague employed in our vocational dimension said that research doesn't really concern her students and colleagues, it is, in her mind, 'not their businesses'. The statement summarized succinctly a challenge we grapple with, not just at our institute, but more generally in society. Research has, for example, been given a meaning in daily parlance which unfortunately often is coupled with exclusivity, even elitism, and is by politicians, business leaders and the media, often used as a synonym for incomprehensible claims that are used to boost one or another opposing points of view (Scott, 2005). Jafari (2003) reminds us that research forms the basis for education, and goes on to outline the four platforms of tourism research. But research is naturally much more than that, thus, what research is, is of less importance than what meanings are attached to research – because this is the matter that causes some to perceive it to be 'incomprehensible', 'not their businesses' or 'exclusive', and this is why TRN is a provocative term.

A dictionary definition of research tells us that it is a 'careful study or investigation, especially in order to discover new facts or information', or something done to find information for a book or a newspaper article (Crowther, 1995, p. 996). Etymologically the word is borrowed from Middle French, and is made up of '*re-* intensive form + *cercher* to seek for', taking on the meaning 'careful hunting for facts' by 1639 in English (Barnhart, 2003, p. 915). Both explanations are on the surface quite plain and seem to suit our daily use of the concept, but this is exactly the challenge – a careful investigation, or fact find, means in different occupations different things, not due to the action, but due to the outcome. A newspaper reporter researches matters in order to produce news stories, a marketer researches in order to learn about the segments intended for their business, a school teacher researches what to include in a syllabus, and a person involved in higher education might join the field to make new discoveries and having a quest for knowledge, but find themselves doing research in order to gain a competitive grant or to publish an article in highly ranked scientific journals due to predominantly neoliberal agendas. It is therefore no surprise that people are disappointed in research outcomes, or consider some research elitist, if by doing the 'right' action an individual reaches the 'wrong' outcome; then the fault naturally lies with that individual (Peters and Olssen, 2005).

TRN is in actual fact almost a tautology: teaching – in its broadest definition – is always led by research – in its broadest definition. Healey states that the broader the definition is of the two, the easier they are to integrate (2005). Thus, let us move on to a literature review of TRN to examine the different debates surrounding the matter, with all I have said in our minds. Ontology, or the study of being, creates the framework for how we, as individuals, connected in societies, make sense of reality. By unraveling the etymologies of teaching and research I have simultaneously created the reality within which this chapter acts: its ontology. By accepting that different stakeholders have different ontological understandings of the concepts examined, we simultaneously accept that they are acting in different parallel realities, and this gives us the keys to understand why debates rage about the issues.

2. LITERATURE

Several authors reflect critically on the discourses used by university management and administrators relating to teaching and research relations (for example Coate et al. 2001; Healey, 2005; Mayson and Schapper, 2012; Schapper and Mayson, 2010). They highlight how the terms 'teaching' and 'research' are used in a dichotomous manner as separate issues that need to be connected for different reasons, whereas these connections are simultaneously made difficult by creating structures that strongly keep them apart.

2.1   Feeding Birds

The background to the need for an engagement between research and teaching stands in
the reasons for higher education institutions to exist worldwide: we conduct research, we
teach, and we provide services to the wider community (Scott, 2005). There is nothing new
or controversial in this, this is a mantra that is repeated worldwide, and academics' work
models are to a different extent allocated to these tasks in different proportions: some
individuals have more of one than others, some institutions emphasize the directions differently, and some nation-states create funding models that forge the field to adapt to a
politically set rationale by which the practice evolves. One could, as a metaphor, see this
as 'feeding birds'.

   You can all probably imagine a person feeding birds in a park or by a pond; it is a
common view globally: a person throwing pieces of old cooked rice or stale bread for birds
to eat. It is naturally first and foremost a picture of affluence and waste, something that
I call global, but let's be honest, relates to societies with more than enough to eat, where
birds, that are generally not intended to become the person's food later, are fed sustenance
that could have fed a person. The direction the crumbs are thrown in catches the attention
of surrounding birds, and more arrive to feast on the food on offer. The person feeding the
birds might favor some birds, and try to throw the pieces in ways that allow those birds to
catch more than other birds. Shy birds might survive by eating the leftovers that pushier
birds miss in their frenzy to catch new larger pieces thrown. Some bread pieces are so big
and dense that certain birds don't even try to eat them and others gulp them down greedily.
The person feeding the birds can change direction of the feeding and can thereby allocate
different feeding grounds for different birds, closer to the feeder or farther away, to the
left or to the right – you can see it quite vividly, can't you? But what does all of this have
to do with our daily lives as teachers in TH&E?

2.2   Teaching–Research Nexus

The metaphor in the previous section illustrates how government funding models work
for educational institutions. The birds are metaphorically an illustration of how we act as
critical, reflective, highly educated and intelligent teachers – we jump, and scream, and fly
for all our wings carry us to different places where we are fed. The crumbs are competitive
grants, and efficiency outcomes, they are student enrolment and graduation numbers, or
the number of citations we count on our differently ranked publications. Schapper and
Mayson call presumptions about the TRN by which decision makers act 'myths' and warn
that the myths can in an unchallenged way simply perpetuate how practice is formed even
though it could be useful to change it (2010, p. 643). They outline four debates that form
the basis for how we engage with TRN.

Debate 1: Can research and teaching be brought together?
The first debate is naturally building on the understanding that teaching and research are
two separate entities, and that they therefore need 'bridges' to meet and overlap (Scott,
2005). Much research states that there is a negligible relationship between the two (Kinchin
and Hay, 2007). By talking about concepts with commas or the word 'and' between them,
a dualistic separation has already been performed. 'A teacher's job is teaching, research,

and services to the community' is the creation of reality – an academic ontology. Job applications, work models, performance reviews, applications for promotions, and other devices to measure and compare people to one another, are commonly divided in the same three sectors, and are measured separately based on separate criteria (Scott, 2005).

Asking whether research and teaching can be brought together is like asking if water and oil can be brought together – of course they can, but as long as no emulsifier is added, they will continue existing side-by-side as two separate entities. Research shows that it is a myth that the two are entwined, the reality is that there is an ongoing desire to bring them together, and this is the reason it remains a policy imperative at many places (Schapper and Mayson, 2010, p. 646), but as long as they are treated as separate matters they will continue to stay separate.

Debate 2: Are there mutual benefits between teaching and research?
Research quality is to a great extent assessed by publication channels and output, and universities distinguish themselves as being 'research focused' in comparison to other modes of education (Boyd et al., 2012). An argument for TRN is that students value being taught by the researcher producing the material, but findings suggest that teachers' research engagements can reduce student interaction (Jiang and Roberts, 2011), and a negative correlation might be created between research output and quality teaching methods (Breen and Lindsay, 1999; Breen et al., 2002). A good teacher is not by necessity a good researcher, and vice versa (Ball and Mohamed, 2010; Healey, 2005). Ramsden and Moses (1992) found, for example, that there is no evidence to indicate that there would be a correlation between getting effective teaching outcomes and producing a large research output. The presumption that teachers will teach what they research is unfounded; curriculum restrictions force teachers to take on a much wider focus in their teaching load (Coate et al., 2001). However, Boyd et al. (2010, p. 16) found that there are benefits in overtly emphasizing the connection between the two as 'the nexus becomes the catalyst to encourage the merging of boundaries between teachers and learners'; this is examined in the model presented in the outcomes below.

The restrictions caused by the curriculum will be discussed in the next section of this chapter, but it is important already here to acknowledge the individual teacher's research interests, and the opportunities those form in shaping learning experiences. A chaotic curriculum for the student, but potentially very fulfilling for the teacher, would be one that is built around different staff members' own interests. A streamlined curriculum, for society and the organization, might satisfy neither the student nor the teacher. A curriculum built around students' interests might lead to instantaneous gratification for them, but neither serve society or teachers' interests or knowledge. These mismatches are further compounded when institutions specializing in certain research areas employ researchers with similar research interests, whereby research might be enhanced, but the link to a broad teaching spectrum becomes ever more elusive. The question of whether teaching and research benefit one another might therefore be of less relevance than whether it is feasible.

Debate 3: Which is more important, research or teaching?
The Western ordering of matters in grade of importance (Franklin, 2008) leads to heated debates about what should be emphasized, and how. I call this chapter 'TRN' based on

my definitions above, but I acknowledge also that other names for the concept exist. A research–teaching nexus, or a teaching–research nexus highlight different assumptions (Pearce, 2005), and so does the difference between research-led teaching and research*er*-led teaching (Schapper and Mayson, 2010). If the most important feature comes first, then it is always a matter of who is in power, or what goals are expected to be achieved, when the order between teaching–research or research–teaching are stated. The other difference, research or researcher, is more important in my mind. Here the former sees that the research that informs teaching doesn't have to be carried out by the person doing the teaching, but the teaching can lean on the findings of research. All too often this distinction is neglected, and TRN is perceived as being researcher-led – and something that only exists in institutions of higher education, whereas this does not have to be the case (Reid and Petocz, 2003).

Debate 4: Is the relationship between teaching and research the same in all disciplines?
A simplistic view of the relationship would suggest that it is the same for all disciplines, but a closer inspection reveals large differences depending on what epistemological foundations the stakeholders act from. Different relationships are not only discipline based but also cultural (Jenkins et al., 2007). As extreme examples, one could look at fields such as law, or medicine, and compare these to sociology, or TH&E. On the one extreme are sciences that are forced by their practice to only act based on accepted findings, and practitioners are certified to be able to work in their chosen field (Guerin and Ranasinghe, 2010). On the other extreme are sciences where the questioning of previous practices is encouraged, and where knowledge is fluid and theory follows practice as often as practice follows theory (Daruwalla and Malfroy, 2002).

Herein lies also one of the great challenges TH&E studies experience in becoming accepted as a 'serious' academic science. If a person decides to quit school to train her/himself to become a medical doctor by practice, you can immediately foresee a range of pitfalls; the same goes for engineering, physics and many other fields. Experiments like this have taken place in modern times, such as the atrocities carried out by the Khmer Rouge in Cambodia, with disastrous consequences (see, for example, Annear, 1998). The research that has been collected and is transmitted to students allows them to go out and practice in a way that will lead to bridges that stay intact for centuries, inflamed appendices that are removed efficiently and safely, or nuclear reactors that produce energy without endangering future generations' lives – at least in theory. Practice is necessitated by theory.

On the other hand, if a person quits school to start work in TH&E, then it is possible, without endangering too many lives or future generations, to achieve a certain competency without knowing any theories. As a TH&E teacher, I can hear your vocal opposition to this claim, and arguments are raised of how much better practices are conducted thanks to theoretical underpinnings, and therein lies the core: What we do in TH&E research is to create *better* practice, not to create the foundation for it all, or are we really?

When politicians, industry stakeholders, or the media criticize research, and teaching that is based on research in TH&E, then this is the ambiguity we are faced with – what is research in people's minds, and how do they assume that this research should affect their expected outcomes. This is where I will move on to my empirical case study, the institute I am employed at, and to theoretical frameworks that will allow us to appreciate the pitfalls of TRN in a simplistic, old-fashioned manner. The opportunities we have by unraveling the multiple realities different stakeholders act within, and the expectations those realities carry with them are also analyzed.

3.   CASE STUDY

3.1   The Multidimensional Tourism Institute (MTI)

The Multidimensional Tourism Institute (MTI) is a strategic alliance instigated in 2009 between three educational organizations: Rovaniemi educational municipality coopera-tion (RKK), Lapland University of Applied Sciences (LaplandUAS), and University of Lapland (Ulapland).

   MTI is both a virtual and a physical alliance; some education takes place at the same physical locations, some virtually, but in either case very different educational philoso-phies are brought together. The three organizations involved act under different legisla-tions, have different funding models, have different student intakes, different curricula, and different educational outcomes. Connecting different entities is always fraught with dangers, and this is naturally the case also here – the distinction between different educa-tional modes is a matter of identity, operations and strategy, combining different things is not as automatic as addition.

   Students apply to study at one of the three organizations. Vocational certificates, diplo-mas and advanced diplomas are on offer at Lapland Tourism College, upheld by RKK. Applied bachelor's and master's degrees are on offer at the Department of Tourism and Hospitality at Lapland UAS. Research-focused bachelor's, master's and doctoral degrees in social sciences, with a major in tourism, are on offer in the School of Tourism Research at Ulapland. The curriculum students follow is the one set by their respective organiza-tion, and when they graduate their official papers are from that chosen organization. Cooperation happens inside the institute, and enrolled students are offered a selection of courses from across the spectrum, participate in classes with peers from the three organizations, and have their studies credited back to their own diploma or degree. The different organizations' education is not referred to as 'levels' because that is a hierarchical word presuming higher and lower levels. The word 'dimensions' is instead used to indicate the different capabilities and knowledge needed in the TH&E industries, with which the different kinds of education equip students.

3.2   The Finnish Educational System – Three Dimensions

Finland has maintained an educational structure past compulsory education divided into three separate dimensions: *first* the secondary dimension compromising 3–4 years either at (theoretical) high schools or alternatively at (practical) vocational schools – offering education up until EQF 5; *second* comes the universities of applied science dimension, which is comparable with polytechnic institutions of Europe – up until EQF 7; *third* comes the classic research university dimension – up until EQF 8. The second and third dimensions are in an international comparison seen as providing degrees that are equal to one another – EQF 6 and 7, bachelor's and master's degrees. Since the 1990s students have been able to move through the system in a flexible way based on the premise that no education should hinder students continuing their studies. In terms of democratizing the system, and allowing young people to find a study path that fits their interests, this is a positive development generally encouraged by educational institutions.

The Finnish Government maintains a policy of state-funded education as a priority. Education is historically seen as a means of equaling social differences and providing all members of the community an opportunity to further their own careers without restrictions based on background. Education in Finland is therefore free of charge, that is, no tuition fees for either domestic or international students. There are, however, strict caps placed on numbers of students being admitted to different institutions. Calculations are made of how many professionals are needed in any one field, and institutions can apply to offer education in different fields. The caps functioned up until recently also as the funding rationale: institutions were funded based on the number of students admitted and studying on a full-time basis. However, new result-based funding models have been brought into Finnish HE and VET during 2012–15, whilst simultaneously making the caps even stricter. These changes are forcing the providers to reposition themselves in terms of student selection, curriculum design and efficiency of the syllabus.

3.3   The Curriculum Space

Teaching around the world follows pre-set curricula. The rationale for this is for stakeholders involved in a particular field to agree on the issues that are of importance to students. The achieved outcome might prepare the student for the next dimension of formal education, or for a work-task in a chosen field. The curriculum that is created is by necessity a compromise between competing interests. The amount of topics, data and skills that are considered to be needed depend on the stakeholder group involved, and because of this, some things have to be sacrificed in order to create a workable whole.

The diverse viewpoints in TH&E have been described by many researchers as a balance between the highly practical expectations of graduates expressed by employers in the industries on the one hand, and the far-reaching liberal humanistic goals set by academia on the other (for example Tribe, 2002). Research carried out in Australia offers a model that portrays the space within which curricula are formed, bordered by skills (*techne*) on one axis, and knowledge (*episteme*) on the other (Dredge et al., 2012). The different internal and external pressures in action that shape the curriculum are analyzed, and the end product aimed for is for graduates to achieve a level of practical intelligence (*phronesis*). This theoretical curriculum space offers a way to map components of curricula in order to investigate the predominant valorization done within different institutions.

The Multidimensional Tourism Institute (MTI) incorporates a multitude of tasks, organizations, geographies, practices and expectations that are combined. Practices used at MTI need to take into consideration the diverse organizations involved in the institute. A way of visually representing how the dimensions differ from one another, but simultaneously overlap other dimensions, is offered in Figure 32.1 (adapted from Dredge et al., 2012).

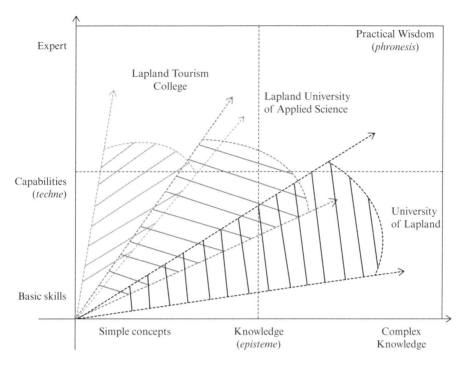

Source: Adapted from Dredge et al. (2012, p. 2167).

Figure 32.1   *The curriculum space applied on the Multidimensional Tourism Institute (MTI)*

3.4   The Curriculum Space Applied at MTI

Students enter the different organizations making up MTI for utilitarian purposes, to get an education, training and skills, and to be able to act successfully in different roles in society. The TH&E industries demand flexible and multi-skilled employees, and in order to prepare students for this, it is important that they are offered opportunities to select learning paths from the whole range of the education spectrum. The majority of enterprises in the field are small and medium sized, and it is therefore integral that graduands have a holistic under-standing not only of their own vocation, but also of how that task plays an important role in creating the individual experiences each customer has. Financiers, the government, project funders and different NGOs have all different ways of measuring the effectiveness of the finances provided – these measurements create different expectations that MTI, through its operations, aims to fulfill, whilst offering flexible, lifelong learning pathways.

The curricula at MTI follow national guidelines, as well as international frameworks, such as those developed through the Bologna Process, and Lifelong Learning initiatives. This means that the education provided needs to be internationally comparable at dif-ferent EQF levels, and a throwback to highly hierarchical thinking is forced upon the institute from the outside. Skills and capabilities are practiced and fine-tuned rather differently from knowledge and complex thoughts. Different types of TRN are therefore developed in the different educational dimensions, something I will describe in detail below in section 4: Outcomes.

3.5 The Curriculum Design TRN Model

The TRN focuses on teaching and research, but an important third component needs to be considered too: learning. Whilst the presumptions in education are that one leads to another (research–teaching–learning), this is not self-evident by any means. Different kinds of teaching suit different learners, but much research proves that the less integrative the methods, the smaller the number of students who learn the presented matter (Allin, 2010). Healey (2005) created a model in which he combined three axes of teaching and learning relations: Student-focused vs. Teacher-focused; Students as participants vs. Students as audience; Emphasis on research content vs. Emphasis on research processes and problems, and he mapped out how research is related to these different forms of interaction; see Figure 32.2.

The four types of TRN in the model were adapted by Healey from Griffiths (2004), and they describe how research can be integrated into teaching, and what kind of learning experiences this offers to learners. Starting from the bottom-left corner, 'Research-led',

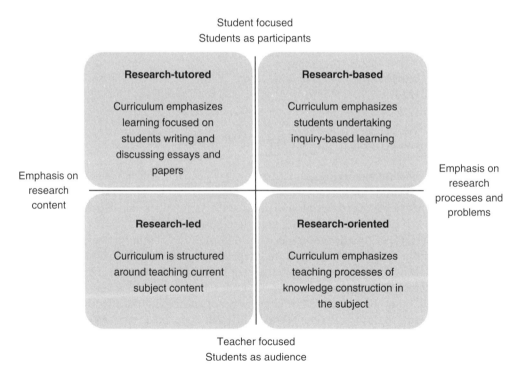

Source: Healey (2005, p. 70).

Figure 32.2 Curriculum design and the TRN

one finds a didactic approach where the teacher is transmitting data to a relatively passively receptive audience. The bottom-right corner, 'Research-oriented', maintains the relatively passive role for learners, but moves the emphasis from knowledge as a constant that is pre-constructed to be transmitted, towards an emphasis of progressively constructed knowledge where students learn how to find answers themselves. The top-left corner, 'Research-tutored', sees again data / knowledge as a constant, but learners are active in small groups and peers can act as teachers to one another. Finally, the top-right, 'Research-based', is where knowledge is created as a process and learners are leading it. Each learning experience above presupposes research in different ways, and makes assumptions on learners' receptiveness too. It could be suggested that formal learning often has to start from research-led teaching to create a common ontology, but then move on in different directions to allow learners to gain expertise to teach themselves and others in simulated real-life situations. Here again, differences in how different fields create accepted epistemologies, and axiological foundations for learning emphasis will restrict or expand the curriculum design and TRN differently.

4.   OUTCOMES

The development of TH&E teaching starts, globally, often from vocational education, so that the industries can access trained staff. This is followed by a small lag by higher education, often with the presumption that it will offer society useful 'research', and staff at supervisory and management levels. The decline in TH&E programs in Western countries in recent years is commonly connected to macro-level changes, such as changes in funding models, or integration into other sciences to take advantage of higher ranked publication channels, to name some. However, it should also be recognized that university-level TH&E programs are not always meeting the expectations and assumptions by the industries that originally lobbied for them.

   Research is still requested, but not necessarily academic research, rather practical reports and market research (Croy, 2011). Teaching and education is still in demand, but there is pressure on universities to design curricula that meet the industries' practical daily needs, not by necessity the fields' long-term development and future trends (Dredge et al., 2012). However, when 'birds are fed', then they eat at the place the feeding happens, not elsewhere, regardless of what the community wishes for. This is exactly the challenging context in which we are acting today, and where we need to understand how teaching practices could be formed, and new innovative ways of putting TRN into practice are needed.

   The education offered in the different dimensions at MTI is aiming at different outcomes. Students enter study pathways to reach personal goals; teaching and research therefore take different shapes:

- Vocational education and training (VET) aims at practical skills – students are learning how to use hands and minds in technical and operational tasks. MTI/VET staff need to be practical experts in the vocational field they teach, they need to know how to do things, as well as why that manner is efficient and how to improve practices. Learning outcomes are competencies and skills that are often learned in smaller groups in a hands-on, personal manner. The research conducted by VET staff is practical, and by immersing themselves in the industries they teach they stay on top of their respective field. This in turn allows staff to create and select learning resources that will allow students chances to achieve the competencies set for the diplomas in question. Research is thus conducted, but not with a theoretical goal in mind, and not the kind of research my colleague from the VET college referred to when she stated that 'research is not her students' and colleagues' businesses' – nor the research mostly found in literature that discusses TRN. However, with a broader definition, teaching is based on, tutored, or led by research here too.

- The University of Applied Science (UAS) aims at applying theoretical knowledge in practical situations – students are learning about best practice and know how to work and lead others in practical situations. MTI/UAS staff have solid experience in the field and have educated themselves further (minimum master's degree) in order to learn how tasks can be done in different ways, and to learn how similar problems have been solved in different manners elsewhere. Theories are applied to practical situations in businesses and communities. The UAS dimension of MTI has adapted problem-based learning (PBL) as their main teaching method, and are thus giving learners responsibilities to research necessary sources themselves to solve given simulated or industry-ordered situations themselves. The research conducted by UAS staff is applied; it involves DMOs and businesses that want help with practical research tasks where student groups, or individuals, are engaged. Outcomes are often study credits tied to regional engagement, which is a funding criterion for UAS institutions, or alternatively reports to the organization asking for the research. TRN is self-evident in UAS studies, both academic and applied research.

- Higher Education (HE) aims at developing research skills that help students think critically about the TH&E field, the people working in it, and their joint impact on well-being in society. Teaching is therefore often research-oriented. MTI/HE staff are experts in research (a majority holding a PhD in a related field), and students are from early on challenged to use theories to critically analyze current events and query their rationale. Research conducted by HE staff comes closest to a conventional definition of academic research, published in peer-reviewed channels, often written in English, and seldom read by the local stakeholders in the field. The reason for this is the funding model that emphasizes publications in high status research outlets. All Finnish bachelor's and master's degrees require research components and these assessable items are supervised by staff; teaching is therefore often research-tutored and research-based in order to prepare students for these keystone components of their degrees.

If the two curriculum models presented above could be merged, then it could be possible to outline how teaching at MTI is meant to be conducted, and also to provide a model for how to emphasize different TRN modes depending on the intended outcomes. Dredge et al.'s (2012) Curriculum Space Framework and Healey's (2005) Curriculum Design Nexus work surprisingly well together even though the matters they reflect come from different backgrounds. Research, teaching and learning do relate to one another, but are not frictionless as long as the ontologies, epistemologies and axiologies they are based on

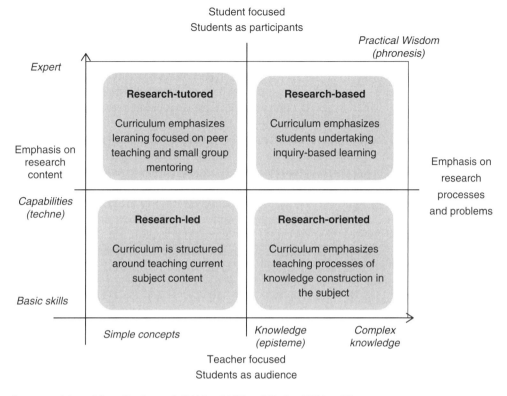

Sources: Adapted from Dredge et al. (2012, p. 2167) and Healey (2005, p. 70).

Figure 32.3   The Curriculum Space and Design TRN Model

exist in different realities. The different dimensions of the TH&E field require different dimensions of teaching to be offered for different learning outcomes to be reached.

The changes I have made to Healey's model are mainly in the top-left space, where I have taken the emphasis off research as written work, and expanded it to also suit skills and competencies (see Figure 32.3). A skill is reached through practice, and expert skills are achieved through trial, error, repetition and reflection. Theoretical leaps can arguably be taken more easily than practical leaps; it requires that the learner unravel research as a process, away from data as a constant entity, and rather perceived as an abstraction with fluid borders. The force-field within which any one curriculum is shaped will remain as fiercely contested as before, but by having a model that allows teachers to include research in different manners and modes, as data and as processes, as learning aim and as learning method, overall goals can be reached more easily.

5.   FUTURE DIRECTIONS

The first future direction we need to set as our goal is to lobby for a wider understanding of research and of TH&E studies generally. The old ontological statement of 'Tourism is . . .' leads us nowhere. The moment people hear a sentence starting with those words, they turn into 'experts' themselves, because they have all been tourists at one or another time – just like we do when teaching comes up, because we have all been students at some stage. We need to learn to state the ontology of tourism through sentences starting with: 'Tourism does . . . ', because then we become the experts of the discussion. A first step towards this new ontology of TH&E is to acknowledge the different meanings that concepts such as research and teaching have in society. Open dialogues remain futile, as long as people are stuck in separate realities.

One way of creating common realities is by openly viewing funding models in place as 'feeding birds'. This is done by telling stakeholders of the field how and where 'breadcrumbs are thrown' for teachers to eat. If an important 'crumb' for us is to produce 'incomprehensible' peer-reviewed articles, without which we will not be able to provide education for new professionals, then the fault is not lying in the birds fighting for the crumbs, but in the hand deciding where to throw what crumbs. TRN is improving practice, but we also need to acknowledge for ourselves that different types of research are required to meet different learning competencies. A top ranked journal article might, but also might not, be the best basis to create the teaching that will prepare a future TH&E professional – here again, it is important that the way 'birds are fed', and what we define as research, are transparent.

My suggestion is thus that TRN should be implemented in all dimensions of the education spectrum. Putting this suggestion on the table also means that we need to critically reflect on teaching resources in use in all stage of TH&E education. How many of you have looked through the learning resources for your local VET in the field? Well, let's extend that question: how many of you have any form of contact with your local VET provider, and how have you developed your curriculum in response to that? Let me guess that it is a minority of you who have done this, and let me congratulate those of you who have – please contact me and tell me about your outcomes. And whilst I wait for my email to fill up, let me go on to suggest that the rest of us, yes I include myself, need to take this as a task for ourselves. It is only since my colleague said that research 'is not VET's businesses' that I started to map out teaching resources in use throughout the institute. Yes, textbooks might not be highly ranked in the environment you 'eat your crumbs in', but they are a major way to impact future professionals in our field.

Would I recommend MTI's model for other institutions? Well, I guess I would say yes to this, because I see it as a natural way of creating an open dialogue between different educational providers. Do not get me wrong, it is not easy, and it is not without challenges, and it requires an enormous amount of buy-in amongst the highest decision makers in participating organizations. My bosses are the rectors of the HE organizations and the director for the educational consortium; they make up the management board of MTI together with TH&E stakeholders, and I report directly to them. The funding is provided for some joint administration but is otherwise channeled purely to operations, and depends on results from previous years. The administrative burden is at times a nightmare, but it is well worth it when seeing the concrete results: joint courses for students, co-teaching between organizations, joint projects and grant funding building on expertise from different organizations' staff, joint research publications and jointly authored textbooks. But best of all, now I have a response when talking to external TH&E stakeholders about outcomes, and about research conducted:

> Right, so you think the research our university teachers conduct is far removed from the day-to-day business; well, I hope so. You see, our vocational arm is involved in the daily operations; they do research about the latest trends and prepare students for it. Our UAS arm applies theories from elsewhere on practical development projects in the region, and the research they conduct together with their students is directly available for you. And, our university staff conduct research about the future of our field, about what we need to prepare ourselves for in the coming five to ten years – the research they do is creating the future of our field, and they teach their students to become experts who will be prepared for changes to come by learning how to do critically reflexive research.

As you can imagine, this makes many of the headaches worthwhile, and this could indeed be a future direction for other organizations too.

6.   CONCLUSIONS

This chapter has been focused on TRN, from a highly philosophical perspective, and I hope you have felt that the indulgences I have taken in using the first person, and metaphors sketched, have helped to make this a readable chapter. I have analyzed TRN from the viewpoint that it is more important to understand what research is *perceived to be*, than what it *is*, according to definitions. The reason for this is that we need to know what kind of outcomes stakeholders are yearning for from research conducted, in order to provide appropriate teaching.

I have discussed the debates surrounding TRN, and suggested that teaching and research stay separated as long as they are treated separately. One of the few matters that connected all TRN research was that it so far only relates to higher education, and my suggestion that it should equally be a matter of interest for VET institutions might be considered controversial – it is often seen as one of the distinguishing features of higher education that it is research-based. I have, however, presented an empirical case, MTI, in the light of Finnish education policies, and I have shown how the institute successfully straddles several dimensions of education. My hope is that this case would allow for a wider interpretation to be done of what research and what teaching is when the TRN is debated.

There is arguably always a nexus involved when teaching and learning is planned and executed, but the question is the depth, extent and mode of research conducted, who it is conducted by, and if it works as a teaching method, or simply provides the data and the skills that are taught. In preparing future professionals of our fields to take on work tasks, we need to prepare them by deciding what dimensions to emphasize – this is where models such as the *Curriculum Space*, the *Curriculum Design TRN* and the *Curriculum Space and Design TRN* that I proposed above are of use. What are the skills that are taught, what knowledge is included – and what type of *phronesis* is aimed for?

The models can be used as a plotting map for collegium thinking about what graduate outcomes their diploma or degree is aiming for. It can be used as a reflexive tool to analyze the assessment methods in use in the program. It can also be used as a positioning map for strategies comparing curricula at different institutions to one another. Student learning is always shaped by the assessable items that they will be graded by, teaching is in similar ways shaped by the curriculum it exists in, but not as overtly – the presented models gives a chance to do that.

REFERENCES

Allin, L. (2010), 'Linking research, teaching and learning within the discipline: Evaluating student learning through real life research in sports development', *The Journal of Hospitality Leisure Sport and Tourism*, **9** (1), 92–100.

Angelo, T. and C. Asmar (2005), 'Towards a new definition of research-led teaching – and learning – at VUW', accessed 24 April 2015 at www.utdc.vuw.ac.nz/research/rlt/rlt.pdf.

Annear, P. (1998), 'Health and development in Cambodia', *Asian Studies Review*, **22** (2), 193–221.

Ball, S. and A.T. Mohamed (2010), 'Insights on how students perceive the research–teaching nexus: A case study of hospitality management students', *Journal of Hospitality, Leisure, Sport and Tourism Education*, **9** (2), 89–102.

Barnhart, R.K. (ed.) (2003), *Chambers Dictionary of Etymology*, Edinburgh: Chambers.

Boyd, W.E., M. O'Reilly, D.J. Bucher, K. Fisher, A. Morton, P.L. Harrison, E. Nuske, R. Coyle and K. Rendall (2010), 'Activating the teaching–research nexus in smaller universities: Case studies highlighting diversity of practice', *Journal of University Teaching & Learning Practice*, **7** (2), 1–18.

Boyd, W.E., M. O'Reilly, K. Rendall, S. Rowe, E. Wilson, K. Dimmock, W. Boyd, E.M. Nuske, J.R. Edelheim, D.J. Bucher and K. Fisher (2012), 'Friday is my research day: Chance, time and desire in the search for the teaching–research nexus in the life of a university teacher', *Journal of University Teaching & Learning Practice*, **9** (2), 1–17.

Breen, R. and R. Lindsay (1999), 'Academic research and student motivation', *Studies in Higher Education*, **24** (1), 75–93.

Breen, R., R. Lindsay and A. Jenkins (2002), 'Academic research and teaching quality: The views of undergraduate and postgraduate students', *Studies in Higher Education*, **27** (3), 309–27.

Coate, K., R. Barnett and G. Williams (2001), 'Relationships between teaching and research in higher education in England', *Higher Education Quarterly*, **55** (2), 158–74.

Crowther, J. (ed.) (1995), *Oxford Advanced Learner's Dictionary*, Oxford: Oxford University Press.

Croy, W.G. (2011), 'Undergraduate tourism student research skills: Preparation for lifelong learning', Proceedings of the 2011 National Conference: 'Tourism: creating a brilliant blend': Council for Australian University, Tourism and Hospitality Education, CAUTHE.

Daruwalla, P. and J. Malfroy (2002), 'Diversity, doctrine and discourse: Internationalising a postgraduate hospitality management subject', *Journal of Teaching in Travel & Tourism*, **2** (3–4), 61–79.

Dredge, D., P. Benckendorff, M. Day, M. Gross, M. Walo, P. Weeks and P. Whitelaw (2012), 'The philosophic practitioner and the curriculum space', *Annals of Tourism Research*, **39** (4), 2154–76.

Franklin, A. (2008), 'The tourism ordering: Taking tourism more seriously as a globalising ordering', *Civilisations*, **57** (1–2), 25–39.

Griffiths, R. (2004), 'Knowledge production and the research–teaching nexus: The case of the built environment disciplines', *Studies in Higher Education*, **29** (6), 709–26.

Guerin, C. and D. Ranasinghe (2010), 'Why I wanted more: Inspirational experiences of the teaching–research nexus for engineering undergraduates', *Journal of University Teaching & Learning Practice*, **7** (2), 2010.

Healey, M. (2005), 'Linking research and teaching: Exploring disciplinary spaces and the role of inquiry-based learning', in Ronald Barnett (ed.), *Reshaping the University: New Relationships Between Research, Scholarship and Teaching*, Maidenhead: McGraw-Hill Education, pp. 67–78.

Jafari, J. (2003), 'Research and scholarship: The basis of tourism education', *The Journal of Tourism Studies*, **14** (1), 6–16.

Jenkins, A., M. Healey and R. Zetter (2007), *Linking Teaching and Research in Disciplines and Departments*, York: The Higher Education Academy.

Jiang, F. and P.J. Roberts (2011), 'An investigation of the impact of research-led education on student learning and understandings of research', *Journal of University Teaching & Learning Practice*, **8** (2), 1–14.

Kinchin, I.M. and D.B. Hay (2007), 'The myth of the research-led teacher', *Teachers and Teaching: Theory and Practice*, **13** (1), 43–61.

Mayson, S. and J. Schapper (2012), 'Constructing teaching and research relations from the top: An analysis of senior management discourses on research-led teaching', *Higher Education*, **64** (4), 473–87.

Pearce, P.L. (2005), 'Australian tourism education: The quest for status', *Journal of Teaching in Travel & Tourism*, **5** (3), 251–67.

Peters, M.A. and M. Olssen (2005), 'Useful knowledge: Redefining research and teaching in the learning economy', in Ronald Barnett (ed.), *Reshaping the University: New Relationships Between Research, Scholarship and Teaching*, Maidenhead: McGraw-Hill Education, pp. 37–47.

Ramsden, P. and I. Moses (1992), 'Associations between research and teaching in Australian higher education', *Higher Education*, **23** (3), 273–95.

Reid, A. and P. Petocz (2003), 'Enhancing academic work through the synergy between teaching and research', *International Journal for Academic Development*, **8** (1), 105–17.

Schapper, J. and S.E. Mayson (2010), 'Research-led teaching: Moving from a fractured engagement to a marriage of convenience', *Higher Education Research & Development*, **29** (6), 641–51.

Scott, P. (2005), 'Divergence or convergence? The links between teaching and research in mass higher education', in Ronald Barnett (ed.), *Reshaping the University: New Relationships Between Research, Scholarship and Teaching*, Maidenhead: McGraw-Hill Education, pp. 53–66.

Tribe, J. (2002), 'The philosophic practitioner', *Annals of Tourism Research*, **29** (2), 338–57.

33 Supervising a tourism doctorate: roles, realities and relationships
Philip L. Pearce

1. INTRODUCTION

It is perhaps informative to preface the contents of this chapter with a personal position. I write as an active, experienced, tourism supervisor in Australia working with the predominantly thesis-driven PhD model. I earned my own full thesis-based doctorate in psychology at Oxford University, where I studied tourists and tourist behavior. I have, though, spent some time in the United States, Italy and Asia, and have worked with students in systems where coursework was a big part of their higher degree induction into the academic research world. My prevailing view is that both systems work and supervisors matter almost equally in both styles, though they may be marginally more important to the thesis-only degrees where the principal supervisor rather than a team of advisers often has a greater influence.

There is plenty of broad advice offered to students and their supervisors about doctoral education. Kearns and Gardiner (2013) provide a 150-page booklet for students suggesting positive and proactive steps for their PhD progress. Morrell (2009), amongst others, maintains a comprehensive website with strategies and scenarios for student success. Considerable advice also exists for supervisors. For example, James and Baldwin (1999) offer eleven practices for effective postgraduate supervision. In just one of many more recent accounts, Grant et al. (2014) suggest key and positive metaphors to guide successful supervision.

Examining the commonalities in these and many similar documents, it is hard to find fault with their advice. The broad commentaries frequently recommend that supervision is structured and well planned, and that supervisors must be capable of integrating empathy with sustained efforts to control the quality of the work. Nevertheless, as Becher and Trowler (2001) pointed out over a decade ago, academic tribes and territories are different from one another. The nuances, traditions and practices across study areas vary due to a complex amalgam of paradigms, acceptable methods, cross-national variations and the status drivers of any academic group. Additionally, doctorates typically belong to a whole university rather than being awarded and administered exclusively by one sub-community in an institution. This factor, too, provides a Foucault-like master gaze on the work of supervisors, and arguably affects the reporting of the activities and the quality control issues for all who supervise at the doctoral level.

In this mix of advice, educational studies and institutional influences, the supervisor tasked with monitoring the work of a PhD student in tourism is a somewhat lonely academic. Little has been written about the supervision process within the tourism tribe and its affiliates. The present chapter seeks to offer a clear internal voice on the topic of PhD supervision in tourism. The chapter is structured by introducing the importance of supervision and then noting the origins and variability of doctorates. The key sections then deal with the roles and the critical position of the supervisor; the topic of gaze and the views of others; and the intriguing challenge of the required forms of emotional labor. Further pivotal issues are then illustrated though the presentation of micro-case studies.

Existing educational writing about the generic supervision process will be used to inform the discussion. Additionally and more creatively, the chapter applies some of the analytical frameworks of tourism study itself, including critical theory (Ateljevic et al., 2012), gaze (Urry, 1990) and labor in the experience economy (Bryman, 2004), to the topic of supervising higher degree students.

2.   LITERATURE

2.1   Historical Context

The young William Shakespeare was a pretty ordinary playwright (Forsyth, 2013). His early manuscripts and the plays built on them were dull and confusing. They lacked eloquence, power and purpose. No one remembers his first five efforts, no one reads them, and they were not performed much in the past and hardly at all today. Shakespeare clearly needed a supervisor. The early struggles of the world's most famous playwright speak to the essence of supervision; there is often a need for guidance from an experienced and supportive mind who can facilitate the acquisition of knowledge, skills and know-how to assist the neophyte function successfully in a professional world.

Shakespeare did not have a PhD-level supervisor because doctorates and their stewardship had not yet been 'invented' in the late sixteenth century. To account for the rise in importance of the PhD in the field of tourism and hence the task of supervision we need to conduct our own short travel story. The origins of the PhD are based in the use of the nearly equivalent terms 'master' and 'doctor' for the role of teacher in Italy in the post-Renaissance period. The term 'doctor' then traveled to Germany in the mid-nineteenth century where it came to mean high levels of competence in fields apart from law and medicine. The older meaning of a doctor as a skilled first-level teacher and graduate has persisted most obviously within the field of medicine. The PhD journey itself moves from Europe in the late nineteenth century to the United States, where the doctorate became institutionalized, initially at Yale University, as the title for the highest level of academic study prior to the launching of a career in any field (Pearce, 2004).

In the middle of the twentieth century the PhD was exported back to the United Kingdom and Europe and, in time, on to the former colonies connected to those countries. The rise of higher educational institutions in Asia, Africa and South America further stimulated the demand for educators and researchers with elite qualifications. The worldwide growth of universities ignited this late twentieth-century demand for international doctoral education.

The migration of the doctorate from the United States back across the Atlantic and on to other continents did not produce a uniform set of outcomes. Some transplants, notably the British/Commonwealth model, emphasized essentially the production of one very large piece of work. Another style now prevalent in Asia follows the current North American model more closely. It consists of a strong coursework component with a substantial but not huge research thesis. The more recently developed professional doctorates, where the term 'philosophy' is removed from the doctoral nomenclature, also conform to this pattern. The merits of these systems remain under scrutiny; arguably the British/Commonwealth approach produces more independence and control of a research program, while the coursework plus thesis approach offers a fuller and more complete grounding in skills but less independence and autonomy with a smaller and closely controlled project. For the purposes of this chapter and analysis, the multiple roles of the supervisor in these two systems are quite similar.

Those undertaking a PhD explicitly in the field of tourism are very much the late arrivals to this travel story. As revealed in the autobiographies of tourism scholars, nearly all researchers in the field before 1990 studied the phenomenon of tourism from their base in another discipline, most often economics, geography, sociology and anthropology (Nash, 2007; Smith, 2011; Dwyer, 2011). A few had a grounding in psychology, politics or other social science fields (Pearce, 2011). Together with colleagues, I have labeled the new wave of individuals with an entirely tourism-based undergraduate education Generation T (Filep et al., 2013). The essence of a tourism phenomenon-centered education is that Generation T graduates have an awareness of the issues of interest but not necessarily a conceptual approach to the problems being raised. In the earliest days of PhD studies in tourism, supervisors lent their own disciplinary expertise to their students, offering a guide to an older field of study with its own quirks, battles and traps. Undoubtedly some supervisors still operate predominantly in this way, but the rise of accessible reviews, the considerable growth of tourism journals and books, and the availability of Internet materials and search engines offer fast access to traditional fields and benefit students and their advisers (Pearce and Packer, 2013). All importantly, there is a developing cadre of studies from within tourism which pursue tailored mini-theoretical positions and conceptual models which are beginning to serve as their own pathways for problem analysis. The growth of some distinctive conceptual perspectives in tourism is not a cause for complacency nor a denial of the ongoing need to be aware of developments in allied areas. It is, however, a pragmatic response to the always overly ambitious view that tourism should have its own large-scale and grand theories (Aramberri, 2010) and that scholars should feel a sense of despair if this was not eventuating. Small steps, too, sometimes make for an effective journey.

A tourism PhD is a recognizable entity: its purpose is to illuminate an aspect of the tourism phenomenon building centrally on a broad understanding of tourism linked forces. Such a thesis stands in opposition to research work implicating tourism but essentially pursuing a topic in geography, sociology or a parent field of interest. There are of course many PhD studies still conducted in that older way, but the core of the difference is captured by the following two signature cases. Consider the issue of water quality in tourism resort swimming areas. The context is tourism, but the water quality problem is explained by reference to analytical techniques, benchmarks and research done in biochemistry. By way of contrast, consider the experience and use of tourism resort swimming pools. The context is again tourism but the problems need to be considered by techniques and studies which consider tourism marketing, the dynamics of market change, tourist experience and behaviors, and resort management. In brief, one study requires almost no awareness of the wider frame of tourism topics, while the other demands such knowledge. Building on these historical points, it is now appropriate to ask

---

BOX 33.1   POSTDISCIPLINARY CONFERENCE ANNOUNCEMENT

We operate within systems of disciplinary powers and in an era where knowledge is power. Habermas showed us how knowledge production is interest bound. While knowledge can be emancipatory, it is often used for domination and control. Foucault invited us to reflect upon which subjects do we turn into objects of knowledge and what are our techniques of domination, governance and discipline. In this conference we ask: Who do we serve with our knowledge? Who do we have at heart when producing tourism research? What are the consequences of disciplinary strictures? What do we want tourism education for? Postdisciplinarity invites us to question different voices in the research process and search for the silences and the absences in our academic systems. This conference is an invitation to engage with these questions and to reflect upon the dimensions of power and ethics, which are embedded in our knowledge production and our lives.

Sources: Trinet conference announcement: 24/09/2014: 2nd Tourism Postdisciplinarity Conference: 'Freedom. Art. Power', 22–24 June 2015.

---

how research topics and problems are framed. The particular issue of 'whose problem is it anyway?' leads to an important discussion on roles and relevance.

2.2   Roles

The core literature on supervision can be usefully approached using the critical theory perspective now current in tourism studies (Ateljevic et al., 2012). The recent conference announcement shown in Box 33.1 summarizes the concerns.

In short, what do supervisors (and tourism researchers generally) think they are doing, for whom and to what end? The questions are easy to ask. Trying to answer these questions can be difficult but stimulating. The answers are heavily dependent on the researcher's culture, personality and institutional strengths. All of this matters for supervision because at some point in the supervision process, the doubts of students about the value of what they are doing are likely to emerge. The supervisor needs to encourage students to answer these challenges. The answers may vary. A PhD may be about personal intellectual growth, community enlightenment, or business profitability. It may be justified as an intellectual quest, a document which supports minorities and seeks justice, or less altruistically, as a building block for a career. All importantly the supervisor's role here is best underpinned by an overriding belief that the doctorate, even if driven by different goals, is worthwhile. It can be argued that this needs to be an unshakeable, unwavering and non-negotiable position of faith and support (Crompton, 2005). If you do not believe the doctorate is worthwhile, then do not supervise. Students need a commitment to match their own (Halse and Honey, 2005).

The political and contested nature of the role of tourism research is likely to surface and then again resurface at several times during the trajectory of a supervision. It may start with the funding for a project. Stimulated by the perennial drought in funding for tourism study, universities may be able to persuade companies to fund a specific project which serves business interests and offers a study opportunity. But the very development or initiative being studied may have considerable impacts on environments, or on communities and their options for other development goals. Supervisors are effectively intermediaries in this process, trying to marry the needs of different stakeholders in ways that fit ethical principles with which they and the student are comfortable. Students have a right to ask: whose needs am I serving here, and will my findings and recommendations benefit a wealthy few but limit the lives of many others?

Such ethical issues have been a topic of discussion among tourism researchers for some time (Fennell, 2005; MacBeth, 2005). Moscardo (2010) reported that there were no explicit codes of ethical conduct for tourism researchers. That situation has not changed. There is, though, an active discussion of the rights of research participants and the responsibilities of researchers (Higgins-Desbiolles, 2006; Tribe, 2006). The philosophical traditions which underpin these ethics-oriented discussions often refer to a deontological position, a view which prompts a focus on consequences. Alternative perspectives include a virtue-oriented approach which defines the ambitious goal of acting in a right or principled way in the present, irrespective of later outcomes (Pearce et al., 2011).

These more abstract conceptualizations of ethical issues find specific expression in the approval processes for conducting research which operate in many (not all) countries where PhD work is carried out (Moscardo, 2010). The guidelines used by committees to assess the ethics of research in many universities combine the two philosophical traditions as they seek to do no harm, or at least very little (a concept labeled non-maleficence), and provide a positive ledger for the overall good of the research when compared to the costs it may produce (a view captured in the term 'beneficence'). These concerns are supplemented by a desirable reflexive awareness of the researchers' role and a call for the respectful treatment of others. Additionally, there is an imperative for researchers to be trustworthy and show personal integrity in dealing with all parties. The key notion that in some timescale the work will benefit a set of people other than the researcher is also an important consideration. The student and the supervisor may spend quite some time reviewing these issues, but as will be suggested in a later section, much of what happens in practice on this topic is often communicated by the actions of the supervisor in their own studies.

The challenges to tourist research may confront the student and their supervisor in a different way, notably through the rejection of a paper or critical remarks at a conference. The technical issues may be easier to handle than the value-based concerns. The perennial question quickly adopted by some sharp critics and reviewers is: how is this relevant? Sometimes it is fellow researchers and academics who ask the question. Industry practitioners and persons in government, as well as curious friends and family members also may require that the PhD student is being useful and relevant in the work they do (Fuchs, 1992). For supervisors and their students, analyzing the term 'relevance' can offer value for their responses to this persistent challenge. There is a time dimension for relevance in tourism study and indeed for research work in general. The work conducted may be applicable in the immediate, mid-term or long-term future. There is sector and sub-sector relevance, with some studies only applying, for example, to the hotel/accommodation sector, the transport sector or the attractions sector. Further, there is relevance of spatial scale, with some work being of local applicability, some of regional consequence while other analyses have import at a national or international scale. Additionally, there may be a focus on single units of operation or broader aggregations (such as one hotel or a hotel chain). As another component of relevance, the PhD student may be studying a topic relating to an economic, socio-cultural or environmental perspective: the three recognized tenets of the triple bottom line (Elkington, 1997). Recent writing on sustainability tends to add an administrative or managerial dimension to sustainability discussions as this dimension identifies capacity in a location to manage sustainability (Bramwell and Lane, 2014). Finally, there is the relevance of style where either the approach to the topic (a way of conceptualizing and assessing problems) or the immediacy and pragmatism of the data and results are the chief contributions.

When the relevance or the 'so what' question is asked at a conference, or sometimes in a scholarly review, it is often a sub-text demanding that the work be short term, local, sector specific, unit oriented, economic and results driven. These are not inherently poor criteria; it is simply that other criteria also matter. Supervisors can fulfill their role as supporters of their student work by having discussions about relevance and purpose, including the ethical dimensions already discussed, before students are confronted with these queries in more public spaces.

Roles and the topic of relevance reappear in another guise. The media often provide PhD students with an inviting opportunity to publicize their work. At its best, the student enjoys the public exposure of their work as it can seem like an affirmation that people care about what they do. Nevertheless, this activity does not always go well. Most members of a community understand that the media want a story and that this need supplants the desire to deliver the caveats which accompany academic and postgraduate work. Clearly, the student's public voice needs to be a well-rehearsed one, desirably checked by the supervisor and media liaison officers to make sure that statements are not easily misinterpreted. A willingness to make a controversial and challenging statement built on good evidence is a contribution to communities. By way of contrast, a fracas arising from false interpretations of media stories damages the student's morale, and beyond that affects the supervisor, the area of study and the university. The role of the supervisor in previewing the media contacts and content for students may avoid the five minutes of fame becoming five days of anguish.

The roles of a supervisor extend beyond being a rock of support for the PhD process and student in the turbulent currents of critical discussion. Supervisors need to fill the roles of both being a knowledge provider and a technical adviser. Two of Aristotle's terms to classify knowledge were *episteme* – theoretical knowledge, and *techne* – a skills-based competence; both can be readily understood as central to good supervision (Flyvbjerg, 2001). Wise counsel and good judgment, the third of Aristotle's components of knowledge (*phronesis*), is also needed. For example, the ability to select the right examiners, to recognize likely impediments to student success and to have a repertoire of convincing arguments to dissuade the student from getting lost are guide-like skills where *phronesis* matters. One of the metaphors commonly discussed for supervision is indeed that of a guide (Grant et al., 2014) and, like guides everywhere, those who take others on the PhD journey have increased responsibilities in the last decade (Weiler and Kim, 2011). These responsibilities are dependent on the realities of working in twenty-first-century universities.

2.3   Realities

The role of the supervisor is subject to the reality that others are watching. The term 'gaze' has been used and reworked many times in tourism studies (Jordan and Aitchinson, 2008;

Maoz, 2006; Moufakkir and Reisinger, 2013; Urry, 1990). In its most complete use it encompasses a coherent social representation of how a setting or situation is interpreted due to cultural conditioning. The term in tourism study can connote uplifting private magical moments when looking at the world, or joyful collective immersion in the crowd. It can also characterize wary reactions and unfounded prejudices towards others. The gaze toward tourism researchers and supervisors is often of this less positive character (Airey et al., 2014). It can be suggested that tourism researchers, postgraduate students and their supervisors are unwittingly caught up in longstanding and suspicious views of fun and entertainment.

In the early Middle Ages enjoying oneself too much was often condemned as dangerous and irreverent, especially among the religious orders (Le Goff, 1997). There were times when even laughter was perceived as a vice. In England this perception that life had to be serious became even more robust after the Protestant Reformation, a period during which enjoying good times was treated with suspicion and disdain (Morreall, 1983). Often the social institutions dampening the flames of laughter, enjoyment and passion have been the churches with the sober and funless creeds of the Protestants, the Lutherans, the Methodists and the Presbyterians, foremost amongst many (Blainey, 2000). The great Protestant work ethic is not matched by a great Protestant laugh and leisure ethic. While the world is no longer in the grip of this single view of work and non-work, it is a modest step to see that studies of a fun-oriented activity such as tourism may not always be assessed as worthwhile. Universities and their personnel do see themselves as serious places and no one would deny that many important research topics demand enormous commitment and are not inherently entertaining. Status considerations matter in most human activities (De Botton, 2004) and for those seeking status in the serious stakes of research, the perceived fun topics of tourism are a low-level marker for asserting personal superiority. These lingering and long-held doubts are more likely to appear when tourism researchers travel frequently and attend conferences in attractive destinations, irrespective of the benefits to their teaching and work (Witsel, 2014).

It can be suggested, therefore, that there is an initially suspicious glint in the eyes of those who gaze upon the activities of tourism supervisors and the work they oversee. There are consequences arising from this kind of gaze. The quality of the work being supervised may receive extra attention from internal multidisciplinary review panels, especially from those in business, management and marketing fields who often deal with parallel concerns in less exciting sectors. Methodological and statistical features of the studies supervised in tourism may be targets for criticism, and it is a supervisory skill to develop high levels of student competence when this kind of work is being conducted while not being overly obsessed with defending what has been achieved.

The suspicious gaze also works to the detriment of tourism studies when it comes to the world of funding. Few non-tourism academics truly appreciate that the business of tourism is largely a world of small and micro-businesses. Both in terms of having time to articulate their research interests and the money to support such activities, small-scale businesses are looking to their own survival rather than to the expansive interests of researchers, supervisors and students. There are of course some big companies, but their interest in research is extremely narrow, functional and profit driven, and conducted in house or by pliant consultants. Corporate social responsibility is a currency in which companies do trade, but little research is fostered under this often marketing-oriented umbrella. The irony in these realities of tourism research funding is that many academic granting bodies believe that the amorphous entity of 'the industry' should fund tourism research. It is a misdirected view, and while small partnerships are possible, most supervisors and students struggle to fund the projects they initiate. Dealing with this reality, and not being dismayed by it, is a supervisory task and, indeed, it can be a liberating one if the view is adopted that the research is therefore desirably independent and not tied to the critical gaze of a funding body.

2.4 Relationships

In his detailed analysis of the processes underlying the success of the Disney theme parks and media world, Bryman (2004) highlights three aspects of labor. The key components are emotional, performative and aesthetic labor. These forms of labor are the bases for the all-important relationship which shapes the adequacy of the short-, medium- and long-term contacts between supervisors and their students. The analysis is congruent with educational research and commentary on supervision as professional work (Halse and Malfroy, 2010).

Aesthetic labor at its simplest level is how supervisors appear to and present themselves to their students. At core, one of the covert questions being addressed here can be framed as: 'Is this supervisor the kind of person (neglecting for the minute the cross-gender issues) I aspire to be?' The issues of appearance include both matters of style and the supervisors' behaviors. Students are often attentive to how supervisors maintain their public persona, as well as their offices, files, books and effects. Aesthetic labor can be a problematic presentation issue if students can see ready contradictions between supervisory advice and personal behavior.

The aesthetic labor works at several subtle levels. During the immediate contact between supervisor and student, the 'supervisory face' and non-verbal expressions can be revealing to students in a way that the words may not. The analogy with Bryman's work and the Disney world can be made. An overweight, blonde, Snow White with a sour expression does not work. For some students there may be a parallel; the approach of supervisors in the style of the sharp, menopausal lady or the grumpy, old man whose first responses are to criticize rather than appreciate their students' latest efforts are also styles which do not work. Another equally ineffective style is to blandly support the student's work with no subtle commentary or directions for improvement. Such limited attention by supervisors may end badly; the happy fantasyland created by the always accepting supervisor may be disrupted by a fierce storm of rejection by reviewers and examiners.

One important component of aesthetic labor is the way the supervisor appears to treat others, and most especially other students. Such information is quickly used as a benchmark for determining the student's own standing and treatment. Many postgraduate students work and co-exist in small tight spaces, interacting daily with others in shared rooms or close proximity. Hints of supervisory favoritism and special attention are picked up quite readily, and it may require explicit discussion with students to inform them that others have specific tailored interactions to meet special needs and these contacts are going to persist over time. This kind of clear communication can help students see the role of the supervisor beyond their own frame of reference.

Performative labor is about having the skills and the knowledge and being able to communicate and share that knowledge effectively with students. Halse and Malfroy (2010) label this component of professional work scholarly expertise, and see it linked to the Aristotelian category of *episteme*. It is important to interpret performative labor broadly. Performative labor can usefully be seen as including currency in personal publishing as well as the theoretical knowledge of knowing about how to conduct and write up research. The role model function of the supervisor is evident at this point. As suggested earlier, the way the supervisor deals with ethical issues in their own studies and with the work of other students provides a resource and a style which many supervisees will observe and monitor for their own research (Neumann, 2007).

Emotional labor is complex and arguably as important as performative labor in many supervision settings. As Bryman reports, emotional labor is a powerful communication tool which builds trust and rapport among personnel in the workplace. It can be enhanced by humor, but also requires empathy, kindness and diplomacy, all of which build the trust and sincerity of the relationship. Halse and Malfroy (2010) partly capture the meaning of the term when they refer to the learning alliance, an agreed pact to pursue a difficult goal together with all its emotional highs and lows. For the supervisor there is also the considerable issue of a duty of care, although the formal legal meaning of that term may be supplanted here by a stronger moral and ethical imperative. The student who leaves their own community, whether that be in another country or from a neighboring city, is often doing so at great personal and emotional cost and is understandably anxious and adrift in their new circumstances. Additionally, they are faced with the largest and longest lasting scholarly task they are yet to attempt. Supervisors have an ethical and moral obligation to give them a chance to succeed through offering the best emotional support relevant to their work and life. This is not to suggest that supervisors need to be entangled in complex psychological problems or medical matters; those areas are for professional support, but an emotional contract of enthusiastic support is a must-have supervisory attribute.

3.   CASE STUDIES

One way of illustrating and providing specificity to this discussion of supervision in tourism lies in providing examples from personal experience. Using the experiences of supervising some forty PhD students I have drawn on the interactions from both the past and present to profile some points about supervision. The cases are constructions and amalgamations of traits and do not describe a single student but blend the characteristics of those I have directly supervised, as well as others I have known. The names are fictitious, in keeping with the fabrication and synthesis of the student characteristics. The number of cases is set as 10 as this is a sample size which often appears to generate saturation in these kinds of qualitative accounts of processes (cf. Yin, 2009). For the readers who seek advice about supervision, these cases can be examined and your personal inductive generalizations can be drawn from the material. The micro-cases and my own appraisals are presented in Box 33.2.

BOX 33.2   MODIFIED MICRO-CASES AND INSIGHTS FOR SUPERVISION

Case 1 'Blake' was an American student with a Master's degree already employed as a junior lecturer. He was skilled in statistics and computer work, sociable and popular with a large range of friends. His thesis work proceeded smoothly, chiefly requiring supervisory advice and support in terms of endorsing some creative application of methods. He completed on time, co-authored a book almost immediately, and has continued to have a successful academic career.

Supervision insight: If you have been fortunate to have had a good supervisor yourself and your first student or set of students are talented and smart, supervision can seem easy – more of a sustained, collegial helping hand and friendship than a major educational challenge. This is a good way to start being a supervisor, with a person who is almost a peer but somewhat junior and in need of the mechanics of constructing a PhD. The principal challenge is to be demanding at times to achieve the highest standards possible.

Case 2 'Susan' was a mature aged mother with dependent children. The PhD was the stepping stone to a new solo career after a successful return to university as an undergraduate. Always thorough, but frequently anxious that her abilities and work met the standards, her time was always pressured and her achievement in completing the PhD considerable.

Supervision insight: Supervising people in very different life stages and personal circumstances requires genuine emotional labour, but being task oriented can be more functional than deep immersion in the student difficulties when you are an inexperienced supervisor. Faith in the value of a PhD matters a lot to these 'career changing' students.

Case 3 'Bob' was an older student and had been a teacher for many years. Seeking a career change, he was persistent with his studies and was finally admitted to a PhD. Always interested in computers and technology, he struggled to have empathy with those who were not so fascinated, including supervisors. His limitations were a modest ability to work with the conceptual material but he graduated partly due to strong time management and organizational skills.

Supervision insight: Some highly independent students can appear to challenge or be disrespectful to the advice offered. It is all important to know and assert the university thesis examination criteria, which is the material which goes to the markers. Students and supervisors have to work to what is actually required, not what some students think is required.

Case 4 'Adrian' was the prototypical bright student, progressing through the undergraduate steps directly into a doctorate supported by the highest level of scholarship. Quirky at times and possibly serious beyond his years, he quickly worked at the required level. He continued to be a high achiever throughout the doctoral degree, publishing well and finding an academic position.

Supervision insight: For some of the very able students you impart less in terms of knowledge and technical skills but you can, by example, demonstrate how academic life can be managed to be a productive all round scholar. There is often an opportunity to learn together in some new areas of the field.

Case 5 'Austin' was a dedicated Korean student and pioneered the way for many Asian students in terms of alerting a whole group of supervisors to the nuances of working with students from a different national background and cultural heritage. Respectful, gregarious, funny and popular, Austin represented the best of Asian international students but very sadly he died of an aggressive cancer before completing his work.

Supervision insight: The attractiveness and depth of relationship possible with some students extends the work-based relationship into novel and mutually rich learning outcomes; it is an experience to be valued when it occurs because it can be ephemeral. These kinds of sad experiences bring a focus to the role of being a supervisor and a commitment to be available and helpful in the immediate present due to the uncertainty of the future.

Case 6 'Fleur' was a student in tourism but worked simultaneously with another area of the university. Committed to strong personal opinions, her time was spent manipulating others to her personal advantage and while her abilities carried her through the PhD, there was never any prospect of long-term trust and further work.

Supervision insight: Some moderately smart people have few people skills and the traditional PhD process can do little to enhance the skills of those who are highly self-interested and exploitative of others. Regrettably, one student like this can sour the supervision experience and it is vital to turn to the rewards from others to maintain enthusiasm for the task. Like any sampling problem it is critical not to be overly influenced by one case or an outlier.

Case 7 'Chrissie' was a delightful Chinese student, funny, always mildly flirtatious, very fluent in English and socially very smart. Her written work and conceptual ability were not her strengths but some students are simply a pleasure to work with on a long-term basis and any supervision which proceeds over 3–4 years without many difficult moments is a rare and positive experience.

Supervision insight: Some international students repay a high level of supervisor involvement especially help with planning the conceptual trajectory of their work and improving their English expression. Such youthful energy and enthusiasm can embrace social activities and be formative in building a positive culture among the whole PhD cohort. Some care must be taken, especially but not exclusively for male supervisors with young female students, to manage public appearance and issues of respectability. The gaze of other students and outsiders may misconstrue the close contact and intimacy as having favorites or even inappropriate sexually motivated behavior.

Case 8 'Janine' was an international student from India, motivated but married and living with her out-of-work husband. Managing a relationship and young children in another country is not an easy context in which to do a PhD. As an emotional person, supervision sessions often varied between tears and laughter as her struggle to be a superwoman was at times overwhelming. Finally successful, students like this may not become major future co-authors but grateful and warm members of a supervision diaspora.

Supervision insights: Students with these major personal life issues and concerns, and indeed all those with troubling relationships and personal problems, need a special kind of supervisory attention. A slow, gentle but persistent pushing of the work agenda is often useful with respect for the issues but an unwillingness to see the problems as insurmountable barriers to doing adequate work. Above all, it is important not to let the life issues dominate the interaction and focus instead on providing high quality, engaging, scholarly advice and encouragement.

Case 9 'Maggie' was a conscientious and very bright Chinese student, intent on being successful and accustomed to success in her academic work. Like many students from a different background, the change in her self-presentation from a quiet serious scholar, steeped in her cultural traditions, to a critical thinker with a powerful personality and sharp mind was a visible transition to those around her.

Supervision insights: Students who make cross-national transitions and adapt to the academic systems from different cultures can have outstanding futures as leaders in both locations. Through their talent and productivity they earn respect and can be very committed academic partners. For a few such key students the relationship can have enduring benefits including productive publishing partnerships.

Case 10 'Kim' was an American student, flamboyant and fashionable. Her work was not her first love but she was good enough to get the tasks done and lead an expansive extra-curricular life.

> Some students' lifestyle and social world can quickly make a supervisor feel older and out of touch with the trends of the times. Cordiality, and clear critical feedback rather than any close bond were enough to ensure success.
>
> *Supervision insights: With some students the kind of connection you have changes considerably over time. Initially, the relationship may be quite limited in its dimensions and student and supervisor initially share little outside of the work focus. Perhaps after some years the relationship may change as the student's career develops and the supervisor becomes a point of reference in their life.*

4. OUTCOMES

This chapter has not been written as a manual or as another 'how to supervise' portfolio. The cases constructed and built on the lives and work of real students in Box 33.1 indicate that any uniformity in such recommendations has to be at the most generic level to cater for the diversity of students being supervised for tourism PhD degrees. As noted before, readers can review the cases and extract their own tailored, take home messages for the unique personal, age, gender, experience level, and institutional contexts in which they work.

Some links between these examples and the educational literature which are not immediately apparent can be made. All of the supervisions underpinning the hybrid examples in Box 33.1 were conducted with a pre-set agenda, meeting notes and delivery of those notes at the next supervisory meeting. Importantly, as supervisor I receive the agenda and the notes from the prior contact the day before the scheduled meeting, so that I can be primed for and, as necessary, prepare for the interaction. The notes are a valuable ongoing file and set of documents, and both supervisor and student keep copies. The material effectively records both the small and big decisions for the trajectory of the PhD. They can be a source of strength when later decisions are forgotten or misremembered or the advice of the day contradicts that of the past. Nevertheless, while the notes are valuable, it is important to stress that supporting documents like this should be quite simple and easy to produce and should not be a goal in themselves or consume the time needed for detailed discussion. My process is a personal precursor to the recommendations in the literature on structuring and organizing good supervision (Kearns and Gardiner, 2013). The approach can help in solving dilemmas about repeating instructions and mutual frustrations about forgotten advice (Delamont et al., 1998).

In the micro case studies, the theme of publication and co-publication by students was only briefly noted. Lee et al. (2007) link the desire for student and staff publication activity with the other theme of emotional labor. They assert that infectious enthusiasm for publishing, whether that is independent efforts by the students or joint work, is the glue that maintains supervisors' passion for the job and builds the students' careers. The concept of specifying the likely authorship of the work is considered differently in different countries and of course varies across departments, but a pragmatic view of what can be a tricky ethical dilemma is to encourage the student to publish jointly at first and later independently.

A challenging issue related to the pressure by managers of institutions for postgraduate students to publish lies in the timing of that activity. Should it be during or after the PhD? While the institutional view typically favors as much as possible and as fast as possible, for the supervisor dealing with less able students, publishing during the PhD can be quite disruptive, especially if there are a number of cycles of reviewer comments to consider and the students are not used to criticism. Again supervisors with confidence in their own abilities can be helpful. It is possible to reveal to students that the supervisor's work is also often subject to the vagaries of the refereeing process and then explain in detail how some specific published articles have had their own long history of revision, and phases of rewriting before acceptance.

5.   CONCLUSION

This examination of the PhD supervision process has covered several key issues: the historical context of tourism PhDs, the critical challenges to the roles of research in our communities, the gaze of others on what we do, and the kinds of labor supervisors are required to perform. It has been argued that supervisors who are to pass the examination of their own behavior need to have a list of desirable traits: reliably supportive, enthusiastic about the whole PhD process and notably publishing, possessing a substantial knowledge base and technical skills but keen to expand these abilities, aware of how to manage external and institutional pressures, and organized but flexible in their approach to different student needs. It is a daunting list for a beginner but it is now possible to read a great deal about supervision in general while learning how to supervise at the pre-doctoral level. In tourism there is an active world of postgraduate study and those who are keen or required to work in this form of education can garner insights and build skills both from the experiences of others with whom they may co-supervise, and perhaps from the perspectives offered in reviews such as this chapter.

   In the introduction to the literature review it was pointed out that Shakespeare was not initially a very capable playwright. Like PhD students, his work of course got better with practice. Supervisors too can get better with practice but desirably their own supervision was at a high standard so students do not have to suffer too much through their on the job learning. It is perhaps appropriate to choose one of Shakespeare's more famous quotations to characterize the end of the supervision process and its emotional labor which have been central to this chapter. The quote comes from Juliet saying to Romeo: 'Good night, good night! Parting is such sweet sorrow.' Certainly the parting did not end well for Romeo and Juliet, but for students and their supervisors the conclusion of long, intense periods of study can also have its own emotional conclusion: graduation finalizes the process and there is sometimes an emotional separation for both parties. Fortunately, the acquaintances can be renewed, and for the successful and best relationships the work and contact can continue for a very long time.

REFERENCES

Airey, D., J. Tribe, P. Benckendorff and H. Xiao (2014), 'The managerial gaze: the long tail of tourism education and research', *Journal of Travel Research*, **54** (2), 139–51.

Aramberri, J. (2010), 'The real scissors crisis in tourism research', in D. Pearce and R. Butler (eds), *Tourism Research: A 20:20 vision*, Oxford: Goodfellow Publishers, pp. 15–27.

Ateljevic, Irena, Nigel Morgan and Annette Pritchard (eds) (2012), *The Critical Turn in Tourism Studies Creating an Academy of Hope*, London: Routledge.

Becher, Tony and Paul Trowler (2001), *Academic Tribes and Territories: Intellectual Enquiry and the Cultures of Disciplines* (2nd edn), Milton Keynes: The Society for Research into Higher Education.

Blainey, Geoffrey (2000), *A Very Short History of the World*, Camberwell, VA: Penguin.

Bramwell, Bill and Bernard Lane (eds) (2014), *Tourism Governance: Critical Perspectives on Governance and Sustainability*, London: Routledge.

Bryman, Alan (2004), *The Disneyization of Society*, London: Sage.

Crompton, J. (2005), 'Issues related to sustaining a long-term research interest in tourism', *Journal of Tourism Studies*, **16** (2), 34–43.

De Botton, Alain (2004), *Status Anxiety*, London: Penguin.

Delamont, S., O. Parry and P. Atkinson (1998), 'Creating a delicate balance: The doctoral supervisor's dilemmas', *Teaching in Higher Education*, **3** (2), 157–72.

Dwyer, Larry (ed.) (2011), *The Discovery of Tourism Economics*, Bingley: Emerald.

Elkington, John (1997), *Cannibals with Forks: The Triple Bottom Line of 21st Century Business*, Oxford: Capstone.

Filep, S., M. Hughes, M. Mostafanezhad and F. Wheeler (2013), 'Generation tourism: Towards a common identity', *Current Issues in Tourism*, **18** (6), 511–23.

Fennell, David (2005), *Tourism Ethics*, Clevedon: Channel View.

Flyvbjerg, Bent (2001), *Making Social Science Matter*, Cambridge: Cambridge University Press.

Forsyth, Mark (2013), *The Elements of Eloquence*, London: Icon Books.

Fuchs, Stephan (1992), *The Professional Quest for Truth: A Social Theory of Science and Knowledge*, Albany, NY: State University of New York.

Grant, K., R. Hackney and D. Edgar (2014), 'Postgraduate research supervision: An agreed conceptual view of good practice through derived metaphors', *International Journal of Doctoral Studies*, **9**, 43–60.

Halse, C. and A. Honey (2005), 'Unravelling ethics: Illuminating the moral ethics of research supervision policy', *Signs*, **30** (4), 2142–61.

Halse, C. and J. Malfroy (2010), 'Retheorizing doctoral supervision as professional work', *Studies in Higher Education*, **35** (1), 79–92.

Higgins-Desbiolles, F. (2006), 'More than an "industry": The forgotten power of tourism as a social force', *Tourism Management*, **27** (6), 1192–208.

James, Richard and Gabrielle Baldwin (1999), *Eleven Practices of Effective Postgraduate Supervisors*, Melbourne: Centre for the Study of Higher Education and the School of Graduate Studies, University of Melbourne.

Jordan, F. and C. Aitchison (2008), 'Tourism and the sexualisation of the gaze', *Leisure Studies*, **27** (3), 329–49.

Kearns, Hugh and Maria Gardiner (2013), *Planning your PhD*, Adelaide: Thinkwell.

Lee, A., C. Dennis and P. Campbell (2007), 'Nature's guide for mentors', *Nature*, **447**, 791–7.

Le Goff, Jacques (1997), 'Laughter in the Middle Ages', in Jan Bremmer and Herman Roodenberg (eds), *A Cultural History of Humour: From Antiquity to the Present Day*, Cambridge: Polity Press, pp. 40–53.

MacBeth, J. (2005), 'Towards an ethics platform for tourism', *Annals of Tourism Research*, **32** (4), 962–84.

Maoz, D. (2006), 'The mutual gaze', *Annals of Tourism Research*, **33** (1), 221–39.

Morreall, John (1983), *Taking Laughter Seriously*, Albany, NY: State University of New York Press.

Morrell, K. (2009), 'Doing a PhD in the social sciences: Myths, tips and strategies', accessed 29 September 2014 at www.kevinmorrell.org.uk/PhDTips.htm.

Moscardo, G. (2010), 'Tourism research ethics: Current considerations and future options', in Douglas Pearce and Richard Butler (eds), *Tourism Research A 20:20 vision*, Oxford: Goodfellow, pp. 203–14.

Moufakkir, Omar and Yvette Reisinger (eds) (2013), *The Host Gaze*, Wallingford: CABI.

Nash, Denison (ed.) (2007), *Anthropology of Tourism*, Bingley: Emerald.

Neumann, R. (2007), 'Policy and practice in doctoral education', *Studies in Higher Education*, **32** (4), 459–73.

Pearce, P.L. (2004), 'History, practices and prospects for the PhD in tourism', *Journal of Teaching in Travel & Tourism*, **4** (3), 31–49.

Pearce, P.L. and J. Packer (2013), 'Minds on the move: New links from psychology to tourism', *Annals of Tourism Research*, **40**, 386–411.

Pearce, Philip (ed.) (2011), *The Study of Tourism: Foundations from Psychology*, Bingley: Emerald.

Pearce, Philip, Sebastian Filep and Glenn Ross (2011), *Tourists, Tourism and Well Being*, New York: Routledge.

Smith, Stephen (ed.) (2011), *The Discovery of Tourism*, Bingley: Emerald.

Tribe, J. (2006), 'The truth about tourism', *Annals of Tourism Research*, **33** (2), 360–71.

Urry, John (1990), *The Tourist Gaze*, London: Sage.

Weiler, B. and A. Kim (2011), 'Tour guides as agents of sustainability: Rhetoric, reality and implications for research', *Tourism Recreation Research*, **36** (2), 113–25.

Witsel, Mieke (2014), 'Walking the talk: Positive effects of work-related travel on tourism academics', in Sebastian Filep and Philip Pearce (eds), *Tourist Experience and Fulfilment*, Abingdon: Routledge, pp. 37–53.
Yin, Robert (2009), *Case Study Research: Design and Methods*, London: Sage.

34 From dialogue to 'being in and of' a qualitative research culture: lived experiences of research students

Gayle Jennings, Olga Junek, Mary-Anne Smith, Sandra Kensbock and Ulrike Kachel

1. INTRODUCTION

> The development of the cultural self occurs, . . ., interactively, as Vygotsky (1978) describes, in collaboration with those already familiar with the way to do and know things in the culture. (Daiute and Lightfoot, 2004, p. xv)

As students enroll in research higher degree programs, they enter a new culture – a research culture, which is both institutionally situated and professionally specific. For the majority of beginning researchers, experiences of institutional research cultures are tangential to the educational cultures of their core undergraduate or postgraduate course-related degree programs. To varying extents, beginning research students will have engaged with some of the cultural 'artifacts' (Schein, 2010, p. 24) of a research culture, such as, models, theories, journal articles, research technologies and laboratories, research and/or statistics courses. However, the behaviors, practices and mores of a research culture as a lived experience will have eluded most. It is in this domain of lived experiences that this chapter situates itself. Specifically, the focus of this chapter is on the lived experiences of four research students who variously engaged in research dialogue sessions over a two-and-a-half-year period. These sessions were designed by their university research-student supervisor to enable collective learning and sharing of research experiences, enculturation into a university-research culture and acculturation into a qualitative research profession. In the process of engaging in the qualitative research sessions, students learnt how to 'be in and of' a qualitative research culture and how to professionally be a qualitative researcher.

Why a focus on lived experiences of research students? Because such a focus addresses an 'under-theorized area' (Jennings et al., 2009a) as well as 'gives voice . . . [to] research students' experiences' (Jennings et al., 2010, p. 3).

In this chapter, our reference to lived experience encapsulates 'the nature or meaning of everyday experiences' (Van Manen, 1990, p. 9). While we acknowledge that '[c]ulture refers to complex, inaccessible, fuzzy, holistic phenomena' (Kunda, 1992, p. 8 in Alvesson, 2002, p. 3), herein we refer to culture as 'a system of common symbols and meanings. It provides the shared rules governing cognitive and affective aspects of membership in an organization, and the means whereby they are shaped and expressed' (Kunda, 1992, p. 8 in Alvesson, 2002, p. 3).

Of particular relevance to the study of research cultures is the work of Edgar Schein (2010) regarding the nature of organizational cultures. Schein (1996, p. 11) proffers that organizational 'culture is the basic tacit assumptions about how the world is and ought to be that a group of people share and that determines their perceptions, thoughts, feelings, and, their overt behavior'.

For Schein (2010), organizational cultures have three levels. At the surface level are the easily detectable elements, the 'artifacts', although the meanings of these are mostly obscure to a newcomer (Schein, 2010, p. 24). Beginning research students, as already noted, have differing lived experiences of these 'artifacts' before entering a research degree program. Their engagement with such 'artifacts' would have primarily incorporated specific directed, conscious knowledge acquisition, that is, explicit learning experiences. Below the surface level of organizational culture sit the 'espoused beliefs and values' (Schein, 2010, p. 24). The 'espoused beliefs and values' are reflected in an organization's or in this chapter, an institution's espoused 'ideals, goals, values, aspirations, ideologies and rationalizations' (Schein, 2010, p. 24). It is through lived experiences that beginning researchers are able to gain understanding of the 'espoused beliefs and values' of research cultures. Herein, again, research student learning involves explicit learning experiences. Below this second level of culture sits the core of an organizational culture, that is, its 'basic underlying assumptions' (Schein, 2010). These latter are the cornerstones of cultures and explain the whys of the ways things are done.

According to Schein (2010), such assumptions are primarily unconsciously learnt and often 'taken for granted' (Schein, 2010). Learning tacit assumptions may occur via unintentional and unconscious knowledge generation, that is, implicit learning and/or through knowledge generation by doing, participating and experiencing, that is, tacit learning. Importantly, learning tacit assumptions is predicated on social learning and participation.

Social learning theories acknowledge that learning is a social process (Vygotsky, 1978) of meaning-making founded on dialogue. Social learning theories also advocate hands-on learning (Piaget, 1973) or experiential learning as described by Dewey (1938) and Kolb (1984) requiring active participation by learners, use of action learning principles (Revans, 1980), and scaffolding to support learning (Vygotsky, 1978) by engaging learners, in this instance research students, with knowledge, supervisors and peers. Social learning is best facilitated by conducive learning environments founded on seven conditions of learning: real world 'immersion', 'demonstration', 'approximation', 'practice', 'responsibility', 'expectation' and 'feedback' (Cambourne, 1984). Relatedly, profession-based learning (Jennings et al., 2007) involves students in real-world framed learning-engagements. Students rehearse, apply and refine profession-based knowledges, practices and skills in settings that engender culture and belonging – *communitas* (Jennings et al., 2009b) – associated with the profession into which they will enter.

Above all, '[any] social theory of learning must . . . integrate the components necessary to characterize social participation as a process of learning and of knowing' (Wenger, 1998, pp. 4–5). Important for research students is that their learning engages them in lived experiences and social learning processes, which offer access to the 'basic underlying assumptions' of a research culture and the profession associated with the conduct of research.

2.   LITERATURE

[K]nowing how something is put together is worth a thousand facts about it. (Bruner, 1984, p. 183)

There is a burgeoning body of research associated with higher degree research student experiences. This research has coalesced around supervision models (Blumberg, 1974; Anderson, 1988; Gurr, 2001; Manathunga, 2012); research student–supervisory relationships and their impact on learning outcomes, the 'rules of the game' (Wisker, 2001; Eley and Murray, 2009); the nature of supervision, which in the main has focused on a one-to-one supervisory model (Delamont et al., 2004; Eley and Murray, 2009; Walker and Thomson, 2010); collective approaches to research student supervision (Simons, 2005; Nordentoft et al., 2013; Manathunga and Goozee, 2007); research culture (Stracke, 2010; Conrad, 2006; Hortsmanshof and Conrad, 2003); use of communities of practice (Caffarella and Barnett, 2000; Janson et al., 2004); peer support groups (Fisher, 2006; Janson et al., 2004) as well as experiences related to becoming an academic researcher, culture and professionalization (Malfroy, 2005).

2.1   Research Supervision

Within the literature, there has been a strong focus on research supervision. Of primary importance to research student success is the supervisor and supervisory style along with the student–supervisor relationship (Ives and Rowley, 2005; Morgan and Sprenkle, 2007; Ezebilo, 2012). The traditional supervisor–student relationship has been formal and controlling (Hemer, 2012), as in the 'master-apprentice' [*sic*] mode derived from the Von Humboldt model of doctoral training (Taylor, 2012). In this model, the student-apprentice conducts research by mirroring the practice of the supervisor while simultaneously engaging in supervisor-related research under the 'master's' [*sic*] supervision (Dysthe, 2002). Another model is the teaching model wherein the teacher orchestrates, directs and corrects the student's research (Dysthe, 2002). More recently, the partnership model has emerged. This model is founded on dialogue and mentoring (Dysthe, 2002). The partnership model mirrors the peer-to-peer model espoused by Wang and Li (2011). Within these latter supervisory models, research students have differing opportunities to be enculturated into a research culture and acculturated as research professionals, wherein the process of enculturation involves the progressive learning over time of norms and mores of a culture – the rules of the game, and acculturation is associated with the adoption of those norms, mores and practices, that is, playing by the rules of the game.

2.2   'Rules of the Game'

When students enroll in higher degree research programs, they encounter new 'rules of the game' (Wisker, 2001; Eley and Murray, 2009). The rules of the game associated with doing research within a university research culture have to be understood and/or learnt. To facilitate the learning of the rules of the game, research students may be assisted by supervisors, graduate research schools, research centers, seminars, and other research students using explicit learning engagements. Rules of the game may also be acquired through collective learning engagements, which encompass both tacit and explicit learning. Emphasis on tacit learning engagements is critical for enculturation into a university research culture.

Of the three supervisory models, the Von Humboldt model and the teaching model primarily rely on explicit learning of the rules of the game. The nuances and finesse, as in the 'basic underlying assumptions', of a research culture may not be completely understood and certainly are not acquired through contextualized or socialized learning unless these are supplemented by graduate research school or research center activities and seminars. In these two models, the supervisor is the mediator and arbiter of research culture learning, which is usually accompanied by the use of written texts as information sources: 'artifacts'. On the other hand, the partnership or peer-to-peer model, which is predicated on dialogue and mentoring, provides real world learning engagements that immerse and demonstrate research culture in context and enable basic tacit assumptions 'to be revealed'. This model as part of its suite of learning experiences may draw on collective learning engagements since the overall model is predicated on social learning theories. The model may also be complemented by institutional activities to engender an inclusive research culture.

2.3   Collective Learning

Opportunities for collective learning engagements are important as extant literature notes that research student learning experiences suffer from 'a lack of cohort experiences', limited 'sense of belonging to a research culture', as well as an absence of 'strong and supportive research cultures' (Jennings et al., 2009a, p. 139). One avenue to address these three issues is to engage in collective learning experiences.

Collective learning experiences involve dialogue. 'The Greek roots of dialogue are *dia* (through) and *logos* (meaning)' (Ellinor and Gerard, 1998, p. 19). By engaging in dialogue, we are able to rehearse, approximate and practice as well as receive feedback on skills and behaviors in meaningful contexts. This is especially important for learning the rules of the game and research culture enculturation. Through regular dialogue sessions, 'the faster the behaviors, norms, and thinking patterns' of a culture are acquired (Ellinor and Gerard, 1998, p. 15). The essence of dialogue is meaning and sense making in a supportive environment. As Ellinor and Gerard (1998, p. 26) note, engaging in dialogue is associated with:

- Suspension of judgment
- Release of the need for specific outcomes
- An inquiry into and an examination of underlying assumptions
- Authenticity
- A slower pace with silence between speakers
- Listening deeply to self, others, and for collective meaning.

A community of practice has similar attributes. At its base, a community of practice is concerned with providing meaningful experiences that offer opportunities for practice of skills and behaviors, which are of interest to the community. These experiences and opportunities enable community members to shape their identity in the community – to become one of the community and, thereby, belong. The key phrases associated with communities of practice are meaning (experiences); practice (doing); identity (becoming); and community (belonging) (Wenger, 1998). Using research dialogue sessions, research communities can be built. Such communities 'develop profession-based [research] learning experiences and skilling for' early career researchers, which contemporaneously embed 'culture and cohort belongingness in their praxis' (Jennings et al., 2009b, p. 140). Additionally, the significant role of socially contextualized processes in profession-based learning (Jennings et al., 2009b) is complemented by Wenger's (1998) communities of practice.

2.4 Back to the Rules of the Game

As already noted, learning the rules of the game can be a lonely and isolating experience (Janson et al., 2004; Simons, 2005; Conrad, 2006). For research students wishing to engage in qualitative research, understanding the rules of the game can be additionally challenging. The dominant research paradigm in tourism and hospitality research has long been a positivistic or post-positivistic one (Walle, 1997; Riley and Love, 2000; Jennings, 2010). Engaging in qualitative research can be an alienating experience and one that is open to negative critique from other researchers and peers who are steeped in a quantitative research ideology.

   The chapter now focuses on the process of using collective learning engagements, specifically, research dialogue sessions, as a means to familiarize beginning researchers with the nuances and subtleties and the 'basic underlying assumptions' of a qualitative research culture as well as into the profession of qualitative research.

3. TEACHING APPROACH/METHOD

> When teachers inquire into their own teaching they are both participants and observers, researchers and clients. (Boomer, 1982, p. 83)

One way to inquire about the effectiveness of a learning/teaching engagement is through the use of narrative inquiry. Narrative inquiry involves 'meaning making through the shaping or ordering of experience' (Chase, 2011, p. 430) associated with 'an interest in life experiences as narrated by those who live them' (Chase, 2011, p. 421). We have used narrative inquiry because 'the urgency of storytelling arises from the need and desire to have *others* hear one's story.' (Chase, 2011, p. 427). We want this 'hearing' in order to improve the research cultures in which students live and study as well as to enable a sense of becoming and belonging to a research culture profession. Our choice of narrative analysis resonates with the reasons for its development in the 1970s (Czarniawska, 2004) – an absence of human storying in social sciences research.

   Our method of narrative inquiry involved the writing of reflections associated with each research higher degree student's experiences of participation in qualitative research dialogue sessions, over a period of 18–30 months at a metropolitan, east coast, Australian university. The number of participants attending the sessions fluctuated based on need. The sessions usually had between 7 and 12 participants. There was always a core of five PhD students, three internal and two external students, associated with the supervisor, who instigated the research dialogue sessions. The core also included an external supervisor who jointly supervised the two external PhD students with the research sessions' instigating supervisor. Based on dialogue focuses, various other internal research students and supervisors as well as established researchers participated in research sessions. There were a number of sessions, which drew up to 20 participants. In the main, the sessions focused on qualitative research, the profession of being a qualitative researcher as well as some of the more generic uncertainties associated with being a PhD student.

At the commencement of the first session and thereafter at the start of each year in which the sessions were held, the research session facilitator sent an email to potential research dialogue participants. This email outlined the principles and practices of the research dialogue sessions. Box 34.1 provides an example of one of those emails.

In the spirit of sustaining communities of practice, and in order to maintain integrity of the research dialogue sessions and their functioning, every session was summarized and shared with all possible participants. This meant that everyone was 'kept in the loop' with regard to happenings and were able to follow up with any participants if further clarification was required. This practice meant the group constantly kept moving forward and did not have to go over old ground if someone missed a session. New participants were also briefed by community members to bring them up to speed, as well as being given access to any written communications by the community. New members were also encouraged to seek out existing members for face-to-face dialogue prior to joining the research dialogue community. Box 34.2 provides an example of a session summary.

One of the intents of the research dialogue sessions was that over time the facilitation would move from a supervisory facilitator to a student facilitator and this did occur. This intent was pursued to evenly share power and to give the group a 'flatter' structure and functionality. Box 34.2 demonstrates the shift from a supervisor to a research student facilitator.

While dialogue was the overall intent of the sessions, as already noted, the nature of the sessions was orchestrated by participant needs. The trigger for dialogue was manifold. It included exemplars of student work, research articles, books, a guest researcher sharing their research, a question or a series of questions. Some students wanted to rehearse their confirmation presentations and then to engage in dialogue following their presentation; others expressly desired feedback on their research tools and technologies. Dialogue was the key element to assist participants to become a qualitative researcher and to 'be in and of' a qualitative research culture. Examples of dialogue starters are presented in Box 34.3.

The research dialogue sessions also generated additional profession-based learning activities, such as group journal article writing resulting in a number of published research articles.

3.1   Narratives: The Storying of Lived Experiences of Research Dialogue Sessions

The four narratives that inform this chapter were written after the research dialogue sessions ceased operating in 2010. The narratives did not focus on 'the moment-by-moment lived experience (Erlebnis)'; instead the narratives focused on 'the evaluated experience (Erfahrung), which is subject to reflection and prescribed meaning (Highmore, 2002)' (Cutler and Carmichael, 2010, p. 3). Prior to writing this chapter, the four research students were given the opportunity to review and revise their narratives. They undertook

BOX 34.1   EXAMPLE OF WELCOMING EMAIL

Hello everyone

A number of you have been asking when the qualitative research dialogue sessions would start again this year. So I figure that now is as good a time as any. For those of you who haven't heard about the sessions or haven't participated in one of the sessions, here is a bit about them.

The sessions have been running for approximately two years now. They are definitely not lectures, they are dialogue sessions that enable us to get together collegially to discuss our qualitative research interests, projects, queries, to practice qualitative methods of empirical material collection and interpretation, to seek feedback, support, reassurance, to write together in groups, and to have fun!! and to celebrate people's milestone achievements. We link in colleagues from an External Regional University and an External City University by teleconference.

You don't have to have a research project underway – you may just be interested in qualitative research and want to learn more about it via the dialogue sessions. The sessions operate on the principle of a supportive collective/community of qualitative researchers with a wide variety of experiences, including those who have never used it before but are interested in it as well as established qualitative researchers. Everyone is welcome.

We set our dialogue topics at the beginning of each year. Topics that we have dialogued in the past have included: theoretical paradigms that influence research designs; qualitative empirical materials interpretation; mixed methods, cross-cultural research, indigenous methodologies, grounded theory, interviews, focus groups.

We tend to have monthly sessions once we begin. Each session is usually two hours long; sometimes we go out together for dinner afterwards. Some of our colleagues located at distance have visited the Host University and have been able to join the Host University group for dinner. We usually take turns in providing afternoon tea at the sessions. In the past, the sessions have been held between 3 and 5 pm. The days of the week change over the semesters. At the beginning of the year, we canvas people's preferred times and then choose the best fit with regard to everyone's schedules.

We usually start the year with a session in which we get together, introduce and re-introduce ourselves to each other, discuss our interests, and/or research as well as make suggestions for topics for the year based on our specific needs. If a topic has been considered before, it can still be considered again.

The sessions are for us and the sessions need to meet our needs – so we set the agenda and we ask all sorts of questions of each other about qualitative research. Every question is respected; there are 'no wrong questions' to ask.

If you can't attend one of the sessions or it clashes with your other commitments, we provide everyone with a summary of each of the sessions so you are kept informed. We also encourage you to catch up with those of us who did go to the session – we let you know in the summary who was there so you can do this.

Based on last year's sessions we have two topics/focuses for our first two focused sessions: . . . So start thinking about what you want to know, learn, practice with regard to qualitative research and/or what you are interested in having others help you with and/or you want to help others with.

In order to get us started, ...

If you know of others who you think may be interested in the dialogue sessions, please let them know about the sessions and encourage them to come along and join in.

If you are new and have further questions, please ask any of the group members noted in the email address for information and background.

Kind regards
Facilitator

BOX 34.2   EXAMPLE OF EMAIL COMMUNICATION PROVIDING WRITTEN
SUMMARY OF A DIALOGUE SESSION

Nov 15, 2007
Good evening everyone

1. Please find below the summary of today's session.

Research dialogue session 7 summary: Update on research

- **Participants:** One MPhil student, 4 PhD students, 2 supervisors (Internal to University), One PhD student (External Regional University).
- **Apologies:** Two supervisors, 3 PhD students (Internal to Host University), One PhD student (External City University 1), One supervisor (External Regional University).

a. Personal updates on research activities
Today's session started off with a catch-up on everyone's research projects. Out of this sharing a number of reoccurring themes, reflections and dialogue arose from our lived experiences:

- Emergent nature of qualitative research design
- Emergence versus forcing grounded theory
- Tourism studies and other disciplinary theories, frameworks and constructs
- Grounded theory and literature and other disciplines, such as, social psychology, environmental sciences, organizational behavior, organizational psychology
- Role of reflexivity throughout research processes
- Counterpoints to Western ontologies and epistemologies – alternative ontologies and epistemologies – different ways of knowing and naming
- Insider and outsider research
- Interviews, conversations, . . .
- Reciprocity and research
- Reciprocity and rapport building
- Positionality and axiology and influences on research design
- Role of gatekeepers and gatekeeper processes
- Qualitative research and writing of chapters

b. Considerations for the next session: Mixed methods . . . and literature review considerations

2. **Next session details:** Session 8: Mixed methods . . . and literature reviews, [Date]. Please advise PhD student facilitator of your availability **PhDfacilitator@InternaltoUniversity.edu.au**

She will be communicating further with you regarding this session.

Kind regards

Facilitator

---

the review process as qualified PhD researchers and were established in the profession of qualitative research.

The four narratives now follow, in full form, so readers can 'hear' the 'research student' voices and co-interpret the texts. Interpretation always involves 'negotiations between the

---

BOX 34.3   EXAMPLE OF RESEARCH DIALOGUE TOPICS

Proposed agenda for 2009 based on 2008:

Session One: Welcome, (re)connecting and setting our dialogue topics for 2009.
[Date] in the Centre Room and via teleconference mode.
Session Two: Confirmation rehearsal, PhD student (Internal to Host University).
Session Three: (a) Critical approaches to tourism and hospitality; (b) Memory-work – research method (Guest facilitator, External City University 2).
Session Four: Proposed confirmation rehearsal, details to be advised.
Session Five: Research online platform dialogue session: PhD student (Internal to University).
Session Six: As per Session One outcomes.

If you know of others . . .

If you are new and have further questions, . . .

Kind regards
Facilitator

---

intention of the reader (*intentio lectoris*) and the intention of the text (*intentio operis*)' (Czarniawska, 2004, p. 68). As Eco (1992) noted, in making such interpretations, readers usually respect *intentio operis*. For researchers undertaking an interpretation, the act of interpreting is always 'a political act of totalizing' regardless of the 'faithfulness' of the interpretation (Czarniawska, 2004, p. 61). To counter totalizing, we have chosen to use polyphony. Polyphony presents a multi-voiced storying so differing perspectives of the research dialogue sessions can be 'read' without any 'Othering' through translation by an 'interpreter'. An alternative to polyphony is the use of 'variegated speech', wherein traces (Bakhtin (1928[1985]), in Czarniawska, 2004, p. 62) and excerpts of narratives echo 'realities'. In this chapter, rather than present echoes, we present multiple perspectives.

To assist readers with their readings and their interpretations, the narratives are framed in the genre of a tale, embedded with the appropriate 'repertoire of reading clues' (Czarniawska, 2004, p. 69). By nature of their length, the tales apply minimal emplotment, that is, 'the passage from one equilibrium to another' (Todorov, 1971[1977], p. 111, in Czarniawska, 2004, p. 19). And, as befits the genre of a tale, the presence of 'heroes' resonates in the research student journeys.

3.1.1   From dialogue to being: affect, learning and heroes without

Over the period of approximately 18 months my supervisor organized and facilitated research dialogue sessions for PhD students using qualitative research. Every four to six weeks interested PhD students gathered to discuss a particular topic that related to the process, methods and experiences of each of us.

In the beginning, I felt quite awkward, being unsure what I was supposed to do and of the processes and protocols. I was also a little uncomfortable with the other students in the room that I had previously not met. I did not wish to appear foolish in front of my peers and so to begin with I was quite reserved. I then felt that others were the same, particularly the international students from various Asian nations, who would rather maintain silence to 'save face'.

Our supervisor (through chatting and inviting us to share our experiences) soon made me feel more comfortable so I took the attitude that I can make mistakes as this is supposed to be a learning environment.

I particularly enjoyed hearing the experiences of two students who were ahead of me in the PhD journey. Their topics were so interesting and it was reassuring to learn how they had overcome certain difficulties.

I learned about different methodologies and better understood the philosophical underpinnings that make a sound PhD.

After a few meetings the group had bonded to such an extent that we occasionally met socially. I believe the success of these sessions was entirely due to my supervisor's encouragement and facilitation skills. I miss these sessions for the shared collective knowledge and learning.

3.1.2   From dialogue to being: sharing/learning with others and the hero within

As a researcher who discovered qualitative research relatively late in life, my experience in developing my research capabilities and in becoming a qualitative researcher has been a very steep learning curve. However, a steep learning curve in this case does not mean rushing through the many aspects of qualitative research, but rather learning, absorbing and finding out which particular methodologies and methods of qualitative research appeal and feel right for the researcher and the research at hand. It was with time and the guidance of others that I developed into a more confident and knowledgeable researcher.

My experience with learning how to develop as a grounded theory researcher and developing a passion for this methodology was very much influenced and fostered by my PhD supervisors. It was their initial guidance, suggestions and their own experience with this methodology and its methods that made me see the potential and appropriateness of it for my own research. So the learning began – the many books, articles, reviews, trying to make sense of it all and feeling confident that I had finally understood – not all, but at least some. As with any research methodology it is only when one starts doing it that many of the unclarities, problems and challenges come to the fore. In the initial stages of undertaking research using grounded theory I certainly wasn't feeling very confident in using this methodology and had many misgivings about being on the right track. One of the causes of this was the fact that there were not many people close by in my own university that had experience in this methodology.

Joining the online and teleconferenced research dialogue sessions was a major step towards my becoming a more confident qualitative researcher and it wasn't until the second or third of these sessions that I realized how much I had actually developed in my knowledge and skills in using grounded theory as a methodology and its methods. By talking to other researchers through this online and teleconferenced community of practice I was able to share my experiences and knowledge of qualitative research but also to further develop my skills in a number of different areas. Through these sessions I was able to give some guidance to researchers who had just started using grounded theory and it was by verbalizing the challenges but also the positive aspects of using this methodology that made me realize, through their questions and responses, how much I had developed as a researcher in this field. These sessions also made me realize the importance of communicating and sharing with other, like-minded researchers, whether it be online or in real time, the knowledge, skills and experiences of research.

Even though I did find the online and teleconferenced sessions beneficial I would have liked to have had the opportunity to interact with members of the group in 'real life' and believe this would have benefited my PhD, and in particular the timely completion of my PhD.

3.1.3 From dialogue to being: heroes without

My participation in a research dialogue group at university involved meetings on a monthly basis over several years. My initial involvement was a 'go and see' adventure and this casual approach quickly changed to a highly anticipated time of great personal value. There were obvious immediate practical advantages of knowledge acquisition, and I found an ongoing opportunity for my professional development. Of particular significance was the formation of long-term fellowships with other group members.

During our meetings that lasted over two hours we would take a round table open-dialogue format where we discussed many topics, and all group members had input into the selection of discussion issues that they would find personally useful. This allowed for input from a broad base of needs and experiences, such as the provision of advice related to many philosophical and technical issues that arose during development of the methodology for my PhD thesis.

A very positive aspect of being part of a research community of practice was the 'snowballing' of participants' contacts that enabled contribution and linkage to diverse research students and encouraged their participation in meetings. This passing on of knowledge was enhanced by the generous support of other PhD students who were further along the research journey from my position. Explanations and considerations from all group members led to construction of shared understandings of epistemological perspectives and theoretical approaches in qualitative research.

My engagement with this research dialogue group, which was composed of a practicing research community, provided opportunities for my professional development. For example, I was encouraged to present a methodology seminar explaining my intended research analysis tools. The group feedback provided a valued critique in my development of this presentation as a teaching tool.

I found participation in the research dialogue group provided a non-threatening environment, where I became more articulate in discussing topics such as ontology and epistemology. I also found participation enriched my learning through observation, such as the action of a role model who chaired many of the sessions, and as a very competent academic, her abilities to succinctly yet comprehensively cover over two hours of dialogue was inspiring. Also, the considered critical understanding from the diverse experiences of the group contributed to my own construction of understanding of the many discussed issues.

There was also a strong social aspect in that as we shared our research difficulties and successes, the developing inter-personal knowledge enabled acknowledgment of birthdays and we had many instances of shared humor. A rapport, empathy and camaraderie developed and this was enhanced by refreshments (tea, coffee, juice and nibbles), which created an informal atmosphere. My involvement in the research dialogue sessions resulted in warm friendships, and I hold the greatest respect for the integrity of character of the people who helped me on my journey by freely sharing their knowledge in this community of practice.

3.1.4　From dialogue to being: affect and heroes in the same boat

When I started my PhD journey in February 2007, I felt excited and scared at the same time. Excited to start a new possible career path, and scared, because I felt as if I knew nothing about what this might entail. My supervisor was organizing regular research dialogue sessions that particularly focused on qualitative research aspects, and joining these sessions, for me, was an important step for not just learning the language of qualitative research but also becoming a qualitative researcher.

Although already a long time ago, I still remember clearly my first session. I felt overwhelmed listening to fellow PhD students who were able to discuss and argue at a much higher level, leaving me thinking that I never would be able to reach such a level. Of course some of these fellow PhD students had more research experiences than I had, and of course they already seemed to know all the 'big words'.

Over the next two years, these research dialogue sessions accompanied my PhD journey and became an important aspect of developing as a qualitative researcher. In each session we focused on different aspects of qualitative research. Although not all of these aspects were applicable to my research, they certainly widened my understanding of qualitative research. These sessions provided a friendly and supportive environment in which I could ask questions or just state that I didn't understand what someone just said. There was no fixed structure on how these sessions were run, therefore allowing everyone to join in, contribute, or just listen. I soon realized that I was not alone on this journey and that everyone else in the group, including established researchers, was still learning.

The research dialogue sessions opened up a whole new world of qualitative research approaches, challenges and possibilities, and even though we were doing different projects, by just discussing the similarities and differences, I learned a lot more than a book or seminar could teach me. We talked about our individual research projects, reflected on what we read in the literature, engaged in interpretation exercises, or just shared ideas on how to overcome challenges. There seemed to be an unspoken, mutual understanding of 'we are all in the same boat', which also might have been influenced by the fact that qualitative research was (is?) often seen as a less accepted approach within academia. These sessions linked us together as a group and although in the meantime we have all moved on, I still feel part of this group.

3.2　Interpretation of the Four Tales

> Some researchers study narrative *as* lived experience, as itself social action. These researchers are as interested in *how* people narrate their experiences as in what their stories are about. (Chase, 2011, p. 422)

In order to find out what the stories were about, after the 'research students' were satisfied with their texts, the narratives were interpreted using thematic analysis rather than structural analysis (Reissman, 2008). Thematic analysis involves researchers identifying and clustering themes within narrative texts, whereas structural analysis focuses on the way narratives are put together as well as the cultural and textual use of language (Reissman, 2008). The principal supervisor of the students conducted the 'thematic analysis' and in order to further counter the totalizing effect of her interpretations, the interpretations were then shared with the students. The students checked the faithfulness of the interpretations in relation to their own individual lived experiences of the research dialogue sessions. Part of this interpretation is reflected in the titling of each of the tales.

The narratives were interpreted using Hernadi's hermeneutic triad (1987), specifically, the guiding questions of 'what does this text say?'; 'why . . . or how does this text say what it does?'; 'what do I, the reader, think of all this?' (Czarniawska, 2004, p.60). Using Hernadi's triad integrates interpretation and explanation (Czarniawska, 2004). These three questions drove the thematic analysis. In processing the three questions, areas of text were highlighted and textual comments were added to the margins of the texts. From the highlighted textual references, themes were elicited. These themes were 'sense of self', 'structural elements of the sessions', 'learning environment', 'nature of the sessions', 'role of supervisors', 'role of student peers'.

The question 'why/how do the texts say what they do?' was related to the nature of the tale and the process of emplotment used in each of the tales. The students' tales storied shifts between equilibrium and disequilibrium in relation to their affective domains, the setting of the tales – the dialogue sessions, learning, ownership of the journey, the social nature of learning, the hero within and the heroes without.

The question 'what do we, the readers, think of all this?' was queried specifically using two questions: 'how do research dialogue sessions benefit participants?' and 'how do research dialogue sessions facilitate profession-based learning?'. These interpretations were viewed through theoretical lenses of communities of practice and collective learning engagements as well as profession-based learning. Table 34.1 details the interpretation/explanation processes.

For us, one of the issues of using narrative inquiry and thematic analysis was not to interpret until the tales were lost. Having distilled the essence of the tales, we now re-narrate the tales.

4.   FINDINGS/OUTCOMES

> To interpret means to react to the text of the world or to the world of text by producing other texts (Umberto Eco, 1990, p. 23)

Enrolling in a PhD program of study is a daunting experience. Despite having various experiences with the 'artifacts' of research and some of the 'espoused beliefs and values' through the conduct of research, in the main the 'basic underlying assumptions' of a research culture remain removed from students. This can be further exacerbated if students chose to undertake qualitative research in the fields of tourism and hospitality studies.

Coming together in collective environments, students fear risk of exposure, of being considered 'charlatans', or not as knowledgeable as they should be or as knowledgeable as others. The use of research dialogue sessions conducted using supportive and conducive learning environments, wherein students are able to be immersed in demonstrations and

Table 34.1   Interpretations/explanations of the 'From dialogue to being' tales

'What do the texts say?'		'Why/How do the texts say what they do?'	'What do we the readers think of all this?'	
Narrative Themes	Textual references	Emplotment: Equilibrium disequilibrium in the tales	How do research dialogue sessions benefit participants?	How do research dialogue session facilitate profession-based learning?
Sense of self	Initially unsure, uncertain, lacking confidence, awkward, uncomfortable, hesitant.	Affective domain	Identity (becoming)	Becoming professionalized as qualitative researchers
	Knowing what don't know, but willing to keep learning.	Learning		
	Moving to confidence and certainty.	The 'hero' within		
Structural elements of the sessions	Time period over 2 years, 2 hour session times, monthly, by telephone and face to face, online connectivity.	The setting of the tales	Meaning (experiences); and practice (doing)	Practice – the language and profession of the how of qualitative research
Learning environment	Collegial, conducive, inclusivity, dialogue, sharing, spill over into other student life – other social activities.	Social nature of learning	Meaning (experiences); practice (doing); and community (belonging)	Practice – the language and profession of the how of qualitative research
	Supportive, risk taking, asking questions no matter what.	The setting of the tales		
	Locus of control – content of sessions, topics and activities, leadership.	Ownership of the journey		
Nature of sessions	Collaborative, sharing, dialogue, social aspects.	Affective domain	Community (belonging)	Practicing and being a qualitative researcher
	Learning is a social process.	Learning	Meaning (experiences); and practice (doing)	

Table 34.1 (continued)

'What do the texts say?'		'Why/How do the texts say what they do?'	'What do we the readers think of all this?'	
Narrative Themes	Textual references	Emplotment: Equilibrium disequilibrium in the tales	How do research dialogue sessions benefit participants?	How do research dialogue session facilitate profession-based learning?
	Critical constructive feedback, regular contact, immersion in all things qualitative, demonstrations and models.			
Role of supervisors	Collaborative, constructive, facilitate learning, flatter model of 'power and influence', rapport, empathy and camaraderie.	Heroes without	Meaning (experiences); identity (becoming); and community (belonging)	Mentoring and coaching re: the profession of qualitative research
Role of research-student peers	Collaborative, supportive, facilitate learning, social aspects.	Heroes without	Meaning (experiences); identity (becoming); and community (belonging)	Co-learning, mentoring and coaching re: the profession of qualitative research.

models of qualitative research, rehearse and practice the skills, knowledge sets and principles of qualitative research while receiving timely feedback, enables research students to gain confidence and personal power by taking responsibility for their own learning as well as the learning of others through and by the provision of constructive dialogue and feedback. Simultaneously, research students are able to gain access to the 'basic underlying assumptions' of associated research cultures and the profession of qualitative research.

Of critical influence in the PhD journey is the role of affect and how the affective domain shapes and reshapes a PhD student's identity. Participation in and joint ownership of the learning processes, where power is distributed equally in dialogue sessions and locus of control is experienced by students, helps frame PhD students' identities as qualitative researchers. Learning processes founded on the social nature of learning undertaken in supportive, collegial settings and environments result in learning that is more meaningful, timely and relevant. Over time, such learning processes and settings harness the power of the heroes within and foster recognition by the students of themselves as competent qualitative researchers. The involvement of heroes without, student peers and supervisors,

facilitate enculturation into institutional and qualitative research cultures and acculturation into the profession of qualitative research.

5.   FUTURE DIRECTIONS

> By reflecting on what it is that human beings do when they learn, it is possible to arrive at
> principles of learning, which can then be transformed into principles of teaching. Practice based
> on these principles focuses in the first place on *what the learner is doing* and only secondarily on
> *what the teacher must do*. (Boomer, 1982, p. viii, emphasis in original)

What can be learnt from the four tales of research students participating in qualitative
research dialogue sessions?

First, we learn that the affective domain is an important influence in a PhD research
student's experience of both the conduct of qualitative research and the overriding university research culture. This domain is one that is not easily addressed using the 'master-
apprentice' [*sic*] or 'teaching model' (Dysthe, 2002; Taylor, 2012). The 'partnership model'
(Dysthe, 2002) is most able to address issues associated with the affective domain as this
model is based on dialogue and mentoring. It is an 'equals' model.

Second, social learning principles and practices need to inform PhD student learning experiences. Pedagogical principles of supervisors determine the nature of whether,
and how, connections between PhD students are formed. Supervisors are especially
instrumental in fostering connections between PhD students at various stages of their
research. Pedagogically, the partnership model supports social learning theories.

Third, the role of supervisors is paramount for the success of research dialogue
sessions. Much has been written regarding 'supervision styles' and 'relationships' (Ives
and Rowley, 2005; Morgan and Sprenkle, 2007; Ezebilo, 2012). In particular, Janson
et al. (2004) emphasize the vital role supervisors play in the establishment of collective
learning groups, specifically, communities of practice. Subsequently, supervisors are one
of the heroes without.

Four, the use of dialogue in collective learning experiences as a regular component of
PhD learning and culture building practices supports the development of *communitas*
upon which social learning is actualized. Through dialogue, students realize how much
they have in common, how much they themselves know and how much they can and
do learn from each other. While some dialogue members may not be able to be physi-
cally present at sessions, telephone and electronic participation still engenders a sense of
communitas as long as facilitation is founded on inclusivity.

Five, in collective learning experiences, locus of control needs to be relinquished from
supervisors and assumed by research students. It is important for students to be responsible for dialogue session activities and tasks and to alternate facilitation amongst members.
Dialogue sessions then become a platform for learning and progression regarding the
profession of qualitative research. Of the three supervision models, master-apprentice
[*sic*], teaching and partnership, again, the latter is best suited to achieve this outcome.

Six, research dialogue sessions support enculturation of institutional research cultures
through tacit learning of the rules of the game as well as acculturation experiences which
enable research students to play by the rules of the game associated with the profession
of qualitative research.

6. SUMMARY/CONCLUSION

A primary responsibility of educators is that they not only be aware of the general principle of the shaping of actual experience by environing conditions, but that they also recognize in the concrete what surroundings are conducive to having experiences that lead to growth. (Dewey, 1938, p. 40)

This chapter focused on the narratives of four tourism and hospitality research students who variously engaged in research dialogue sessions over a two-and-a-half-year period. The students drew on the narrative genre of 'tales' with minimal equilibrium/disequilibrium emplotments to narrate their individual lived experiences of these sessions. The narrative inquiry method of thematic analysis was used for interpretation/explanation of the student tales. Key themes elicited were 'sense of self', 'structural elements of the sessions', 'learning environment', 'nature of the sessions', 'role of supervisors', and 'role of student peers'. The tales moved between equilibrium and disequilibrium regarding: the students' affective domains; the setting of the tales, that is, the dialogue sessions; learning; ownership of the journey; the social nature of learning; the hero within and the heroes without.

Narrative inquiry facilitated reflection on the effectiveness of learning/teaching engagements; in this chapter, research dialogue sessions. These sessions were instigated by the four research-students' university research-supervisor. The sessions were predicated on dialogue to enable collective learning and sharing of research experiences, enculturation into a university-research culture and acculturation into a qualitative research profession. The sessions resonated with communities of practice principles, specifically, identity (becoming), meaning (experiences), practice (doing) and community (belonging). Simultaneously, the dialogue sessions contributed to the research students 'becoming professionalized as qualitative researchers'; provided 'practice of the language and profession of the how of qualitative research'; gave opportunities for 'practicing and being a qualitative researcher'; 'mentoring and coaching by supervisors re: the profession of qualitative research' as well as 'co-learning, mentoring and coaching by research student peers re: the profession of qualitative research'.

Based on the interpretation/explanation of the four research student tales, we encourage others involved in PhD research programs to use a partnership model of supervision and to supplement this model with research dialogue sessions as an effective means for collective learning and sharing as well as enabling enculturation and acculturation. Importantly, in the process of engaging in the qualitative research dialogue sessions, research students learn how to 'be in and of' a qualitative research culture and how to professionally be a qualitative researcher.

REFERENCES

Alvesson, Mats (2002), *Understanding Organizational Culture*, London: Sage Publications.
Anderson, Jean L. (1988), *The Supervisory Process in Speech Language Pathology and Audiology*, San Diego, CA: College Hill Press.
Blumberg, Arthur (1974), *Supervisor and Teaching: A Private Cold War*, Berkeley, CA: McCutchan.
Boomer, Garth (1982), *Negotiating the Curriculum: A Teacher–Student Partnership*, Sydney: Ashton Scholastic.
Bruner, Jerome. S. (1984), *In Search of Mind: Essays in Autobiography*, Alfred P. Sloan Foundation Series, New York: HarperCollins.

Caffarella, Rosemary, S. and Bruce G. Barnett (2000), 'Teaching doctoral students to become scholarly writers: The importance of giving and receiving critiques', *Studies in Higher Education*, **25** (1), 39–52.

Cambourne, Brian (1984), 'The origins of teachers' doubts about "naturalising" literacy education. And some suggestions for easing them', in *Reading: 1984 and Beyond, Selected Key Papers of the 10th Australian Reading Conference 1984*, Vol. 2, pp. 17–39.

Chase, Susan E. (2011), 'Narrative inquiry: Still a field in the making', in Norman Denzin and Yvonna Lincoln (eds), *The Sage Handbook of Qualitative Research*, 4th edn, Los Angeles: Sage, pp. 421–34.

Conrad, Linda (2006), 'Countering isolation: Joining the research community', in Carey Denholm and Terry Evans (eds), *Doctorates Downunder: Keys to Successful Doctoral Study in Australia and New Zealand*, Camberwell, Victoria: Australian Council for Educational Research, pp. 34–40.

Cutler, Sarah Q. and Barbara A. Carmichael (2010), 'The dimension of the tourist experience', in M. Morgan, P. Lugosi and J.R.B. Ritchie (eds), *The Experience of Tourism and Leisure: Consumer and Management Perspectives*, Clevedon: Channel View, pp. 3–26.

Czarniawksa, Barbara (2004), *Narratives in Social Science Research*, London: Sage.

Daiute, Colette and Cynthia Lightfoot (2004), 'Editors' introduction: Theory and craft in narrative inquiry', in Colette Daiute and Cynthia Lightfoot (eds), *Narrative Analysis: Studying the Development of Individuals in Society*, Thousand Oaks, CA: Sage, pp. vii–xviii.

Delamont, Sara, Paul Atkinson and Odette Parry (2004), *Supervising the Doctorate: A Guide to Success*, 2nd edn, New York: Open University Press.

Dewey, John (1938), *Experience and Education*, New York: Collier Books.

Dysthe, Olga (2002), 'Professors as mediators of academic text cultures: An interview study with advisors and masters' degree students in three disciplines in a Norwegian University', *Written Communication*, **19** (4), 493–544.

Eco, Umberto (1990), *The Limits of Interpretation*, Bloomington, IN: Indiana University Press.

Eco, Umberto (1992), *Interpretation and Overinterpretation*, Cambridge: Cambridge University Press.

Eley, Adrian and Rowena Murray (2009), *How to be an Effective Supervisor: Best Practice in Research Student Supervision*, New York: Open University Press.

Ellinor, Linda and Glenna Gerard (1998), *Dialogue: Rediscovering the Transformative Power of Conversation*, New York: John Wiley and Sons.

Ezebilo, Eugene E. (2012), 'Challenges in postgraduate studies: Assessments by doctoral students in a Swedish university', *Higher Education Studies*, **2** (4), 49–57.

Fisher, Kath (2006), 'Peer support groups', in Carey Denholm and Terry Evans (eds), *Doctorates Down Under: Keys to Successful Doctoral Study in Australia and New Zealand*, Camberwell, Victoria: ACER Press, pp. 41–9.

Gurr, G.M. (2001), 'Negotiating the "rackety bridge": A dynamic model for aligning supervisory style with research student development', *Higher Education Research and Development*, **20** (1), 81–92.

Hemer, Susan R. (2012), 'Informality, power and relationships in postgraduate supervision: Supervising PhD candidates over coffee', *Higher Education Research and Development*, **31** (6), 827–39.

Hernadi, Paul (1987), 'Literary interpretation and the rhetoric of the human sciences', in John S. Nelson et al. (eds), *The Rhetoric of the Human Sciences*, Madison, WI: University of Wisconsin Press, pp. 263–75.

Hortsmanshof, L. and L. Conrad (2003), 'Postgraduate peer support programme: Enhancing community', in Proceedings of HERDSA (Higher Education Research and Development Society of Australia), *Learning for the unknown future: research and development in higher education*. University of Otago, Christchurch, New Zealand, 6–9 July.

Ives, G. and G. Rowley (2005), 'Supervision selection or allocation and continuity of supervision: PhD students' progress and outcomes', *Studies in Higher Education*, **30** (5), 535–55.

Janson, Annick, Laurie Howard and Michele Schoenberger-Orgad (2004), 'The odyssey of PhD students becoming a community of practice', *Business Communication Quarterly*, **67** (2), 168–81.

Jennings, G.R. (2010), *Tourism Research*, 2nd edn, Brisbane: John Wiley & Sons.

Jennings, Gayle, Michael Scantlebury and Kara Wolfe (2009b), 'Tertiary travel and tourism education: Using action research cycles to provide information on pedagogical applications associated with reflexivity, team-based learning and communities of practice', *Journal of Teaching in Travel and Tourism*, **9** (3), 193–215.

Jennings, Gayle R., Ulrike Kachel, Sandra Kensbock and Mary-Anne Smith (2009a), 'Tourism and hospitality research student experiences: How to achieve quality, inclusivity and belongingness', *Journal of Hospitality and Tourism Management*, **16**, 139–47.

Jennings, Gayle R., Sandra Kensbock, Olga Junek, Kylie Radel and Ulrike Kachel (2010), 'Lived experiences of early career researchers: Learning about and doing grounded theory', *Journal of Hospitality and Tourism Management*, **17** (1), 21–33.

Jennings, Gayle R., Glen Hornby, Gary Allen, Carl Cater, Kristine Toohey, Scott Richardson and Millicent Kennelly (2007), 'Business ethics and responsible practice: A profession-based learning approach in tertiary education', paper presented at the Asia Pacific Academy of Business in Society conference, Port Vila, Vanuatu.

Kolb, David A. (1984), *Experiential Learning: Experience as the Source of Learning and Development*, Upper Saddle River, NJ: Prentice-Hall.

Malfroy, Janne (2005), 'Doctoral supervision, workplace research and changing pedagogic practices', *Higher Education Research and Development*, **24** (2), 165–78.

Manathunga, Catherine (2012), 'Supervisors watching supervisors: The deconstructive possibilities and tensions of team supervision', *Australian Universities Review*, **54** (1), 29–37.

Manathunga, Catherine and Justine Goozee (2007), 'Challenging the dual assumption of the always/already autonomous student and effective supervisor', *Teaching in Higher Education*, **12** (3), 309–22.

Morgan, M. and D. Sprenkle (2007), 'Towards a common factors approach to supervision', *Journal of Marital and Family Therapy*, **33**, 1–17.

Nordentoft, Helle Merete, Rie Thomsen and Gitte Wichmann-Hansen (2013), 'Collective academic supervision: A model for participation and learning in higher education', *Higher Education*, **65** (5), 581–93.

Piaget, J. (1973), *To Understand is to Invent: The Future of Education*, New York: Grossman Publishers.

Reissman, Catherine K. (2008), *Narrative Methods for the Human Sciences*, Thousand Oaks, CA: Sage.

Revans, Reginal W. (1980), *Action Learning: New Techniques for Management*, London: Blond and Briggs.

Riley, R.W. and L.L. Love (2000), 'The state of qualitative tourism research', *Annals of Tourism Research*, **27** (1), 164–87.

Schein, Edgar (1996), 'Three cultures of management: The key to organizational learning', *Sloan Management Review*, **38** (1), 1–20.

Schein, Edgar (2010), *Organizational Culture and Leadership*, 4th edn, San Francisco, CA: John Wiley and Sons.

Simons, Penny (2005), 'An issue of isolation', in Adrian Eley and Roy Jennings (eds), *Effective Postgraduate Supervision: Improving the Student/Supervisor Relationship*, New York: Open University Press, pp. 7–11.

Stracke, Elke (2010), 'Undertaking the journey together: Peer learning for a successful and enjoyable PhD experience', *Journal of University Teaching and Learning Practice*, **7** (1), Article 8.

Taylor, Stanley (2012), 'Changes in doctoral education', *International Journal for Researcher Development*, **3** (2), 118–38.

Van Manen, M. (1990), *Researching Lived Experience: Human Science for an Action Sensitive Pedagogy*, London, Ontario: State University of New York Press.

Vygotsky, Lev S. (1978), *Mind in Society: The Development of Higher Psychological Processes*, trans. A.R. Luria, M.M. Lopez-Morillas, Michael Cole and J. Wertsch, Cambridge, MA: Harvard University Press.

Walker, Melanie and Pat Thomson (eds) (2010), *The Routledge Doctoral Supervisors Companion: Supporting Effective Research in Education and the Social Sciences*, London: Routledge.

Walle, A.H. (1997), 'Quantitative versus qualitative tourism research', *Annals of Tourism*, **24** (3), 524–36.

Wang, T and L.Y. Li (2011), '"Tell me what to do" vs. "guide me through it": Feedback experiences of international doctoral students', *Active Learning in Higher Education*, **12** (2), 101–12.

Wenger, Etienne (1998), *Communities of Practice: Learning, Meaning, and Identity*, Cambridge: Cambridge University Press.

Wisker, G. (2001), *The Postgraduate Research Handbook*, London: Palgrave.

PART VII

CONTEMPORARY ISSUES IN TEACHING AND LEARNING

35 Standards, benchmarks and assurance of learning
David Airey and Pierre Benckendorff

1. INTRODUCTION

Two of the greatest changes in higher education over the past few decades have been the sheer growth in scale and the shift in funding from the state to the learners. Student enrolments in an expanded higher education system in the UK increased from about 600 000 in 1970 (Office for National Statistics, 2002) to nearly 2.5 million in 2014 (Higher Education Statistics Agency, 2015). Similar growth is also seen in Australia where the shift to a demand-driven higher education funding system has fueled an increase in student numbers from 161 455 in 1970 (Department of Education Training and Youth Affairs, 2001) to over 1.3 million in 2013 (Department of Education and Training, 2015; Norton, 2014). As Airey et al. (2015a, p. 3) put it, 'After a few decades of expansion, higher education sectors in most countries have transitioned from elite to mass providers of programs with significant implications for the consumption of public resources'. On the subject of resources, Airey et al. (2015b, p. 141) suggest that 'not only has funding become tighter but, through the introduction of fees, students (and their parents) have increasingly become responsible for funding universities rather than the taxpayer'. At the same time public funding of higher education has been subsidized by increasing numbers of international students and in some countries this has positioned higher education as a key source of export earnings. In some cases, this focus on economic outcomes has been accompanied by the growing presence of private institutions specializing in areas such as business, hospitality and tourism.

These changes have brought in their wake a range of consequences for higher education for tourism, not the least of which has been increased scrutiny, from governments on behalf of the taxpayer, the students, as well as the employers and other stakeholders. They have also led to increased competition, consumerism and the marginalization of non-revenue-generating disciplines and programs (Shahjahan, 2012). The aim of this chapter is to explore the background, nature and implications of some of these consequences, particularly as they relate to standards and quality assurance for tourism education. The focus is largely on teaching and learning standards, although reference will be made to other standards. The chapter draws particularly on the experience of the UK and Australia, which are the home locations of the two authors, but it also includes other parts of the world as well as some of the international developments influencing higher education. Although regulation of the higher education sector first emerged in the USA in the late nineteenth century (Jarvis, 2014), the UK and Australia have progressed much further than most countries in experimenting with national academic standards and quality assurance frameworks (Dill, 2014).

2.   REGULATORY RESPONSES TO CHANGE

The changes in higher education participation and funding have had two fairly obvious consequences for tourism education. First, they have brought increased scrutiny, especially by government agencies. In many cases, as noted later in this chapter, this scrutiny has developed alongside that of other agencies such as voluntary accreditation bodies as well as professional associations and regulatory and statutory bodies. In brief, the growth in student numbers brought with it increased public expenditure and it is not surprising that governments became increasingly interested in the value for money that was being provided as well as in the level and consistency of quality of provision across the growing number of higher education providers. This interest was also compounded by government interest in the link between a highly educated workforce and economic prosperity (Airey, 2005). It has been estimated that at least half of the world's governments have instituted higher education quality assurance systems or regulatory agencies tasked with setting standards, monitoring performance and ensuring compliance (Jarvis, 2014). In the UK this took the form of the creation of The Quality Assurance Agency for Higher Education (QAA) in 1997, replacing two predecessor bodies that had already begun to address quality assurance issues from the late 1980s. The QAA is not itself a government body, rather it is an independent agency set up to ensure standards and improve quality, but it nevertheless works closely with the government department and agencies for higher education.

Similar developments have occurred in Australia, where the Australian Universities Quality Agency (AUQA) was established in 2000 to promote, audit and report on quality assurance in higher education. The AUQA investigated the extent to which institutions achieved their missions and objectives through a cycle of institutional audits. These audits assessed the adequacy of an institution's quality assurance arrangements in teaching and learning, research and management. The 2008 *Review of Australian Higher Education* found that 'Australia must enhance its capacity to demonstrate outcomes and appropriate standards in higher education if it is to remain internationally competitive and implement a demand-driven funding model' (Bradley et al., 2008, p. 128). A shift from an audit-based system focused on inputs and processes to an outcomes-based standards framework that included not only the universities, but also other education providers was initiated to protect the reputation of Australia as an international education provider. In 2011 the AUQA was replaced by an independent statutory authority known as the Tertiary Education Quality Standards Agency (TEQSA).

TEQSA's objects are articulated in the *Tertiary Education Quality and Standards Agency Act 2011* and create clear links between higher education quality, market protection and economic competitiveness. The TEQSA registers and evaluates the performance of higher education providers against the Higher Education Standards Framework (HESF) developed and maintained by the Higher Education Standards Panel (HESP). The purpose of these higher education standards is to ensure that the quality of the teaching and research infrastructure is sufficient to ensure appropriate outcomes for graduates. The establishment of a national accreditation and quality assurance system and the setting of external national standards removed the institutional discretion and control previously enjoyed by universities.

The second consequence is that higher education began to operate in an increasingly competitive environment, especially to attract students whose fees now account for the bulk of higher education funding. In this setting information from quality assurance agencies as well as a range of other metrics have become important indicators of higher education provision and sources of competitive advantage. This in turn has prompted independent guides to universities as well as national and international league tables and rankings using various metrics. One study suggests 'student recruitment, student quality, teaching quality, research income, research outputs, research impacts are just a few of the metrics used' (Airey et al., 2015b, p. 141).

So in a fairly short period of time universities have moved from an environment in which the major control over their operations was through public funding mechanisms, with governments, for example, putting a ceiling on total funding or student fee levels, to one in which such funding controls are being relaxed, as in Australia, but at the same time explicit and implicit controls over operations are being introduced. The explicit controls relate, above all, to external scrutiny of quality and standards. Implicit influences flow from the various metrics and performance indicators that are now publicly available. Together these provide a fairly formidable set of controls that are not only determining the shape and operations of higher education institutions but also pose threats to the future of those institutions and subjects that show signs of underperformance. The combination of external scrutiny and competitive pressures has transformed the standards and quality assurance environment for all aspects of higher education, including tourism education.

3.   STANDARDS-BASED QUALITY FRAMEWORKS

Although there are frequent references to standards in the higher education context there is little consensus about what they are. Thompson-Whiteside (2012) explains that academic standards can be viewed either as a set of general principles and processes or as a set of explicit thresholds. Although most education systems use a combination of principles and thresholds, he observes that anglophone countries have tended to emphasize explicit threshold standards. This emphasis may have historic origins, as the notion of standards appears to originate from the use of the 'Kings Standard' in sixteenth-century England (Thompson-Whiteside, 2012). In spite of this, when applied to an academic context the meaning of the term is often opaque and not well understood outside the academic discourse.

According to Sadler (1987, p. 194) academic standards can be defined as 'a definite level of excellence or attainment or the recognized measure of what is adequate for some purpose, established by authority, custom or consensus'. The UK QAA (2013b, p. 5) defines threshold academic standards as 'the minimum acceptable level of achievement that a student has to demonstrate to be eligible for an academic award'. This definition is more focused on student achievement but the QAA then go on to define academic standards as being 'the standards that individual degree-awarding bodies set and maintain for the award of their academic credit or qualifications' (p. 5). Academic 'quality' can be defined in many ways and varies according to the perspective of different stakeholders (Harvey and Green, 1993). However, in the UK higher education context academic quality is 'concerned with how well the learning opportunities made available to students enable them to achieve their award' (Quality Assurance Agency for Higher Education, 2013a, p. 1).

In Australia, the HESP describe threshold standards as codifying the minimum standard of provision of higher education that is acceptable in Australia, but offers no definition for 'standards'. However, the TEQSA (2015, p. 1) does define academic standards as 'an agreed specification (such as a defined benchmark or indicator) that is used as a definition of a level of performance or achievement, rule, or guideline'. The agency further notes that standards may be applied to academic outcomes, such as student or graduate achievement of core discipline knowledge and skills (usually referred to as threshold learning outcomes), or to academic processes such as student selection, teaching, research supervision, and assessment. The key operational elements of most academic standards are criteria (or qualities) and specified minimum levels of performance (Sadler, 2014). These concepts of standards and quality provide the key starting points for the assurance of education provision, whether by national bodies or accreditation agencies. In setting out their dimensions and the expected performance levels the various agencies have a major influence on university operations.

In the case of the UK, the QAA has created a three-part quality code relating to standards, quality and information. For standards this has involved setting out a Framework for Higher Education Qualifications (FHEQ) at a number of levels, from Certificate to Doctoral, each of which represents a distinct level of intellectual achievement based on outcomes and illustrated by a qualification descriptor for that level. For the UK these in turn are aligned with the *Framework for Qualifications of the European Higher Education Area* (the QF-EHEA) (Quality Assurance Agency for Higher Education, 2013b). The generic framework is then supplemented by what are referred to as subject benchmark statements that 'make explicit the nature and characteristics of awards in a specific subject area and set out the attributes and capabilities of graduates in that subject' (Quality Assurance Agency for Higher Education, 2013b, p. 18). Although, notwithstanding various critiques (Botterill and Tribe, 2000), as the QAA emphasizes (2013b, p. 19):

> Subject benchmark statements . . . describe what gives the subject its coherence and identity, the main characteristics of programmes, and the nature of teaching, learning and assessment in that subject or subject area . . . they do not represent a national curriculum in a subject area; rather, they allow for flexibility and innovation in programme design within an overall framework.

For tourism, the current benchmark statement makes the comment that 'Most programmes have broadened from their vocational origins to embrace wider social science issues relating to the nature, impacts and meanings of tourism' (Quality Assurance Agency, 2008, p. 12), as reflected in the broad statement about the content of degree programs in tourism. The UK Tourism Benchmark Statement (Quality Assurance Agency, 2008, p. 13) states that degrees in tourism often involve the following:

- a consideration of the concepts and characteristics of tourism as an area of academic and applied study;
- an examination of the nature and characteristics of tourists;
- an analysis of tourism in the communities and environments that it affects;
- a study of the products, structure, operations and interactions within the tourism industry.

Turning to quality, the QAA (Quality Assurance Agency for Higher Education, 2013a) has established an 11-part Quality Code for Higher Education that sets out the: '*Expectations* that higher education providers are required to meet to ensure: that appropriate and effective teaching, support, assessment and learning resources are provided for students; that the learning opportunities provided are monitored; and that the provider considers how to improve them.'

These include for example the requirement that universities have systems in place for the sound design, development and approval of programs and their subsequent monitoring and review as well as for the recruitment, selection and admission of students and arrangements to deal with appeals and complaints. As a key part of this, the expectations include the requirement that institutions use external reference points, including the involvement of external examiners and advisers. Specifically, in relation to learning and teaching, the code includes the expectation that:

> Higher education providers, working with their staff, students and other stakeholders, articulate and systematically review and enhance the provision of learning opportunities and teaching practices, so that every student is enabled to develop as an independent learner, study their chosen subject(s) in depth and enhance their capacity for analytical, critical and creative thinking. (Quality Assurance Agency for Higher Education, 2012a)

The final part of the QAA quality code relates to the provision of information with the 'expectation that higher education providers make available valid, reliable useful and accessible information about their provision' (Quality Assurance Agency for Higher Education, 2012a).

Together, these three elements provide a very full quality assurance context for universities in the UK. In operational terms the process involves a self-evaluation followed by a visit by QAA appointed auditors, typically senior academics from other institutions, who make judgments about the provision against the various expectations, and resulting in a published report. This has led one commentator to suggest that 'it is difficult to overestimate the influence of QAA' (Robbins, 2005, p. 451).

Australia has also developed a tripartite quality assurance system consisting of the Higher Education Standards Framework (HESF), the Australian Qualifications Framework (AQF) and discipline-based threshold learning outcomes (TLOs). The AQF plays a similar role to the UK's FHEQ and both frameworks are examples of the various national qualifications frameworks (NQFs) that have been established in over 140 countries around the world (Jarvis, 2014; McBride and Keevy, 2010). The AQF establishes a standard for Australian qualifications by setting out a taxonomy of levels and qualification types defined by learning outcomes. The HESF plays a similar role to the UK Quality Code for Higher Education. The HESF was established in 2011 and consisted of 'threshold' and 'non-threshold' standards. The threshold standards included provider registration standards, provider category standards, provider course accreditation standards and qualification standards. These were revised in 2015 to remove the concept of non-threshold standards and to introduce a new framework consisting of the seven major domains summarized in Table 35.1.

As was the case in the UK, Australia also set out discipline-specific TLOs, which fulfill a similar role to the subject benchmark statements. The Learning and Teaching Academic Standards (LTAS) Project was established in 2009 by the Australian Learning

Table 35.1   Australian Higher Education Standards Framework

Domain	Description
Student participation & attainment	The education-related experiences of students from admission through to attainment of a certified qualification(s)
Learning environment	The nature and quality of the learning environment provided, whether physical, on or off campus, virtual or blended
Teaching	The academic activities of the higher education provider that guide
Research and research training	and facilitate learning and, in the case of research and research training, contribute to new knowledge as well.
Institutional quality assurance	The mechanisms that are established by the higher education provider to assure itself of the quality of the higher education it provides, and
Governance and accountability	to maintain effective governance of its operations.
Representation, Information and Information Management	The higher education provider's representation of itself to prospective students and others, the provision of information to prospective and enrolled students to enable informed participation in their educational experience, and the information management systems that support the higher education provider's higher education operations.

Source: Higher Education Standards Panel (2014).

and Teaching Council (ALTC), now the Australian Government Office for Learning and Teaching (OLT), with the aim to develop threshold learning outcomes across nine disciplines. The threshold learning outcomes for tourism, hospitality and events were developed with the support of the OLT in 2015 and include descriptors for each field arranged into five domains: service and experience design, interdisciplinary inquiry, problem solving, collaboration and professional responsibility (see Table 35.2). Unlike the UK Benchmark Statements, the Australian TLOs were developed for both bachelor's and master's coursework qualifications. The Australian approach also places greater emphasis on capabilities and the application of skills rather than knowledge. The development of discipline-based standards and benchmarks provides an opportunity to legitimize newer fields such as tourism by delineating similarities and differences with other fields of study.

The Australian threshold learning outcomes and the UK benchmark statements both describe academic standards in terms of learning outcomes and therefore focus only on the achievement of skills and capabilities of graduates. In addition to these national systems, there are other agencies such as accreditation and international bodies that have their own systems and quality assurance regimes. Some tourism programs operating in business schools and departments for example are accredited by the Association to Advance Collegiate Schools of Business (AACSB) and/or the EFMD Quality Improvement System (EQUIS). AACSB has been accrediting programs since 1919 and currently operates with 14 standards designed to 'to drive innovation, engagement, and impact with students, employers, and the communities they serve' (AACSB, 2013). The standards relate to strategic management and innovation; students, faculty and professional staff; learning and teaching; and academic and professional engagement. For its part, EQUIS covers similar aspects but places a stronger emphasis on internationalization. Turning to international

Table 35.2   Australian threshold learning outcomes for tourism

Domain	Bachelor's Graduates	Master's Graduates
Service and Experience Design	Graduates will be able to apply knowledge and skills to design and deliver sustainable tourism services and experiences.	Graduates will be able to apply advanced knowledge and skills to design and deliver meaningful, high-quality, sustainable tourism services and experiences.
Interdisciplinary Inquiry	Graduates will be able to integrate a broad and coherent elementary, theoretical and operational knowledge of tourism as an interdisciplinary field of research and practice.	Graduates will be able to demonstrate a critical, advanced, contemporary and integrated theoretical and operational knowledge of tourism as an interdisciplinary field of research and practice.
Collaboration	Graduates will be able to work together with key stakeholders to acquire and convey knowledge and ideas effectively to achieve shared goals.	Graduates will be able to work together with diverse stakeholders to integrate complex knowledge and convey ideas effectively to achieve shared goals in ambiguous contexts.
Problem Solving	Graduates will be able to apply cognitive skills to collect, analyze and synthesize information to develop and evaluate solutions for straightforward tourism problems.	Graduates will be able to apply cognitive, creative and reflective skills to collect, analyze and synthesize information to generate, implement and evaluate new solutions for complex tourism problems.
Professional Responsibility	Graduates will be able to critically reflect on their own conduct, to improve their own interpersonal and operational skills and knowledge, in light of their role in tourism and its impact on the economy, environment and society.	Graduates will be able to critically reflect on the performance of self and others, and demonstrate initiative and professional responsibility in dynamic settings, in light of their role in tourism and its impact on the economy, environment and society.

Source: Whitelaw et al. (2015).

systems in tourism, TEDQUAL (Tourism Education Quality) is the longest established. This was created in 1998 by the UNWTO specifically to provide a quality accreditation system for the growing number of institutions offering tourism programs, with the specific objective to improve the quality of tourism education, training and research programs. This uses five areas of analysis to evaluate the programs:

> the coherence of the plan of studies; infrastructure and pedagogical support; policies, tools and support mechanisms for administrative management; the existence of transparent mechanisms for the selection of the faculty and favourable conditions for their professional development; and the relevance of the content of the programme of studies with respect to the needs of the tourism sector. (UNWTO Themis Foundation, n.d.)

The last point about the needs of the tourism sector provides a distinctive feature of this accreditation, with an obvious emphasis on the vocational aspects of tourism education.

This point is also present in the other international tourism accrediting body, THE-ICE, established in 2004. As Airey et al. (2015b, p. 141) report:

> The International Centre of Excellence in Tourism and Hospitality Education based in Australia has also emerged as an international accreditation body that provides 'confidential benchmarking and raising awareness of the quality of our accredited members to future students. Accreditation . . . focuses on an institution's mission, goals, and aims and how these are delivered through its programs, graduate attributes, facilities, teaching staff, internationalization policies, and industry engagement.' (THE-ICE, 2012)

Like the other accrediting bodies identified here, THE-ICE operates through self and peer review involving a form of written self-evaluation against the criteria or standards followed by a peer visit. Attaining one or more of these international professional accreditations is often seen as a proxy measure for reputation and quality.

4. THE STUDENT VOICE

As a part of the work on standards and quality, most accreditation agencies and systems pay particular attention to the views of the students. For example, the Quality Code of the QAA in the UK includes a specific section on student engagement (Quality Assurance Agency for Higher Education, 2012b), which outlines expectations about the institutions' activities in collecting, reporting and responding to the comments made by students. The rights and needs of students in Australia are also explicitly acknowledged in the TEQSA's objects and the Higher Education Standards Framework. Similarly, most accreditation visits will spend time gathering the views of students. This engagement with students has also been taken a stage further in some jurisdictions in the form of national student surveys in which students are asked to comment on various aspects of their university experience, with the results published nationally. For example, the Higher Education Funding Council for universities in England introduced such a survey for all final year undergraduates in 2005 (Higher Education Funding Council for England, 2014). In this, students are asked to rate the performance of their institution on a number of criteria: teaching; assessment and feedback; academic support; organization and management; learning resources; personal development; and overall satisfaction. Similarly, Graduate Careers Australia surveys students four months after graduation in that country, and other initiatives such as the International Student Barometer, which, as its name suggests, surveys and makes comparisons internationally, are used extensively by education providers.

Given the increasingly competitive environment, such surveys, published nationally and internationally and widely used by the press and other agencies to construct league tables, have begun to play a major part in the operation of universities. As with accreditation they form a part of the controlling environment within which institutions operate, and as with accreditation exercises, institutions cannot afford to perform badly. As a result, great attention is paid to the various criteria against which institutions are assessed, with some institutions including achievement in the associated league tables as a part of their strategic objectives.

5. THE RESEARCH DIMENSION

Increased scrutiny is not confined solely to learning, teaching and students. For similar reasons associated with the growth of higher education, its higher profile in government and public consciousness, and increased competition for funding, the research activities of universities have also come in for greater scrutiny. In the UK this has taken the form of a series of Research Assessment Exercises (RAE). The most recent version in 2014 was named the Research Excellence Framework (REF). These exercises were started in the UK in 1986 to provide a basis for the allocation of research funding for universities at a time when budgets were restricted. Subsequently they have been repeated by the UK Higher Education Funding Councils approximately every five years. The criteria on which the peer judgments are made have varied across the years but have regularly included the quality of research outputs, especially in academic journals, success levels in research funding and the research environment, including that for PhD students, and for 2014 the impact of research was included. Similar research quality assessments are conducted in many other countries, including Australia, where tourism research is evaluated as part of the Excellence in Research for Australia (ERA) initiative. A related process includes the ranking of tourism journals based on a range of quality indicators. Well established rankings related to tourism include the UK Association of Business Schools Journal Rankings and the Australian Business Deans Council Rankings.

6. HOW IS TOURISM PERFORMING?

The scrutiny from accreditation bodies, by students and in connection with research activities noted above all provide a lot of data about universities. To these must be added a range of other information required notably by government bodies. So in addition to headline information such as student satisfaction, accreditation results and research income, universities now also produce a wealth of other data on, for example, student entry qualifications, student performance, progression and degree results, student progression to employment, faculty profiles, qualifications, publications, citations and awards and levels and patterns of university spending. For the UK many of these data are collected and regularly reported by the Higher Education Statistics Agency (HESA) (Higher Education Statistics Agency, 2014). Together they provide the basis for the various league tables that purport to measure and compare performance by universities and it is on the basis of such data that attempts can be made to explore how different subjects are performing.

In their recent study of this topic for tourism, Airey et al. (2015b) point to the extent to which, in a competitive environment, the relative performance of disciplines and fields will influence their survival simply because heads of institutions will not be supportive of areas that weaken overall university performance. Using the metrics of student numbers, quality and satisfaction, research outputs and income and impact, they come to the conclusion that the performance of tourism is mixed. While there are some tourism centers that are performing well with strong recruitment, good levels of student satisfaction, good research outputs and student employment success, generally student quality, research income and impacts are relatively poor and in their words tourism also 'suffers from a long tail of relatively poor performance' (Airey et al., 2015b, p. 147).

The outcome of the increased scrutiny and competition for tourism therefore is challenging. Student satisfaction with tourism programs is generally not out of line with other subjects, a fact which Airey et al. (2015b, p. 144) suggest may be influenced by 'the attention given over many years by tourism teachers to the development of the curriculum and to their approaches to learning and teaching'. The QAA has now ended its scrutiny of individual programs, focusing instead on whole institutions, but in its last overview report related to tourism programs, produced in 2001 and based on 109 institutions, they also came to the view that the field performed strongly in learning and teaching. In one of their conclusions they commented: 'The quality of teaching is consistently high. It is characterized by a rich diversity of approaches, including many industry supported initiatives' (Quality Assurance Agency, 2001, p. 1). In the meantime, the increased scrutiny has exposed some of the weaknesses of the subject area. At a time of intense competition between institutions, weaknesses that affect reputation are dangerous.

7.   IMPLICATIONS FOR TEACHING AND LEARNING IN TOURISM

It is obvious that higher education now operates within a complex network of quality frameworks and controls. Table 35.3 attempts to summarize these with a number of international examples. Some of these quality frameworks are voluntary and provide reputational benefits but others are mandatory, in the sense that governments can withdraw funding, impose quotas and in some cases revoke an institution's right to issue diplomas and degrees.

These observations and examples have significant implications for the ways in which universities operate – not least in the resources that have had to be devoted by institutions to ensuring that the requirements of the accrediting bodies are met. This is no easy task, since a single academic program may be subject to several different accreditation and national standards frameworks. For example, programs in Australia must demonstrate alignment with the AQF, the HESF and the recently developed tourism, hospitality and event TLOs. Given that some tourism programs are structured as majors within a broader business degree, there may also be a need to attend to TLOs developed for accounting, finance, marketing and economics. In addition, many programs are subject to AACSB, EQUIS, UNWTO and/or THE-ICE accreditation. However, the remainder of this discussion will explore the implications of national qualifications frameworks and discipline-based standards as these impact most directly on teaching and learning. These implications relate broadly to the activities of setting the standards, integrating these standards into the curriculum, assessing student achievement of standards and evidencing this achievement.

Brennan et al. (1996) have argued that the setting of national and international standards has implications for power, control and autonomy in higher education. Indeed, following Foucault (2007) it could be argued that regulatory quality assurance frameworks and standards create a mechanism for exercising political power, control and surveillance. As a result, externally imposed standards, performance-based evaluations and quality

Table 35.3   Quality assurance frameworks and controls in higher education

Instrument	Examples
National Quality Assurance Standards	Quality Code for Higher Education (UK)
	Higher Education Standards Framework (Australia)
Qualifications Frameworks	Framework for Higher Education Qualifications (UK)
	Australian Qualifications Framework
	New Zealand Qualifications Framework
	Canadian Degree Qualifications Framework
	National Qualifications Framework (South Africa)
	European Qualifications Framework
Discipline-based Benchmarks and Standards	Subject Benchmark Statements (UK)
	Discipline Threshold Learning Outcomes (Australia)
	ANECA Título de Grado en Turismo (Spain)
	Tuning Tourism Competences (Russia, Middle East & North Africa)
Market Feedback Instruments	Times Higher Education World University Rankings
	QS World University Rankings
	Academic Ranking of World Universities (ARWU)
	National Survey of Student Engagement (NSSE) (USA)
	Course Experience Questionnaire (Australia)
	International Student Barometer
National Research Assessments	UK Research Excellence Framework (REF)
	Excellence in Research for Australia (ERA)
	Performance-Based Research Framework (PBRF) (New Zealand)
	Evaluation of Research Quality (Italy)
	Fundação para a Ciência e a Tecnologia (FCT) (Portugal)
Accreditation Systems	EFMD Quality Improvement System (EQUIS)
	Association to Advance Collegiate Schools of Business (AACSB)
	United Nations World Tourism Organization – Tourism Education Quality (UNWTO-TEDQUAL)
	Tourism and Hospitality Education International Centre for Excellence (THE-ICE)

assurance audits are often perceived as a threat to institutional autonomy and academic professionalism and there are several accounts of academic resistance (Anderson, 2006; Lucas, 2014; Newton, 2002). Individual academics may feel that they have lost control over the setting of assessment tasks and the awarding of grades. The counter argument to this view is that standards should be developed, monitored and assessed by the academic community to ensure a shared understanding of what the standards are and how they can be situated in the curriculum. This raises further issues regarding the codification and interpretation of standards (Sadler, 2014). According to Sadler (2014, p. 287), academic standards 'are inherently fuzzy and open to interpretation, and the minimum required levels are invariably expressed in relative rather than absolute terms'.

The embedding of standards into the curriculum often requires program-wide curriculum redesign. This entails change and can be difficult to achieve in an academic environment because, as noted earlier, external standards may be perceived as eroding academic freedom and trust. The focus on standards and quality has served to ensure that they are a high priority for those delivering programs but at the same time they have restricted the development of subject areas. For example, with reference to the UK benchmarking exercise, Botterill and Tribe (2000) suggest that this is unduly restrictive, especially for a subject area like tourism, which they see as being in a pre-paradigmatic state. In a similar vein Airey et al. (2015a, p. 7) note the paradox created by this sort of control, commenting that, 'at the time of increasing competition for students during which institutions seek ways to differentiate themselves, much of the international impetus seems to have prompted standardization'. They refer not just to the extent of programs being delivered in English rather than in local tongues but also to all the national and international accreditation initiatives that almost inevitably tend toward a standardizing template against which to judge programs with the result that all programs become very similar and operate within a restrictive framework. They also point to the international dimension of this, with initiatives such as the Tuning Project producing a European Qualifications Framework linking the qualification systems of participating countries (Tuning, 2010). This international context has also been picked up by Harrison (2015) from the perspective of non-Western countries which also follow a similar heavily Western-oriented model.

These concerns about standardization are entirely valid and they raise some interesting questions about the level of detail specified in threshold learning outcomes and bench-mark statements. Less prescriptive statements allow for greater diversity but outcomes that are too liberal may not allow for meaningful benchmarking and comparison. The approach adopted in Australia when designing the tourism, hospitality and events TLOs was guided by a mantra of 'standards not standardization'. To understand this, consider that most countries have strict standards for road vehicles and yet streets and highways are filled with a wide variety of roadworthy vehicles of different shapes, colors and sizes. The *raison d'être* for the creation of the Australian academic standards in tourism was to ensure that graduates, and by implication their qualifications, met clearly defined minimum benchmarks in terms of knowledge, skills and capabilities. Graduates must be 'fit for purpose' and this was determined by seeking consensus amongst key stakeholders (that is, educators, government agencies and employers). This approach emphasizes outcomes rather than processes and inputs and is therefore not concerned with how the standards are achieved, provided they are being met.

With this in mind, the development of the Australian TLOs for tourism, hospitality and events was guided by the following eight principles:

1. The learning standards reflect threshold not aspirational outcomes.
2. The learning standards will not provide guidance about either the design or how learning outcomes will be assessed.
3. The number of learning standards will be limited to the minimum necessary to avoid compromising provider diversity while still assuring public confidence.
4. The learning standards will acknowledge the authority of the AQF and international standards.
5. The learning standards will be developed using an evidence-based approach relevant to contemporary practice and will be appropriately documented.
6. The process for standards development will be collaborative, iterative and incorporate feedback from multiple sources including industry and academia.

7. Each learning outcome will incorporate an appropriate illustrative example for each field of study.
8. The threshold learning outcomes will be interdependent and interlinked (Whitelaw et al., 2015).

These principles allow individual institutions to differentiate themselves in terms of assessment and pedagogy but do impose some constraints on the curriculum. While institutions can adopt a specialist focus (for example, tropical tourism, destination management, ecotourism) the standards do specify some of the core curriculum areas and the level at which graduates are expected to perform. In Australia, these standards are minimum thresholds and therefore institutions can also differentiate themselves by exceeding the standards in one or more domains.

Once standards are embedded they must be sustained and this necessitates a system of internal monitoring to ensure that the standards are being enacted. This is typically achieved using a curriculum mapping approach. Curriculum mapping usually highlights the points at which the curriculum aligns with the standards and can be a useful tool for identifying gaps, duplication and opportunities for scaffolding learning outcomes. A robust curriculum mapping process usually involves vigorous debate and agreement between educators about how to embed and assess standards across the curriculum.

Careful consideration is needed to determine when and how the achievement of standards is assessed. Curriculum mapping exercises often include assessment mapping, to identify the points at which learners are required to demonstrate the achievement of standards. Given that many standards are now concerned with threshold learning outcomes, standards are often assessed towards the end of a program. In this context, the use of capstone units that allow students to demonstrate the attainment of several standards has become more widespread.

The final activity involves the collection of evidence so that an institution is able to satisfy external quality assurance agencies that graduates have achieved the standards. Various approaches are used in different countries to assure compliance with standards, including external audits, external review, peer review of student assessment, moderation and calibration, benchmarking, performance indicators and surveys of students, graduates and employers (Rowlands, 2012; Sadler, 2014). A full review of these approaches is beyond the scope of this chapter but it is important to note that these assurance of learning processes impose an enormous compliance burden which arguably detracts from time that could be spent on teaching and learning innovation. In a competitive environment an institution cannot afford to fail an accreditation visit. As a result, many academic forums for discussing and debating teaching and learning matters have become more focused on compliance and accountability rather than innovation (Rowlands, 2012).

8. CONCLUSION

In some ways the development of tourism and the development of the regulatory regimes over the past few decades can been seen as representing two almost contradictory processes. Tourism, as a new field of study, developed with the freeing of higher education from its more traditional origins with the creation of new universities, new programs of study, a new and much larger cohort of students and new approaches to teaching and researching. In other words, it developed in a new world of more apparent freedom in universities. On the other hand, the regulatory regimes can be seen as representing an opposite trend of restricting freedoms. Of course, as noted earlier in this chapter, in many ways it was the growth of higher education that prompted the regulation, and all the evidence suggests that both are now permanent features of the higher education environment. The key issue now is how the universities and others involved in higher education respond to their position between these two trends. In stark terms they can use their freedoms, for example, to develop new programs, reach new student groups, provide new approaches to learning, and set up commercial ventures or they can let the regulatory environment restrict their activities, above all by chasing performance metrics.

So far it looks as if the regulatory regime is winning with, for example, many universities setting their future directions to meet particular performance metrics and setting up internal regulatory systems that restrict the scope of academic decision-making and innovation. For a relatively new subject area like tourism this creates a number of dangers and missed opportunities. The dangers come in part from the extent to which many centers of tourism study have not yet established themselves as high performers, especially in relation to research outputs and income. To some extent, the growing emphasis on such output and income sets up a tension between the research and teaching roles of academics, with the former taking priority. The missed opportunities relate to the extent to which tourism's strengths as an interdisciplinary and multi-method area of study are being underexploited in providing an education that addresses the needs of an increasingly complex post-industrial world. This is a theme picked up by Dredge et al. (2015, p. 547) who, recognizing the constraints that they describe as 'the marketization of higher education, the industrialization of teaching and the neoliberal zeal for performance measures, audits and rankings', nevertheless remain hopeful of tourism as a subject that can 'break down disciplinary boundaries, professional program structures, and the artificial divides between theory and practice, classroom and field work, student and teacher, town and gown'. For them, this is where the strength of tourism lies in the academy. There is a real risk that the wrong approach to standards, benchmarks and quality assurance will provide a hostile environment for this new world of tourism education. Standards and benchmarking activities must balance the need for quality assurance with the need for differentiation and innovation. Quality assurance standards must be framed so that they empower tourism educators to innovate and improve the outcomes of teaching and learning.

Standards-based regulatory frameworks have been more successful in some countries than others but are unlikely to be disbanded in the near future. The frameworks in countries like the UK and Australia now have a long history of evolution and they continue to be tweaked and refined to reduce some of the problems identified in this chapter. Attention has also moved to the international harmonization of standards and attempts to create regional and supranational qualifications frameworks (Jarvis, 2014). The most ambitious of these have been the Tuning Project, the European Qualifications Framework (EQF), and the OECD's Assessment of Higher Education Learning Outcomes (AHELO). Future refinement will also need to be responsive to the growing presence of private education providers, off-shore campuses and hybrid models of education and business (Coates, 2014). These developments provide a backdrop for the big challenges facing tourism education as it enters its sixth decade of development. The academic community should be given an opportunity to contribute to the setting and maintenance of standards to ensure that interdisciplinary fields such as tourism are clearly delineated and not restricted by old disciplinary paradigms. At the same time, the standards themselves provide a basis for robust academic discussion and debate about the performance of our graduates. Scrutiny and competition have brought the subject's strengths and weaknesses to the fore. The challenge is to ensure that the strengths are appropriately acknowledged and the weaknesses are addressed.

REFERENCES

AACSB (2013), '2013 standards: A bold evolution for the global business revolution', accessed 15 August 2014 at http://www.aacsb.edu/en/accreditation/standards/2013-standards.aspx.

Airey, D. (2005), 'Growth and development', in D. Airey and J. Tribe (eds), *An International Handbook of Tourism Education* (pp. 13–24), Oxford: Elsevier.

Airey, D., Dredge, D. and Gross, M. (2015a), 'Tourism, hospitality and events education in an age of change', in D. Dredge, D. Airey and M. Gross (eds), *The Routledge Handbook of Tourism and Hospitality Education* (pp. 3–14), Abingdon: Routledge.

Airey, D., Tribe, J., Benckendorff, P. and Xiao, H. (2015b), 'The managerial gaze: The long tail of tourism education and research', *Journal of Travel Research*, **54** (2), 139–51.

Anderson, G. (2006), 'Assuring quality/resisting quality assurance: Academics' responses to "quality" in some Australian universities', *Quality in Higher Education*, **12** (2), 161–73.

Botterill, D. and Tribe, J. (2000), 'Benchmarking and the Higher Education Curriculum', The National Liaison Group for Higher Education in Tourism Guideline No. 9, London, accessed 15 March 2009 at http://www.athe.org.uk/publications/.

Bradley, D., Noonan, P., Nugent, H. and Scales, B. (2008), *Review of Australian Higher Education*, Canberra: Department of Education Employment and Workplace Relations.

Brennan, J., Frazer, M., Middlehurst, R., Silver, H. and Williams, R. (1996), *Changing Conceptions of Academic Standards*, Milton Keynes: The Open University.

Coates, H. (2014), 'Threshold quality parameters in hybrid higher education', *Higher Education*, **68** (4), 577–90.

Department of Education and Training (2015), 'Selected higher education statistics: 2013 student data', accessed 16 March 2015 at https://education.gov.au/selected-higher-education-statistics-2013-student-data.

Department of Education Training and Youth Affairs (2001), *Higher Education Students Time Series Tables*, Canberra: Commonwealth of Australia.

Dill, D.D. (2014), 'Ensuring academic standards in US higher education', *Change: The Magazine of Higher Learning*, **46** (3), 53–9.

Dredge, D., Airey, D. and Gross, M.J. (2015), 'Creating the future: Tourism, hospitality and events education in a post-industrial, post-disciplinary world', in D. Dredge, D. Airey and M.J. Gross (eds), *The Routledge Handbook of Tourism Education* (pp. 535–50), Abingdon: Routledge.

Foucault, M. (2007), *Security, Territory, Population: Lectures at the College de France, 1977–78*, Basingstoke: Palgrave Macmillan.

Harrison, D. (2015), 'Educating tourism students in the South Pacific: Changing cultures, changing economies', in D. Dredge, D. Airey and M. Gross (eds), *Routledge Handbook of Tourism and Hospitality Education* (pp. 225–34), London: Routledge.

Harvey, L. and Green, D. (1993), 'Defining quality', *Assessment and Evaluation in Higher Education*, **18** (1), 9–34.

Higher Education Funding Council for England (2014), 'National student survey', accessed 16 August 2014 at http://www.hefce.ac.uk/whatwedo/lt/publicinfo/nss/.

Higher Education Statistics Agency (2014), 'Higher Education Statistics Agency', accessed 16 August 2014 at https://www.hesa.ac.uk/.

Higher Education Statistics Agency (2015), 'Statistical release 210: Student enrolments and qualifications, higher education student enrolments and qualifications obtained at higher education providers in the United Kingdom 2013/14', Cheltenham: Higher Education Statistics Agency, accessed at https://www.hesa.ac.uk/sfr210.

Jarvis, D.S.L. (2014), 'Regulating higher education: Quality assurance and neo-liberal managerialism in higher education – A critical introduction', *Policy and Society*, **33** (3), 155–66.

Lucas, L. (2014), 'Academic resistance to quality assurance processes in higher education in the UK', *Policy and Society*, **33** (3), 215–24.

McBride, V. and Keevy, J. (2010), 'Is the national qualifications framework a broken promise? A dialogue', *Journal of Educational Change*, **11** (2), 193–203.

Newton, J. (2002), 'Views from below: Academics coping with quality', *Quality in Higher Education*, **8** (1), 39–61.

Norton, A. (2014), *Unleashing Student Demand by Ending Number Controls in Australia: An Incomplete Experiment*, Oxford: Higher Education Policy Institute.

Office for National Statistics (2002), *Students in Further and Higher Education: By Type of Course and Gender, 1970–71 to 1997/98, Social Trends 30*, London: Office for National Statistics.

Quality Assurance Agency (2001), *Subject Overview Report*, Gloucester: Quality Assurance Agency for Higher Education.

Quality Assurance Agency (2008), 'Subject benchmark statement, hospitality, leisure, sport and tourism', accessed 13 March 2014 at http://www.qaa.ac.uk/Publications/InformationAndGuidance/Pages/Subject-benchmark-statement-Hospitality-leisure-sport-tourism-2008.aspx.

Quality Assurance Agency for Higher Education (2012a), 'UK Quality Code – Part C: Information about higher education provision', accessed 15 August 2014 at http://www.qaa.ac.uk/assuring-standards-and-quality/the-quality-code/quality-code-part-c.

Quality Assurance Agency for Higher Education (2012b), 'UK Quality Code for Higher Education – Chapter B5: Student engagement', accessed 16 August 2014 at http://www.qaa.ac.uk/en/Publications/Documents/quality-code-B5.pdf.

Quality Assurance Agency for Higher Education (2013a), 'Safeguarding standards and improving the quality of UK higher education: UK Quality Code – Part B assuring and enhancing academic quality', accessed 14 August 2014 at http://www.qaa.ac.uk/assuring-standards-and-quality/the-quality-code/quality-code-part-b.

Quality Assurance Agency for Higher Education (2013b), *UK Quality Code for Higher Education Part A: Setting and Maintaining Academic Standards*, Gloucester: QAA.

Robbins, D. (2005), 'Quality assurance', in D. Airey and J. Tribe (eds), *An International Handbook of Tourism Education* (pp. 451–68), Oxford: Elsevier.

Rowlands, J. (2012), 'Accountability, quality assurance and performativity: The changing role of the academic board', *Quality in Higher Education*, **18** (1), 97–110.

Sadler, D.R. (1987), 'Specifying and promulgating achievement standards', *Oxford Review of Education*, **13** (2), 191–209.

Sadler, D.R. (2014), 'The futility of attempting to codify academic achievement standards', *Higher Education*, **67** (3), 273–88.

Shahjahan, R.A. (2012), 'From "no" to "yes": Postcolonial perspectives on resistance to neoliberal higher education', *Discourse: Studies in the Cultural Politics of Education*, **35** (2), 219–32.

TEQSA (2015), 'TEQSA glossary of terms', accessed 15 March 2015 at http://www.teqsa.gov.au/glossary.

THE-ICE (2012), 'International Centre of Excellence in Tourism and Hospitality Education (THE-ICE)', accessed 12 September 2012 at http://www.the-ice.org/about-us/who-we-are.

Thompson-Whiteside, S. (2012), 'Setting standards in Australian higher education?', *Journal of Institutional Research*, **17** (1), 27–38.

Tuning (2010), *Tuning Sectoral Framework for Social Sciences*, Bilbao: University of Deusto.

UNWTO Themis Foundation (n.d.), 'Certification System TedQual', accessed 15 August 2014 at http://dtx-tq4w60xqpw.cloudfront.net/sites/all/files/docpdf/tqcertificacion-en_0.pdf.

Whitelaw, P.A., Benckendorff, P., Gross, M., Mair, J. and Jose, P. (2015), *Tourism, Hospitality and Events Standards*, Sydney: Australian Government Office for Learning and Teaching.

36 Quality versus standards: challenges in quality assurance in tourism education
Georgios C. Papageorgiou

1. INTRODUCTION

For all the tools, theories, examples, analyses, knowledge, direction, guidelines and resources that are at the disposal of tourism academics and educational establishments, it is perhaps a frequent realization that somehow designing an effective tourism education system, or even program, is difficult not only due to the inherent complexity of the task, but also to potentially conflicting priorities among the several stakeholders involved (Dredge et al., 2012). Research on the wider subject of tourism education, and indeed several of the chapters in this volume, attest to the various viewpoints that, according to different studies and authors, need to be considered – yet are not necessarily compatible. As a brief indication, key perspectives and considerations should include the orientation of the educational establishments, the regulatory framework within which these operate, the needs of the tourism and hospitality industry, the characteristics of the learners themselves, the definition and design of educational content, its effective delivery by qualified faculty, the assurance of quality throughout the educational process, the consistency and comparability of educational standards and outcomes across systems and establishments, and the dual imperative of commercial as well as educational success. The intentionally convoluted character of the above list should highlight that a realistic understanding of the influence and concomitant implications of such factors is essential in the design and delivery of a tourism education 'product' that will be deemed appropriate or successful on numerous different counts. Consequently, the criteria by which success is judged will vary wildly among the different stakeholders involved, while the fact that many of the highlighted factors are outside the direct control of educational establishments adds further complexity.

Mapping the web of influences, priorities, restrictions and challenges that interfere with the effectiveness of academic practice could lead to potentially useful prescriptions about tourism education design and management, and so the first part of the chapter is primarily intended to introduce the context within which the key area of discussion is located. However, the main focus of the discussion is on the conceptual as well as practical distinction between academic quality standards and the ideal outcomes that these standards aim to promote. The chapter argues that there are various reasons why this distinction occurs, partly related to the complex context within which tourism higher education operates, at times related to the standards themselves, but most often relating to the ability of institutions and academics to apply and foster them competently. The discussion illustrates different facets of this perceived challenge, hopefully highlighting the potential implications for both education management and academic practice.

2.   STANDARDS AND CONSISTENCY AS COMPONENTS OF QUALITY

2.1   The Tourism Education Context: Academia, Industry and Policy Perspectives

The argument of the potentially conflicting perspectives determining approaches to tourism education is not novel. Early thinking as well as recent research has identified influences on shaping the tourism and hospitality curriculum (cf. Pollock and Ritchie, 1990). The emphasis is most often placed on a perceived dichotomy between a vocational orientation, favoring hands-on, practical training for skills that are in demand in the tourism industry, and a liberal approach to tourism education (cf. Cooper et al., 1994; Tribe, 2002). University brochures often highlight the distinction between schools or programs of study that are focused mostly on providing vocationally relevant, operational skills, and those that address tourism as a field of study at a higher/wider, perhaps more academic level – usually combined with subjects such as sociology, urban and regional planning, and environmental studies (Wang et al., 2010). Irrespective of orientation, one of the principal considerations by prospective students and parents when choosing an institution or program of study is the career potential it can guarantee (Hsu, 2013). The sheer volume of tourism research concentrating on this desired match between knowledge supply and demand highlights this point as a priority in the design and delivery of tourism programs (for example Stanciulescu and Bulin, 2012; Testa and Sipe, 2012; Rodríguez-Antón et al., 2013).

This renders the tourism and hospitality industry a crucial stakeholder (Roberts, 2009; Dredge et al., 2012), representatives of which are often invited to participate as expert advisors in procedures such as a new program creation or a periodic review. The benefit is twofold: higher education institutions receive practical recommendations for program design, and at the same time a tacit promise of industry advisors becoming future employers for the institution's students and graduates. There is also a commercial angle to this, as the involvement of industry advisors is used for promotional purposes as a guarantee of currency and employability. The commercial dimension of education highlights measures of success for universities that are quite distinct from educational attainment: at least from a business perspective, enrolment figures and revenues take precedence over academic merit. The promise of employability in the tourism industry is key in this – if not for prospective students, then, it could be argued, for their parents and sponsors. Placing emphasis on an industry-driven curriculum is therefore regarded as a positive feature of many institutions. Knowledge transfer protocols between academia and industry can add substance as well as glamour to tourism programs of study (Roberts, 2009), and applied rather than conceptual research is often perceived to add more value (and marketability) to the education product, at the same time generating revenues through research funding.

An industry-relevant curriculum is also seen as an essential component of many countries' tourism education systems. National tourism strategies often recognize education and training as vital resources and success factors on a par with hard tourism infrastructure and destination marketing activities (Hall et al., 2002). While tourism policy seldom interferes directly with the tourism curriculum, public policy may do so indirectly by regulating education in general and setting standards for private (primarily) as well as public educational establishments. The specification of these standards again relies on the perception of economic as well as social benefits that tourism education can and is expected to yield (Ispas, 2008; Yusop Ab.Hadi et al., 2013). A systems approach is proffered in creating a purposeful framework to guide the design, planning and deployment of national tourism training strategy (Mayakka and Akama, 2007), while Cuffy et al. (2012) also consider the temporal element and propose a tourism education policy model that fosters a lifelong learning approach to education and training, especially for destinations that rely heavily on tourism for their viability (see also the chapter by Cuffy, this volume). Without going into the distinction between education and training, it is clear that one of the mandates of tourism education is to offer industry-relevant skills in order to satisfy demands imposed by tourism and hospitality employers (for example Wang et al., 2009; Jaykumar et al., 2014). Not surprisingly, Ayikoru et al. point to the fundamental challenges posed to tourism educators by the fact that 'different stakeholders have specific tourism education needs they deem appropriate for their own purposes' (2009, p.192). The study of tourism for its own sake, that is, out of a drive towards knowledge per se rather than employability at some level, seems to be on the brink of extinction – although it would be difficult and perhaps inappropriate to rule for or against this trend.

As such, one potential downside of the emphasis on the industry perspective that permeates the design, delivery and evaluation of tourism programs, as well as of other external factors dictating educational priorities, is that they may favor a results-oriented approach at the expense of a more philosophical nature of study and inquiry (Barnett, 1994; Busby and Huang, 2012). It should be pointed out that this issue is not unique to tourism studies, with similar debates occurring in other business-related fields (cf. Holman, 2000; Goodrick, 2002; Roksa, 2006; Paisey and Paisey, 2007).

One element of the tourism curriculum whose importance seems to be reduced to a peripheral rather than central role is the development of higher-order capacities such as critical thinking, abstract synthesis and theory conceptualization (Biggs, 2003). Despite its undeniable pedagogical value, it is perhaps telling that the importance of this deep approach to learning through critical engagement needs to be defended (for example Bianchi, 2009; Belhassen and Caton, 2011; Fullagar and Wilson, 2012). This discrepancy is often discussed in tandem with the disciplinary orientation of the tourism curriculum. Common practice rather favors placing tourism as a subject of study in a business and management context (Scott et al., 2007), with many early academics (for example Jafari and Ritchie, 1981; Leiper, 1981; McIntosh, 1983) as well as more recent commentators (for example Tribe, 1997; 2005; Coles et al., 2006; Liburd and Hjalager, 2010; L'Espoire Decost and Grunewald, 2011; Dredge et al., 2012; Caton, 2014) striving for the recognition of a need towards a multi-, inter- or meta-disciplinary approach to understanding and teaching tourism. Indeed, several other chapters in this volume also argue for a more liberal curriculum that includes critical studies, sustainability, ethics and research skills.

2.2 The Academic Management Context: Standardization as the Proposed Solution

Centered on the importance of industry-relevance and employability, the above discussion points to a number of interlinked influences on educational priorities and academic practice. While not constituting opposite sides of the same coin, and while a balanced approach is often proposed (cf. Fidgeon, 2010), nevertheless the various priorities and approaches may seem to be creating tension rather than consensus. From an education management viewpoint, satisfying all stakeholders seems to be of paramount importance but also riddled with considerable complexity. One type of prescription seems to be the application of a uniform, standardized approach to tourism education in terms of content (Airey and Johnson, 1999; Zagonari, 2009), while at times administrative structure and organization is seen as a determinant of education quality (Pirnar, 2014). It is understandable that in order to avoid any one perspective or concern taking center stage in shaping academic practice at the expense of others, a set of guidelines and safeguards must be developed and applied consistently.

The guiding authority in the UK higher education system is the Quality Assurance Agency in higher education (QAA), which provides guidelines for higher education establishments and programs through its Quality Code. The Quality Code acts as an agreed reference point for 'setting and maintaining' academic standards among different institutions, and 'assuring the quality of the learning opportunities they provide for students'. One of the aims of the Quality Code is 'to ensure that higher education provision and learning outcomes are comparable and consistent at a threshold level across the UK' (QAA, 2014, p. 4). The specified standards also address the content of the Hospitality, Leisure, Sport and Tourism curriculum, through the articulated subject benchmark statements devised by teams of experts on tourism as a subject area.

As a starting point, such educational standards provide valuable prescription aimed at consistency, offering a rather welcome sense of security. From a pedagogical viewpoint, decisions relating to the quality of the learning experience – including what should be taught, at what level, in what way, at what depth and so on, as well as how student learning should be monitored, supported and evaluated, and, even further, how the overall learning experience should be examined for its relevance and currency with regard to the knowledge, skills and attitudes desired in the industry and society as a whole – should not be arbitrary (Robbins, 2005). Furthermore, the implementation of these decisions at 'ground' level, that is, by individual lecturers, program leaders and academic directors, should be in line with those decisions. Such an approach aimed at guaranteeing a degree of consistency is adopted in many educational systems (Srikanthan and Dalrymple, 2007). Its implementation relies on monitoring any institution's and individual academic's practices by qualified third parties based on widely agreed standards specifying all of the above elements.

This ensures that academic practices are not arbitrary, because they are verified by independent observers who confirm the reliability and validity of most aspects of our practice. At the same time, the documentation of quality assurance procedures provides proof against claims of unfair treatment by students. An additional benefit is that QAA standards and benchmark statements can make it easier to design appropriate educational systems and programs due to the prescribed specifications they set.

On the other hand, despite their usefulness, quality assurance procedures may be regarded as a nuisance rather than a facility, as they translate into significant time and effort in terms of the paperwork they involve at all levels and functions – the time devoted to them often kept to a minimum. And it can be argued that this is exactly the point that might raise a concern with quality assurance and standardization practices unless they are embraced and implemented appropriately.

3. MINIMUM VERSUS OPTIMUM: ACADEMIC AND ADMINISTRATIVE ISSUES IN QUALITY ASSURANCE

3.1 Potential Challenges in Employing a Standardization Approach

When attempting to establish and apply quality standards through academic specifications and regulations, there is a danger that the resulting provisions will tend to ascertain a *minimum* common denominator rather than a guiding approach aimed at enhancing learning and teaching practice. It must be clarified that this is not criticism towards standards themselves, but towards the manner in which they are often interpreted and applied.

Quality assurance mechanisms aim to set standards, that is, both benchmarks and guiding approaches that can promote a degree of consistency and allow for performance comparisons on different aspects of academic practice. However, when the primary concern is over consistency as a prerequisite of quality rather than on excellence, and on accountability rather than enhancement, a standards approach may tend to decrease rather than increase performance goals and aspirations (Harvey and Green, 1993). To use an analogy from hospitality, what often wins customers over is not the service standard achieved by imposing specifications through standard operating procedures documents and training (which are rather taken for granted), but the fact that service delivery in some cases will go *beyond* these specifications. Both in the case of hospitality service and academic practice, a quality assurance approach in the form of specifications can help prevent instances of poor performance or arbitrary action (Teng et al., 2013). Yet it can also stifle initiative that might be beneficial for the recipients of the service. This dilemma is at the heart of 'threshold standards', which represent minimum standards of attainment rather than being aspirational. On the other hand, threshold standards allow for institutions to differentiate themselves when they can competently exceed the set standards.

The above points form a brief indication of the differing arguments that can be provided both for and against a standardization approach to education, which may suggest that merely the existence of standards and control mechanisms is not sufficient in promoting the goals these are intended to achieve. Indeed, there may be instances where we seem to forget that quality assurance mechanisms are a means rather than an end – perhaps blinded by the investment in time and effort they require on the part of institutions as well as individual academics. They are a means for ensuring the best possible level of educational quality measures such as consistency, fairness, transparency, relevance, currency, rationale and so on – all geared towards fostering a quality learning and teaching environment that is conducive of educational merit and pedagogic attainment. Or are they?

3.2 Quality Assurance Aims, Misunderstood

A potential pitfall of quality assurance mechanisms lies in the potential for misinterpretation or incompetent application of standards. The author is a firm believer in the value of quality assurance in higher education (Biggs, 2003; Ramsden, 2003) and especially the value it can offer to students directly or indirectly (for example through standards on student and staff selection, student and staff support and development, curriculum design and review, teaching practice, assessment, marking, feedback and so on). This is on the condition, that is, that academics are appropriately chosen and trained for understanding, applying and supporting the *spirit* rather than merely the letter of quality assurance mechanisms. Mechanisms, as related to education, should never be merely mechanistic – their application not routine or simply compulsory practice.

An analogy from music will be adopted to aid the explanation of the above point. In order to develop the necessary agility for competent performance in an instrument, most students receive the largest part of their instruction through the study of musical scales and other exercises. This contributes to reaching a level of technical ability that should enable students to apply their mechanical and auditory skill in any genre and style. Yet the result is very often the opposite: 'boxing' students into particular 'shapes' on the guitar fingerboard, limiting their inventiveness largely to a reproduction of those scales and exercises rather than creative musical expression. This is a case where performing to standards (pun intended) may produce slaves to technique rather than help students flourish to their musical potential. The answer that's offered by more mature instructors? You must learn how to play scales, and then you must forget them – otherwise all you ever do is play scales rather than play music. Back to our field, this example hopefully emphasizes that it is important for academics to be proficient in the application of quality standards, but not lose sight of the bigger purpose these serve: they are a means towards a desirable end, that is, educational quality.

This approach has also served the author well during lecturing and dissertation supervision, when encouraging students to develop a critical appreciation of the value of different theoretical concepts and frameworks, as opposed to merely reciting serious-sounding terminology and reproducing models (Papageorgiou, 2007). Critical thinking, or perhaps more specifically critical engagement with any topic of study and material available, seems to be a pursuit at the heart of the British and other higher education systems. Accreditation, validation and periodic review panels, external examiners and moderators rightly treat this element as a prerequisite for the award of any higher education degree. The gradual progression across levels of study towards the attainment of this higher-order capacity must be explicitly embedded in the curriculum, as well as evidenced in student performance. Academics are instructed to foster critical thinking through their classroom delivery, reading suggestions and assessment design (Biggs, 2003).

Yet unfortunately for many academics, fostering critical thinking as a quality assurance prescription is practically limited to utilizing Bloom et al.'s (1956) taxonomy keywords with almost religious zeal while composing module descriptors or assessment briefs, directing students to the latest journal articles as opposed to textbooks, and even setting a minimum number of sources to be cited in projects and dissertations – another example of standardization at the low end. As argued earlier, merely having a standard is a far cry from reaching the results it is intended to achieve. While there is no argument against adopting quality assurance standards that help specify the imperative for fostering critical thinking, applying this principle often falls short of expectations due to a number of complications. Wang (2010) identifies potential gaps in, and respective opportunities for, faculty development: appropriate emphasis should be placed on creating an accurate understanding of academic quality principles as part of a comprehensive professional development strategy. This hints at the often limited ability of academics themselves to understand, explain, support and evaluate critical engagement. However, lack of experience or qualifications (Wu et al., 2014) or lack of clear direction may only be one part of the problem, with academics' perceptions of their own role posing a conceptual barrier (Grey and French, 1996).

3.3 Operationalizing Academic Quality Assurance

As the chapter posited in the introduction, a number of influences interfere with academic practice, often shadowing its centrality to the wider purpose of education. One influence that has already been dealt with is the frequent inability on the part of academic administration to foster the development of an ethos of enhancing academic quality – instead striving for consistency through the basic coverage of minimum, not optimum, standards. Poignantly as always, Wheeller's reflection on 'the ever tightening vice of conformity that is gripping education' (2005, p. 309) captures the recurring chasm between educational/pedagogical principles and the mechanical manner in which these are often prescribed. Notions such as benchmarking, blueprinting, terms of reference, checklists and the ubiquitous Excel worksheet prevail at the expense of a thoughtful rather than routine, purposeful rather than obligatory, insightful rather than 'results-driven' approach to academic quality assurance. It is argued here that when the emphasis of quality assurance mechanisms is mostly on accountability rather than on quality then there is a danger that the system will not yield an optimal outcome.

At the same time, an inescapable influence that academics recognize but often have trouble coming to terms with is the commercial dimension of education as a business. This directly or indirectly permeates the full range of scholarly and academic-related functions: from student enrollment to staff remuneration, from learning resources to funding for extracurricular activities, from teaching loads to research output requirements, from faculty development opportunities to funding for conference attendance and from admissions criteria to pass or failure rates. The latter is perhaps the most frustrating example of a clash between the commercial and academic imperatives – with overtones of 'quality versus quantity' and 'students as customers'. Well-defined standards pertaining to the fulfillment of learning outcomes, demonstrating critical engagement, and preventing and treating instances of academic misconduct often fall prey to an unduly lenient attitude centered on not disappointing the customer, or not giving the institution a bad name among prospective students ('too tough' to get in or get out).

Tangentially to the above point, a further issue for consideration is the degree of flexibility that must be built into any quality assurance system in order to allow for appropriate pragmatic discretion to be exercised when necessary. This is particularly relevant in the context of the relatively recent trend towards student-centered learning, that is, the consideration of the learner as the object of education. This, however, entails placing student needs, characteristics, particularities and even preferences at the center of academic practice (Ivanič et al., 2007; Kim and Davies, 2014). By inference this leads to a change of paradigm in accommodating various learning styles, teaching modes, classroom activities, assessment methods and learning outcomes (Maher, 2004). Any quality assurance system should be able to cater for any such shift since, at heart, it would provide for the same principles: fairness, transparency, development opportunities – all centered on the learner.

This, however, calls for a critical understanding of the spirit of quality assurance mandates and an ability by academic administrations as well as lecturers to exercise their judgment while applying them. Unfortunately, at times there is neither clarity of thought nor perspicacity to negotiate the letter of academic regulations – for fear of the consequences of, for example, departing from the use of traditional or 'approved' assessment methods, or introducing improvements to a module mid-semester to suit student/ cohort needs. Consistently applying quality assurance standards is a prerequisite for fairness and accountability across students, cohorts, programs and schools. However, wasting opportunities to enhance (individual) student learning and the overall student experience simply out of inexperience or inability to reasonably and fairly deviate from regulations that are deemed counter-productive, rather contradicts this turn towards a student-centered approach to education. The issue highlighted here raises an implication for academic/education management practice that, it is believed, merits further study.

3.4   Back to the Tourism Context: Critically Reflecting on our Practice as Tourism Academics

So far the discussion has referred mostly generically to education rather than specifically to education for tourism. Due to the service element inherent in the tourism product (Teboul, 2006), as well as its international nature, tourism and hospitality academics often stress the particularities of the profession (cf. Ladkin, 2005) primarily in the sense that a specific disposition is essential for employees to perform well and progress effectively. In addition to technical skills and knowledge that interns and graduates must possess, the inference is that the tourism profession is 'not for everyone'. Serving a customer and designing/offering an experience-based product presupposes a degree of empathy and understanding that is not so central in the case of tangible consumer products.

   However, out of the multitude of positions involved in tourism, only a relative minority will involve a service interaction. Additionally, despite the special, 'superior' qualities this view seems to allude to, it can be argued that the same assertion can be made for most professions – as each may require a mindset conducive to that profession's goals and practices. And perhaps to move the thought process one step further, the academic profession, itself a service, too (Roberts, 2009) should certainly involve people of a specific mindset and special abilities: a student-first approach, an emphasis on effective communication, a commitment to lifelong learning, a critical mind, a philosophic attitude. And we know that unfortunately this is not always the case – with institutions as well as lecturers themselves giving priority to other elements (Wheeller, 2005).

   Perhaps contrary to the perception that tourism is such a peculiar and distinctive profession and field of study, the tendency in most relevant research as well as the design of most tourism education programs seems to be towards a cohesive approach. If we adopt Tribe's (2002) categorization of tourism curricula along two axes, that is, the vocational– liberal axis and the reflection–action axis, contemporary approaches most often endeavor to incorporate elements of all four 'ends'. This actually reflects rather than contradicts the feedback often received from industry professionals regarding their expectations for a range of managerial competencies that encompass communication, marketing, financial, legal, socio-cultural, and environmental knowledge.

   While this should be a reassuring trend – of academia pursuing both educational and vocational objectives, thus not being separate from the reality of the professional arena – Tribe's (2002) framework could also be employed in evaluating our own practice as academics. And in worryingly numerous cases it might be argued that the realities of our day-to-day duties, as well as the orientation and priorities of the institutions that employ us, place the emphasis towards the 'action' and 'vocational' ends. Getting things done seems to take precedence over reflecting on how things should be done, or how they could be improved. And concentrating on offering applied knowledge is in itself a commendable quest, but is often pursued at the expense of developing our own, and our students', mental faculties and skills of a more liberal nature. As this chapter focuses on a conceptual treatment of the subject, strictly speaking this is an unsupported generalization. However, it is suspected that it might strike a chord with at least some of the readers of this volume.

To tie this viewpoint with the chapter's overall focus on quality learning and teaching practices, it can be argued that a preoccupation with standardizing our practice – whether imposed by mere obligation to apply quality assurance procedures or by institutional inability to manage diversity – may in fact induce indifference and passivity rather than diligence on the part of motivated academics, as well as condone and mask the inexperience or limited ability of some colleagues. In this not so extreme scenario, standardization can be perceived to offer a disservice to students as the supposed object of our efforts, by moving the focus away from quality, enhancement and excellence, and placing it on conformity, reproducibility and verification. And that would be defeating the purpose. The famous epigram by Karl Kraus that 'psychoanalysis is that spiritual disease of which it considers itself to be the cure' (Janik and Toulmin, 1973, p. 77) seems alarmingly apposite here. But perhaps that's just a matter of perspective.

4.   CONCLUSION

The chapter has attempted to reflect on academic quality assurance in relation to tourism education through the conceptual discussion of a number of factors and influences that interfere with its application. While the principles and mandates of quality assurance frameworks make a decisive contribution towards establishing a desired approach to academic practice, their implementation may not, for various reasons, yield the expected results in terms of educational quality. Undoubtedly, competent direction on the use of quality assurance standards is essential in fostering an appropriate approach centered on quality, rather than on standards. However, such mechanisms are often seen as a nuisance due to the (perceived) bureaucracy they involve, and the principles are applied mechanistically rather than purposefully. The task is not made easier by the fact that (tourism) academics are called to satisfy success criteria dictated by factors that are outside their educational remit and control. Furthermore, different institutional priorities and policies may often exert pressure on faculty time, which makes it harder for academics to embrace what are often regarded as 'additional' procedures in the appropriate spirit.

In this light, a number of conceptual contradictions were identified and discussed, notably between consistency (shared practice) and conformity (uniform practice); between setting optimum standards (aimed at enhancing quality) as opposed to setting minimum standards (aimed at satisfying base requirements); and between focusing on the spirit (principles) rather than the letter (procedures) of quality assurance mechanisms. The analysis employed analogies that pointed to practical as well as more philosophic implications for academics and educational establishments. Effective faculty training and development are of paramount importance, but there is a discernible distance between 'knowing what to do' and actually engaging in the relevant procedures in the spirit they are intended. The various reasons behind this form an issue worth investigating further through primary research.

However, the chapter has also inferred that the discrepancy between having a standard and yielding the full benefit of its application is perhaps a matter of attitude rather than aptitude. But then, that is the case with all the functions academics are called to perform: teaching, supervision, research, administration and so on. As the popular maxim goes, 'if your heart isn't in it . . .', no amount of prescription can guarantee a quality outcome. Especially in the case of tourism education, attempting to bridge all perspectives or identify a single right approach might be overambitious, or even redundant. The chapter posits that it is worth investing in further work, both conceptual and evidence-based, that could contribute to the enhancement of our curriculum and practice. It is hoped that the thoughts expressed here may illuminate perhaps neglected considerations, thereby contributing to current thinking on the issue.

REFERENCES

Airey, D. and S. Johnson (1999), 'The Content of Tourism Degree Courses in the UK', *Tourism Management*, **20** (2), 229–35.
Ayikoru, M., J. Tribe and D. Airey (2009), 'Reading Tourism Education: Neoliberalism Unveiled', *Annals of Tourism Research*, **36** (2), 191–221.
Barnett, R. (1994), *The Limits of Competence: Knowledge, Higher Education and Society*, Buckingham: Open University Press.
Belhassen, Y. and K. Caton (2011), 'On the Need for Critical Pedagogy in Tourism Education', *Tourism Management*, **32** (6), 1389–96.
Bianchi, R.V. (2009), 'The "Critical Turn" in Tourism Studies: a Radical Critique', *Tourism Geographies*, **11** (4), 484–504.
Biggs, J. (2003), *Teaching for Quality Learning at University* (2nd edn), Buckingham: Open University Press.
Bloom, B.S., M.D. Engelhart, E.J. Furst, W.H. Hill and D.R. Krathwohl (1956), *Taxonomy of Educational Objectives: The Classification of Educational Goals. Handbook I: Cognitive Domain*, New York: David McKay Company.
Busby, G. and R. Huang (2012), 'Integration, Intermediation and Tourism Higher Education: Conceptual Understanding in the Curriculum', *Tourism Management*, **33** (1), 108–15.
Caton, K. (2014), 'Underdisciplinarity: Where are the Humanities in Tourism Education?', *Journal of Hospitality, Leisure, Sport & Tourism Education*, **15**, 24–33.
Coles, T., C.M. Hall and D.T. Duval (2006), 'Tourism and Post-Disciplinary Enquiry', *Current Issues in Tourism*, **9** (4&5), 293–319.
Cooper, C., R. Shepherd and J. Westlake (1994), *Tourism and Hospitality Education*, Guildford: University of Surrey.
Cuffy, V., J. Tribe and D. Airey (2012), 'Lifelong Learning for Tourism', *Annals of Tourism Research*, **39** (3), 1402–24.
Dredge, D., P. Benckendorff, M. Day, M.J. Gross, M. Walo, P. Weeks and P. Whitelaw (2012), 'The Philosophic Practitioner and the Curriculum Space', *Annals of Tourism Research*, **39** (4), 2154–76.
Fidgeon, P.R. (2010), 'Tourism Education and Curriculum Design: A Time for Consolidation and Review?', *Tourism Management*, **31** (6), 699–723.
Fullagar, S. and E. Wilson (2012), 'Critical Pedagogies: A Reflexive Approach to Knowledge Creation in Tourism and Hospitality Studies', *Journal of Hospitality and Tourism Management*, **19**, 1–6.
Goodrick, E. (2002), 'From Management as a Vocation to Management as a Scientific Activity: An Institutional Account of a Paradigm Shift', *Journal of Management*, **28** (5), 649–68.
Grey, C. and R. French (1996), 'Rethinking Management Education: An Introduction', in R. French and R. Grey (eds), *Rethinking Management Education*, Thousand Oaks, CA: Sage, pp. 1–16.
Hall, K.O., J.S. Holder and C. Jayawardena (2002), 'Caribbean Tourism and the Role of UWI in Tourism and Hospitality Education', *Social and Economic Studies*, **51** (1), 145–65.
Harvey, L. and D. Green (1993), 'Defining Quality', *Assessment and Evaluation in Higher Education*, **18** (1), 9–26.

Holman, D. (2000), 'Contemporary Models of Management Education in the UK', *Management Learning*, **31** (2), 197–217.

Hsu, L. (2013), 'Work Motivation, Job Burnout, and Employment Aspiration in Hospitality and Tourism Students: An Exploration Using the Self-Determination Theory', *Journal of Hospitality, Leisure, Sport & Tourism Education*, **13**, 180–89.

Ispas, A. (2008), 'The Role of Education in Romania's Tourism Sector: From Level Descriptors to Learning Outcomes', *Tourism and Hospitality Management*, **14** (1), 115–28.

Ivanič, R., R. Edwards, C. Satchwell and J. Smith (2007), 'Possibilities for Pedagogy in Further Education: Harnessing the Abundance of Literacy', *British Educational Research Journal*, **33** (5), 703–21.

Jafari, J. and J.R.B. Ritchie (1981), 'Toward a Framework for Tourism Education: Problems and Prospects', *Annals of Tourism Research*, **8** (1), 13–34.

Janik, A. and S. Toulmin (1973), *Wittgenstein's Vienna*, New York: Simon and Schuster.

Jaykumar, V., L. Nitin Fukey and K. Balasubramanian (2014), 'Hotel Managers Perspective of Managerial Competency Among Graduating Students of Hotel Management Program', *Procedia – Social and Behavioral Sciences*, **144**, 328–42.

Kim, A.K. and J. Davies (2014), 'A Teacher's Perspective on Student Centred Learning: Towards the Development of Best Practice in an Undergraduate Tourism Course', *Journal of Hospitality, Leisure, Sport & Tourism Education*, **14**, 6–14.

Ladkin, A. (2005), 'Careers and Employment', in D. Airey and J. Tribe (eds), *An International Handbook of Tourism Education*, Oxford: Elsevier, pp. 437–50.

Leiper, N. (1981), 'Towards a Cohesive Curriculum Tourism: The Case for a Distinct Discipline', *Annals of Tourism Research*, **8** (1), 69–84.

L'Espoir Decosta, J-N.P. and A. Grunewald (2011), 'Logies of Tourismology: The Need to Include Meta-Theories in Tourism Curricula', *Journal of Teaching in Travel & Tourism*, **11** (3), 289–303.

Liburd, J. and A-M. Hjalager (2010), 'Changing Approaches Towards Open Education, Innovation and Research in Tourism', *Journal of Hospitality and Tourism Management*, **17**, 12–20.

Maher, A. (2004), 'Learning Outcomes in Higher Education: Implications for Curriculum Design and Student Learning', *Journal of Hospitality, Leisure, Sport & Tourism Education*, **3** (2), 46–54.

Mayaka, M. and J.S. Akama (2007), 'Systems Approach to Tourism Training and Education: The Kenyan Case Study', *Tourism Management*, **28** (1), 298–306.

McIntosh, R.W. (1983), 'A Model University Curriculum in Tourism', *Tourism Management*, **4** (2), 134–7.

Paisey, C. and N.J. Paisey (2007), 'Balancing the Vocational and Academic Dimensions of Accounting Education: The Case for a Core Curriculum', *Journal of Vocational Education & Training*, **59** (1), 89–105.

Papageorgiou, G.C. (2007), *Learning to Supervise*, unpublished PGCert Learning Portfolio, University of Surrey.

Pirnar, I. (2014), 'Tourism Education Universities in Turkey: Comparison of Different Structures and Related Effects on Education Quality', *Procedia – Social and Behavioral Sciences*, **116**, 5070–74.

Pollock, A. and J.R.B. Ritchie (1990), 'Integrated Strategy for Tourism Education/Training', *Annals of Tourism Research*, **17** (4), 568–85.

QAA (2014), *The UK Quality Code for Higher Education: A Brief Guide*, Gloucester: The Quality Assurance Agency for Higher Education.

Ramsden, P. (2003), *Learning to Teach in Higher Education* (2nd edn), Abingdon: RoutledgeFalmer.

Robbins, D. (2005), 'Quality Assurance', in D. Airey and J. Tribe (eds), *An International Handbook of Tourism Education*, Oxford: Elsevier, pp. 451–68.

Roberts, E. (2009), 'Mind the Gap: Aligning Learning and Graduate Outcomes through Industry Partnerships', *Journal of Hospitality and Tourism Management*, **16** (1), 130–38.

Rodríguez-Antón, J.M., M.M. Alonso-Almeida, L.R. Andrada and M. Celemín Pedroche (2013), 'Are University Tourism Programs Preparing the Professionals the Tourist Industry Needs? A Longitudinal Study', *Journal of Hospitality, Leisure, Sport & Tourism Education*, **12**, 25–35.

Roksa, J. (2006), 'Does the Vocational Focus of Community Colleges Hinder Students' Educational Attainment?', *The Review of Higher Education*, **29** (4), 499–526.

Scott, N.M., V.A. Puleo and J.C. Crotts (2007), 'An Analysis of Curriculum Requirements among Hospitality and Tourism Management Programs in ACSB Colleges of Business in the United States', *Journal of Teaching in Travel & Tourism*, **7** (4), 71–83.

Srikanthan, G. and J.F. Dalrymple (2007), 'A Conceptual Overview of a Holistic Model for Quality in Higher Education', *International Journal of Educational Management*, **21** (3), 173–93.

Stanciulescu, G.C.J. and D. Bulin (2012), 'Shaping Tourism Higher Education Curriculum: Strategy to Develop Skills for Tomorrow's Jobs', *Procedia Economics and Finance*, **3**, 1202–207.

Teboul, J. (2006), *Service is Front Stage: Positioning Services for Value Advantage*, Basingstoke: Palgrave Macmillan and INSEAD Business Press.

Teng, C.C., J.S. Horng and T. Baum (2013), 'Academic Perceptions of Quality and Quality Assurance in

Undergraduate Hospitality, Tourism and Leisure Programs: A Comparison of UK and Taiwanese Programs', *Journal of Hospitality, Leisure, Sport & Tourism Education*, **13**, 233–43.

Testa, M.R. and L. Sipe (2012), 'Service-leadership Competencies for Hospitality and Tourism Management', *International Journal of Hospitality Management*, **31** (3), 648–58.

Tribe, J. (1997), 'The Indiscipline of Tourism', *Annals of Tourism Research*, **21** (3), 638–57.

Tribe, J. (2002), 'The Philosophic Practitioner: A Curriculum for Tourism Stewardship', *Annals of Tourism Research*, **29** (2), 338–57.

Tribe, J. (2005), 'Tourism, Knowledge and the Curriculum', in D. Airey and J. Tribe (eds), *An International Handbook of Tourism Education*, Oxford: Elsevier, pp. 47–60.

Wang, J., H. Ayres and J. Huyton (2009), 'Job Ready Graduates: A Tourism Industry Perspective', *Journal of Hospitality and Tourism Management*, **16** (1), 62–72.

Wang, J., H. Ayres and J. Huyton (2010), 'Is Tourism Education Meeting the Needs of the Tourism Industry? An Australian Case Study', *Journal of Hospitality & Tourism Education*, **22** (1), 8–14.

Wang, M. (2010), 'Faculty Development in China: An Essential Strategy for Tourism Education Service', *Journal of China Tourism Research*, **6** (4), 428–38.

Wheeller, B. (2005), 'Issues in Teaching and Learning', in D. Airey and J. Tribe (eds), *An International Handbook of Tourism Education*, Oxford: Elsevier, pp. 309–18.

Wu, B., A.M. Morrison, J.K. Yang, J.L. Zhou and L.L. Cong (2014), 'Cracks in the Ivory Tower? A Survey-Based Analysis of Undergraduate Tourism Education and Educators in China', *Journal of Hospitality, Leisure, Sport & Tourism Education*, **14**, 26–38.

Yusop Ab.Hadi, M., R. Roddin, A.R. Abdul Razzaq, M. Zaid Mustafa and J. Abd Baser (2013), 'Poverty Eradication through Vocational Education (tourism) among Indigenous People Communities in Malaysia: Pro-Poor Tourism Approach (PPT)', *Procedia – Social and Behavioral Sciences*, **93**, 1840–44.

Zagonari, F. (2009), 'Balancing Tourism Education and Training', *International Journal of Hospitality Management*, **28** (1), 2–9.

37 The role and responsibilities of industry advisory boards in enhancing the educational experience
Ady Milman

1. INTRODUCTION

Industry advisory boards are external support groups for universities, colleges, schools, departments or other academic institutions. They bridge the gap between industry and academia by supporting the institution's strategic direction and helping it achieve its educational, research and community partnership goals (Conroy and Lefever, 1996; Dorazio, 1996). Advisory boards serve as sources of information and advice to academic administrators and assist students, faculty, and trustees to realize broader, more objective perspectives on academic matters. They typically monitor the academic program's effectiveness and provide quality improvement guidelines (Taylor et al., 2010). Some advisory boards also provide academic institutions with beneficial contacts to government officials, businesses, industry and professional associations (Carnegie Mellon University, 2014).

The rationale for establishing advisory industry boards lies in the premise that 'great institutions are created and sustained with the guidance of experts who bring to them new perspectives and ways of thinking' (University of Miami, 2014). Some scholars suggest that advisory boards are crucial for the survival of an academic program, as administrators ought to be well-informed about the industry needs of the educational program and its human resources management (Hicks et al., 2011; Rhea, 2009).

Advisory boards are not expected to lead an organization (National Council on Family Relations, 2014); however, they provide prestige, legitimacy, market information, access to data, business know-how, financial and human resources for the academic programs they serve on (Zahra et al., 2011). Their role may vary from one academic institution to another and from one academic unit to another. For example, the goal of the School of Architecture at the University of Texas' advisory board is to promote the value and importance of architecture, planning, and design by supporting the mission, values and interests of the university and the school (The University of Texas at Austin School of Architecture, 2014).

Advisory boards are usually comprised of accomplished expert volunteers who contribute their time, knowledge, perspective, advice and industry experience to enhance and improve a specific academic unit in an institution of higher learning (Nagai and Nehls, 2014; Stautberg and Green, 2007). A well-selected board aligns with the institution's common interests by active participation, and by influencing all stakeholders involved with the academic program (Taylor et al., 2010).

Some academic institutions or units have several advisory boards. For example, the School of Business Administration at the University of Dayton (Ohio) has seven advisory boards: a board that assists the Dean and other school administrators in improving the quality of the school's programs, activities and long-term strategy, a board that supports the director and other entrepreneurship faculty members, and a board that advises the Portfolio Management Center, a learning environment of Wall Street investment activities. Other school boards assist faculty and administrators in the areas of accounting, management information systems, operations management, and small business administration (University of Dayton School of Business Administration, 2014).

2.   STRUCTURE AND MEMBERSHIP OF INDUSTRY ADVISORY BOARDS

Industry advisory boards typically consist of eight to twenty members, depending on the need and size of the academic unit. Membership varies, as some academic institutions have advisory boards composed of alumni while others are composed exclusively of industry members or a combination of alumni and industry members. For example, the advisory board members of the University of Texas at Austin School of Architecture represent a variety of professional and community roles, including architecture, planning, interior design, engineering, education, real estate development, foundations, law, investments and civic leadership (University of Texas at Austin School of Architecture, 2014). Advisory boards usually include a few representatives from the academic institution, one of whom typically co-chairs the board with an industry representative.

Board members are typically appointed to a fixed term and are expected to be active as ambassadors of the academic unit, to strengthen the institution's academic reputation and, in some cases, to increase its financial resources (University of Miami, 2014). The appointment procedure may vary from formal to informal. Some universities developed detailed guidelines for the appointment of advisory board members, while others appoint members in a more untailored way. For example, the University of North Carolina at Greensboro developed a formal document that specifies the purpose, composition of board members, length of service and approval, procedures for appointment at the university, college and departmental levels, and organization in terms of meeting cycle, meeting schedules and venues (University of North Carolina at Greensboro, 2014).

3.   LITERATURE REVIEW

Academic research on the operation, make-up, and effectiveness of advisory boards is limited. Zahra et al. (2011) concluded that the academic literature on the role and composition of industry–academic advisory boards is 'sparse and fails to inform us about the factors that influence the contributions of these boards in general and student learning in particular' (Zahra et al., 2011, p. 117). The literature addressed several relevant topics including typology of boards, the role of advisory boards in a variety of disciplines, membership characteristics, members' motivation to serve on the board, the impact of the boards' activities on students' learning outcome and skill development, and obstacles faced by board members while serving (Genheimer and Shehab, 2009; Hicks et al., 2011).

Most of the studies have had methodological challenges; in particular, relatively low sample sizes coupled with low response rates. For example, Genheimer and Shehab (2009) studied 43 directors from 42 different engineering programs around the US who shared their perception of their industry advisory boards. A significantly higher sample was secured by Zahra et al. (2011) who collected data from 208 industry professionals who served on 31 advisory boards, representing about 63 percent of their sample.

While most of the studies applied quantitative methodologies, several studies employed qualitative approaches. In their study of non-alumni hospitality board members at the University of Nevada Las Vegas, Nagai and Nehls (2014) conducted ten in-depth semi-structured interviews with board members, university administrators, faculty members and other stakeholders. A different approach was adopted by Baker et al. (2008b), who summarized the various opportunities for industry–academic partnerships and the major benefits and drawbacks associated with each type of alliance. They acknowledged that the data presented in the paper was an outcome of 'combined years of experience' (Baker et al., 2008b, p. 98) working as faculty members, university administrators, industry professionals and as consultants (Baker et al., 2008b).

No matter what the methodological orientation adopted, the limited research provided the groundwork to continue studying significant issues pertaining to industry advisory boards serving academic institutions. The following is a short summary of the major findings presented in the literature.

3.1 Typology of Industry Advisory Boards

Penrose (2002) identified three types of industry advisory boards: (1) Business education boards whose major role is to make recommendations to teaching institutions regarding the educational needs of the future labor force (Roach, 1999) and to suggest community or social responsibility improvement programs; (2) vocational, technical or industry boards that advise educational institutions in skills-based vocational programs. Typically, legislatures require the educational institutions to establish these boards so their members can ensure skills acquisitions by the students; and (3) university, college or departmental advisory boards that assess the academic programs and make recommendations for improvements. Usually, these boards provide scholarship support, theoretical foundations or adequacy in student laboratories.

Zahra et al. (2011) suggested that advisory boards could be categorized to either hands-off ceremonial boards or more hands-on and engaged boards. Ceremonial boards place greater emphasis than engaged boards on examining and assessing the existing curriculum, offer guidance and suggestions on new course development and serve as allies and supporters on issues pertaining to curriculum change. On the other hand, engaged boards typically put higher emphasis on 'probing general trends that could affect the student learning environment, identify areas where new courses and programs could be developed, and analyzing the usefulness and applicability of new pedagogy in enhancing student learning' (Zahra et al., 2011, p. 121). The study concluded that the type of board 'can profoundly influence students' learning experiences' (Zahra et al., 2011, p. 121).

3.2 The Process of Establishing Industry Advisory Boards

The literature suggests several standards and logistics for establishing the advisory boards. Dorazio (1996) suggested that prior to establishing an advisory board, it is necessary to set up the guidelines for its operation, including how often and where the board will meet, what would be the exact role of its members, or what should be the bylaws or the charter for the group. Genheimer and Shehab (2009) concluded that effective boards should have a clear understanding of their role and limitations in impacting the curriculum, engagements with students, active involvement in accreditation processes, and their alignment with the educational institution's goals and objectives.

3.3   Industry Advisory Boards: Membership Characteristics, Recruitment, and Obstacles to Serve

Dorazio (1996) recommended choosing carefully the individuals who will serve on the board. Members should represent a variety of related disciplines, bring prestige to the program, and 'must genuinely want to help' (Dorazio, 1996, p. 102), committing to invest time and effort. Genheimer and Shehab (2009) concluded that board members with close ties to the academic institution would be more likely to attend meetings consistently and be advocates for the program. In addition, effective board members would often be alumni of the program who were also more likely to be financial contributors to the academic institution.

Recruiting individuals to advisory boards could be challenging. The literature suggests developing a short document to be distributed to prospective members. The document would serve as basic guidelines describing the specific relationships, duties, and responsibilities of all stakeholders involved (Dorazio, 1996). Once identified, the prospective members should receive formal appointment letters. Most advisory boards limit membership for several terms, while others adopt a policy of staggered terms of two or three years, rotating membership accordingly. This rotating membership mix allows new members to be cultivated while maintaining communication with experienced members who had served on the board (Dorazio, 1996).

Several studies explored why members, typically volunteers, chose to serve on industry advisory boards. Nagai and Nehls's (2014) study concluded that board members were motivated to commit their time to serve on the board because of 'ideological incentives' (Nagai and Nehls, 2014, p. 13) and intangible rewards such as satisfaction and fulfillment (Nagai and Nehls, 2014). Some board members were motivated to serve because they had an interest in education, respect, loyalty and connection to the university or college, or just being involved in the community and industry affairs. A number of board members chose to serve on advisory boards to gain professional development or to meet the expectations of their employers (Nagai and Nehls, 2014).

A few studies looked at board members' experiences, their level of engagement, and the obstacles they face while serving on the board. Nagai and Nehls (2014) concluded that engaged board volunteers were more likely to contribute their time and financial support to the university.

Zahra et al. (2011) identified four major obstacles to advisory boards' contribution: (1) lack of clear and complete information about the overall curriculum; (2) lack of understanding where the specific academic program fits into the overall student curriculum; (3) board members' busy work schedules that do not allow continuous participation with the program; and (4) the board members' perception that their involvement was not part of their job.

3.4   The Role of Industry Advisory Boards

A number of studies looked at the roles and responsibilities of industry advisory boards. Nagai and Nehls (2014) concluded that boards' functions vary according to the type of academic program the board members are affiliated with and the board's formal structure. Genheimer and Shehab's (2009) study provided insight into the patterns and trends of various advisory boards. They concluded that both academic administrators and advisory board members thought that boards were effective in attaining the academic program's objectives (Genheimer and Shehab, 2009).

Genheimer and Shehab (2009) identified eight objectives for industry advisory boards. Participants in their study were asked to evaluate the importance of each objective and the effectiveness of the board in accomplishing these objectives. The most important objectives identified were curriculum input and feedback to meet accreditation criteria. Health and development opportunities, as well as advocacy for the program with the academic institution's administration, the community, industry, and alumni were also perceived as important objectives. While many academic institutions are seeking fundraising opportunities, Genheimer and Shehab (2009) suggested that boards can be effective with or without involvement in fundraising.

Baker et al. (2008a, 2008b) highlighted the role of industry advisory boards in facilitating industry–academic research partnerships, including joint and industry-sponsored research projects that would help disseminate science-based information about the industry. They distinguished between long-term, in-depth graduate student-centered projects with the industry and short-term student-centered projects like individual or group class projects, company visits and management interviews (Baker et al., 2008a, 2008b).

The facilitation of industry hands-on sabbatical leave programs for faculty members was another responsibility identified in the literature (Baker et al., 2008a, 2008b). Contemporary research on sabbatical leaves suggests that sabbaticals are a positive tool for enhancing faculty morale and allowing faculty to study, carry out research, and travel. Overall, sabbaticals also have a positive impact on the institution (Kang and Miller, 1999).

The literature also suggests that industry advisory boards can facilitate short faculty internships with various businesses and corporations associated with the academic programs they serve on. Hales et al. (2007) suggested that faculty internships are an interesting and cost-effective way to provide current and useful experiences and information to help meet these responsibilities.

In the hospitality industry, for example, Hyatt, Marriott, Darden and Sodexho companies offer faculty internships through the Council on Hotel, Restaurant and Institutional Education (CHRIE) (Hales et al., 2007). The Club Foundation Faculty Internship Program is another example of a faculty internship program with the goal of increasing club management expertise among faculty members in established colleges and universities' hospitality programs (Club Foundation, 2014). Similar faculty internships could be developed and executed with the assistance of advisory boards at their respective organizations.

Members of industry advisory boards could help design more personal or individualized faculty internships that could be arranged with a specific business or a corporation. Dealing directly with a particular business provides the benefit of specialization and the ability to focus on a few specific training areas (Hales et al., 2007).

Finally, the literature suggested that industry advisory boards could provide a springboard for faculty consulting. Faculty members at universities have a unique opportunity to share their intellectual property with the industry as they bring value through their analytical techniques, precise methodologies and objectivity (Baker et al., 2008a, 2008b). Faculty members could benefit from industry consulting because it impacts their understanding of the industry, provides an insight into how businesses operate and examines the problems companies face (Baker et al., 2008a, 2008b).

A limited number of studies solicited advisory board members to identify specific skills that students should gain in the classroom. In their study of entrepreneurship centers' advisory boards, Zahra et al. (2011) summarized board members' priorities of the expertise that students should gain. The board members that participated in the study identified leadership, sales, communication, innovation, problem solving and decision-making as the most important skills that students should acquire (Zahra et al., 2011).

Zahra et al. (2011) also concluded that *ceremonial* board members placed higher importance on student teaching evaluations of their professors, whereas *engaged* board members valued more feedback from employers following students' internship or full-time employment (Zahra et al., 2011). Table 37.1 summarizes the various roles and responsibilities assumed by industry advisory boards as identified in the literature.

4.   CASE STUDY: THE ROSEN COLLEGE'S THEME PARK AND ATTRACTION MANAGEMENT ADVISORY BOARD

The Theme Park and Attraction Management Advisory Board at the Rosen College of Hospitality Management was crucial in the process of developing a new academic program that currently serves over 600 students. The following section will describe the industry and academic settings that led to the development of the advisory board and its current major role and responsibilities. A short brainstorming exercise activity with board members and other stakeholders of the academic program will be reported. The activity not only helped enhance the curriculum but also enhanced the board members' engagement.

4.1   Orlando's Tourism and Hospitality Industry

The rationale for developing a theme park and attraction management track at the Rosen College was an outcome of the structure and product composition of the Orlando tourism and hospitality industry. The metropolitan Orlando area spreads over 2538 square miles with a 2011 population of over 2.1 million residents. In 2013, Orlando welcomed 59 million visitors, representing a 3 percent increase over the previous year. The Orlando International Airport is located within 15 miles of the Orange County Convention Center, the main hotel area and major theme parks and attractions. It serves more than 35 million passengers annually, with non-stop service from more than 100 domestic and international destinations (Visit Orlando, 2014b).

The metropolitan Orlando area has 454 hotels, with over 118000 rooms, demonstrating 2014 year-to-date average annual occupancy of 77 percent (Visit Orlando, 2014b). Orlando's Orange County Convention Center is ranked second in the US in

Table 37.1   The roles and responsibilities assumed by industry advisory boards identified in the literature

Industry Board Role	Source
Advise program on curriculum content to meet industry needs ● Assess the existing curriculum, including individual courses ● Offer guidance on new course development and ● Serve as allies and supporters on issues pertaining to curriculum change	Genheimer & Shehab (2009); Zahra et al. (2011); Penrose (2002)
Provide input and feedback to help meet accreditation requirements	Genheimer & Shehab (2009); Penrose (2002)
Provide input on program health and development opportunities ● Search general trends that could impact student learning environment ● Identify areas where new courses and programs could be developed ● Analyze the usefulness of new teaching methodologies	Genheimer & Shehab (2009); Zahra et al. (2011)
Serve as an advocate for the program with administration, community, industry, alumni, etc. ● Add credibility to the program ● Share advice regarding hiring trends or skills needed among graduates ● Support through politicians or lobbying groups	Genheimer & Shehab (2009); Penrose (2002)
Assist with student enrichment activities like seminars, design projects, facility development, technology resources, graduate placement, mentoring, etc. ● Internships ● Mentoring ● Site visits ● Guest speakers ● Assess graduates' readiness	Genheimer & Shehab (2009); Penrose (2002); Baker et al. (2008a, 2008b)
Help promote and coordinate research opportunities with industry ● Joint and industry-sponsored research projects ● Long-term, in-depth student-centered projects with the industry ● Short-term student centered projects	Genheimer & Shehab (2009); Baker et al. (2008a, 2008b)
Raise funds for school use from board member individual contacts (scholarships, professorships, research funds, gifts in kind)	Genheimer & Shehab (2009); Baker et al. (2008a, 2008b); Penrose (2002)
Use board member contacts and influence to raise funds from other sources	Genheimer & Shehab (2009)
Assist coordination of sabbatical leave with the industry	Baker et al. (2008a, 2008b)
Assist faculty in research project or consulting opportunities	Baker et al. (2008a, 2008b)
Interaction with students outside the board meetings ● Participate in classroom experience	Nagai & Nehls (2014); Penrose (2002)
Interaction with faculty outside the board meetings ● Advise on contemporary issues	Nagai & Nehls (2014); Penrose (2002)
Interaction with fellow board members outside the board meetings	Nagai & Nehls (2014)

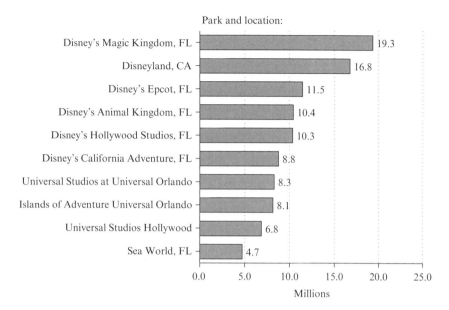

Source: Rubin (2015).

Figure 37.1   Top North American amusement/theme parks: 2014 estimated visitor attendance

terms of exhibition space, with more than 2.1 million square feet. Conference hotels and freestanding-event facilities offer an additional 3.4 million square feet of meeting space (Visit Orlando, 2014b). Visit Orlando is the official tourism association for the destination, with 1200 member organizations, representing all segments of the tourism, travel, and hospitality industry. The association has representation in more than a dozen countries around the world (Visit Orlando, 2014c).

The North American theme park and attraction industry has exhibited continuous growth in the past several years. In 2014, the top 20 theme parks in North America attracted 138.1 million visitors, 2.2 percent more than the previous year (Rubin, 2015). The Orlando area claimed the largest visitor market share (Figure 37.1). In 2014, Disney's Magic Kingdom maintained its position as the most visited theme park in the world, hosting 19.3 million visitors, an increase of 4 percent over the previous year (Rubin, 2015). Visit Orlando membership includes ten major theme parks and 66 tourist attractions (Visit Orlando, 2014a). Orlando's major theme parks comprise the four Walt Disney World parks, two Universal Orlando parks, and two Sea World parks (Figure 37.1).

In the past several years, Orlando has experienced one of the most significant expansion periods in the destination's history. In 2013, SeaWorld Orlando opened *Antarctica: Empire of the Penguin*, the biggest expansion in the company's history, while Walt Disney World Resort completed a multi-year project that doubled the size of the *Magic Kingdom's Fantasyland*. In 2014, Universal Orlando Resort opened the world's first centrally themed, multi-park experience by expanding *The Wizarding World of Harry Potter* across both of its theme parks (Visit Orlando, 2014b). A recent study of visitors' motivation for attending theme parks in Orlando identified six factors that inspired visitors to attend the Orlando theme parks: 'fantasy and myth', 'learning', 'excitement', 'science and technology', 'rides' and 'small-town America' (Park et al., 2009).

4.2   The Theme Park and Attraction Advisory Board's Academic Institution Setting

The University of Central Florida (UCF) is the second largest university in the US, offering 212 degree programs. The university has become an academic and research forerunner in numerous fields, such as optics, modeling, and simulation, engineering and computer science, business administration, education, science, hospitality management and digital media (University of Central Florida, 2014).

The university's 1415-acre main campus provides modern facilities and has 12 colleges. More than 60 000 students attend classes on UCF's main campus and its nine regional campuses located throughout Central Florida, including the Rosen College of Hospitality Management (University of Central Florida, 2014). The Rosen College of Hospitality Management is situated in the heart of Orlando's tourism industry, within a short distance from some of Orlando's top theme parks, attractions, hotels and resorts, restaurants and meeting venues. The off-main campus facility is a 159 000-square-foot, Mediterranean resort-style campus and is the largest facility ever built for hospitality management education (Rosen College, 2014).

The college offers six academic degrees, including undergraduate degree programs in Hospitality Management, Event Management, and Restaurant & Foodservice Management. Graduate degree programs include a Master's in Hospitality & Tourism Management and a doctoral program in Hospitality Management. In addition to the academic programs, students benefit from industry partnerships that include guest speakers, internships, memberships in industry associations, scholarships and networking opportunities (Rosen College, 2014).

The Rosen College's theme park and attraction management track is an outcome of the reputation and attractiveness of the industry among students and the industry's recruitment needs. The track offers one theme park and attraction introductory class required by all undergraduate students who are enrolled in the hospitality program. In addition, the program offers six elective classes in the areas of guest experience management, employee experience management, risk management, contemporary operational issues, amusement technology, and entertainment, arts, and events (Rosen College, 2014).

4.3   Membership and Activities of the Rosen College Theme Park and Attraction Advisory Board

The college's advisory board is composed of theme park and attraction operational and human resource executives representing the Walt Disney World Company, Universal Orlando, Sea World Parks, and Herschend Family Entertainment that manages smaller theme parks, attractions, aquariums and dinner shows throughout the US. While most of the board members represent local attractions, several members are affiliated with theme parks and attractions outside Florida. This has provided the college and the board a nationwide exposure and the opportunity to engage and recruit more members from different types of attractions located throughout the US. Furthermore, a nationwide board may also expose the academic program to more potential students and employers.

The board's charter emphasizes its role as a source of industry feedback regarding the theme park and attraction management educational experience, industry recruiting needs, and hiring and retaining top talent. The board typically meets two to three times a year in rotating locations at Orlando's theme parks or the Rosen College. While the board is composed of 16 official members and two faculty members, the meetings typically include about 25–28 attendees including industry representatives, alumni, current students and two representatives of the Future Theme Parks Leaders Association's (FTPLA) student organization. Industry guests have the opportunity to experience several meetings, and in some cases to join the board officially following their observation of the meetings. The board's charter also requires its members to be experienced in their field of work, willing to commit to ongoing participation and able to articulate on issues and needs for the educational program. Members are chosen in a manner to maintain a balance of representation from the different theme park industry players, and the various lines of business within the industry.

Members are appointed to the board at the discretion of the board's chair and the Rosen College faculty advisor. Members are expected to serve a minimum term of two years, although this may be extended at the discretion of the board chair and the faculty advisor. Members are expected to participate in all advisory board meetings and may be contacted by email or phone as needed to provide additional input on specific issues or strategies. From time to time, members may be asked to solicit input from others within their organization or the industry or to serve on subcommittees for the development of specific projects.

The board has been active for 13 years, since the inception of the theme park and attraction management track. The initial representatives were recruited using a snowball effect (Atkinson and Flint, 2001) where members were recruited by other members through personal contacts. The initial meeting had the following objectives: (1) assistance in the new curriculum development, in particular identifying required knowledge areas, skill competencies, and on-the-job experience for prospective students who were interested in developing a career in the theme park and attraction management; (2) input on theme park and attraction research needs; (3) guidance on student experiential learning, internships and placement; and (4) development of strong relationships between the college and its external stakeholders.

In spite of the variety of the theme park and attractions companies represented on the board, its members adopted a strategy of cohesion and unity. The costs to members of its respective organizations have been relatively insignificant; while the college hosts a board meeting at least once a year, meetings have been sponsored and rotated between the various members who represent the Central Florida theme park and attraction industry. Research indicated that indirect costs of an advisory board can outweigh the benefits (Kane and Jisha, 2004).

4.4 Enhancing the Role of the Industry Advisory Board: A Board Engagement Exercise

Dorazio (1996) suggested that developing activities for collaborative relationships between board members and the academic institution is the most important principle for establishing a successful advisory board. Activities keep the board members interested and maintain the board's function in the program's development (Dorazio, 1996).

Furthermore, Genheimer and Shehab (2009) recommended that overall effectiveness of an advisory board depends on the academic institution's culture, values, and priorities. They suggested that the board leadership should ensure clear member understanding of the institution's educational mission and the institution's expectations of the advisory board role. They also suggested developing formal procedures for board involvement in accreditation processes or other university activities, engagement of board members with students, and coordinating the board's activity with the rest of the college and the university (Genheimer and Shehab, 2009).

To enhance the board's engagement, an interactive brainstorming session was planned during a recent advisory board meeting. The goals of the interactive session were to enhance communication among board members, students, alumni and other industry members who are involved in the educational program and to provide comprehensive feedback to the college about the academic program.

The exercise involved 26 participants, who were randomly divided into four groups of five to seven participants each and were given the task of generating ideas regarding the program's curriculum and enhancing the relationships with the advisory board. Each group was assigned a task in the form of a question relating to the four areas of curriculum enhancement, development of students' competencies, enhancement of the board's engagement with the academic institution, and interaction with students through guest lectures. The specific questions are indicated in Table 37.2.

Following the groups' discussion, each group reported their recommendations to the board in an informal way, using the information recorded on flip charts. The interactive brainstorming exercise provided opportunities for the participants to use their knowledge, experience, skills and perspectives to identify new trends in the industry that could be reflected in the curriculum, student experiential learning, and research (Hicks et al., 2011). Table 37.3 provides a summary of the board's recommendations.

Table 37.2   Industry advisory board task questions

Board recommendation topics	Specific question presented to the board
Curriculum Enhancement	What are new contemporary topics that should be introduced in the theme park and attraction curriculum? Please indicate specific sub-topics in each of the recommended topics.
Development of Student Competencies	What competencies should we incorporate in the theme park and attraction curriculum?
Enhancement of the Board's Engagement with the Academic Institution	How can we better engage the theme park and attraction board in the college and the theme park track in the area of teaching, research and service?
Interaction with Students through Guest Lectures	What topics should guest speakers introduce to create a thought-provoking interactive experience to the students?

Table 37.3   Industry advisory board recommendations for improvement

Board recommendation topics	Examples of specific suggestions
Curriculum Enhancement	• The impact of technology, in areas like marketing, smartphones and Apps, security, risk management, etc. • Project Management proficiency • Contemporary issues in the theme park and attraction industry
Development of Student Competencies	• Industry-specific know-how skills • Guest-centric orientation skills • Management skills • Personal development skills • Ability to challenge self-status quo • Confident humility
Enhancement of the Board's Engagement with the Academic Institution	• Sit in classes and evaluate the content of instruction • Become more involved with student organizations • Facilitate research between the college and the industry. • Improve communication channels between and among board members, as well as between board members and the college
Interaction with Students through Guest Lectures	• Understand the 'whys?' • Evolution and continuous changes in the theme park and attraction industry • Operational applications • Crisis management • Leadership • Be practical • The impact of technology • Promote diverse perspectives

Industry participants in the four groups represented different theme parks and attractions and different experiences. Nevertheless, some of the issues raised by the different groups were similar across several groups. In general, the groups recommended the development of student skills and competencies in three major areas: industry know-how, management and leadership skills, and personal development. Some specific recommendations that should be noted included the suggestions of putting more emphasis on the impact of technology, understanding the guest experience, recognizing the importance of safety and crisis management, and the understanding of contemporary issues that face the theme park and the attraction industry.

The exercise was an attempt to engage the board members and to make them feel more proactive in the design and delivery of the academic program and student internship and placement. This type of activity could also enhance the agenda of future board meetings and contribute to a stronger commitment to the academic institution.

5. CONCLUSIONS

Industry advisory boards can be an important resource for administrators, faculty, and students. While many board members are eager to be engaged with students, many academic programs continue to face several challenges in recruiting, retaining and making effective use of their advisory boards.

The chapter provided a general overview of the role and responsibilities of industry advisory boards in academic settings, including the type of boards, the process of establishing a board, recruitment and membership, and board members' motivation to serve on such boards. While the literature is rather limited, previous research addressed practical issues like the various roles of advisory boards, their impact on student skill development, and obstacles facing board members when serving the academic institution.

The chapter also presented the case of the industry advisory board at the Rosen College of Hospitality Management at the University of Central Florida in Orlando and reported a short case study of a brainstorming exercise undertaken by members of the theme park industry advisory board affiliated with the Rosen College of Hospitality Management. The interactive exercise was implemented during a recent advisory board meeting and enhanced the sense of ownership among board members, as well as providing extensive information regarding curriculum development, enhancement of students' competencies, overall board engagement, and effective industry interaction with students.

The case study presented was a report of a single industry advisory board at one institution and its role, responsibilities, and ongoing activities may not be applicable to all academic institutions. It could serve, however, as a framework for developing and enhancing other industry advisory boards in other academic institutions. Enhancement of board engagement may be attained through regular meetings, events, and activities that would make board members feel that they contribute to the academic program specifically and the community at large.

Due to the limited size of industry advisory boards, future research should include more qualitative methodologies to better understand the perception of advisory board members in a particular academic discipline. Furthermore, research should not only address board members but should also include more relevant groups that work with boards like administrators, faculty, students and other community groups that are involved with the academic program. Since the goals and objectives of each academic institution vary, different research goals should be adopted.

Future research should also add new knowledge on the role and responsibilities of industry advisory boards, including exploring the complex motivations of volunteers serving on boards (Nagai and Nehls, 2014), meeting the members' needs and expectations (Nagai and Nehls, 2014), or how to better engage them with the various stakeholders of the academic institution.

REFERENCES

Atkinson, R. and Flint, J. (2001), 'Accessing Hidden and Hard-to-reach Populations: Snowball Research Strategies', *Social Research Update*, **33** (1), 1–5.

Baker, G.A., Wysocki, A.F. and House, L.O. (2008a), 'Industry–Academic Partnerships: The View from the Corner Office', *International Food and Agribusiness Management Review*, **11** (3), 57–79.

Baker, G.A., Wysocki, A.F., House, L.O. and Batista, J.C. (2008b), 'Industry–Academic Partnerships – Benefit or Burden?', *International Food and Agribusiness Management Review*, **11** (1), 97–117.

Carnegie Mellon University (2014), 'Advisory board', accessed 12 December 2014 at http://www.cmu.edu/engineering/estp/about-us/advisory-board.html.

Club Foundation (2014), 'Faculty Internship Programs', accessed 14 September 2014 at www.clubfoundation.org/facultyInternship.htm.

Conroy, P.A. and Lefever, M.M. (1996), 'The value of college advisory boards', *Cornell Hotel & Restaurant Administration Quarterly*, **37** (4), 85–90.

Dorazio, P. (1996), 'Professional Advisory Boards: Fostering Communication and Collaboration between Academe and Industry', *Business Communication Quarterly*, **59** (3), 98–104.

Genheimer, S.R. and Shehab, R.L. (2009), 'A Survey of Industry Advisory Board Operation and Effectiveness in Engineering Education', *Journal of Engineering Education*, **98** (2), 169–80.

Hales, J.A., Wiener, P. and Lynn, C. (2007), 'Faculty Internships for Hospitality Instructors: Internships can Help Hospitality Faculty Build Industry Relationships while also Ensuring the Best and Most Current Training for their Students', *Techniques: Connecting Education and Careers (J3)*, **82** (4), 36–9.

Hicks, L., Vansickle, J., Hancer-Rauch, H. and Satterblom, A. (2011), 'Creating a Program Advisory Board: A Key Advocacy and Marketing Strategy for Longevity in Turbulent Times', *JOPERD: The Journal of Physical Education, Recreation and Dance*, **82** (3), 46.

Kane, J.J. and Jisha, J.E. (2004), 'An Analysis of Sport Management Clubs and Advisory Boards in Sport Management Programs across North America', *International Sports Journal*, **8** (1), 132–8.

Kang, B. and Miller, M. (1999), *An Overview of the Sabbatical Leave in Higher Education: A Synopsis of the Literature Base*, Ipswich, MA: ERIC.

Nagai, J. and Nehls, K. (2014), 'Non-Alumni Advisory Board Volunteers', *Innovative Higher Education*, **39** (1), 3–16.

National Council on Family Relations (2014), 'Function and Value of Advisory Boards for Academic Programs', accessed 14 September 2014 at www.ncfr.org/ncfr-2012/thursday/function-and-value-advisory-boards-academic-programs.

Park, K., Reisinger, Y. and Park, C. (2009), 'Visitors' Motivation for Attending Theme Parks in Orlando, Florida', *Event Management*, **13** (2), 83–101.

Penrose, J.M. (2002), 'Strengthen Your Business Communication Program with an Alumni Advisory Board', *Business Communication Quarterly*, **65** (4), 73–85.

Rhea, D.J. (2009), 'The Physical Education Deficit in the High Schools', *JOPERD: The Journal of Physical Education, Recreation and Dance*, **80** (5), 5–9.

Roach, T.D. (1999), 'Corporate Relationships with Business Education Programs', *National Business Education Yearbook*, **1999**, 152–61.

Rosen College of Hospitality Management (2014), 'About us', accessed on 1 September 2016 at https://hospitality.ucf.edu/about-rosen-college/.

Rubin, Judith (ed.) (2015), *2014 Theme Index: The Global Attractions Attendance Report*, Themed Entertainment Association/Economics Research Associates, accessed 28 June 2015 at http://www.teaconnect.org/images/files/TEA_103_49736_150603.pdf.

Stautberg, S. and Green, N. (2007), 'How an advisory board drives innovation: Procter & Gamble offers a strong example of how to create an advisory board, how to manage it successfully, and how to apply its recommendations for bottom-line results', *Directors & Boards*, **3**, 53–5.

Taylor, E., Marino, D., Rasor-Greenhalgh, S. and Hudak, S. (2010), 'Navigating Practice and Academic Change in Collaborative Partnership with a Community Advisory Board', *Journal of Allied Health*, **39** (3), 103–10.

University of Central Florida (2014), 'About UCF', accessed 15 September 2014 at www.ucf.edu/about-ucf/.

University of Dayton School of Business Administration (2014), 'Advisory Boards', accessed 14 September 2014 at www.udayton.edu/business/about/advisory_boards.php.

University of Miami (2014), 'School of Business Administration Advisory Boards', accessed 14 September 2014 at www.bus.miami.edu/explore-the-school/development/boards/.

University of North Carolina at Greensboro (2014), 'Administrative Guidelines for the Appointment of Advisory Boards', The University of North Carolina at Greensboro, accessed 14 September 2014 at provost.uncg.edu/documents/personnel/advisory.pdf.

University of Texas at Austin School of Architecture (2014), 'UTSOA Advisory Council', accessed 14 September 2014 at soa.utexas.edu/about/support-donate/utsoa-advisory-council.

Visit Orlando (2014a), 'Things to do in Orlando', accessed on 1 September 2016 at http://www.visitorlando.com/things-to-do/.

Visit Orlando (2014b), 'Fast facts about Orlando meetings', accessed on 1 September 2016 at http://trade.

visitorlando.com/includes/content/images/media/docs/MeetingsOrlando%20Mtgs%20Fact%20Sheet%20 2014%20(2).pdf.

Visit Orlando (2014c), 'Orlando announces record 59 million visitors in 2013', accessed on 1 September 2016 at http:// www.visitorlando.com/blog/index.cfm/2014/4/8/Orlando-Announces-Record-59-Million-Visitors-in-2013/.

Zahra, S.A., Newey, L.R. and Shaver, J. (2011), 'Academic Advisory Boards' Contributions to Education and Learning: Lessons from Entrepreneurship Centers', *Academy of Management Learning and Education*, **10** (1), 113–29.

38 Networks for social capital building in tourism higher education
Florian Aubke and Anja Hergesell

1. INTRODUCTION

Higher education institutions form a micro-cosmos in which students build social connections both inside and outside of the classroom. Some relations can be considered affective (for example, friendships), some can be considered functional (for example, group work). Some relations are formed voluntarily, some are induced. Some relations endure beyond the university context and reach into the private sphere; some relations are of limited duration. At any point in time, students engage in multiple social relationships and the networks these relationships form have, in turn, a significant effect on student academic performance (Baldwin et al. 1997; Cho et al. 2007; Rizzuto et al. 2009).

The interdependence of social relationships and academic performance builds on the theory of social capital. The mastery of building and using relationships and thereby social capital has been defined as a key element of (higher) education and thus should find a place in modern curricula (Wilson 1997). Preparing students to become responsible leaders in tourism requires that students get the opportunity (1) to learn how to build social capital and use it to their own and society's benefit; and (2) to develop and capitalize on a range of relations with each other at present and in the future.

In order for universities to match this expectation, they need to go beyond a revision of classroom teaching and get a thorough understanding of the characteristics of student networks and the effects these features have on the network members before being able to actively encourage social capital building. The exploratory study presented in this chapter touches on these questions examining an intercultural tourism student setting and the characteristics of selected student networks. It also considers the impacts of those network characteristics on student performance. While the case study is context-specific and exploratory in nature, it can provide indicative insights into the interplay of network features and network development and highlights the opportunities of applying social network analysis (SNA) to investigate social capital building.

2. SOCIAL CAPITAL BUILDING IN HIGHER EDUCATION

The role social interaction plays for the learning process has long been acknowledged (Bandura 1977; Vygotsky 1978), and contemporary pedagogies propose collaborative approaches to problem solving rather than an individualized accumulation of knowledge (Johnson and Johnson 2009). Social interactions can lead to higher levels of cognition (Schrire 2006) and provide the opportunity to reflect on one's own understanding, alternative views of the learning content and the effectiveness of learning approaches (Hadwin and Järvelä 2011). Today, there is a general consensus in the literature that social interactions not only increase student satisfaction, but also have a positive effect on academic performance (Akyol and Garrison 2011; Haythornthwaite et al. 2000; Hommes et al. 2012; Johnson et al. 2008; Mayer and Puller 2008; Yuan et al. 2006).

The concept of social capital describes the opportunities imbedded in social relations. It is defined as 'resources embedded in one's own social network that can be accessed or mobilized through ties in networks' (Lin 2001, p. 51). In this concept, the resources of others, paired with social relations to these others, occupy critical significance. Social relations enable individuals to generate returns for themselves by capturing and accessing these second order resources. A theory of social capital therefore describes the process of investing in social relations in order to utilize others' resources.

Naturally, social capital is contingent on social networks. However, the mere existence of networks does not constitute a sufficient condition for social capital. Rather, certain network characteristics may increase or decrease the flow of a certain quantity and quality of resources between actors (Sparrowe et al. 2001). In other words, networks are considered important antecedents exogenous to social capital (Lin 2001). Network size, number of connections relative to the size, and degree of clustering in the network are examples of network characteristics.

The question prevails as to which network structures foster or hinder the access to social capital. The closure argument states that dense networks, that is, networks of strongly connected individuals, provide sources of social capital (Burt 2001; Coleman 1988). Conversely, the 'weak tie' argument (Granovetter 1983) suggests that networks can profit from individuals who are more loosely connected (weak ties), since knowledge exchange tends to be more informative. The 'structural hole' argument (Granovetter 1983), in turn, suggests that social capital emerges when individuals hold a brokerage function between two otherwise unconnected groups (structural holes).

The importance of social capital has long been recognized in the organizational behavior literature, where it has been understood as a quality created between people based on network mechanisms (Burt 1997; 2000). Networks commonly under investigation are affiliation, communication, friendship, trust and advice networks (Jansen 2006). Research on student networks across disciplines confirms that connectedness among students and the structural position taken in networks affect student satisfaction, academic performance, the degree of commitment to the institution and persistence (Thomas 2000). The studies imply that relationship building boosts the return on an individual's human capital as networks influence knowledge creation and dissemination but also creativity and innovation (Burt 1997; 2000; TEFI 2010). Social capital thereby offers benefits both to the individual and society.

Wilson (1997, p. 756) recognizes the consequential necessity to actively support social capital building within the educational system, summarizing:

> Those professionals who learn the tools, skills and values of social capital building will lead their communities and their professions. Those schools and universities that educate their students with the values and skills to build social capital, both in the work-place and in the community, will help to set the standards, the pace and the vision.

The study presented here aims to encourage educators in tourism to recognize the value of social capital building. It provides some insights on a selection of networks that are created among students and discusses the extent to which network characteristics influence student performance, which is one of the main concerns of educators and an immediate return on social capital building.

In a first step, the underlying structure of the tourism student networks is uncovered by describing (a) the networks with regard to their size and density, and (b) the actors in the networks. In a second step, the effect of network structure on student performance is examined. The size of a network is described by the number of actors forming this network. The density of a network describes the number of existent ties relative to all ties possible. The density (or sparseness) of a network has profound effects on the resource flow within the network. Caution should be exerted when interpreting density. For one, density measures should really only be interpreted in comparison with other, equivalent networks. Second, whether high network density is advantageous or detrimental is highly context specific. In some cases, higher densities allow, for example, for better information flows (Reagans and Zuckerman 2001), in other cases it was found that maintaining high numbers of relationships places a burden on actors (Boyd and Taylor 1998), thus limiting the innovative capabilities.

Most actor-level variables revolve around the concept of centrality, describing an individual's position in a network. Several measures of centrality have been proposed, including degree (Nieminen 1974), betweenness (Freeman 1977) and eigenvector centrality (Bonacich 1987). Degree centrality is a useful measure when the relative number of incoming and outgoing ties is examined, that is, it allows actors to be classified on the basis of their network activity and general connectedness. Betweenness centrality describes the power of actors to function as bridges between actors. These actors are also known as brokers, as they are able to control the resource flow between actors or groups of actors. The eigenvector centrality additionally considers the centrality of actors one is connected to. In other words, connections to other central actors are considered more valuable than those to less central actors.

A central concept in the analysis of actors and ties in the network is homophily (Bourdieu 1986; Kilduff and Tsai 2003). It describes the phenomenon that individuals who share similar characteristics are more likely to form social relationships with one another. In their review of homophily concepts appearing in social networks, McPherson et al. (2001) outline that, in diverse networks, race and race-like ethnicity is the most prevailing mediator of homophily. Further, sex, age and religion are also apparent as having an influence on one's tendency to form relationships, whereas an effect of occupation, network position, behaviors and intrapersonal values could only be found in certain types of networks.

In most accounts on homophily, it is seen as an antecedent to network development, yet it seems equally interesting to investigate whether homophilic relationships have an effect on other out-of-network behaviors. This instrumentalization of the homophily concept seems particularly appropriate for research in educational settings, where the heterogeneity of the group under investigation is apparent, and where diversity is embedded in the educational concept of the institution.

3.   METHOD

Social network analysis (SNA) has established itself as a methodological toolkit available to researchers who focus on the analysis of relational data. Its focus is the structure, emergence and consequences of connections, which is in contrast to traditional statistical approaches.

Grounded in graph theory mathematics, the study of social networks has seen a considerable increase in popularity over the last decade. A range of accessible and comprehensible statistical procedures, both descriptive and inferential, have gained acceptance in the scientific community (Scott and Carrington 2013). Since attributes are at least in part responsible for the emergence of ties, most models of social dynamics include both relational as well as attribute data.

The study data was gathered from a cohort of students of a private university in Vienna in 2009. The university's international orientation was deemed a suitable context for studying the effects of social networks on student academic performance and the role of homophily. For the study, all 62 first-year students of the undergraduate program in tourism and hospitality management were contacted shortly after the commencement of their studies and were asked to voluntarily respond to an online survey on social network effects among university students. This point in time was chosen since most of the relationship building occurs during the first semester. Network information was gathered regarding five different types of social interaction contexts: friendship, advice, lunch, leisure time and student work groups (see Table 38.1 for complete network questions). The reason for measuring different networks simultaneously lies in the fuzziness of some of the underlying constructs, and the fact that perceived networks are measured (as opposed to actual, objective exchanges). Friendship, for example, is perceived differently across the respondent group for cultural but also personal reasons. A lunch-network or leisure-network, on the other hand, is a more 'objective' measure and, thus, can function as a validation of the initial friendship-network. Given that students generally did not know each other before the beginning of the semester, the friendship network was the main focus with respect to building sustainable social capital. Network data comprise the reported relationships (incoming and outgoing ties) in each of the aforementioned contexts. Respondents were also asked some demographic questions as well as measures of happiness (Ahrendt 2003). Finally, the average grade from the first semester was used as a measurement of academic performance.

As with any data, social network data usability is dependent on the quality and completeness of the dataset. However, relational data is particularly sensitive to inaccuracies, and missing data cannot simply be computed. The interdependency of subjects means that one inaccurate or missing tie immediately affects the overall structure of the network. Unfortunately, 'no failsafe solution to the missing data problem exists' (Knoke and Kuklinski 1982, p. 35), yet one needs to be aware that some statistical procedures are more vulnerable to working with incomplete data matrices than others.

In this case, a total of 40 students out of 62 took part in the survey, corresponding to a completion rate of 64.5 percent. Three students opted out and were completely removed from the study population. The remaining students were treated as non-respondents, meaning they remained active nodes in the network (and could thus be related to), but they did not report on connections to other nodes.

As opposed to 'traditional' data collection, respondent anonymity is, by the very nature of the data collected, difficult to observe. Acknowledging privacy concerns, all names were immediately deleted from the file, but an identification number was added to enable the network nodes to be connected properly. That way, anonymity of respondents was ensured for the data analysis and presentation phases.

As noted before, SNA works with relational data, which has a profound effect on the statistical analysis applied. Traditional statistical methods for hypothesis testing are not to be used, since relational data is inherently interdependent and therefore does not satisfy the requirement for independent observations, normally distributed populations, residuals, standard errors and so forth. As an alternative, a large set of specific analytical procedures have developed over the last decades, among those the Quadratic Analytic Procedure (QAP) (Hubert and Schulz 1976). Ucinet (Borgatti et al. 2002), a specialized software for network analysis, was applied. It allows for the calculation of QAP correlations and computes the p-values by applying a bootstrap algorithm, thus circumventing the problem of dependencies.

Among the respondents, the share of females is 65 percent, whereas it is 61 percent in the population, which is a non-significant deviation. Similarly, the proportion of Austrians in the sample (55 percent) does not deviate markedly from that in the population (61 percent). Half the sample was born between 1989 and 1991. In the sample, 33 students reported not having regular employment besides their studies; the rest worked part-time between 5 and 30 hours. Six of the students are only children, 11 are eldest siblings, 7 in-between, and 16 youngest siblings. Median student performance by the time of the assessment was 74 percent, in which female students performed significantly better than males (medians 80 percent vs. 64 percent, one-tailed $p = 0.006$); the latter are more heterogeneous in their performance (standard deviation 23 instead of 14, one-tailed $p = 0.03$).

4.   FINDINGS

As depicted in Table 38.1, the friendship network is the largest in total number of ties. Given the binary nature of the networks, this does not provide any indication of tie strength, yet it means that the friendship network has the highest density (13 percent) of all networks observed. At the same time, the advice network shows the lowest density, with just below 4 percent of all possible ties. This may be explained by the fact that students who have just commenced their studies may not have had the opportunity or, in fact, see the need to build such an advice network. However, students will have had the opportunity to form friendship ties during the first weeks of their studies. The density of the network needs to be read with caution though, since in fact only 23 percent of all the reported ties in the friendship network are reciprocated, suggesting that most respondents hold a more flexible view of friendship.

Differences in friendship ties were noted between actors of different gender and nationality. Figure 38.1 depicts the friendship network by gender. A Multidimensional Scaling (MDS) display was chosen, which puts actors in proximity based on structural equivalence. The most central actors in the network are placed in or near the center; the less connected an actor is, the more on the periphery he can be found. Circles represent female

Table 38.1   Overview of tie distribution in networks

Type of Network	Number of Ties[1]	Network Density[2]	Reciprocity[3]
Advice			
Who do you turn to for advice regarding student life in general?	117	0.0354	N/A
Friendship			
Who would you consider to be your friend?	443	0.1340	0.2340
Leisure			
Who do you regularly meet outside university for leisure activities?	176	0.0532	0.2308
Lunch			
With whom do you regularly spend your lunch break when you are at university?	272	0.0823	0.2252
Workgroup			
With whom would you prefer to work on a group project?	333	0.1007	0.1978

Notes:
[1]   Total number of ties found in respective network.
[2]   The density of a binary network is the total number of ties divided by the total number of possible ties.
[3]   Percentage of ties that are reciprocated in a network. (Note: in an advice network, ties are directed.)

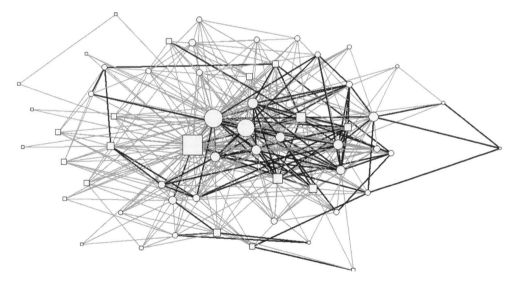

Figure 38.1   MDS display of friendship network entailing gender and actor centrality

students and squares male students. The size of a node is determined by their network centrality (in this case eigenvector centrality). Bold lines show reciprocal ties, that is, two actors have named each other as friends.

In this case it can be seen that female actors have many more reciprocal ties than their

Table 38.2   Associations' demographic matrices and networks (Jaccard coefficients and p-values)

Matrices	Leisure Network		Friendship Network		Workgroup Network		Lunch Network		Advice Network	
	Jac.	p	Jac.	p	Jac.	p	Jac.	p	Jac.	p
What is your nationality?	0.07	0.003	0.15	0.001	0.12	0.003	0.10	0.002	0.04	0.015
Which language is spoken at home?	0.07	0.018	0.14	0.005	0.13	0.001	0.10	0.001	0.05	0.008
Do you hold a regular job besides your studies?	0.08	0.001	0.16	0.001	0.11	0.014	0.10	0.002	0.05	0.017
What is your gender?	0.07	0.009	0.12	0.005	0.11	0.005	0.10	0.002	0.04	0.015

male counterparts, suggesting that female students have a more balanced understanding of friendship. This may trigger researchers to further investigate gender effects on network formation and possibly (in the case of longitudinal network research) network stability.

To assess the effect of homophily on network structure, attribute data (gender, ethnicity, language spoken at home, and employment besides studies) were first transformed into matrices. Table 38.2 shows the results of the QAP. The significant correlations suggest similarities in the structure of the networks. For example, actors who form ties in the gender network (that is, they are of the same sex) are also more likely to form ties in the friendship network. It can be noted that all associations are significant at $p < 0.05$, thus suggesting that homophily is a characteristic of tourism student networks at the beginning of their studies. This, in turn, questions whether a mixed student cohort (with regard to gender, nationality, and so on) really mingles.

One of the key issues for educators is the effects of social relations and, in consequence, individual network positions on academic performance. In other words, if social capital is understood as a metaphor for advantage (Burt 2000), can this advantage be turned into academic success? Intuitively, most educators would support this notion, thinking that well connected students have an advantage in selecting study partners, can benefit from alternative views of a subject matter and may be generally more positively attuned to their studies.

In this study, degree centrality (indegree/incoming ties and outdegree/outgoing ties) was computed for each actor in all of the five networks. The correlations with centrality scores and end-of-semester average grades showed that indegree centralities have a much stronger predictive power than outdegree centralities. Formulated as linear regressions, the average grade could be predicted with adjusted $r^2 = 0.25$ ($p = 0.007$) by the four centralities of incoming workgroup, incoming advice, incoming friendship and incoming leisure activity ties. This means that, in our sample, social selection processes are in line with academic performance. High achievers are more sought after as social contacts, which is interesting given the fact that network data was collected during the first semester. Whether the social selection processes occur as a result of strategic study behavior of students remains a topic of further study, as does the question of whether social influence processes emerge over time. To get a more complete picture of the social dimensions at work within student cohorts, researchers may be advised to collect longitudinal network data.

5.   FUTURE DIRECTIONS

The case study undertaken provides ideas to further investigate social capital building in tourism education by extending the research focus and by using further SNA analyses.

While the case study only looked at a few selected networks within one student cohort at one moment in time, future research could extend with regard to time, networks examined and actors included. Longitudinal studies would help to better understand cause–effect relationships. They would also provide a more complete picture of the social dimensions at work within student cohorts.

Examining more types of networks would provide insights into how friendship and work relationships interactively develop, and thus provide ideas for educators about how to support social capital building in the classroom by strategically setting up work relationships between students. Special attention could be given to how homophily within networks could be overcome, if indeed homophily is a 'problem', in using the full potential of social capital building provided by international tourism student cohorts. The question is how far homophily emerges from social selection or social influence processes, in other words whether similarity triggers the formation of ties or whether similarity is a consequence of a social relationship. If the former is the case, and acknowledging that tourism provides international careers for its students, homophily may restrict career development. However, further research would be needed to examine such a long-term cause–effect relationship.

Finally, including more actors such as other student cohorts, friends outside of university but also friends of friends, would recognize that human agents are not only affected by their immediate friends, but also friends of friends and possibly those even further away, beyond their horizon of observability (Friedkin 1998).

Extending the research focus could be combined with the application of more advanced SNA tools such as Exponential Random Graphs (ERGMs), which allow researchers to test more sophisticated hypotheses by considering the existence of multiple, parallel relations between nodes (multi-level), the relations between events and nodes (bipartite), or relations between nodes, events and organizations.

This study could be replicated (a) in other tourism programs to corroborate the findings, and (b) in other disciplines of higher education to examine whether the particularities of the study, its contents, teaching mode and delivery style but also the characteristics of the students enrolled in a program influence networking and social capital building. Comparisons could also help to identify best practice examples from which tourism educators could learn how to actively encourage networking in a way that boosts social capital building.

While there are a vast number of research questions unanswered with regard to tourism student networks, researchers might be cautious to enter this field of study and educators might be reluctant to examine their university networks in detail to improve social capital building. The biggest challenge in studying such networks is anonymity issues in the data collection. Privacy concerns will remain so that benefits of such studies and the methodology applied will have to be convincingly presented to university ethics committees.

6.   CONCLUSION

The objective of this chapter was to raise awareness among tourism educators of the importance of social capital building among students, and to provide some insights on network formation among students at the start of their tourism studies. The study looked, on the one hand, at network architecture by describing selected student friendship networks and examining differences in social relationship formation by selected actor characteristics (for example are two individuals more likely to become friends if they share certain traits, such as nationality or gender?). On the other hand, the study investigated how the network structure influences student academic performance (for example can academic performance of one student be explained by the number of connections this student maintains with other students of different achievement levels?).

The case study, focusing on an international tourism and hospitality management cohort, suggested that the understanding of the term 'friendship' differs between students, which may partially be linked to the limited time passed since the start of their studies. It also confirms that the researchers' simultaneous examination of various friendship networks was justified. All friendship networks showed homophily with regard to gender, nationality, language spoken at home, and employment status, thus confirming the proverb 'Birds of a feather flock together', and questioning whether offering international and otherwise diverse study settings could really be capitalized on. The study also showed that network structure and student performance are associated, in other words that the students who are sought after in friendship networks (that have more incoming ties) perform better in their academic studies.

It should be noted that the present study only provides a small glimpse on network formation, structure and capital building among tourism students. Longitudinal studies during and beyond the time of tourism studies would be helpful in better understanding the development of networks and the range of opportunities provided by social capital building for individuals, their future employers and society at large. Also comparative studies would be helpful in understanding the determinants of network characteristics and their effects in order to develop best practice examples and provide guidelines for tourism educators, particularly program managers.

In summary, tourism educators faced with an increasingly heterogeneous and international student base seem to be eager for solutions to engage the student body and foster social relations in the classroom to benefit the study experience and social capital building. Empirical research in this context is sparse and thus educators often rely on their own professional experience and anecdotal evidence. Maybe this chapter encourages some educators to look more closely at social relationships and their effects on student experience, not just to extend educational research, but to inform academic practice and provide more community-centered instruction.

REFERENCES

Ahrendt, D. (2003), *The Quality of Life Survey*, Fieldwork Technical Report, Hilversum: GfK INTOMART.
Akyol, Z. and D.R. Garrison (2011), 'Understanding cognitive presence in an online and blended community

of inquiry: Assessing outcomes and processes for deep approaches to learning', *British Journal of Educational Technology*, **42** (2), 233–50.

Baldwin, T.T., D.M. Bedell and J.L. Johnson (1997), 'The social fabric of a team-based MBA program: Network effects on student satisfaction and performance', *Academy of Management Journal*, **40** (6), 1369–97.

Bandura, A. (1977), *Social Learning Theory*, Englewood Cliffs, NJ: Prentice-Hall.

Bonacich, P. (1987), 'Power and centrality: A family of measures', *American Journal of Sociology*, **92**, 1170–82.

Borgatti, S.P., M.G. Everett and L.C. Freeman (2002), *Ucinet for Windows: Software for Social Network Analysis*, Harvard, MA: Analytic Technologies.

Bourdieu, P. (1986), 'The forms of capital', in J.G. Richardson (ed.), *Handbook of Theory and Research for the Sociology of Education*, New York: Greenwood, 241–58.

Boyd, N.G. and R.R. Taylor (1998), 'A developmental approach to the examination of friendship in leader–follower relationships', *Leadership Quarterly*, **9** (1), 1–25.

Burt, R. (1997), 'The contingent value of social capital', *Administrative Science Quarterly*, **42**, 339–65.

Burt, R. (2000), 'Decay functions', *Social Networks*, **22**, 1–28.

Burt, R. (2001), 'Structural holes versus network closure as social capital', in N. Lin, K.S. Cook and R. Burt (eds), *Social Capital: Theory and Research*, New Brunswick, NJ: Transaction Publishers, 31–56.

Cho, H., G. Gay, B. Davidson and A. Ingraffea (2007), 'Social networks, communication styles, and learning performance in a CSCL community', *Computers & Education*, **49** (2), 309–29.

Coleman, J.S. (1988), 'Social capital in the creation of human capital', *American Journal of Sociology*, **94**, 95–120.

Freeman, L. (1977), 'A set of measures of centrality based on betweenness', *Sociometry*, **40** (1), 35–41.

Friedkin, N.E. (1998), *A Structural Theory of Social Influence*, New York: Cambridge University Press.

Granovetter, M. (1983), 'The strength of weak ties: A network theory revisited', *Sociological Theory*, **1**, 201–33.

Hadwin, A. and S. Järvelä (2011), 'Introduction to a special issue on social aspects of self-regulated learning: Where social and self meet in the strategic regulation of learning', *Teachers College Record*, **113** (2), 235–9.

Haythornthwaite, C., M.M. Kazmer, J. Robins and S. Shoemaker (2000), 'Community development among distance learners: Temporal and technological dimensions', *Journal of Computer-Mediated Communication*, **6** (1).

Hommes, J., B. Rienties, W. Grave, G. Bos, L. Schuwirth and A. Scherpbier (2012), 'Visualising the invisible: A network approach to reveal the informal social side of student learning', *Advances in Health Education*, **17** (5), 743–57.

Hubert, L. and J. Schulz (1976), 'Quadratic assignment as a general data analysis strategy', *British Journal of Mathematical and Statistical Psychology*, **29** (2), 190–241.

Jansen, D. (2006), *Einführung in die Netzwerkanalyse*, Wiesbaden: VS Verlag für Sozialwissenschaften.

Johnson, D.W. and R.T. Johnson (2009), 'An educational psychology success story: Social interdependence theory and cooperative learning', *Educational Researcher*, **38** (5), 365–79.

Johnson, R.D., S. Hornik and E. Salas (2008), 'An empirical examination of factors contributing to the creation of successful e-learning environments', *International Journal of Human-Computer Studies*, **66** (5), 356–69.

Kilduff, M. and W. Tsai (2003), *Social Networks and Organizations*, London: SAGE Publications.

Knoke, D. and J.H. Kuklinski (1982), *Network Analysis*, Beverly Hills, CA: SAGE Publications.

Lin, N. (2001), 'Building a network theory of social capital', in N. Lin, K. Cook and R. Burt (eds), *Social Capital: Theory and Research*, New York: Aldine de Gruyter, 3–30.

Mayer, A. and S.L. Puller (2008), 'The old boy (and girl) network: Social network formation on university campuses', *Journal of Public Economics*, **92** (1–2), 329–47.

McPherson, M., L. Smith-Lovin and J.M. Cook (2001), 'Birds of a feather: Homophily in social networks', *Annual Review of Sociology*, **27** (1), 515–44.

Nieminen, J. (1974), 'On the centrality in a graph', *Scandinavian Journal of Psychology*, **15** (1), 332–6.

Reagans, R. and E.W. Zuckerman (2001), 'Networks, diversity, and productivity: The social capital of corporate R&D teams', *Organization Science*, **12** (4), 502–17.

Rizzuto, T. E., J. LeDoux and J.P. Hatala (2009), 'It's not just what you know, it's who you know: Testing a model of the relative importance of social networks to academic performance', *Social Psychology of Education*, **12** (2), 175–89.

Schrire, S. (2006), 'Knowledge building in asynchronous discussion groups: Going beyond quantitative analysis', *Computers & Education*, **46** (1), 49–70.

Scott, J. and P. Carrington (eds) (2013), *The SAGE Handbook of Social Network Analysis*, London: SAGE Publications.

Sparrowe, R.T., R.C. Liden, S.J. Wayne and M.L. Kraimer (2001), 'Social networks and the performance of individuals and groups', *Academy of Management Journal*, **44** (2), 316–25.

TEFI (2010), *A Values-Based Framework for Tourism Education: Building the Capacity to Lead*, accessed 28 November 2014 at www.tourismeducationfutures.org/publications/TEFI%20White%20Paper%20Aug%20 2010.pdf?attredirects=0&d=1.

Thomas, S.L. (2000), 'Ties that bind: A social network approach to understanding student integration and persistence', *The Journal of Higher Education*, **71** (5), 591–615.

Vygotsky, L.S. (1978), *Mind in Society: The Development of Higher Psychological Processes*, Cambridge, MA: Harvard University Press.

Wilson, P.A. (1997), 'Building social capital: A learning agenda for the twenty-first century', *Urban Studies*, **34** (5/6), 745–60.

Yuan, Y.C., G. Gay and H. Hembrooke (2006), 'Focused activities and the development of social capital in a distributed learning community', *The Information Society*, **22** (1), 25–39.

39 Innovation and change in tourism education with special focus on India
Babu P. George

1. INTRODUCTION

The debate about the nature of tourism knowledge has not settled and we have not yet any consensus about the status of tourism as a single and unified academic discipline of inquiry (Cooper and Shepherd, 1997). On the contrary, such debates in the international tourism academic circles have accelerated in the recent past which, in my view, is an indicator of the health and vibrancy of an emerging science of tourism. A handful of international journals devoted to the study of human resource development in tourism and tourism education have emerged in the recent past (Ayikoru et al., 2009). The number of conferences on tourism education and related themes has also seen a concurrent surge.

Research by Ladkin (2014) indicates that not every country or region is at the same stage of the tourism education life cycle. The present author has been conducting extensive interviews with tourism education experts in a sample of countries from around the world in connection with a grant funded research project and has plotted his inferences about the status of tourism education in these countries on a bell curve (George, 2013). While the major thrust area of his research was the adoption of e-learning technologies by tourism schools around the world, parallels with the general tourism education arena cannot be missed. Based on factors like popularity and the degree of disciplination, the product life cycle stage of tourism education in some countries is in decline whereas in some other countries it is just in the launch phase. The nascence and vibrancy in some of the newcomers is evident with the formation of new departments, faculties, programs and even entire universities dedicated to tourism. There is huge government and industry support and students are enthused as well. Yet some of the early movers in the USA and UK have already reached stagnancy and some are in decline. With few sources of external finance and dwindling student enrolments, some of the pioneering tourism schools have either closed down or repositioned themselves in radically different ways. Interestingly, Sciarini et al. (2012) reach similar conclusions about the historical development of online tourism education in selected countries.

It must be specially noted that some of the early movers overcame 'decline' by internationalization. For example, Australian universities either went overseas (direct export or via partnerships) or promoted home campuses overseas (via educational fairs, educational consultants and so on). While engaging in multinational expansion, the Australian universities also restructured their curricula to distinguish them and make them stand out. Historically, many of these programs were modeled on the early pioneers (UQ, JCU, VU), which meant that there was very little market differentiation among these programs.

In many countries, tourism education evolved from trade schools and polytechnics. In the US, tourism education started in 'home science' schools, later absorbed by b-schools.

Even today, independent tourism schools are rare unless there is significant local industry support. Historical focus was more on skills (knowledge utilization) than knowledge creation (research) or knowledge sharing (education). Also, historically, tourism education in many countries has experienced a slow start, followed by abrupt (unsustainable) expansion. What does this imply? Lack of direction, premature death, or absorption by other disciplines? Many trends are emerging, but it is still too early to say something concretely.

2. DISCOVERING AND TEACHING TOURISM KNOWLEDGE

It is difficult to judge if tourism knowledge is a body of complexified simplicities or that of simplified complexities. Many tourism practitioners, and even researchers in consumer sciences, still think that tourism is not worthy of special academic attention. Thus, the initial growth of tourism knowledge was by the rebels who revolted against the system. Jafari (1990) noted that early studies featured mostly economic prospects of tourism, emphasizing its benefits. Gradually, this unilateral economic view gave way to a wave of studies focusing on the socio-cultural aspects of tourism and brought the benefits of tourism under scrutiny. After the waves of economic and socio-cultural research, academic interest began to focus on alternative forms of tourism development which were purportedly sustainable (this era marks the beginning of growing out of disciplinary boundaries). These events by and large resulted in significant cumulative changes in tourism knowledge. Yet, such knowledge did not find its way into educational programs until the push came from various powerful quarters. The need for tourism educational programs was felt as a result of the compounding effect of multiple forces: these forces include the need for developing a technologically progressive industry, the need for raising the image of tourism careers, and increasing need for technically trained staff, among others (Amoah and Baum, 1997).

The process of educational program development based on tourism knowledge was not straightforward. Confusion about target markets and nomenclature has continued to be a key contentious issue. Most common degree titles include Tourism Management and Tourism Studies, yet a huge diversity is evident. Many programs are prefixed with terms like 'international', 'global' and so on, while some amalgamated their titles with leisure, recreation, sports, and/or hospitality. Variety in terms of BS / BA / BBUS / MSc / MA / MBA nomenclature can also be seen, while the content remained almost the same. A vocational vs. more liberal focus was another contentious issue (see Dredge et al., 2012). Such variety confuses the students and the employers alike. When it comes to the identification of target markets for tourism employment, the unanswered question is: should tourism degrees enable students to seek employment outside of the industry (Barron et al., 2007; McKercher et al., 1995)?

Problems in teaching tourism have been multifold. Again, this is due to the complexity of the venture. Tourism is the most wide-ranging industry in the world, in terms of disciplinary contributions required to understand it; it is the most culturally diverse industry in the world, in terms of guests and hosts involved; it is the most politically charged industry in the world, in terms of inter-stakeholder strains; and, last but not the least, it is still the most neglected industry in the world, in terms of developmental priorities.

3.   THE INTERNET AS A 'DESTABILIZER'

Bricks-and-mortar classroom-based instruction is no longer the Holy Grail of tourism education. Hybrid, blended, fully online, and Massive Open Online Classroom (MOOC) options are increasingly being considered by the educational providers as well as the learners. Contemporary educational technologies provide economies of scale and scope. The promise of gaining globally valid diplomas without leaving your doorstep is enticing many back to the (virtual) classrooms. Tourism, given its transnational nature, has the scope as a special subject for such studies. Also, there is a heightened understanding among everyone that 'webification' is not merely digitizing content and that it requires understanding of the underlying cultural drives.

Even the industry is beginning to re-understand that having an employee with a 'degree certificate' is relatively less important than having one with actionable knowledge. This coincides with the proliferation of MOOCs. Thanks to disruptive internet-based technologies, educators' role as knowledge sharers is almost gone: this time-honored role is replaced by their emerging role as information complexity/overload reducers. Also, educators now have their role as content creators for open audiences: Yes, 'share and thou shalt receive' is the norm.

With the declining 'teaching' role, what is discernible is the increasing weighting of faculty research in performance measurements. However, many counter-currents are visible, too. For instance, a herd of academicians have been evangelizing the agenda of 'active learning' as a strategy to reduce the blind assault of technology. Finally, the impact of technology upon tourism education cannot be understood in isolation: it is mixed with the impacts of globalization, demographic–psychographic shifts, and that of complex market forces.

4.   THE INDIAN FOCUS

Tourism education in India is of a relatively recent origin and Indian academia is yet to become a major part of the brewing debate. Yet, leaders of tourism education in India have been organizing in the form of conclaves and think tanks to discuss pressing issues like curriculum planning, stakeholder integration, and the molding of future tourism educators. For the sheer fact that the country cannot find itself anywhere in the list of major tourism revenue recipients despite its inimitably superlative natural and cultural heritage, the central government of India has taken the cause of tourism education very seriously. In order to attract the best students and to ensure their employment placements, educational institutions have increasingly begun to embrace a marketing orientation to their program design and delivery. However, there are many prickly problems afflicting tourism higher education in India. Some of these problems are noted internationally as well, while the rest are very India specific.

This chapter is an attempt to identify some of the issues slowing down the advancement of tourism education in India. The present author worked as a faculty member in one of the Central Universities of India teaching tourism before he migrated to the United States six years ago, providing the unique vantage point of an ex-insider. While no grand design is offered as a panacea, it is hoped that the discussion contained here will help clarify the issues better, which is the first major step in identifying meaningful solutions. Valid and peer-reviewed empirical research into the issues and challenges faced by the tourism educational system in India is scarce. The author would like to forewarn readers that the observations contained herein are mostly based on own experiences and anecdotal evidence and hence the inferences drawn from them should be treated with an additional grain of salt.

4.1   The Discourse of Constituency Disputes

By the term 'constituency disputes', what I mean is the petty quarrels about the boundaries of knowledge that define tourism. While this is a global issue, it is strikingly visible in the Indian scenario. For the most part, I attribute it to the historical development of tourism education in India. In the past, tourism programs in India were conceived, developed and run by pure social science faculties whose focus was primarily to provide a vocational track for their otherwise unemployable graduates. For instance, history departments in many Indian universities tweaked their undergraduate and graduate programs to include a few courses in the history of tourism, cultural tourism and so on, in order to make these programs 'job oriented'. However, it didn't take long to realize that the graduates of these programs could not excel in the industry. While many of them got industry placements at the entry level and began to work alongside those who graduated out of the 'trade mills' that were tasked with imparting training on only certain specific job-related Knowledge-Skill-Attitude (KSA) set, their career advancement was severely hampered due to the inherent skewness of their disciplinary orientations (Sheldon et al., 2011; Singh, 1997). Most of them could not advance to higher levels in the hierarchy due to their complete unfamiliarity with the principles and practices of management (Echtner, 1995).

   If some of these graduates excelled in the profession, that was mostly due to their self-learning in entrepreneurship and management or at times given the niche nature of business they were into (say, a tourism business that focuses on historical interpretation and guiding). The intention I have in narrating this situation is not that I am against a liberal arts-humanities orientation to tourism studies. In fact, critical approaches to tourism have resulted in significant benefits – not only for theory but also in containing various unethical and illegal tourism-related practices.

   My purpose is to show the negative effects of the *disciplinization of tourism*. I believe that tourism can better be taught with an inter-disciplinary, multi-disciplinary, trans-disciplinary, or even a counter-disciplinary approach. In Australia this is often called the 're-disciplining of tourism' (or, disciplinary colonization). I think a distinction also needs to be made here between the intellectual goals and institutional goals of tourism. The intellectual goal of research informed by disciplines is sometimes confused with institutional goals to prepare students for employment. Suggesting that we should teach what we research leads to all sorts of problems (I thank Pierre Benckendorff, the co-editor of the present volume, for this valuable insight).

   The above-mentioned state of affairs prompted some professors belonging to the business faculties of Indian universities to reformulate tourism programs in the manner of typical business programs. By the early 1990s, university business departments were already beginning to see avenues for diversified growth, with some of them launching bachelor's and master's programs focusing on industrial domains such as banking, healthcare, shipping and telecommunications, and tourism was a popular choice in this list. To be fair, these initiatives were taken up mostly by the enterprising second-rung faculty members of the business departments who were motivated primarily by the chance to prove their administrative capabilities and enjoy the perks of being an administrator than by their 'love for tourism' as a field of inquiry. Thanks to a combination of (1) the lukewarm support they got from their faculty colleagues who did not get to enjoy a piece of the pie; (2) the fear of the existing academic administrators who feared a loss of controlling rights; and (3) the sluggishness of national higher education approval-accreditation bodies like Universities Grant Commission of India (UGC) and All India Council for Technical Education (AICTE), the new programs could not be christened after MBAs and BBAs and were run as second grade programs. Often, these programs were self-financed and were variously named as BTS, BA-Tourism, MTA, MTM and so on. It took a court verdict later that allowed universities to name and run technical programs without AICTE approval for this state of affairs to change.

4.2 What (or Who) Makes a Tourism Educator in India

The inauguration of tourism degree programs with the 'Master of Business Administration' title augmented what I prefer to call the 'caste differences' within tourism academia. Given the generally perceived superiority of MBA programs over other applied social science degree programs, MBA (Tourism) assumed the status of the most favored program title. Interestingly, in many cases, it was just a rechristening of the older names and these programs continued to be housed in the faculties where they were originally launched. This led to the strange scenarios of history, geography, or even biology departments of Indian universities running MBA programs. As is known, a rose by any other name cannot smell like jasmine or lavender. Yet faculty members and students associated with the MBA programs soon became part of an Ivy League. Or, that was the way their image management efforts were directed. Page (2003) throws some light on how such business orientation has extracted the vital juices out of a diverse range of tourism studies programs when many schools accepted the 'tourism is (just/only) a business' creed.

For an observer of Social Darwinism in the academic institutional context, the excitement is not yet over. The dialectical process took a turn after the early 2000s, with the induction of a new breed of faculty members to teach tourism programs at all levels. Yes, for the first time the presence of graduates with tourism PhDs was felt in the ranks of tourism academia. They began to identify themselves as 'core tourism' faculty and had the support of senior academic administrators who found in them hope to liberate tourism education from the hold of various detractors. Since most of this new blood entered the sector at the lecturer/assistant professor level, senior faculty members who had conveniently strayed into the tourism education landscape did not find them a threat.

However, by the late 2000s, the young blood consolidated itself to fully challenge the existing order. Some of them rose to the levels of program coordinators, department heads, and a few to the level of faculty deans. Increasingly, one can observe instances of tourism PhD holders administering the deanship of an entire disciplinary or interdisciplinary area. These changes resulted in the reversal of currents. The caste system I described before took a U-turn in direction. The new dynamics reconfigured things in such a way that the core tourism faculty are now the upper class in the tourism academic caste system.

   This section cannot be wound up without giving a glimpse into the situation of affiliated college faculty. A vast majority of universities in India still follow the age-old system wherein the university conducts its various academic programs through affiliated colleges. While the qualifications required of the professors of these colleges are the very same as those of the university professors, the former class is perceived to be of lower stature. Except for a few autonomous institutions among the affiliated colleges, the rest are supposed to follow the syllabus and student examinations imposed upon them by the affiliating universities. Such overbearingness of university administration and university-based faculty results in resentment and lack of morale among their affiliated college counterparts. Pritchard and Morgan (2007) elaborate at length about tourism's gatekeepers of knowledge and how these gatekeepers potentially kill a lot of buds before they blossom into roses. The Indian scenario I described above might be a good case in point.

4.3   Careers in Tourism for Graduates in India

What do aspiring students expect from a tourism degree program? A job, for sure. But, what kind? Studies show that, internationally, aspiring tourism students expect to receive high-paying, alluring, and glamorous jobs (Pearce, 2005). I am not aware of any published research that addresses this topic in the Indian context. Based on my personal experiences (mostly as a member of student admission committees), the expectations of Indian students are not any different. Unfortunately, most aspiring students do not have the opportunity to see the rich diversity of the kinds of enterprises and employment opportunities available to them in the tourism industry. More unfortunately, the glamorous jobs on which they build their dreams are just the tip of an iceberg. By the final semester, these students are invariably presented with this reality: what they encounter is not a lack of employment opportunities but a lack of the kinds of jobs they dreamed of. Barring a few, schools that offer higher education programs in the area of tourism do not sensitize students to the myriad opportunities and associated challenges of starting careers in the tourism industry.

   In the West, a substantial number of freshmen (and the vast majority of master's degree aspirants) come to the campus with a good deal of work experience. For them, a college degree will ensure faster progression up the career ladder. Given the prior experience factor, it is more likely that they will reach their expectations more closely once they graduate. In India, in contrast, most students join undergraduate and graduate programs without any noteworthy work experience. Despite the best efforts by educational institutions to correct this by means of instituting internship requirements and action learning projects, lack of prior work experience remains a major impediment for proper industry placements – especially since the tourism industry gives a high premium for within-industry experience (Ladkin, 2000). Against this backdrop, the present author is reminded of a joke made by a former colleague: *tourism is probably the only professional educational program in India where students aspire more to become professors than to excel in the industry.* This is a no-brainer since the starting salaries of those placed in the industry on an average are lower than those of an assistant professor.

   There is no overnight solution to this problem. As a nation, India needs to encourage the presence of young high school and higher secondary school graduates in the part-time workforce. This way, students going to colleges will have an income and at the same time get an opportunity to learn about life in the workplace (remember, 'self-reliance' is something Gandhi stressed a lot!). In the short run, intensification of industry interactions during the course of study undertaken by the students is probably the only way to deal with this problem.

Another employment-related issue is the heterogeneity of the industry, mentioned elsewhere in this chapter. It is almost impossible to prepare a student to be an expert in every segment-activity spectrum that constitutes the tourism industry. Two years spent on a master's degree program in tourism would make someone a jack of most tourism-related trades but a master of none. In this regard, it is encouraging to see that many institutions have started offering specializations. It is understandable that some institutions adopt a cautious stance when it comes to micro-specializations (since tourism itself is a specialization): their fear is that such micro-specializations would reduce the chances for their graduates to find employment elsewhere outside of the chosen cocoon.

Finally, as a nation, India is currently in the headlines of the international news media for all the wrong reasons. Thanks to the all-pervasiveness of the social media, reports of violence against women and minorities are increasingly coming to light. Tourism is a culturally diverse industry and if it has a gender, most would call it feminine. Despite this hallmark femininity, guardians of college-going students are unwilling to send them to tourism-related programs. Typical tourism jobs are 24/7/365 and safety and security of the female workforce are always a concern. Women face harassment, not only in the workplace but also in the public spaces. Added to this is the perception in rural India that tourism jobs demand 'loose morals'. It takes time and concerted efforts to change such perceptions.

4.4   Industry–Institution Interface in Indian Tourism Institutes

Employment placement is the number one reason for most students joining tourism degree programs and the perception of the tourism industry regarding the employability of graduates should therefore be one of the most important considerations (Seth, 2007). Of late, there have been serious attempts to invite and integrate industry views into the curriculum. Many university tourism departments/centers have an advisory board drawn from the industry. These advisory boards meet at least once a year and provide input on a variety of issues ranging from curriculum improvement to campus placements. Anecdotal evidence suggests that these inputs are not always used in the best possible manner. For many tourism institutes, advisory boards are just a lifeline to their placement efforts. This might be the reason why advisory board meetings are often held during the placements season.

In some Western universities, there is a dedicated track for practitioners to join academics. Variously called clinical professors, adjunct professors, or professors of practice, this track ensures that professional educational programs get a feeder line of practitioner inputs on a regular basis. Also, this is an exclusive channel for the accomplished business practitioners to come back to join the academics and enrich it. Tourism education in India is certain to benefit from similar initiatives: however, the enthusiasm among the rank and file faculty to do this is minimal. Also, given the insistence upon a PhD for career advancement, the chances are that industry practitioners can join only at the entry level or as temporary guest faculty – this does not motivate even the well-intentioned practitioners.

If academic institutions are not able to produce graduates who meet the standards expected by the industry, the latter's role should be examined as well. Historically, the tourism industry has been lackluster in its approach towards higher education. This includes the fragmented nature of the industry, the small size (and limited scope) of typical tourism businesses, and the importance of in-house training to sustain and perpetuate brand uniqueness. Also, many industry players (quite wrongly) assume that the job profiles are not complex enough to demand the presence of college and university graduates in the managerial workforce (Evans, 2001). These factors result in the lack of proactive interest in the industry to engage with educational institutions constructively and in a continuous manner.

While discussing human resource development, my attention has been largely on the traditional students. Universities tend to neglect an increasingly large segment of potential learners – those who have been working in the industry but want to return to study to earn a higher degree. Universities like Indira Gandhi National Open University (IGNOU) offer them a chance to pursue their educational aspirations by means of distance education programs. However, the current level of e-learning technologies being used by these universities does not facilitate synchronous meetings. Not being about to experience an intensely personal and rich classroom experience which the traditional schools provide can be a disappointing experience for some students.

It is common in the West to see traditional universities restructuring their higher education programs into hybrid fashion with a few face-to-face sessions (mostly during the evenings and the weekends) and the rest consisting of online sessions. This has two benefits for the traditional student base: one, they can directly learn from the experiences of their classmates who have industry experience; two, they get time to do part-time jobs during their free time. Being able to network with those who already work is an added advantage, especially when it comes to employment placements later. The instructors too benefit out of such a scheme: they get a chance to directly know the current issues and challenges in the workplace. In the same spirit, an experiment at Alaska Pacific University deserves special mention. We are developing thick collaborations with some of the key local businesses in consultation with their human resource experts. We follow something close to the agile/Scrum project management methodology (Schwaber, 2004) and, out of these collaborations, develop custom-made courses for their workforce. Many such courses are eligible for credits that could be applied towards a BS or MBA if participants choose to pursue such programs later. The tourism department of a university could identify major employers in the vicinity, initiate similar processes, and explore possibilities for developing such custom made courses (I am told Flinders University in Australia uses a similar approach).

4.5   Quality Assurance Issues

When it comes to evaluating the claims of quality made by tourism educational institutions in India, an absolute lack of peer approved and rational standards cannot escape one's notice. The All India Council for Technical Education (AICTE) accredits general MBA degree programs and some MBA (Tourism) programs might have been accredited by them as well. However, AICTE's expected learning outcomes are too generic and do not reflect the quality expected of tourism educational programs. Also, many quarters express serious criticism of the role that bodies like AICTE play in the bureaucratization of education and stifling educational innovations (Gupta, 2008; Henthorne et al., 2010). Most universities and institutions like the Institute of Hotel Management and Catering Technology (IHMCT) and the Indian Institute of Tourism and Travel Management (IITTM) have developed their own internal standards of quality; however, these standards are not easily comparable with one another.

With the number of institutions offering programs and the number of students enrolling in those programs ever increasing, tourism has emerged as a mainstream graduating field in India. I am told of at least two new tourism-focused universities that are going to be launched in the near future. Since international accreditation bodies have much more stringent standards and there are national priorities to be protected, a national-level accreditation body for the quality assurance of tourism and allied programs is the need of the hour.

An interesting observation about quality initiatives in the Indian educational scenario is that most schools expend a great amount of their efforts in student grading. Very little attention is paid to what is to be taught. More striking is the sheer neglect in ensuring instructor quality. It is encouraging to see more and more Faculty Development Programs and Refresher Programs in the tourism area. But again, many such programs are done just because 'it is a requirement' and instructor evaluation criteria are rarely research based (George, 2007). That apart, in the public university system, getting employment by itself is an assurance of lifelong employment. In other words, except for those with an intrinsic motivation to excel in teaching, research and service, professors can be absolutely carefree about their expected roles and still ensure that they continue to be on the payroll. Unfortunately, a lot of them waste the opportunity to excel in their teaching and research roles and become parasites on the system.

The way to enhance quality is to enrich the process: spending too much on evaluation will not increase quality. When it comes to tourism education, this means enriching the learner experiences with everything that matters to tourism. Studies show that inter-institution partnerships create better opportunities for sharing knowledge and experiences. It is an encouraging trend to see Indian tourism educational institutions establishing international partnerships and organizing international study tours and placement initiatives. However, this is not feasible for a vast majority of second and third tier institutions. India is very diverse in terms of tourism products and opportunities and there is a clearly visible demand for partner programs among educational institutions within India. The Finnish University Network for Tourism Studies is a great model for this. The emphasis of such an arrangement is on leveraging the shared knowledge of a network of universities in order to empower students with multi-professional skills. It synergizes the resources; even if a partner university does not have all the required resources, the collaboration ensures that students can obtain them from one of the other universities (FUNTS, 2015). Such partnerships with industry conglomerates will also be valuable.

Being an outsider of the Indian tourism education system who used to be an insider once bestows upon me a unique vantage point. While I have portrayed a largely gloomy picture of the state of affairs, I must admit that most of the observations made here are highly personal and hence contestable. On the positive side, I have taken care to address the malice in a constructive way and possible solutions have been offered. Also, I do not intend to neglect some of the drastic initiatives being taken by a few leading institutions to bring forth meaningful change.

5.   TOWARDS AN INTEGRATIVIST MODEL OF TOURISM EDUCATION

While many models have been proposed, one that I feel offers significant promise in the Indian scenario is an adaptation of the three domains model developed by Dale and Robinson (2001). This model classifies tourism programs into generic (for example tourism management), product/market focused (for example cultural tourism; Asian tourism), and functional (for example tourism marketing; tourism planning). It also identifies a wide range of (conflicting) issues in curriculum design and gives important pointers for educational program planners and curriculum designers. But it should be noted that it misses the target when there is need to classify programs by academic, professional, vocational or entrepreneurial criteria. In the current form, it is silent on the issue of academic rigor vs. practical relevance (Professor John Tribe discusses at length the need for 'philosophic practitioners' in the tourism industry: see Tribe, 2002). Also, it is silent on what kind of individuals and individual identities these types of programs aim to carve out. I suggest an improvement upon this model, in the light of the wider global and more local trends discussed in this article (see Figure 39.1: (a) is the original model; (b) is the improvement).

The improved conceptual model recognizes the need for building self-awareness and individual identity in a highly globalizing world. Such individual identity is also the basis of creativity and innovation. It also recognizes the importance of knowing/knowledge and doing/skills. Again, in the revised model given in the figure, I have included two new approaches (supply focus, issue focus) and have eliminated one (generic focus). Tourism by nature is a micro-specialization: the term 'generic tourism degrees' is a misnomer. It's like someone saying he is a generic neurosurgeon. The supply side is an existing thrust area (for example destination management, tour operation management and so on) whereas issue focus in an emerging thrust area (for example sustainable development in tourism, accessible tourism and so on).

6.   CONCLUDING REMARKS

The World Tourism Organization identified early on the need to establish educational institutions in order to achieve tourist satisfaction and to increase national competitiveness in tourism by means of the availability of qualified manpower in a country (Fayos-Solá, 1997). The good news is that India is known globally for its large pool of technically qualified manpower. But the existing systems cannot efficiently and effectively tap into this manpower (Kaul, 2009). Due to technological innovations and radical changes in the consumption patterns of tourists, human resource development experts have been calling for a reexamination of tourism higher education.

Tourism educational programs have thus far lagged behind other business programs in terms of the adoption of new formats of delivery as well. You don't find many MOOCs or hybrid format programs in the tourism area. Given the need for continuous re-training

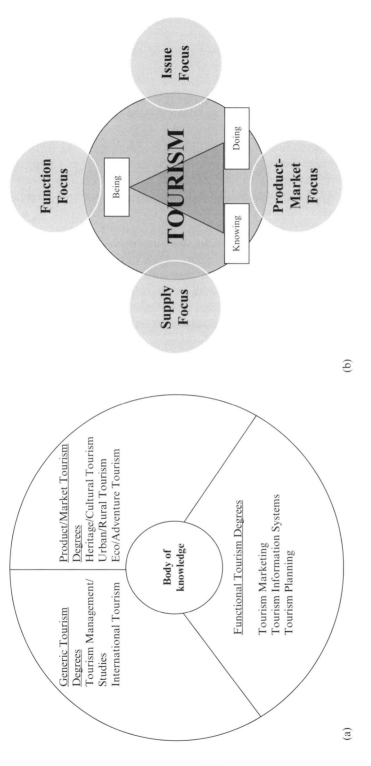

Figure 39.1   (a) Dale and Robinson's (2001) model and (b) George's (2013) model

and development of the workforce and their non-standard hours on work-roles, flexibility in higher educational offerings will add a lot of value. Tourism programs could emulate some of the educational innovations that have emerged in the more mainstream MBA track. Two good examples are the *Carnegie Mellon FlexMBA* and *Rutgers Mini-MBA* (Carnegie Mellon, 2013; Rutgers, 2013).

Despite their modernity orientation, business educational programs are also resistant to change (Mintzberg and Gosling, 2002); Kuhnian dominant design can threaten and kill even a high-spirited call for changes. Within this realization, excellent educational offerings in business studies should hope to develop in the learners knowing (knowledge), doing (skill), and being (developing sense of personal identity and purpose, expressed as attitude and behavior), according to David Garvin, Associate Dean of Academics at Harvard Business School. Tourism as a practice, especially when we look at the demand side of it, is the process of discovering the self by means of the 'other' (Urry, 1990). Understanding own identity is critical in understanding another's and being passionate about serving others. While knowledge, and to some extent skills, are comprehensively imparted by tourism programs, the third component has not been given its due weight. Skill development also has to move beyond the mechanics that have dominated curriculum design. Drawing from Datar and colleagues (2010), tourism schools may find some benefit in mimicking medical schools. The more the fieldwork/action learning, the better the value addition for the tourism graduates. Insistence on MBAs taking an oath before they can practice are gaining increasing momentum.

The search for solutions should not be restricted to the education system – it should extend to the industry and also to the myriad interconnections among other stakeholder groups such as the government, the media, and pressure groups in the non-profit sector. Torn between the need for structural stability and ideational change, it fails to deliver the unique needs of emerging professions like tourism. The worst hit in the demands of the changing times are affiliated colleges – with very little intellectual life of their own and as remnants of the bygone British colonial system (Altbach and Umakoshi, 2004). Industry insiders do not have the luxury to expect the required KSAs in the fresh recruits and most new recruits would admit only that 'what you learn in the classroom cannot be applied on the job'. If they learn anything relevant to their professional life in the industry, it is more than likely through shadow learning from their co-workers.

Using research to shape tourism education policy is rarely heard of. The utilization of research-based knowledge promises greater success in achieving objectives for a rich and prosperous society, as noted by Toffler (1970). This chapter is concluded with the sincere hope that tourism educational policy makers will critically examine the observations contained herein and incorporate appropriate elements into policy and practice.

REFERENCES

Altbach, P.G. and Umakoshi, T. (2004), *Asian Universities: Historical Perspectives and Contemporary Challenges*, Baltimore, MD: Johns Hopkins University Press.

Amoah, V.A. and Baum, T. (1997), 'Tourism education: policy versus practice', *International Journal of Contemporary Hospitality Management*, **9** (1), 5–12.

Ayikoru, M., Tribe, J. and Airey, D. (2009), 'Reading tourism education: Neoliberalism unveiled', *Annals of Tourism Research*, **36** (2), 191–221.

Barron, P., Maxwell, G., Broadbridge, A. and Ogden, S. (2007), 'Careers in hospitality management: Generation Y's experiences and perceptions', *Journal of Hospitality and Tourism Management*, **14** (2), 119–28.

Carnegie Mellon (2013), 'Carnegie Mellon FlexMBA', accessed 16 March 2015 at www.tepper.cmu.edu/mba/mba-curriculum/mba-programs-coursework/flexmba/index.aspx.

Cooper, C. and R. Shepherd (1997), 'The relationship between tourism education and the tourism industry: Implications for tourism education', *Tourism Recreation Research*, **22** (1), 34–47.

Dale, C. and Robinson, N. (2001), 'The theming of tourism education: A three-domain approach', *International Journal of Contemporary Hospitality Management*, **13** (1), 30–35.

Datar, S.M., Garvin, D.A. and Cullen, P.G. (2010), *Rethinking the MBA: Business Education at a Crossroads*, Boston, MA: Harvard Business School Press.

Dredge, D., Benckendorff, P., Day, M., Gross, M., Walo, M., Weeks, P. and Whitelaw, P. (2012), 'Crises, conundrums and curricula: A new golden age for tourism, hospitality and event management education?', paper presented at the CAUTHE National Conference, Melbourne.

Echtner, C.M. (1995), 'Tourism education in developing nations: A three pronged approach', *Tourism Recreation Research*, **20** (2), 32–41.

Evans, N. (2001), 'The development and positioning of business related university tourism education: A UK perspective', *Journal of Teaching in Travel and Tourism*, **1** (1), 17–36.

Fayos-Solá, E. (1997), *An Introduction to TEDQUAL (Tourism Education Quality)* (1st edn), Madrid: World Tourism Organization.

FUNTS (2015), *Finnish University Network for Tourism Studies*, accessed 31 January 2015 at www.uef.fi/en/funts/in-english.

George, B.P. (2007), 'Participation of teacher participants during the in-service faculty training programs and student–teacher interaction in the regular classrooms: A study conducted in India', *Journal of In-service Education*, **33** (3), 377–81.

George, B.P. (2013), 'The culture of technology: Differences in the use of e-learning technologies among Asian vs. North American tourism instructors and students', paper presented at the Lily Arctic 2013 conference on Innovations and Excellence in Teaching and Learning, accessed 27 February 2013 at www.uaf.edu/lillyarctic/information/presenters.

Gupta, A. (2008), 'International trends and private higher education in India', *International Journal of Educational Management*, **22** (6), 565–94.

Henthorne, T.L., George, B.P. and Williams, A.J. (2010), 'The evolving service culture of Cuban tourism: A case study', *Tourismos*, **5** (2), 129–44.

Jafari, J. (1990), 'Research and scholarship: The basis of tourism education', *Journal of Tourism Studies*, **1** (1), 33–41.

Kaul, S. (2009), 'Higher education in India: Seizing the opportunity', Working Paper No. 179, New Delhi: Indian Council for Research on International Economic Relations, accessed 27 February 2013 at dspace.cigilibrary.org/jspui/handle/123456789/20974.

Ladkin, A. (2000), 'Vocational education and food and beverage experience: Issues for career development', *International Journal of Contemporary Hospitality Management*, **12** (4), 226–33.

Ladkin, A. (2014), 'Employment and career development in tourism and hospitality education', in D. Dredge, D. Airey and M. Gross (eds), *The Routledge Handbook of Tourism and Hospitality Education* (pp. 395–407), Abingdon: Routledge.

McKercher, B., Williams, A. and Coghlan, I. (1995), 'Career progress of recent tourism graduates', *Tourism Management*, **16** (7), 541–5.

Mintzberg, H. and Gosling, J. (2002), 'Educating managers beyond borders', *Academy of Management Education and Learning*, **1** (1), 64–76.

Page, S.J. (2003), 'Evaluating research performance in tourism: The UK experience', *Tourism Management*, **24** (6), 607–22.

Pearce, P. (2005), 'Australian tourism education: The quest for status', in C.H.C. Hsu (ed.), *Global Tourism Higher Education: Past, Present and Future*, (pp. 251–67), Binghamton, NY: Haworth Press.

Pritchard, A. and N. Morgan (2007), 'Decentering tourism's intellectual universe or traversing the dialogue between change and tradition', in I. Ateljevic, A. Pritchard and N. Morgan (eds), *The Critical Turn in Tourism Studies: Innovative Research Methodologies*, (pp. 11–28), Oxford: Elsevier.

Rutgers (2013), 'Rutgers Mini-MBA', accessed 27 February 2015 at cmd.rutgers.edu/subject-area/mini-mba.

Schwaber, K. (2004), *Agile Project Management with Scrum*, Redmond, WA: Microsoft Press.

Sciarini, M., Beck, J. and Seaman, J. (2012), 'Online learning in hospitality and tourism higher education worldwide: A descriptive report as of January 2012', *Journal of Hospitality and Tourism Education*, **24** (2/3), 41–4.

Seth, Y. (2007), 'CII to focus on education, tourism reforms', *The Times of India*, 28 May.

Sheldon, P.J., Fesenmaier, D.R. and Tribe, J. (2011), 'The tourism education futures initiative (TEFI): Activating change in tourism education', *Journal of Teaching in Travel and Tourism*, **11** (1), 2–23.

Singh, S. (1997), 'Developing human resources for the tourism industry with reference to India', *Tourism Management*, **18** (5), 299–306.
Toffler, A. (1970), *Future Shock*, New York: Random House.
Tribe, J. (2002), 'The philosophic practitioner', *Annals of Tourism Research*, **29** (2), 338–57.
Urry, J. (1990), *The Tourist Gaze: Leisure and Travel in Contemporary Societies*, Newbury Park, CA and London: Sage Publications.

PART VIII

CONCLUSIONS

40 The nature of innovation in tourism higher education: an institutional innovation approach
Janne J. Liburd and Anne-Mette Hjalager

1. INTRODUCTION

Understood as a phenomenon, a vision or work methods, innovation is increasingly applied in relation to tourism (Hjalager, 2010; Pikkemat, 2008; Williams and Shaw, 2011). Over the past decade, research has scrutinized tourism businesses and destinations to enhance knowledge on innovation results, innovation capacities, spin-offs, networks and alliance building, as well as implications of innovative behavior (Liburd et al., 2013; Novelli et al., 2006; Sørensen, 2007). The term 'institutional innovation' occurs infrequently in tourism innovation studies, with a few examples found in Hjalager (2002) and Van Wijk et al. (2015). Fairly systematically, although with some reservations, tourism is still characterized as an industry and activity that, compared to other sectors, lags behind in terms of innovation (Camison and Monfort-Mir, 2012; Hall, 2009; Sundbo et al., 2007).

Any innovative industry sector relies not only on its own capacities, but on related infrastructures and services. Thus, the amount of innovative businesses and destinations may correlate with innovations in, for example, public governance and educational services, including higher education. The subtle synergies and dynamics are shown for example in Silicon Valley (Casper, 2006), the wine industry in Australia (Aylward, 2004), and the timber industry in Sweden (Carrie, 2000). Studies indicate that permeable structures contribute to multi-directed knowledge flows and innovation diffusion (Hamdouch and Moulaert, 2006). Experimentally oriented universities tend to achieve significant recognition in the business sectors for their ability to challenge paradigms and spur developments in open and collaborative manners (Asheim et al., 2006: Clark, 2000; Leydesdorff and Etzkowitz, 1996; Liburd, 2013).

Tourism higher education has received only marginal attention as a subject of comprehensive innovation studies based on the above. An analytical linking of industry innovation with creative capacities and learning in the educational sector has escaped critical attention. As tourism increases the level of socio-economic importance, which calls for increased professionalism, mutuality and ethical behavior (Sheldon et al., 2008), it is essential to reassess the nature of innovation higher tourism education and relationships with the industry.

The aim of this contribution is to present a model of institutional innovation and apply it to tourism higher education. The chapter first introduces the concept of institutional innovations. Next the underlying changes in tourism higher education and the curriculum are explained. There are a multitude of ways to analyze and categorize how innovation occurs in tourism higher education. In this chapter, an institutional innovation perspective will be pursued. Other focuses could have been applied, but taking into consideration the longstanding, essential and collaborative elements of tourism higher education, an institutional innovation focus serves well to capture the contexts and complex relations at stake. Institutional innovations are addressed as intuitive and strategic and whether these approaches are aligned or detached. Offering a macro-perspective with innovative examples on tourism education and learning, this chapter dissects trends and issues for contemporary developments in tourism higher education by reference to the many contributions of this volume.

2.   DEFINING INSTITUTIONAL INNOVATION

Leaning on seminal work of Joseph Schumpeter (1942), innovation comes in different formats: product innovations, process innovations, marketing innovation and organizational innovation. These distinctions are still widely applicable and instructive, but later research has supplemented the list with other innovation forms, so as to be able to include more recent types of innovation and innovations in complex contexts. Institutional innovation is one of these.

Institutions can be defined as organizational constructs that create meaning and guide the behavior, roles and relationships of individuals. Institutions are formal organizations with a specific purpose (Raffaelli and Glynn, 2015). But institutions are also the established customs, laws and more or less formal associations in a society or a community, and they are assemblages of historically and socially constructed practices and understandings that are somehow taken for granted (DiMaggio, 1988). Institutions put activities and interactions of social systems in recognizable order. Tourism higher education is usually embedded in universities, which are formal institutions in their own respect. However, institutionalization and institutional arrangements are ubiquitously found in all the details of a single organization (Hargrave and Van de Ven, 2006). The particular view depends on the emphasis of inquiry, as explained in greater detail below. Tourism higher education is also implanted in institutional constellations with the surrounding world, including for example the industry, the state, or communities that affect interactions, negotiations and innovative possibilities.

Institutions are subjects of change in which some are fast and others evolve at a slower pace in response to shifting environments, users or new ideas. Institutional change can be seen as any substantial alteration in the dominant mode of coordination and organization of relationships in or between organizations. The innovation literature often sees institutional change as a prerequisite or cause for other types of innovation. Institutional innovations are, however, in their own respect reformations of the proportions of the organizations, their meanings and structures. Interpreted in this way, institutional innovation is about improving the 'software' of an organization: the belief and values, the frameworks of understanding, formal and informal rules, organizational patterns, and regular patterns of behavior (Hargrave and Van de Ven, 2006). Changes may be related to shifting societal norms, government policies and market incentives, and institutional innovations can therefore appear to be rather fuzzy.

To elaborate and point to changes in higher education, institutional innovation can be brought about in a way that redefines the rationale of the activities and the institution per se. In many parts of the world universities are increasingly challenged to be accountable, to reform or modernize practices and perform at multiple levels, which are combined with new forms of governance (Liburd, 2013). Tied to central government for much of their finance, universities compete in a struggle for reduced public funding. In order to attract other sources of revenue (through increasing tuition fees, industry research contracts, sale of patents and intellectual property rights, and so on), many universities are becoming more obviously capitalistic, competitive and market orientated (Bok, 2003). Bringing about new institutional relationships can be a matter of transformations that tie institutions together in novel ways and with different objectives. Some institutional innovations are constructed to disrupt existing performance, trade-off patterns and privileges whereby resources otherwise bound in rigid structures are released. Institutional innovations can be a means to create and harness scalable efficiency.

Research in institutional innovation is substantial and growing, but fairly little is directed to issues in tourism, and apparently none to tourism higher education. The rationale of this chapter is to explore and open up a path for future, in-depth inquiry.

3. INNOVATIONS IN TOURISM HIGHER EDUCATION

The growth, complexity and socio-economic significance of tourism as a globalized phenomenon played important parts in prompting universities to meet the demands and opportunities created by the tourism industry (Airey, 2005). Tourism higher education continues to stimulate academic reflection and learning about the meaning of tourism to tourists (for example MacCannell, 1976; Urry, 1990), tourism as a means to development (for example Pearce, 2005; Smith, 1977; 1989), strategic management (for example Ooi, 2002; Tribe, 2010), and on the relations of tourism to complex phenomena such as mobility, globalization, motivation, consumption, governance, identity, technology, social networks, sustainability, quality of life, among others (Liburd et al., 2012). The following will briefly illustrate how innovations in tourism higher education have evolved in response to, but also in isolation from the larger society and socio-economic contexts in and by which tourism exists, which tacitly points to the presence and absence of institutional innovation at multiple levels.

Applying a broad-brush approach, innovations in tourism as a field of study will be outlined in the relation to the four research platforms described by Jafar Jafari (1989; 1990; 2001). Capturing the contours of how tourism education and research have changed over the past five decades, considerations will point to the main changes in knowledge and the influence on curriculum. This will set the context for subsequent analysis of institutional innovations in tourism higher education.

To capture the changes in higher tourism education since the 1950s, Figure 40.1 is intended to highlight the defining characteristics and interrelations between research platforms underpinning tourism higher education, the disciplines informing the curriculum, and development stages in tourism higher education.

Jafari's (1989; 1990) four research platforms are based largely on motives as a key rationale of scholars in tourism, hence the classifications as advocacy, cautionary, adaptancy and knowledge. Airey (2008: 2) notes that it was not until the knowledge platform approach that a broader and more mature state of tourism as a field of study was achieved. Graphically simplified in Figure 40.1, the horizontal and vertical relations should be depicted by arrows pointing in both directions to emphasize how scientific knowledge

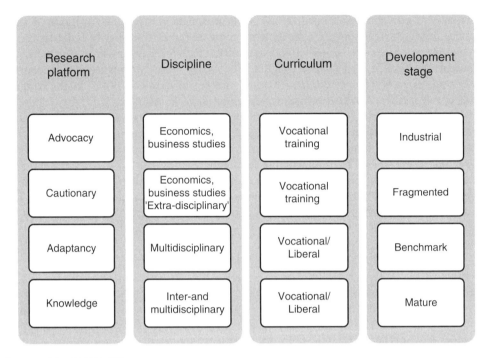

Source: Liburd (2013: 87).

Figure 40.1   Changes in tourism higher education and research

is always predicated on existing knowledge. The four development stages thus represent artificial divides, which fail to take into account overlapping practices and epistemologies in the incremental changes of tourism higher education and research over time.

Here, a slight discrepancy between Airey's (2008) time periods for the development stages and Jafari's (1989; 1990) research platforms should be noted. Aligning the industrial stage with Jafari's advocacy platform and research disciplines in the following section denotes the 1950s–1960s. Airey's (2008) division of stages includes the 1970s in the industrial period, thus merging Jafari's advocacy and cautionary platforms. The analysis will next disclose the connections and interrelations between the stages and domains, rather than addressing these as separate, chronological entities. Indeed, Jafari (2001: 29–32) identifies all four platforms as co-existing in the twenty-first century, as in 1989 when conceptualizing each platform as reflecting a growing complexity in the field of tourism since World War II. The analysis will not consider subsequent development stages, such as the 'ethics platform' proposed by Macbeth (2005), as the level of maturity in tourism higher education and research remains open to question (Airey, 2008).

3.1   The Industrial Phase

The industrial development stage was characterized by close links between academia and industry, and broader societal interest in the seemingly endless growth and development potentials of tourism. Early research was dominated by economists advocating the fiscal importance of tourism with sporadic contributions from geography. In Western Europe, as in many parts of North America, employment had started shifting from manufacturing to the service industries (of which tourism was one of the fastest growing) in the 1950s (Taylor, 1979).

Early institutional interest was prompted by the substantial expansion of the number of students enrolling in higher education, fueling the creation of the mass university. Tourism's internal placement in departments of hotel and catering management was reinforced by the external environment. With close links to industry and to equip graduates to operate in their chosen career, framing of the tourism curriculum was essentially business-oriented and highly vocational in origin. A highly vocational tourism curriculum was geared to leave students 'surprise free' about what they would find in employment. Airey (2005: 15) describes how business studies embraced tourism as a vocational 'add-on' to provide a specific focus on practice and operation of the industry.

3.2   The Fragmented Stage

A prevailing representation of tourism informing higher education and research since the 1970s is the impacts of tourism at the destination level (Archer et al., 2005; Patullo, 1996; Smith, 1977; 1989; Smith and Brent, 2001). At this stage, economics continued to dominate tourism research but disciplinary interest from anthropology, sociology, psychology and again geography contributed to a more fragmented tourism knowledge domain. Both the advocacy and the caution platforms enjoy academics subscribing to respective standpoints which contend that those conducting such surveys may have too often imposed their own perceptions of tourism's impacts on respondents (Moscardo and Pearce, 1999).

Framed by sustained reliance on extra-disciplinary knowledge combined with business studies, the curriculum of the fragmented stage was hardly surprising. It indicated the interests of those producing and using such knowledge. Extra-disciplinary materials also found their way into one of the early influential textbooks by Burkhart and Medlik (1974). This framing prevailed in spite of the burgeoning evidence of the less than admirable impacts of tourism, especially in the less developed countries.

3.3   The Benchmark Stage

The 1980s were characterized by a quest for alternatives to the negative impacts of mass tourism around the world. Subsequent calls to ensure a balance between civic, recreational use and conservation were captured by the umbrella term of 'alternative tourism development' (Mowforth and Munt, 1998; Smith and Eadington, 1989). Multidisciplinary attention gradually focused on forms of tourism that were responsive to local host communities and their needs, while developing the product base to please tourists (Macbeth, 2005). Thus appearing only as a partial remedy to the societal ills caused by mass tourism, Jafari (1990) contended that the adaptancy platform failed to fully develop its strategies to address the steadily growing volume of international tourism.

In addition to satisfying the demand of business, a more liberal approach to the tourism curriculum included critical reflections of the role of tourism in society and the world. Emerging multidisciplinary research was evident in how the different kinds of knowledge and methodologies sought to influence the curriculum space during the benchmark stage. First, the contest between differing interests and subject areas seeking space in the curriculum unsettled what the tourism curriculum should contain. Second, the means and aims of the tourism curriculum were contested. While the vocational origin represented a stabilizing force for the majority of programs, the strictly vocational view of the curriculum was challenged by a more liberal and reflective approach (Airey, 2008).

3.4 The Mature Stage

The worldwide presence of tourism as a mega-industry and socio-cultural phenomenon broadened the scope of tourism higher education and research beyond concerns regarding impacts, unequal service exchanges, and superficial, socio-cultural encounters. The knowledge-based platform appeared less preoccupied with justifying or criticizing the existence of tourism and its place in the wider debates of the social sciences (Airey, 2008; Liburd et al., 2012). Engagements with wider debates and critical reflections about the aims and stance of tourism education and research further reflect a maturation of the field, marked by the establishment of internationally distinguished research journals (*Annals of Tourism Research, Journal of Travel Research, Tourism Management*) (Graburn and Jafari, 1991).

These changes resonated in the curriculum space. The contribution of tourism to distant effects, changes and actions, which involve not just business operations and tourists but individuals, communities, governments and environments in the vocational curriculum, is a given, rather than subject to questioning of its existence and occurrence (Koh, 1995). Tribe (2002) developed new aims and principles for ordering of the curriculum, introducing four key domains of vocational action, vocational reflection, liberal reflection, and liberal action to educate philosophic practitioners in tourism. Philosophic practitioners are graduates who deliver effective tourism services, seek holistic understandings of the tourism phenomenon while simultaneously satisfying the role of stewardship for the development of the world in and of which tourism exists (Tribe, 2002). The epistemological underpinning is multidisciplinary and draws on business interdisciplinary studies as well as extra-disciplinary knowledge that may exert dominance over vocational studies, while respectful of pluralistic values and interests (Tribe, 2002: 353).

Other tourism scholars have since expressed less confidence in the maturity of tourism and have argued that the tourism curriculum fails to educate graduates who are able to work in, innovate and engage in co-creating uncertain futures (Liburd and Hjalager, 2010; Ring et al., 2009; Sheldon et al., 2008; 2011). Moreover, the incremental innovations illustrated above only to a lesser extent reveal whether these are aligned with institutional strategies, for example in response to a larger student intake and industry demands for skilled labor, or if changes occur in detached, intuitive forms where tourism academe offers a platform to critique the impacts of tourism.

4.   A MODEL OF INSTITUTIONAL INNOVATIONS IN TOURISM HIGHER EDUCATION

Illustrated through the lens of tourism research platforms and the curriculum, innovations in tourism higher education occur gradually and may be reflected in institutional innovations. While these have received scant research attention, this volume and its contributions provide ample opportunity to map the field of institutional innovations. Taking as a vantage point the arguably mature stage of tourism higher education, the analysis will demonstrate connections among and presence of several stages and domains. For this purpose, a conceptual model has been established, illustrated in Table 40.1.

The statement in the model is that institutional innovation may be observed under two main investigative perspectives. Inspired by Weick and Quinn (1999), on the horizontal axis the innovation approach distinguishes between *intuitive* and *strategic* change:

- *Intuitive* is a continuous and reflexive mode of change. Changes are 'bottom-up' with a significant participative power of entities and individuals. Changes are rapid, but partial, and can be related to occurring opportunities. Institutional innovations vary, but often comprise reconceptualization of social systems and interpretative models that introduce new ways of integration and inclusion/exclusion.
- *Strategic* is an episodic effort, mainly 'top-down', initiated and engineered with a predetermined purpose of change based on institutional objectives and vision. After a change period with considerable turbulence and ambiguity, the institutional patterns are stabilized and reconstituted. Members of staff are expected to adapt and work with the institutional arrangement, until the event of the next strategic, institutional restructuring.

On the vertical axes, Table 40.1 is also divided in two groups, *detached* and *aligned*, to describe the level of external permeability:

- *Detached* describes a situation with significant freedom of action, and where directions of change are guided by 'inside' perspectives. These are largely determined by the needs and wants of the institution and its participants. This indicates a high level of trust in the ability of its participants to judge the needs of the users (including students) and determine the direction of future steps. Institutional innovations can be contained without substantial external interference or consultation.
- *Aligned* is a more external approach, where institutional innovations take into account the variety of stakeholders in openly inviting manners by drawing on external capacities and creating relational values and operational logics. This part of the figure illustrates the dependencies and influences, where any institution will have to mirror itself in external organizations and institutions.

Table 40.1 provides details of the track of analysis by indicating the nature of the institutional innovation for tourism higher education in a metaphorical way (Christensen and Eyring, 2011). Innovations are described in terms of management, course and curriculum designs, technology, relationships, and values about rites of passage for tourism students.

Table 40.1   Framework for institutional innovations in tourism higher education

	Innovation approach	
	Intuitive	Strategic
Detached	*Metaphor:* Intellectual playground. Tourism as a phenomenon, a creative field of inquiry.	*Metaphor:* Mass production, Fordism. Higher education is a standardized commodity where academic knowledge is for sale.
	Innovation management: Relatively self-governing subject units. Strong elements of student participation, freedom. Inquiry-based learning, disruptive, criticality, values-based. Economics of scope.	*Innovation management:* Neo-liberalism, new public management, benchmarks, quality control mechanisms to ensure excellence in research, employability, values. Economics of scale.
	Innovating course and curriculum design: Problem Based and Experimental Learning: E-tivities, peer assessment and integrity, life-wide learning, collaborative and team learning.	*Innovating course and curriculum design:* E-learning, embedding research skills, lifelong learning, M- and U-Learning, online learning, teaching–research nexus.
	Innovating technology: Technology enhanced learning, e-Portfolios, Students in Action. Co- and self-authorship development.	*Innovating technology:* BlackBoard, Continuous Dynamic Feedback Systems. Visual Approaches. Online Learning Simulations.
	Innovating the rites of passage: Celebrating extraordinary creativity, diversity, but mainly in small groups, communities, emphasizing being and belonging. Portfolio of celebrations part of the assessments. Ethics, indigenous knowledge, narratives and perspectives.	*Innovating the rites of passage:* Celebrating extraordinary standards of performance, symbols given at symbolic events. Final assessment as the only valid and valuable part of the rite.
Aligned	*Metaphor:* Collaboration. Knowledge co-creation, communicative action and engagement.	*Metaphor:* Growth. Global competitiveness, market shares. An engine to help drive the economy forward.
	Innovation management: Social media-based management, open systems, those who are present decide on the course content, outcomes, students, staff, enterprises alike.	*Innovation management:* Internationalization. Control of all aspects of the higher education business. Industry engagement and advisory boards.
	Innovating course and curriculum design: Communities of teaching and learning. Problem-Based Learning, the Flipped Classroom. Experiential Learning. Case studies, fieldtrips.	*Innovating course and curriculum design:* Work-integrated learning, applied thesis. Student mobility. Negotiation skills.
	Innovating technology: INNOTOUR, BEST EN Lecture Series.	*Innovating technology:* MOOCs.
	Innovating the rites of passage: Celebrating the extraordinary creativity, diversification, with the wider community. Portfolio of celebrations part of the assessments, but the narratives and quality of collaboration as main issues.	*Innovating the rites of passage:* The performance as strategic–detached (above), supplemented with students in alumni, ambassador functions. Special celebrations by invitation only, social media document 'we-are-the-good-guys'.

The division should not be perceived as juxtapositions but different approaches and forms of institutional innovation.

In the following, each of the four quadrants of Table 40.1 will be elaborated in greater detail by drawing on notable examples from this *Handbook*.

4.1 Intuitive and Detached Forms of Innovation

The following examines innovation approaches related to the situation where university actors can operate independently and without decisive control from external governmental or stakeholder bodies. It is a condition where developments of individual choice can be undertaken. The *Intellectual Playground* works as a metaphor for this approach to institutional innovation.

The assumption is that tourism departments and units have wide sovereignty in decision making. They are allowed, if not outright expected, to explore and exploit teaching innovations, provided that the steps taken are well articulated and according to the overall institutional framework. In this type of set-up, innovation is regarded as a privilege and a responsibility. It is envisaged that teaching at university level is an improvisational performance (Sawyer, 2004), and creativity is an existential prerequisite and an operational target for both students and staff (Gibson, 2010).

Tourism is seen as a phenomenon rather than an industrial sector with rigid employability requirements to be met by higher education. Likewise, tourism is a field of study rather than a discipline (Tribe, 1997), which invites continual and critical exploration of boundaries and desirable futures.

Innovation management is characterized by participatory styles, openness and inviting processes. All members of the institution – students, staff and administrative personnel – have the power respectfully to challenge the state of affairs. The institutional system possesses material and immaterial resources to support open innovation fields, partly as a consequence of significant commitment, voluntary action and feelings of belonging.

This book provides several examples of the intuitive and detached approach. Aubke and Hergesell (Chapter 38) discuss the classroom dynamics and relational attributes between students as carriers of wider educational and developmental benefits. Birkle et al. (Chapter 8) confirm that student motivation is highly influenced by other students, and that the management of the classroom and interactive processes is as important as the curricular content.

The disciplinary challenges are addressed by Carreira and Bingre do Amaral (Chapter 28), Cotterell et al. (Chapter 25) and Young and Maguire (Chapter 31). When teaching sustainability issues or social cohesion in tourism they emphasize the need to stimulate students to engage in novel interpretations by bringing in cross-disciplinary approaches. The authors note how nurturing responsibility and ethical behavior among students depends on their active involvement throughout the program.

Course and curriculum design embraces new ways of activating students and promoting never-ending reflections with strong ethical elements (Crossley, Chapter 29). Edelheim (Chapter 32) argues that a robust teaching–research nexus is a means progression. Ideas are transformed into models and eventually tested to be successful in benefiting student learning as well as the esteem of tourism as a professional field. In order to align student learning and research, curricula can be creatively designed in different ways. As noted by

Edelheim, not all students aim to become researchers, and the challenge is therefore to include practice elements as many students face careers as future managers in tourism.

Innovating technology: technology has become a facilitator to enhance creativity and stimulate intuitive learning processes. In this volume, Holladay (Chapter 10) sees online teaching and blended learning as deeply integrated with the transformative processes in the classroom. In his opinion, technical instruments may change both teachers and students radically, not to mention the interrelationships between them. He refers to the flexibility of teaching and learning and the adaptability to students' particular circumstances and needs. In addition, students may construct their own learning space and add value to the totality of class processes.

ePortfolios are discussed by Mössenlechner (Chapter 12), who sees the ePortfolio as an integrated learning instrument with a clear perspective towards students' future careers. She talks about ePortfolio pedagogy, suggesting that the ePortfolio has a far wider ranging position in the totality of the learning environment. This efficiently illustrates the intrinsic values of the learning processes and learning outcomes, and may be used to prepare for labor market interaction. ePortfolios are an instrument that is subject to continuous innovative progression.

Rites of passage refer to how institutions appreciate and celebrate good student and staff performance. Rites of passage are also matters of continuous innovation. Crossley (Chapter 29) suggests that the threshold of ambition must be high in student evaluation, particularly when it comes to abilities of critical thinking and personal, value-based judgment. Subtle competences such as creativity, disruptive learning and participatory reflection are difficult to expose in rigid rites of passage. ePortfolios may be considered particularly relevant. They maintain process-oriented perspectives and respect the individual as well as the collective learning spaces in which the student acquires his or her competences.

Rites of passage could also be a means to celebrate steps for achievements in difficult procedures or exhibitions to build student engagement and celebrate learning. Celebrating stepwise progress is seen in workplace teambuilding activities, and recognized as beneficial for integrative learning processes.

4.2   Intuitive and Aligned Forms of Innovation

The metaphor for this type of innovation is *collaboration*. Collaboration rests on the hypothesis that the sum of the work is more than its individual parts (Liburd, 2013: 13). The concept of collaboration suggests the joint effort of individuals to achieve a common goal, ostensibly for the purpose of widening the boundaries of knowledge (Anandarajan and Anandarajan, 2010). Collaboration at institutional levels is not new. Reliance on individual knowledge production to uphold epistemologies, disciplinary practices, assessment and reward criteria continues to exert a significant influence. This volume is a significant testament to changing and innovative practices in tourism higher education and learning, where external stakeholders are allowed to contribute substantially to the learning processes.

Innovation management has a significant focus on gatekeeping: inviting select partners in and controlling their contributions and influence. Management ensures a continuous balance of resource and the trimming of incentives. It is essential for the university heads of departments to be on empathetic terms with industry leaders and to ensure mutual value of engagement. The dissemination of knowledge is regarded as a two-way process, where industry benefits from the university, and where real-life practice positively affects the teaching and learning environments.

Universities may pursue deliberate strategies of investing in work-based learning. Wiltshier and Rawlinson (Chapter 19) describe a university learning laboratory where stakeholders engage in shared teaching and learning projects to meet core needs and development of the students. They report on strong correlations between student achievement, graduate recruitment, partners' satisfaction, research and consultancy prospects.

Innovating course and curriculum design. Several examples on integration of sustainability in the tourism curriculum are found in this publication. Cotterell et al. (Chapter 25) examine the potential for teaching more complex understandings of sustainability. Wearing et al. (Chapter 27) explore the potential of work integrated learning in promoting cultural and environmental awareness through sustainable tourism education and authentic practices. Carreira and Bingre do Amaral (Chapter 28) report on multidisciplinary ecotourism education in Portugal, which includes courses in agro-sciences, forestry and environmental studies. Ecotourism students participate in activities in areas as diverse as the natural resource management (including woodlands and wild game), the processing of agrifood products in rural contexts, the design of tourist routes, food and wine tourism, equine sports and management, organic agriculture, bird watching, nature conservation, and entrepreneurship, among others.

Examples including innovative approaches to teaching as well as learning can be found in Higgins-Desbiolles's (Chapter 30) shared experiences of embedding indigenous content in the tourism curriculum. She demonstrates how indigenous perspectives and worldviews shift the line of focus from conventional tourist demand and product development to the rights of host communities and social justice of tourism. Caldicott and Wilson (Chapter 16) argue that the development of self-authorship, described as the capacity to internally generate beliefs, identity and social relationships, encourages learners to be more critical in their approaches to knowledge and decision making processes. Exploring 147 hospitality employers' expectations of higher education in Poland, Kachniewska and Para (Chapter 2) expose an educational gap of entrepreneurial skills, understandings of service quality and organizational culture. In order to reconnect with industry, the authors see the need to include these competencies in the merit and didactic dimensions of tourism and hospitality education.

Innovating technology: emphasizing technology in the co-construction and mobilization of knowledge, Morellato (Chapter 9) advocates the need for attention to the learning process and ethical dimensions of digital competence. The example from a New Zealand university takes a critical stance towards the glorification of technology by engaging students as active producers in the co-construction and mobilization of knowledge. INNOTOUR is a web 2.0 platform for tourism education, research and business innovation (www.innotour.com). Launched in 2009, it is an open resource based on content created by its users. The BEST EN Sustainability Series is the latest addition to INNOTOUR. The series is part of a larger movement of institutions adopting Open Educational Resources as a tool to promote learning in society at large.

Innovating the rites of passage may involve celebrations of how institutions evaluate, acknowledge and reward good student performances. Rather than making assessment based on final, individual papers that typically involve worrying situations for the students, Barth (Chapter 3) reports on the use of collaborative examinations as evaluation tools. The two-stage collaborative exams furthermore support examination validity by reducing plagiarism, cheating and academic misconduct in less stressful conditions. Jennings et al. (Chapter 34) narrate and interpret the lived experiences of four research students based on a series of research dialogue sessions over several years. Through the process, students learn how to 'be in and of' a qualitative research culture and how to professionally 'be' a qualitative researcher.

4.3   Strategic and Detached Forms of Innovation

The metaphor used for this category of innovations is *Fordism*. In this context, universities as whole institutional entities are principally considered to be units of production (Lorenz, 2012). They operate in commercial or semi-commercial markets for knowledge under neo-liberal governance (Barnett, 2013). In order to create profits or in order to survive within squeezed public budgets, each university department will have to rationalize and innovate in its delivery systems on a continuous basis, increase efficiency and control, and nurture the product brand.

Directions for the future are matters consolidated in strategic management processes, where tourism programs compete with other universities and with internal actors who compete for the same resources. In this context, mass production and standardization of programs are the solution. The death of mass tourism has been proclaimed many times (Claver-Cortés et al., 2007; Poon, 1993) but in many destinations tourism still relies on fairly standardized products and services. Related competences can be taught and learned in similarly Fordist ways.

Innovation management: managerial bureaucratic changes are dominant in strategic and detached innovation. Methods applied in manufacturing reflect those undertaken in tourism higher education (Murphy et al., 2015). Innovation is about trimming, organizing and controlling. Students and employers consider education a product with particular attributes. When applied in practice it will give specific, even guaranteed benefits. Therefore, significance is placed on full transparency of the delivery process and the educational elements, so that any buyer can assess the value for money on a continual basis during courses and after graduation. An example of innovative management through international student mobility is provided by Vertesi (Chapter 24). Vertesi explains how returning students are assisted in deconstructing their experience to contribute to the internationalization of those who stay at home.

Innovative course and curriculum design: in this category, innovation of course content and teaching methods might be given less attention as existing models have proved to be sufficiently efficient and productive. In a detached strategy, there are financially good reasons to narrow down the pace of change in course and curriculum design, and to reuse and employ existing models. The status quo is brought to a level of perfection and then frozen. Crossley (Chapter 29) paraphrases this as 'pragmatic management competencies' delivered to the students, in contrast to critical skills.

An accurate understanding of the qualification needs of the industry is regarded as essential for the employability of the students as illustrated by Crotts (Chapter 4), and Kachniewska and Para (Chapter 2). Stergiou and Airey (Chapter 1) identify the potential gaps between the understanding of competences in the industry and at the university. Ways to close the gap are yet to be found.

The Fordist model may employ a range of in- and extra-curricular methods and facilities. This is not at the core of the contributions in this volume, where most authors have an emphasis on the other innovation models. However, as suggested by George (Chapter 39) in the case of India, there might be good reasons for a developing country to address curriculum and course development in a highly standardized approach. Moreover, Airey and Benckendorff (Chapter 35) suggest that there is a risk that a Fordist approach to standards may be misinterpreted as standardization. A similar theme is also found in Papageorgiou (Chapter 36).

Innovating technology: technology, including online learning, matches the ideas of the Fordist detached innovation system. Holladay (Chapter 10) mentions that technologies and blended learning can enhance the use of the curricular rationale while increasing the reach and efficiency of learning. Technologies also apply to learning management systems, such as a Blackboard, which supports learning, for example, by complementing, substituting and duplicating situations where face-to-face teaching fails. In this context innovative efforts in technology can be a means to ensure self-service, benefiting the student through a greater flexibility and the institution through saved resources.

Online Business Simulations have more recently gained interest in higher education. Business simulations offer authentic learning experiences that mirror real world problems and enable students to practice and develop graduate capabilities, technical skills and strategic decision making skills. A comprehensive overview and evaluation of relevant tools, cases and pedagogies to enhance learning outcomes are provided by Benckendorff et al. (2015).

Rites of passage: the main rites of passage are prudently formulated and integrated in procedural order, with nothing left to the casual handling of outsiders or coincidental actors. The control element is essential. Exceptional students may be recognized for their achievements, and ceremonies are strategically included in institutional communication strategies. Examples of artifacts are spectacular written certificates, uniform clothing, hats and so on, to represent the solemnness of the academic learning process.

4.4   Strategic and Aligned Forms of Innovation

The metaphor capturing this form of institutional innovation is *Growth*. Using higher education to help drive the economy forward, governments play a key role in controlling most if not all aspects of the higher education business.

Innovation management: managerial innovations consist of a range of instruments. Airey and Benckendorff (Chapter 35) provide an overview of the full extent of the neo-liberal instruments applied in higher education. This includes the implementation of standards that efficiently render grades comparable and transferable between universities and across national borders. Certification bodies are set up outside the individual institutions (Papageorgiou, Chapter 36). Bureaucratic innovativeness includes a range of Internet Communication Technologies-based measurement systems and tools. They support the perpetual pursuit of positive benchmarks internally and against competing institutions. Milman (Chapter 37) discusses the role, responsibilities and impacts of industry advisory boards. Here industry is involved in an all-encompassing manner, including curriculum development, student competencies, student interactions through guest lecturers and other classroom activities. Institutions concentrate efforts on applying and monitoring the standards, and efficiently following up, adapting, shaping and not the least communicating the achievements.

Innovating course and curriculum design: inquiry learning is the pedagogical approach of the Haaga-Helia Porvoo Campus in Finland (Edelheim, Chapter 32). Motivation and interest are the key elements of inquiry learning, where students are required to take responsibility for their own learning processes in real life development projects. The Hong Kong Polytechnic University promotes experiential service-learning with notable reference to Hotel ICON. Owned and operated by the university, Hotel ICON is a teaching and research hotel. King and Zhang (Chapter 14) explain how the mandating of a four-year curriculum for public universities by the Hong Kong Government provided an opportunity to extend the scope of learning. In Scotland, the Scottish Curriculum for Excellence is the main government instrument for providing education for life, work and industry. Cuffy (Chapter 6) reports on how two Scottish universities are presently responsible for advancing the lifespan of a national tourism curriculum. This illustrates how tourism higher education is utilized to advance a government agenda of lifelong learning. As Blackman and Benckendorff observe (Chapter 15), similar opportunities exist to acknowledge and connect the skills that learners develop through paid part-time employment with the formal curriculum.

Innovating technology: Murphy et al. (Chapter 11) remind us that Massive Open Online Courses (MOOCs) draw on a trajectory of online pedagogy. The path began with cognitive-behaviorist approaches that were followed by social learning, connectivism and community learning. Outlining the main MOOC pedagogies, critical attention is paid to MOOCs' abysmal completion rates. While viable MOOC business models remain unknown, and with very few examples from tourism and hospitality, they point to exciting opportunities for mass education at a hitherto unprecedented scale.

Innovating the rites of passage: the rites mirror the strategic–detached approach (above), in addition to having students in alumni ambassador functions. Elite programs, such as the European Master in Tourism Management (EMTM), celebrate extraordinary achievements at VIP events. Only select industry leaders and university management are invited to the annual EMTM graduation ceremony in addition to the next generation EMTM students. The 'EMTM key' is handed over to the next generation of EMTM students who get a glimpse of the hard work and ceremonial traditions. The EMTM graduates do not wear gowns but traditional national costumes, where in use. The event is meticulously organized by the graduates but closely controlled by the university. Streaming of the event showcases to the elite that 'we-are-the-good-guys'. Celebrations are carefully integrated in the marketing strategy. Students and graduates are protagonists in the external positioning and reputation of the university.

5.   CONCLUSION AND FURTHER PERSPECTIVES

This chapter addresses institutional innovations in tourism higher education. As demonstrated throughout this volume and in this analysis in particular, a multitude of institutional innovations have emerged over the past decades. There is a fascinating amount of creativity in the field, potentially benefiting students as well as tourism enterprises and destinations. These activities may signal the emergence of innovative universities (Christensen and Eyring, 2011).

Across the four units of analysis, some major conclusions can be drawn. Convincing examples illustrate how tourism higher education is a phenomenon that cannot meaningfully be captured by a single form of innovation. Referred to here as the 'intellectual playground', there are elements of intuitive and detached behavior where teachers and students explore their own alleys of teaching and learning. Simultaneously it is evident that institutions strategically control academic freedom and bottom-up anarchy through an industrial, Fordist approach. Each stance, and the balances, is a matter of innovative institutional endeavor.

Examples in this volume also demonstrate that tourism higher education continues to recognize the importance of addressing external needs and industry requirements. Engaging stakeholders may be serendipitous, acknowledging that creative inspiration is multi-dimensional and unpredictable. Other exemplars of institutional innovation utilize external relationships in advisory functions to help underpin growth and rational decision making. The strategic use of external stakeholders, notably the industry, was mostly seen in innovation management, but also found in several instances of curriculum design.

Ideas travel and so do institutional innovations. Diffusion across universities and countries of institutional innovations in tourism higher education are expected to take place, depending on the conditions and motivations (Blättel-Mink and Kastenholz, 2005). The examples in this volume suggest a remarkable uniformity and convergence across countries and continents in two aspects. One is the evidence of capitalistic and market oriented operations in tourism higher education. The new Holy Trinity of impact, assessment and funding (Collini, 2012) means that many institutions engage private sector management strategies, such as new public management and neo-liberal managerialism (Taylor, 2013). Tensions easily arise from requirements to do more with less. Added to the mass production of students are pressures to maintain individual student satisfaction and meeting institutional requirements, such as professional accreditations, research excellence frameworks, league table rankings and competitive funding schemes. It is hardly surprising that many tourism educators and researchers find themselves working harder and harder, simply to stand still (Liburd, 2013: 8).

The other uniformity is found in the past five decades of development in the disciplines and tourism curriculum space, illustrated in Figure 40.1. The present influence of inter- and multi-disciplinarity and a vocational/liberal curriculum are detected in innovative examples curriculum content and design from across the world. Are these to be seen as a refinement of institutional demands on what to teach through predefined learning outcomes, and in some instances the definition of core curricula and skills objectives? Are these innovations simply means that fail to critically engage with the ends of tourism higher education?

This study illustrates that institutional innovation is a suitable and promising field of inquiry in tourism higher education. Further research is needed, especially to gain better understandings of the procedural aspects of institutional innovations, the viability of specific institutional innovations, and how gradual adaptions may occur. Tapping into the more extensive literature of institutional change, such inquiries may also address issues about path dependency and institutional convergence, which are well-recognized concepts in neo-institutional and innovation research (Powell and DiMaggio, 2012). It will be crucial to investigate the applicability of Powell and DiMaggio's (2012) mechanisms of isomorphism: *Coercive*, where formal and informal pressures lead to standardization, and where external governmental forces and financial necessities are leading to isomorphism, whereas *Mimetic* isomorphism concerns an imitation of fashions and practice; to judge from the contributions in this volume also something that appears to be in operation in higher tourism education. Eventually, Powell and DiMaggio (2012) mention *normative processes* that mainly refer to the immanent professionalization. Impacts of student satisfaction, state and industry relations can also be suggested, as can the nature of legitimization processes. Finally, diffusion patterns and logics of institutional innovations may also be matters for further examination.

REFERENCES

Airey, D. (2005), 'Growth and development', in Airey, D. and Tribe, J. (eds), *An International Handbook of Tourism Education*, Advances in Tourism Research Series, Oxford: Elsevier, pp. 13–24.

Airey, D.W. (2008), 'Tourism education: Life begins at 40', accessed 14 May 2015 at epubs.surrey.ac.uk/cgi/viewcontent.cgi?article=1039andcontext=tourism.

Anandarajan, A. and Anandarajan, M. (2010), *e-Research Collaboration*, Berlin and Heidelberg: Springer-Verlag.

Archer, B., Cooper, C. and Ruhanen, L. (2005), 'The positive and negative impacts of tourism', in W.F. Theobald (ed.), *Global Tourism*, Burlington, MA: Elsevier Butterworth-Heinemann, pp. 79–102.

Asheim, B.T., Cooke, P. and Martin, R. (eds) (2006), *Clusters and Regional Development: Critical Reflections and Explorations*, London: Routledge.

Aylward, D. (2004), 'Working together: Innovation and export links within highly developed and embryonic wine clusters', *Strategic Change*, **13** (8), 429–39.

Barnett, R. (2013), *Imagining the University*, London and New York: Routledge.

Benckendorff, P., Lohmann, G., Pratt, M., Reynolds, P., Strickland, P. and Whitelaw, P. (2015), *Online Business Simulations: Good Practice Guide*, Sydney: Australian Government Office for Learning and Teaching.

Blättel-Mink, B. and Kastenholz, H. (2005), 'Transdisciplinarity in sustainability research: Diffusion conditions of an institutional innovation', *The International Journal of Sustainable Development and World Ecology*, **12** (1), 1–12.

Bok, D. (2003), *Universities in the Market Place: The Commercialization of Higher Education*, Princeton, NJ: Princeton University Press.

Burkhart, A.J. and Medlik, S. (1974), *Tourism: Past, Present and Future*, London: Heinemann.

Camison, C. and Monfort-Mir, V.M. (2012), 'Measuring innovation in tourism from the Schumpeterian and the dynamic-capabilities perspectives', *Tourism Management*, **33** (4), 776–89.

Carrie, A.S. (2000), 'From integrated enterprises to regional clusters: The changing basis of competition', *Computers in Industry*, **42** (2), 289–98.

Casper, S. (2006), 'Exporting the Silicon Valley to Europe: How useful is comparative institutional theory?', in J. Hage and M. Meeus (eds), *Innovation, Science, and Institutional Change*, Oxford: Oxford University Press, pp. 483–504.

Christensen, C.M. and Eyring, H.J. (2011), *The Innovative University: Changing the DNA of Higher Education from the Inside Out*, San Francisco: Jossey-Bass.

Clark, B.R. (2000), 'Collegial entrepreneurialism in proactive universities: Lessons from Europe', *Change: The Magazine of Higher Learning*, **32** (1), 10–19.

Claver-Cortés, E., Molina-Azorı, J.F. and Pereira-Moliner, J. (2007), 'Competitiveness in mass tourism', *Annals of Tourism Research*, **34** (3), 727–45.

Collini, S. (2012), *What are Universities for?* London: Penguin Books.

DiMaggio, P. (1988), 'Interest and agency in institutional theory', in L. Zucker (ed.), *Institutional Patterns and Organizations: Culture and Environment*, Cambridge, MA: Ballinger Publishing, pp. 3–21.

Gibson, R. (2010), 'The "art" of creative teaching: Implications for higher education', *Teaching in Higher Education*, **15** (5), 607–13.

Graburn, N.H.H. and Jafari, J. (1991), 'Introduction: Tourism social science', *Annals of Tourism Research*, **18** (1), 1–11.

Hall, C.M. (2009), 'Innovation and tourism policy in Australia and New Zealand: Never the twain shall meet?', *Journal of Policy Research in Tourism, Leisure and Events*, **1** (1), 2–18.

Hamdouch, A. and Moulaert, F. (2006), 'Knowledge infrastructure, innovation dynamics, and knowledge creation/diffusion/accumulation processes: A comparative institutional perspective', *Innovation: The European Journal of Social Science Research*, **19** (1), 25–50.

Hargrave, T.J. and Van de Ven, A.H. (2006), 'A collective action model of institutional innovation', *Academy of Management Review*, **31** (4), 864–88.

Hjalager, A.M. (2002), 'Repairing innovation defectiveness in tourism', *Tourism Management*, **23** (5), 465–74.

Hjalager, A.M. (2010), 'A review of innovation research in tourism', *Tourism Management*, **31** (1), 1–12.

Jafari, J. (1989), 'An English language literature review', in J. Bystranowski (ed.), *Tourism as a Factor of Change: A Socio-cultural Study*, Vienna: Centre for Research and Documentation in Social Sciences, pp. 17–60.

Jafari, J. (1990), 'Research and scholarship: The basis of tourism education', *The Journal of Tourism Studies*, **1** (1), 33–41.

Jafari, J. (2001), 'The scientification of tourism', in V. Smith and M. Brent (eds), *Hosts and Guests Revisited: Tourism Issues of The 21st Century*, Elmsford: Cognizant Communications, pp. 28–41.

Koh, K. (1995), 'Designing the four-year tourism management curriculum: A marketing approach', *Journal of Travel Research*, **34** (1), 68–72.

Leydesdorff, L. and Etzkowitz, H. (1996), 'Emergence of a triple helix of university–industry–government relations', *Science and Public Policy*, **23** (5), 279–86.

Liburd, J.J. (2013), *The Collaborative University: Lessons from Tourism Education and Research*, Professorial Dissertation, University of Southern Denmark: Odense Print and Sign.

Liburd, J.J. and Hjalager, A-M. (2010), 'Changing approaches towards open education, innovation and research in tourism', *Journal of Hospitality and Tourism Management*, **17**, 12–20.

Liburd, J.J., Benckendorff, P. and Carlsen, J.C. (2012), 'Tourism and quality of life: How does tourism measure up?', in M. Uysal, R. Perdue and J. Sirgy (eds), *Handbook on Tourism and Quality of Life Research,* Dordrecht, Heidelberg, London and New York: Springer Business, pp. 105–32.

Liburd, J.J., Carlsen, J. and Edwards, D. (eds) (2013), *Networks for Sustainable Tourism Innovation: Case Studies and Cross-case Analysis*, Melbourne: Tilde University Press.

Lorenz, C. (2012), 'If you're so smart, why are you under surveillance? Universities, neoliberalism, and new public management', *Critical Inquiry*, **38** (3), 599–629.

Macbeth, J. (2005), 'Towards an ethics platform for tourism', *Annals of Tourism Research,* **32** (4), 962–84.

MacCannell, D. (1976), *The Tourist*, New York: Schocken.

Moscardo, G. and Pearce, P.L. (1999), 'Understanding ethnic tourists', *Annals of Tourism Research*, **26** (2), 416–34.

Mowforth, A. and Munt, I. (1998), *Tourism and Sustainability: New Tourism in the Third World*, London: Routledge.

Murphy, J., Kalbaska, N., Horton-Tognazzini, L. and Cantoni, L. (2015), 'Online learning and MOOCs: A framework proposal', in J. Murphy, N. Kalbaska, L. Horton-Tognazzini and L. Cantoni (eds), *Information and Communication Technologies in Tourism 2015*, Lugano: Springer International Publishing, pp. 847–58.

Novelli, M., Schmitz, B. and Spencer, T. (2006), 'Networks, clusters and innovation in tourism: A UK experience', *Tourism Management*, **27** (6), 1141–52.

Ooi, C.S. (2002), 'Contrasting strategies: Tourism in Denmark and Singapore', *Annals of Tourism Research*, **29** (3), 689–706.

Patullo, P. (1996), *Last Resorts: The Cost of Tourism in the Caribbean*, London: Cassell.

Pearce, P. (2005), *Tourist Development*, Harlow: Longman.

Pikkemaat, B. (2008), 'Innovation in small and medium-sized tourism enterprises in Tyrol, Austria', *The International Journal of Entrepreneurship and Innovation*, **9** (3), 187–97.

Poon, A. (1993), *Tourism, Technology and Competitive Strategies*, Wallingford: CAB International.

Powell, W.W. and DiMaggio, P.J. (eds) (2012), *The New Institutionalism in Organizational Analysis*, Chicago: University of Chicago Press.

Raffaelli, R. and Glynn, M.A. (2015), 'Institutional innovation: Novel, useful, and legitimate', in C.E. Shalley, M.A. Hitt and J. Zhou (eds), *Oxford Handbook of Creativity, Innovation, and Entrepreneurship*, Oxford: Oxford University Press.

Ring, A., Dickinger, A. and Vöeber, K. (2009), 'Designing the ideal undergraduate program in tourism', *Journal of Travel Research*, **48** (1), 106–21.

Sawyer, R.K. (2004), 'Creative teaching: Collaborative discussion as disciplined improvisation', *Educational Researcher*, **33** (2), 12–20.

Schumpeter, J.A. (1942), *Capitalism, Socialism and Democracy*, New York: Harper and Brothers.

Sheldon, P., Fesenmaier, D. and Tribe, J. (2011), 'The Tourism Education Futures Initiative (TEFI): Activating change in tourism education', *Journal of Teaching in Travel and Tourism*, **11** (1), 2–23.

Sheldon, P., Fesenmaier, D., Woeber, K. Cooper, C. and Antonioli, M. (2008), 'Tourism education futures, 2010–2030: Building the capacity to lead', *Journal of Teaching in Travel and Tourism*, **7** (3), 61–8.
Smith, V.L. (ed.) (1977), *Hosts and Guests: The Anthropology of Tourism*, 1st edn, Philadelphia, PA: University of Pennsylvania Press.
Smith, V.L. (ed.) (1989), *Hosts and Guests: The Anthropology of Tourism,* 2nd edn, Philadelphia, PA: University of Pennsylvania Press.
Smith, V.L. and Brent, M. (2001), *Hosts and Guests Revisited: Tourism Issues of the 21st Century*, New York: Cognizant.
Smith, V.L. and Eadington, W.R. (1989), *Tourism Alternatives: Potentials and Problems in the Development of Tourism*, Philadelphia, PA: University of Pennsylvania Press.
Sørensen, F. (2007), 'The geographies of social networks and innovation in tourism', *Tourism Geographies*, **9** (1), 22–48.
Sundbo, J., Orfila-Sintes, F. and Sørensen, F. (2007), 'The innovative behaviour of tourism firms: Comparative studies of Denmark and Spain', *Research Policy*, **36** (1), 88–106.
Taylor, M. (2013), 'Shared governance in the modern university', *Higher Education Quarterly*, **67** (1), 80–94.
Taylor, P.A. (1979), 'Jobs through tourism', *Tourism Review*, **34** (4), 17–18.
Tribe, J. (1997), 'The indiscipline of tourism', *Annals of Tourism Research,* **24** (3), 638–57.
Tribe, J. (2002), 'The philosophic practitioner', *Annals of Tourism Research*, **29** (2), 338–57.
Tribe, J. (2010), 'Tribes, territories and networks in the tourism academy', *Annals of Tourism Research*, **37** (1), 7–33.
Urry, J. (1990), *The Tourist Gaze: Leisure and Travel in Contemporary Societies*, London: Sage Publications.
Van Wijk, J., Van der Duim, R., Lamers, M. and Sumba, D. (2015), 'The emergence of institutional innovations in tourism: The evolution of the African Wildlife Foundation's tourism conservation enterprises', *Journal of Sustainable Tourism*, **23** (1), 104–25.
Weick, K.E. and Quinn, R.E. (1999), 'Organizational change and development', *Annual Review of Psychology*, **50** (1), 361–86.
Williams, A.M. and Shaw, G. (2011), 'Internationalization and innovation in tourism', *Annals of Tourism Research*, **38** (1), 27–51.

41 The future of teaching and learning in tourism
Pierre Benckendorff and Anita Zehrer

1. INTRODUCTION

The universities of today bear little resemblance to the universities of the 1970s and 1980s. A number of forces continue to shape the future of higher education and our approaches to teaching and learning. In this chapter we review some of the megatrends impacting on the future and we use these as a foundation to provide an original synthesis of the future of teaching and learning in tourism at the macro level. We also discuss meso- and micro-level trends by summarizing and extending the key themes that emerge from a number of the chapters presented in this volume. While several books have been devoted to tourism education, the 40 chapters presented prior to this final chapter represent the most comprehensive attempt to address the more focused topic of teaching and learning. However, in spite of the range of contributions and topics included, there are some important topics that were not able to be covered either because appropriate contributors were not available or because the topic has not received sufficient consideration to warrant a lengthy discussion. Therefore, we attempt to extend on the work already presented by not only summarizing key themes but also adding additional commentary and analysis.

2. MEGATRENDS

While many methods could be used to provide strategic foresight of the future, many analyses begin with an assessment of key megatrends. In this chapter we start with the major trends and challenges confronting our planet and the future of humanity. These are often referred to as megatrends and can be divided into socio-demographic, techno-logical, environmental, economic and political trends. This division should not imply that these trends operate independently of each other. On the contrary, they often interact in complex and unpredictable ways, making predictions about the future difficult. Education is not immune from these trends. As Selwyn (2014, p. 21) observes: 'any aspect of higher education is enmeshed with shifts in global economics and national politics, as well as various societal and cultural (re)formations'. While a full review of key trends in each of these areas is well beyond the scope of this book, we touch on a few trends that we believe have important implications for teaching and learning.

Socio-demographic megatrends are often complex, but an array of data sources ranging from traditional census and population statistics to increasingly pervasive 'big data' provide a number of indicators for further discussion. Exponential population growth is without a doubt the major social trend of the last two centuries. Projections predict that the world population will reach 9.7 billion by 2050 and 11.2 billion by 2100 (United Nations, 2015). Most of this growth is expected to take place in developing nations, with most of the world's future population likely to live in urban rather than rural settings. At the same time, we have seen a concerted effort through the United Nations Millennium Development Goals (MDGs) and the more recent Sustainable Development Goals (SDGs) to reduce the proportion of the population living under extreme poverty. Education is regarded as a key pillar in achieving these goals, leading to increasing participation in secondary and tertiary education. While there is some concern about this 'massification' of higher education, these developments provide an opportunity to re-evaluate approaches to teaching and learning (Altbach et al., 2009). A second major social trend in wealthy developed countries is the ageing of the population. In most developed nations this growth coincides with the exit of the baby boomer generation from the tourism workforce. While current graduates in many developed economies face high levels of youth unemployment, demographers generally agree that by 2020 the ageing population will result in a labor shortage in many industries. The tourism academy will undergo similar generational changes, propelling so-called 'Generation Tourism' academics into senior leadership positions (Filep et al., 2015). These academics are likely to face pressure to lead their institutions to deliver higher quality education to increasingly diverse student cohorts at a lower cost.

Information technologies and new media are arguably amongst the most pervasive drivers of innovative disruption in higher education systems (Selwyn, 2014; Walsh, 2015). New technologies have supported new business models and innovative approaches to teaching and learning (Chapter 40). As the contributions in Part II of this volume indicate, tourism educators have been at the forefront of using technology to enhance teaching and learning. Recent advances have resulted in the rapid rise of Massive Open Online Courses (MOOCs) promising free open-access mass online education (see Chapter 11). The *NMC Horizon Report: 2016 Higher Education Edition* identifies the increasing use of blended learning designs as a major short-term trend (Johnson et al., 2016; Zehrer and Schuckert, 2016). Advances in learning analytics, adaptive learning, gamification, artificial intelligence and virtual reality are likely to make blended learning pedagogies even more compelling. Technological developments also impact on how educators work and interact. The growing availability of high-quality open-access content challenges the current need to replicate content for local delivery. There seems little to be gained from hundreds of educators all duplicating the same content in different locations. Some education futurists have speculated that rather than being tenured to a single institution, educators in the future are likely to operate as freelancers earning fees for expert content adopted by learners across many institutions. The implication for learners is that future programs may be made up of online knowledge delivered by experts from around the world, with class time reserved for activities that build social capital.

Economic trends are complex and difficult to separate from some of the other trends discussed in this chapter. In the economic sphere, trends and forecasts have largely focused on economic growth and wealth generation. It is increasingly apparent that the increases in resource consumption that underpin economic growth are not sustainable. It is likely that the economic system will make a transition from fossil fuel-dependent economies to renewable energies. Some economies are already well advanced in this transition, while others remain reliant on non-renewable energy sources. This transition coincides with unsustainable levels of debt that will constrain the ability of some countries to transition to more sustainable economic systems. Austerity measures in many developed nations mean that government funding of higher education is increasingly constrained.

In some countries, the constrained funding environment has resulted in institutional consolidation, rationalization and concentration. In contrast, the new economies of Asia have increased their investment in higher education in an effort to create internationally competitive universities. Similarly, in Europe greater wealth and higher levels of taxation have ensured continued support for universal free tertiary education. At the same time, higher education is increasingly enmeshed in a number of globalized processes (Wilson, 2010). The globalization of education brands is likely to facilitate global mobility for both learners and educators. In Part IV, several chapters of this volume are devoted to different aspects of internationalization and the ramifications for teaching and learning. At the curriculum level, globalization and increased mobility creates increasing pressure to harmonize learning standards and outcomes (see Chapter 35). Globalization has also created an environment conducive to off-shore campuses, multinational universities, global partnerships, and global networks of private education providers.

In the area of environmental trends there is little doubt that climate change is the major challenge of our times. The threat of climate change is inextricably linked with environmental issues such as resource depletion, pollution and species extinction. These trends mean that the world of 2050 will be dramatically different from the world of 2016. For educators the challenge is how to educate graduates to meet the challenges of tomorrow. An obvious response is to ensure that the curriculum provides students with opportunities for the deep learning required for complex topics such as climate change adaptation and mitigation. This also implies a curriculum that is multidisciplinary in nature. However, the challenges posed by climate change extend beyond content and curriculum to the development of skills and competencies to deal with change, complexity and uncertainty (Zehrer and Mössenlechner, 2009). In this context, the TEFI values proposed by Sheldon and Fesenmaier (2015) provide some direction for developing graduates who are socially and environmentally responsible. The threshold learning outcomes (TLOs) developed in Australia also seek to address some of these skills by highlighting the importance of inter-disciplinarity, professional responsibility, collaboration and the design of sustainable tourism services and experiences (see Chapter 35).

The future of higher education cannot be divorced from political trends. Many of the changes faced by universities over the last three decades can be linked with changes in government policy and political ideology. Most governments have pursued an agenda of increasing participation in higher education. As we have noted earlier, this agenda is linked to the notion of education as a driver of economic growth and poverty alleviation. Higher participation rates have been partly achieved by increasing the supply of higher education. A second political trend, partly driven by so-called 'neo-liberalism', is the gradual deregulation and privatization of higher education. In many countries this has resulted in the growth of private education providers. The private education sector has undergone a period of consolidation, with many private education brands now managed by a handful of global education conglomerates. In some countries political rhetoric has increasingly portrayed higher education as a private good rather than a public good. This has shifted the emphasis from 'education for society' to 'education for the labor market' and has transferred the funding burden from taxpayers to institutions and their students (Ayikoru, 2015). Public institutions have been under increasing pressure to generate alterative revenue streams to offset diminishing government funding. Inevitably these revenue streams involve more commercial or entrepreneurial activities.

3.   IDENTIFYING KEY THEMES FOR TEACHING AND LEARNING IN TOURISM

While our brief analysis of megatrends may be superficial and underdeveloped, our aim was to present a selection of trends to demonstrate how complex interactions at the macro level can impact teaching and learning at the coalface. However, to gain further insight into the future of teaching and learning it is useful to reflect on developments at the meso (for example institutional) and micro (for example curriculum, pedagogy, learning outcomes) levels. When preparing chapters for this volume, authors were asked to provide some commentary on any future directions pertaining to their contribution. Most authors took the opportunity to do this and as a result this volume offers many insights into how teaching and learning in tourism is likely to change in the future. We offer an overview of developments at the meso and micro levels in the next section by contemplating some of the key themes that have emerged from the contributions in this volume.

To identify key themes, each of the chapters in this volume was included in a Leximancer analysis. Leximancer is a computer assisted content analysis tool that uses proximity values and artificial learning to automatically identify and map themes and concepts in textual data (Smith and Humphreys, 2006).

The technique combines both conceptual and relational content analysis. The conceptual analysis identifies the presence and frequency of concepts in a body of text whereas the relational analysis measures how the concepts are related to each other. A 'concept' consists of sets of words that are used in close proximity to each other in the same review. Leximancer identifies key concepts by using word frequencies and co-occurrence to identify families of terms that tend to be used together in a body of text. The words that make up each concept are then placed in a 'thesaurus' that contains the set of associated words and weightings that indicate the relative importance of each word. This approach to weighting concepts goes well beyond simple word frequency counts and co-occurrence counts because the software differentiates between words and concepts, with concepts being the most semantically significant words (Rooney et al., 2009).

Leximancer produces a concept map which provides an overview of the conceptual structure of a body of text. Concepts that co-occur frequently within a two-sentence block are likely to be closer together when the map is produced, resulting in similar concepts clustering together in close proximity. Clusters of concepts are grouped by theme circles to summarize the main ideas in particular clusters. Therefore, the concept map presents a conceptual overview of the semantic structure of the text by visually presenting the associations between concepts. The concept map shown on Figure 41.1 summarizes the key concepts and themes found in this volume.

The most frequent concepts identified by the analysis included students, tourism, education, study, learning and research. Following careful reading of the text, the four key themes were labeled as 'institutions', 'curricula', 'social pedagogies' and 'students'. The following discussion is arranged according to these themes. The aim is not to summarize or repeat the content presented in the book, but rather to use the themes as a starting point for further discussion about future teaching and learning trends and issues at the meso and micro levels. Some links are made to specific sections and chapters of the book.

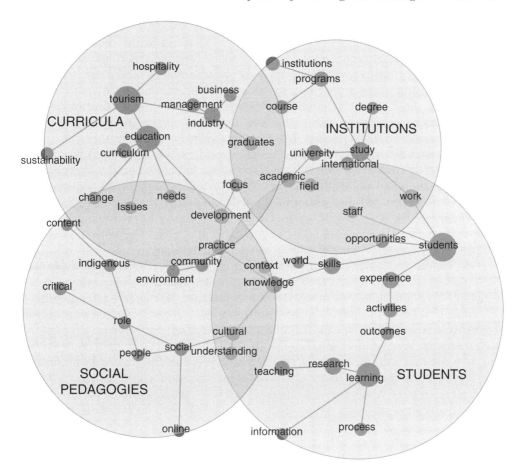

Figure 41.1   Key themes and concepts discussed in this volume

4.   INSTITUTIONAL FUTURES

The 'institutions' themes included a wide range of concepts related to study, work, universities and institutions, programs and courses. In this section we try to extend on the many issues presented in this volume by focusing on three major topics linked to the future of educational institutions. These topics include institutional structures and forms, the role of teaching and learning in the knowledge economy and the influence of new media and information technologies on teaching and learning.

4.1   Transforming Institutional Structures and Forms

Just as the universities of today bear little resemblance to the universities of the 1970s and 1980s, the universities of the future are likely to look markedly different. Several themes emerge from attempts by various commentators to predict how the higher education institutions of the future will look. As we have noted already, the growth of private education providers has altered the dynamics of the sector in many countries. It seems likely that the private education sector will continue to experience both growth and consolidation. The worldwide surge in private higher education and the funding models for this sector have important implications for educators, students and society more broadly (Altbach et al., 2009). For some educators, this means a more diverse range of potential employers with a variety of different goals and objectives, ranging from purely commercial enterprises to traditional research-intensive universities. Other educators will view the rise of commercially oriented private education providers with some suspicion. Private education brands are likely to consolidate around a small number of global conglomerates, creating new opportunities for student and staff mobility. Some private providers will seek out partnerships with well-established public university partners to reinforce their own reputations. However, given high levels of casualization in the private sector it seems unlikely that such institutions would develop significant research capability.

Privatization combined with declining government funding of universities is likely to place middle and lower-tier universities and colleges under considerable pressure. These pressures lead to several strategic responses. An institution may rationalize the breadth of programs it delivers in an effort to specialize in fields where it is competitive. This strategy is likely to result in niche institutions, with some specializing in tourism, hospitality, leisure, events, sports and related fields. An alternative strategic response, given the increasing cost of conducting research, is to become a teaching-focused institution. In some educational contexts it may be practical for several smaller institutions to merge into a larger university that is capable of competing with well-established research-intensive universities. A variation of this approach may involve alliances between public or private education providers. Some institutions may also seek to lower their cost base by outsourcing administrative support functions such as human resource management, marketing, financial management, travel and information technologies (Ernst and Young, 2012). An institution in this situation may also seek to diversify its revenue base by tapping into new markets.

Many of these strategic responses are already evident in some countries but the strategic options available to a particular institution are likely to be contingent upon national regulatory and quality assurance frameworks. These observations are particularly relevant to the future of tourism education because many well-known tourism research groups are located in less well-ranked universities (Airey et al., 2015). Tourism educators in these institutions often find themselves in a vulnerable position, either as a result of rationalization processes or due to the increasing workload associated with generating new partnerships and revenue streams. Tenured positions in these institutions are likely to become the exception rather than the norm as constrained funding will favor casualization (Gappa, 2000). However, the more applied, vocational orientation and the teaching and learning focus of some institutions will provide fertile opportunities for innovative tourism education (Chapter 40).

The world's top-tier elite universities are likely to come under immense pressure to offer a comprehensive suite of high-quality programs while continuing to fund world-class research. While their endowments and reputation are likely to offer some protection from the forces impacting on other higher education institutions, these institutions will also experience change. New competitors will emerge from China, the Middle East and India.

A sound strategic direction for these universities is to generate new funding streams by commercializing research discoveries. In the teaching and learning area, these universities are likely to use their global brands to build partnerships with other reputable providers to generate revenue from education.

In summary, while some commentators have questioned whether there is a future for 'public intellectuals' (Posner, 2003), the work of Ernst and Young (2012) and Barber et al. (2013) points to a higher education landscape that will consist of a variety of different institutions, including:

- *Elite providers:* broad-based research and teaching institutions with global reputations that will continue to offer a comprehensive range of programs. The teaching and learning focus is likely to be on integrating cutting-edge research with education. Only a handful of the world's tourism programs are based in institutions that rank amongst the top 100 universities in the world (Airey et al., 2015). Examples include Cornell University and The University of Queensland.
- *Mass providers:* large teaching-focused universities and colleges with research expertise in specialized areas. Many of the world's tourism groups are found in these institutions. The teaching and learning focus is likely to be on combining applied research with innovative pedagogies and blended learning to create a competitive advantage. Examples include Virginia Tech, Griffith University and Hong Kong Polytechnic University.
- *Niche providers:* institutions specializing in specific locations, markets or disciplines. The teaching and learning focus is likely to be on industry-based vocational pedagogies. This model is already common in Europe, with the famous business schools and Swiss hotel schools offering good examples of this approach. Other examples include MODUL University in Vienna and the Management Center Innsbruck.
- *Private providers:* private institutions or global conglomerates focusing on high-yield, industry-focused programs. The teaching and learning focus is likely to be on educational 'products' that can be repacked in different formats for commercial goals. Examples of large private providers offering tourism programs include Pearson Education, Apollo Global and Laureate.

There are of course some providers that defy categorization and others that straddle several of these archetypes – a good example is Taylor's University in Malaysia. The diversification of institutional models will intensify competition for talented students and educators. It is critical to the long-term viability of the field to ensure that tourism research and education continues to be represented across the full spectrum of education providers. As Dredge et al. (2015) observe, a broad spectrum of institutions offering different programs and pathways creates ample room for a range of different learning styles and pedagogic approaches in tourism education.

4.2 The Role of Teaching and Learning in the Knowledge Economy

The knowledge economy refers to 'the increasing significance of the production and manipulation of information and knowledge rather than the production and consumption of goods and services' (Selwyn, 2014, p. 23). Implicit in this notion of the knowledge economy is the role of universities as catalysts for the creative endeavor that underpins economic competitiveness and employability (Besley and Peters, 2013). One outcome of the knowledge economy is the availability of vast amounts of online 'knowledge'. This 'democratization of knowledge' and the massification of higher education represent a major change in the role of universities as the producers and keepers of knowledge (Ernst and Young, 2012). At the same time, the cost of education is increasing while the value of a degree is decreasing, especially in fields like tourism and hospitality where a tertiary qualification is not a prerequisite for professional accreditation or practice. If universities are to remain relevant and useful, it becomes increasingly important for educators to contemplate how tourism education can add value to the vast amounts of information already available online. Barnett's (2015) notion of the 'creative university' may provide a schema for thinking about universities as more than producers and keepers of knowledge. The many chapters in this volume on graduate capabilities (Part I), technology enabled learning (Part II), experiential learning (Part III), and critical perspectives (Part V) provide useful examples of creativity in teaching and learning. They also offer future insights for navigating the changing role of education in the knowledge economy.

In a globalized knowledge economy it is important to attend to the competencies, dispositions and different cultural contexts of learners. Thus we have to deal with new environments and have to build identity with and compassion for multiple cultures. Knowledge can therefore be progressively regarded as a cultural artifact with multi-dimensional collaborative characteristics which consistently need to be tested. The question of 'knowledge cultures', which embody cultural ways of doing things developing over generations, must be examined at micro, meso and macro levels. These 'knowledge cultures' thus ultimately depend upon cultural concepts and analyses. Following this logic, education, teaching and learning need to be redefined to focus on capabilities that individuals develop in their lifetime based on their cultural backgrounds.

4.3   Rethinking Teaching and Learning in the Digital Age

It is somewhat disarming to see that technology does not feature prominently in the concept map presented in Figure 41.1. Much has been written about the demise of the traditional university in the face of technological innovation in teaching and learning. As we have noted earlier in this chapter, there can be no doubt that technological changes represent significant megatrends that have disrupted traditional approaches to teaching and learning. However, many commentators also argue that the death of the traditional university at the hands of technology is greatly exaggerated (Altbach et al., 2009; Ernst and Young, 2012; Selwyn, 2014). Most claims that information technologies will displace traditional universities are based on the premise that technology can be used as a direct substitute for traditional teaching and learning approaches. Although there are examples where technology does play a substitution role (for example video lectures, spell checkers, online media), many of the technologies used by contemporary higher education institutions are complementary to traditional models of learning.

Puentedura (2006) argues that technology can be used not only as a substitute but also to augment, modify or redefine learning tasks. Thus, as Morellato notes in Chapter 9, technology is not a threat to the traditional university but rather provides new opportunities for creativity in teaching and learning. Despite the growth of distance education and

MOOCs, it is increasingly clear that the most effective applications of technology involve blended learning rather than purely digital channels of delivery. Innovative technology enhanced learning techniques increasingly rely on a 'bring your own device' model supported by ubiquitous Wi-Fi access for learners, removing the need for universities to invest in hardware that ages rapidly. Subsequent chapters in Part II of this book indicate that tourism educators are experimenting with creative technology-enhanced learning techniques. Improvements in the quality of online simulations are also likely to offer improved opportunities for learners to practice and demonstrate capabilities requiring integration, analysis and problem solving (Benckendorff et al., 2015).

The growth of online education and personal mobile devices demands that tourism educators keep abreast of new developments in technology-enhanced learning. While technology can be intimidating to educators who are more comfortable in traditional classrooms, technology-enhanced teaching and learning can be mastered with appropriate support and professional development. However, it is increasingly apparent that technology is not an antidote for poorly conceived teaching and learning techniques. Learners are remarkably diverse in their responses to the use of technology in teaching and learning, challenging the veracity of claims made by some commentators about the expectations of largely non-existent cohorts of 'digital natives' (Henderson et al., 2015). The most widely adopted technologies afford learners with greater flexibility and convenience in modes of learning but do not always lead to more novel learning opportunities. Henderson et al. (2015) argue that contemporary debates about technology and pedagogy should occur in the context of content and curriculum design, expectations of assessment, student diversity and assumptions about engagement and learning. When discussing the role of technology in pedagogy and assessment, the question should always be about the principles that underpin learning design. The principle of constructive alignment suggests that technology-enhanced learning approaches should deliver learning outcomes that are more efficient or effective than the traditional approaches they replace. Otherwise, what is the point of adopting a new technology? This observation highlights the need not only for creativity and experimentation, but for robust research and evaluation of technology-enhanced learning outcomes.

As we look to the future, there is little doubt that tourism educators will have to consider learning in a new light, with technology being a catalyst for teaching and learning. Traditional campuses are likely to remain important centers for learning, but technologies such as mobile devices, augmented and virtual reality, artificial intelligence and learning analytics will transform the 'value' proposition and the way in which education is delivered by higher education providers (Ernst and Young, 2012). Part of this value proposition may well involve the dissolution of the boundaries between culture, knowledge and understanding as technology becomes a tool for lifelong learning both inside and outside formal education institutions (Selwyn, 2014). Reflecting some of the ideas in Bauman's (2000) 'liquid modernity', the literature in this area variously refers to this new fluidity between universities and society as the 'borderless university' (Cunningham et al., 1998), the 'edgeless university' (Bradwell, 2010), and the 'networked university' (Standaert, 2012). These ideas highlight the need for more effective models of learning to inform the role of technology in teaching and learning.

5.   THE TOURISM CURRICULUM

The disciplinary focus and design of the tourism curriculum continues to be a source of ongoing debate in the broader literature (Dredge et al., 2012; Tribe, 2001; Koh, 1995). The key concepts in the 'curriculum' theme presented in Figure 41.1 included concepts such as tourism, education, industry, development, practice, curriculum, graduates and management. Many of the chapters in this volume touch on the issue of curriculum design and content to varying degrees. Tourism is a rich and rewarding inter-disciplinary field of inquiry. This is evident not only in the range of disciplinary approaches to research but also the diverse range of disciplinary approaches to teaching and learning reported in this volume. In presenting the work of tourism educators from different disciplines we have taken some care to ensure that the varied styles of discourse were not diluted for the sake of consistency. These disciplinary voices are important to the presentation of teaching and learning techniques, approaches and challenges.

The chapters emphasizing the importance of industry engagement and student mobility are particularly pertinent and highlight an ongoing tension between a more vocational focus that meets the needs of the labor market and a more liberal focus that emphasizes the needs of society (Dredge et al., 2012; Tribe, 2002). As Dredge et al. (2012) observe, the balance between vocational and liberal education in tourism programs becomes an issue because the curriculum space is crowded and decisions about what to include in the curriculum are influenced by a complex network of forces emanating from various stakeholders. A major concern within the tourism academy is that many tourism programs are dominated by business and management perspectives that emphasize economic sustainability and growth (Wilson and Von der Heidt, 2013). However, these critiques neglect the fact that management education itself is undergoing the same debates and transformations as tourism education. Within business schools there is increasingly a view that learners should receive a more liberal education. This is most evident in the discourses about service learning in business education (Godfrey et al., 2005), education for sustainability in business (Stubbs and Cocklin, 2008; MacVaugh and Norton, 2012), critical management studies (Grey, 2004; Reynolds and Vince, 2004) and social entrepreneurship (Tracey and Phillips, 2007). More recently, Tribe and Liburd (2016) have also acknowledged that the boundaries between business and the social sciences in tourism are permeable. These observations are not intended to dilute the role of other disciplinary perspectives in the tourism curriculum, but rather offer opportunities to integrate these various disciplinary perspectives to produce graduates with the capacity to solve post-disciplinary challenges. However, there is a justifiable concern that even within business programs the curriculum does not offer enough space for learners to explore the complexity of concepts such as sustainability (Von der Heidt and Lamberton, 2014). This is an important concern that will be explored further in the next section.

The challenge for educators in the future will be to determine the most suitable balance between vocational and liberal education in tourism. There are likely to be many different approaches, ranging from purely vocational programs to programs that are almost entirely focused on the liberal and social arts. Vocational and liberal education are of course not mutually exclusive and as educators continue to develop the curriculum many hybrid models are likely to emerge. The multidisciplinary nature of tourism would suggest that rather than defining an optimal or 'standard' curriculum for all tourism programs, it might be better for individual institutions to work towards meeting the needs of their stakeholders. This would result in a more diverse range of programs catering to different student markets and industry needs. However, there is a risk that the development of national standards and benchmarks may limit diversity. Therefore, the emphasis should be on developing threshold standards or benchmarks that provide a broad framework of learning outcomes and indicators of quality without specifying standardization of curriculum, pedagogy or assessment (see Chapters 35 and 36).

The role of industry in curriculum design and delivery is also related to the discussion about vocational and liberal education. Institutions will be under pressure to build stronger links with industry to differentiate their teaching and learning programs and support the funding of research. Here the contribution by Milman (Chapter 37) provides a number of valuable insights about the roles and responsibilities of industry advisory boards in curriculum design. However, there is a tension between industry and academia. The role of education is not to teach students to do things the way industry has always done them, but to challenge conventions and traditions. This can sometimes be difficult to convey to industry partners. The contributions presented in Part III offer a number of different approaches to facilitate learner and industry engagement. Tourism, perhaps drawing on its long association with hospitality, has tended to rely on traditional internships to provide learners with an opportunity to apply their knowledge and to develop workplace skills. Some more vocationally focused programs have provided training facilities such as hotels, restaurants, aircraft cabins and other simulated environments where students can develop operational skills. However, these pedagogies are becoming increasingly untenable because they are resource intensive and may not always provide optimal learning outcomes for an increasingly diverse study cohort. Craggs et al. (Chapter 18) demonstrate how educators can move beyond traditional internships by involving students in an active collaborative learning environment that includes local industry, industry groups as well as civic and broader community members as key components of the destination.

We anticipate that further innovation will result in a more diverse range of opportunities for students to engage with industry through a mix of pedagogies including fieldtrips (Chapters 20 and 21), learning laboratories (Chapter 19), study tours, immersion programs, shadowing programs, internships (Chapters 16 and 17), consultancy projects, service learning, community-based learning, social entrepreneurship, and virtual work integrated learning. The examples provided in Chapter 14 by King and Zhang illustrate how several experiential learning methods can be combined in novel ways across an entire program.

6. SOCIAL AND CRITICAL PEDAGOGIES IN TOURISM EDUCATION

It is perhaps not surprising, given the sociological and anthropological origins of tourism (Benckendorff and Zehrer, 2013), that there is clear interest in social and critical pedagogies. A consistent message across all of the chapters in Part V of this volume is that tourism education should foster critical awareness and concern about economic, social, cultural, political and ecological interactions in tourism. The position of this theme between the 'curricula' and 'students' themes (Figure 41.1) highlights that the development of social awareness and critical skills is not only about what is *taught* in the curriculum but what is *learned* by students. As Cottrell, Arcodia and and Ferreira note in Chapter 25, it is critical for educators to develop learners' skills in critical thinking and foreseeing the implications of their actions, along with a sense of ethics and empathy. This requires a fundamental change in the nature of education and shifts the focus to education as a transformative experience for learners (Benckendorff and Moscardo, 2015). Teaching and learning approaches that are particularly germane to this goal include reflective learning (see Chapter 7), inquiry-based learning (Chapter 8), service learning and community-based learning, social entrepreneurship, education for sustainability, and opportunities for socially constructed learning. Often these critical pedagogies are combined with critical reflexivity that requires both extrinsic evaluation and introspection in order to challenge the assumptions, discourses and practices that shape reality (Fullagar and Wilson, 2012; García-Rosell, 2015).

Service learning is based on the premise of extending learning beyond the classroom and into the community by providing experiential learning opportunities that include meaningful community engagement. Furco (2003) identifies four types of service learning arranged according to the beneficiary (the recipient or the learner) and the focus (balance between service and learning). His schema includes volunteerism, community service, field education and internships as examples of service learning, although he aligns service learning more closely with community service and field education. Service learning is not widely used in tourism education but Wearing et al.'s contribution (Chapter 27) provides one example of embedding students with local communities. Their approach also incorporates some of the features of social entrepreneurship in education (Tracey and Phillips, 2007). Other examples include studio learning (Bosman and Dredge, 2015), real consultancy projects (Buijtendijk and Van der Donk, 2015), problem-based learning (García-Rosell, 2015), technology-enabled learning (Jennings and Kachel, 2015; Schott, 2015), fieldwork and contextual learning. Many of the features of Education for Sustainability in Tourism proposed by Benckendorff and Moscardo (2015, p.272) are relevant to this discussion.

Given the pervasiveness of tourism in rural and regional areas and in developing economies, the scope for learning experiences that build community capacity and social capital seems enormous. These experiential learning opportunities would be particularly well suited to fostering engagement with Indigenous perspectives and worldviews (see Chapters 30 and 31). As Crossley observes in Chapter 29, when combined with critical reflexivity, these experiences have enormous scope for developing more critical perspectives that position the learner as an empowered social actor. Similarly, Caldicott and Wilson (Chapter 16) demonstrate how a self-authorship perspective of Work Integrated Learning can encourage learners to be more critical in their decision-making processes.

Perhaps, as technological innovations such as MOOCs and vodcasts become the norm for transmitting knowledge, there are new opportunities to use classroom time for social interaction. The term 'classroom' here is used both literally and figuratively to help readers consider how learning opportunities can be designed to facilitate socially constructed learning. In this context, Aubke and Hergesell (Chapter 38) make an important contribution by using network theory to illuminate how social capital impacts on student performance. Other approaches involve inviting members of the community into the classroom to share perspectives or sending learners to the field to participate in meaningful learning activities that have a clear community benefit. While some institutions have a strong commitment to communities and Indigenous peoples, it seems that the desire to foster graduate capabilities such as social and civic responsibility is a more recent consideration for most institutions. As Boyle notes in Chapter 26, this may be because educators face a range of impediments and barriers in using critical pedagogies as transformative learning experiences. Yet there is clearly an opportunity for further development of teaching and learning approaches that promote critical reflexivity in tourism.

7.   STUDENTS AND LEARNING OUTCOMES

The final theme identified in Figure 41.1 relates to students, learning outcomes, skills, knowledge and experience. Just as our institutions and curricula face ongoing changes, our students and the learning outcomes that they are required to demonstrate also continue to change. We have already touched on learning outcomes on several occasions in this chapter because they are inextricably linked with our discussions about curricula and social and critical pedagogies. We believe that four developments in particular will impact on the relevance of learning outcomes in the future. These developments include changes in the way we view learners; shifts in our understanding of what it means to 'be' a tourism graduate; the rise of program level, national and supranational learning outcomes; and the promise of a brave new world of personalized learning underpinned by learning analytics and adaptive learning systems.

There has been an increasing tendency toward treating students as customers rather than apprentices of the academy. Another less common view is that graduates are the 'product' and employers are the 'customers'. There are clearly benefits to viewing students as customers, including focusing attention on how the entire student experience can be improved (Benckendorff et al., 2009). Similarly, the 'employers as customers' perspective focuses attention on the needs of industry. However, taking these analogies too far can lead to the commodification of higher education (Ball, 2012). A student as customer, or employer as customer emphasis gives a stronger voice to a single stakeholder (that is, the student or the employer) at the expense of other stakeholders (that is, educators, society, taxpayers, government). At core, this raises the question of whether the goal of tourism education should be to produce graduates to meet the needs of society or graduates that meet the needs of the labor market. A more cynical analysis might question whether the goal of education is to generate a profit for education providers. Perhaps these goals overlap and are not mutually exclusive as implied here, but the question serves to focus debate around the learning outcomes that tourism graduates should be able to demonstrate.

The graduates of the future must be equipped to solve the problems of the future. Earlier in this chapter we provided a brief review of megatrends likely to impact on tourism and higher education. The key question is: what can tourism education do to prepare graduates for this future? What skills, knowledge and capabilities do we need to develop? If we are going to equip learners with the ability to solve the problems of tomorrow we will need to move them beyond 'knowing' (facts) and 'doing' (skills) to 'being' (Barnett and Coate, 2005). This requires educators to ask the question: what does it mean to 'be' a tourism graduate? Some answers to this question are provided in the chapters in Part I of this volume. It should be apparent from the discussion so far that the answer to this question is likely to be diverse, and that this diversity leads to a wide range of potential learning outcomes at the institutional level. Various attempts have been made to identify threshold learning outcomes that are common to any tourism degree. As Airey and Benckendorff explain in Chapter 35, educators in the UK, Australia and Spain have attempted to identify threshold learning outcomes and competencies at the national level, while various iterations of the Tuning Project have resulted in the development of competencies in Russia, the Middle East and Africa. Developments in other disciplines would suggest that attempts will be made in the future to harmonize various national and regional standards to identify a set of universally accepted learning outcomes for tourism graduates. While this ambition may never be fully achieved, progress toward such a goal would stimulate useful debate about what it means to be a tourism graduate as well as conversations about innovative teaching and learning approaches that allow learners to develop and demonstrate learning outcomes.

Institutions are increasingly adopting a constructive alignment approach to ensure that intended learning outcomes (ILOs) at the individual unit level are scaffolded, mapped and assessed to achieve program learning outcomes (PLOs). PLOs are then mapped against national standards and benchmarks. The emerging field of big data and learning analytics is likely to support this process by using increasingly sophisticated systems to provide real-time insight into the performance of learners. While initial efforts have focused on using a range of indicators to identify learners who might be at risk, there is considerable potential to use big data and learning analytics to provide learners with a personalized dashboard of progress toward particular learning outcomes (Charleer et al., 2014). This personalized information about progress toward personal goals or performance relative to peers can be useful in motivating and encouraging learners (Siemens and Long, 2011; Gašević et al., 2015). When these technologies are combined with other developments, such as badging and credentialing (Gibson et al., 2015), MOOCs (Chapter 11), ePortfolios (Chapter 12), ubiquitous personal devices, online simulations and virtual environments, there is immense potential for personalized learning pathways in which the pace and the approach are scaffolded to meet the needs of individual learners and in which the learning is tied to personal interests and experiences (Culatta, 2016).

8.   CONCLUSION

While the future of teaching and learning includes many challenges, there are also many exciting opportunities to improve the learning experience for tourism graduates. The chapters provided in this volume indicate a healthy interest in teaching and learning innovation on the tourism field. The multi-disciplinary nature of tourism is reflected in both the diversity of content and range of teaching and learning approaches used by educators in the field. There is every reason to believe that the intersection of two of the world's most exciting post-industrial industries, tourism and education, provides many opportunities for innovation and disruption of traditional systems and models. It is our hope that the chapters included in this volume will be a source of inspiration for educators who, through their graduates, strive to make the future a better place than the past.

REFERENCES

Airey, D., Tribe, J., Benckendorff, P. and Xiao, H. (2015), 'The managerial gaze: The long tail of tourism education and research', *Journal of Travel Research*, **54** (2), 139–51.

Altbach, P.G., Reisberg, L. and Rumbley, L.E. (2009), *Trends in Global Higher Education: Tracking an Academic Revolution*, Paris: UNESCO.

Ayikoru, M. (2015), 'Neoliberalism and the new managerialism in tourism and hospitality education', in Dredge, D., Airey, D. and Gross, M.J. (eds), *The Routledge Handbook of Tourism and Hospitality Education*, Abingdon: Routledge, pp. 118–29.

Ball, S.J. (2012), *Global Education Inc.: New Policy Networks and the Neo-liberal Imaginary*, Abingdon: Routledge.

Barber, M., Donnelly, K. and Rizvi, S. (2013), *An Avalanche is Coming: Higher Education and the Revolution Ahead*, London: Institute for Public Policy Research.

Barnett, R. (2015), 'Towards the creative university', London: Institute of Education, accessed 12 November 2015 at www.ronaldbarnett.co.uk/assets/docs/talks2015/Towards%20the%20Creative%20University%20-%20Buenos%20Aires%20-%2028%20April%202015.pdf.

Barnett, R. and Coate, K. (2005), *Engaging the Curriculum in Higher Education*, New York: Open University Press.

Bauman, Z. (2000), *Liquid Modernity*, Cambridge: Polity Press.

Benckendorff, P. and Moscardo, G. (2015), 'Education for sustainability futures', in Moscardo, G. and Benckendorff, P. (eds), *Education for Sustainability in Tourism*, Heidelberg: Springer-Verlag, pp. 271–83.

Benckendorff, P. and Zehrer, A. (2013), 'A network analysis of tourism research', *Annals of Tourism Research*, **43**, 121–49.

Benckendorff, P., Ruhanen, L. and Scott, N. (2009), 'Deconstructing the student experience: A conceptual framework', *Journal of Hospitality and Tourism Management*, **16** (1), 84–93.

Benckendorff, P., Lohmann, G., Pratt, M., Reynolds, P., Strickland, P. and Whitelaw, P. (2015), *Online Business Simulations: Good Practice Guide*, Sydney: Australian Government Office for Learning and Teaching.

Besley, A.C. and Peters, M.A. (eds) (2013), *Re-imagining the Creative University for the 21st Century*, Rotterdam: Sense Publishers.

Bosman, C. and Dredge, D. (2015), 'Teaching in a post-disciplinary teaching context', in Dredge, D., Airey, D. and Gross, M.J. (eds), *The Routledge Handbook of Tourism and Hospitality Education*, Abingdon: Routledge, pp. 265–78.

Bradwell, P. (2010), *The Edgeless University: Why Higher Education must Embrace Technology*, London: Demos.

Buijtendijk, H. and Van der Donk, M. (2015), 'Sustainability in tourism: A corporate perspective', in Moscardo, G. and Benckendorff, P. (eds), *Education for Sustainability in Tourism*, Heidelberg: Springer-Verlag, pp. 239–70.

Charleer, S., Klerkx, J. and Duval, E. (2014), 'Learning dashboards', *Journal of Learning Analytics*, **1** (3), 199–202.

Culatta, R. (2016), 'What are you Talking about?! The need for common language around personalized learning', *EDUCAUSEreview*, **51** (2), 1.

Cunningham, S., Tapsall, S., Ryan, Y., Stedman, L., Bagdon, K. and Flew, T. (1998), *New Media and Borderless Education: A Review of the Convergence between Global Media Networks and Higher Education Provision*, Canberra: Department of Education, Training and Youth Affairs.

Dredge, D., Airey, D. and Gross, M. (2015), 'Creating the future: Tourism hospitality and events education in a post-industrial, post-disciplinary world', in Dredge, D., Airey, D. and Gross, M.J. (eds), *The Routledge Handbook of Tourism and Hospitality Education*, Abingdon: Routledge, pp. 535–50.

Dredge, D., Benckendorff, P., Day, M., Gross, M.J., Walo, M., Weeks, P. and Whitelaw, P. (2012), 'The philosophic practitioner and the curriculum space', *Annals of Tourism Research*, **39** (4), 2154–76.

Ernst and Young, (2012), *University of the Future: A Thousand Year Old Industry on the Cusp of Profound Change*, Australia: Ernst and Young.

Filep, S., Hughes, M., Mostafanezhad, M. and Wheeler, F. (2015), 'Generation tourism: Towards a common identity', *Current Issues in Tourism*, **18** (6), 511–23.

Fullagar, S. and Wilson, E. (2012), 'Critical pedagogies: A reflexive approach to knowledge creation in tourism and hospitality studies', *Journal of Hospitality and Tourism Management*, **19** (1), 1–6.

Furco, A. (2003), 'Service learning: A balanced approach to experiential education', in *Introduction to Service-learning Toolkit*, Providence, RI: Campus Compact, pp. 11–14.

Gappa, J.M. (2000), 'The new faculty majority: Somewhat satisfied but not eligible for tenure', *New Directions for Institutional Research*, **2000** (105), 77–86.

García-Rosell, J-C. (2015), 'Promoting critical reflexivity in tourism and hospitality education through problem-based learning', in Dredge, D., Airey, D. and Gross, M.J. (eds), *The Routledge Handbook of Tourism and Hospitality Education*, Abingdon: Routledge, pp. 279–91.

Gašević, D., Dawson, S. and Siemens, G. (2015), Let's not forget: Learning analytics are about learning', *TechTrends*, **59** (1), 64–71.

Gibson, D., Ostashewski, N., Flintoff, K., Grant, S. and Knight, E. (2015), 'Digital badges in education', *Education and Information Technologies*, **20** (2), 403–10.

Godfrey, P.C., Illes, L.M. and Berry, G.R. (2005), 'Creating breadth in business education through service-learning', *Academy of Management Learning and Education*, **4** (3), 309–23.

Grey, C. (2004), 'Reinventing business schools: The contribution of critical management education', *Academy of Management Learning and Education*, **3** (2), 178–86.

Henderson, M., Selwyn, N., Finger, G. and Aston, R. (2015), 'Students' everyday engagement with digital technology in university: Exploring patterns of use and "usefulness"', *Journal of Higher Education Policy and Management*, **37** (3), 308–19.

Jennings, G. and Kachel, U. (2015), 'Online learning: Reflections on the effectiveness of an undergraduate sustainability tourism module', in Moscardo, G. and Benckendorff, P. (eds), *Education for Sustainability in Tourism*, Heidelberg: Springer-Verlag, pp. 187–200.

Johnson, L., Adams Becker, S., Cummins, M., Estrada, V., Freeman, A. and Hall, C. (2016), *NMC Horizon Report: 2016 Higher Education Edition*, Austin, TX: The New Media Consortium.

Koh, K. (1995), 'Designing the four-year tourism management curriculum: A marketing approach', *Journal of Travel Research*, **34** (1), 68–72.

MacVaugh, J. and Norton, M. (2012), 'Introducing sustainability into business education contexts using active learning', *International Journal of Sustainability in Higher Education*, **13** (1), 72–87.

Posner, R.A. (2003), *Public Intellectuals: A Study of Decline,* Cambridge, MA: Harvard University Press.

Puentedura, R.R. (2006), 'Transformation, technology and education', accessed 23 November 2015 at http://www.hippasus.com/resources/tte/.

Reynolds, M. and Vince, R. (2004), 'Critical management education and action-based learning: Synergies and contradictions', *Academy of Management Learning and Education*, **3** (4), 442–56.

Rooney, D., Paulsen, N., Callan, V., Brabant, M., Gallois, C. and Jones, E. (2009), 'A new role for place identity in managing organizational change', *Management Communication Quarterly*, **24** (1), 44.

Schott, C. (2015), 'Digital immersion for sustainable tourism through a critically reflexive approach', in Moscardo, G. and Benckendorff, P. (eds), *Education for Sustainability in Tourism*, Heidelberg: Springer-Verlag, pp. 213–28.

Selwyn, N. (2014), *Digital Technology and the Contemporary University: Degrees of Digitization*, Abingdon: Routledge.

Sheldon, P. and Fesenmaier, D. (2015), 'Tourism education futures initiative: Current and future curriculum influences', in Dredge, D., Airey, D. and Gross, M.J. (eds), *The Routledge Handbook of Tourism and Hospitality Education*, Abingdon: Routledge, pp. 155–70.

Siemens, G., and Long, P. (2011), 'Penetrating the fog: Analytics in learning and education', *EDUCAUSEreview*, **46** (5), 30.

Smith, A.E. and Humphreys, M.S. (2006), 'Evaluation of unsupervised semantic mapping of natural language with Leximancer concept mapping', *Behavior Research Methods*, **38** (2), 262–79.

Standaert, N. (2012), 'Towards a networked university', in Barnett, R. (ed.), *The Future University: Ideas and Possibilities*, Abingdon: Routledge.

Stubbs, W. and Cocklin, C. (2008), 'Teaching sustainability to business students: Shifting mindsets', *International Journal of Sustainability in Higher Education*, **9** (3), 206–21.

Tracey, P. and Phillips, N. (2007), 'The distinctive challenge of educating social entrepreneurs: A postscript and rejoinder to the special issue on entrepreneurship education', *Academy of Management Learning and Education*, **6** (2), 264–71.

Tribe, J. (2001), 'Research paradigms and the tourism curriculum', *Journal of Travel Research*, **39** (4), 442–8.

Tribe, J. (2002), 'The philosophic practitioner', *Annals of Tourism Research*, **29** (2), 338–57.

Tribe, J. and Liburd, J.J. (2016), 'The tourism knowledge system', *Annals of Tourism Research*, **57**, 44–61.

United Nations (2015), *World Population Prospects: The 2015 Revision, Key Findings and Advance Tables*, New York: United Nations Department of Economic and Social Affairs, Population Division.

Von der Heidt, T. and Lamberton, G. (2014), 'How academics in undergraduate business programs at an Australian University view sustainability', *Australian Journal of Environmental Education*, **30** (2), 215–38.

Walsh, L. (2015), 'The tail wagging the dog? Emergent trends and drivers of international digital education', in Hayden, M., Levy, J. and Thompson, J. (eds), *The SAGE Handbook of Research in International Education* (2nd edn), London: Sage Publications, pp. 233–45.

Wilson, E. and Von der Heidt, T. (2013), 'Business as usual? Barriers to education for sustainability in the tourism curriculum', *Journal of Teaching in Travel and Tourism*, **13** (2), 130–47.

Wilson, M. (2010), 'The impact of globalization on higher education: Implications for globally networked learning environments', *E-Learning and Digital Media*, **7** (2), 182–7.

Zehrer, A. and Mössenlechner, C. (2009), 'Key competences of tourism graduates: The employers' point of view', *Journal of Teaching in Travel and Tourism*, **9** (3–4), 266–87.

Zehrer, A. and Schuckert, M. (2016), 'Online learning formats in tourism and hospitality higher education', *Zeitschrift für Tourismuswissenschaft*, **8** (1), 85–94.

Index